Marvel: the Characters and Their Universe

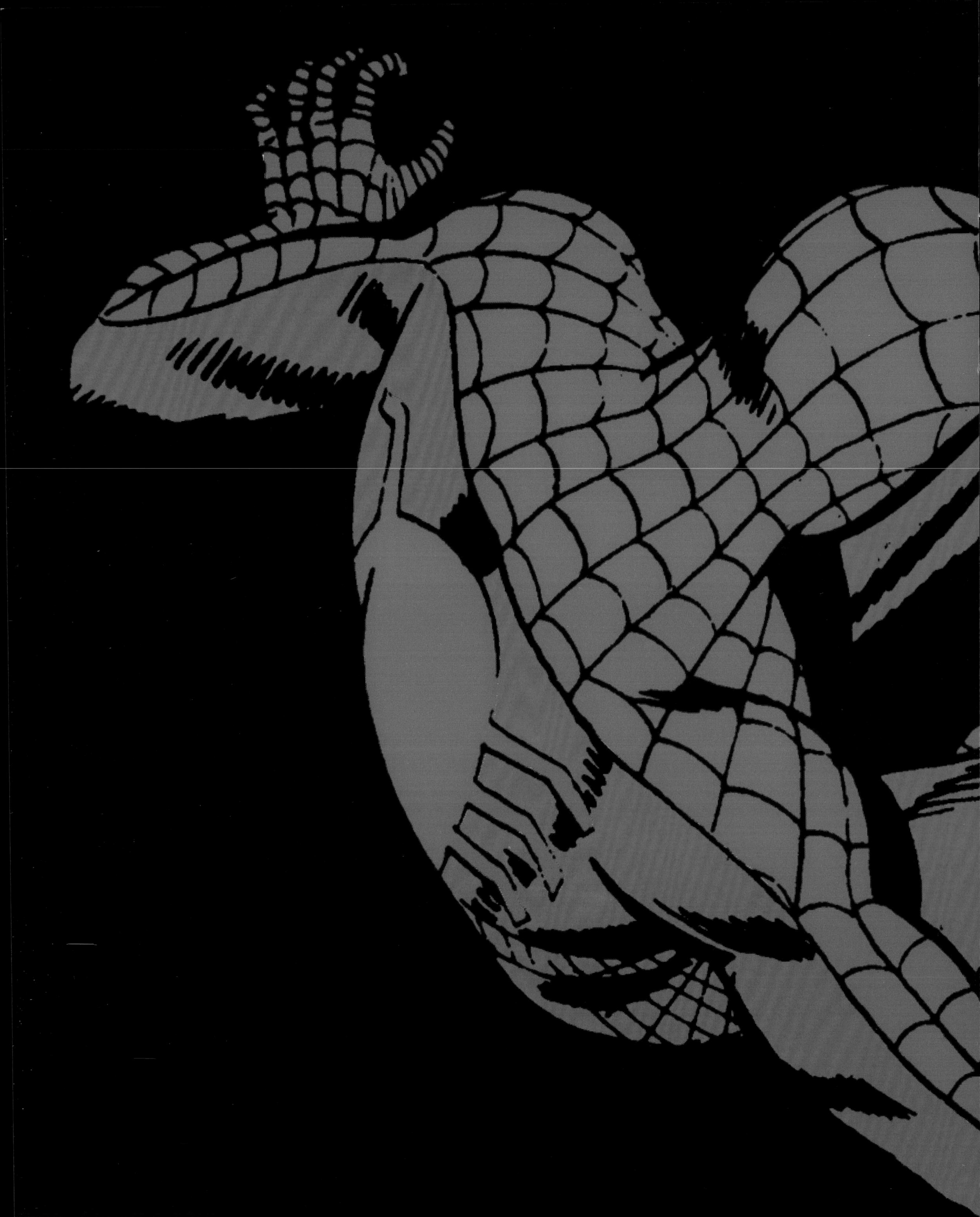

MAR

THE CHARAC

AND TH

VEL
TERS
IR UNIVERSE

MICHAEL MALLORY

MARVEL CHARACTERS, INC.
CHARTWELL BOOKS

ACKNOWLEDGMENTS:

Many people generously contributed their time, reminiscences, personal photographs, and artwork to make this book possible, and the author would like to express heartfelt thanks to the following:

Avi Arad, Ralph Bakshi, Jerry Beck, Jodi Benz, Tom Brevoort, Linda Buckley, John Buscema, Chris Claremont, Dave Cockrum, Gene Colan, Robin Davids, Michael Diaz, Tom De Falco, Philip De Guere, Claire Dodridge, Sean Dudas, Joe Everett, Lou Ferrigno, David S. Goyer, Stephanie Graziano, Kenneth Johnson, Heidi Keller, Neal Kirkman, Mitch Lasky, Mary Ann Lataif, Larry Lieber, Margaret Loesch, Carlos Lopez, Jean McFaddin, Michael McLane, JoAnn McLaughlin, Lili Malkin, Helen Mallory, Brendan Mallory, Jim Moore, Patrick Nally, Michelle Orsi, Ray Patterson, June Patterson, Randy Poe, Sam Raimi, Mia Rehm, Eric Rollman, John Romita, Jr., Bob Rutan, Leigha Schmidt, Alfie Scopp, Joe Simon, Joe Sinnott, John Smith, Paul Soles, Flo Steinberg, Matt Sullivan, Victoria Tapscott, Mike Thomas, Roy Thomas, Scott Trowbridge, John Vernon, Fred Waugh, and Steve Worth.

Special thanks to Mike Stewart of Marvel; Jim Muschett of Rizzoli International Publications, Inc.; John Romita, Sr., whose artistry is exceeded only by his generosity; Claire Brandt and the staff of Eddie Brandt's Saturday Matinee, the best video store in the world; Mark Bishop of Jerry Ohlinger's Movie Material Store; and John Marshall, collector extraordinare (who can be found at jmars@toyzilla.com). And last, though anything but least, special thanks to Stan Lee.

The photos credited to John Marshall/Schiffer Publishing are taken from *Comic Book Hero Toys* (Schiffer Publishing, 1999), copyright 1999, John Marshall, and are used with permission.

This edition published in 2014 in arrangement with Universe Publishing, a division of Rizzoli International Publications, Inc., by

CHARTWELL BOOKS
an imprint of Book Sales
a division of Quarto Publishing Group USA Inc.
142 West 36th Street, 4th Floor
New York, New York 10018
USA

2016 2017 2018 2019 / 10 9 8 7 6 5

ISBN-13: 978-0-7858-3165-5

Printed in China

CONTENTS

THE WO
OF M

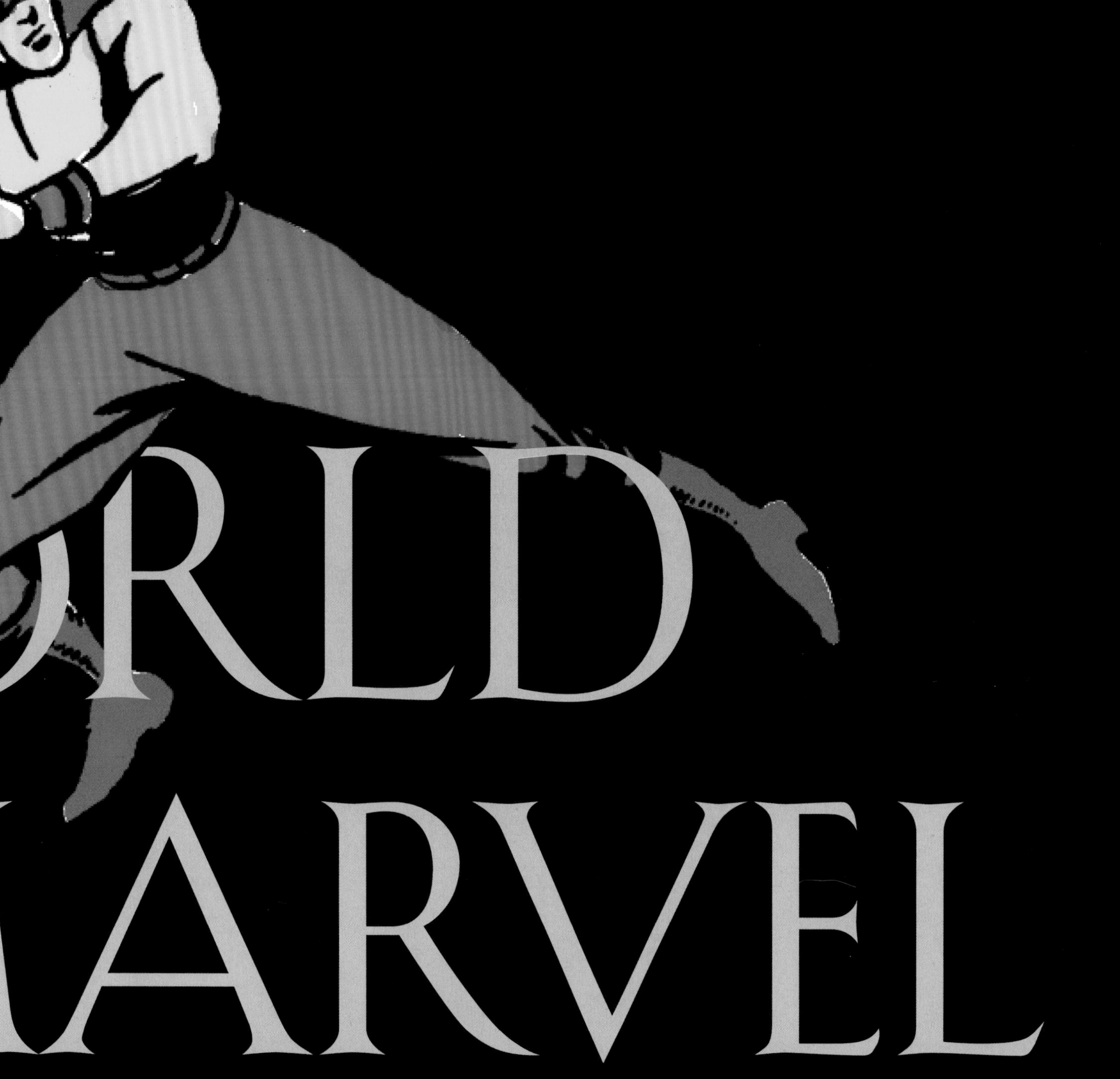
ORLD
ARVEL

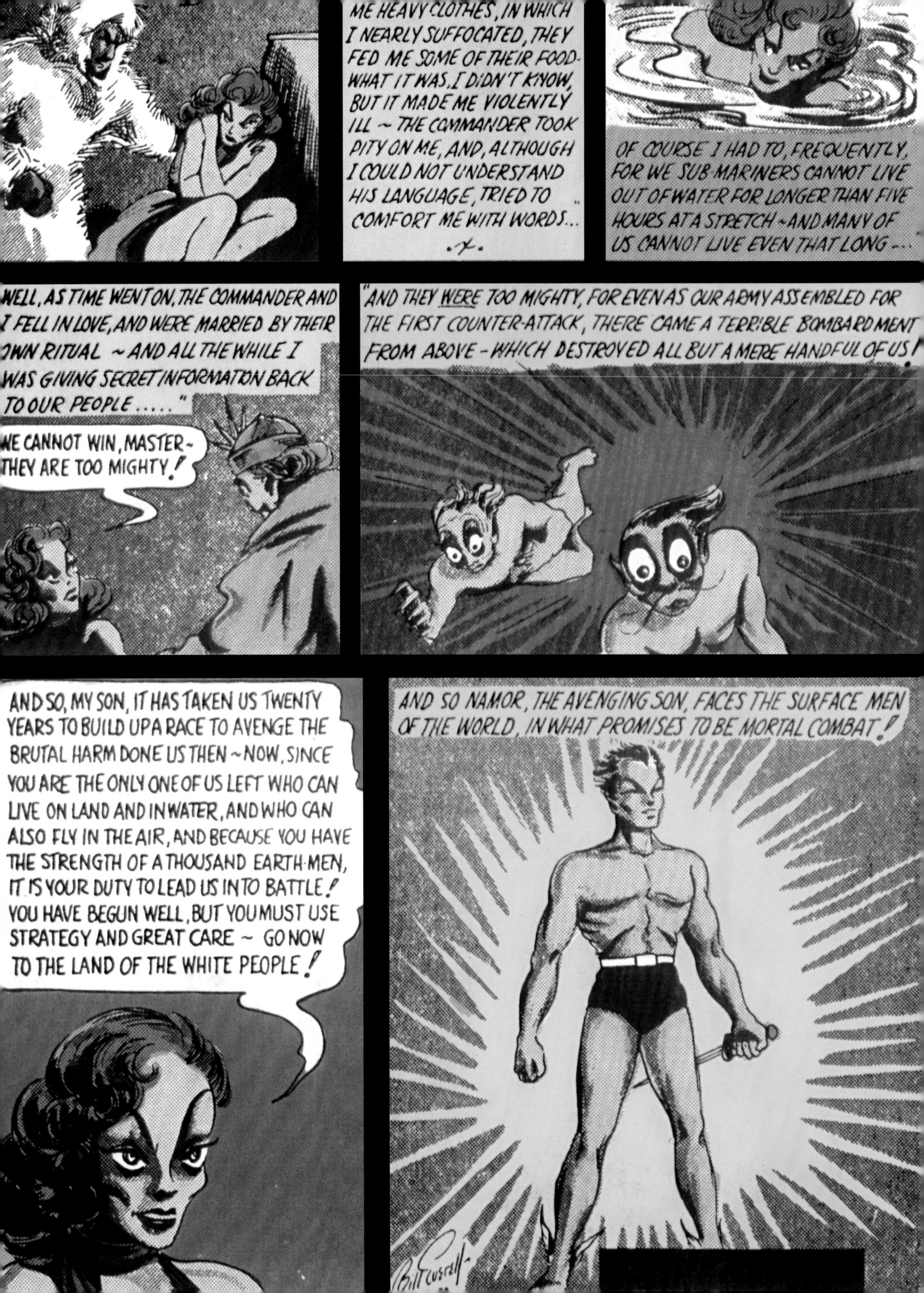
ME HEAVY CLOTHES, IN WHICH I NEARLY SUFFOCATED, THEY FED ME SOME OF THEIR FOOD - WHAT IT WAS, I DIDN'T KNOW, BUT IT MADE ME VIOLENTLY ILL ~ THE COMMANDER TOOK PITY ON ME, AND, ALTHOUGH I COULD NOT UNDERSTAND HIS LANGUAGE, TRIED TO COMFORT ME WITH WORDS..."
OF COURSE I HAD TO, FREQUENTLY, FOR WE SUB-MARINERS CANNOT LIVE OUT OF WATER FOR LONGER THAN FIVE HOURS AT A STRETCH ~ AND MANY OF US CANNOT LIVE EVEN THAT LONG...
WELL, AS TIME WENT ON, THE COMMANDER AND I FELL IN LOVE, AND WERE MARRIED BY THEIR OWN RITUAL ~ AND ALL THE WHILE I WAS GIVING SECRET INFORMATION BACK TO OUR PEOPLE....."
WE CANNOT WIN, MASTER - THEY ARE TOO MIGHTY!
"AND THEY WERE TOO MIGHTY, FOR EVEN AS OUR ARMY ASSEMBLED FOR THE FIRST COUNTER-ATTACK, THERE CAME A TERRIBLE BOMBARDMENT FROM ABOVE - WHICH DESTROYED ALL BUT A MERE HANDFUL OF US!
AND SO, MY SON, IT HAS TAKEN US TWENTY YEARS TO BUILD UP A RACE TO AVENGE THE BRUTAL HARM DONE US THEN ~ NOW, SINCE YOU ARE THE ONLY ONE OF US LEFT WHO CAN LIVE ON LAND AND IN WATER, AND WHO CAN ALSO FLY IN THE AIR, AND BECAUSE YOU HAVE THE STRENGTH OF A THOUSAND EARTH-MEN, IT IS YOUR DUTY TO LEAD US INTO BATTLE! YOU HAVE BEGUN WELL, BUT YOU MUST USE STRATEGY AND GREAT CARE ~ GO NOW TO THE LAND OF THE WHITE PEOPLE!
AND SO NAMOR, THE AVENGING SON, FACES THE SURFACE MEN OF THE WORLD, IN WHAT PROMISES TO BE MORTAL COMBAT!
[redacted]

THE WORLD OF MARVEL

TWENTIETH CENTURY GODS

When early astronomers turned their gazes to the majesty of the night sky, they projected upon the stars images of the gods, goddesses, and fantastic creatures that inhabited the mythology of their culture. For these ancient peoples, it was a way of defining their universe. If that process were for some reason to take place today, the constellations would not bear such classical names as Andromeda, Hercules, or Cassiopeia, but would most likely be named Spider-Man, Hulk, and Wolverine.

In ages of so-called enlightenment, mythology becomes increasingly fictional, and no fictional form so perfectly fits the mold of mythology as comic book stories. Like classical mythology, comics offer colorful, larger-than-life figures—some of whom represent all that is good while others represent all that is evil—interacting in the world with normal men and women, battling opponents on a level far above the mortal realm. The need for such stories in our lives seems to be a constant of the human condition. And in the twentieth century, no entertainment company entity has been better at fulfilling this basic need than Marvel Comics.

For forty years now, the world has been under the spell of the Marvel Universe, which is not so much a parallel universe to our own but a larger, greater universe that encompasses an enhanced version of our reality, set against other worlds created not by physical laws, but by the forces of imagination. Taken on a surface level, the Marvel Universe is an immensely complex matrix of time and space that encompasses the stories of thousands of characters and manages to interweave them into a single, solid quilt (John Romita, one of Marvel's greatest artists, calls these travail-filled character paths "convoluted journeys"). While the character mythologies established by other comic book publishers tend to operate as a series of linear sagas that rarely interrelate, the Marvel Universe is as far reaching and comprehensive as the known universe. There are far fewer than six degrees of separation from one Marvel character to any other.

The romantic, heroic Prince Namor, The Sub-Mariner, as introduced in *Marvel Comics* #1 (October 1939).

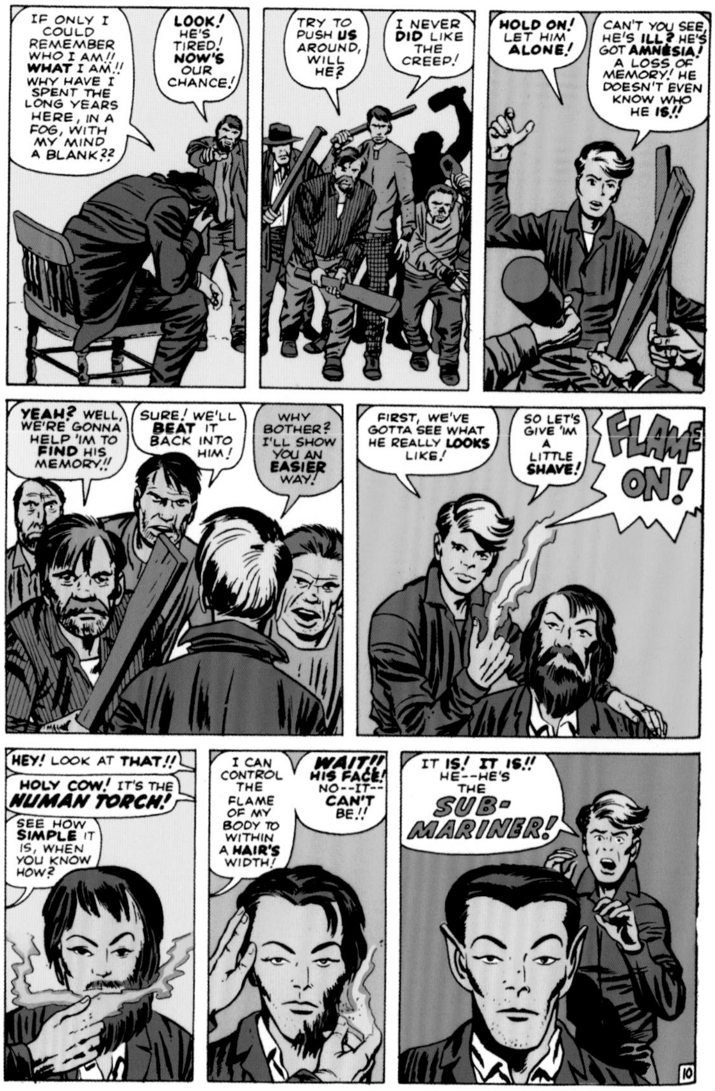
IF ONLY I COULD REMEMBER WHO I AM!! WHAT I AM!! WHY HAVE I SPENT THE LONG YEARS HERE, IN A FOG, WITH MY MIND A BLANK??
LOOK! HE'S TIRED! NOW'S OUR CHANCE!
TRY TO PUSH US AROUND, WILL HE?
I NEVER DID LIKE THE CREEP!
HOLD ON! LET HIM ALONE!
CAN'T YOU SEE, HE'S ILL? HE'S GOT AMNESIA! A LOSS OF MEMORY! HE DOESN'T EVEN KNOW WHO HE IS!!
YEAH? WELL, WE'RE GONNA HELP 'IM TO FIND HIS MEMORY!!
SURE! WE'LL BEAT IT BACK INTO HIM!
WHY BOTHER? I'LL SHOW YOU AN EASIER WAY!
FIRST, WE'VE GOTTA SEE WHAT HE REALLY LOOKS LIKE!
SO LET'S GIVE 'IM A LITTLE SHAVE!
FLAME ON!
HEY! LOOK AT THAT!!
HOLY COW! IT'S THE HUMAN TORCH!
SEE HOW SIMPLE IT IS, WHEN YOU KNOW HOW?
I CAN CONTROL THE FLAME OF MY BODY TO WITHIN A HAIR'S WIDTH!
WAIT!! HIS FACE! NO--IT--CAN'T BE!!
IT IS! IT IS!! HE--HE'S THE SUB-MARINER!
10

Johnny Storm recognizes Prince Namor through reading Sub-Mariner comics. From The Fantastic Four #4 (May 1962).

One of the more interesting things about this fantastic realm is that it completely coexists with our own real world. Spider-Man and The Fantastic Four, for instance, have not set up shop in some stand-in metropolis that serves as metaphor for a major American city. Instead they live and work in Manhattan, appearing against the same recognizable landmarks that are seen every day by the city's real inhabitants. One of the most dramatic moments in the entire Marvel canon, the climactic and deadly showdown between Spider-Man, his love Gwen Stacy, and the evil Green Goblin (recounted in *Spider-Man* issue #121), takes place atop a tower of the Brooklyn Bridge.

The two worlds are even connected by their appreciation for comic books. As early as 1941, in the first issue of *Captain America,* President Franklin D. Roosevelt himself is depicted ribbing two military leaders who are confessing their failure to contain enemy espionage. "What would you suggest, gentlemen?" the commander in chief asks. "A character out of the comic books? Perhaps The Human Torch in the army would solve our problem!" An interesting parallel occurs some twenty years later, in *The Fantastic Four* issue #4, when Johnny Storm, a.k.a. The Human Torch (albeit a different Human Torch than the one mentioned by FDR) would recognize a heavily disguised Sub-Mariner, suffering from amnesia, after having read one of his old comic books. As time went on, Marvel would become renowned for such touches of self-satire, even to the point of placing the comics' creators themselves into the action, as with the cameo appearances by Stan Lee and Jack Kirby in *The Fantastic Four* #10 (January 1963), who are confronted in the Marvel offices by mega-villain Doctor Doom.

The expansion of the Marvel Universe has been in part a result of the unique nature of comic books themselves. With the exception of television soap operas, no other entertainment format continues along not simply for years, but for decades, constantly challenging its creators to come up with new angles, new twists, and

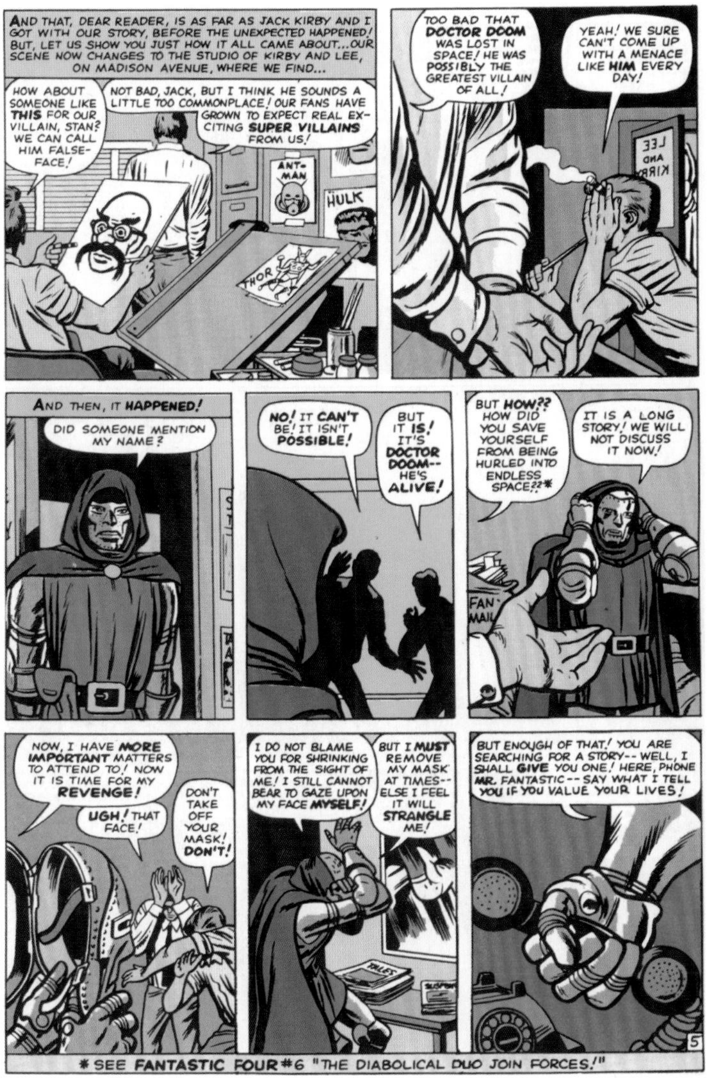
AND THAT, DEAR READER, IS AS FAR AS JACK KIRBY AND I GOT WITH OUR STORY, BEFORE THE UNEXPECTED HAPPENED! BUT, LET US SHOW YOU JUST HOW IT ALL CAME ABOUT... OUR SCENE NOW CHANGES TO THE STUDIO OF KIRBY AND LEE, ON MADISON AVENUE, WHERE WE FIND...
HOW ABOUT SOMEONE LIKE THIS FOR OUR VILLAIN, STAN? WE CAN CALL HIM FALSE-FACE!
NOT BAD, JACK, BUT I THINK HE SOUNDS A LITTLE TOO COMMONPLACE! OUR FANS HAVE GROWN TO EXPECT REAL EXCITING SUPER VILLAINS FROM US!
ANT-MAN
HULK
THOR
TOO BAD THAT DOCTOR DOOM WAS LOST IN SPACE! HE WAS POSSIBLY THE GREATEST VILLAIN OF ALL!
YEAH! WE SURE CAN'T COME UP WITH A MENACE LIKE HIM EVERY DAY!
AND THEN, IT HAPPENED!
DID SOMEONE MENTION MY NAME?
NO! IT CAN'T BE! IT ISN'T POSSIBLE!
BUT IT IS! IT'S DOCTOR DOOM-- HE'S ALIVE!
BUT HOW?? HOW DID YOU SAVE YOURSELF FROM BEING HURLED INTO ENDLESS SPACE??*
IT IS A LONG STORY! WE WILL NOT DISCUSS IT NOW!
FAN MAIL
NOW, I HAVE MORE IMPORTANT MATTERS TO ATTEND TO! NOW IT IS TIME FOR MY REVENGE!
UGH! THAT FACE!
DON'T TAKE OFF YOUR MASK! DON'T!
I DO NOT BLAME YOU FOR SHRINKING FROM THE SIGHT OF ME! I STILL CANNOT BEAR TO GAZE UPON MY FACE MYSELF!
BUT I MUST REMOVE MY MASK AT TIMES-- ELSE I FEEL IT WILL STRANGLE ME!
BUT ENOUGH OF THAT! YOU ARE SEARCHING FOR A STORY-- WELL, I SHALL GIVE YOU ONE! HERE, PHONE MR. FANTASTIC-- SAY WHAT I TELL YOU IF YOU VALUE YOUR LIVES!
5
* SEE FANTASTIC FOUR #6 "THE DIABOLICAL DUO JOIN FORCES!"

Universes collide as Stan Lee and Jack Kirby (faces carefully hidden) are confronted by Doctor Doom himself, who coyly exposes his ruined face, in *The Fantastic Four* #10 (January 1963).

new roads down which to take the characters. As a result, a character's backstory is open for continuous embellishments, additions, even outright reversals. It is safe to say that when Marvel's creator-in-residence Stan Lee sat down and conceived The Incredible Hulk four decades ago, he could not predict the kind of complex psychodrama that future comic book writers would put the character through. On the other hand, without the groundwork laid down by Lee in the early days, these later permutations would have been impossible. Characters must be born with strength before they can develop flexibility.

The characters that inhabit the Marvel Universe have ceased to be simply comic book characters, and have become pop culture icons, figures so deeply ingrained in our collective consciousness that it is startling to realize that many of them have only been around for the last thirty or forty years. They are as much a part of Americana as Paul Revere and Buffalo Bill.

A BRIEF HISTORY OF MARVEL COMICS

The company that would become known to the world as Marvel was formed in 1932 by a young (then only twenty-two) entrepreneur named Martin Goodman, who started up a publishing house to turn out pulp fiction magazines, an immensely popular form of escapist entertainment in the early part of the century. Goodman's publications included the titles *Marvel Science Stories.* a science-fiction magazine, and *Marvel Tales,* which leaned more in the direction of fantasy and horror, but the bread and butter of the company—which was then identified as Red Circle—were Western and detective magazines. In 1938, however, the world of escapist publishing was set on its ear by a character created specifically for the fairly new format comic books: a fellow in blue tights and a cape called Superman. Before long, Goodman moved into the field of comic books.

Goodman's first effort, published in October of 1939, was prophetically called *Marvel Comics* and

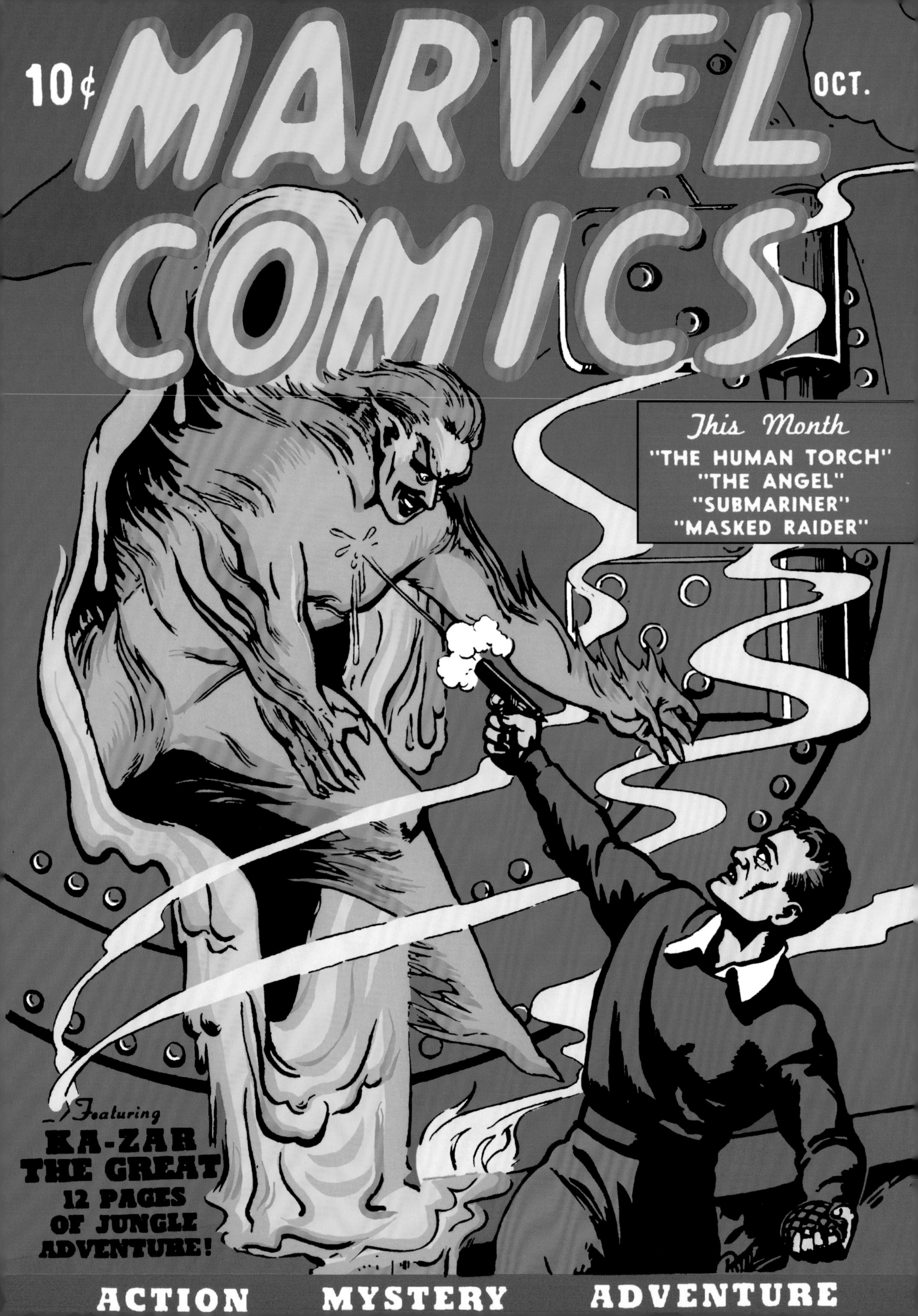
10¢
MARVEL COMICS
OCT.
This Month
"THE HUMAN TORCH"
"THE ANGEL"
"SUBMARINER"
"MASKED RAIDER"
Featuring
KA-ZAR THE GREAT
12 PAGES OF JUNGLE ADVENTURE!
ACTION MYSTERY ADVENTURE

featured one of comicdom's most enduring characters, Prince Namor, The Sub-Mariner, the creation of a young artist and writer named Bill Everett. Born in Cambridge, Massachusetts, in 1917, Everett began his career in commercial art before turning to comics. Initially, Everett created The Sub-Mariner for *Motion Picture Funnies Weekly,* which appeared a few months prior to *Marvel Comics.* His passion for submergible superheroes would lead him to create three other aquatic do-gooders in the years to come: Hydroman, The Fin, and Namora. In the early fifties, Everett drew many of the horror comics Martin Goodman was then publishing, and a decade later he returned to Marvel to draw the first issue of *Daredevil* in 1964, and resume work on the Sub-Mariner series. He continued to draw his creation, Prince Namor, until a short time before his untimely death in 1973.

Another featured character in that first issue of *Marvel Comics* (which also included two of comicdom's *least* enduring creations, The Angel—not to be confused with the X-Men character of many years later—and The Masked Raider) was the original Human Torch, created by Carl Burgos. A New York City native, Burgos (who was born either in 1917 or 1920, depending on the source) would have limited association with Marvel throughout the years, chiefly returning to the company in the 1950s, like Everett, to draw horror comics, and then again in the mid-sixties where he worked with the characters Giant-Man and the new Human Torch. Burgos died in 1984.

Everett had come to Goodman's company, which was now operating under the company name Timely, by way of a comic book packager called Funnies, Incorporated, which marketed stories and art for a host of publishers. Before long, two more young artist/writers would come Timely's way through Funnies, Inc., young men who were destined to have a major impact on the company. Their names were Joe Simon and Jack Kirby.

Today, Simon and Kirby are rarely thought of as a team, except in the case of their signature creation,

The original Human Torch was among the very first that would become a Marvel Superhero. From *Marvel Comics* #1 (October 1939).

Captain America. But the fact is, they were partnered for more than fifteen years, during which time they worked on a variety of comic book projects at many different companies.

Joe Simon, who was born in Rochester, New York, in 1915, had worked as a newspaperman before entering comics. Prior to signing on with Timely, Simon worked as an editor for Fox Comics, an outfit run by one Victor Fox, whom Simon describes as "no Twentieth Century [Fox], he was like Twelfth Century!"

Jack Kirby (born Jacob Kurtzburg in New York City in 1917) came to comic books by way of newspaper cartooning and animation, having worked briefly for the Max Fleischer Studios in New York. Kirby was earning fifteen dollars a week at Fox and picking up free-lance work through Funnies, Inc., at the time he and Simon began their partnership. That union would carry them in and out of Timely and on to National (DC), Harvey Comics, and some smaller independent companies, before going their separate ways in the mid-1950s. "We were very close friends for many years," Simon says of his former partner. "But I think Jack's problem was that he was self-destructive. He'd sign everything away and give anything for a paycheck. But he was always very sweet, very nice, and we worked together very well. We had great fun working together."

After the split Simon went on to a stint with Archie comics and in the late 1960s became editor of the satire magazine *Sick*, a job he loved. Kirby, meanwhile, realigned with Timely (now called Atlas) in the late 1950s, where he was, in a sense, rediscovered. Long before his death in 1994, Kirby had achieved legendary status among comic book fans.

For its first year or so, Timely featured such superheroes as Simon's The Fiery Mask, who is in reality Jack Castle, a man who develops super strength (and a glowing face) after being jolted with the power of the elements by a demented scientist's raygun; The Red Raven, who is raised from infancy by a strange, alien race of bird-men then dispatched to fight crime on his native

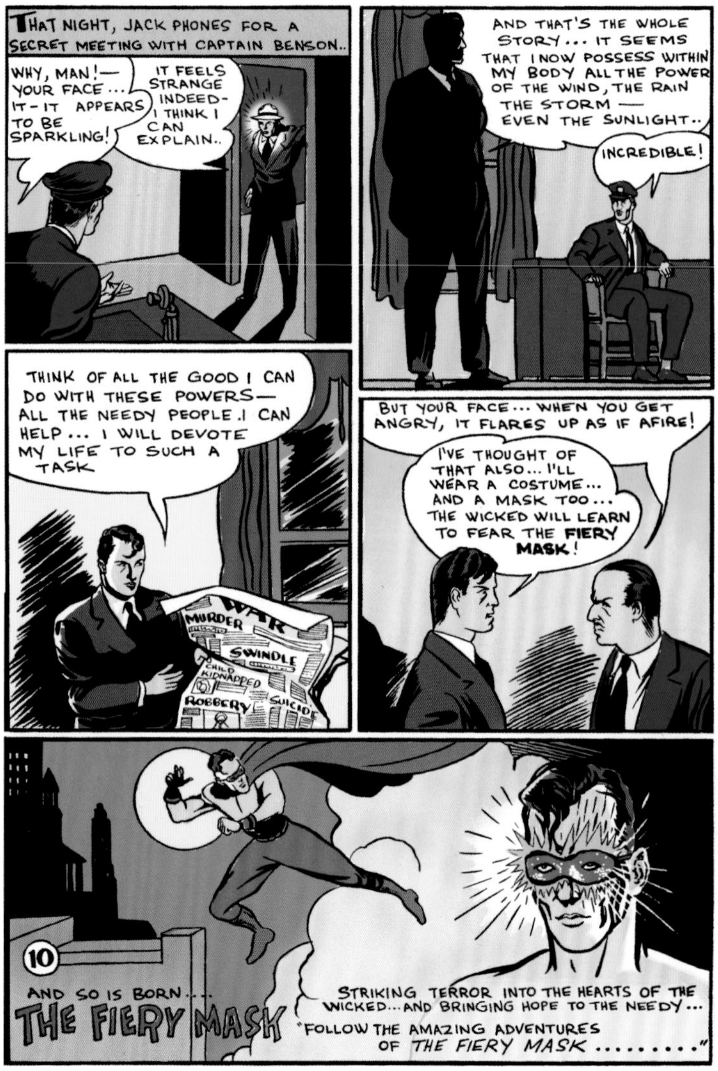
THAT NIGHT, JACK PHONES FOR A SECRET MEETING WITH CAPTAIN BENSON..
WHY, MAN!— YOUR FACE... IT-IT APPEARS TO BE SPARKLING!
IT FEELS STRANGE INDEED- I THINK I CAN EXPLAIN..
AND THAT'S THE WHOLE STORY... IT SEEMS THAT I NOW POSSESS WITHIN MY BODY ALL THE POWER OF THE WIND, THE RAIN THE STORM — EVEN THE SUNLIGHT..
INCREDIBLE!
THINK OF ALL THE GOOD I CAN DO WITH THESE POWERS— ALL THE NEEDY PEOPLE. I CAN HELP... I WILL DEVOTE MY LIFE TO SUCH A TASK
WAR
MURDER
SWINDLE
CHILD KIDNAPPED
ROBBERY
SUICIDE
BUT YOUR FACE... WHEN YOU GET ANGRY, IT FLARES UP AS IF AFIRE!
I'VE THOUGHT OF THAT ALSO... I'LL WEAR A COSTUME... AND A MASK TOO... THE WICKED WILL LEARN TO FEAR THE FIERY MASK!
10
AND SO IS BORN... THE FIERY MASK
STRIKING TERROR INTO THE HEARTS OF THE WICKED... AND BRINGING HOPE TO THE NEEDY...
"FOLLOW THE AMAZING ADVENTURES OF THE FIERY MASK........"

The Fiery Mask was one of the many characters developed by Joe Simon. From *Daring Mystery Comics* #1 (January 1940).

(Opposite) The Red Raven (whose creator remains unknown) was unusual in that he had no secret identity. From *Red Raven Comics* #1 (August 1940).

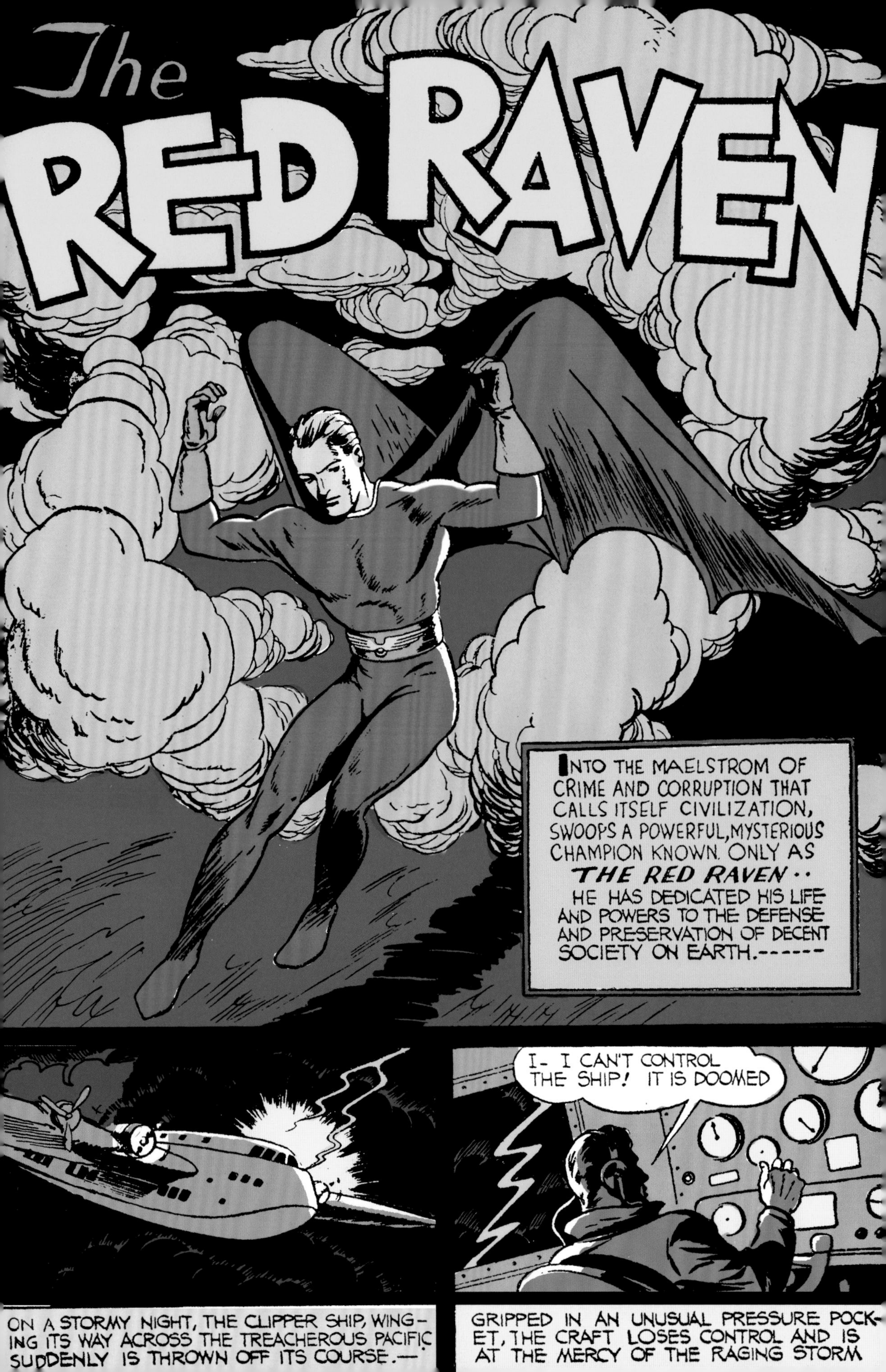

The RED RAVEN
INTO THE MAELSTROM OF CRIME AND CORRUPTION THAT CALLS ITSELF CIVILIZATION, SWOOPS A POWERFUL, MYSTERIOUS CHAMPION KNOWN ONLY AS THE RED RAVEN.. HE HAS DEDICATED HIS LIFE AND POWERS TO THE DEFENSE AND PRESERVATION OF DECENT SOCIETY ON EARTH.------
ON A STORMY NIGHT, THE CLIPPER SHIP, WING-ING ITS WAY ACROSS THE TREACHEROUS PACIFIC SUDDENLY IS THROWN OFF ITS COURSE.—
I- I CAN'T CONTROL THE SHIP! IT IS DOOMED
GRIPPED IN AN UNUSUAL PRESSURE POCK-ET, THE CRAFT LOSES CONTROL AND IS AT THE MERCY OF THE RAGING STORM

Earth; and Kirby's The Vision, a green-skinned, supernatural crimefighter with a large, domed head and eerie, pupil-less eyes. It was a more down-to-earth character, though, that really resonated with readers. Captain America, as rendered by Simon and Kirby, first appeared in his own magazine in March 1941 (actually earlier, since comic books are invariably postdated by a couple of months) and was an immediate hit.

Simon and Kirby quickly rose to the positions of editor and art director, respectively, and soon found themselves working with a teenaged kid named Stanley Martin Lieber, a junior writer who was related to Goodman's wife. Born in New York City in 1922, Lieber was blessed with a wildly creative spirit and a genius for promotion. By the time he came to work for Goodman at the age of seventeen, his resume included winning the *New York Herald Tribune* essay contest three times, and his ambition was to pen the great American novel, or at least the great American *something*. For that reason he opted to use a pseudonym for his comic book work, splitting his first name into its two syllables: *Stan Lee*. The sudden departure of Simon and Kirby in late 1941, due to a financial dispute, left only Lee to carry on, which he did over the next half-century, with spectacular results.

Three more artists who would become key figures in the history of Marvel put in brief stints at Timely in the late 1940s and early 1950s: John Buscema (born in New York City in 1927), whose brother Sal would also make his mark as a Marvel artist, John Romita (born in Brooklyn in 1930), and Gene Colan (another NYC native, born in 1926). "I had all the different stories thrown at me," recalls Colan. "It was really baptism by fire. I flew by the seat of my pants, and whatever they threw at me, I had to make something good out of it. There were romance stories, western stories, war stories, it was a good education." But not necessarily a good education for drawing superheroes, since the trend for costumed crimefighters had started to decline after the war, in part because of the downsizing of military bases,

Stan Lee in the early 1940s.

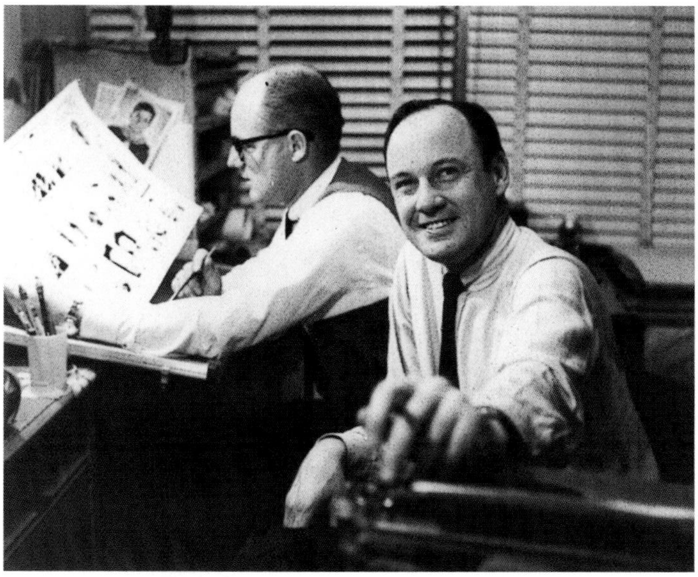

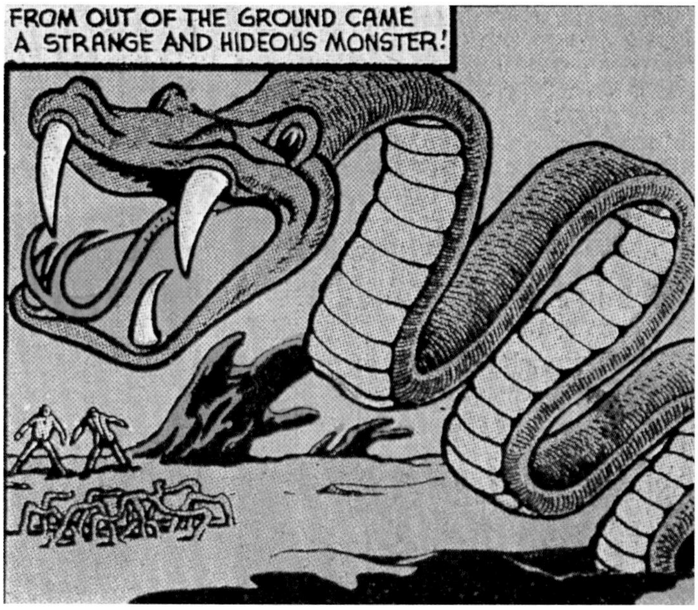
FROM OUT OF THE GROUND CAME A STRANGE AND HIDEOUS MONSTER!

(Top) Stan Lee (right) with artist Joe Maneely in the mid-1950s.

(Above) A typical BEM ("Bug-Eyes Monster") of the 1950s, from *Adventures into Terror* (December 1951).

where comic books had been immensely popular forms of entertainment.

The decade of the 1950s was a strange, uncertain time in the comic book industry. Timely—which had by then shifted its on-cover identity to Atlas—tried to revive Captain America, The Sub-Mariner, and The Human Torch, but the efforts were short lived. What's more, gritty crime melodramas and gruesome horror stories—which had supplanted superhero books in the first place—were coming under attack from the United States government, which had convinced itself that "violent" comic books were the root of every societal problem in the nation.

Atlas survived, but just barely. "When I started working there in June 1958, I asked Martin Goodman how he would describe the industry, and he said, 'I'd call it a dying industry,'" recalls artist and writer Larry Lieber, who is the younger brother (by nine years) of Stan Lee. Prior to Lieber's arrival, Lee, who was by then also serving as editor and art director, was the only writer Goodman had. The company's output at that point largely consisted of Western titles or science-fiction magazines featuring "BEMs"—Bug-Eyed Monsters.

"Things were extremely bad from '58 to '61," recalls artist Joe Sinnott, one of the industry's most accomplished inkers, who joined Timely in 1951 at the age of twenty-five, fresh out of Cartoonists and Illustrators School. "We were doing monster books, you know, 'Gordo,' characters like that. It was a fun period but we weren't making much money at that point and they weren't all that popular. It was in '61 when the superheroes came back that pulled us out of the doldrums."

Not only was Marvel pulled from the doldrums, so was the entire comic book industry.

THE BIG BANG

Inspired by the success rival publisher National (DC) was having with *The Justice League of America*—a superhero team made up of DC's first-string heroes, including Batman, Superman, The Flash, and Wonder Woman—Goodman suggested that Stan Lee create a similar superhero team. Lee was game, particularly after realizing that this was his chance to do something about a pet peeve of his: superheroes who acted and spoke identically, cookie-cutter do-gooders that were virtually interchangeable underneath their rainbow leotards. The team Lee wanted to develop was one whose members possessed individual personalities and who suffered from recognizable, everyday problems. This would become the hallmark of Marvel comics, whose heroes not only had to save the world from incredible supervillains, but had to do it while worrying about how many months they were behind on the rent.

To create the graphic vision for the new superhero team, Lee turned to Jack Kirby, who was one of three artists—Steve Ditko and Don Heck were the others— that Lee was striving to keep busy at the time. While Ditko and Heck would each make brilliant contributions to the growing Marvel Universe over the next several years, it is Jack Kirby who must be considered the godfather of Marvel Comics. It was he who visually created most of the company's classic superheroes, deploying a deceptively simple yet amazingly powerful style that set the standard for the industry for decades to come. Kirby's talent for staging action had been revealed in his earliest work for Timely in the early 1940s, but now he was to be given the kind of canvas that would establish him as a legend of the medium.

With issue #1 of *The Fantastic Four*, which debuted in November 1961 under the imprint of Marvel Comics Group, a new revolution in comics was officially underway.

In staging Marvel's return to the superhero genre, Lee consciously or unconsciously hit upon several potent ideas. One was the concept of the ongoing story. "Back in the '50s the stories were short stories, five or six pages, and they all concluded," says Sinnott. "There was no continuity. You didn't have to buy the following month's

(Top) Perhaps Marvel's most important artist, Jack "King" Kirby.

(Above) Why is this man smiling? Maybe because he's revolutionized the comic book industry. Stan Lee, c. 1965.

COMIC BOOKS UNDER FIRE

I SPECIAL COMICS INFORMATION	APPROVED FOR ALL READERS

In the seven-decade history of comic books, no single force has had as great an impact on the industry as the 1954 hearings before the Subcommittee to Investigate Juvenile Delinquency of the Committee on the Judiciary of the United States Senate. The centerpiece of the hearings was a book by a psychiatrist named Dr. Fredric Wertham, titled *Seduction of the Innocent,* which pinpointed crime and horror comics as the primary cause for the rise in juvenile delinquency. Even though the hearings themselves petered out after only a few sessions, the resulting fallout is felt to this day.

Marvel, then Atlas, came under scrutiny not only for content—an issue of *Strange Tales,* which had offended the subcommittee's executive director, Richard Clendenen—but also for its business structure (the subcommittee seemed determined to find something sinister in the fact that some comic book companies, Atlas included, were made up of many individually registered corporations). While no official government sanctions were ever imposed on any company—in fact, the hearings were never even completed—a direct result was the establishment of the Comics Magazine Association of America, which thereafter issued the Comics Code seal of approval for every magazine published by a member organization. Marvel's courageous decision to defy the Comics Authority guidelines and publish anti-drug stories in the early 1970s actually caused those guidelines to be amended.

Sample Comics Code seal established by the Comics Magazine Association of America.

book in order to continue with the story. So when the superheroes came into being they were twenty-one, twenty-two-page stories, and I still think this is the reason we were able to turn out more books with better quality."

Another idea was revolutionary: the now-famous "Marvel Method" of creating a story. Instead of typing out a full script and then giving it to the artist to illustrate, Lee would prepare a synopsis or simply explain the gist of the story he wanted, then leave it up to the artist to plot it out over the course of the requisite pages. Once the story was drawn out in panels, Lee, or one of his growing stable of writers, would supply the dialogue and captions. "That started just as a method of expediency, because I could only write one script at a time," Lee says, "but I found out that we actually got better stories that way, because the artists were then able to use their total imagination."

Better stories and artwork make for better magazines, but it takes something else to transform a line of comic books into an international phenomenon. In the case of Marvel, it was the ability to connect directly, almost personally, with the reader. "I tried to establish a friendly relationship between the readers and ourselves, so they didn't feel like they were just readers," notes Lee. "I wanted them to feel like they're friends and that we're all sharing a fun time together that the outside world isn't privy to." Readers were encouraged to participate in such fan clubs as the Merry Marvel Marching Society (which came with its own 45-rpm record to march to) and later, F.O.O.M., "Friends Of Ol' Marvel," which came with its own specially produced fan magazine.

The idea that the Marvel Bullpenners were as familiar as classmates was further fostered by the personal nicknames Lee devised for the stable of writers and artists, such as "Jolly" Jack Kirby (later dropped in favor of the more regal Jack "King" Kirby), "Dazzlin'" Don Heck, "Jazzy" John Romita, and in a moment of supremely hysterical hyperbole, John "Blood 'n Guts" Buscema ("Stan just happened to be a little

THE MERRY MARVEL MESSENGER

"FACE FRONT, MARVELITES"

Season's Greetings

BLASTS AND BRAVOS ON TV SUPER-HEROES

Response to our bombastic boob-tube venture have been so overwhelming the past few weeks that the Post Office is threatening to make Irv Forbush help them deliver all of your letters!

But, at least we know that somebody out there must be tuning us in – 'cause Smilin Stan hasn't been able to dig his way through last week's mail! And, by now, the letters are piled up so high in front of his door that it looks like he may be confined to his office for eternity!

Just before we went to press, though, he did send up a smoke signal to let us know that a majority of you frantic fanatics think the show is a gas. Of course, on the other hand – a lot of you have spotted a few fumblin' flaws in the show, and you should see how many *we* found, ourselves!

Just like many of you, your brain-bustin' Bullpen realizes that the animation isn't up to Walt Disney, yet–and one or two of your respective hosts may be playing up a bit much to the bubble-gum brigade–but just wait till next season! All in all, we think old Wing-Head, Fish-Face, Green Skin, Goldilocks, and Shell-Head come off pretty well in videoville!

And we're mighty glad that enough of you agree with us to make Marvel Super-Heroes a top-rated show in its time-slot in most areas of the country! ★ ★ ★

WE NEED HELP, O, TRUE BELIEVER

Clutch your MMMS membership button to your bosom – keep calm, and, above all, don't fool with your cool! 'Cause this is your chance to become an important part of our glitzy little group!

Starting right now, pussycat, the MMMS needs you! No, not as a member! If you're reading this, we've already got you hawgtied! What we need from you is news! We want you to write and tell us what's going on among the rank and file of your own cavortin' chapters!

Get the picture? Good! Now, all you have to do is send your reports to Marvel Comics Group, News Dept., 625 Madison Avenue, New York, N. Y. 10022! We'll print the best of your batty bulletins in each future issue along with the name, address and MMMS number of the reporters who submitted them.

Ready? Then rush to your typewriters and get with it! After all, we can't print the news until you've made it!

And, in case your chapter hasn't made any news lately (and we shudder at the thought), we might suggest a few worthwhile projects! You might take a green-skinned monster to the cafeteria for lunch– or you might arrange for one of your classmates to be bitten by a radio-active spider! But, if neither of those ideas grab you, why not march on city hall in your Thing

INTRODUCING: OUR NEWEST BULLPEN BOMBSHELL!

Hang loose, frantic ones – and feast your eyes on the latest labor of love from your blushin' Bullpen!

We've been promising all of you a regularly-published newsletter for a long time now–and, like the man said, here it is!

After many long hours of sleepless brain-searching, we decided that the best way to print news is in – wouldja believe a newspaper? So, we've created the Merry Marvel Messenger for MMMS members only–to keep you clued-in on all the latest happenings in and around the Marvel Madhouse!

And, that's not all. We're gonna give all you madcap marchers a chance to tell us–and all the rest of Marveldom–what's cooking with your local chapters! You send us the news, and we'll do our best to print it–right on the pages of this, your exclusive club bulletin! But, we'll tell you how to go about sending in your nutty news elsewhere in this frantic first ish!

Now, in addition to telling you what's cooking in the Bullpen, we're also gonna toss in some crazy contests, frenzied features about all the Marvel Maniacs and a gob of other goodies too numerous to mention right now! And, if any of you have ideas of things you'd like to see in the Marvel Messenger–don't hesitate, let us hear about it! Got it? Got it!

So, before you get so excited about jotting down all of your scintillatin' suggestions that you forget to read the rest of the paper, we're gonna cool it–and just tell ya to feast your eyes and enjoy! After all, we did all'a this just for you, tiger! ★ ★ ★

and Hulk sweat shirts. (Marvel T-shirts should be permissible dress for those few Marvelites who are still dwelling in the last century and haven't ordered their sweat shirts yet!) ★ ★ ★

(Above) A holiday edition of *The Merry Marvel Messenger*, one of the publications that kept fans connected.

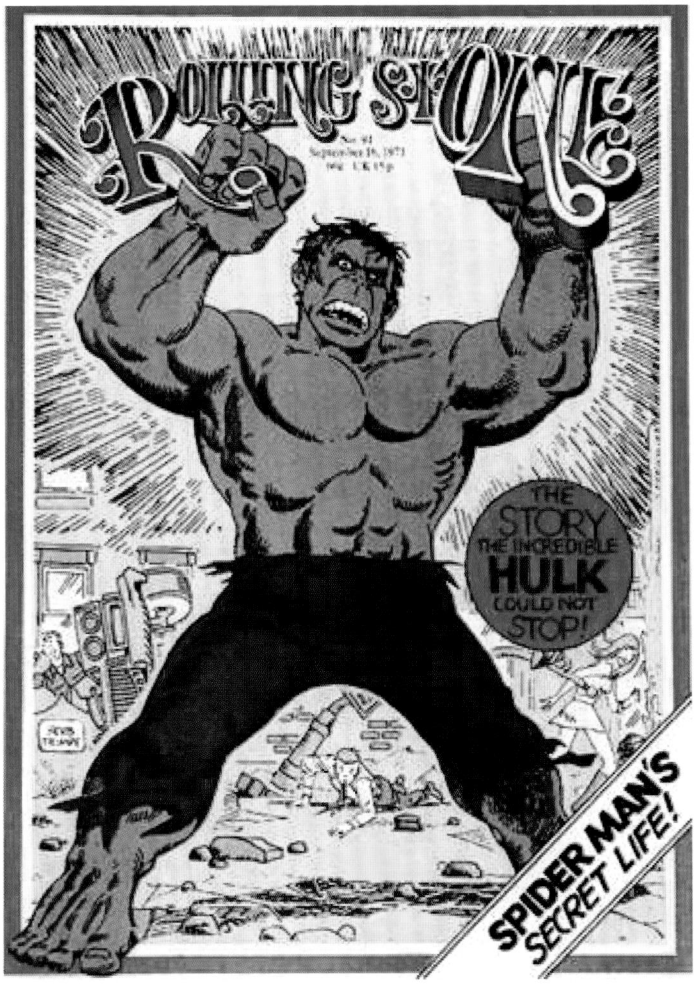
ROLLING STONE
THE STORY THE INCREDIBLE HULK COULD NOT STOP!
SPIDER MAN'S SECRET LIFE!

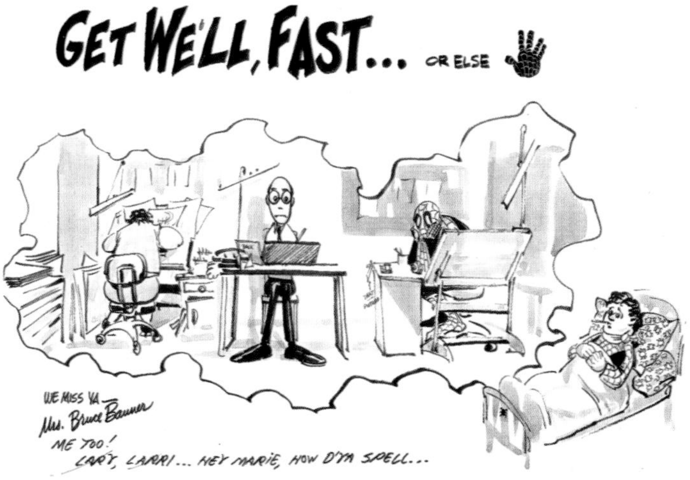
GET WELL, FAST... OR ELSE
WE MISS YA—
Mrs. Bruce Banner
ME TOO!
LARY, LARRI... HEY MARIE, HOW D'YA SPELL...

(Top) Gonzo journalism meets gamma radiation: Among the startling revelations in this *Rolling Stone* cover story from September 1971 was the truth about Stan Lee's mod style hairpiece.

(Above) The talented Marie Severin drew this homemade get-well ultimatum, which shows writer Larry Lieber and Spidey himself pining for the return of ailing John Romita. (Courtesy of John Romita)

melodramatic that day, I guess," comments Buscema, who was normally dubbed "Big John" on the title pages). By the late sixties, Marvel's way of turning outsiders into insiders made the company not just popular but increasingly hip, even to America's growing counter-culture, as was clearly demonstrated when *Rolling Stone* magazine made Marvel its cover story on September 16, 1971.

While Marvel's reader base exploded with the Big Bang, the company itself did not—at least not at first. "When I first started, it was just Stan and me in the office," notes Flo Steinberg, who served as Lee's assistant from 1963 to 1968 (and who is back with Marvel today as a proofreader). "By the time I left it was like a little bullpen, maybe four or five people." One of those in the bullpen wasn't even a bull: the talented Marie Severin, who was not only one of the most versatile artists the company had, capable of working in almost any capacity from pencil art to color styling to art direction, but also one of the very few female artists working in the male-dominated comic book industry.

Roy Thomas joined the company in 1965 as a staff writer, "but in a few days I was proofreading things and started to be referred to as 'assistant editor,'" he says. Born in Missouri in 1940, Thomas had been a comic book fan from childhood, and even co-founded one of the industry's first fanzines, *Alter-Ego,* in 1961. He began his working career as a teacher, but found more fulfillment in writing comics, first for National (a very brief stint), then for Marvel. Thomas replaced Lee as editor in chief in 1972, while Lee became the publisher. That same year, Martin Goodman, the man who started it all, retired from the company.

During the 1970s and into the '80s, the New York offices of Marvel were in an almost constant state of flux, no place more so than in the editor's chair, which became something of a musical chair in the mid-1970s. Writers Len Wein, Gerry Conway, Marv Wolfman, and Archie Goodwin all put in brief editorial stints before Jim Shooter took over the post in 1978. That same year also saw Stan Lee relocating to Los Angeles to oversee the expansion of the Marvel Universe into television and film. This kicked off a period that was one of the company's most visible, with a rash of prime-time television projects based on Marvel characters, including "Spider-Man," "The Incredible Hulk," "Dr. Strange," and "Captain America," which brought the characters (albeit in varying degrees of fidelity) to audiences that extended far beyond the reaches of comic book fandom. Spider-Man even crossed the ocean for a weekly television series produced in Japan. This media boom was further strengthened in 1980 when Marvel Productions, Ltd., was formed. Based in Los Angeles, Marvel Productions was created to develop and produce all of the company's media spin-offs, particularly the growing Marvel presence in Saturday morning animation.

However, Marvel's huge creative boom of the 1970s had not translated into a huge financial boom. That would begin in the late '80s, which was another time of change for the company. In 1987 Marvel was bought by an entertainment company called New World, and that same year Tom DeFalco took over as editor in chief, replacing Jim Shooter. Marvel's fortunes at this time were greatly improved by the success of two movies, but ironically, they were not Marvel movies.

"The Batman movie and the Teenage Mutant Ninja Turtle movie came out and helped to promote comics by bringing people into the comic book stores," explains DeFalco, who stayed in the editor's chair until 1994, at which time Bob Harras took over. "Marvel didn't have any movies coming out, so we came up with a defensive publishing plan, figuring that everybody's going to be coming into these comic book stores looking for Turtles and Batman. DC didn't do a lot of publishing behind the first Batman movie, and Turtles didn't have a lot of extra publishing either, but we got a lot of stuff out, so when people came into the comic book stores, having seen the movies, the only thing they could buy was Marvel product."

(Top) Art director John Romita and traffic manager Virginia Romita work out of a converted broom closet in Marvel's Manhattan offices, c. 1975. (Courtesy of John Romita)

(Above) Marvelites party hearty—left to right: Gene Colan, Marie Severin, John Romita, Sr., Marvel president James Galton, John Buscema, Mike Esposito (a.k.a. Mickey Dimeo), and John Tartaglione. (Courtesy of John Romita)

MARVEL ON WALL STREET

2 SPECIAL COMICS INFORMATION | APPROVED FOR ALL READERS

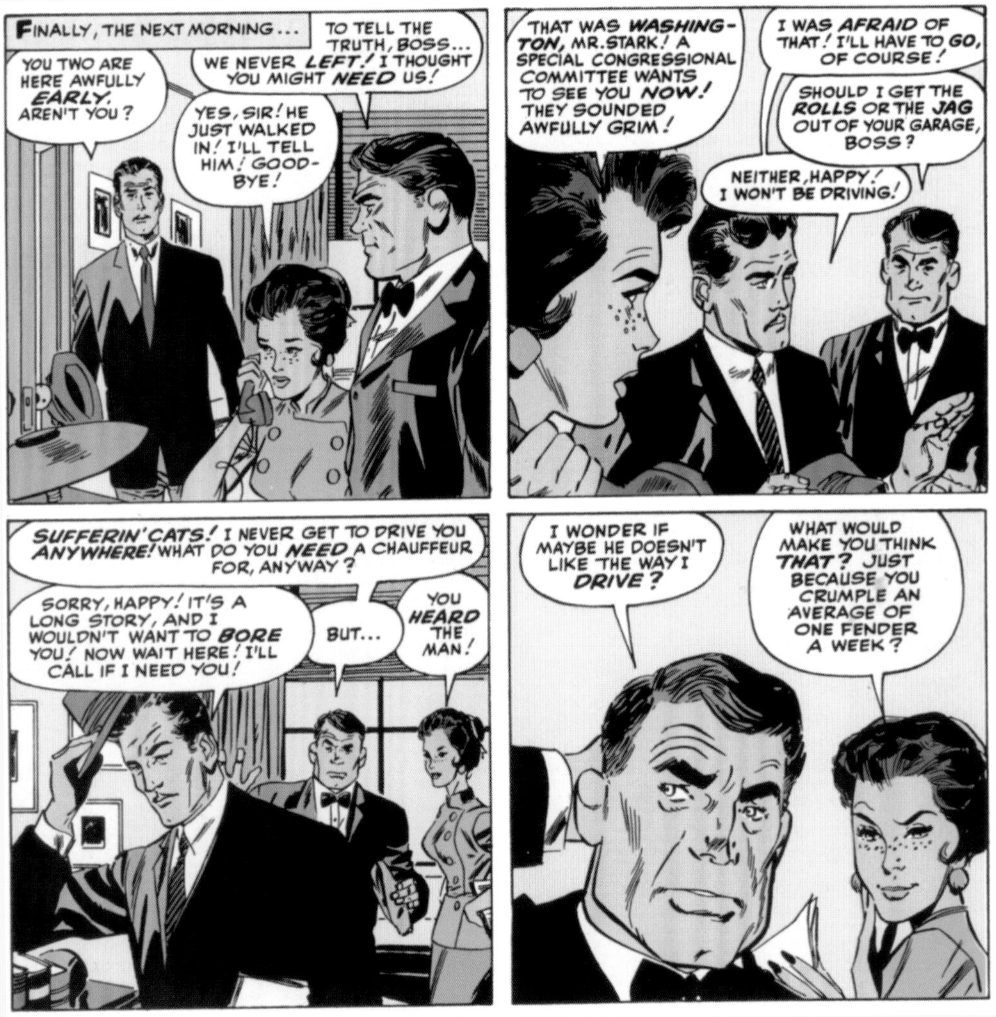
FINALLY, THE NEXT MORNING...
YOU TWO ARE HERE AWFULLY EARLY. AREN'T YOU?
TO TELL THE TRUTH, BOSS... WE NEVER LEFT! I THOUGHT YOU MIGHT NEED US!
YES, SIR! HE JUST WALKED IN! I'LL TELL HIM! GOOD-BYE!
THAT WAS WASHING-TON, MR. STARK! A SPECIAL CONGRESSIONAL COMMITTEE WANTS TO SEE YOU NOW! THEY SOUNDED AWFULLY GRIM!
I WAS AFRAID OF THAT! I'LL HAVE TO GO, OF COURSE!
SHOULD I GET THE ROLLS OR THE JAG OUT OF YOUR GARAGE, BOSS?
NEITHER, HAPPY! I WON'T BE DRIVING!
SUFFERIN' CATS! I NEVER GET TO DRIVE YOU ANYWHERE! WHAT DO YOU NEED A CHAUFFEUR FOR, ANYWAY?
SORRY, HAPPY! IT'S A LONG STORY, AND I WOULDN'T WANT TO BORE YOU! NOW WAIT HERE! I'LL CALL IF I NEED YOU!
BUT...
YOU HEARD THE MAN!
I WONDER IF MAYBE HE DOESN'T LIKE THE WAY I DRIVE?
WHAT WOULD MAKE YOU THINK THAT? JUST BECAUSE YOU CRUMPLE AN AVERAGE OF ONE FENDER A WEEK?

Tony Stark (a.k.a. Iron Man) out of costume, in his office, and representing Big Business.

Marvel Comics became big business in the 1990s due to the company's purchase by billionaire investor Ronald O. Perelman, who paid in excess of $82 million for Marvel and its assets. In 1991, for the first time in its history, the company went public when Perelman offered forty percent of Marvel for sale to investors. Under Perelman, the company also became linked to New World Productions and Toy Biz—both of which were already in his stable of holdings. Realizing the immense marketability of the characters, Perelman made licensing a top concern for the company, and as a result, Marvel's licencing revenues rose to $50 million by 1995.

But just as Stark Industries ran into previously unthinkable financial problems within the Marvel Universe, so did life imitate art in the real world. Through a confluence of over-extended investments, costly development of films that were never produced, and a downturn in the comics industry, the company went into a financial tailspin that ended with its filing for bankruptcy at the end of 1996. The company was taken over by bondholder Carl Icahn in June of 1997 and emphasis was once more put on Marvel's core businesses—the comic books, licensing, and media—which resulted in, if not a rainbow bridge to Asgard, at least the road to recovery.

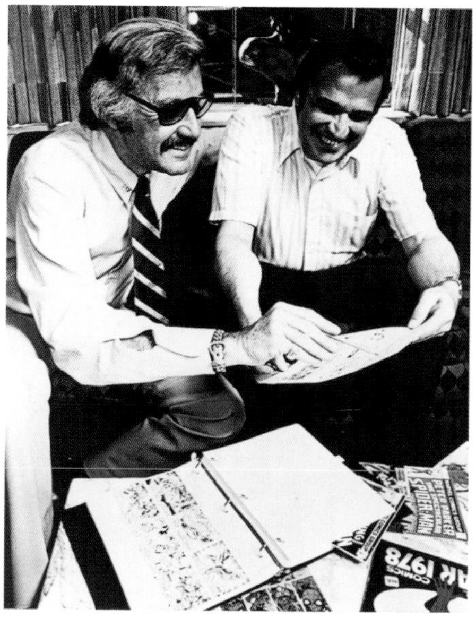

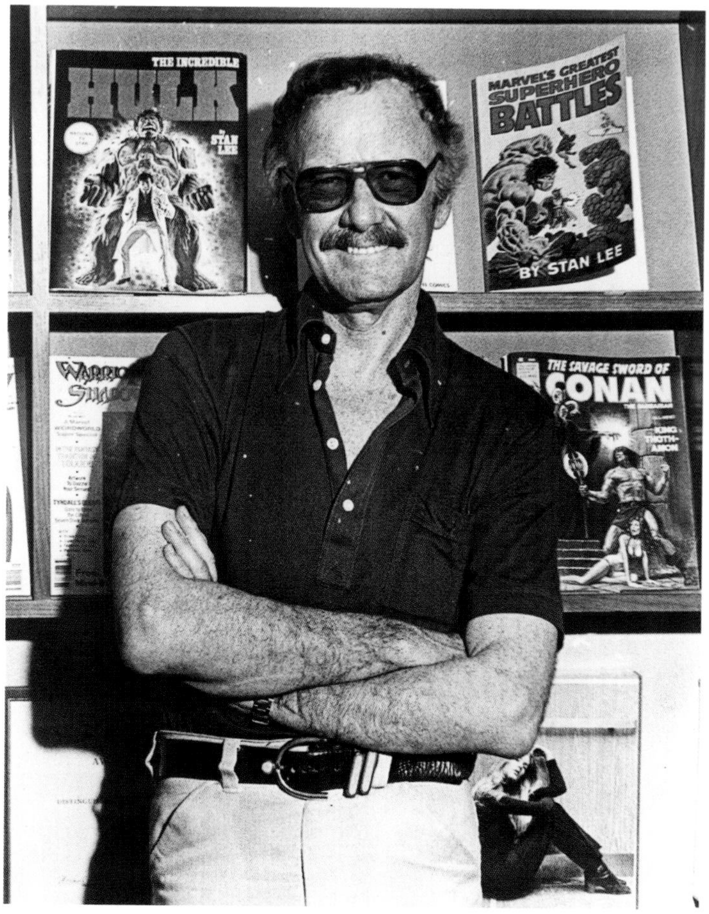
THE INCREDIBLE
HULK
MARVEL'S GREATEST
SUPERHERO
BATTLES
BY STAN LEE
THE SAVAGE SWORD OF
CONAN

(Top) Stan Lee and John Romita, Sr., from the late 1970s.

(Above) 'Nuff said.

The decade of the 1990s was one of financial ebb and flow for the comic book industry, in part because of changes in distribution outlets: specialized comic book stores had largely replaced the ubiquitous corner newsstand of old. Still, Marvel has not only survived the roller coaster ride brought by changes in the industry, it has leapt into the twenty-first century with its creativity, ambition, and influence undimmed.

To say that Marvel has revolutionized the comic book industry is to speak the obvious, but it has accomplished something even more remarkable than that: the characters inhabiting the Marvel Universe have captured not only the minds of its readers, but their hearts as well. This was driven home to John Romita, Sr., a number of years ago while working on a Spider-Man story at home. "My youngest son, who is now one of the best artists in the business, was looking over my shoulder seeing me rule up the pages, and I'm starting to draw Peter Parker, and he asks why we don't give Peter Parker an issue where everything goes right for him," Romita recalls. "And it struck me right then and there that this kid wanted Peter Parker to have a better life. I said, 'Wow, that's the grab—this kid cares about what happens to a paper character.'"

That kid still cares about Spider-Man, and continues to prove it by carrying Spider-Man into the new century. "Here I am full cycle," says John Romita, Jr. "When I was a kid I was immersed in it, and here I am a professional and doing it the same way." In fact many of the artists and writers who would come to the Marvel House of Ideas from the 1960s on were comic book lovers who grew up in the Marvel Universe. They would continue the tradition with almost unlimited imagination and style.

No one who worked on the first issue of *The Fantastic Four* forty years ago could have predicted that it was destined to change the direction of popular culture in the twentieth century. But the last panel of that first issue says it all: "And so was born 'The Fantastic Four!!' And from that moment on, the world would never again be the same!!"

THE MARVEL PRODUCTION METHOD IN THE TWENTY-FIRST CENTURY

3 SPECIAL COMICS INFORMATION | APPROVED FOR ALL READERS

As any reader can attest, the look of comic books have greatly changed over the past decade and a half. Improvements in color separation and "dot screen" printing have taken what was once an exclusively hand-crafted artform and brought it into the computer age. Whereas in the past colorists painted directly on photostats of the original artwork and were restricted to a palette of only sixty-four colors, today's colorists more often than not work on a computer that has thousands of shades and hues at its disposal, as well as the ability to create texturing and color effects, such as simulated airbrushing. The lettering process, once the most specialized skill in comics, has now also been computerized, with letterers creating fonts based on their hand lettering and digitally comping the dialogue and captions to stats of the artwork. Likewise, paste-up is done digitally.

How does this affect the artwork itself? According to Marvel editor Tom Brevoort, many artists "are a little more aware of the impact of the coloring and they leave more of a given image to be rendered by a color artist than they would have in the past." But for artist John Romita, Jr., the traditional basics of comic book storytelling remain unchanged. "It does help to have better quality in production, paper, and coloring," he says, "but if you're not a good artist or writer, it doesn't do any good."

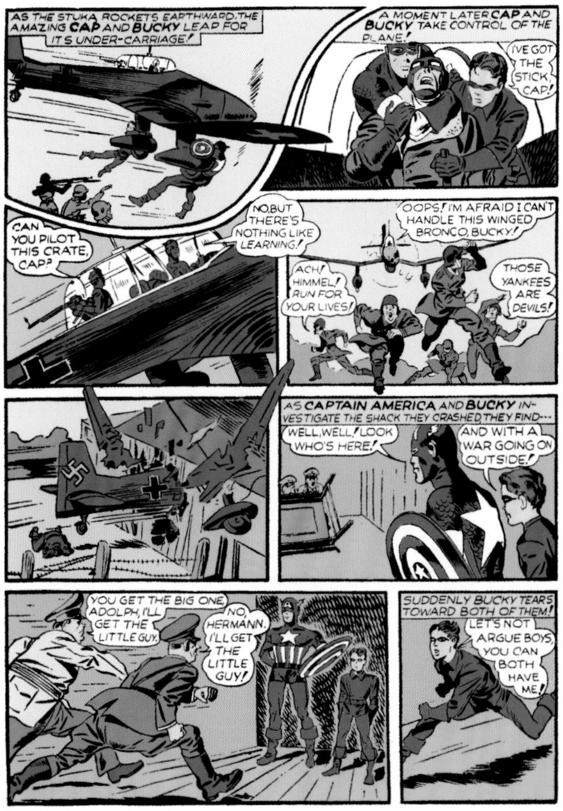
AS THE STUKA ROCKETS EARTHWARD, THE AMAZING CAP AND BUCKY LEAP FOR ITS UNDER-CARRIAGE!
A MOMENT LATER CAP AND BUCKY TAKE CONTROL OF THE PLANE!
I'VE GOT THE STICK, CAP!
CAN YOU PILOT THIS CRATE, CAP?
NO, BUT THERE'S NOTHING LIKE LEARNING!
OOPS! I'M AFRAID I CAN'T HANDLE THIS WINGED BRONCO, BUCKY!
ACH! HIMMEL! RUN FOR YOUR LIVES!
THOSE YANKEES ARE DEVILS!
AS CAPTAIN AMERICA AND BUCKY INVESTIGATE THE SHACK THEY CRASHED, THEY FIND---
WELL, WELL! LOOK WHO'S HERE!
AND WITH A WAR GOING ON OUTSIDE!
YOU GET THE BIG ONE, ADOLPH, I'LL GET THE LITTLE GUY!
NO, HERMANN, I'LL GET THE LITTLE GUY!
SUDDENLY BUCKY TEARS TOWARD BOTH OF THEM!
LET'S NOT ARGUE BOYS, YOU CAN BOTH HAVE ME!

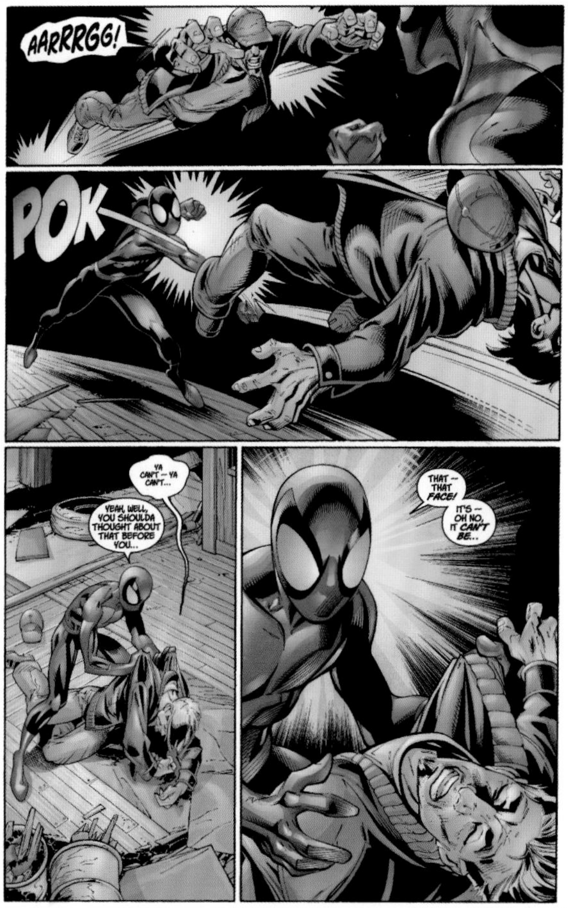
AARRRGG!
POK
YA CAN'T—YA CAN'T...
YEAH, WELL, YOU SHOULDA THOUGHT ABOUT THAT BEFORE YOU...
THAT—THAT FACE!
IT'S—OH NO, IT CAN'T BE...

Panel sizes and color styling has changed over the years, but the Marvel brand of storytelling remains the same.

THE M

NFLUEN

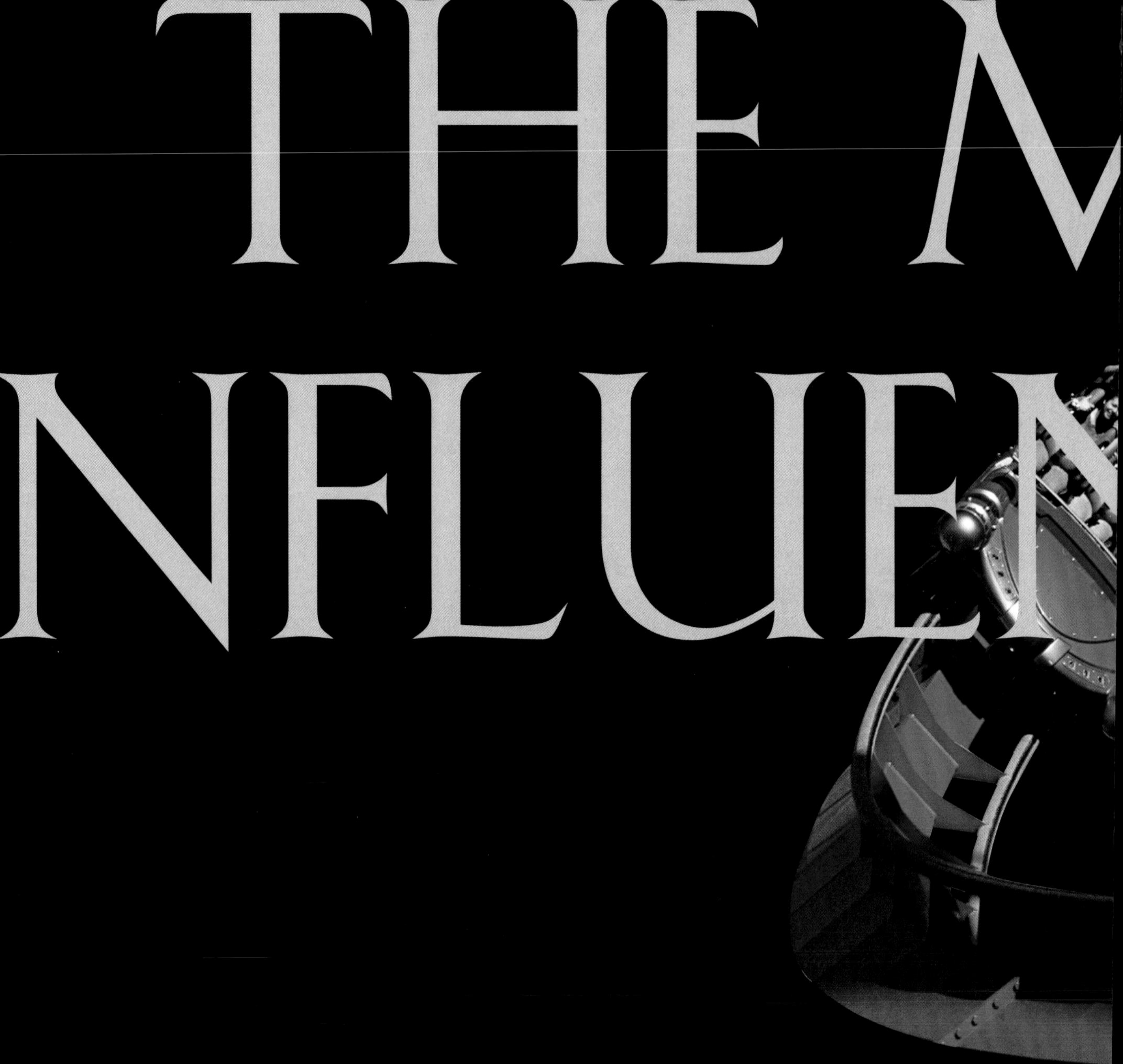

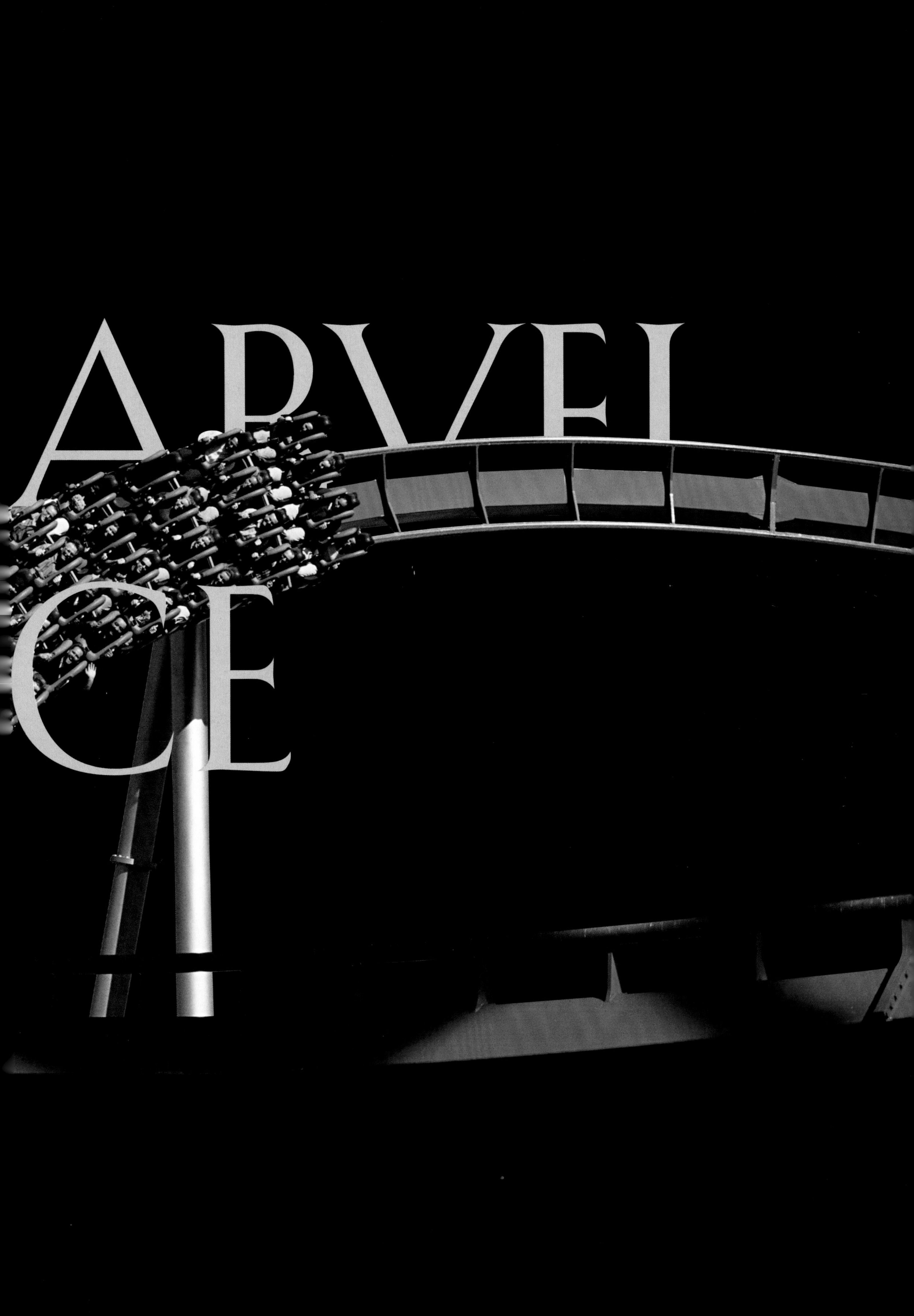
ARVEL
CE

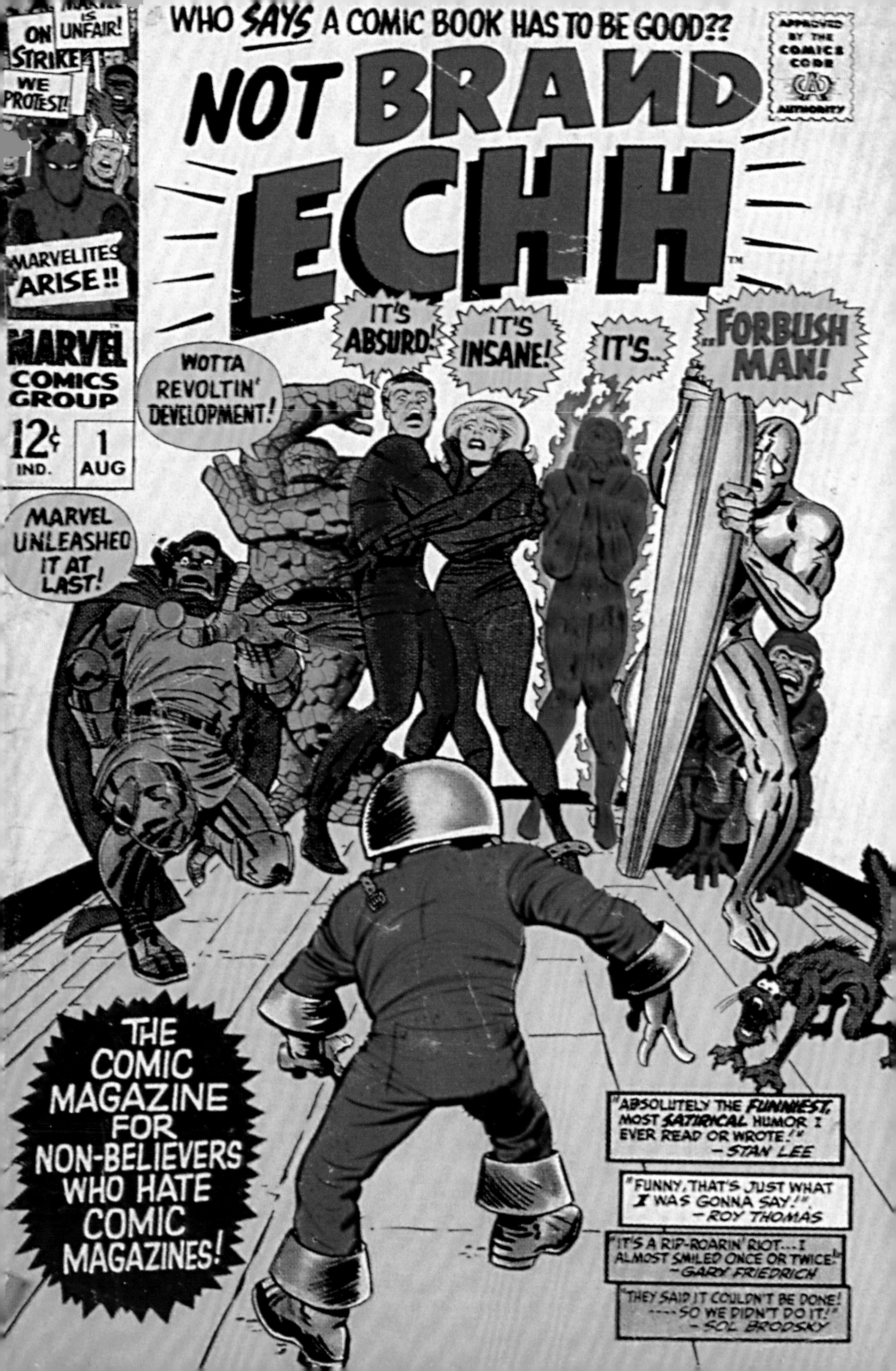
WHO SAYS A COMIC BOOK HAS TO BE GOOD??
NOT BRAND ECHH™
APPROVED BY THE COMICS CODE AUTHORITY
IS UNFAIR!
ON STRIKE
WE PROTEST!
MARVELITES ARISE!!
MARVEL COMICS GROUP
12¢ IND.
1 AUG
IT'S ABSURD!
IT'S INSANE!
IT'S...
...FORBUSH MAN!
WOTTA REVOLTIN' DEVELOPMENT!
MARVEL UNLEASHED IT AT LAST!
THE COMIC MAGAZINE FOR NON-BELIEVERS WHO HATE COMIC MAGAZINES!
"ABSOLUTELY THE FUNNIEST, MOST SATIRICAL HUMOR I EVER READ OR WROTE!" —STAN LEE
"FUNNY, THAT'S JUST WHAT I WAS GONNA SAY!" —ROY THOMAS
"IT'S A RIP-ROARIN' RIOT... I ALMOST SMILED ONCE OR TWICE." —GARY FRIEDRICH
"THEY SAID IT COULDN'T BE DONE! ----SO WE DIDN'T DO IT!" —SOL BRODSKY

THE MARVEL INFLUENCE

MARVEL AT YOUR FINGERTIPS

The Marvel Universe is everywhere. It is part of our culture, part of our heritage, even part of our language. Catch phrases like The Thing's "It's Clobberin' Time!" or "Your Friendly Neighborhood Spider-Man," and even the terse editorial comments "'Nuff said!" and "Excelsior!" have entered the lexicon. During the 1970s and '80s run of television's "The Incredible Hulk," "hulking out" became the slang term for losing control. And there is probably not a baby-boomer alive who cannot sing at least part of the theme song from the 1967 "Spider-Man" animated series.

The impact on popular culture of characters such as Spider-Man and The Hulk can be fully appreciated when one stops to realize that these are characters who have existed only since the 1960s, yet they remain in our consciousness as though they have been around forever. Evidence that the Marvel Universe touches people of all ages can easily be discerned by visiting a comic book store. Today's fan is just as liable to be a young professional with a cell phone strapped to his belt and a meeting to get to as a kid with a spiky haircut and a skateboard.

The influence of Marvel Comics resonates in many of today's leading pop culture figures, including filmmakers such as George Lucas, James Cameron, and Quentin Tarantino, all of whom are confessed Marvel fans. In the case of Lucas, the influence seems clear: without the precedents set by such mythology-rich properties as X-Men, and characters such as Phoenix, who after a largely noble history, allied with the dark side of the cosmos, could there have been *Star Wars* and such a complex villain as one-time Jedi Darth Vader?

Academy Award–winning actor and Marvel fan Nicolas Cage owes his nom de film to Marvel. The actor, who was born Nicolas Coppola (he's the nephew of filmmaker Francis Ford Coppola), took his last name from Marvel's 1970s/80s African-American hero Luke

Bullpenners get it out of their system with *Not Brand Ecch,* a short-lived self-spoofing magazine from the late 1960s.

Cage, a.k.a. Power Man. Even sports figures reflect the Marvel influence. Andre Reisen of the Kansas City Chiefs has taken as a nickname "Spider-Man," while pro wrestler Terry Hogan based his ring persona on a certain green bad/good guy, emerging as "Hulk" Hogan.

Even those who are not comic book fans are touched by the Marvel Universe every year on that most quintessentially American of holidays, Thanksgiving, when Spider-Man flies down Broadway in all his glory in the Macy's Thanksgiving Day Parade. Introduced in 1987, the balloon has become one of the hallmarks of the Macy's parade, so much so that when the parade was depicted in Steven Spielberg's 1993 animated film *We're Back: A Dinosaur's Story,* the Spidey balloon (in cartoon form) was chosen as the identifying icon.

By the same token, Marvel has come to represent the comic book industry in general in the eyes of popular media. In the 1990 motion picture *The Ambulance,* for instance, Eric Roberts plays a comic book artist who becomes involved in a mysterious medical conspiracy. The scenes of Roberts at work are set in the Marvel offices, and Stan Lee appears in the film as himself.

If imitation is truly the sincerest form of flattery, Marvel's superheroes must be blushing. The characters themselves have inspired direct parodies and/or imitations in every medium—even within the Marvel Bullpen itself. *Not Brand Echh,* a short-lived magazine that premiered in August 1967, was a broad lampoon of the company's own superheroes, perpetrated by the very wizards who made them super, including Stan Lee, Roy Thomas, Jack Kirby, and Marie Severin. Each issue bore the banner: "Who *says* a comic magazine has to be good??", while the first issue declared itself to be "the comic magazine for nonbelievers who hate comic magazines!" The magazine's recurring character was Forbush Man—a.k.a. Irving Forbush, an in-house gag character who had previously turned up in the news pages of the comic called *Bullpen Bulletins*—though it also featured the exploits of the Echhs-Men.

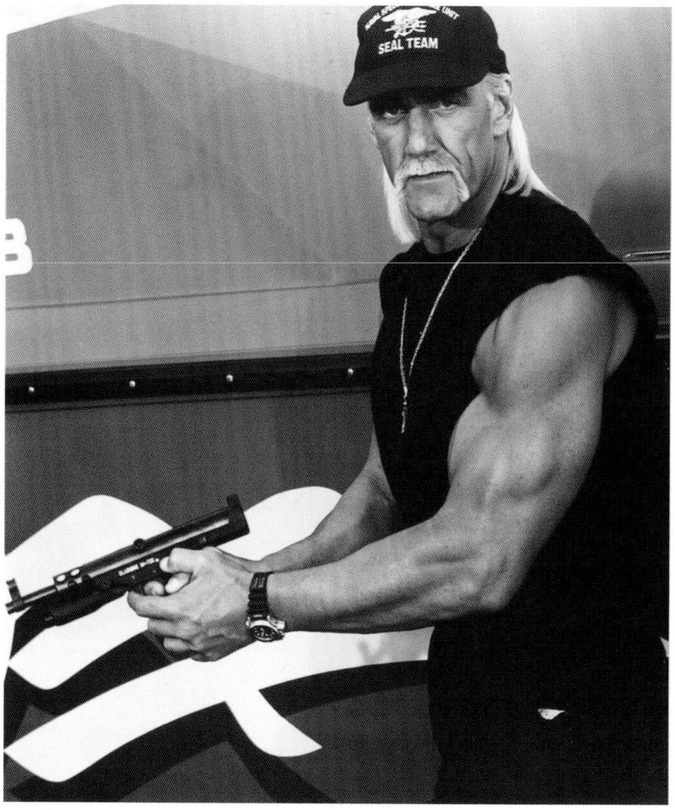
SEAL TEAM
(Top) Pro wrestler and occasional actor Terry "Hulk" Hogan took his moniker from Marvel's resident green giant.

Hmm, who are these guys supposed to be? Major Glory, The Infraggable Krunk, and The Valhallan from Cartoon Network's hit animated series "Dexter's Laboratory."

Marvel's original Avengers were also spoofed in the popular Cartoon Network series "Dexter's Laboratory." A regular feature of the show was "Justice Friends," a kind of cross between a superhero team and MTV's "Real World," in which the heroes The Infraggable Krunk, Major Glory, and The Valhallan find that saving the world is not as difficult as co-habitating peacefully. One does not even have to see the skewed character designs; all that is required is to read the names to know upon whom the three heroes were based.

The intrinsic richness and complexity of the Marvel superhero characters have enabled them to make the leap from comic books to novels. In 1978 and '79, a time when the Marvel characters were also exploding onto television screens, Pocket Books released a series of paperback novels featuring Captain America, Dr. Strange, Spider-Man, The Hulk, The Fantastic Four, and The Avengers. These books, which were alternately (in some cases jointly) written by authors Joseph Silva, William Rostler, Paul Kupperberg, and Richard S. Meyers, as well as Marvel scribes Stan Lee, Len Wein, and Marv Wolfman, represented the first major attempt to translate comic book characters into novel form. Then, in the mid 1990s, another major publishing push came as a result of the collaboration between Marvel, Byron Preiss Multimedia, and Berkeley Publishing Group. A series of illustrated novels featuring Marvel's Magnificent Seven—Spidey, The Hulk, X-Men, Generation X, Daredevil, The Fantastic Four, and Iron Man—were published as paperbacks under the Boulevard Books imprint. Many of these novels were also penned by Marvel writers, such as Lee, Peter David, Scott Lobdell, David Michelinie, Danny Fingeroth, and Eric Fein.

It is little exaggeration to say that one cannot spend time in a shopping mall without encountering the image of a Marvel character somewhere, on products as varied as school notebooks, clothing (including adult fashion), and candy dispensers. That Marvel has been a dominant force in the toy business for nearly thirty-five

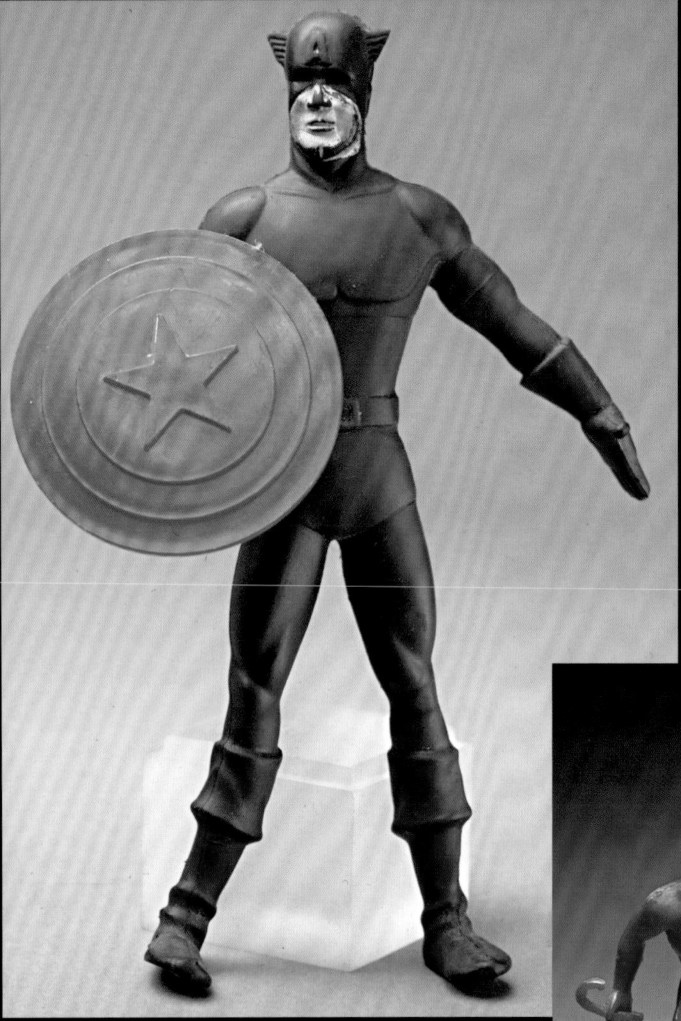

(Left) A truly classic action figure: the Captain America "bendy" figure by Lakeside from the 1960s. (Courtesy of Scott Talis, Play With This)

(Below) Dare Devil, Thor, and Incredible Hulk cut dashing figures in monochrome in this series by Marx from the 1960s. (Courtesy of Paul Levitt)

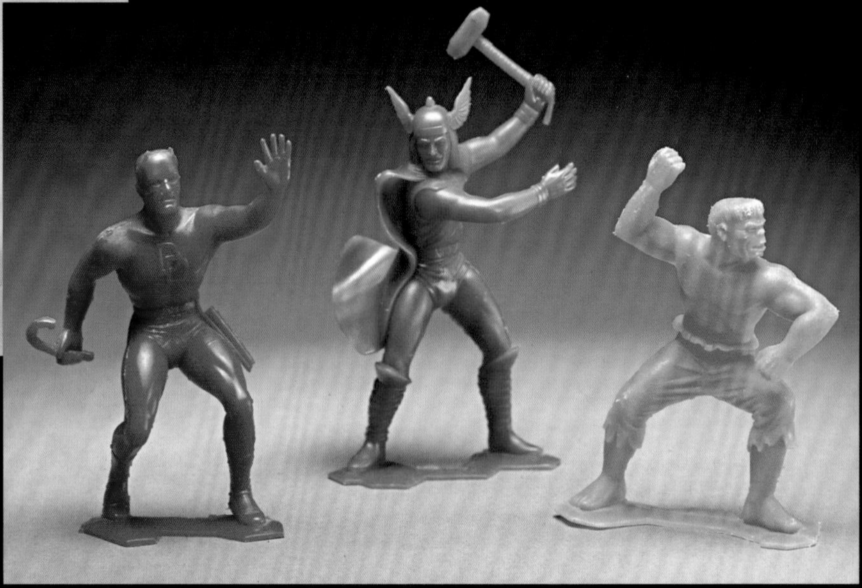

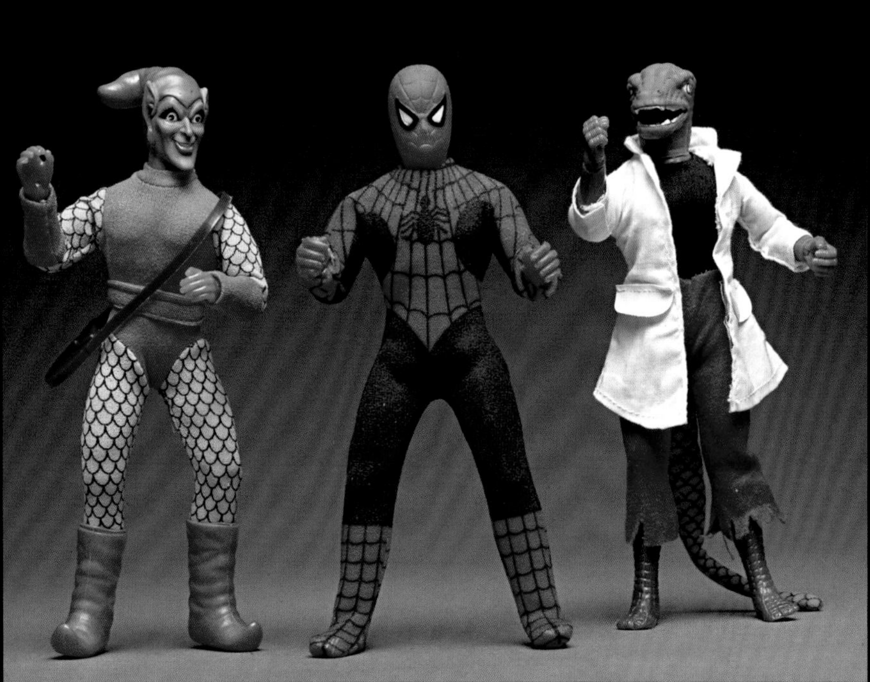

(Left) Spider-Man is flanked by his enemies—Green Goblin (left) and The Lizard—as 9-inch Mego action figures, from the 1970s. (Courtesy of Scott Talis, Play With This)

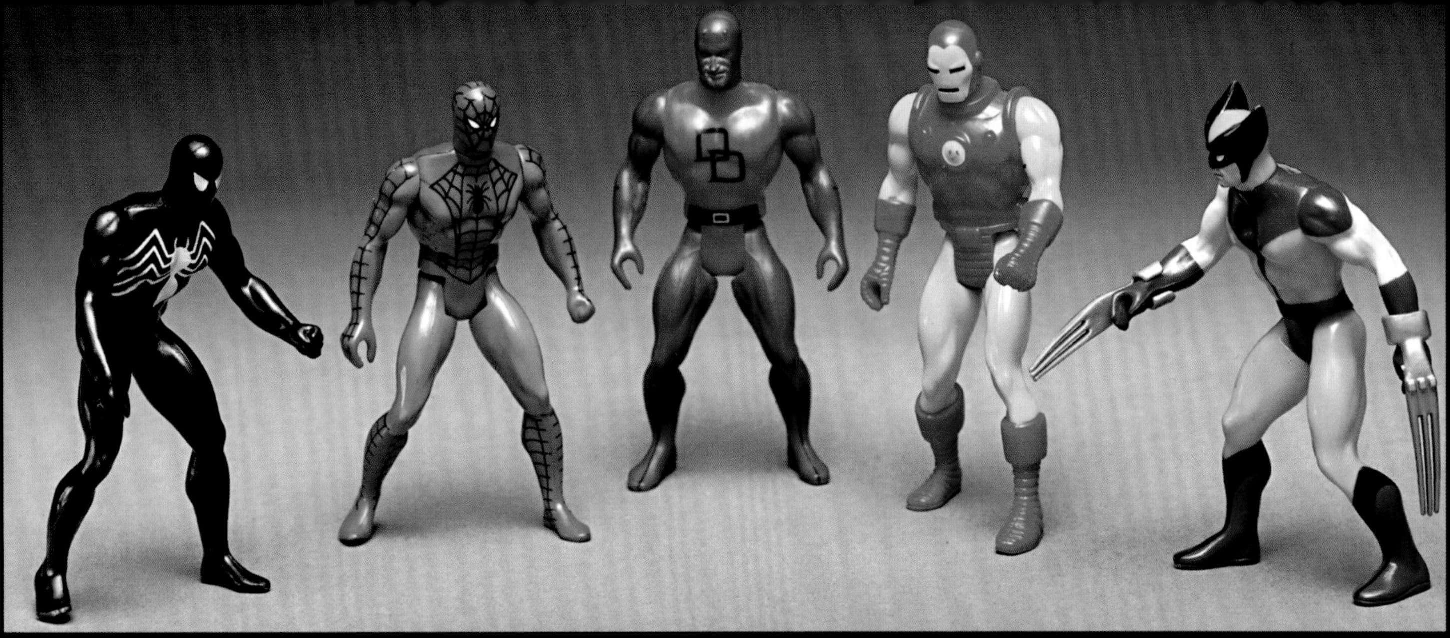

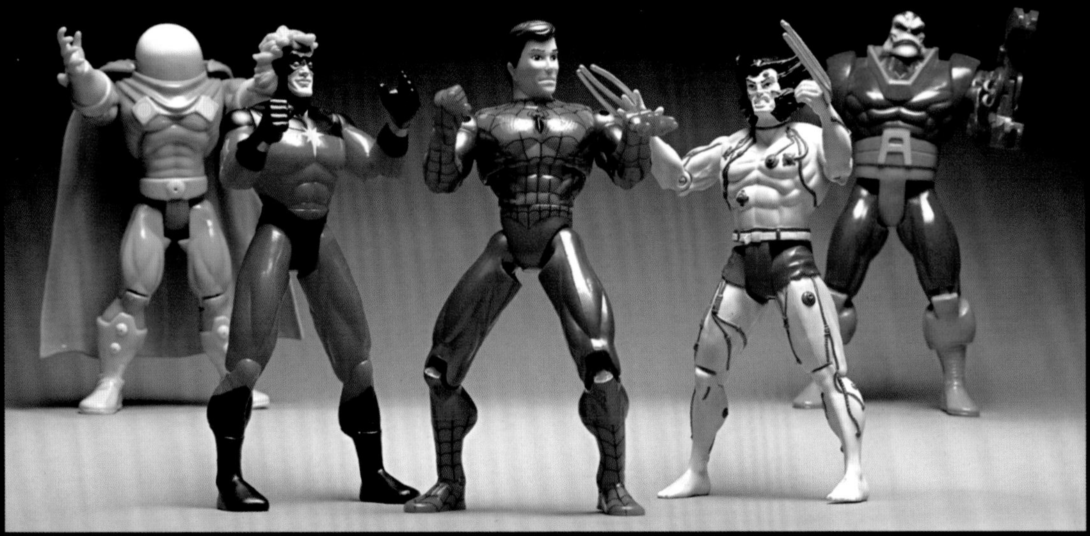

(Top) A super hero forum: figures from the 1980s Secret Wars collection by Mattel (left to right) Black Spider-Man, Spider-Man, Dare Devil, Iron Man, and Wolverine. (Courtesy of John Marshall and Scott Talis, Play With This)

(Above) The 12-inch action figures by Toy Biz included (left to right): Mysterio, Captain Marvel, Spider-Man with Peter Parker head, Wolverine, and Apocalypse. (Courtesy of Paul Levitt)

(Right)Silver Surfer strikes a familiar pose as a 9-inch action figure by Toy Biz, 1990s. (Courtesy of Paul Levitt)

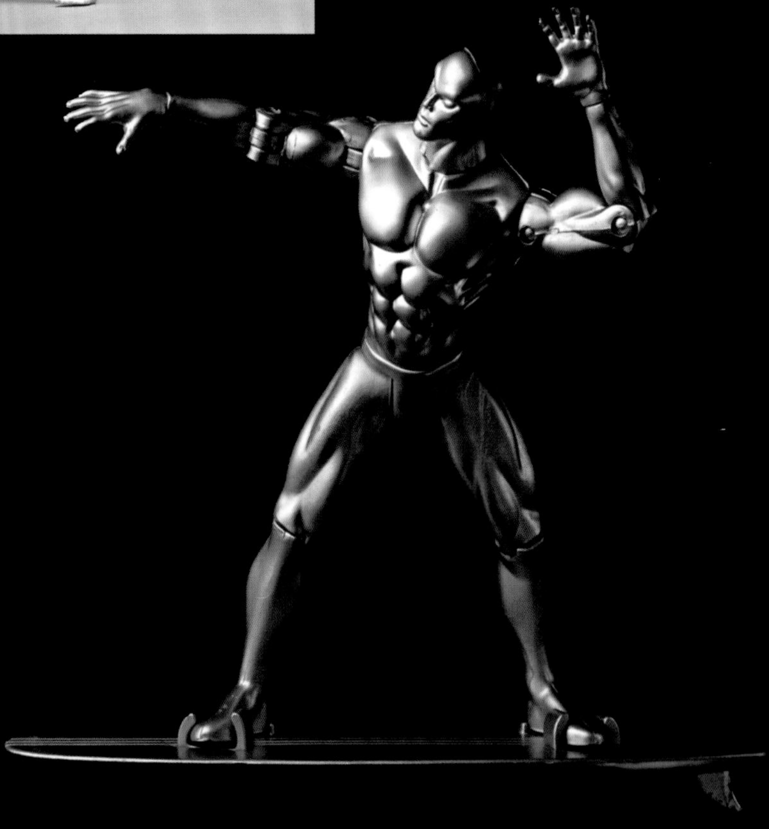

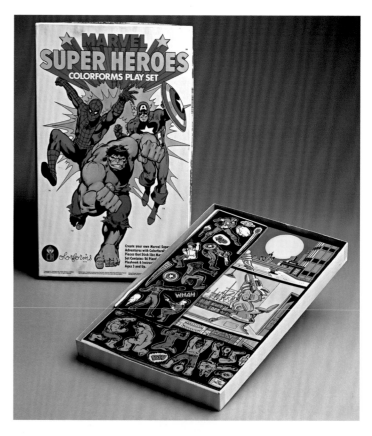

years should come as no surprise. In 1967, Marx Toys released its first line of Marvel character figures. (Spider-Man, The Hulk, Captain America, Thor, Iron Man, and Daredevil were in that first batch.) That same year also saw Milton Bradley come out with the first Marvel-related game, The Amazing Spider-Man Game. Since then literally thousands of products from roller skates to Halloween costumes to wallets have been manufactured and sold with Marvel identification.

This made for busy days for the Marvel artists, who were increasingly asked to provide product promotional artwork in addition to their comic book duties. As Marvel's former art director John Romita, Sr., recalls: "Editorial and promotion used to be at loggerheads many times and I would be caught in the middle. Promotion would come to me and say, 'We've got to get this done!' and then editorial would come to me and say, 'These people are not getting our books out!' There must have been dozens of toy-connected things I did Spider-Man adaptions on."

Ironically, as with the case of artist Neal Adams's box artwork of The Hulk and Spider-Man for Aurora's plastic model kits of the mid-1960s, the original packaging for toys is often worth more in today's collectors market than the toy itself!

In the early 1970s, Mego launched a series of very popular lines of action figures, starting with Captain America and Spider-Man, then expanding to include Iron Man, The Incredible Hulk, The Fantastic Four, Thor, and two villains, The Green Goblin and The Lizard. By the next decade, action figures would become the backbone of the toy industry and the popularity of Marvel action figures would be confirmed by a series of four-and-a-half-inch figures made by Mattel that were based on the now-classic *Secret Wars* saga from 1984. *Secret Wars* starred an honor roll of heroes—Captain America, Iron Man, Daredevil, Spider-Man, Wolverine, The X-Men, The Avengers, and The Fantastic Four—all pitted against a rogues' gallery of supervillains, including Magneto, Galactus, Doctor Doom, Doctor Octopus,

MARVEL
SUPER HEROES
COLORFORMS PLAY SET
WHAM

DR.DOOM

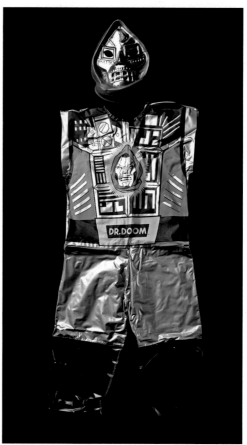

(Top) New Marvel worlds were easy to create with the Marvel Super Heroes Colorforms Play Set, 1980s. (Courtesy of Paul Levitt)

(Above)Trick or treat? Who wouldn't look good in this Dr. Doom Halloween costume? (Courtesy of Paul Levitt)

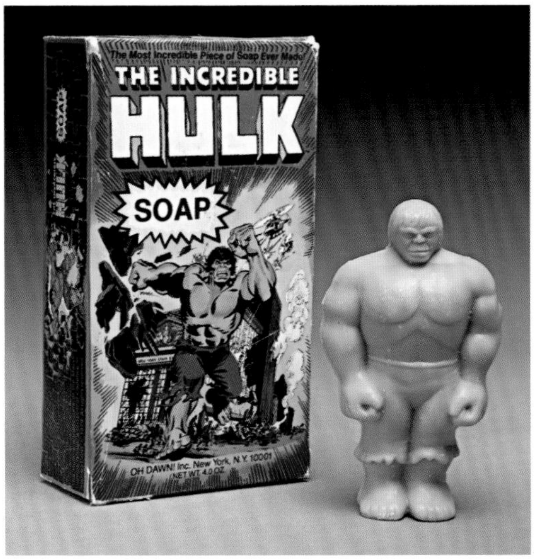
THE INCREDIBLE
HULK
SOAP

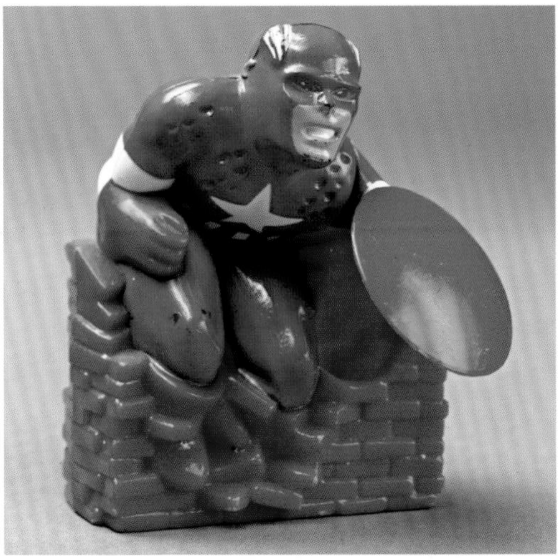

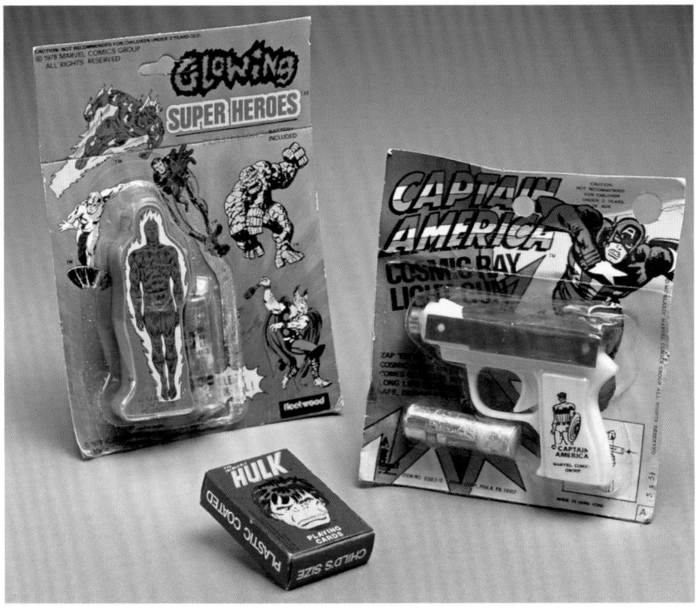
Glowing
SUPER HEROES
CAPTAIN AMERICA
HULK
PLAYING CARDS
PLASTIC COATED
CHILD'S SIZE

(Top) Get mean, green, and clean—all at once—with the Incredible Hulk soap from 1979. (Courtesy of Paul Levitt)

(Middle) The Captain America gumball dispenser delivers the goods in heroic style, 1980s. (Courtesy of Scott Talis, Play With This)

(Above)"Fun" took many different forms during the 1970s: a glowing Torch night light, Captain America Cosmic Ray light gun, and a pack of Incredible Hulk playing cards. And batteries included! (Courtesy of Paul Levitt; Captain America ray gun courtesy of John Marshall)

Baron Zemo, and the Hobgoblin. Both the good and bad guys were represented in Mego's line, which included two separate versions of Spidey, one in his traditional costume and one in the all-black suit that later spawned the supervillain Venom.

Equally popular have been "vehicle" toys, which depict the superheroes driving around in everything from a motorcycle to a rail dragster. While often fanciful (outside of The Fantastic Four's flying "Fantasticar," Silver Surfer's boogie board, and the villainous Green Goblin's jet-ski, Marvel superheroes are not known for their vehicles) these toys have certainly been plentiful. Beginning in the 1970s Corgi produced a series of sometimes whimsical Marvel-related vehicles, including a Hulkmobile and a Spiderbuggy. In 1984 toy manufacturer Buddy L came out with a line of vehicle toys tied into the *Secret Wars* saga, which included a Wolverine helicopter, a Spider-Man motorcycle, a Doctor Octopus van, and a Doctor Doom race car.

It was in 1990 that Marvel became associated with a young company called Toy Biz (which is now a sister company of Marvel Comics under the Marvel Enterprises umbrella), an association that has gone on to become one of the most successful and lucrative in the toy industry. For the toymaker, the attraction of a company like Marvel is its familiarity with consumers. "You don't necessarily need a movie or an animated show to do these characters," says JoAnn McLaughlin, Senior Vice President of Product Development for Toy Biz. "They have been established for over thirty years and have a big collector fan base."

The very first series of Marvel Superheroes action figures from Toy Biz included the usual suspects, Cap, Spidey, Hulk, and Daredevil, as well as the Silver Surfer and villains Doctor Doom and Doctor Octopus. Iron Man, Thor, The Punisher, Venom, and The Green Goblin would soon be added. But it was a new line of X-Men figures introduced in 1992 that revolutionized the action figure industry. "We introduced our X-Men action figures in great poses and built up their muscles,"

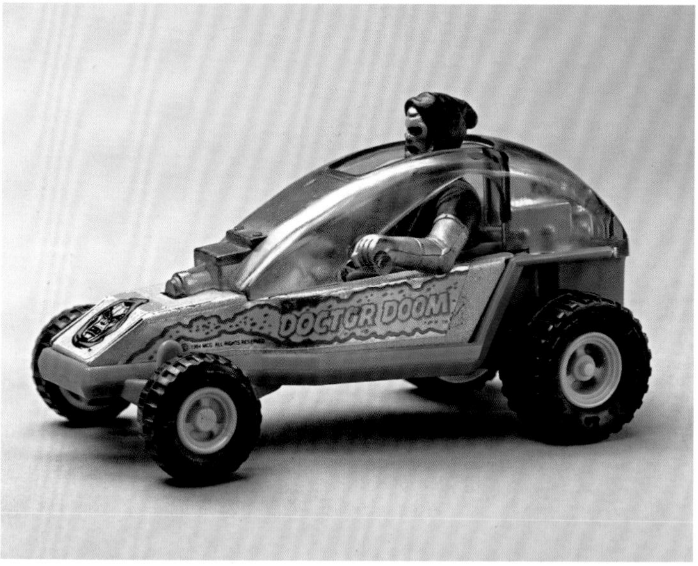
DOCTOR DOOM

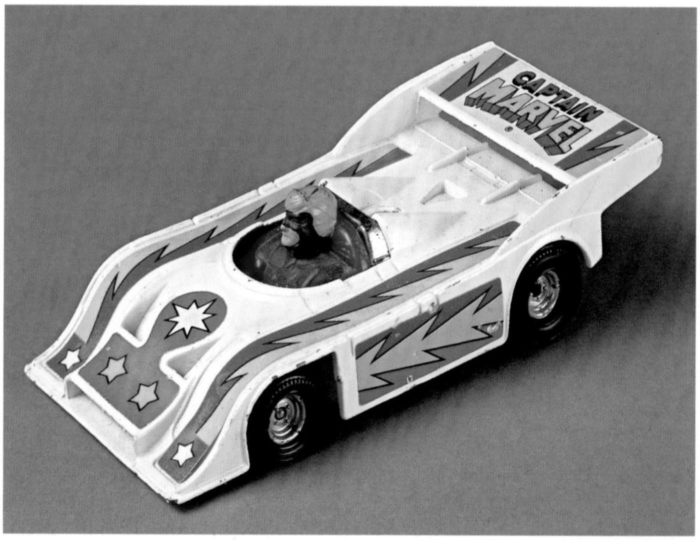
CAPTAIN MARVEL

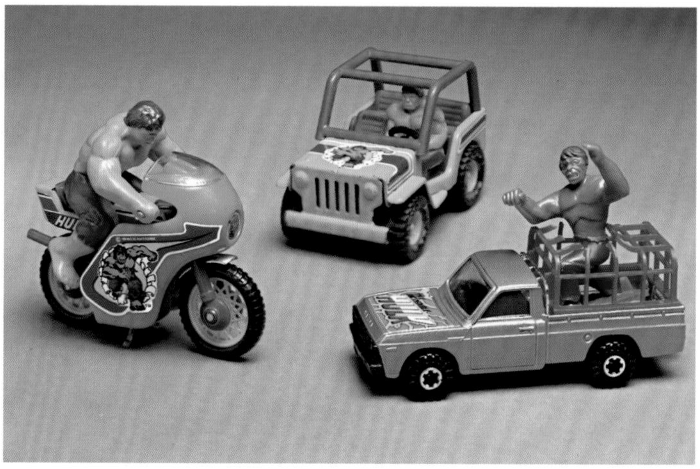

(Top) Race from the scene of the crime with Dr. Doom in his 1980s custom vehicle by Buddy L. (Courtesy of Paul Levitt)

(Middle) Race to the scene of the crime with Captain Marvel in his 1970s sports car by Corgi. (Courtesy of Paul Levitt)

(Above) "Traffic jam" takes on a whole new meaning when the Incredible Hulk is driving: Hulk Motorcycle and Jeep by Buddy L from the 1970s and the Hulk truck by Corgi from the 1980s. (Courtesy of Paul Levitt)

McLaughlin explains. "They weren't stiff-looking figures like the ones done by every other company, and previously by Toy Biz as well. Everybody started to make their action figures larger and more dynamic." In 2000, Toy Biz released a special X-Men line derived from the feature film, utilizing the likenesses of the actors and the new costumes, as well as another line related to the Kids WB animated series *X-Men: Evolution.* In addition to action figures, the company has manufactured many other Marvel-related products, such as a Spider-Man Web-blaster that shot canned string.

The explosion of video games in the late 1980s and into the '90s further revolutionized the play industry, and the Marvel characters have been translated into games covering virtually every platform from the industry's earliest days, when Atari was the brand of choice, to the present, which has seen the technical sophistication and artistry of video games increase to an amazing level. In 1998, Marvel partnered with leading software publisher Activision to produce "X-Men Academy," an arena fighting game, and a Spider-Man action/adventure game for the PlayStation console, both of which utilize 3-D computer-generated graphics. For Activision the attraction of Marvel characters was in their complexity. "Our audience is somewhat more sophisticated and somewhat more demanding of depth in character, and there is a lot of depth and complexity to the Marvel Comics characters," says Activision's Mitch Lasky, Executive Vice President, Studios. "Spider-Man, for instance, has a lot of internal conflict about what he's doing, and that is very attractive to us and our audience.

Activision's Spider-Man game allows the player to experience what it is like to climb walls and swing through the city along with Spidey as he pursues his quarry, a format that the company plans to utilize for

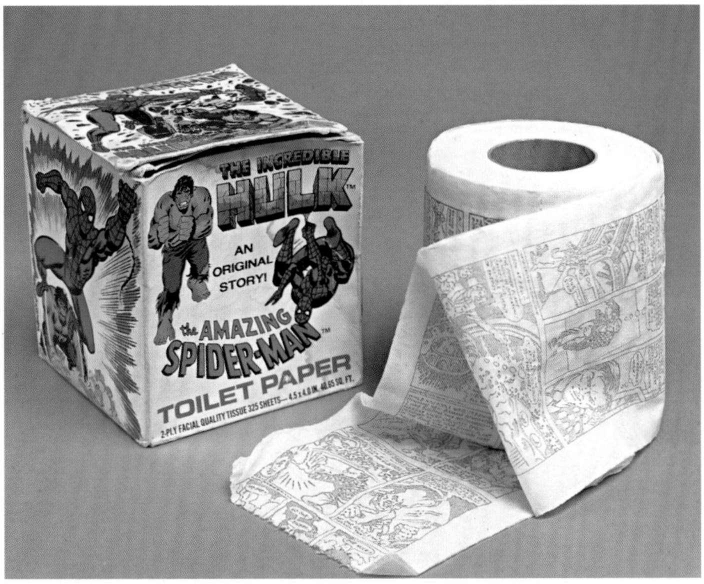
THE INCREDIBLE
HULK
AN ORIGINAL STORY!
the AMAZING
SPIDER-MAN
TOILET PAPER

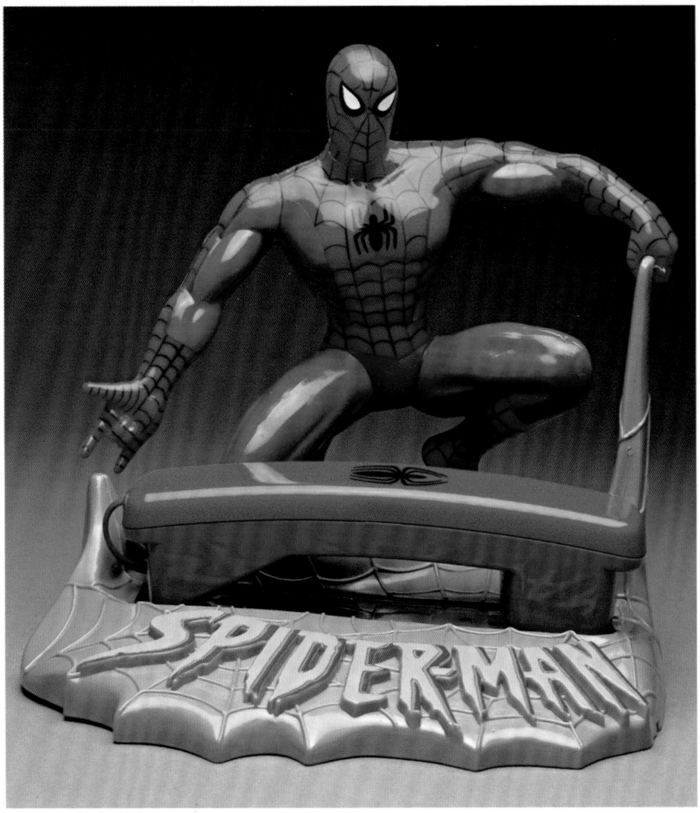
SPIDER-MAN

(Top) Multi-tasking was never easier than when The Incredible Hulk and Amazing Spider-Man toilet paper hit the stores in 1979. Each roll had an original story! (Courtesy of Paul Levitt)

(Above) A call to action was never more exciting than on the Spider-Man telephone by Rec Sound, 1994. (Courtesy of Scott Talis, Play With This)

an upcoming Blade action/adventure game and a second X-Men game.

The Marvel Universe has even extended to the recording industry, most notably with a series of records released in the mid-1970s by Power Records. These mini-albums contained anywhere from one to five adventure stories inspired by the Marvel characters, and are now sought-after collectors items. In 1977, Peter Pan Records, which specialized in children's disks, brought out a record version of Spidey Super Stories as part of an arrangement between Marvel and public television's "The Electric Company." The record jacket featured a dynamic cover drawing by John Romita, Sr., and the disk itself contained eight stories acted out by the cast of "The Electric Company." The album is notable today for another reason: one of the young, unknown performers on the show was future Academy Award–nominee Morgan Freeman.

Restaurant patrons in recent years have discovered Marvel-on-the-menu both in fast food venues—notably a campaign with the Hardees hamburger chain—and through a prototype themed restaurant called Marvel Mania, which opened in 1998 at Universal Studios City Walk in Hollywood. Created in partnership with Planet Hollywood, Marvel Mania boasted an elaborate themed decor and offered a menu that included "Doc Ock's Wok," "Defenders Tenders," "Cap's Battle Burger," and a full line of "Stanwiches." Marvel fans certainly had plenty to chew on. The Marvel Universe has even extended to the musical stage. In 1999 England's Butlins Family Resorts, a chain of "holiday camps" (British for vacation resorts), launched the production of a full-scale, Broadway-style two-act musical, *Spider-Man On Stage,* which played exclusively as part of Butlins' "Centrestage" program that offers original musicals geared to family

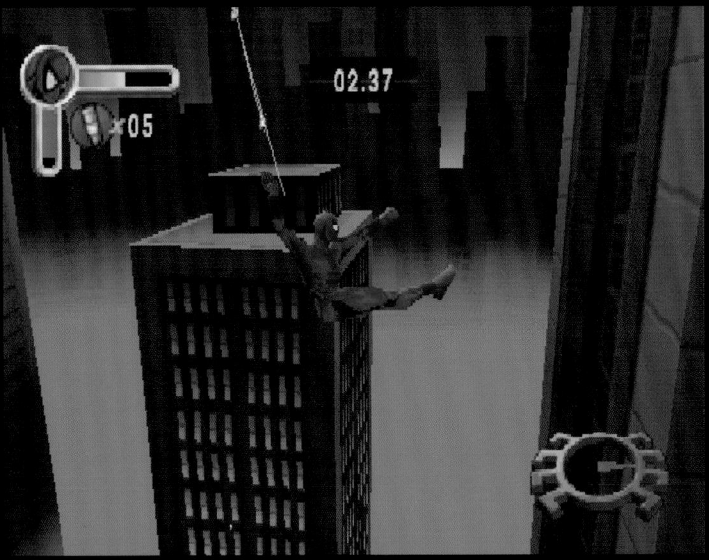
02.37
x05
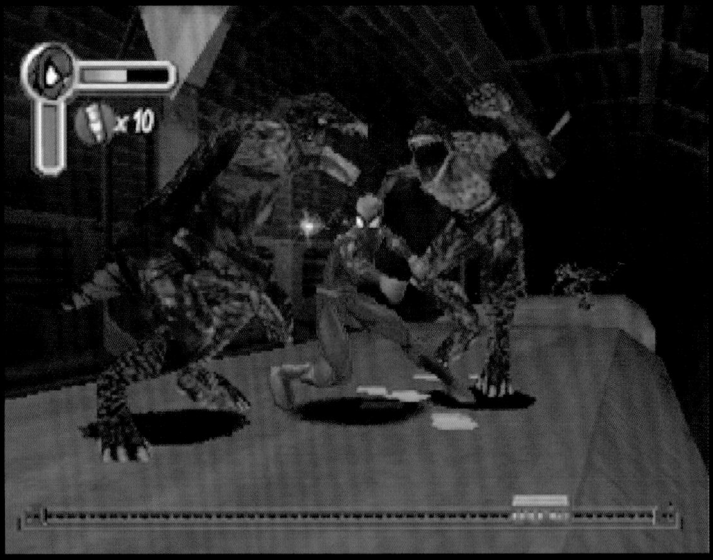
x10

Spidey swings into action in advanced computer graphics in Activision's Spider-Man video game, created for the PlayStation console.

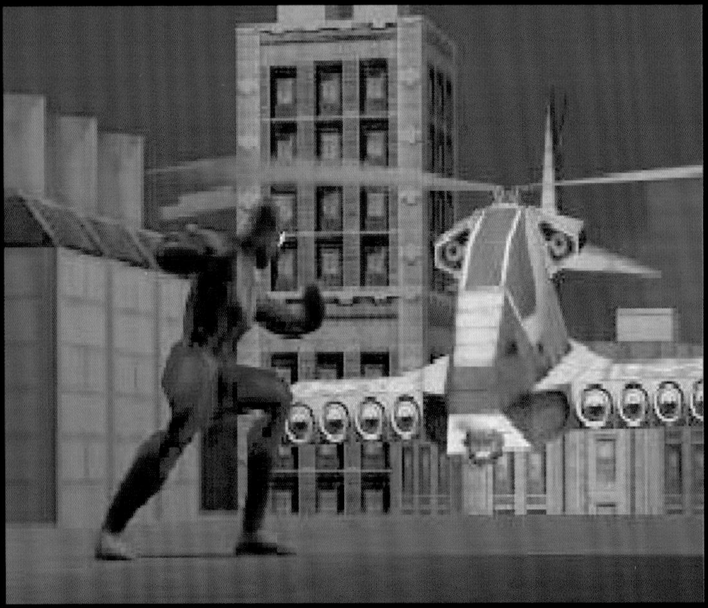
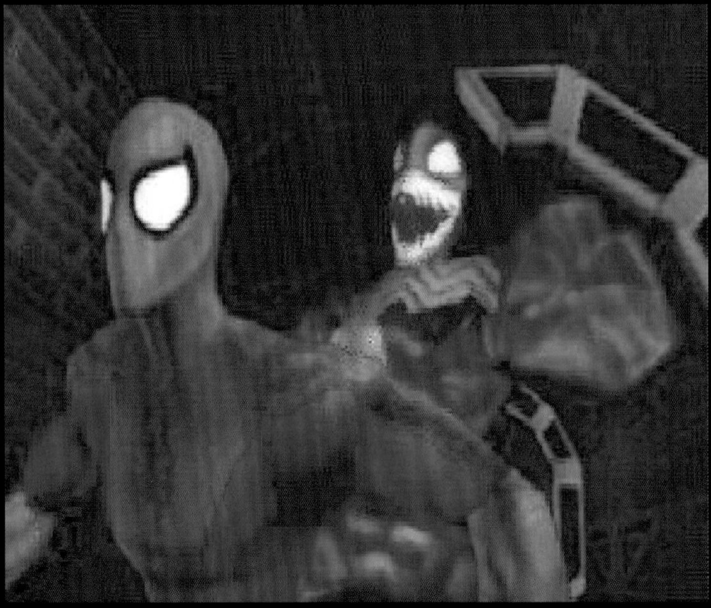

Players of Activision's Spider-Man video game get to swing and climb along with Spidey in a realistic big-city setting.

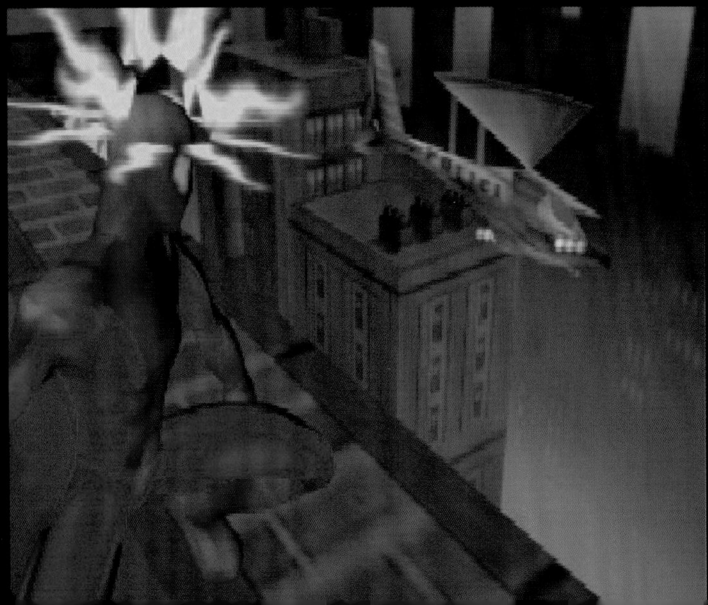
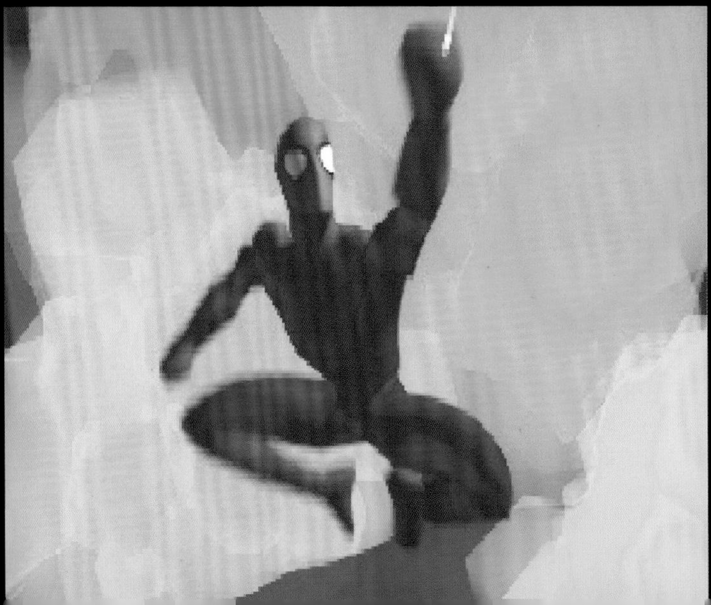

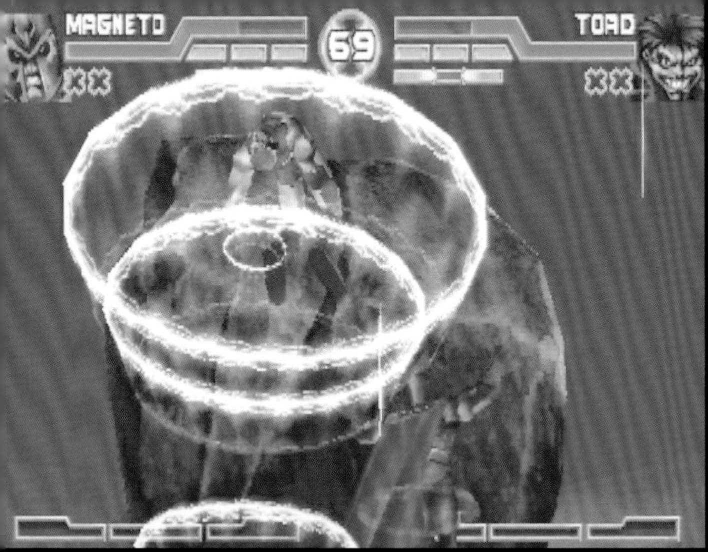
MAGNETO
69
TOAD

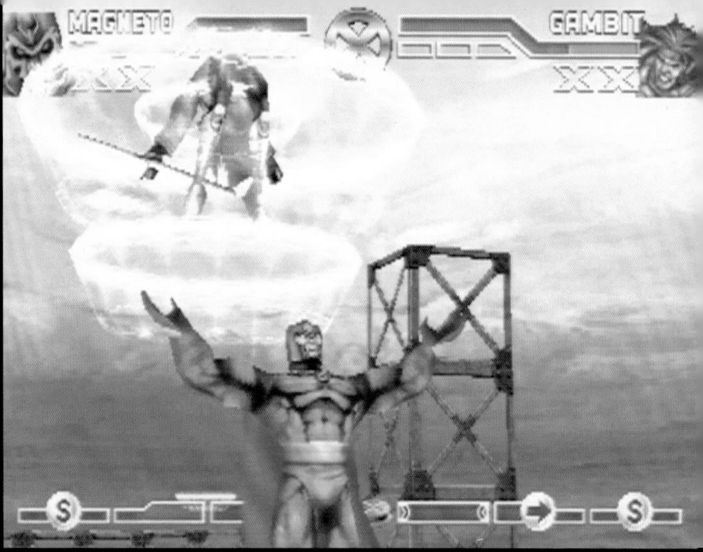
MAGNETO
GAMBIT

The many worlds and battles of the X-Men and their foes are brought to life in Activision's X-Men Mutant Academy video game, for the PlayStation console.

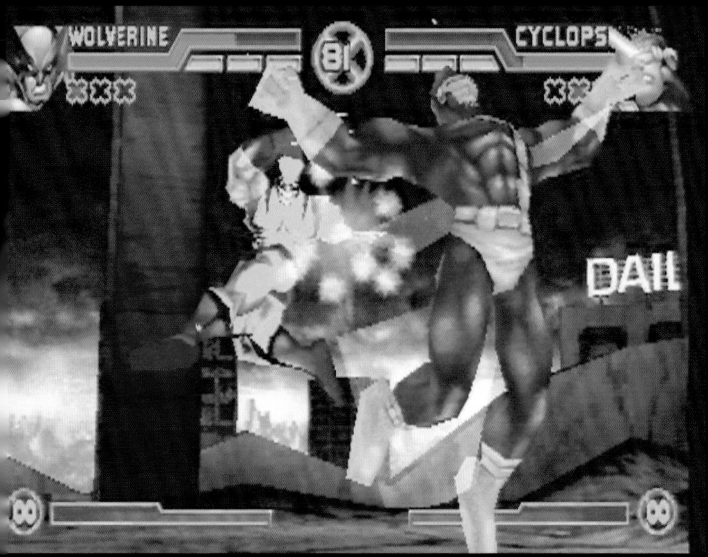
WOLVERINE
81
CYCLOPS
DAIL

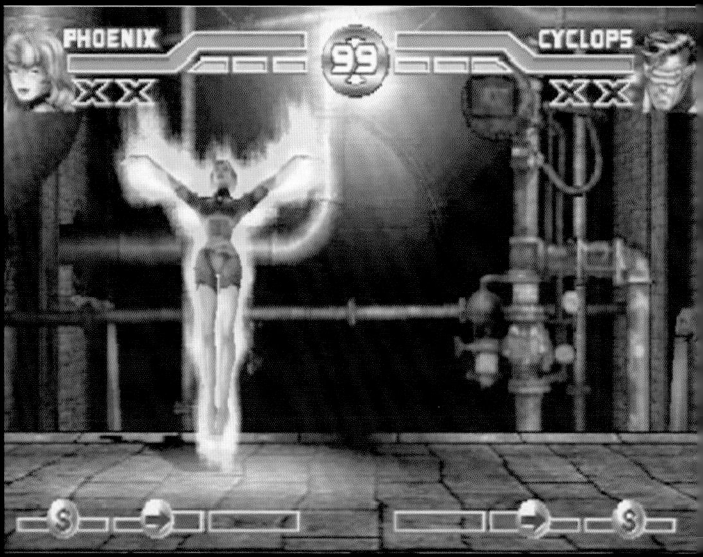
PHOENIX
99
CYCLOPS

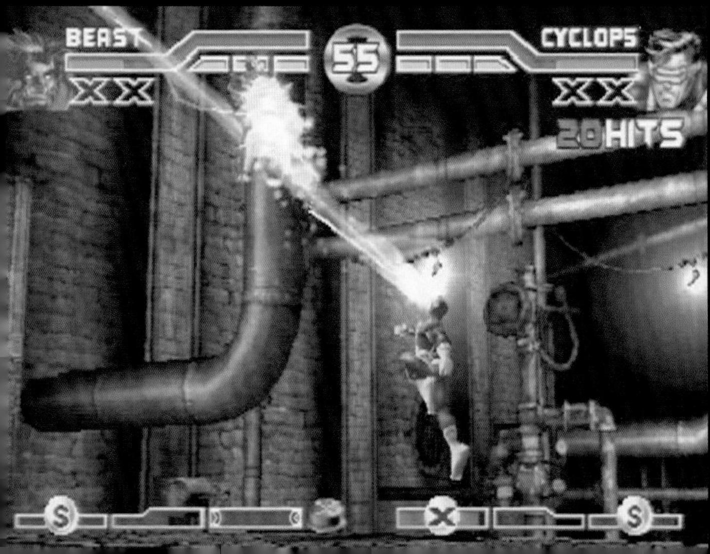
BEAST
55
CYCLOPS
20 HITS

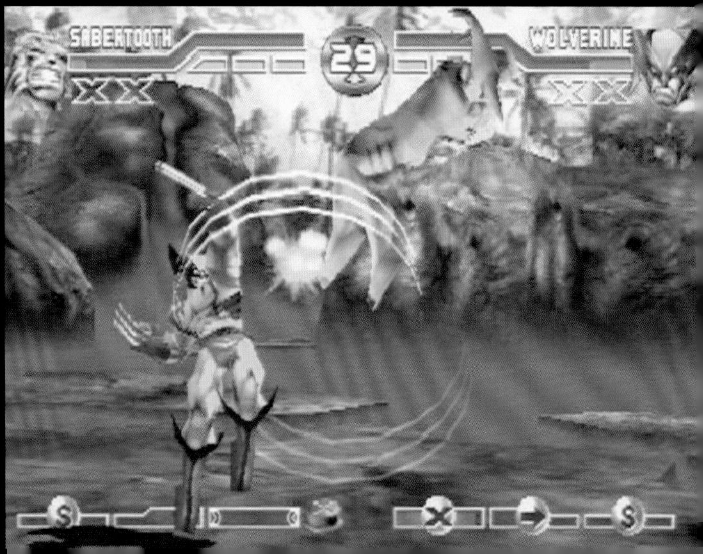
SABERTOOTH
29
WOLVERINE

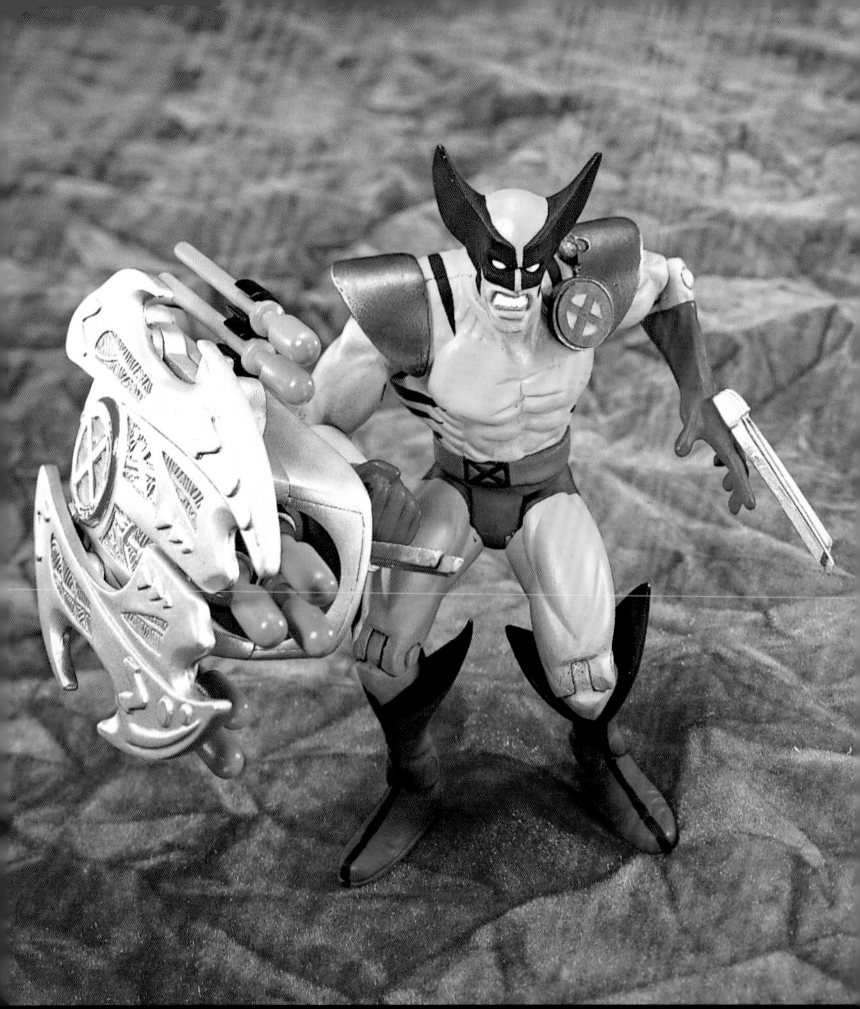

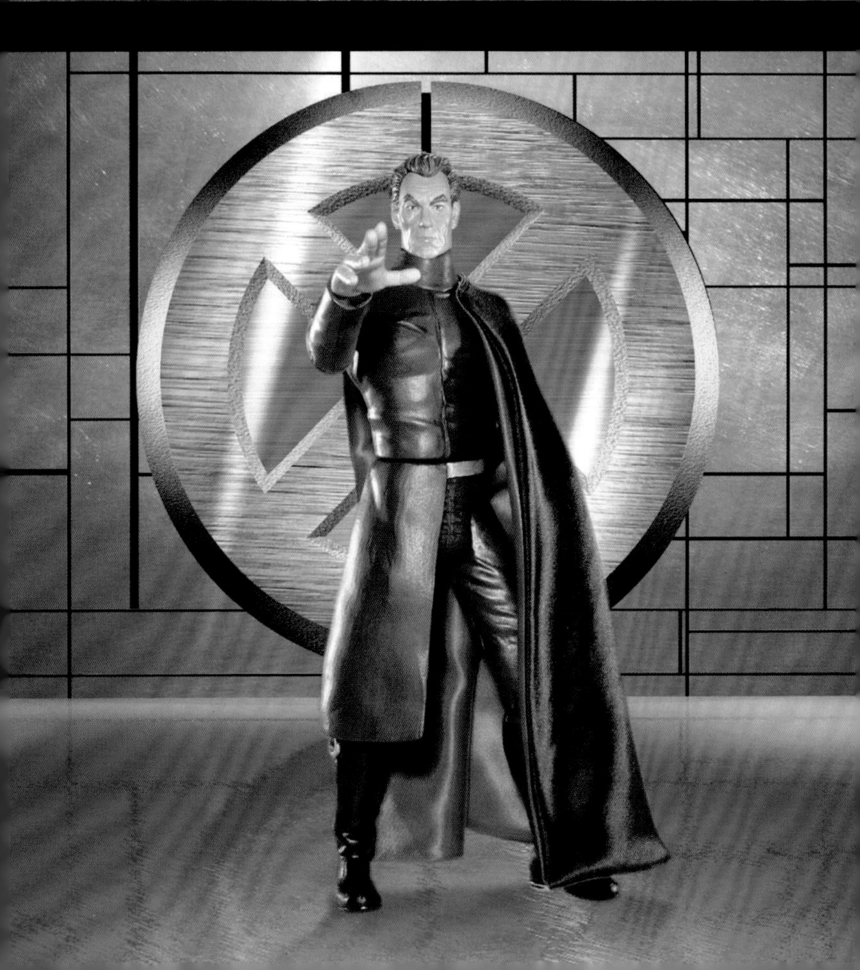

(Top) Tim Oxbrow as Peter Parker in Spidey's only legit theatrical appearance to date, *Spider-Man: On Stage,* produced in Britain.

(Above) The Lizard (Victor Pellegrino, somewhere inside the suit/puppet) explains his demented plans to Betty Brant (Natalie Regan) in *Spider-Man: On Stage.*

(Opposite top) The *X-Men* line based on the 2000 feature film put the action back into action figures, as the Wolverine and Sabretooth figures demonstrate. Wolverine also came in the slightly less ferocious Logan figure.

(Opposite bottom) A commanding 6-inch figure of Magneto in the image of actor Ian McKellen, as he appears in the film *X-Men.*

audiences. The youthful cast, lead by Tim Oxbrow as Peter Parker/Spider-Man, was made up of a mix of American and British stage, revue, pantomime, and cabaret performers.

Conceived by Patrick Nally, with music by Henry Marsh and Phil Pickett, and book and lyrics by David H. Bell (who also directed and choreographed), the musical took its lead from Spidey's debut story in *Amazing Fantasy* and covered territory that had been ignored in all previous film adaptations of the character: the murder of Peter's Uncle Ben and the guilt trip from which the teenaged superhero suffers as a result. Much of the subsequent action takes place on the campus and in the classrooms of Midtown College, where one-armed professor Dr. Curtis Connors successfully regenerates his missing arm through a science experiment. The experiment takes a turn toward disaster, however, when as a by-product of the regeneration, Connors turns into the reptilian madman The Lizard. (Connors and his scaly alter ego were, of course, staples of the comic books, appearing for the first time in *Spider-Man #6* in 1963.)

While The Lizard (represented in the play by a large puppet) is busy creating a special serum that will turn everybody in the entire world into lizard-people like himself, Spider-Man has to juggle his crimefighting with working at the *Daily Bugle* and preparing for Midtown's Big Homecoming Broadcast that will link together every high school class in America. By the show's end, he has managed to rescue Betty Brant from The Lizard's clutches, saved the entire student body of Midtown from being turned into iguanas, and even cured Dr. Connors of his reptilian affliction in time for the final reprise. With a nod in the direction of earlier teen/nostalgia-oriented rock musicals such as *Grease, Spider-Man On Stage* proved to be a lively, colorful show for the family trade.

The imagination behind Marvel cannot be confined to traditional entertainment media. Spider-Man has also lent his presence to the most technologically advanced theme park ride ever created, "The Amazing

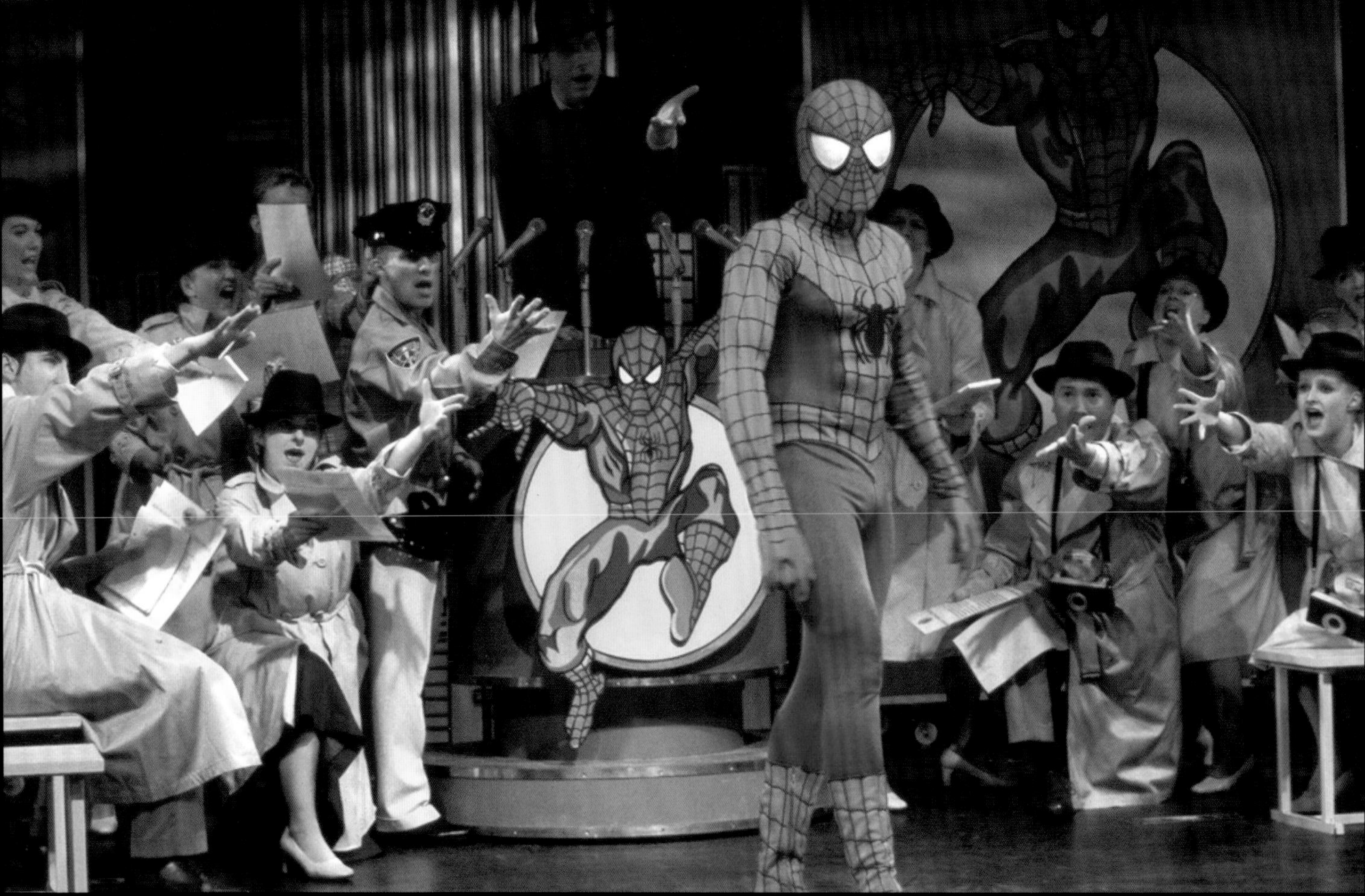

(Above) Spidey plays to the press instead of trying to catch the criminal that moments later will shoot his uncle in *Spider-Man: On Stage*.

(Opposite) What Spider-Man lost in wall climbing ability, he made up for in acrobatics, courtesy of gymnast Andrew Wareham. From Butlins' *Spider-Man: On Stage*.

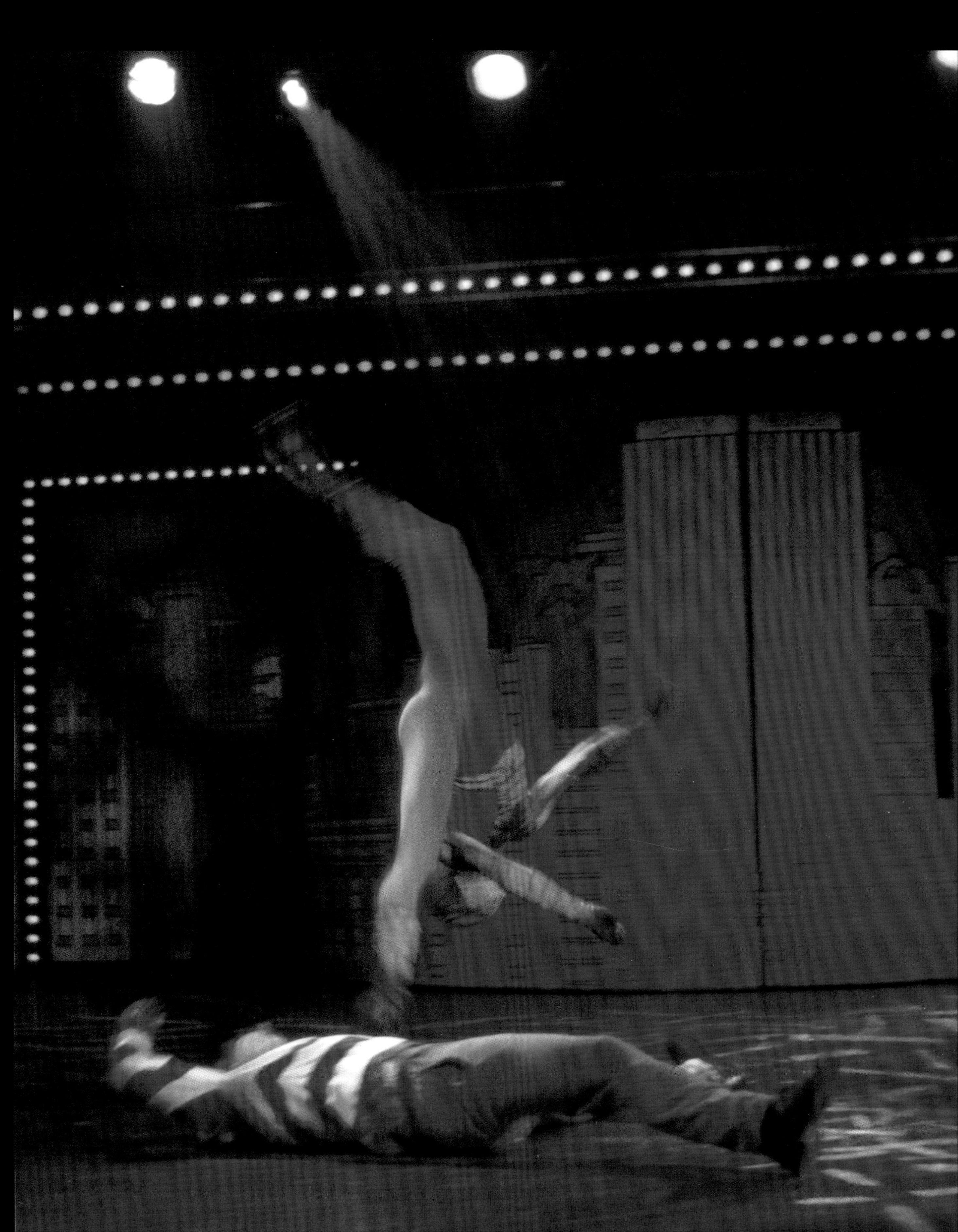

Comin' at ya! Universal Studios Escape's state-of-the-art attraction "The Amazing Adventures of Spider-Man."

Adventures of Spider-Man," built for Marvel Super Hero Island, which is one part of Universal Studios Escape's Islands of Adventure theme park in Orlando, Florida.

How does one translate a comic book hero into a state-of-the-art theme park attraction? "When we decided to partner with Marvel we took a hard look at who some of the iconic characters were and we started thinking about the best way to deliver the story, the character, the feeling of these different characters," says Scott Trowbridge, a producer for Universal Creative, which designed the attraction. "For Spider-Man we felt it should probably be a pretty emersive adventure." "The Amazing Adventures of Spider-Man" combines every known dimension as ride vehicles moving in excess of 60 mph soar through sets representing the streets of Manhattan and interact with action sequences filmed in stereoscopic 3-D, projected by twenty-five large format projectors and a host of smaller ones. The effect is to literally place the guest in the middle of Spidey's world by appealing to all the senses. "When Spider-Man jumps

"The Incredible Hulk Coaster" is part of Marvel Superhero Island at Universal Studios Escape's "Islands of Adventure" in Orlando.

next to you, you can feel him," says Trowbridge. "When Doc Ock blasts you with a flame thrower, you can feel the heat."

The attraction's storyline spotlights the web-spinner's confrontations with the nefarious "Sinister Syndicate," which is made up of Doctor Octopus, the Hobgoblin, Hydro Man, Electro, and Scream, all of whom have united to steal the Statue of Liberty! At one point, attraction guests are "levitated" by Doc Ock's anti-gravity device—in reality, they are shot up to a height of four-hundred feet then plummet back down again in darkness. Even before boarding the ride cars, though, guests are indoctrinated into the world of Spider-Man and Peter Parker through a queue story that sets up the ride and offers a diversion to keep people entertained while waiting in line. In this pre-show, guests enter past the guard shack of the *Daily Bugle* offices and make their way to "J. Jonah Jameson Park," a trumped-up monument to the ego of Peter's employer, where discarded newspapers familiarize the waiting crowd with the story behind the Sinister Syndicate, eventually passing through the newsroom of the *Bugle,* where they are deputized by Jameson as reporters and sent on a wild ride in order to get the story.

Visceral experiences are provided by Marvel Super Hero Island's two other themed attractions, "The Incredible Hulk Coaster" and "Doctor Doom's Fearfall." "The Hulk Coaster" is a massive, bright green thrill ride that renders its riders literally weightless as they race up a 150-foot tunnel at G-force speed ("G" here standing for *Gamma,* of course) and turns them upside-down 110 feet in the air. "For the Hulk, we pretty quickly latched onto the idea that it should be a very physical experience, a kind of out-of-control, driving, primeval experience similar to what it would be like to be The Hulk," says Trowbridge.

"Doctor Doom's Fearfall," which consists of twin two-hundred-foot towers, was designed with a slightly tongue-in-cheek storyline that has the masked menace creating the ultimate weapon, one powered by human fear. In order to obtain that fear, he subjects his guests to a 3 G-force launch to the top of one of the towers, an experience followed by a faster-than-gravity fall back down to the bottom. Whatever the outcome of Doom's previous attempted crimes against humanity, this time it appears he has gotten his wish!

It almost goes without saying that the Marvel Universe has expanded into cyberspace. Marvel.com offers original online comics, featuring such popular characters as Wolverine and Nick Fury, original animated films, such as The Secret Adventures of Captain America (which is presented by a cartoon Stan Lee!), created through Flash animation, and even a Marvel online radio channel.

How much more can the Marvel Universe expand? As with the real universe, the boundaries are limitless, though one thing can be stated with certainty: at the dawn of the twenty-first century, at least, contact with the Marvel Universe in one form or another has become as commonplace as sunshine.

Even the towers of "Doctor Doom's Fearfall," an attraction at Universal Studios Escape's "Islands of Adventure" in Florida, look ominous.

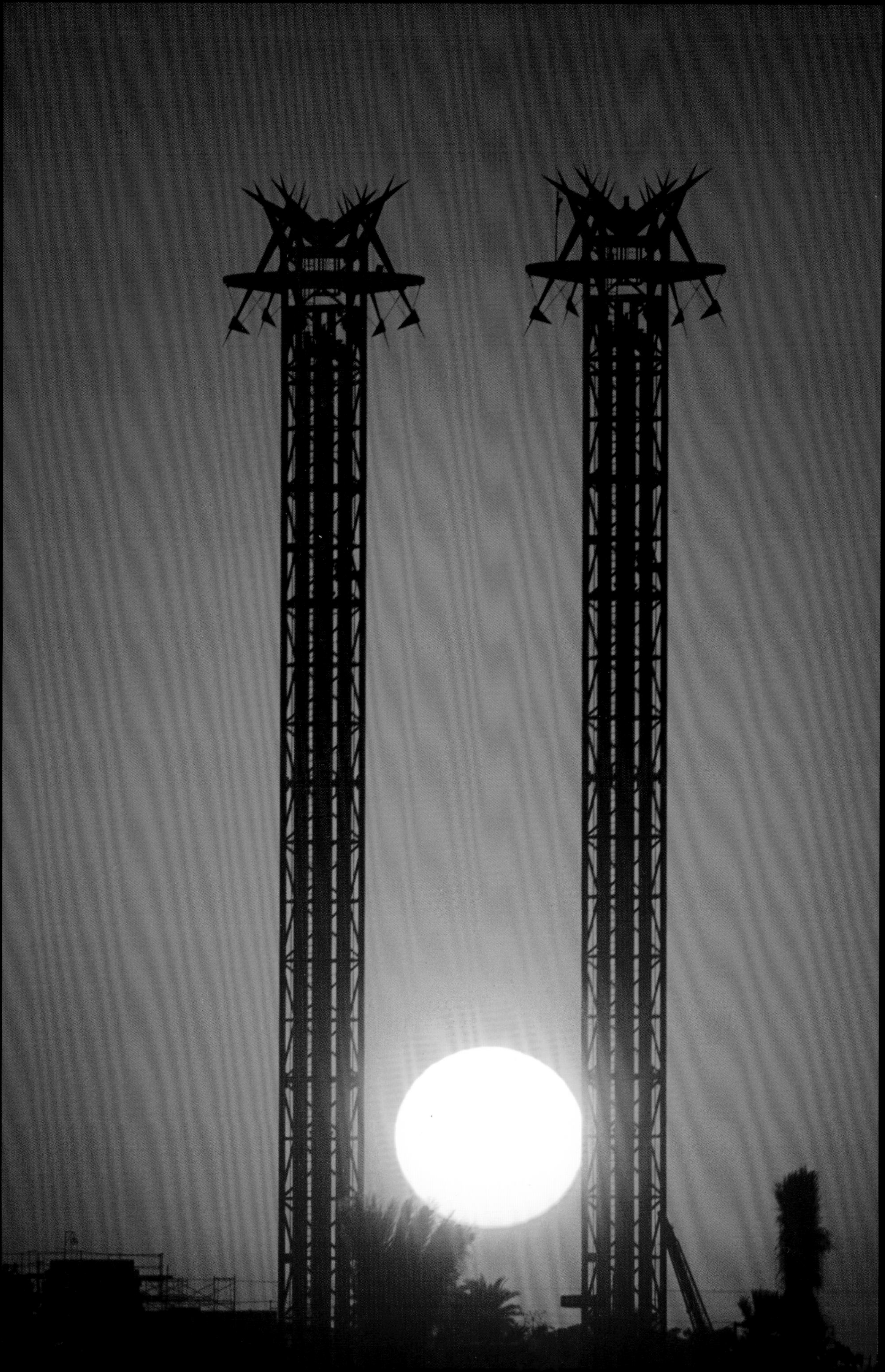

CAPTAI

A

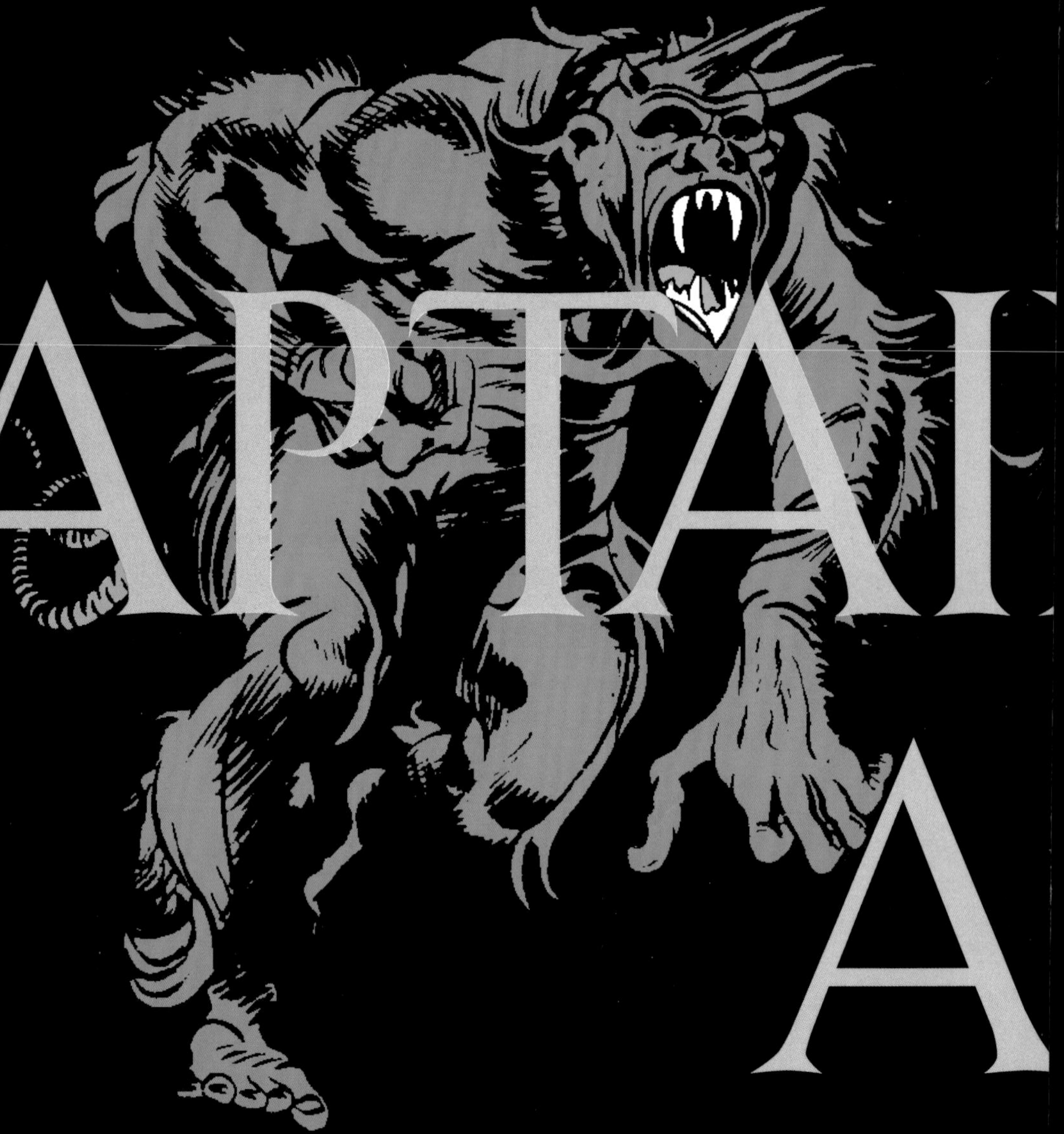

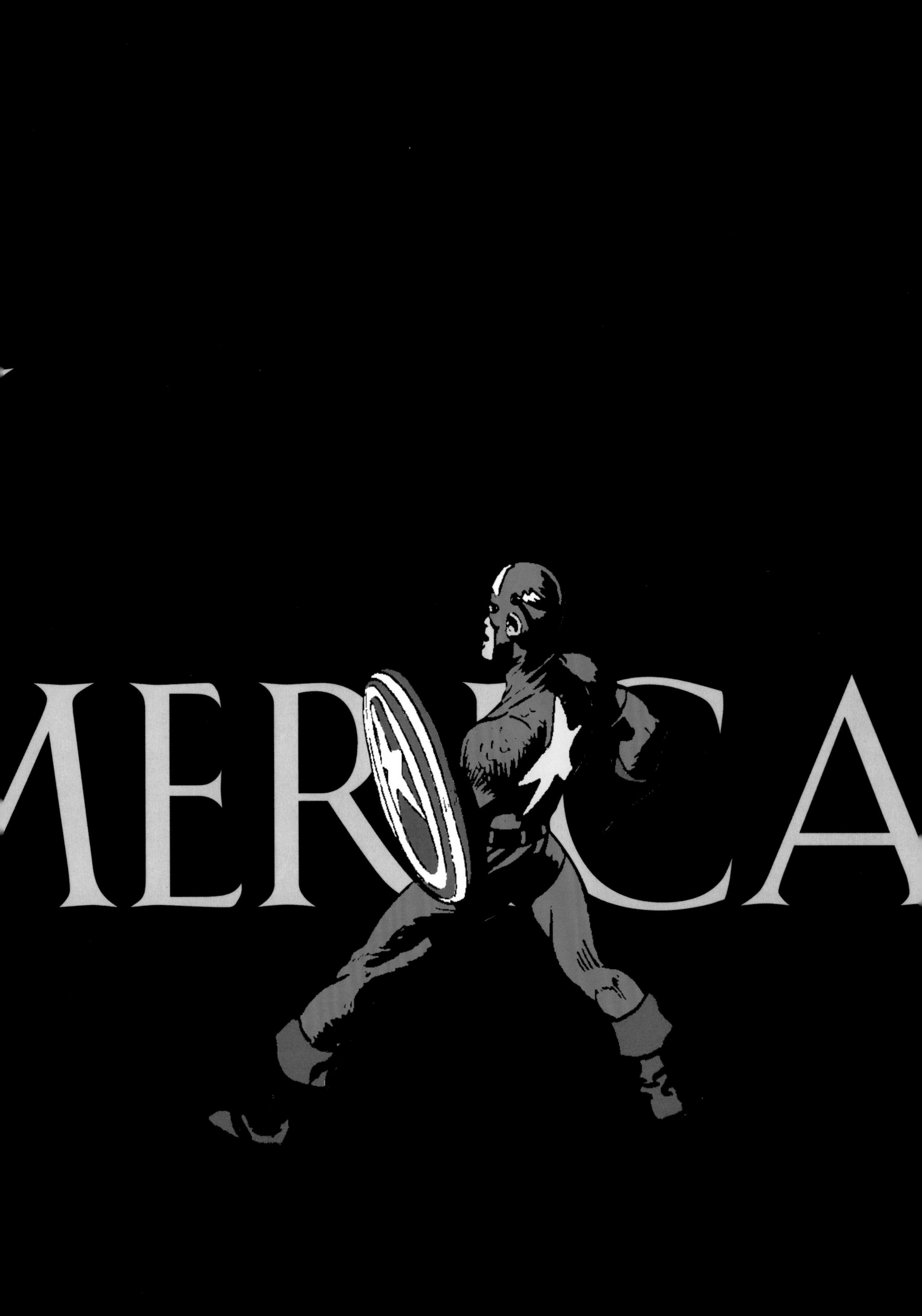
MERICA

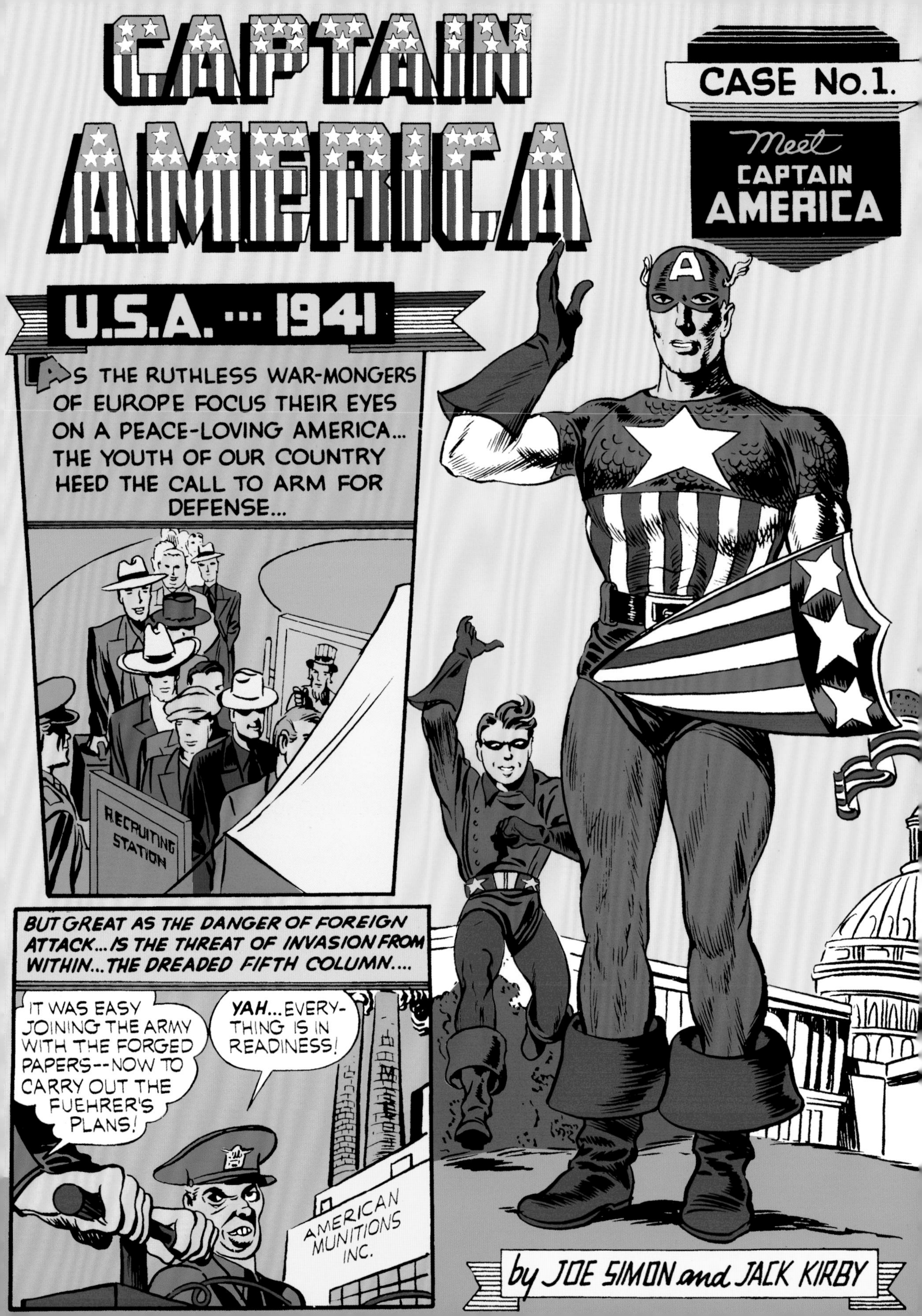
CAPTAIN AMERICA
CASE No. 1.
Meet CAPTAIN AMERICA
U.S.A. ... 1941
AS THE RUTHLESS WAR-MONGERS OF EUROPE FOCUS THEIR EYES ON A PEACE-LOVING AMERICA... THE YOUTH OF OUR COUNTRY HEED THE CALL TO ARM FOR DEFENSE...
RECRUITING STATION
BUT GREAT AS THE DANGER OF FOREIGN ATTACK... IS THE THREAT OF INVASION FROM WITHIN... THE DREADED FIFTH COLUMN....
IT WAS EASY JOINING THE ARMY WITH THE FORGED PAPERS--NOW TO CARRY OUT THE FUEHRER'S PLANS!
YAH... EVERY-THING IS IN READINESS!
AMERICAN MUNITIONS INC.
by JOE SIMON and JACK KIRBY

Captain America

NATIONAL HERO

1941: a time in America when war clouds loomed darkly on the horizon. Even though the United States would not officially become involved in the war that was tearing Europe apart until December of that year, the signs of trouble were approaching. A peacetime draft had been established by the government in 1940, and many were nervously watching and listening to the encroachment of the Axis powers into the free nations of Europe, spurred on by Adolf Hitler. Patriotic fervor was on the rise. The time was right for a national hero to emerge, even if he was to be an imaginary one.

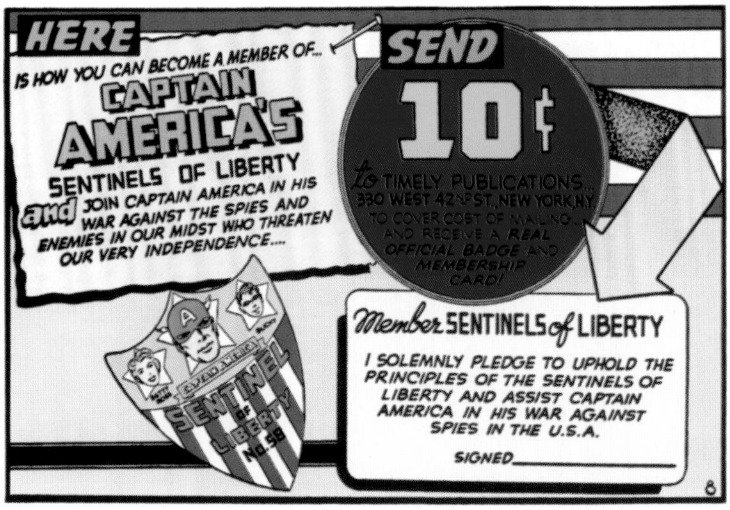
HERE
IS HOW YOU CAN BECOME A MEMBER OF...
CAPTAIN AMERICA'S
SENTINELS OF LIBERTY
and JOIN CAPTAIN AMERICA IN HIS WAR AGAINST THE SPIES AND ENEMIES IN OUR MIDST WHO THREATEN OUR VERY INDEPENDENCE....
SEND
10¢
to TIMELY PUBLICATIONS... 330 WEST 42ND ST., NEW YORK, N.Y.
TO COVER COST OF MAILING... AND RECEIVE A REAL OFFICIAL BADGE AND MEMBERSHIP CARD!
SENTINEL OF LIBERTY
No. 58
Member SENTINELS of LIBERTY
I SOLEMNLY PLEDGE TO UPHOLD THE PRINCIPLES OF THE SENTINELS OF LIBERTY AND ASSIST CAPTAIN AMERICA IN HIS WAR AGAINST SPIES IN THE U.S.A.
SIGNED
8

For the price of a comic book, young readers could feel like they were helping the war effort by joining the "Sentinels of Liberty."

Captain America, who debuted in the pages of his own magazine in March 1941, was that hero. Cap's co-creator Joe Simon recalls: "I was doing *Silver Streak, Blue Bolt, Captain Marvel,* a thing called *Treasury Man.* I was turning out quite a lot of material, some with Funnies, Inc., and some on my own. Eventually Martin Goodman offered me more money than Funnies, Inc., so I sent the sketches directly to him. Captain America was one of the things he loved, so I produced it for him. I brought Jack Kirby into the studio, and Howard Ferguson was my letterer."

Adolf Hitler himself was the impetus that jump-started Captain America to comic book life. "You came up with the villain first," Simon states. "That was the main jumping-off point for the characters. Adolf Hitler was the super, ultra villain, very much hated, stranger than fiction, actually, and I came up with the patriotic hero to fight the villain. That was a time when we were all patriotic. There had been patriotic superheroes before, but they were pretty stiff."

Captain America was anything but stiff. He was passionate about his cause and zealous about defeating the enemies of democracy, and he was devoted to his youthful sidekick, Bucky Barnes, who suits up and fights crime right alongside Cap. Future embellishments to the mythology would rechristen Bucky as James Buchanan Barnes, but in the beginning he was just Bucky—named after Bucky Pearson, a high school classmate of Simon's.

(Opposite) Captain America's first appearance, complete with a triangular shield, which would quickly give way to the more familiar round one. From *Captain America* #1 (March 1940).

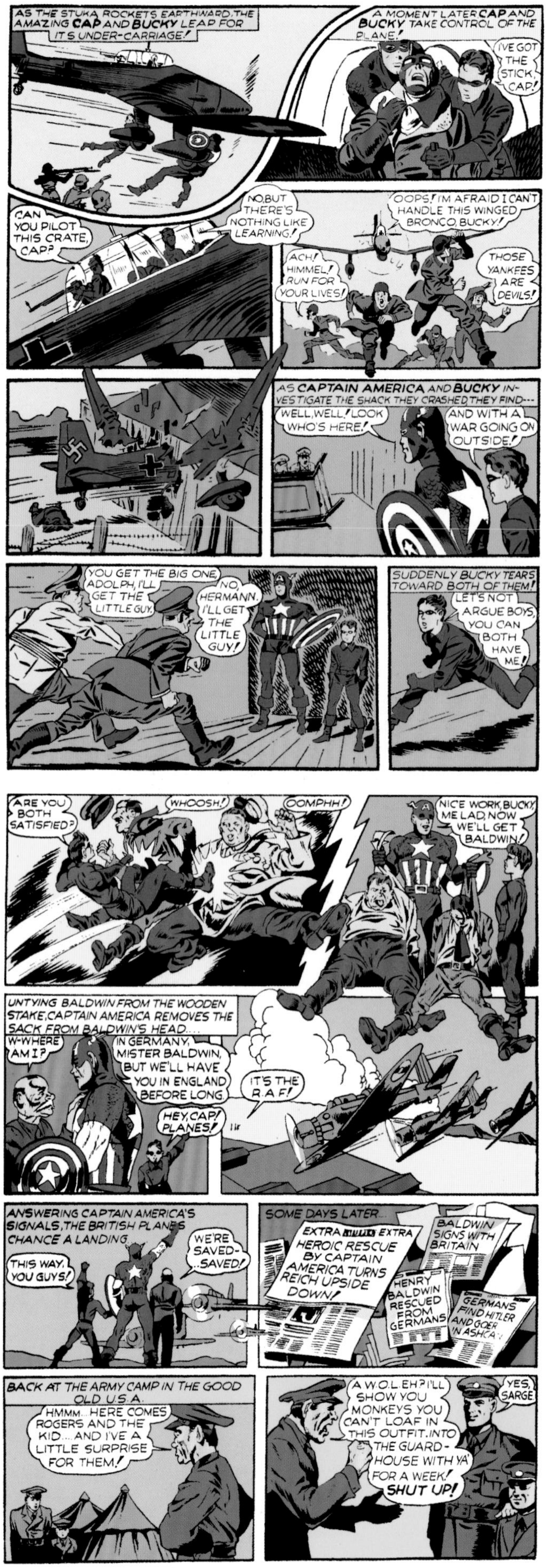

AS THE STUKA ROCKETS EARTHWARD, THE AMAZING CAP AND BUCKY LEAP FOR IT'S UNDER-CARRIAGE!
A MOMENT LATER CAP AND BUCKY TAKE CONTROL OF THE PLANE!
I'VE GOT THE STICK, CAP!
CAN YOU PILOT THIS CRATE, CAP?
NO, BUT THERE'S NOTHING LIKE LEARNING!
OOPS! I'M AFRAID I CAN'T HANDLE THIS WINGED BRONCO, BUCKY!
ACH! HIMMEL! RUN FOR YOUR LIVES!
THOSE YANKEES ARE DEVILS!
AS CAPTAIN AMERICA AND BUCKY INVESTIGATE THE SHACK THEY CRASHED, THEY FIND---
WELL, WELL! LOOK WHO'S HERE!
AND WITH A WAR GOING ON OUTSIDE!
YOU GET THE BIG ONE, ADOLPH, I'LL GET THE LITTLE GUY.
NO, HERMANN, I'LL GET THE LITTLE GUY!
SUDDENLY BUCKY TEARS TOWARD BOTH OF THEM!
LET'S NOT ARGUE BOYS, YOU CAN BOTH HAVE ME!
ARE YOU BOTH SATISFIED?
WHOOSH!
OOMPHH!
NICE WORK, BUCKY ME LAD, NOW WE'LL GET BALDWIN!
UNTYING BALDWIN FROM THE WOODEN STAKE, CAPTAIN AMERICA REMOVES THE SACK FROM BALDWIN'S HEAD...
W-WHERE AM I?
IN GERMANY, MISTER BALDWIN, BUT WE'LL HAVE YOU IN ENGLAND BEFORE LONG
IT'S THE R.A.F!
HEY, CAP! PLANES!
ANSWERING CAPTAIN AMERICA'S SIGNALS, THE BRITISH PLANES CHANCE A LANDING
THIS WAY, YOU GUYS!
WE'RE SAVED-- ..SAVED!
SOME DAYS LATER
EXTRA EXTRA HEROIC RESCUE BY CAPTAIN AMERICA TURNS REICH UPSIDE DOWN!
BALDWIN SIGNS WITH BRITAIN
HENRY BALDWIN RESCUED FROM GERMANS
GERMANS FIND HITLER AND GOER IN ASHCA
BACK AT THE ARMY CAMP IN THE GOOD OLD U.S.A.
HMMM.. HERE COMES ROGERS AND THE KID... AND I'VE A LITTLE SURPRISE FOR THEM!
A.W.O.L. EH? I'LL SHOW YOU MONKEYS YOU CAN'T LOAF IN THIS OUTFIT. INTO THE GUARD-HOUSE WITH YA' FOR A WEEK! SHUT UP!
YES, SARGE!

Hitler himself, along with Herman Goering, made appearances in the second issue of *Captain America* (April, '40)—and both were kayoed by Bucky Barnes.

Cap's premiere adventure, which appeared in *Captain America* issue #1, March 1941, tells the tale of a scrawny, 4-F weakling named Steve Rogers who participates in a secret government experiment conducted by a Professor Reinstein. Rogers is inoculated with a "strange seething liquid" and then bombarded with "vita-rays," which immediately turns him into an Atlas. Reinstein reveals that Rogers is to be "the first of a corps of super-agents whose mental and physical ability will make them a terror to spies and saboteurs," and then dubs him Captain America.

But there is an extra rat in the lab. One of the witnesses to the experiment is a Nazi spy, who shoots Reinstein so that no more American super men can be created. The new and improved Rogers quickly dispatches the traitor by throwing him into an electrical coil. After his transformation, Rogers enlists as a mild-mannered, pipe-smoking buck private stationed at Camp Lehigh, Virginia, the base from which he continues his off-hours duty as Captain America. Rogers sneaks off the base whenever necessary in the company of Bucky, the regiment's "mascot," who has discovered his secret identity. To cover his off-duty activities, Rogers willingly plays the role of company goat for the benefit of those around him, notably Betty Ross, a blonde (occasionally redheaded) special investigator for the U.S. government, and blustery Sergeant Duffy, a thickheaded non-com who is constantly assigning Rogers extra KP duty and other menial tasks because of what he perceives to be tardiness, inattention to duty, and AWOLs, all of which are caused by Rogers's stints as Captain America.

The world of Captain America is one virtually overrun with enemy spies, and through the comics, readers were allowed to get involved in the fight against them. For ten cents youngsters could become one of Captain America's Sentinels of Liberty and receive a shield-shaped badge that bore the likenesses of Cap, Bucky, and Betty Ross, along with a membership card that read: "I solemnly pledge to uphold the principles of the Sentinels of Liberty and assist Captain America in his

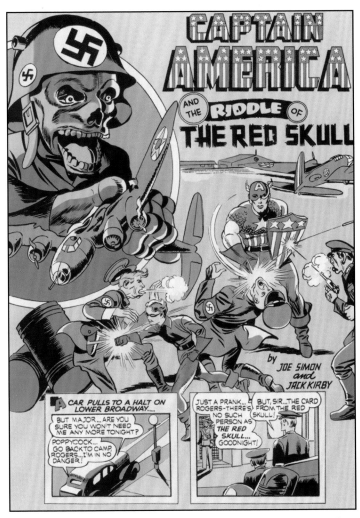

CAPTAIN AMERICA
AND THE RIDDLE OF THE RED SKULL
by JOE SIMON and JACK KIRBY
A CAR PULLS TO A HALT ON LOWER BROADWAY....
BUT MAJOR...ARE YOU SURE YOU WON'T NEED ME ANY MORE TONIGHT?
POPPYCOCK... GO BACK TO CAMP, ROGERS...I'M IN NO DANGER!
JUST A PRANK... ROGERS-THERE'S NO SUCH PERSON AS THE RED SKULL... GOODNIGHT!
BUT, SIR...THE CARD FROM THE RED SKULL!
This title page from the Red Skull's debut story from Captain America *#1 leaves no doubt for* whom the grotesque villain was working.

war against spies in the U.S.A." Whether any of the nation's ten-year-olds actually ferreted out any hotbeds of espionage in their neighborhoods is unlikely, but helping Captain America allowed young readers to feel that they were part of the war effort, while teaching them such necessary wartime practices as material conservation and recycling.

The first issue of *Captain America* magazine also introduced a figure who would become Cap's most durable nemesis: The Red Skull. A grotesquely masked, seemingly supernatural Nazi operative, The Red Skull was said to possess a lethal "look of death" that kills anyone who gazes upon his crimson ugliness. But in his first appearance The Skull turns out to be George Maxon, of the Maxon Aircraft Company, who is sabotaging his own planes, while the look of death is nothing more than magician's misdirection, allowing for a hypo of poison to be secretly administered while the victim's attention is captured by the ghastly mask. During a fight with Captain America, Maxon himself rolls on the hypo and is killed.

The Red Skull was far too potent a villain to die off in his initial appearance, however, so he returned in the third issue of *Captain America* to sneer at the U.S. government officials who thought him dead. This particular story, titled "The Return of The Red Skull," is notable for a particularly chilling panel in which The Red Skull, having caught imposters whom he thinks are Cap and Bucky, lynches them and cackles madly as their bodies swing! In future adventures it would be revealed that the traitorous industrialist George Maxon was nothing more than a pawn in The Red Skull's war against the Allies, and that the "real" Skull was Johann Schmidt, former right-hand man to Hitler.

Hitler himself appeared in some of the early Cap stories (Bucky had the honor of knocking him unconscious in *Captain America* issue #2), though as time went on, Cap's nemeses became increasingly weird, and such stories as "Horror Hospital" from issue #4, in which a nightmarish, demon-like creature called Gorro is unleashed by a mad doctor, approached the realm of H.P. Lovecraft.

Simon and Kirby stayed with *Captain America* only through the magazine's first year, after which Goodman turned the character over to other writers and artists, notably Al Avison and Syd Shores. After the war, though, a change in times and the real-life defeat of the ultimate villain, Adolf Hitler, set *Captain America* and Bucky adrift. For issue #74 in 1949, *Captain America* magazine was changed to *Captain America's Weird Tales* and continued Cap's association with the bizarre. The next issue, #75, featured weird tales, but no Cap! The title was dropped until 1954, when *Captain America Comics* reintroduced America's hero and Bucky as stalwart Communist fighters. This tactic did not catch on with readers and the title folded after only two more issues.

It took an entire decade for Captain America to return to the forefront of comic book heroes. After an exploratory adventure in *Strange Tales* #114, Cap officially returned in *The Avengers* #4, issue date March 1964, once again drawn by Jack Kirby though now written by Stan Lee. Captain America's rebirth comes when he is discovered in a block of ice and thawed out by The Avengers (Iron Man, Thor, Giant Man, and The Wasp), having been in suspended animation for nearly twenty years. His last conscious memory was falling into the freezing waters near the Arctic circle in 1945, after he and Bucky had been carried aloft by a drone plane filled with explosives that had been launched by the evil Nazi scientist Dr. Zemo (also known as Baron Zemo). Cap escaped, but Bucky was not so lucky: in the rethinking of the mythology, Bucky was killed when the plane exploded, a development prompted as much by Lee's disdain for teenaged sidekick characters as its inherent drama.

Two decades in suspended animation have not impaired Cap's abilities, and he proves himself useful to The Avengers. But the intervening years have affected

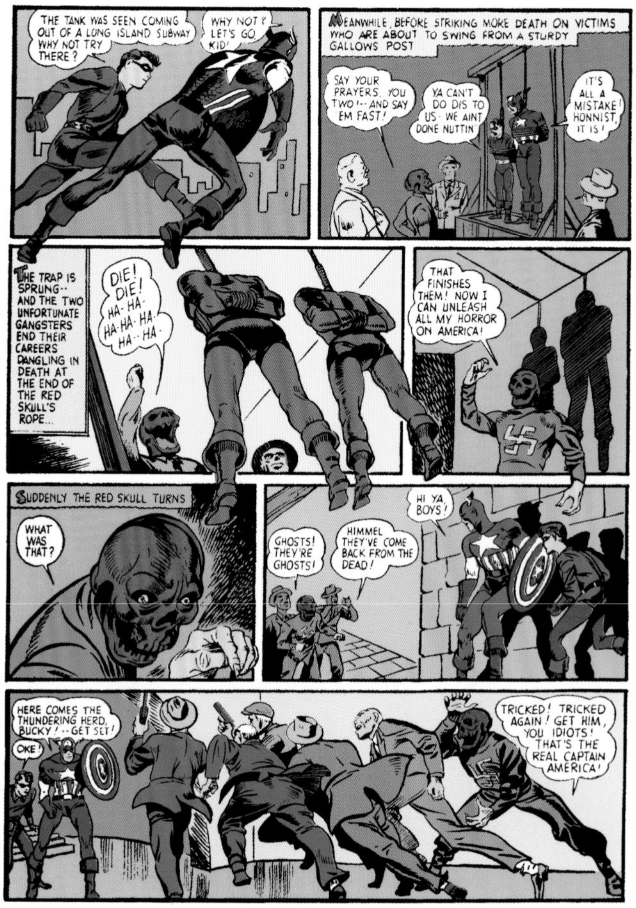
THE TANK WAS SEEN COMING OUT OF A LONG ISLAND SUBWAY WHY NOT TRY THERE?
WHY NOT? LET'S GO, KID!
MEANWHILE, BEFORE STRIKING MORE DEATH ON VICTIMS WHO ARE ABOUT TO SWING FROM A STURDY GALLOWS POST
SAY YOUR PRAYERS, YOU TWO--AND SAY EM FAST!
YA CAN'T DO DIS TO US · WE AINT DONE NUTTIN
IT'S ALL A MISTAKE! HONNIST, IT IS!
THE TRAP IS SPRUNG-- AND THE TWO UNFORTUNATE GANGSTERS END THEIR CAREERS DANGLING IN DEATH AT THE END OF THE RED SKULL'S ROPE...
DIE! DIE! HA-HA- HA-HA-HA HA--HA-
THAT FINISHES THEM! NOW I CAN UNLEASH ALL MY HORROR ON AMERICA!
SUDDENLY THE RED SKULL TURNS
WHAT WAS THAT?
HI YA BOYS!
GHOSTS! THEY'RE GHOSTS!
HIMMEL THEY'VE COME BACK FROM THE DEAD!
HERE COMES THE THUNDERING HERD, BUCKY!--GET SET!
OKE!
TRICKED! TRICKED AGAIN! GET HIM, YOU IDIOTS! THAT'S THE REAL CAPTAIN AMERICA!

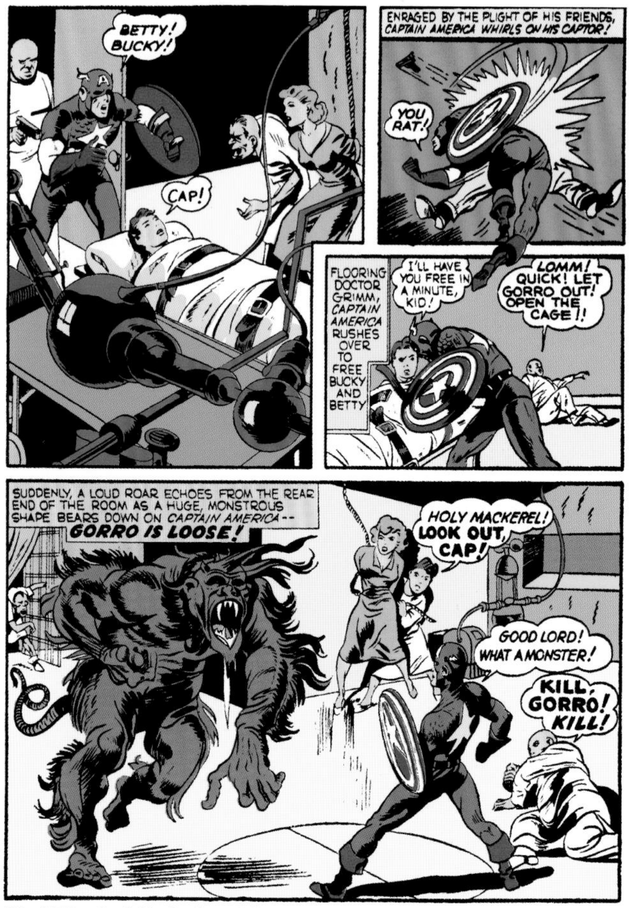
BETTY! BUCKY!
CAP!
ENRAGED BY THE PLIGHT OF HIS FRIENDS, CAPTAIN AMERICA WHIRLS ON HIS CAPTOR!
YOU RAT!
FLOORING DOCTOR GRIMM, CAPTAIN AMERICA RUSHES OVER TO FREE BUCKY AND BETTY
I'LL HAVE YOU FREE IN A MINUTE, KID!
LOMM! QUICK! LET GORRO OUT! OPEN THE CAGE!
SUDDENLY, A LOUD ROAR ECHOES FROM THE REAR END OF THE ROOM AS A HUGE, MONSTROUS SHAPE BEARS DOWN ON CAPTAIN AMERICA-- GORRO IS LOOSE!
HOLY MACKEREL! LOOK OUT, CAP!
GOOD LORD! WHAT A MONSTER!
KILL, GORRO! KILL!

(Top) The Red Skull played for keeps, as this chillingly dramatic page from *Captain America* #3 (May 1940) demonstrates.

(Above) Cap's early stories often pitted him against such nightmarish creatures as Gorro, from *Captain America* #4 (June 1940).

A "BLACK HOLE" IN THE MARVEL UNIVERSE

4 SPECIAL COMICS INFORMATION | APPROVED FOR ALL READERS

SLOWLY, ALMOST HALTINGLY, THE INCREDIBLE TALE BEGINS TO ISSUE FORTH FROM THE LIPS OF THE MIGHTY MAN WITH THE TRAGEDY-HAUNTED EYES...
IT SEEMS LIKE ONLY YESTERDAY--BUT IT WAS MORE THAN TWENTY YEARS AGO THAT MY TEEN-AGE PAL, BUCKY--AND I--WHILE ACTING AS SECURITY GUARDS AT AN E.T.O.* ARMY BASE-- TRIED TO STOP AN EXPLOSIVE-FILLED DRONE PLANE FROM TAKING TO THE AIR!
WE'RE TOO LATE, BUCKY! WE'LL HAVE TO GO AFTER IT IN ANOTHER PLANE!
NO! DON'T STOP! I THINK I CAN REACH IT, CAP!
HAH! THUS DO I TRIUMPH OVER CAPTAIN AMERICA AND BUCKY! IF THEY REACH THE PLANE, THEY DIE! AND IF THEY FAIL, AMERICA LOSES ONE OF ITS NEWEST WEAPONS!
*E.T.O.: EUROPEAN THEATER OF OPERATIONS.
THE BOY WAS CLOSER--HE REACHED THE PLANE! BUT CAPTAIN AMERICA HIMSELF CANNOT HOLD ON!
CAN'T MAKE IT! DROP OFF INTO THE WATER, LAD! DON'T TRY TO GO IT ALONE!
NO! I CAN BRING THE PLANE BACK --I KNOW I CAN!
BUCKY! LET GO! IT MIGHT BE BOOBY-TRAPPED! YOU CAN'T DEACTIVATE THE BOMB WITHOUT ME! DROP OFF!
YOU'RE RIGHT, CAP! I SEE THE FUSE! IT'S GONNA BLOW!
"AND THOSE WERE THE LAST WORDS THAT BRAVE, WONDERFUL LAD EVER UTTERED... MAY THE LORD REST HIS SOUL!
BUCKY!! IT EXPLODED! BUCKY'S GONE!
"AS FOR ME, I DIDN'T CARE IF I LIVED OR DIED! I STRUCK THE WATER OFF THE COAST OF NEWFOUNDLAND AND PLUMMETTED LIKE A ROCK--WITH BUCKY'S FACE ETCHED BEFORE ME! AND THAT IS THE LAST THING I REMEMBER!"
HE'S GONE---AND I---WITH ALL MY POWER--ALL MY STRENGTH--I COULDN'T SAVE HIM!

The Marvel Universe is an amazingly cohesive matrix with an almost Biblical sense of history and lineage. This remarkable achievement is all the more remarkable when once considers the sheer number of editors, writers, and artists who have kept track of the comings and goings within the Universe. During Marvel's production boom of the late 1980s and early 1990s, two staffers, Mark Gruenwald and Peter Sanderson, were responsible for cross-over continuity, making sure that appearances by characters in other series were consistent with that character's own series.

Throughout the years there has been only one blatant shattering of the Marvel Universe's space-time continuum, and that revolves around the death of Bucky Barnes. For his 1964 rebirth, Captain America is haunted by the memory of his young sidekick's death at the hands of Baron Zemo, which was said to have happened at the height of World War II. Yet in the original Cap series, Bucky was alive and well and fighting Commies as late as 1954. What, then, was the cause for the discrepancy? "I think, mainly, I had forgotten about them [the 1950s Cap adventures with Bucky]," admits Stan Lee, "it's as simple as that."

Bucky Barnes's tragic and ultimately mysterious death is seen in flashback in *The Avengers* #4.

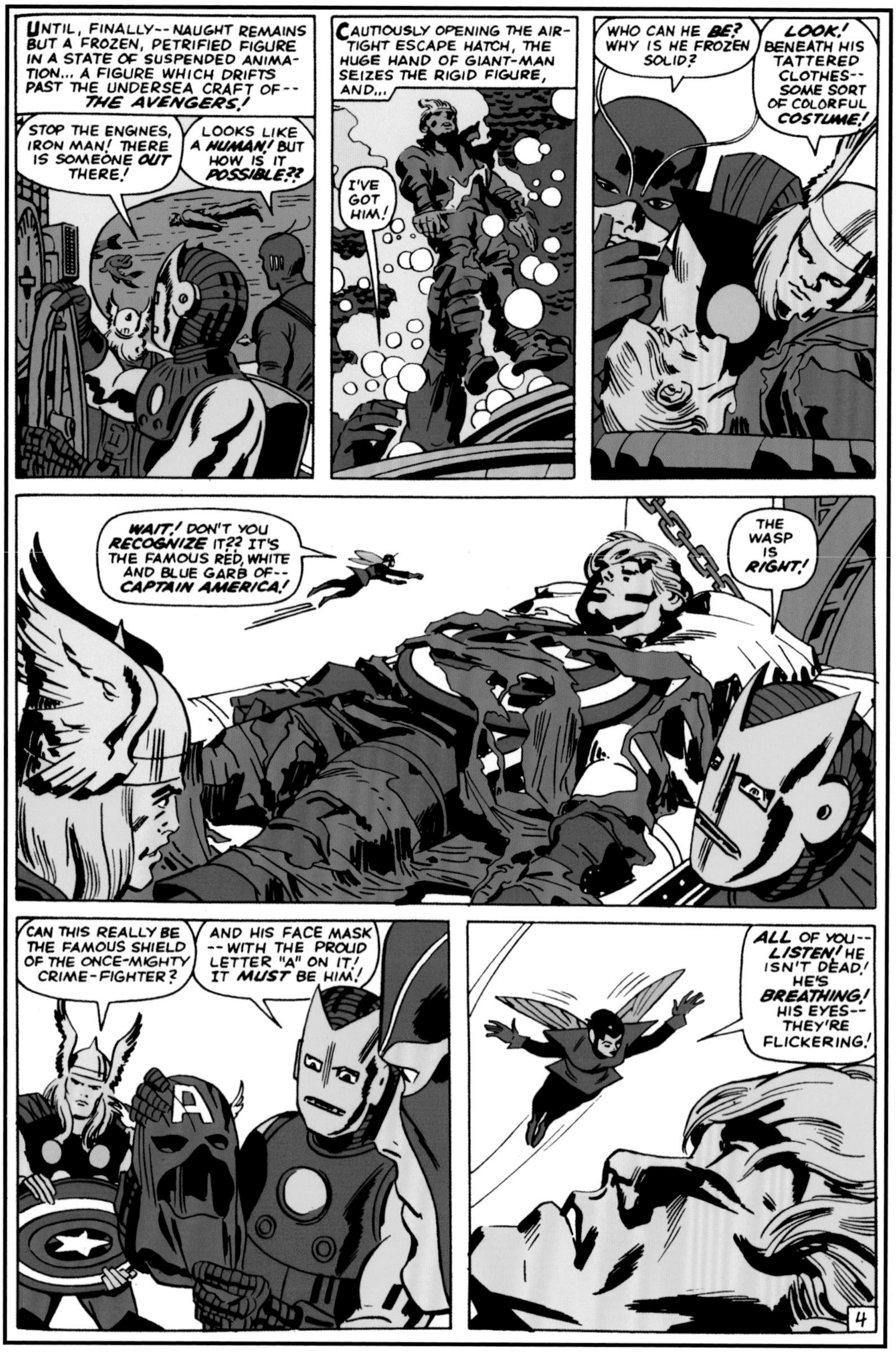
UNTIL, FINALLY-- NAUGHT REMAINS BUT A FROZEN, PETRIFIED FIGURE IN A STATE OF SUSPENDED ANIMATION... A FIGURE WHICH DRIFTS PAST THE UNDERSEA CRAFT OF-- THE AVENGERS!
STOP THE ENGINES, IRON MAN! THERE IS SOMEONE OUT THERE!
LOOKS LIKE A HUMAN! BUT HOW IS IT POSSIBLE??
CAUTIOUSLY OPENING THE AIR-TIGHT ESCAPE HATCH, THE HUGE HAND OF GIANT-MAN SEIZES THE RIGID FIGURE, AND...
I'VE GOT HIM!
WHO CAN HE BE? WHY IS HE FROZEN SOLID?
LOOK! BENEATH HIS TATTERED CLOTHES-- SOME SORT OF COLORFUL COSTUME!
WAIT! DON'T YOU RECOGNIZE IT?? IT'S THE FAMOUS RED, WHITE AND BLUE GARB OF-- CAPTAIN AMERICA!
THE WASP IS RIGHT!
CAN THIS REALLY BE THE FAMOUS SHIELD OF THE ONCE-MIGHTY CRIME-FIGHTER?
AND HIS FACE MASK --WITH THE PROUD LETTER "A" ON IT! IT MUST BE HIM!
ALL OF YOU-- LISTEN! HE ISN'T DEAD! HE'S BREATHING! HIS EYES-- THEY'RE FLICKERING!
4

Cap's dramatic resurrection, as captured by Jack Kirby, in *The Avengers* #4 (March 1964).

his disposition, so that the happy-go-lucky warrior of old is now a brooding man who is haunted by the death of Bucky even as he mentors young Rick Jones, the friend of The Incredible Hulk, who wants to become Cap's permanent sidekick. When Cap learns that Zemo is still alive, and a menace to The Avengers, he swears to avenge Bucky, and finally does so in *The Avengers* issue #15. Cap's popularity with *The Avengers* earned him his own magazine, *Tales of Suspense*, which had started to feature Cap since issue #58, was officially changed to *Captain America* with issue #100 in 1968.

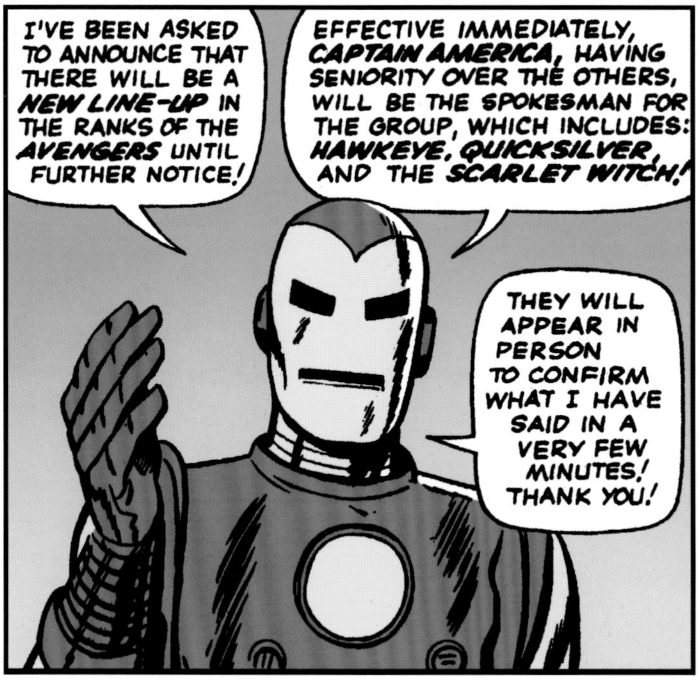
I'VE BEEN ASKED TO ANNOUNCE THAT THERE WILL BE A NEW LINE-UP IN THE RANKS OF THE AVENGERS UNTIL FURTHER NOTICE!
EFFECTIVE IMMEDIATELY, CAPTAIN AMERICA, HAVING SENIORITY OVER THE OTHERS, WILL BE THE SPOKESMAN FOR THE GROUP, WHICH INCLUDES: HAWKEYE, QUICKSILVER, AND THE SCARLET WITCH!
THEY WILL APPEAR IN PERSON TO CONFIRM WHAT I HAVE SAID IN A VERY FEW MINUTES! THANK YOU!

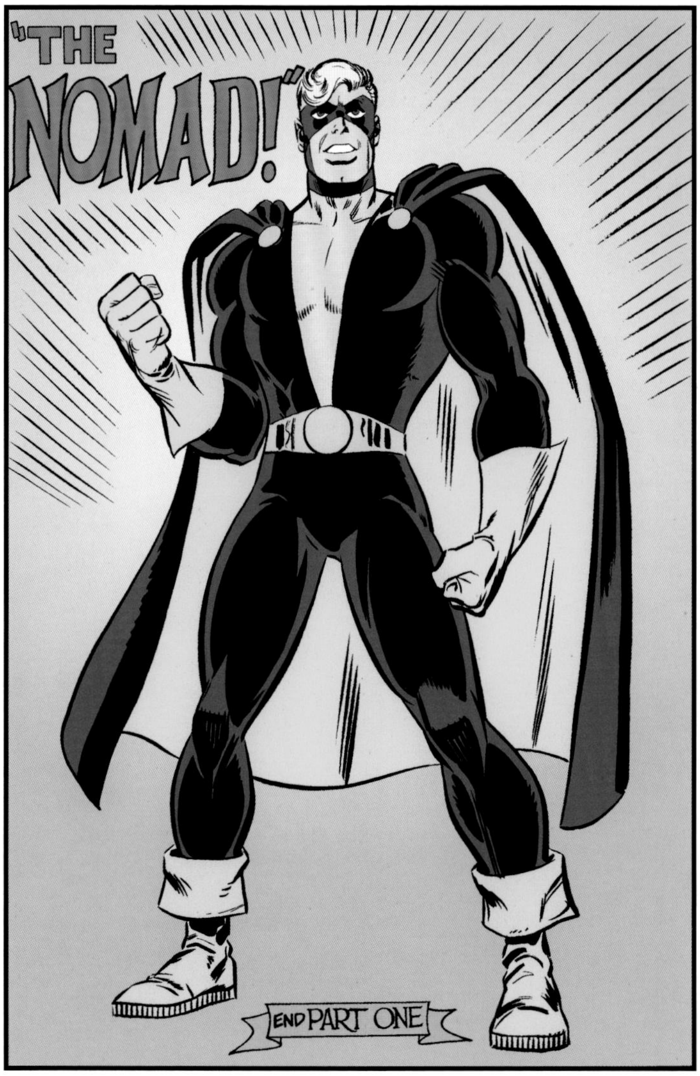
"THE NOMAD!"
END PART ONE

(Top) In *The Avengers* # 16 (May 1965), Captain America is entrusted with the leadership of The Avengers.

(Above) Disillusioned as a symbol of his country, Steve Rogers briefly became "Nomad" in the 1970s.

Captain America would eventually become the leader of a new team of Avengers that included Hawkeye, Quicksilver, and the Scarlet Witch, and would be featured in retro adventures involving a wartime group of heroes called *The Invaders*. But more important, Cap would wage battle with his own internal demons that would sometimes find him questioning his entire ideology. It is this questioning, skeptical dimension to his character that kept him from becoming a flag-draped anachronism in the era of Vietnam and Watergate. "The most important thing is to give a hero a personality, give him things that he philosophizes and agonizes about," Stan Lee points out. "Cap felt he was in the wrong time, living in the 1960s but with a 1930s outlook on everything, and he was aware of that. I had a line—I can't remember what the story was—but he was thinking that the establishment isn't always right, and sometimes you have to think twice before going along blindly with what the establishment says or does. And as he was thinking of himself in the past, he said: 'Maybe I should have acted less and questioned more.' And that sort of set the tone for him when we brought him back."

By 1974, in fact, Steve Rogers (like many in the real world) had become so disillusioned by what was going on in the government that he rejected his Captain America persona and took on a new identity as Nomad, trading in his red-white-and-blues for a new costume of dark blue and yellow. He eventually re-assumed the costume that was the symbol of his country, and in 1980 Cap turned down a bid to make him the official leader of the country when he refused to be drafted as a nominee for president of the United States.

Writers such as Roger Stern and Steve Englehart (whose politically charged *Secret Empire* storyline, outlining a high-level, inside attempt to take over the United States government, provided the set-up for Cap's disillusionment), and artists like Gene Colan, Frank Robbins, and John Byrne have followed Lee and Kirby's lead in giving the character a tradition of realism that equals his tradition of heroics.

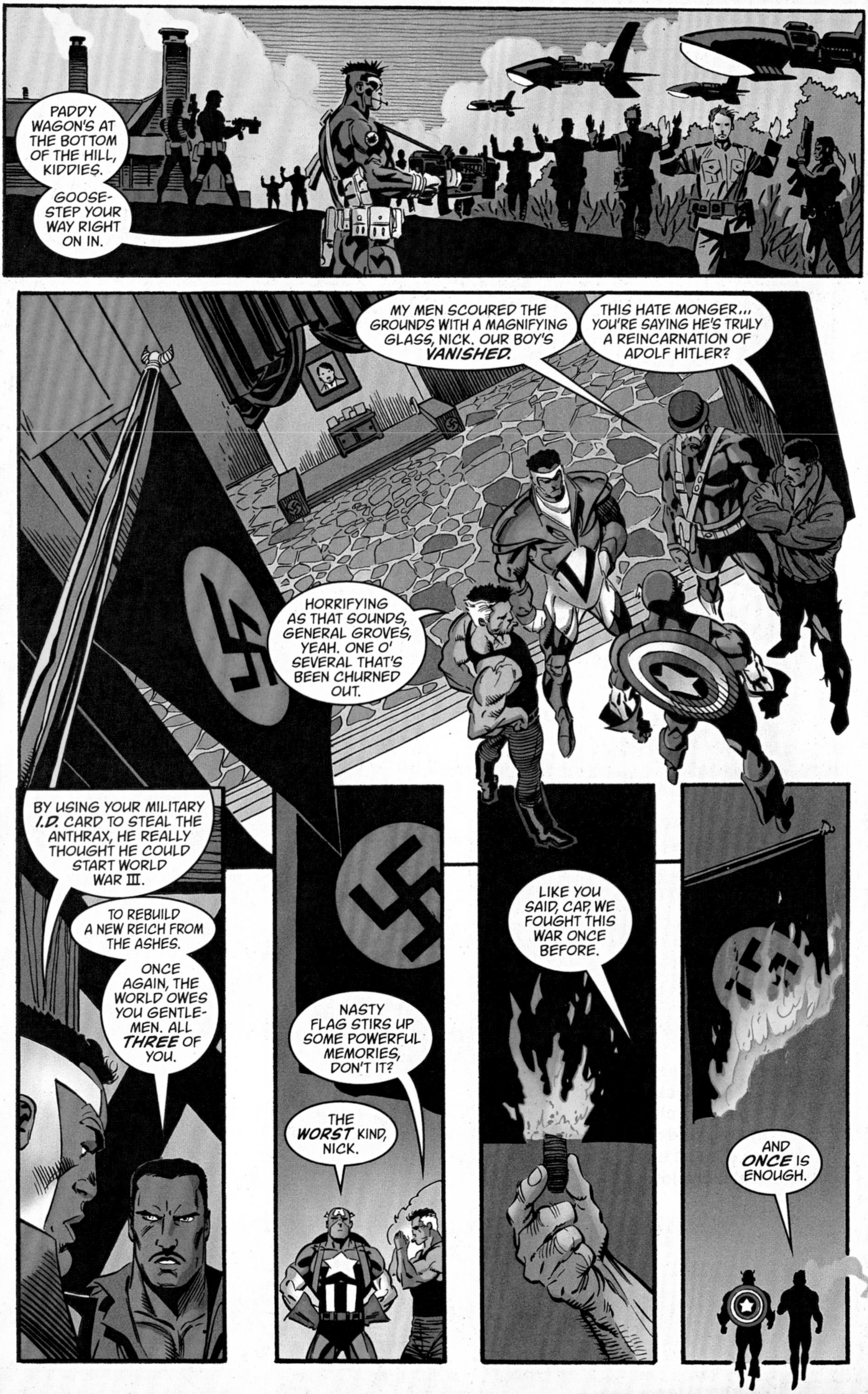
PADDY WAGON'S AT THE BOTTOM OF THE HILL, KIDDIES.
GOOSE-STEP YOUR WAY RIGHT ON IN.
MY MEN SCOURED THE GROUNDS WITH A MAGNIFYING GLASS, NICK. OUR BOY'S VANISHED.
THIS HATE MONGER... YOU'RE SAYING HE'S TRULY A REINCARNATION OF ADOLF HITLER?
HORRIFYING AS THAT SOUNDS, GENERAL GROVES, YEAH. ONE O' SEVERAL THAT'S BEEN CHURNED OUT.
BY USING YOUR MILITARY I.D. CARD TO STEAL THE ANTHRAX, HE REALLY THOUGHT HE COULD START WORLD WAR III.
TO REBUILD A NEW REICH FROM THE ASHES.
ONCE AGAIN, THE WORLD OWES YOU GENTLEMEN. ALL THREE OF YOU.
NASTY FLAG STIRS UP SOME POWERFUL MEMORIES, DON'T IT?
THE WORST KIND, NICK.
LIKE YOU SAID, CAP, WE FOUGHT THIS WAR ONCE BEFORE.
AND ONCE IS ENOUGH.

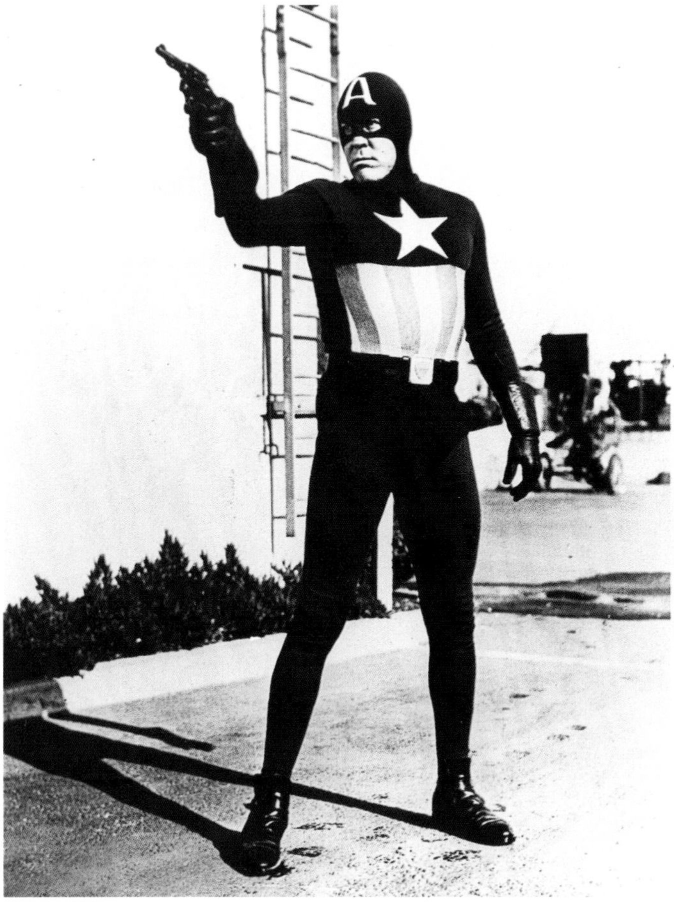

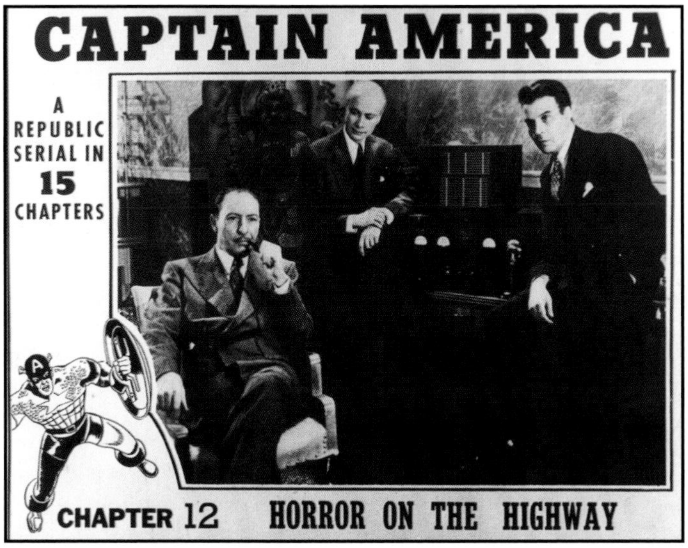
CAPTAIN AMERICA
A REPUBLIC SERIAL IN 15 CHAPTERS
CHAPTER 12
HORROR ON THE HIGHWAY

(Top) For his serial adventures, Cap traded in his trademark shield for a more mundane weapon.

(Above) A lobby card from Republic's 1943/44 serial *Captain America.* Veteran hissable Lionel Atwill (with the pipe) played the villainous Scarab.

(Opposite) Some battles never end, as Cap and Nick Fury learn at the dawn of the twenty-first century. From *Captain America* Vol. 3, #27 (March 2000).

Captain America continues to fight crime in comic books, grimly taking on the kinds of enemies he thought he defeated fifty years ago, neo-Nazis, such as The Hate Monger, who is believed to be an actual reincarnation of Adolf Hitler.

CAPTAIN AMERICA IN THE MEDIA

If any entertainment format seemed a natural for Captain America, it was Saturday afternoon serials. This unique form of moviemaking flourished in the 1930s and 1940s, and was targeted squarely at the same young audience that was reading comic books. Each Saturday afternoon a fifteen-minute chapter of the adventure would screen in theaters (it took three months to get the entire story). Every chapter contained a cliffhanger ending in which the hero or heroine would find themselves in a deathtrap from which it was virtually impossible to escape and the viewer would have to wait until the next Saturday to see how the heroes managed to survive. While several studios produced serials, the undisputed king of the format was Republic Studios.

Unfairly dubbed "Repulsive Studios" by the Hollywood mainstream, Republic was a solid, professional entertainment factory whose watchwords were "Quick," "Cheap," and "Efficient." By the early 1940s the studio had already turned comic characters Captain Marvel and Spy Smasher into well-received chapterplays, and in 1943 Republic optioned the rights to Captain America. The studio spared no expense on the fifteen-chapter serial, lavishing $223,000 on the production (lunch money by today's standards, but the most the studio ever spent on a serial), and placing it in the experienced hands of directors John English and Elmer Clifton. Filmed in the fall of 1943, *Captain America*'s first chapter was in theaters by December of that year. Fans of Republic serials were delighted with the action and thrills and the painstaking miniature work that were hallmarks of the studio. But fans of Captain America comic books could not help but be disappointed with the changes that had been made in the character.

In translating Captain America to the screen, the filmmakers completely dropped the existing mythology from the comics and started from scratch. Instead of being Steve Rogers, Republic's Captain America was crusading district attorney Grant Gardner, a guy with quick fists and a knack for surviving catastrophes. Instead of a blue costume with wings on the hood, the serial Captain America wore black tights, a black sweatshirt with a star and stripes, and a ski-mask hood with an "A" plastered on it. Most noticeably, instead of his trademark shield, this Captain America wielded a gun. Martin Goodman was reportedly very unhappy with the changes wrought by Republic, but there was nothing he could do about it.

No trace of Bucky or Betty is to be found in the serial, either. Instead, Grant Gardner (played by Dick Purcell) is aided by his assistant/secretary Gail Richards (Lorna Gray) and together they battle a mysterious murderer and thief called The Scarab (enacted with sinister glee by Lionel Atwill), who for personal reasons is wiping out the members of a recent South American scientific expedition one by one. Despite Atwill's ripe villainy, The Scarab is definitely a mundane villain when compared to The Red Skull, although The Red Skull's influence can definitely be seen in a later Republic serial, 1946's *The Crimson Ghost,* in which the title villain hides behind a ghastly skull mask until the final chapter.

While the cliffhanger endings were frequently imaginative—one of them had Gail strapped onto an industrial paper cutter, about to be guillotined!—there are few elements of the fantastic in the serial version *Captain America.* Even more surprising, the serial removes Cap from any kind of wartime context, even though other Republic serials of the time capitalized on depicting Axis-controlled villains as the enemy. Then there was Dick Purcell, a short, stocky tough-guy actor who was an odd choice for a hero, even taking into consideration the wartime shortage of leading men. This bit of miscasting was further underscored by the physical difference between Purcell and his action double, Dale

(Top) Cap's uniform in the serial did not quite meet fans' expectations.

(Above) The Red Skull? No, but the influence behind the title villain of Republic's 1946 serial *The Crimson Ghost,* released two years after Captain America, seems obvious.

(Opposite top) Actor Dick Purcell, who played Cap's new alter ego Grant Gardner in the serial version. Purcell's untimely death at thirty-eight came only four months after finishing work on Captain America.

(Middle) Brawny stuntman Dale Van Sickel, seen here, performed all of Cap's action scenes.

(Bottom) Is Captain America coming out of the closet? Or is he simply cleaning up crime.

Van Sickel, who was considerably taller, slimmer, and brawnier. As a result, Captain America appears to lose about fifteen pounds in every long shot. Still, fights, thrills, action and danger were the things that the serial fans of the time demanded, and *Captain America* did not let them down.

If the serial version of *Captain America* rewrote the character from head to toe, a 1966 cartoon series based on Cap's adventures followed the comic book adventures to the letter. Captain America, along with The Sub-Mariner, The Incredible Hulk, Iron Man, and The Mighty Thor, were licensed to producer Steve Krantz for a syndicated cartoon show called "The Marvel Superheroes," which was produced by Grantray-Lawrence Productions, a commercial animation house owned by veteran Hollywood animators Grant Simmons and Ray Patterson, and New York producer Robert Lawrence.

To demonstrate how comic book art could be used as the basis for animated cartoons, Patterson, Simmons, and animator Robert "Tiger" West filmed a test reel using a Classics Illustrated comic adaption of Dumas's *The Count of Monte Cristo.* A follow-up demo was created featuring Captain America and The Red Skull, which resulted in an order for a total of 195 six-minute cartoons, split up among the five characters, with each story told over a series of three cartoons.

Because the budget for this series was extremely low (about $6,000 per cartoon), the animators turned to the technique of xeroxing artwork as the basis for the animation. "We had one of the first Xerox machines among the small studios," Patterson says. "We'd take the black-and-white [comic book] proofs and xerox them on a plate, and if we wanted to animate the mouth, we'd take the mouth off, or an arm, or sometimes we'd move the whole character for a few frames. But it would start with the xerox and we'd use the actual, beautiful drawings." The stationary plates, and any limited animation, would then be inked and painted on cels in the traditional method. Camera movement was

SEE CAPTAIN AMERICA!

As Steve Rogers—a soldier in the service of his country. In his secret identity as CAPTAIN AMERICA with his shining shield, he's a super foe of super-villains.

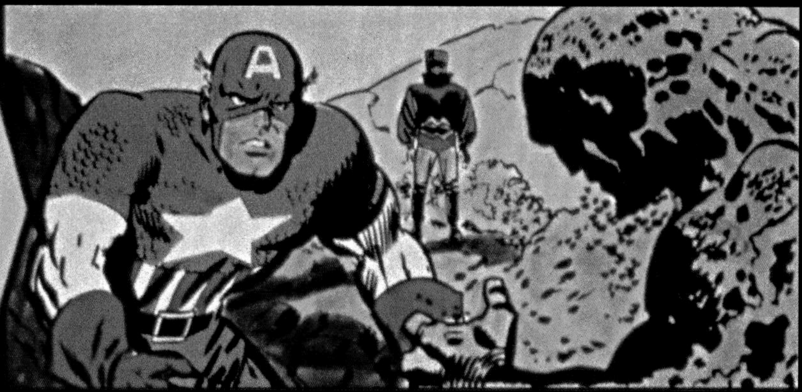

SEE THE MIGHTY THOR!

His real name is Dr. Blake—a serious and dedicated doctor. As THOR—he can cause storms and can fly by swinging his enchanted hammer, letting go and holding on.

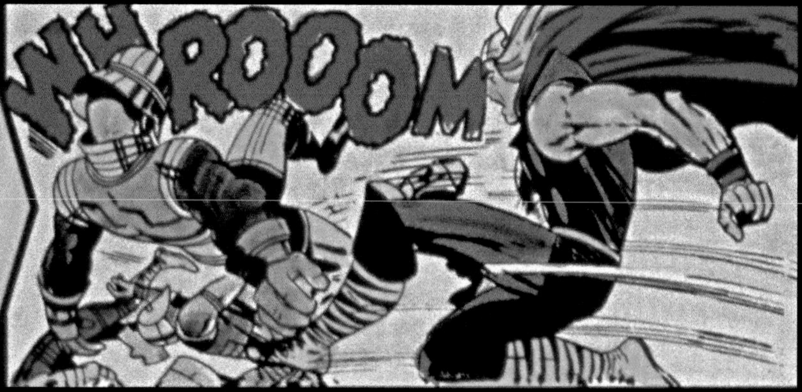
ROOOM

SEE The INCREDIBLE HULK!

His real name is Bruce Banner—but having been belted by gamma rays, he's THE HULK—a sort of Jekyll and Hyde arrangement. The jolly green giant is merely the strongest mortal to walk the earth.

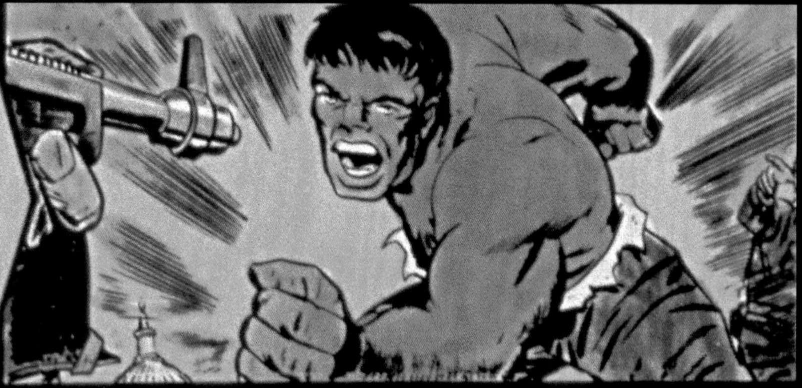

SEE SUB-MARINER!

He is really Prince Namor—half human and half descendant of the underwater kingdom of Atlantis. In the water he is supreme. Strong as a whale. On land, many times stronger than any human. He can fly limited distances as his tasks demand with his offbeat little ankle wings.

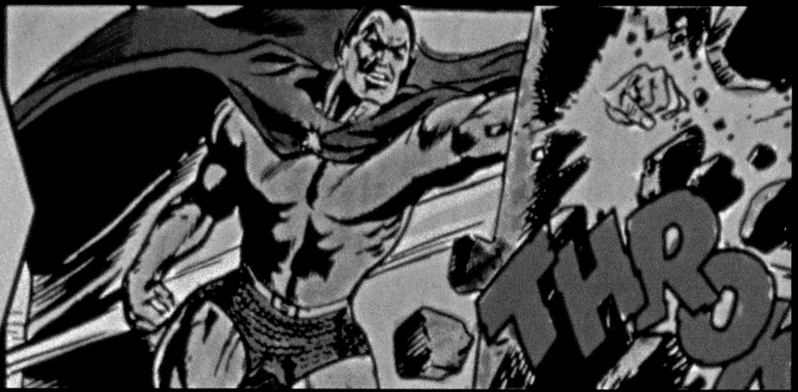

SEE IRON MAN!

As handsome, debonair Tony Stark, he's the world's greatest inventive genius, owning the world's largest armament factory. Donning his suit of armor, with jet power, he can fly and with his transistorized gadgets—he's as strong as a tank.

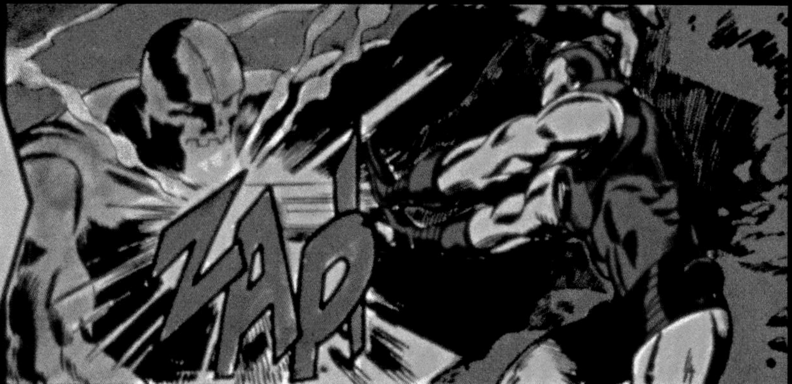
ZAP!

A drawing from the 1966 animated "Captain America," taken directly from the original comic book art.

(Opposite) Captain America arrives on television in 1966 as part of "The Marvel Superheroes."

frequently used to give the illusion of animation on a stationary drawing, and the comic book–inspired "Whaps!" and "Pows!" were drawn in as well.

To further save money, the voice tracks were recorded in Toronto, where producer Lawrence was able to take advantage of a rich pool of radio acting talent, including Bernard Cowan, Henry Ramer, John Vernon, Paul Soles, Peg Dixon, and Paul Kligman, at a fraction of the cost of American actors. The "Marvel Superheroes" cartoons are also fondly remembered today for their catchy, wordplay-filled theme songs (Cap's theme contained an almost Sondheimian exercise in internal rhyming: *"When Captain America throws his mighty shield; All those who chose to oppose his shield must yield ..."*)

Some of the Captain America cartoons were set in the 1940s, and depicted Steve Rogers and Bucky at Camp Lehigh. Many shots are so stationary that the only actual animation might be an eye blink. But after one gets used to the convention, the Grantray-Lawrence cartoons become quite attractive, translating the comic book art to film amazingly well. These cartoons have a visual rhythm all their own, which is abetted by fine voice work and thrilling music. Despite the budgetary limitations, these first translations into animation for the Marvel characters were, in their own way, beautifully done.

Cap's next appearance on television was not until 1979, though in the interim there was another popular series about a guy named Steve who was transformed by government scientists and doctors into a superman, which resulted in his acting as a secret weapon for Washington. In this case, the "Steve" was Steve Austin, and the series, "The Six-Million Dollar Man," ran on ABC from 1974 to 1978. Although the show was officially based on a Martin Caidin novel called *Cyborg*, the shadow that Steve Rogers cast over Steve Austin was easy to detect.

When Captain America himself returned to the small screen it was as part of a package of Marvel properties that had been optioned by Frank Price, then head of Universal Television. In addition to Cap, the group included Spider-Man, The Incredible Hulk, Dr. Strange, The Human Torch (from The Fantastic Four), and Ms. Marvel, who was then starring in a short-lived comic magazine of her own. The latter two never made it beyond development stages. By the time "Captain America" was launched as a pilot for a potential series for CBS, on January 19, 1979, "The Incredible Hulk" and "Spider-Man" had already made it to weekly series status. Captain America, however, proved to be a harder sell.

Once again, Hollywood chose to jettison the established mythology of Captain America, allowing writers Chester Krumholz and Don Ingalls to reinvent his backstory, making the young man who would ultimately become Captain America the son of the 1940s figure. In this adaptation, Steve Rogers is a footloose ex-Marine, motocross champion, and a fledgling artist who is ambling down the California coast in a van with a motorcycle strapped on back, in search of a new, nonmilitary life. But Rogers (played by a former All-American footballer named Reb Brown) learns that he is not master of his own destiny. He is being watched by strange men and receives puzzling telegrams from someone named Simon Mills.

Mills (Len Birman, in an appropriately inscrutable performance) turns out to be a rather mysterious government employee who reports directly to the president. He lures Steve to the U.S. Government National Security Laboratory and informs him that his late father had developed a secret formula for the government called "FLAG"—Full Latent Ability Gain serum—which increases the human body's strength potential from the normal 30 percent to near 100 percent, and which turned the elder Rogers into a super crimefighter who was sneeringly dubbed "Captain America" by the underworld. Since the serum had been synthesized from Rogers's own body fluids, the lab scientists need some of Steve's blood to continue their research and perfect the formula. Steve is initially reluctant to help, feeling that he has already done his

(Top) Television's "Captain America" (1979) offered a greatly changed version of the venerable hero.

(Above) Steve Rogers, as played by Reb Brown in two television movies in 1979, was presented as the son of the "real" Captain America.

(Top) With a modified costume, somewhat closer to the original design, Cap leaps into action.

(Above) The crash helmet for Cap's television appearances reflected his preferred mode of transformation, a souped-up motorcycle.

duty for his country. But he soon learns that he is already involved in a deadly plot launched by a megalomanic oil tycoon named Lou Bracket (a cold-eyed Steve Forrest), who has secretly been developing a neutron bomb. Brackett plans to use the bomb to devastate Phoenix, Arizona, so that he can empty the $1.4-billion gold depository that is located there.

Fearful that Steve will interfere with his plans, Brackett attempts to kill him by forcing his motorcycle off a cliff, and he nearly succeeds. Steve only survives because Mills has decided to use the FLAG serum on him. As a result, Steve develops super strength and super senses, but also the feeling that he's being used as a super pawn. Once again he rejects his government's call. Only when it becomes clear that he is too deeply involved in the strange goings-on to get out does he accept Mills's offer. The government in return gives Steve a souped-up, gadget-laden van, complete with a jet-powered, ultra-silent motorcycle that utilizes a bulletproof Captain America shield for its windscreen, and a "disguise" that is based on Steve's own sketch—a blue, satiny jump suit with a motorcycle helmet and goggles.

Blasting into action as the new Captain America, Steve manages to stop Brackett en route to Phoenix and agrees to sign on full time with Uncle Sam as a "secret weapon," but under one condition: that he is allowed to become the same Captain America his father was. In the film's last few moments, Steve shows up in his father's old costume (the first mention that the elder Rogers had ever worn a costume), which, save for the crash helmet, is closer to the design established in the comic books.

Director Rod Holcomb stages some very effective scenes for "Captain America," particularly one spectacular stunt in which camera angles and skillful editing give the impression that Steve Rogers has run a motorcycle up a ramp, let go at the top, and leapt onto the skid of an overhead helicopter. Taken simply as an example of the kind of television movie that was being produced in the late-1970s, "Captain America" is not bad. As for Reb Brown, while admittedly no Brando, he

displayed a natural charm and played his role with a
sincerity that serves to anchor the film against all the
strangeness that is going on around him. But once again,
legions of comic book fans were disappointed with
"Captain America," chiefly because of the changes made
in the character and the fact that precious little is seen
of Cap himself, as opposed to Steve Rogers.

CBS's second Captain America pilot was aired
later that year and split over two nights, on November
23 and 24, 1979. Titled simply, "Captain America II,"
the script was written by Wilton Schiller and Patricia
Payne, with Ivan Nagy taking over from Rod Holcomb
as director (though Holcomb received a 2nd Unit
director credit).

Now supporting himself as a sketch artist on
Venice Beach in California, Steve is once more drawn
into mysterious proceedings by Simon Mills, who asks
him to investigate the disappearance of a scientist who
had been working on an anti-aging formula. Not so
coincidentally, the mysterious terrorist Miguel (played
by British cult star Christopher Lee) is thought to have
gained entry into the United States, though no one
knows where he is, or even what he looks like.

The trail leads Steve to a small town in Oregon,
where the people remain frightened, secretive, and
unfriendly, and Steve cannot penetrate why. Finally he
learns that the town has been exposed to a quick-aging
formula, which was created by the kidnapped scientist,
and is being used as a test village by Miguel, whose
forces are controlling the town, doling out the antidote
to the residents in return for their silence. From his
hideout cleverly set up in a federal penitentiary in
Oregon, Miguel plans to drop the rapid-aging formula
from an airplane over Portland unless the United States
government pays him $1 billion in cash. The formula
would age each person exposed seventy years in one
month's time.

Despite the fact that the terrorist's audacious
claims have been borne out by a laboratory test, the
president of the United States refuses to do business

Steve Rogers receives a less than warm welcome by townspeople in
"Captain America II" (1979).

(Top) International terrorist Miguel (British horror film veteran Christopher Lee) succumbs to his own aging serum in "Captain America II."

(Above) Cap blasting off into a new adventure.

with the terrorist. So Miguel orders the aging serum dropped from a plane, which writes "SMILE" in skywriting before filtering down as a blanketing fog over Portland. The townspeople are told that they're infected, and the antidote will be made available only when the president ponies up, but now the price has been raised to $2 billion!

From his small town base, Steve discovers that Miguel is holed up in the nearby prison. In Captain America garb, he infiltrates the prison compound and manages to obtain both the aging serum and the antidote from Miguel's lab, while releasing the kidnapped scientist in the process. Leaving the prison on his motorcycle, which transforms into a hang glider, Cap follows Miguel's limo from the air, chasing the car until it stops. Having been forced into a corner, Miguel fights back the only way he can, by pitching a bottle of aging serum toward Cap. But Cap slings his shield at and shatters the bottle midair, and the liquid splashes back onto Miguel. Then in a scene reminiscent of Christopher Lee's previous disintegrations in his many Dracula films, the terrorist ages fifty years in a matter of seconds and dies. Portland fares better—it only ages ten months before Mills arranges to have the antidote sprayed over the city from planes.

"Captain America II" has a much more complex plot, and more important, featured many more scenes of Cap in action, including recurring shots of him blasting out of the back of his van on his jet-cycle, amidst a huge burst of smoke, but the film failed to make much of an impression. In June of 1980 "Captain America II" (now retitled "Captain America") was rebroadcast as a single two-hour movie by CBS. Despite the heavy press fanfare for the rebroadcast, it failed to create interest in any further Captain America television projects.

Throughout the 1980s, big-screen adaptions of *Captain America* were announced several times. The first was in October 1984, at which time ads appeared in Hollywood trade papers announcing a version from Cannon Films written by James R. Silke. Nothing came of that announcement. Then in 1986, another version of *Captain America* was announced, this one to be directed by Michael Winner and utilizing a script by Stan Lee and Lawrence Block. There were even rumors at the time that Marlon Brando was interested in playing The Red Skull, while Elton John was being mentioned in the press as a candidate for the role of Captain America! That turned out to be a hoax (though in the right circumstances, the rock legend might have made a convincing Bucky). Ultimately it did not matter, since the project never got off the ground.

A new script, written by Stephen Tolkin, based on a story by Tolkin and Block, went before the cameras in June of 1989, with Albert Pyun (a one-time assistant to Japanese master filmmaker Akira Kurosawa) directing and former Cannon Films head Menachem Golan producing for 21st Century Film Corporation. Filming of the $12-million production began in Zagreb, Yugoslavia, with location scenes shot in Los Angeles and Alaska. Actor Matt Salinger (the son of writer J.D. Salinger) took the role of Steve Rogers/Captain America, and Scott Paulin played The Red Skull, while a host of more familiar actors, including Ronny Cox, Darren McGavin, Ned Beatty, and former child star Bill Mumy (from "Twilight Zone" and "Lost in Space" fame) rounded out the cast.

To tell the story of Captain America for modern audiences, the filmmakers went back to the original comic book mythology and married it to the rebirth mythology from the 1960s, showing Cap both as a World War II hero and as a man in modern times having been thawed from the ice block.

The film opens in Portovenere, Italy, in 1936, where a young boy is giving a piano recital for his family, a home concert that is being recorded with a wire recorder. With no warning, fascist storm troopers break in, take the boy and slaughter the family. The boy, who has been selected because of his superior intellect, is taken to a foreboding castle called Fortress Lorenzo, where a group of Axis leaders are being shown results of

(Opposite) Matt Salinger made a very convincing Cap in the film *Captain America* (1990).

An appropriately hideous Red Skull (actor Scott Paulin) from *Captain America* (1990).

a ghastly experiment on a common lab rat. The creature has been injected with a special drug that has imbued it with superior intelligence and strength, but it can no longer be considered a rat: it has become a vicious, crimson, skeletal monster. The scientists then plan to perform the same experiment on the young boy. Only one member of the scientific team objects: Dr. Maria Vaselli, who cannot justify torturing the boy. She escapes amidst gunfire from the fortress and listens outside in horror to the boy's agonizing screams.

Seven years later, Dr. Vaselli, who has defected to America, is the creator of "Operation Rebirth," a scientific project that will allow crippled children to be cured and regenerated. But the government is more interested in using it to create super soldiers. The film duplicates intact the original creation story involving Steve Rogers (whose frailty is here depicted as the result of a bout with childhood polio), including having a murderous Nazi spy as a witness to the experiment, but adds the bizarrely creative touch of having the secret experiment take place in a hidden grotto underneath a Southern California diner!

Despite the fact that Rogers—now known only as Captain America, his government code name—has been wounded by the Nazi spy, he is drafted by his government to stop the Nazis, who are believed to have an experimental rocket ready to launch at the U.S. within five days. Clad in his fireproof, brightly colored Captain America costume, which had been made by Dr. Vaselli (and which prompts Steve to quip, "She sure didn't know much about camouflage"), Steve parachutes out behind enemy lines and battles his way into the grim Fortress Lorenzo. There he encounters the result of the horrible Nazi experiment that had been conducted seven years earlier, the hideous, skinless, milk-eyed visage of The Red Skull, who addresses Cap as "my American brother." To his dismay, the powerful Red Skull proves to be a more strategic fighter and easily defeats Cap, then ties him onto a missile, which is launched directly at the White House. Realizing he is doomed, Cap spends what little time he has left in trying to spare Washington. He kicks at the missile's control panel with his heel until he manages to break through and smashes the circuitry, which causes the missile to veer off course at the last minute. It soars over the White House and heads northward to Alaska, where it crash-lands in a frozen wasteland.

The film segues to the present day, when Cap's body is discovered by explorers. As the revived Steve Rogers tries to acclimate himself to the modern world, he is horrified to learn that The Red Skull is still alive. His looks partially restored through plastic surgery (which leaves his face scarred, but no longer sickeningly inhuman), The Skull now operates as an Italian businessman named de Santis, who is really the leader of an international cartel working to take over the world.

An American general named Fleming (who as a young officer had witnessed the experiment that created Captain America decades earlier) is part of the cartel, and he is advocating assassinating the president of the United States. The Red Skull/de Santis, however, has other ideas. "Assassination isn't worth the trouble," he says. "It took two years to find Sirhan, three to find Oswald. The King job alone cost us over twenty-two million dollars. And what do we get for our pains? Saints. Martyrs to the cause." (And while on paper this speech may read tastelessly over the top, Scott Paulin's delivery of it is quite chilling.) De Santis instead recommends kidnapping the president while he's in Rome, hosting an international summit on environmental protection, and putting an implant in his brain in order to control him.

The president is abducted and Steve makes his way to Italy to try and find the Skull. He is accompanied by Sharon, the daughter of his old girlfriend Bernie (a carryover from the comic books), whom he left behind in 1943 when he went to war. Sharon is along for vengeance, since an attempt on Steve's life, directed by de Santis's beautiful but deadly daughter, Valentina, resulted in Bernie's death. Having learned of The Skull's

(Top) Cap battles The Red Skull at his Nazi lair.

(Above) A tattered Cap squares off against a reconstructed Red Skull in *Captain America*.

In 1990's *Captain America* the filmmakers at last got Cap's shield and costume right.

whereabouts in Italy, Rogers dons his tattered Captain America costume one last time to face his Italian "brother" in a fight to the death. De Santis taunts him, sneering, "You remain a clownish symbol that no one cares about." "I care," Cap says. But the former Skull now plays his final hand: he has a secret detonator that will wipe out all of Southern Europe. He refuses to be taken alive, and plans to take Europe down with him. But a well-placed shield fling knocks de Santis off the parapet of Fortress Lorenzo. With the traitorous General Fleming in custody, the president goes on to host his environmental protection summit as planned, and in the film's closing moments, thanks Captain America, "wherever he is." (The film's environmental message was not just a plot point: a note at the end of the closing credits encouraged viewers' support for the Environmental Protection Act of 1990.)

Captain America was picked up for distribution by Columbia in 1990. Posters advertising the release were displayed in New York City, but the film itself never appeared in theaters. Rumors began to fly, some of them coming from the studio itself, that either the film had not been completed or its quality was too poor to warrant a theatrical release. Instead it was distributed as a direct-to-video feature in June 1992.

Despite the rumors of the time, *Captain America* is not a bad film. It is not a *perfect* film—some of the action sequences, for instance, are clumsily filmed and edited—but it's colorful and it does work on the comic book level for which it was designed. Matt Salinger is convincing as both the frail Steve Rogers in the early scenes and the beefed-up, powerful Captain America. Scott Paulin makes The Red Skull/de Santis a believable menace and even makes an appearance without the prosthetic makeup early in a second role in the film as the physician who attends Steve Rogers in the army hospital. Ultimately, though, the film shares a common problem with the 1978 version: there's too much Steve Rogers and not enough Captain America. Cap is seen in costume for only two sequences, both showing his battles with The Red Skull, which is a particular shame since, for once, the filmmakers actually got the costume right. But despite its flaws, the 1990 *Captain America* remains the best live-action treatment of Cap on film to date.

After sixty years, Captain America shows no signs of slowing down. He has most recently been seen in a guest appearance battling his old enemy Baron Zemo on the Saturday morning series "The Avengers," which is produced for Fox Kids Network by Marvel Studios and Saban Entertainment, a creative partnership that has brought many Marvel characters to the small screen. In 1998, plans were made for a full-scale Captain America animated series, which would have taken the character back to his earliest comic book roots by placing he and Bucky against the backdrop of World War II. A short pilot was produced, which revealed dramatic character design and staging, but it did not result in the desired thirteen-episode series.

From that first sketch by Joe Simon, showing Cap waving heroically, to the present, it has been an incredible journey for Captain America—long may he wave.

Development art for a prospective "Captain America" animated series in 1998, which would have returned the character to his World War II roots.

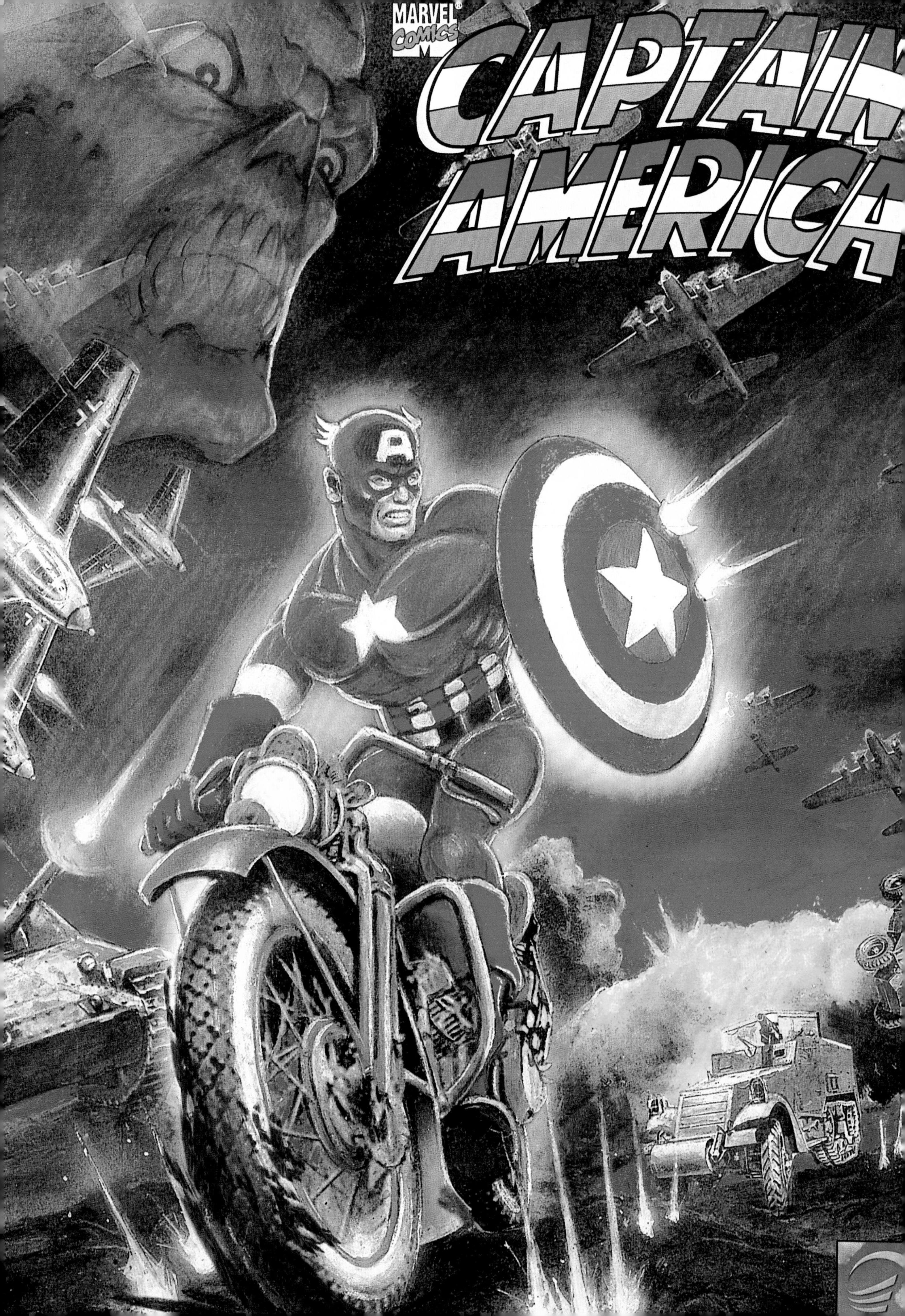
MARVEL COMICS
CAPTAIN AMERICA

SPIDER

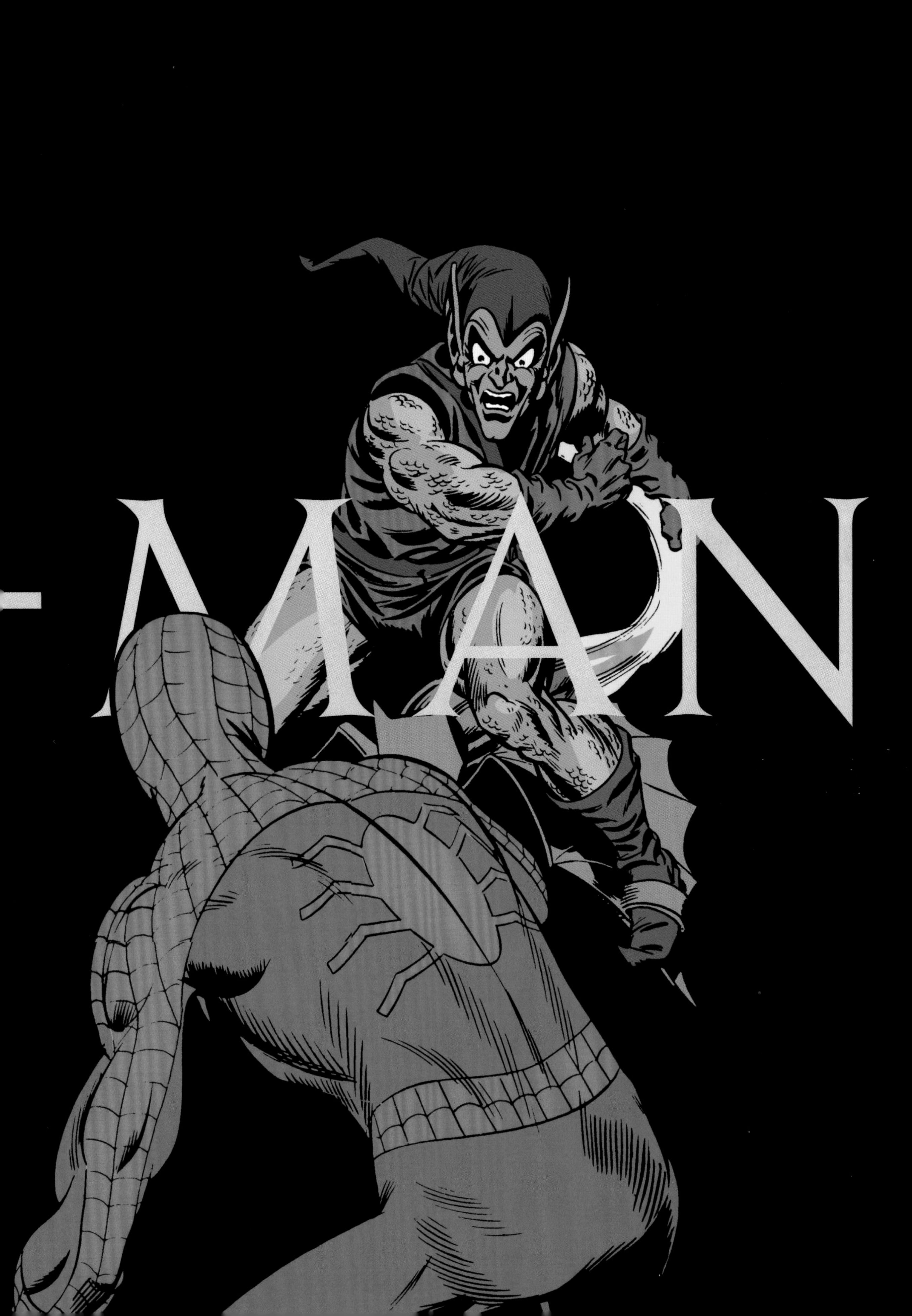
-MAN

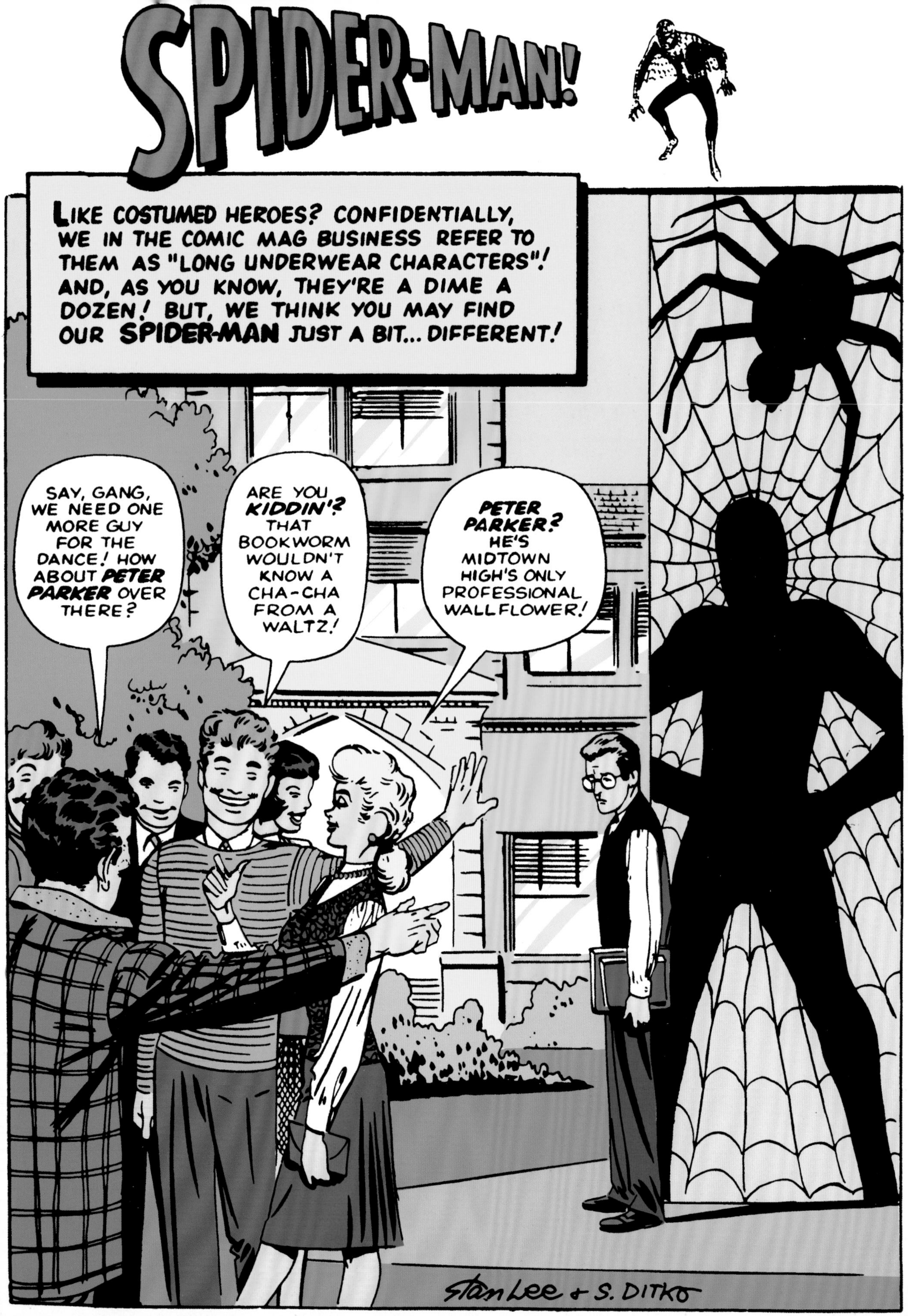
SPIDER-MAN!
LIKE COSTUMED HEROES? CONFIDENTIALLY, WE IN THE COMIC MAG BUSINESS REFER TO THEM AS "LONG UNDERWEAR CHARACTERS"! AND, AS YOU KNOW, THEY'RE A DIME A DOZEN! BUT, WE THINK YOU MAY FIND OUR SPIDER-MAN JUST A BIT... DIFFERENT!
SAY, GANG, WE NEED ONE MORE GUY FOR THE DANCE! HOW ABOUT PETER PARKER OVER THERE?
ARE YOU KIDDIN'? THAT BOOKWORM WOULDN'T KNOW A CHA-CHA FROM A WALTZ!
PETER PARKER? HE'S MIDTOWN HIGH'S ONLY PROFESSIONAL WALLFLOWER!
Stan Lee + S. DITKO

SPIDER-MAN

ARACHNO-PHENOMENON

For many, Spider-Man is THE superhero of the twentieth century.
He has come to symbolize Marvel Comics, and for good reason.
More than any other character, he represents Marvel's unique
approach of creating heroes with real-world problems. Spider-Man's
alter ego Peter Parker suffers from allergies, insecurities, uncertainty
around girls in his early years, and chronic difficulty making ends
meet in later years. Except for his ability to crawl up and down walls,
he could be the nerdy kid next door.

The creation of the character has become the stuff
of legend. The version most commonly told is that when
Stan Lee was trying to come up with a new superhero
idea he spied a fly crawling up the wall of his office.
Inspired by the notion of a wall-climbing comic book
hero, he quickly ran down a list of potential names, such
as "Insect Man" and "Mosquito Man," before settling on
the dramatic sounding "Spider-Man." But Lee adds: "I
always preface that story by saying I've told it so often
that, for all I know, it might even be true." An entirely
different account of Spidey's creation was related by Lee
in the book *Origins of Marvel Comics.* In this version the
character was inspired by an old pulp magazine of the
1930s called *The Spider, Master of Men,* and the name
Spider-Man was offered as a deliberately tongue-in-cheek
parody of Superman.

Regardless of whether it was The Spider or the
fly, Lee realized that he had the opportunity to create a
character that defied the conventional wisdom governing
what made a successful superhero. Furthermore, the fact
that the story was slated to appear in *Amazing Fantasy,* a
magazine that was about to be discontinued, meant that
he had nothing to lose by experimenting. Initially, Jack
Kirby was assigned to draw Spider-Man's debut story,
but it quickly became apparent that, despite Kirby's
talent, the artist was miscast. "I didn't want Peter Parker
to look like a superhero, I wanted him to look like an
average school boy," says Lee. "Jack had a way of drawing
people who looked bigger and bolder than life, and when

Spider-Man's introduction in *Amazing Fantasy* #15 (August 1962), showed
Peter Parker at his most downtrodden.

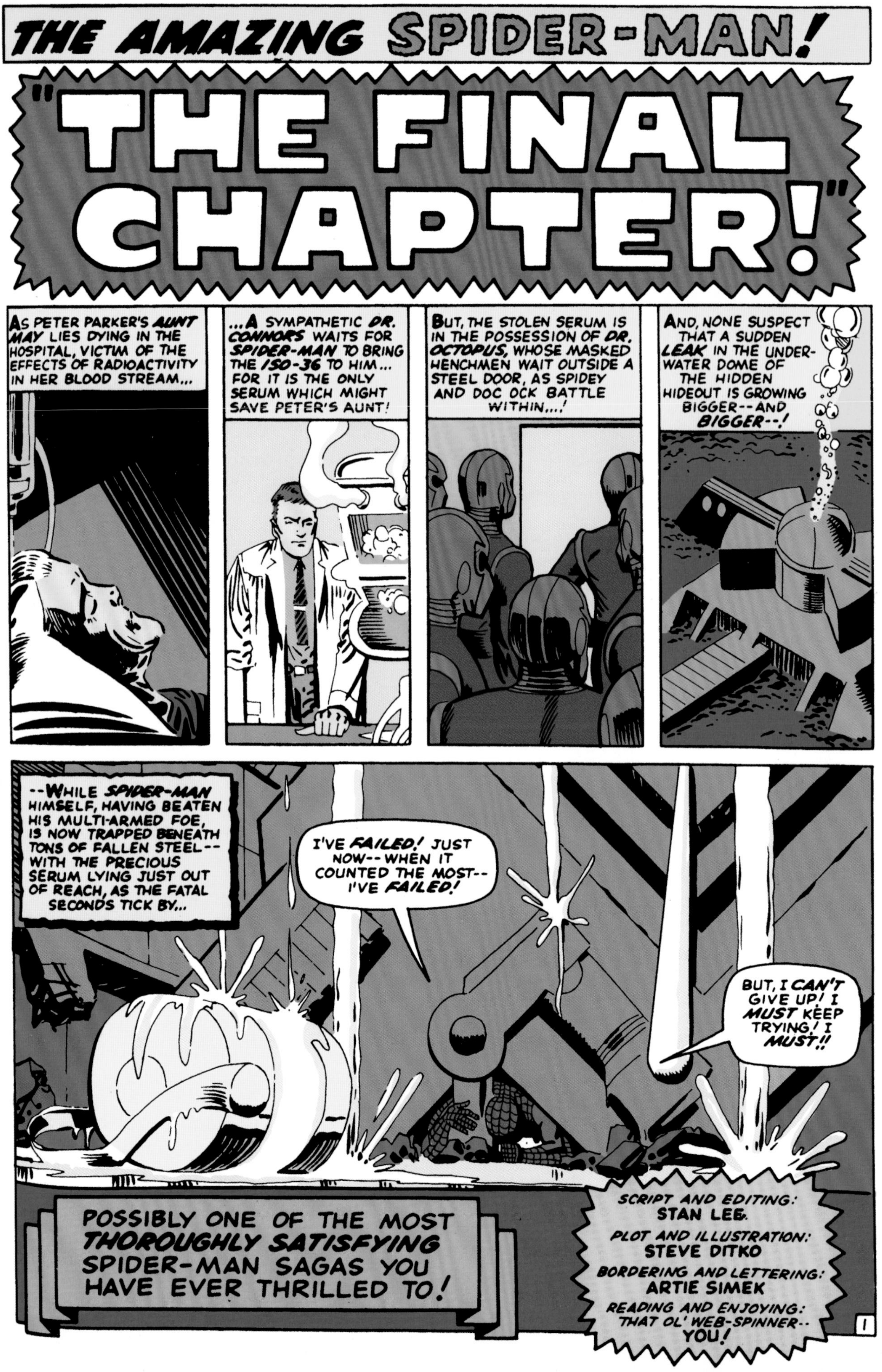
THE AMAZING SPIDER-MAN!
"THE FINAL CHAPTER!"
AS PETER PARKER'S AUNT MAY LIES DYING IN THE HOSPITAL, VICTIM OF THE EFFECTS OF RADIOACTIVITY IN HER BLOOD STREAM...
...A SYMPATHETIC DR. CONNORS WAITS FOR SPIDER-MAN TO BRING THE ISO-36 TO HIM... FOR IT IS THE ONLY SERUM WHICH MIGHT SAVE PETER'S AUNT!
BUT, THE STOLEN SERUM IS IN THE POSSESSION OF DR. OCTOPUS, WHOSE MASKED HENCHMEN WAIT OUTSIDE A STEEL DOOR, AS SPIDEY AND DOC OCK BATTLE WITHIN...!
AND, NONE SUSPECT THAT A SUDDEN LEAK IN THE UNDER-WATER DOME OF THE HIDDEN HIDEOUT IS GROWING BIGGER--AND BIGGER--!
--WHILE SPIDER-MAN HIMSELF, HAVING BEATEN HIS MULTI-ARMED FOE, IS NOW TRAPPED BENEATH TONS OF FALLEN STEEL--WITH THE PRECIOUS SERUM LYING JUST OUT OF REACH, AS THE FATAL SECONDS TICK BY...
I'VE FAILED! JUST NOW--WHEN IT COUNTED THE MOST--I'VE FAILED!
BUT, I CAN'T GIVE UP! I MUST KEEP TRYING! I MUST!!
POSSIBLY ONE OF THE MOST THOROUGHLY SATISFYING SPIDER-MAN SAGAS YOU HAVE EVER THRILLED TO!
SCRIPT AND EDITING: STAN LEE
PLOT AND ILLUSTRATION: STEVE DITKO
BORDERING AND LETTERING: ARTIE SIMEK
READING AND ENJOYING: THAT OL' WEB-SPINNER--YOU!
1

I'VE GOT TO TRY TO FREE MYSELF-- NO MATTER HOW IMPOSSIBLE IT SEEMS!
AND LIFTING IS THE ONLY WAY! THE-- ONLY-- WAY--!
UHHHHH-- I CAN'T!-- SO EXHAUSTED-- AFTER ALL THAT FIGHTING-- I-- I FEEL SO WEAK--!
BUT THEN, THE AMAZING TEEN-AGER GLIMPSES THE LIFE-SAVING SERUM-- SO NEAR, AND YET SO FAR-- SO HOPELESSLY FAR AWAY!
IT'S LYING THERE-- JUST BEYOND REACH-- AS THOUGH MOCKING ME-- TAUNTING ME--
IT'S THE ONE THING-- THE ONLY THING-- THAT MAY SAVE AUNT MAY! AND I CAN'T BRING IT TO HER--!
IF SHE-- DOESN'T MAKE IT-- IT'LL BE MY FAULT! JUST THE WAY I'LL ALWAYS BLAME MYSELF FOR WHAT HAPPENED TO UNCLE BEN*...!
*FROM THE MOMENTOUS TALE OF SPIDEY'S ORIGIN-- REMEMBER?--STAN.
THE TWO PEOPLE IN ALL THE WORLD WHO'VE BEEN KINDEST TO ME! I CAN'T FAIL AGAIN! IT CAN'T HAPPEN A SECOND TIME! I WON'T LET IT-- I WON'T!--
NO MATTER WHAT THE ODDS-- NO MATTER WHAT THE COST-- I'LL GET THAT SERUM TO AUNT MAY! AND MAYBE THEN I'LL NO LONGER BE HAUNTED BY THE MEMORY-- OF UNCLE BEN!

WITHIN MY BODY IS THE STRENGTH OF MANY MEN...!
AND NOW, I'VE GOT TO CALL ON ALL THAT STRENGTH-- ALL THE POWER-- THAT I POSSESS!
I MUST PROVE EQUAL TO THE TASK-- I MUST BE WORTHY OF THAT STRENGTH--
--OR ELSE, I DON'T DESERVE IT!
THE WEIGHT-- IS UNBEARABLE! EVERY MUSCLE-- ACHES--!
MY HEAD-- IT'S SPINNING-- EVERYTHING'S BEGINNING TO --WHIRL AROUND--!
THE STRAIN! IT-- IT'S UNBEARABLE --!

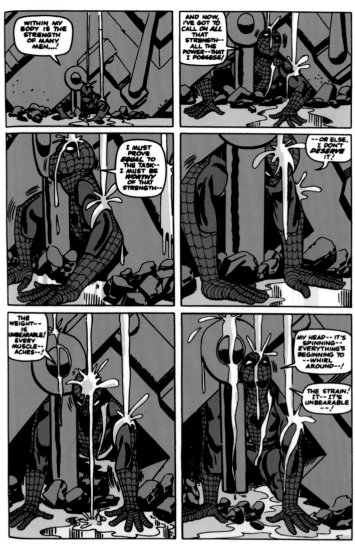

I saw the way [Peter Parker] looked, I said, 'Jack, forget it, I'm going to give it to Ditko instead.'"

Artist Steve Ditko, whose eye leaned more toward drama and realism than fantastic action, proved to be the right choice. Born in 1927 in Johnstown, Pennsylvania, Ditko had entered the comics field in the early 1950s, and by 1956 he was providing art for some of Atlas's horror comics (years later Ditko would return to the genre through Warren Publishing's black-and-white comic magazines *Creepy* and *Eerie*). While Ditko's time at Marvel was relatively brief—he left the company in 1966 and didn't return until 1979 for another short stint—his presence loomed large and his distinctive graphic style made an impact on readers.

Amazing Fantasy #15 (August, 1962) introduced bookish, bespectacled Peter Parker, who is described as "Midtown High's only professional wallflower." While the school athletes are out with their girlfriends, Peter, who lives with his doting Aunt May and Uncle Ben, heads for the school science lab to watch an experiment

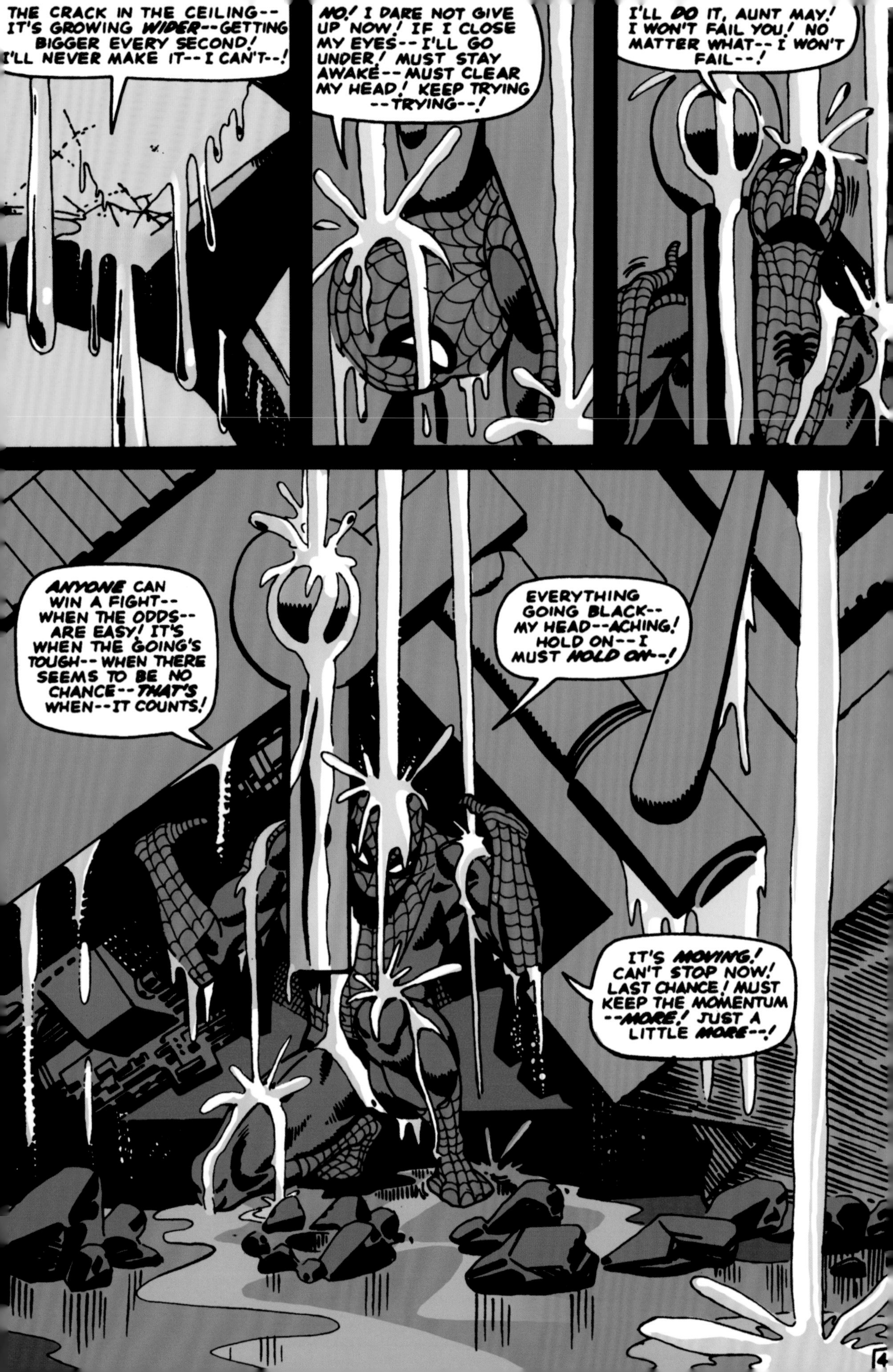
THE CRACK IN THE CEILING-- IT'S GROWING WIDER--GETTING BIGGER EVERY SECOND! I'LL NEVER MAKE IT-- I CAN'T--!
NO! I DARE NOT GIVE UP NOW! IF I CLOSE MY EYES-- I'LL GO UNDER! MUST STAY AWAKE--MUST CLEAR MY HEAD! KEEP TRYING --TRYING--!
I'LL DO IT, AUNT MAY! I WON'T FAIL YOU! NO MATTER WHAT-- I WON'T FAIL--!
ANYONE CAN WIN A FIGHT-- WHEN THE ODDS-- ARE EASY! IT'S WHEN THE GOING'S TOUGH-- WHEN THERE SEEMS TO BE NO CHANCE--THAT'S WHEN--IT COUNTS!
EVERYTHING GOING BLACK-- MY HEAD--ACHING! HOLD ON--I MUST HOLD ON--!
IT'S MOVING! CAN'T STOP NOW! LAST CHANCE! MUST KEEP THE MOMENTUM --MORE! JUST A LITTLE MORE--!
4

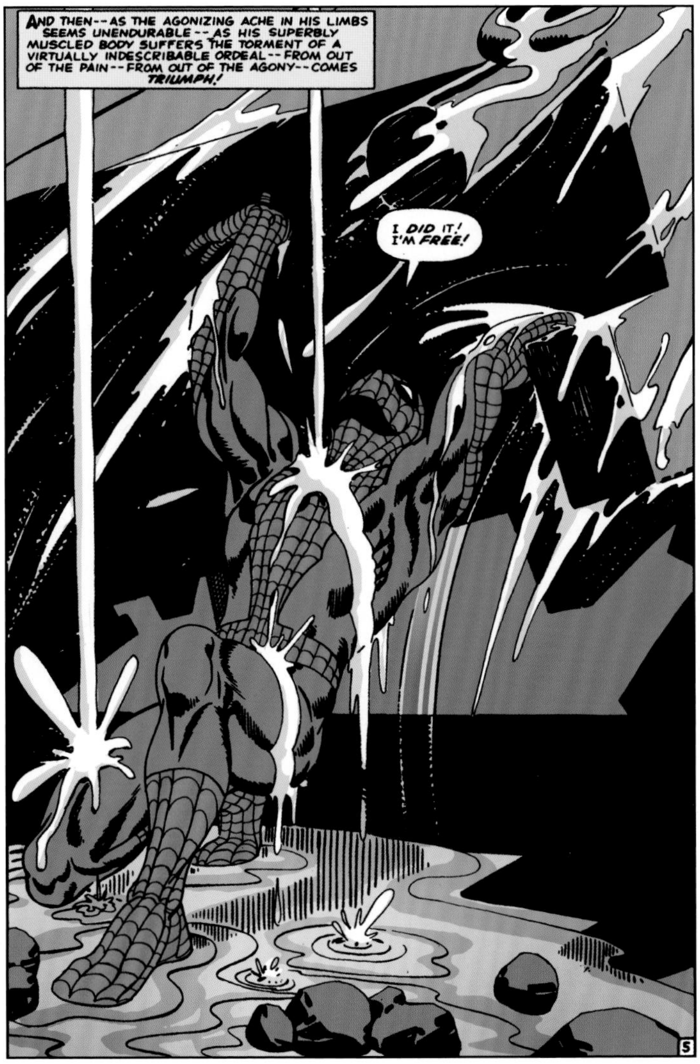
AND THEN--AS THE AGONIZING ACHE IN HIS LIMBS SEEMS UNENDURABLE--AS HIS SUPERBLY MUSCLED BODY SUFFERS THE TORMENT OF A VIRTUALLY INDESCRIBABLE ORDEAL--FROM OUT OF THE PAIN--FROM OUT OF THE AGONY--COMES TRIUMPH!
I DID IT! I'M FREE!
5

(Previous spread, left, above) This now-classic sequence drawn by Steve Ditko, from *Spider-Man* #33 in 1966, in which Spidey agonizes over his life, as well as his predicament, was a turning point for the character and a perfect example of the "Marvel Method" of creation at work.

demonstrating how radioactive rays can be controlled. But during the experiment, a spider comes down from the ceiling and absorbs the rays, then bites Peter on the hand. Very shortly afterward, a startled but excited Peter discovers that he has strange powers, including the ability to crawl up walls and shinny down cables, like a spider. At home he fashions a blue and red costume (which initially featured a wing-like spider web under each arm) and crafts wristbands to wear under his costume that shoot out webs made from liquid cement. "So, they laughed at me for being a bookworm, eh? Well, only a science major could have created a device like this!" he gloats.

Unlike previous superheroes, who immediately put their powers to use for truth and justice, Peter uses his new talents to make a buck, showing off on television. But his initial success goes to his head. When a policeman berates him for not trying to stop a fleeing thief who has just run by him, Peter says: "Sorry, pal! That's your job! I'm thru [sic] being pushed around by anyone. From now on I just look out for Number One–that means–me!"

That moment of self-centeredness will haunt Peter forever. The young man's world is shattered when he discovers that his Uncle Ben has been shot and killed by a burglar, who turns out to be the very same criminal that Peter could have apprehended, but did not. As he wrestles with the guilt over having been an unknowing accessory to his uncle's murder, Peter resolves to stop squandering his newfound powers in frivolous ways and use them only to benefit humanity. In doing so, he reluctantly accepts that with great power there must also come great responsibility.

Copies of *Amazing Fantasy* #15 flew off the newsstands and Spider-Man was rewarded with his own monthly magazine, *The Amazing Spider-Man* (the word "Amazing" retained as a subtle nod to Spidey's debut mag) and allowed to grow up . . . more or less. Upon graduation from high school, Parker entered Empire State University and continued to work as a freelance

I APOLOGIZE FOR MY... UNFORTUNATE LAPSE EARLIER THIS EVENING.
"LAPSE"? YOU MEAN, LIKE TRYING TO KILL ME?
I SWEAR I'M IN CONTROL AGAIN! AND I BEG YOU--

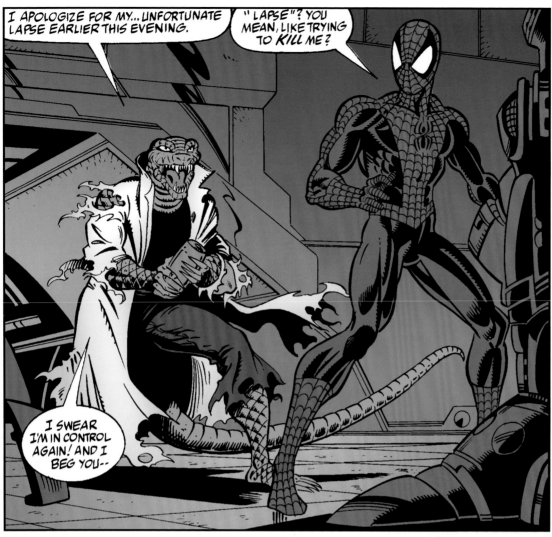

(Left) The Lizard (a.k.a. Curt Connors) would be one of Spidey's most perennial—and most bizarre—opponents.

(Below) Manic publisher J.J. Jameson's hatred for the web-crawler actually caused him to lose his grip in *The Amazing Spider-Man* #72 (1969).

(Opposite) Doctor Octopus, better known as "Doc Ock," was another of Spidey's most fearsome enemies.

AND, SPEAKING OF CONCENTRATION, LET'S SEE WHAT JOLLY JONAH JAMESON IS COGITATING ABOUT RIGHT NOW---
WHAT'S THIS??!!
MY OWN NEWSPAPER CALLING SPIDER-MAN A HERO?!!
BUGLE
DAILY BUGLE
THE WHOLE @X*!!#!%@??!! COUNTRY'S GOING TO THE DOGS!
A MAN CAN'T EVEN ENJOY HIMSELF IN THE HOSPITAL ANYMORE!
I'M GONNA FIRE EVERY NINCOMPOOP ON THAT PAPER!!
MR. JAMESON! YOU'RE DELIRIOUS!
YOU'RE DING DONG RIGHT I AM!
WHEN I FIND OUT WHO WROTE THAT STORY--!!
DOCTOR! DOCTOR! HELP!
YOU CAN'T DO THIS TO ME! GET ME MY LAWYER!
YOU'LL NEED AN UNDERTAKER IF YOU DON'T CALM DOWN!
HELLO! HELLO! GET ME THE BUGLE!
NOT BAGLE, DUMMY!! BUGLE!
NO! I DON'T WANT A DING-BUSTED MUSIC STORE...I MEANT THE DAILY BUGLE!
MR. JAMESON! YOU SIMPLY MUST HOLD STILL!
NO! I DON'T WANT A DAD-BLASTED PET SHOP!!
HOW COME YOU DIDN'T GET ME A PET SHOP... WHERE THEY SELL BEAGLES?!!
GET THAT NIT-WITTED NEEDLE AWAY FROM ME!!
NO! NO! I DIDN'T MEAN YOU!
I THOUGHT I'D NEVER GET THAT TRANQUILIZER INTO HIM!
ONLY WHEN HE'S AWAKE!
IS HE ALWAYS THAT EXCITABLE, DOCTOR?
WHY DID I BECOME A PUBLISHER?
I'M TOO SENSITIVE... TOO GENTLE... FOR ALL THIS!
NOBODY... UNDERSTANDS ME... NOBODY... CARES... NOBODY... ZZZZZ

photographer for the tyrannical J. Jonah Jameson, publisher of the *Daily Bugle.* Ironically, Jameson delights in conducting a Hearst-like smear campaign against Spider-Man, whom he considers a menace to society, despite Spidey's taking the public's side against the likes of such villains as Doctor Octopus and The Lizard, a.k.a. Dr. Curt Connors. While Jameson is far too obtuse to realize that this so-called menace is actually on his payroll, Peter does worry that some of the Bugle's more observant employees, such as Jameson's secretary Betty Brant—who would eventually become Peter's first love interest—and editor Joe "Robbie" Robertson (who was one of the first African-American recurring characters in comic books) might begin to suspect Peter's relationship with Spider-Man is closer than he lets on.

Starting in the mid-1960s, artist John Romita took over the character from Ditko, bringing a smooth, action-packed, kinetic energy to Spidey's adventures. Romita also proved he had a way with the ladies in his depiction of Peter Parker's two love interests, the

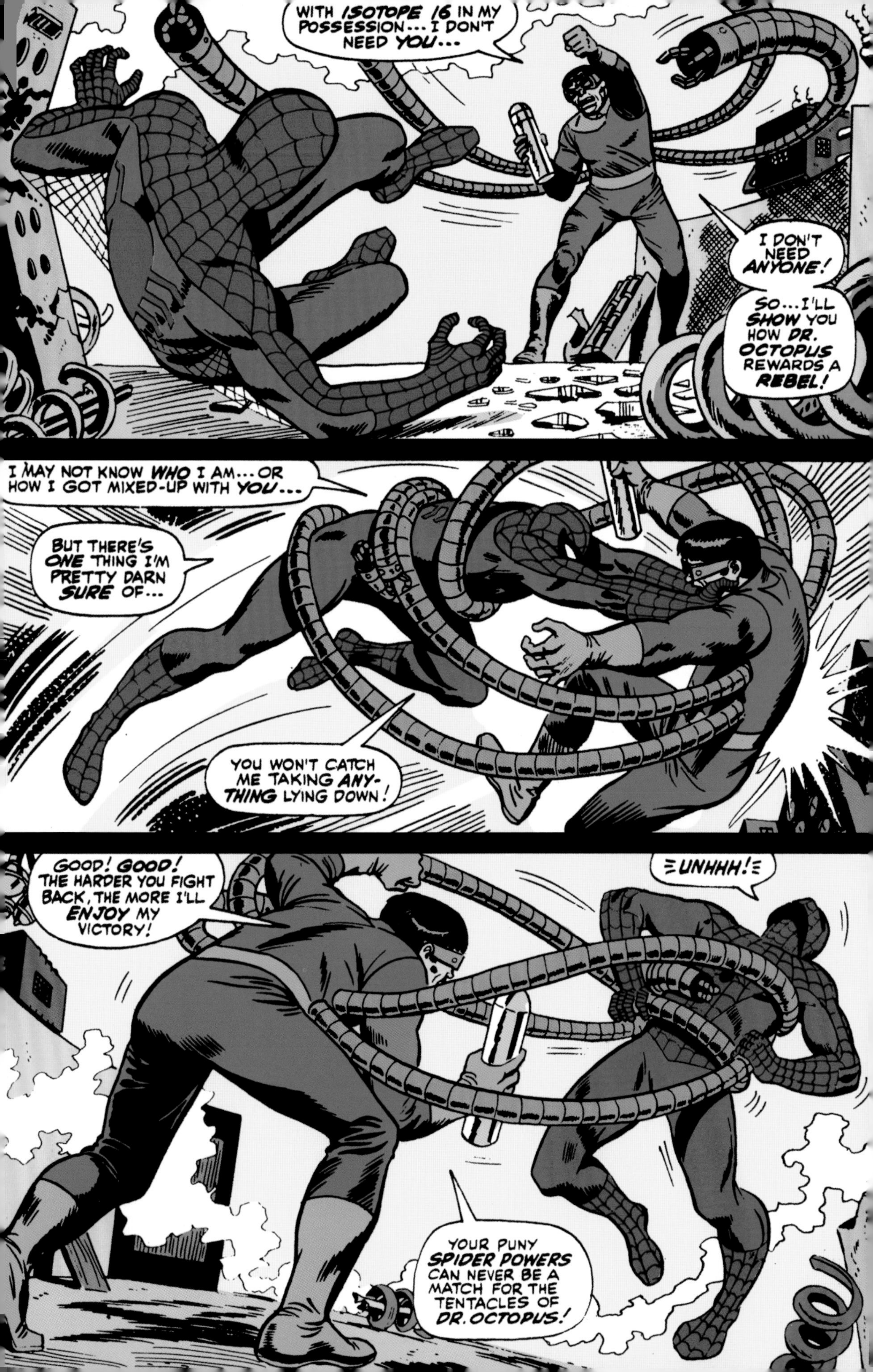
WITH ISOTOPE 16 IN MY POSSESSION... I DON'T NEED YOU...
I DON'T NEED ANYONE!
SO... I'LL SHOW YOU HOW DR. OCTOPUS REWARDS A REBEL!
I MAY NOT KNOW WHO I AM... OR HOW I GOT MIXED-UP WITH YOU...
BUT THERE'S ONE THING I'M PRETTY DARN SURE OF...
YOU WON'T CATCH ME TAKING ANY-THING LYING DOWN!
GOOD! GOOD! THE HARDER YOU FIGHT BACK, THE MORE I'LL ENJOY MY VICTORY!
UNHHH!
YOUR PUNY SPIDER POWERS CAN NEVER BE A MATCH FOR THE TENTACLES OF DR. OCTOPUS!

redheaded Mary Jane Watson and the cool blonde Gwendolyn Stacy. The longing for a normal home life, ideally with Gwen (or, as Peter preciously refers to her, "Gwendy"), even prompts him to abandon his costume and responsibility and give up crimefighting—at least for one issue (*Amazing Spider-Man* #50). In fact, Peter's increasingly complicated life threatened to overwhelm him in a now-classic three-issue (#96–#98) series from 1971, featuring the nefarious Green Goblin, who was in reality Norman Osborne, the wealthy but schizophrenic father of Peter's friend, Harry Osborne (though in later years, after Norman's death, Harry would acquire his father's mental instability and his costume, and become the new Green Goblin).

It wasn't the demented activity of The Goblin, or even the dynamic and dramatic artwork by Gil Kane (pencils) and John Romita (inks) that has made this particular storyline legendary. Instead it was the fact that, for the first time in comic books, the hot-button issue of drugs was addressed head-on. That came about when Stan Lee had been asked by the Department of Health, Education, and Welfare in Washington to do a story about the dangers of drug abuse. He complied by turning out a story in which Harry Osborne (with whom Peter Parker was then rooming because he could no longer afford a place of his own) becomes hooked on pills and eventually becomes bedridden through a bad acid trip. The problem was that the Comics Code, which affixed its seal of approval to every comic book published in the United States, had an ironclad policy that no mention of drugs was permissible.

"I said, 'Look, we're not telling kids to take drugs, this is an anti-drug story,'" Lee recalls. "And they said, 'Yeah, but you're not allowed to mention drugs.' So I said, 'We're going to mention that, we just won't put the seal of approval on the cover of those books.' I felt that the United States Government somehow took precedence over the Comics Authority." When those three issues came out, sans the Comics Code seal, the Comics Authority finally got the message and amended their policy to allow for anti-drug statements.

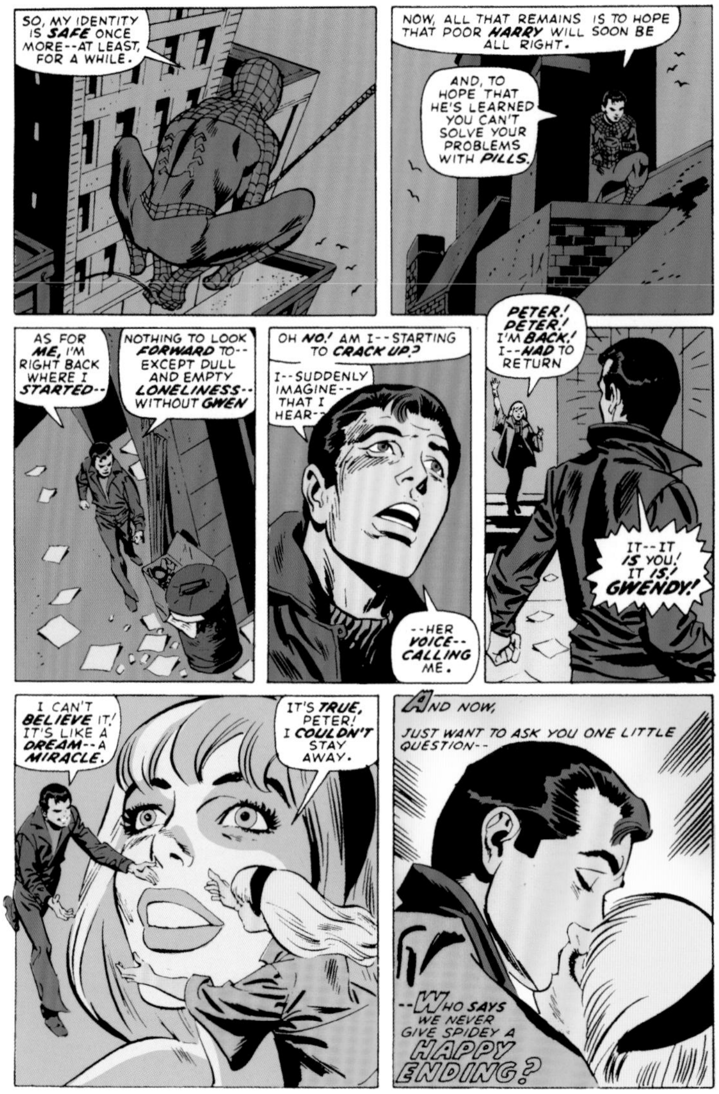
SO, MY IDENTITY IS SAFE ONCE MORE--AT LEAST, FOR A WHILE.
NOW, ALL THAT REMAINS IS TO HOPE THAT POOR HARRY WILL SOON BE ALL RIGHT.
AND, TO HOPE THAT HE'S LEARNED YOU CAN'T SOLVE YOUR PROBLEMS WITH PILLS.
AS FOR ME, I'M RIGHT BACK WHERE I STARTED--
NOTHING TO LOOK FORWARD TO--EXCEPT DULL AND EMPTY LONELINESS--WITHOUT GWEN
OH NO! AM I--STARTING TO CRACK UP?
I--SUDDENLY IMAGINE--THAT I HEAR--
--HER VOICE--CALLING ME.
PETER! PETER! I'M BACK! I--HAD TO RETURN
IT--IT IS YOU! IT IS! GWENDY!
I CAN'T BELIEVE IT! IT'S LIKE A DREAM--A MIRACLE.
IT'S TRUE, PETER! I COULDN'T STAY AWAY.
AND NOW, JUST WANT TO ASK YOU ONE LITTLE QUESTION--
--WHO SAYS WE NEVER GIVE SPIDEY A HAPPY ENDING?
The romance between Peter and Gwen Stacy finally blossomed in issue #98 (1971), though the "happy ending" would not last long.

(Opposite) Longing for a normal life, Peter Parker temporarily abandoned his superhero alter ego in *The Amazing Spider-Man* #50.

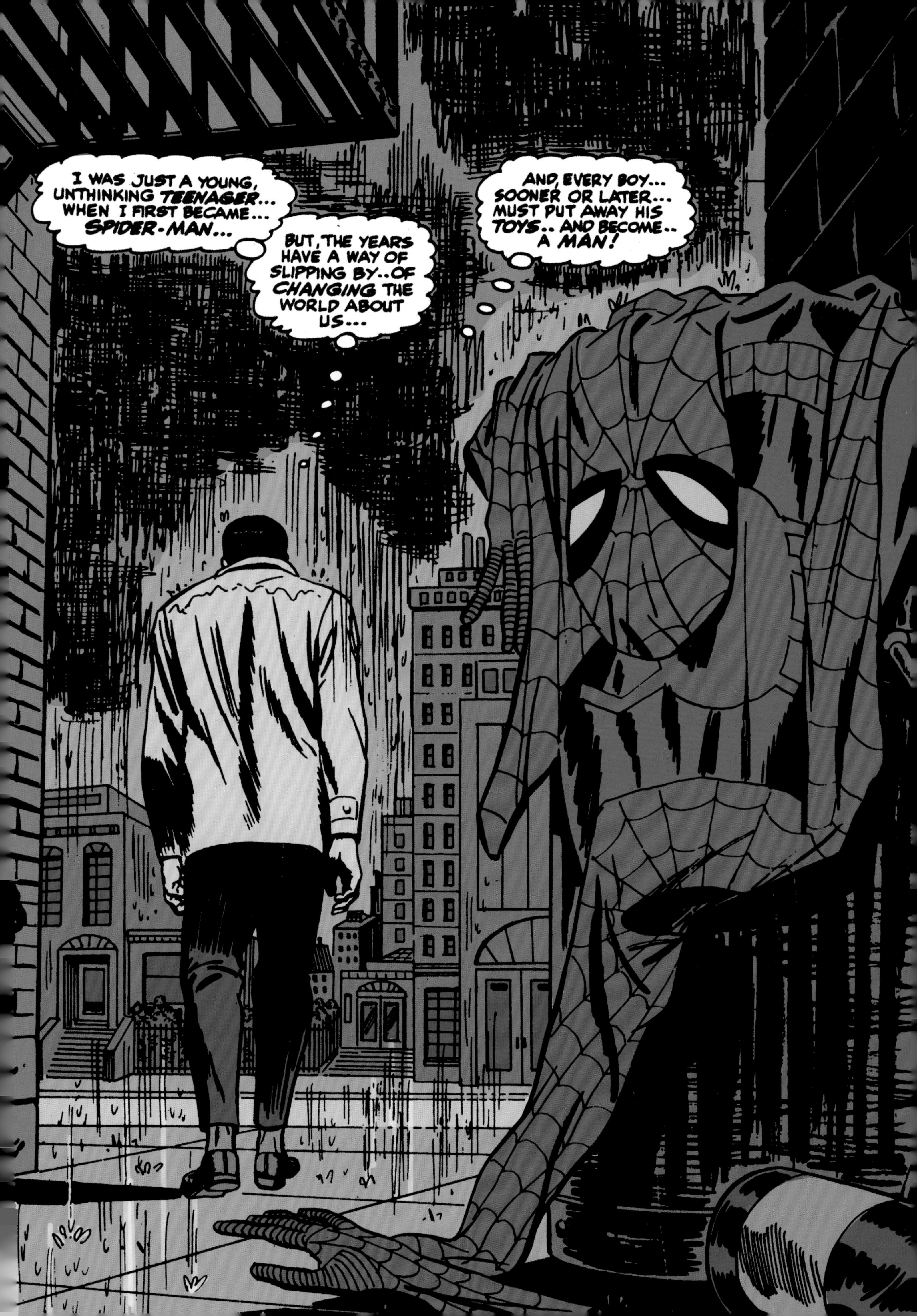
I WAS JUST A YOUNG, UNTHINKING TEENAGER... WHEN I FIRST BECAME... SPIDER-MAN...
BUT, THE YEARS HAVE A WAY OF SLIPPING BY..OF CHANGING THE WORLD ABOUT US...
AND, EVERY BOY... SOONER OR LATER... MUST PUT AWAY HIS TOYS.. AND BECOME.. A MAN!

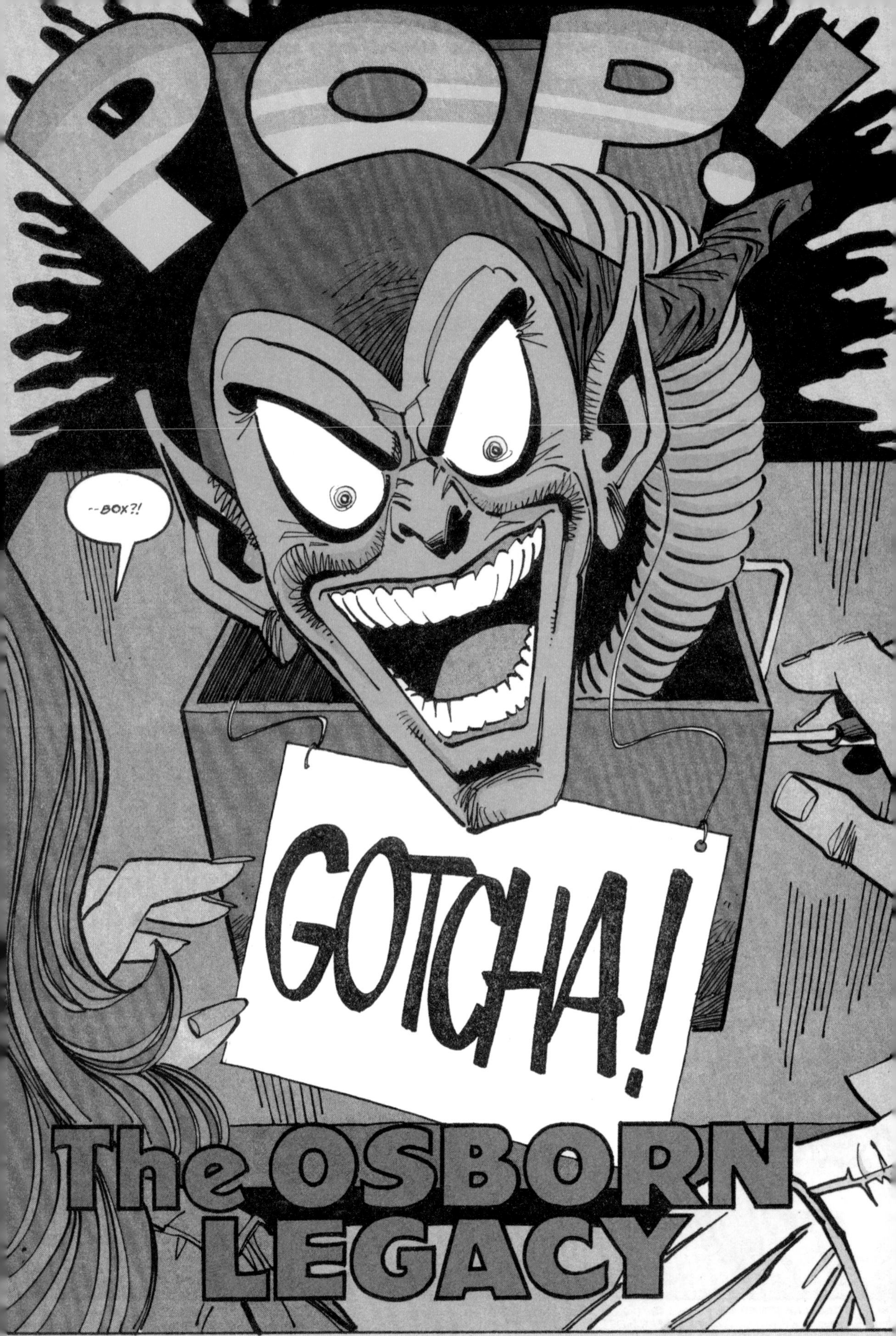
POP!
--BOX?!
GOTCHA!
The OSBORN LEGACY

A DOUBLE-SIZE SHOCKER CELEBRATING THIRTY YEARS OF WEB-SPINNING WONDERMENT-- COURTESY OF:
J.M. DeMATTEIS, WRITER * SAL BUSCEMA, ARTIST * JOE ROSEN, LETTERER * BOB SHAREN, COLORIST *
ERIC FEIN, ASSISTANT EDITOR * DANNY FINGEROTH, EDITOR * TOM DeFALCO, EDITOR-IN-CHIEF

STAN LEE, STEVE DITKO, AND JOHN ROMITA, SR., SOUL & INSPIRATION

THIS STUFF IS REAL NEW-- AND IT AIN'T EASY TO COME BY--
BUT, FOR A GUY WHO CAN USE 'EM, LIKE YOU...
LEMME SEE! WHAT ARE THOSE THINGS?
DON'T TAKE MY WORD FOR IT, OSBORN! JUST TRY A FEW-- AND NOTHING'S GONNA BOTHER YOU.
IT'LL BE WORTH ANY-THING-- TO GET HER OUT OF MY MIND!
SURE, KID --SURE! I KNOW HOW YOU FEEL.
EVERYONE'S GOT A MILLION HANG-UPS NOWADAYS.
THAT'S WHY THIS STUFF I GOT IS JUST WHAT THE DOCTOR ORDERED.
SO HOW ABOUT IT?
OKAY. OKAY.
NICE DOING BUSINESS WITH YOU, OSBORN! SEE YOU AGAIN.
OH NO! THIS IS THE FIRST TIME-- AND THE LAST.
I'M NOT GETTING HOOKED.
YEAH-- THAT'S WHAT THEY SAY.

Comic book history was changed with this presentation of Peter's friend Harry Osborne becoming caught up in the web of drugs. From *The Amazing Spider-Man* #97 (1971).

(Opposite) Of all Spidey's foes, the Green Goblin (originally Norman Osborn, then later his equally unstable son Harry), would have the most negative personal effect on Peter Parker (from *Spectacular Spider-Man #189* c. 1992).

But a far more shocking development was yet to come. Of all the provocative storylines Marvel has produced in the last forty years, none has matched the notoriety achieved by *Amazing Spider-Man* issue #121, scripted by Gerry Conway, pencilled by Gil Kane, and inked by John Romita and Tony Mortellaro, in which Gwen Stacy died at the hands of The Green Goblin. "The hue and cry was tremendous," recalls Romita. "It was one of the first times a [lead] character had died in comic books. People still come up to me at conventions and say, 'You're the guy who killed Gwen Stacy!'" Further playing upon the theme of guilt that surrounds Peter Parker, the subtle, discomforting use of the word *Snap* depicted as coming from Gwen's neck as Spider-Man tries to save her suggests that he was the actual agent of her demise.

While comic book readers were reveling in the increasingly dramatic and adult storylines of the '70s, professional educators were using the character to teach children to read (a reversal of sensibilities that would have choked Dr. Fredric Wertham, the man who tried to drive a stake through comic books in the 1950s). *Spidey Super Stories*, a special comic book series that was produced jointly by Marvel and The Childrens Television Workshop, was launched in 1974 and lasted until 1982. With its simplified stories and graphics that were laid out in accordance with up-to-date scientific evidence as to how a child's eye travels across the page, *Spidey Super Stories* took both time and trouble to produce, but it remains a proud achievement for the Marvelites who worked on it. "Many educators have pointed to that series as the most amazing turnaround in young's people's reading habits," says Romita, "and I have great pride in the fact that we were connected."

From 1984 to 1988, Peter Parker abandoned his traditional red and blue suit for a form-fitting black one with a white spider insignia on the chest, which in turn led to the creation of a remarkable villain. The suit, which Peter acquired from another planet (a story recounted in 1984's twelve-issue special edition series

Secret Wars), is actually a symbiotic alien being. Peter abandons the costume, which is picked up by Eddie Brock, the disgraced former star reporter for the *Daily Bugle,* and an old adversary of Peter's. Brock didn't just wear the costume. He merged with its alien core to become Venom, a nightmarish parody of black Spider-Man with a gaping, shark-like mouth and a hideous grin. Venom—whose ghastly menace was fully realized by the fiercely talented Todd McFarlane (born 1961 in Calgary, Alberta), the artist who took over Spider-Man in the mid-'80s—has the powers of Spider-Man plus a few more, and is dedicated to destroying Spidey.

Fortunately, there were some happy moments amidst all the turmoil. By 1987, Peter Parker had recovered from the tragedy of Gwen Stacy's death sufficiently to wed Mary Jane in a remarkable *triple* ceremony—one held in the Spider-Man newspaper strip, one held in *The Amazing Spider-Man* Giant Sized Annual, and one held in New York's Shea Stadium! In one of the most elaborate publicity stunts ever staged by Marvel (or anyone else, for that matter), Spidey and M.J., represented by actors in costume, were "married" in the baseball stadium by Stan Lee on June 5, 1987, before a jubilant crowd of 55,000 people. The ceremony came complete with an enormous tiered wedding cake, and the "bride" wore a white gown created by fashion designer Willi Smith, while Spidey wore a tuxedo jacket over his traditional costume. The wedding in Shea Stadium remains the most remarkable—and audacious— point of contact between the Marvel Universe and the real one.

However inauspicious Spidey's debut in 1962 might have been (and even that is debatable), his "relaunch" in 1990 was a monumental triumph. In August Marvel released *Spider-Man* (no *Amazing*) #1, hailing the magazine as the "1st All-New Collector's Item Issue!" Whether it was the marketing hype or Todd McFarlane's dynamic artwork and script (he also did the cover), or both, the issue became the top-selling comic book in U.S. history, selling more than *2.5 million*

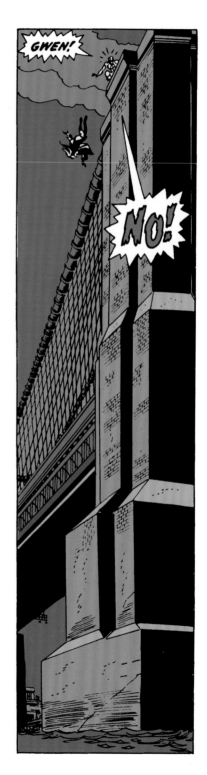

(Above and opposite) Nearly thirty years later, the death of Gwen Stacy remains one of most upsetting of all occurrences in the Marvel Universe. From *The Amazing Spider-Man* issue #121 (1973).

I'VE GOT TO CATCH HER--
--STOP HER FALL BEFORE SHE HITS THE WATER!
I'VE GOT TO!
I'VE GOT TO!
DID IT!
SWIK!
SPIDER-POWERS, I LOVE YOU!
SNAP!
NOT ONLY AM I THE MOST DASHING HERO ON TWO LEGS--

(Following spread left) The deadly Venom, as rendered by artist Todd McFarlane (from issue #317).

(Following spread right) Spider-Man stories never took the easy way out. In *The Amazing Spider-Man* #248, Spidey reveals his secret identity to a young fan dying of leukemia.

copies. Still waggish after all those years, Marvel reintroduced their star character with the declaration: "The Legend of the Arachknight," a take-off on rival Batman's recent repackaging as "The Dark Knight."

The decade of the '90s brought more trauma for Peter Parker, including the apparent death (in *Amazing Spider-Man* issue #400, 1995) of his Aunt May, the fragile mother figure that was probably the most important woman in Peter's life. Not only was Peter devastated by the event, but a considerable number of readers were, too. But in the realm of comic books, reports of a character's death are sometimes greatly exaggerated (Gwen Stacy notwithstanding), and venerable, resilient Aunt May returned, not having died at all, only having disappeared.

Another complicated wrinkle involving Spider-Man's identity was introduced that same year by writer J.M. DeMatteis, who had taken over the scripting of *The Amazing Spider-Man.* It centered around Peter's discovery that he had been cloned some twenty years earlier, and that the clone, named Ben Reilly, had taken on a crimefighting identity as The Scarlet Spider, a kind of clone of Spider-Man. Haunted by the thought that he and Reilly had somehow been switched at the cloning table, Peter ultimately turned his Spider-Man identity over to Reilly and reactivated his old dream of abandoning the responsibility of crimefighting in return for a normal life and family. He and Mary Jane left their home in Queens, New York, and Peter took a job as a scientist. But like many situations within the Marvel Universe, this was just a reality supernova. The fact that a new track of Spidey adventures launched in 1998 was titled *Peter Parker: Spider-Man* indicates that his identity crisis is over (and a related identity mystery involves Peter and M.J.'s daughter, May, who disappeared in the present-day time frame only to be chronicled as Spider-Girl in a magazine set in the future).

After nearly forty years Spider-Man remains as popular as ever. His adventures continue to appear in newspapers across America, scripted by Stan Lee and

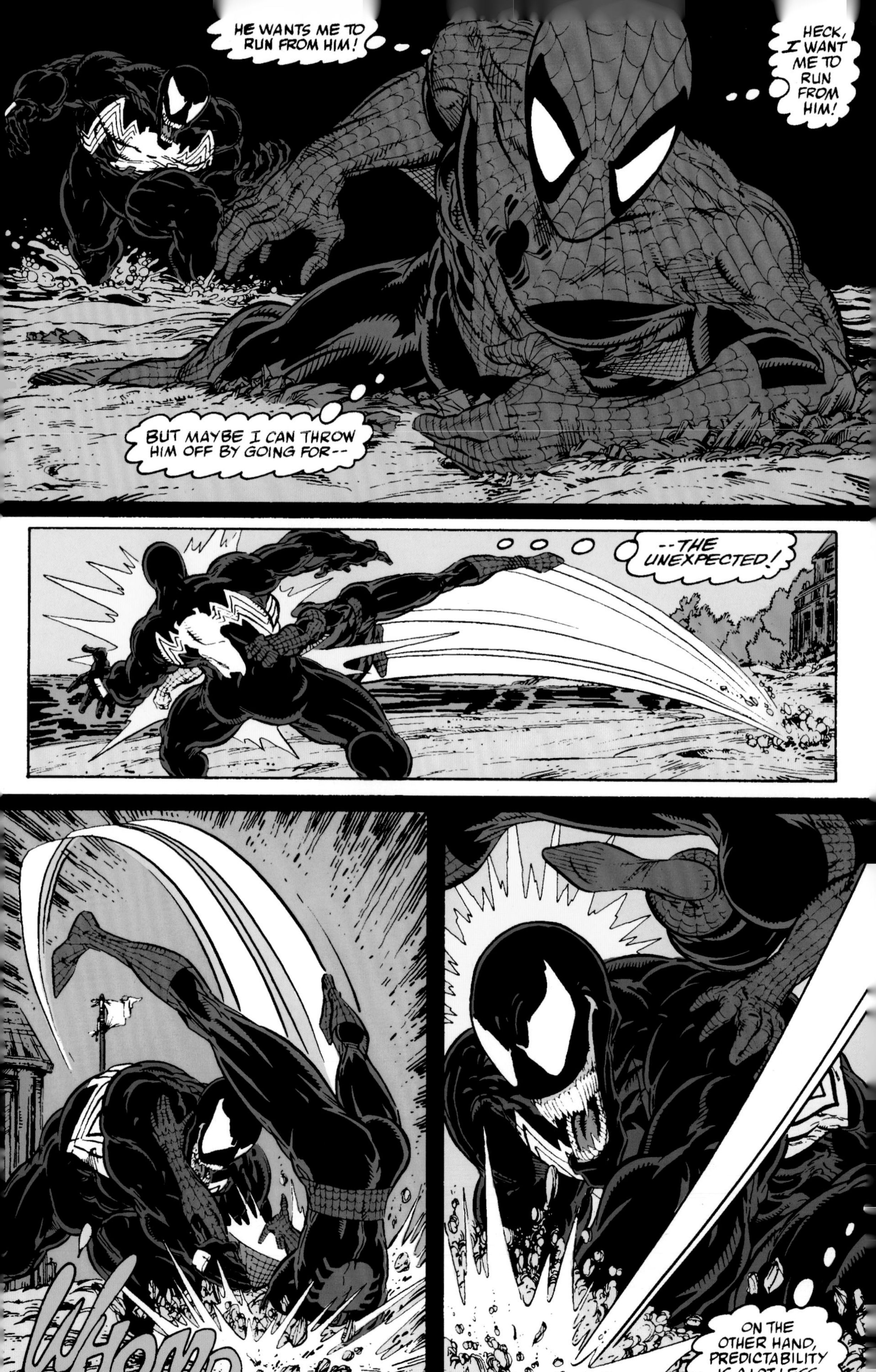
HE WANTS ME TO RUN FROM HIM!
HECK, I WANT ME TO RUN FROM HIM!
BUT MAYBE I CAN THROW HIM OFF BY GOING FOR--
--THE UNEXPECTED!
WHOMP
ON THE OTHER HAND, PREDICTABILITY IS A LOT LESS PAINFUL!

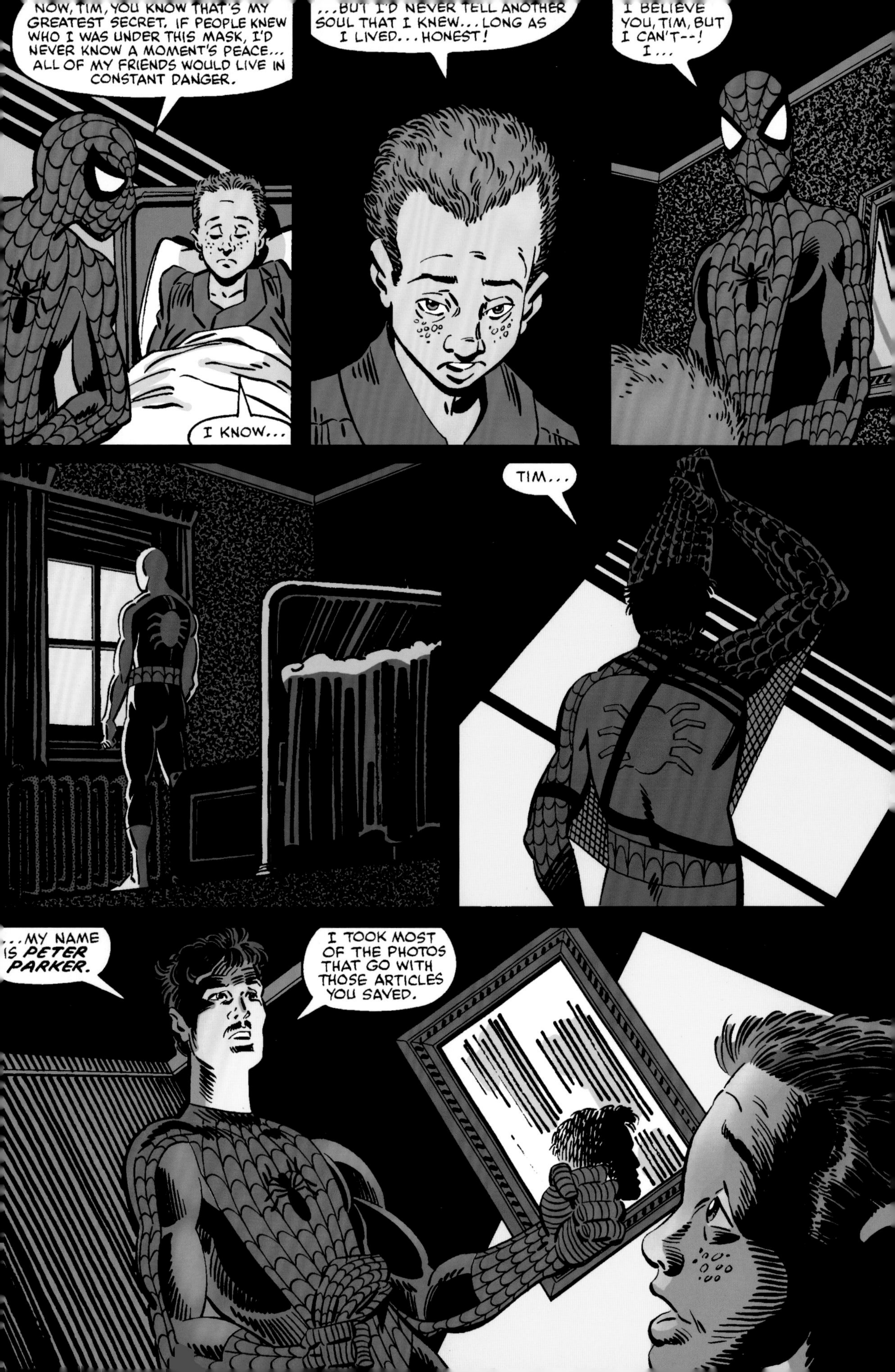
NOW, TIM, YOU KNOW THAT'S MY GREATEST SECRET. IF PEOPLE KNEW WHO I WAS UNDER THIS MASK, I'D NEVER KNOW A MOMENT'S PEACE... ALL OF MY FRIENDS WOULD LIVE IN CONSTANT DANGER.
I KNOW...
...BUT I'D NEVER TELL ANOTHER SOUL THAT I KNEW... LONG AS I LIVED... HONEST!
I BELIEVE YOU, TIM, BUT I CAN'T--! I...
TIM...
...MY NAME IS PETER PARKER.
I TOOK MOST OF THE PHOTOS THAT GO WITH THOSE ARTICLES YOU SAVED.

drawn by Larry Lieber in the dailies and Joe Sinnott for the Sunday strips, the latter working from layouts by Alex Saviuk. It is a popularity that Tom DeFalco attributes to Spider-Man's innate heroism. "This is a very insecure person who goes into almost every battle convinced he's going to lose, but he goes in anyway," says DeFalco. "He's the most heroic character of all."

SPIDER-MAN IN THE MEDIA

The success of "The Marvel Superheroes" in syndication led to Marvel's signature character being translated into animation a year later. Steve Krantz and Grantray-Lawrence were once more behind the project, though unlike "Superheroes," the "Spider-Man" series, which debuted on ABC in September of 1967, did not utilize the original comic book art or stories as a jumping-off point for the animation. While the staging and graphics still show the heavily shadowed, comic book inspiration, a slightly increased budget resulted in more fluid animation.

June Patterson, the wife of animation producer Ray Patterson, served as story supervisor for the series. "We did one and I remember the network went crazy, and Stan Lee went crazy, they were all crazy about it," she recalls. "It was one of those days when I was in a facetious mood or something, and I wrote this thing where Spidey is chasing a villain and he comes into a TV studio where they're shooting a Western, and he chases the villain across the Western bar, and down the breakaway stairs, and it turned out so good that they just loved it!"

The voice tracks were once more recorded in Toronto, with actor Paul Soles taking the roles of Spidey and Peter Parker. "I was often more comfortable doing Peter Parker than Spider-Man," Soles relates, "because in physique and outlook, I never really thought of myself as a superhero. To put myself in the frame of mind of a superhero, that was pretty tough to do. It called for an attitude that was a little above and beyond normal life. But it was fun to do."

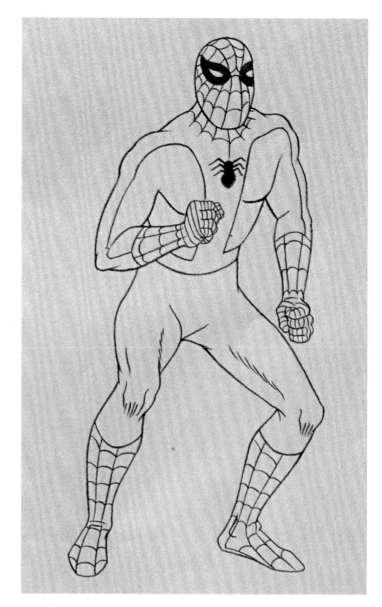

(Top) An animation drawing from 1967's animated "Spider-Man."

(Above) A rough animation drawing showing Spidey in action.

(Opposite, top to bottom) More original animation artwork was done for "Spider-Man" than for the earlier "Marvel Superheroes." An animation rough of Peter in the lab. Original animation drawing of a rather stolid Peter Parker from 1967's "Spider-Man." Say "cheese!" An original animation drawing of Peter, suited-up, plying his trade. The red-lined field indicates the part of the drawing that will be seen on television. The lines of Spidey's costume were painstakingly drawn by Grantray-Lawrence's animators for the 1967 "Spider-Man."

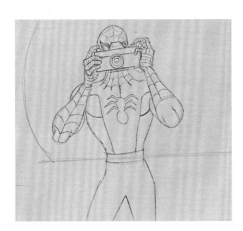

Once the series was underway, however, financial problems caused the production to be moved from Grantray-Lawrence to the New York–based company of animation maverick Ralph Bakshi. A longtime fan of the comic books, as well as one of the most outspoken men in show business, Bakshi had little patience for those who did not share his devotion to the medium. "One writer asked me why [Spider-Man] had to wear a costume," Bakshi recalls. "I said, 'So his mother wouldn't recognize him.' And he believed it! But you have to take the stuff as seriously as you can. A comic book is an honest kind of thing, if you take it seriously." "Spider-Man" ran three seasons on ABC.

While it is easy to animate a character who crawls up the sides of buildings and swings around on web lines, staging that in live action is a daunting prospect. Producer Charles Fries accepted the challenge in 1977, creating a two-hour "Spider-Man" pilot for Universal Television. Veteran television director E.W. Swackhammer cast newcomer Nicholas Hammond as Peter Parker and filled out the cast with more recognizable television faces, including Hilly Hicks as Robbie Robertson, David White (best known to baby-boomers as Larry Tate from "Bewitched") as J. Jonah Jameson, and Thayer David as the villain of the piece, Dr. Edward Byron. Nineteen-forties starlet Jeff Donnell appeared in a cameo as Aunt May.

In the film, the origin story of Spider-Man is interwoven with a bizarre plot involving a crazy self-help guru, Dr. Byron, who is planting post-hypnotic suggestions by way of microwave signals in mechanisms hidden inside lapel pins Byron has given to various professional people to make them commit robberies. Once the crime is committed, and the loot taken away by Byron's henchmen, the zombie-like perpetrator is programmed to self-destruct. This is simply a prologue to a much bigger plot: Byron demands $50 million dollars from the mayor of New York, or else he will instruct ten prominent citizens under his control to destroy themselves! Peter becomes involved in the plot both as a photojournalist and as Spider-Man. Going undercover, he attends one of Byron's abrasive psychological motivation seminars and becomes a walking time bomb, hypnotically programmed to jump off the Empire State Building. At the last minute, Peter loses his lapel pin, which breaks the post-hypnotic control, and after turning into Spidey, finds Byron's microwave transmitter and reverses the beam, turning the mind-control expert into one of his own zombies.

"Spider-Man" was aired September 14, 1977, and scored a ratings hit for CBS. Fans of the comic book character had reason to be satisfied with this television incarnation since, for the most part, the filmmakers took care to stay close to the original. Peter is still a bookish, somewhat nerdy student (though now he's in grad school) who is bitten by the radioactive spider, which in this version was contaminated through contact with a beaker of nuclear waste in the school lab. Nicholas Hammond was an excellent choice for Peter Parker, giving the character just the right touch of youthful immaturity, and Spidey's costume ended up being a faithful rendering of the comic book design, despite initial attempts to change it.

"When they did the first movie, Stan was in California and he called me up and said, 'They don't want to do him in red and blue,'" recalls John Romita. "My first thought was they were thinking red and blue was too much like Superman, but that wasn't it: they said they had to make him red and black—which actually would not have been the end of the world— because against the blue matte he would have turned transparent. And I said, 'Wait a minute, the Childrens Television Workshop solves that problem every day, they put him everywhere! They're probably telling you they've got a blue matte background and they don't want to repaint it.' And that's exactly what it was!"

The shots in question involved Spider-Man climbing around the side and roof of Aunt May's house, and the optical trickery the filmmakers employed was fairly obvious. For most of the scenes involving building,

(Top) An original cel showing Spidey in repose from 1967's "Spider-Man."

(Above) This color key drawing of Peter Parker indicates that, at least in the late 1960s, he had a preference for primary colors.

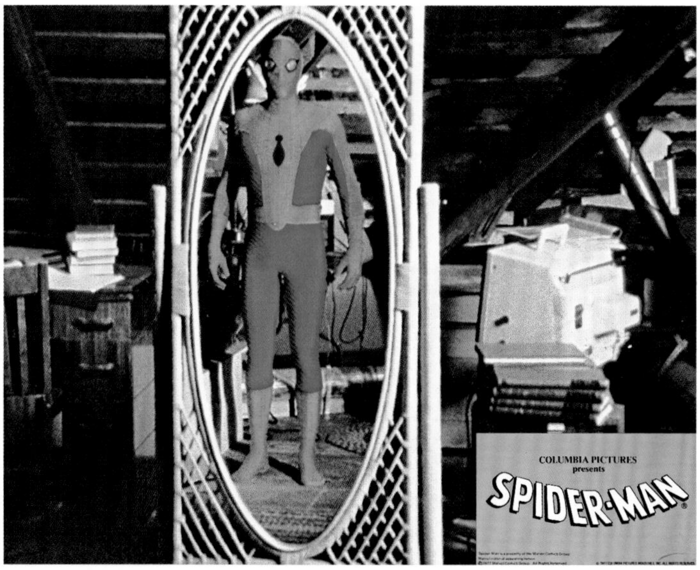
COLUMBIA PICTURES
presents
SPIDER-MAN

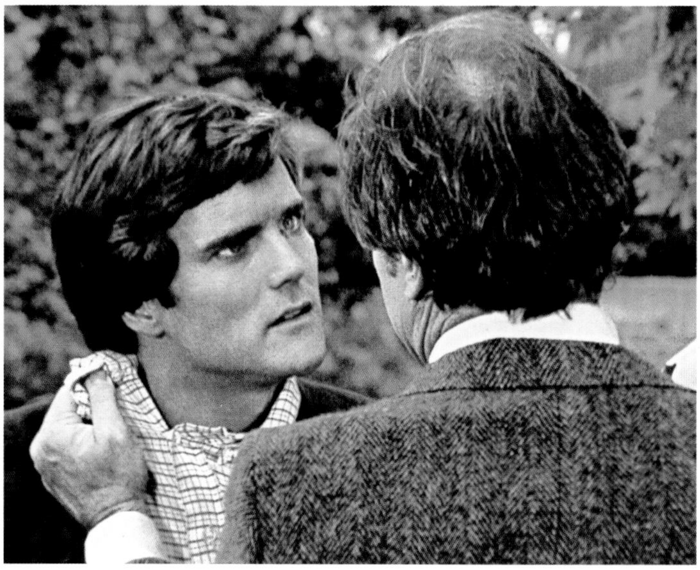

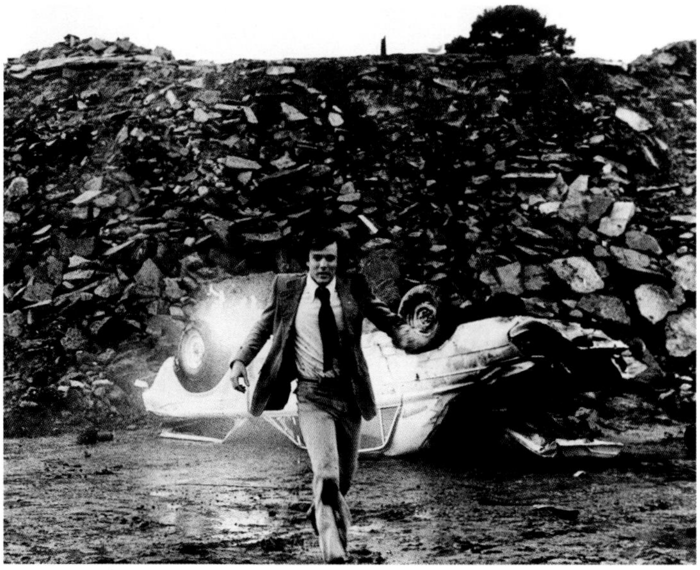

(Top) The first image of Spidey from the 1977 television movie "Spider-Man." (Lobby card from the overseas theatrical release version.)

(Middle) Nicholas Hammond made a slightly older, but still mild-mannered Peter Parker in TV's "Spider-Man."

(Above) On television, Peter Parker got into almost as much trouble out of costume as in.

wall, and ceiling climbing, though, no camera magic of any kind was used. In one truly jaw-dropping shot, Spidey suddenly springs from a standing position to the ceiling, then runs the length of the hallway ceiling upside down—and all of it was filmed without visual effects. For scenes such as this, the man in the Spidey suit was not Hammond, but a stuntman and former trapeze artist named Fred Waugh. "That [shot] was even written up in *Variety*," Fred Waugh states proudly. "They said it was the most unbelievable stunt they'd ever seen, and they couldn't figure out how it was done."

To perform the stunt, Waugh rigged a "traveling track" that contained a roller that allowed a cable to move back and forth above the hallway set. The set's ceiling was then built around it to obscure the track. Under his costume, Waugh wore a harness attached to the cable, which ran up through the rafters of the soundstage and back down, where it was connected to a rope. When a half-dozen stunt grips pulled on the rope, Waugh appeared to fly upside down to the ceiling. "We rehearsed that four or five times," Waugh says, "and each time we did it we pulled a little faster, a little faster, a little faster, and then for the take I said, "All right, let's go for it, guys." So they rolled the cameras and, when I said 'Now!' I was there! I mean, I was on that ceiling *fast!* And then I swung around and crawled down using the slider track, because that pressure was holding me up to the ceiling." Two separate setups and some skillful editing completed the sequence, which shows Spider-Man springing from the ceiling to a wall, and then back down to the floor.

Exterior shots showing Spider-Man climbing up and down the sides of buildings were similarly done with cable rigging, and proved equally eye popping. This is particularly true of Spidey's head-first descents, which, according to Waugh, were actually easier to perform than the ascents. "With all that weight in my harness and my shoulders, I could run sideways down the building," he says. "I could really sell that thing coming down, but going up was hard. I had seven guys pulling me all the time, and I would start to get to the middle of the cable and my feet would start swinging away from the building. I couldn't get any traction." The fact that Waugh was able to closely replicate Spidey's unique crouching stance from the comic books further helped to sell the character.

The success of the "Spider-Man" television movie prompted a limited-run television series on CBS, beginning in 1978. Now called "The Amazing Spider-Man," it brought back Nicholas Hammond as Peter, though Robert F. Simon took over the role of Jameson, who was now played as a grouch-with-a-heart-of-gold. A new recurring character was added: Rita Conway, Jameson's secretary, who was a kind of cross between Betty Brant and Robbie Robertson, and was played by actress Chip Fields. Fred Waugh continued his climbing duties and also served as stunt coordinator and second unit director for the show.

Several changes were made in Spidey's costume for the series, including the addition of a large silver wrist band from which his webs emanated, and a matching silver utility belt, and modifications in the mask that replaced the silvery eye patches with dark, reflective lenses. The latter was done to increase visibility for Waugh, though the effect was to give Spider-Man a bug-like visage. The series lasted only one month, after which further Spider-Man episodes were aired as specials on an occasional basis. Another new character was added, Julie Mason (played by Ellen Bry), who was a friend of Peter's and a photographer for a rival New York newspaper, the *Register.* Some of the later episodes were very elaborate, most notably a two-hour feature titled "The Chinese Web," which was filmed on location in Los Angeles, New York, and Hong Kong, and concerns Peter's attempts to save the reputation and life of a Chinese government official who is being framed and threatened by a wealthy, ruthless American industrialist doing business in Hong Kong. The high point of this film is the sight of Spider-Man scaling the face of a Hong Kong skyscraper.

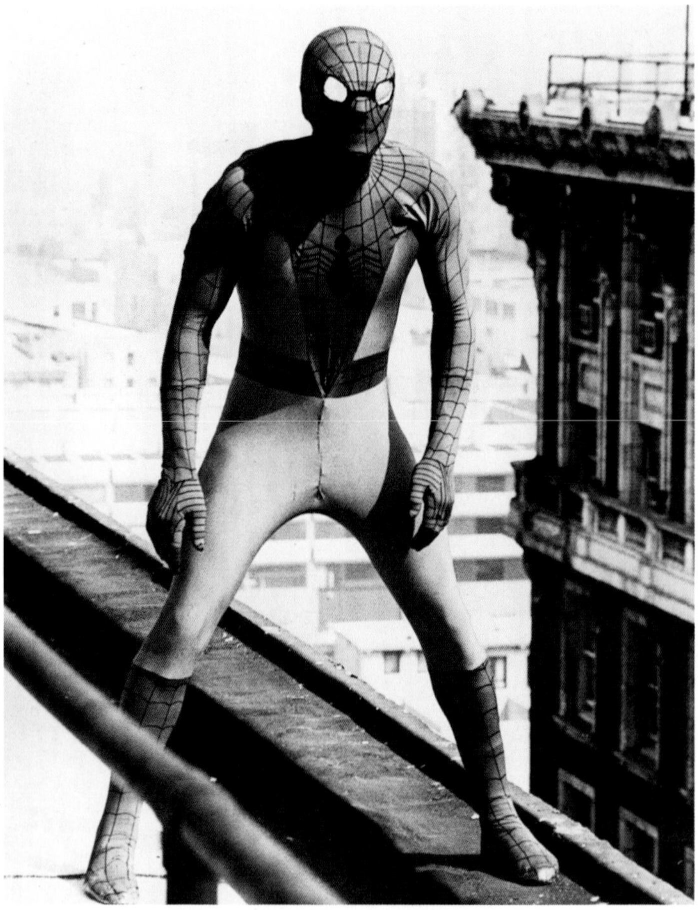

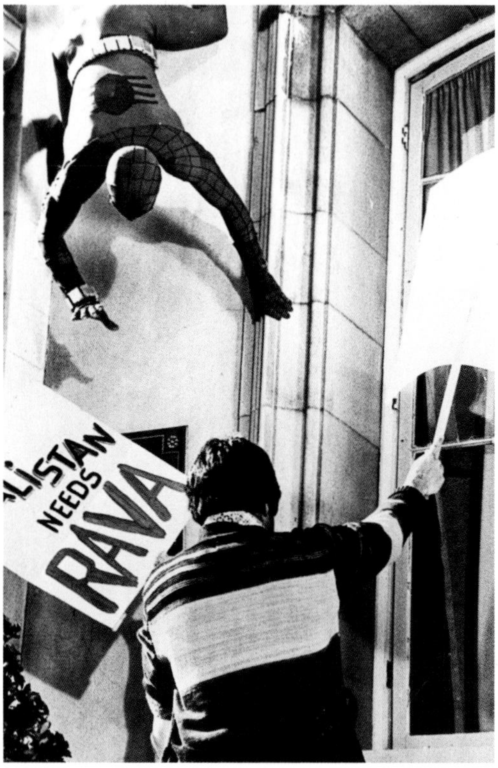
LISTAN
NEEDS
RAVA

(Top) Underneath the Spidey suit is stuntman Fred Waugh, who did all the wall-climbing for the "Spider-Man" television movie and series.

(Bottom) Spidey gets the drop on a protestor.

(Top) The reflective lenses used in Spidey's mask were not only hard to see out of, they occasionally reflected the camera crew.

(Above) The "Spider-Man" television series added a silver utility belt and a web-shooting bracelet to Spidey's costume.

Given the stunt and location budgets, it should come as no surprise that "The Amazing Spider-Man" was one of the most expensive shows on television, which contributed to its being canceled. The last episode was aired by CBS in June of 1979. (A year later, "The Chinese Web" was released theatrically overseas as *The Dragon's Challenge.*)

At the same time as the American series, another live-action series was being produced by Toei Productions for Japanese television. While the Spider-Man costume remained intact, the mythology was completely ignored in favor of the "monster-of-the-week" format that is common in Japanese action shows. Forty-one episodes of Toei's "Spider-Man" were produced and ran on TV Tokyo from May 1978 through the first half of March 1979.

Back in the U.S., Spider-Man was out of the public eye only momentarily, though when he next appeared on television it was in support of Spider-Woman, a character who had debuted in her own magazine in 1978. The animated series "Spider-Woman" premiered on ABC in September 1979.

Clad in a body suit of red with a yellow hourglass design on the front, yellow gloves and boots, and a red and yellow half-mask, Spider-Woman was in reality Jessica Drew (voiced by actress Joan Van Ark), the globetrotting editor and publisher of *Justice* Magazine. As a small girl Jessica was bitten by a poisonous spider, which prompted her scientist father to administer a powerful but untested antidote ("Serum #34") that saved her life, but which also left her with super-spider powers. In addition to spider-intuition and an ability to climb walls rivaling Spider-Man's, Jessica is able to spin and shoot webs from her fingertips, without having to rely on hidden mechanical gizmos. She can also fly, thanks to bat-like wings under the arms of her costume, not unlike the ones that appeared on Steve Ditko's original Spider-Man design.

Jessica changes into Spider-Woman by whirling herself into a mini-tornado, from which she emerges

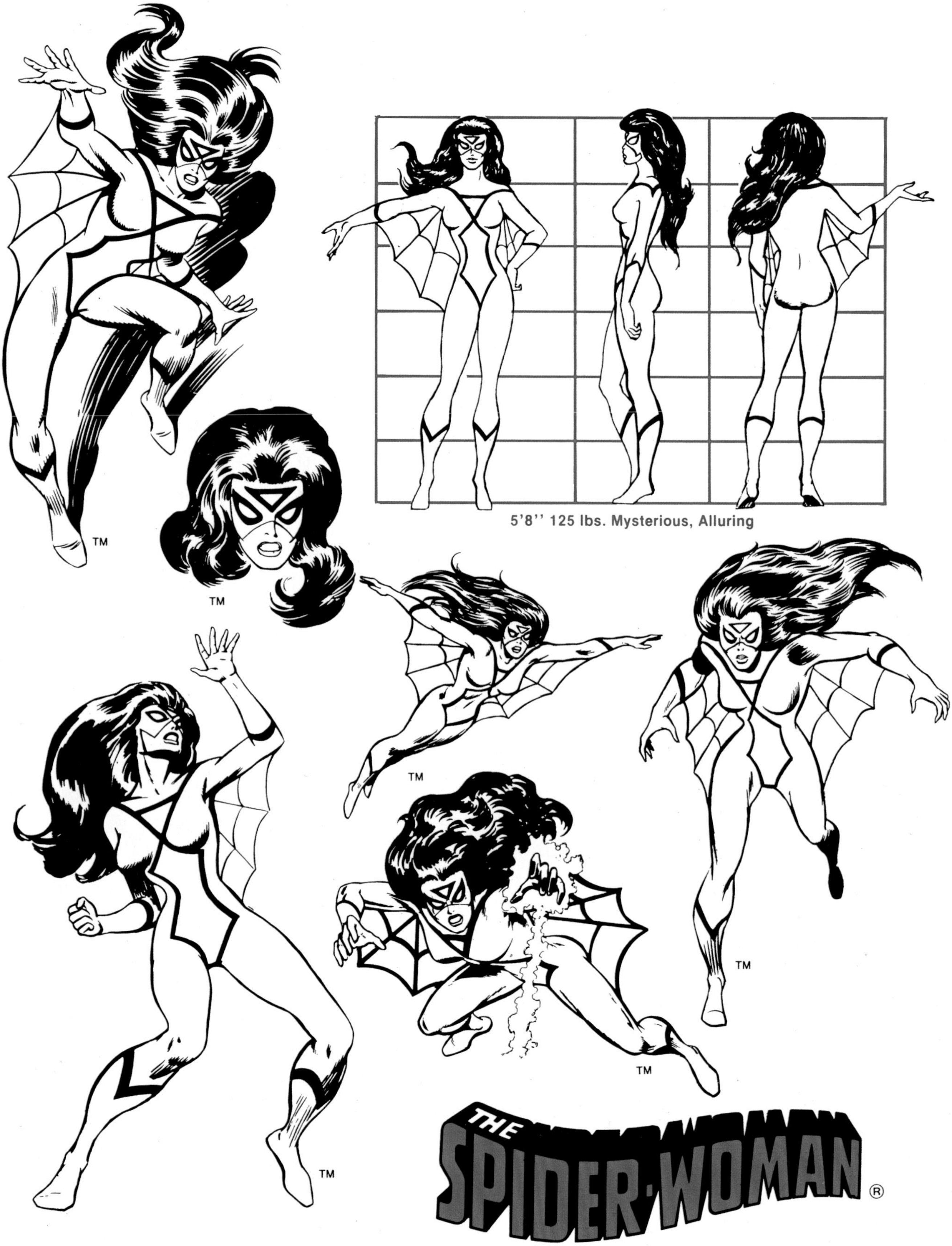
5'8'' 125 lbs. Mysterious, Alluring
TM
THE SPIDER-WOMAN ®

ARP Films, Inc.

342 Madison Avenue / New York, New York 10173 / (212) 867-1700
TWX: 710-581-4362 / CABLE: HILLFILMS

(Top) In animation, Jessica Drew changed into Spider-Woman in a tornado-like spin.

(Above) Spider-Woman was able to shoot webs naturally from her fingertips, rather than relying on a mechanical device.

(Opposite) Advertising character model for the animated "Spider-Woman" series.

fully costumed. While Spider-Woman knows and occasionally helps Spider-Man (who tends to regard her in a cavalier manner, despite the fact that she has rescued him on several occasions), the two of them are not a team. Instead she travels the world over with her photographer and would-be boyfriend Jeff Hunt and her twelve-year-old nephew Billy, ostensibly covering stories for the magazine, but in reality using her job as a cover to investigate matters as Spider-Woman.

All of Spider-Woman's half-hour adventures were rooted in the supernatural (even Eric Rogers's music for the show was at times reminiscent of James Bernard's thundering music scores for Hammer horror films), with the heroine battling such bizarre opponents as alien mummies from the planet Hotep, who fly around in pyramid-shaped space ships, Amazon women from outer space, and Ghost Vikings who rise from the bottom of the ocean. The dread Dormammu, well known to readers of *Dr. Strange,* appears in one episode as a floating mask-like head with a fiery mane. Produced by DePatie-Freleng Productions, "Spider-Woman" lasted only a half-season, disappearing from the Saturday morning schedule in April 1980.

In September of 1981, NBC premiered a new Saturday morning, animated incarnation of the character, this one targeted to a slightly younger audience. The first series to appear under the banner of Marvel Productions, "Spider-Man and His Amazing Friends" was made by many of the same people who had worked on "Spider-Woman," including executive producer David DePatie (who had since become president of Marvel Productions, Ltd.) and directors Gerry Chiniquy, Sid Marcus, and Bob Richardson. The participation of Stan Lee was enhanced as well: in addition to having created the series for TV, he was now also its narrator, communicating directly with viewers in the same personal way he had been connecting with readers for years.

The "Amazing Friends" in question are young Bobby Drake, who as Iceman has the power to freeze anything by creating ice from the moisture in the air, and Angelica Jones, alias "Firestar," who is Iceman's opposite: she can create heat. Both Bobby and Angelica have transferred to Empire State University, which Peter Parker is also attending. Not so coincidentally, the two new superheroes also begin to show up around town, piquing the interest of J. Jonah Jameson, who tells Peter (voiced by Dan Gilvegan) to stop wasting his time with Spider-Man photos and instead photograph Iceman and Firestar. When a fire in the school lab breaks out, Spidey goes into action, setting his automatic camera to capture his daring deeds, but Iceman and Firestar also show up. Later, when he develops the film, Peter discovers he has captured images of Bobby and Angelica changing into their superhero costumes. Peter confronts them and reveals that he is Spider-Man, and convinces them to join with him and create a team of superheroes. To simplify matters, Bobby and Angelica are taken into Aunt May's home as student borders, and the three teens proceed to work out of a secret laboratory that was installed in the house for them by inventor Tony Stark, whom they had earlier helped out of a jam (without realizing that he is in reality Iron Man).

In "Spider-Man and His Amazing Friends," the emphasis was as much on comedy as it was on adventure and heroics. Those who had followed the Marvel comic books for any length of time recognized Bobby Drake/Iceman as one of the original "X-Men," and even though at one point Angelica Jones/Firestar referred to herself as an ex-X-Man, she was a character created specifically for the animated series (though a decade later she would appear on the comic book page as a member of *The New Warriors*).

"Spider-Man and His Amazing Friends" lasted only one season, although its episodes were rerun as part of "The Incredible Hulk/Amazing Spider-Man Hour" on NBC from 1982 until 1984. During its production, however, the same unit produced another animated treatment of Spider-Man, this time for a syndicated series simply titled "Spider-Man." Whereas "Amazing

(Top) In "Spider-Man and His Amazing Friends," the "Spidey Friends" often went to amazing places, like this domain of monsters.

(Above) Spider-Man, Iceman, and Firestar even took on mythological creatures in "Spider-Man and His Amazing Friends."

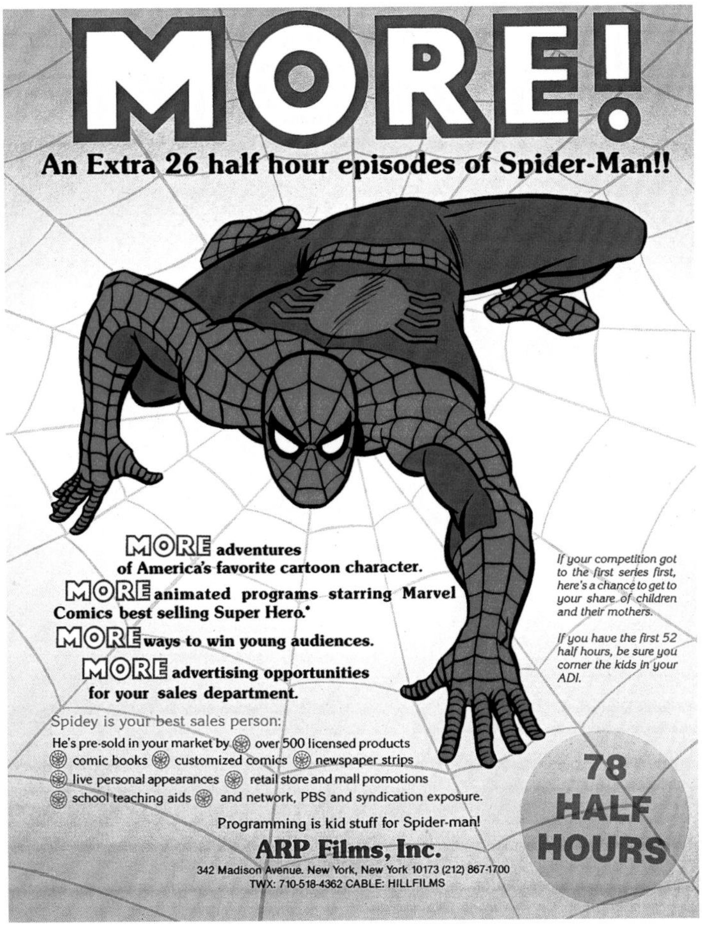
MORE!
An Extra 26 half hour episodes of Spider-Man!!
MORE adventures of America's favorite cartoon character.
MORE animated programs starring Marvel Comics best selling Super Hero.*
MORE ways to win young audiences.
MORE advertising opportunities for your sales department.
If your competition got to the first series first, here's a chance to get to your share of children and their mothers.
If you have the first 52 half hours, be sure you corner the kids in your ADI.
Spidey is your best sales person:
He's pre-sold in your market by over 500 licensed products comic books customized comics newspaper strips live personal appearances retail store and mall promotions school teaching aids and network, PBS and syndication exposure.
Programming is kid stuff for Spider-man!
ARP Films, Inc.
342 Madison Avenue. New York, New York 10173 (212) 867-1700
TWX: 710-518-4362 CABLE: HILLFILMS
78 HALF HOURS

An ad for the 1981 syndicated *Spider-Man* series, produced at the same time as *Spider-Man and His Amazing Friends*.

Friends" was a cute show for kids, the syndie "Spider-Man" (which, along with other episodes of the syndicated "Spider-Man" were re-broadcast in 1988 as part of "The Marvel Action Universe") managed to capture the element of satire and tongue-in-cheek spirit that had long governed the Marvel Universe in print.

A perfect example of the show's grasp of the Spidey spirit was on display in an episode titled "The Capture of Captain America." In it, Spider-Man is teamed with Captain America, the latter being a superhero worshiped by J. Jonah Jameson, who proclaims Cap as "maybe the greatest hero this nation has had since Herbert Hoover" and plans to honor him in New York.

However, the Red Skull (grotesquely elegant in a smoking jacket and ascot, with a boutonniere in his lapel) plans to capture Captain America by taking Jameson's place for the ceremony. When Cap strides up to the podium to accept his award, the Red Skull reveals himself, and Peter Parker (who is envious of Cap's hero status) swings into action as Spider-Man. But instead of saving his fellow superhero from the Red Skull, Spidey only gets in the way and unintentionally facilitates Cap's capture, which prompts the real Jameson to accuse him of traitorous collusion with the Red Skull!

As a result, shouts of anger and hate greet Spider-Man wherever he goes. Kids even throw away their Spider-Man comics. When Spidey accidentally tears an American flag, the crowd views it as an act of desecration, and the citizenry of New York becomes so enraged that he actually has to flee for his life!

Fortunately, he had the foresight to plant a homing device on Cap's shield, but since it's dangerous for him to be seen in his costume, he goes to Stan's Costume Shop (!) and rents an oversized Captain America costume. Disguised as Cap, he convinces a pilot to fly him to the Red Skull's castle, where the homing device has led them, and bails out.

Inside the castle, the Red Skull is showing off a diabolical mind transference machine through which the

Skull will switch places with Cap and in that guise take over the United States! But the sudden appearance of Spider-Man helps thwart the Skull's plans and leaves him an empty shell whose mind has been drained off. The two superheroes return to New York and Captain America Day proceeds without interruption.

Perhaps more than any other individual film or cartoon episode made to that time, "The Capture of Captain America" caught the essence of Spider-Man: his foibles, his insecurities, his plain bad luck, all of which are juxtaposed against his humor and indomitable spirit, resulting in a totally unique brand of heroism. It even manages to poke fun at Captain America without the aftertaste of ridicule (though purists might quibble with the dandified Red Skull).

Beginning in 1987, Spider-Man made the first of his most unique appearances on national television, as a giant balloon in the Macy's Thanksgiving Day Parade. The balloon, which depicts Spidey in classic wall-crawling stance, was constructed by Manford Bass, a specialist in crafting large-sized inflatables, from a design by John Romita.

"Manny Bass is the genius behind those balloons and he deserves the credit for it," Romita says. "What I did was come up with a sketch in the first meeting that was almost the exact thing that was finally done. While we were talking he [Bass] was giving me the aerodynamic necessities, like you need to have the bulk of the helium in the upper part of the balloon so that it would be stable and stay upright. So I put his head and arms down and put his rump and his legs all bunched up in the back and that was the design that was chosen."

Romita was also called upon to paint a plaster model that would be used as a guideline for coloring the balloon itself. "I've done a lot of goofy things since I've worked for Marvel," the artist says, "but this one was interesting because I made this as a guide to show the exact web pattern and how it would translate to 360 degrees around the arms and legs. It was very tricky."

What might be the definitive animated adaptation

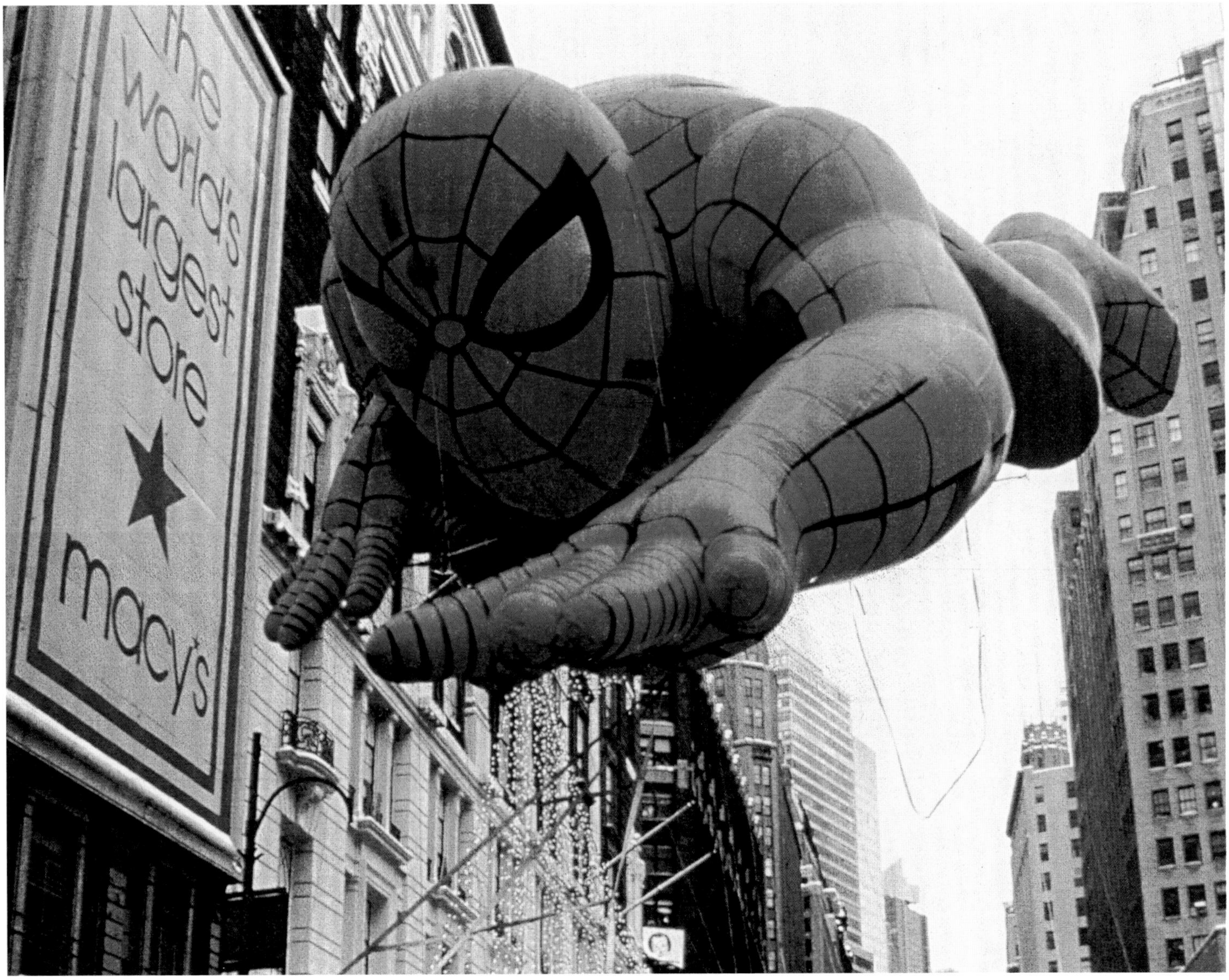
the world's largest store
macy's

Spider-Man doing what most spiders *can't*—flying down Broadway in the Macy's Thanksgiving Day Parade. (© 1997 Macy's East, Inc. All rights reserved.)

of the world's favorite wall climber premiered on Fox Kids Network in 1994. Titled "Spider-Man: The Animated Series," the 65-episode series was a joint production of Marvel Productions, New World Entertainment, Saban Entertainment, and Graz Entertainment, and offered both a heightened sophistication in the storylines and a look that was new to television at that time, thanks to the use of computer generated imagery (CGI) for the backgrounds. A virtual replica of New York City was created in the computer for Spider-Man (now voiced by Christopher Daniel Barnes) to swing through, and CGI was also used to enhance lighting and even add special effects, such as fog. "Since Spider-Man is basically a mythology that takes place in New York, we're real careful about trying to make the city look and feel like New York," said Bob Richardson, who served as supervising producer for the series. "We're trying to create a very effective reality base of the city so that the contrast with the fantasy of Spider-Man and these amazing villains he fights is all the more dramatic."

Spidey poised (and posed) for action, from "Spider-Man: The Animated Series."

The buzz on "Spider-Man: The Animated Series" served to make it one of the most eagerly anticipated animated shows in the history of Saturday morning television. The premiere episode, which aired in November 1994, only whetted the appetite for Spidey fans, who had to wait three more months for the series to appear. The reason given for the delay was that extra time was needed to work on both the complex storylines and the computer graphics. When "Spider-Man: The Animated Series" finally debuted as a weekly series in February of 1995, it immediately became one of Fox's top-rated animated programs and stayed on the air for three years.

Spidey's next animated treatment was a definite departure from everything that had preceded it. Developed for television by Marvel Media president and chief creative officer Avi Arad and writer/producer Will Meugniot, "Spider-Man Unlimited" takes place on the newly discovered planet Counter-Earth, where Spider-Man (voiced by Rino Romano) was marooned while

(Opposite top) Venom was among the villains who made the transition from the page to the screen in "Spider-Man: The Animated Series."

(Opposite bottom) 1995's "Spider-Man: The Animated Series" was one of most eagerly awaited shows in the history of Saturday morning television.

SPIDER-MAN

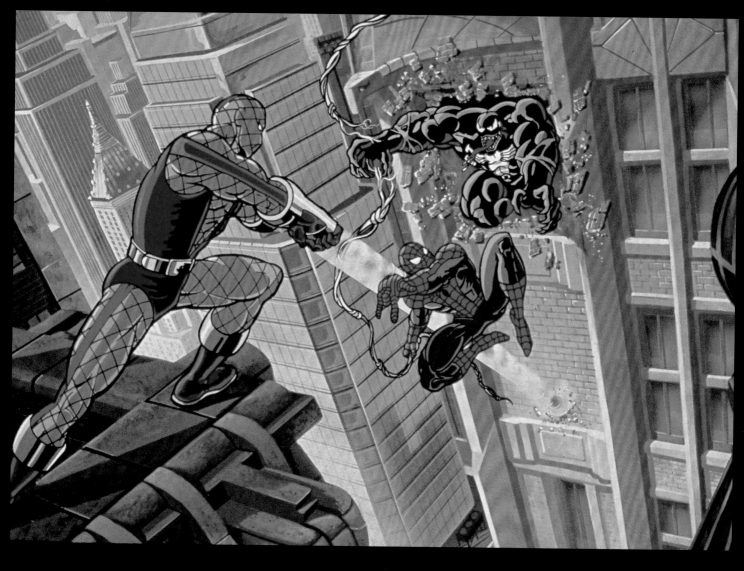

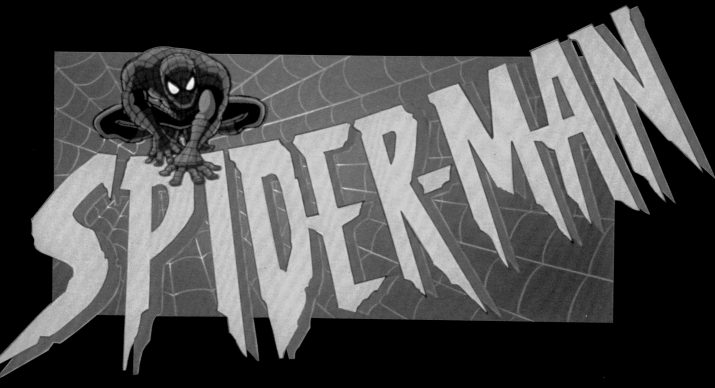

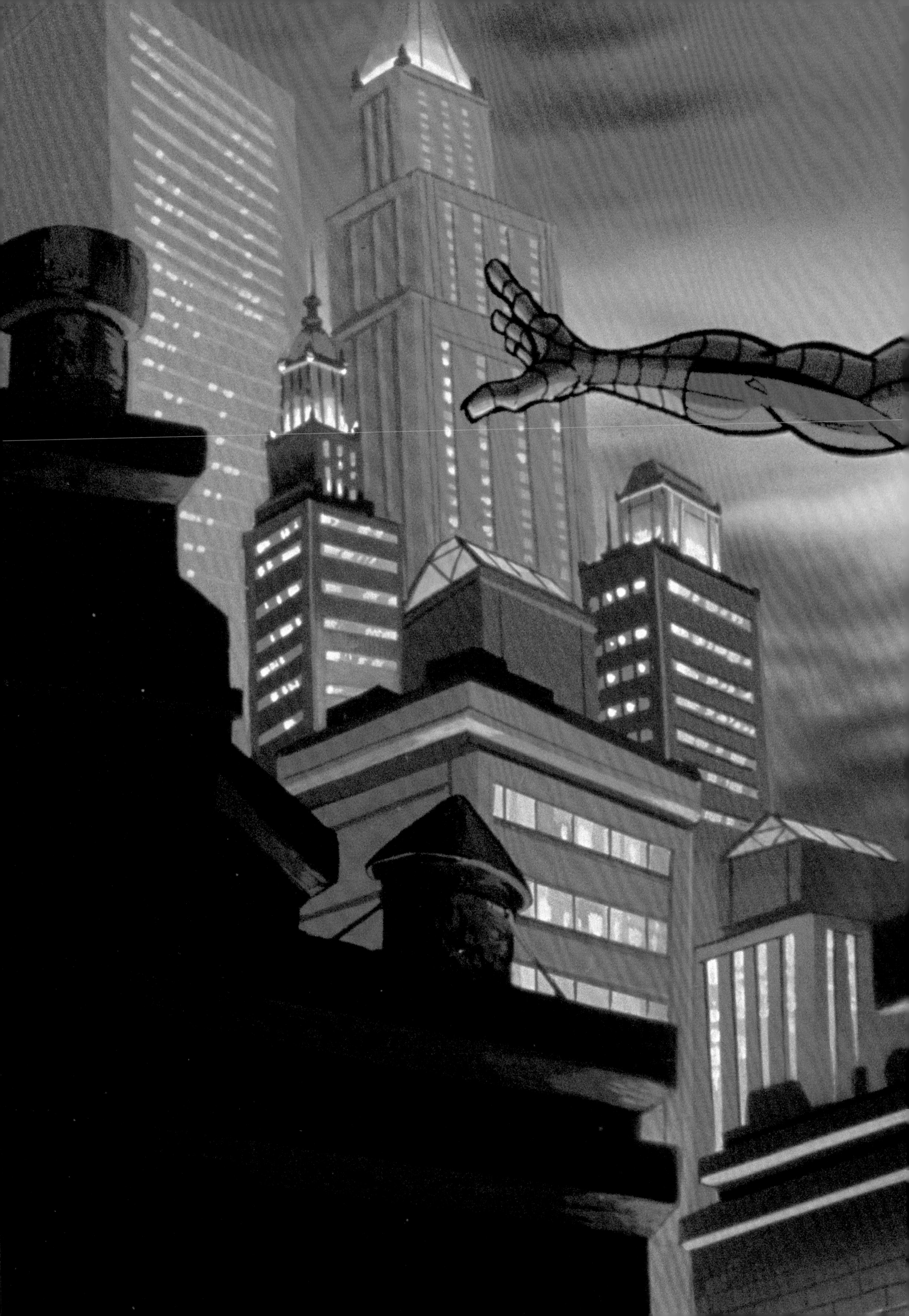

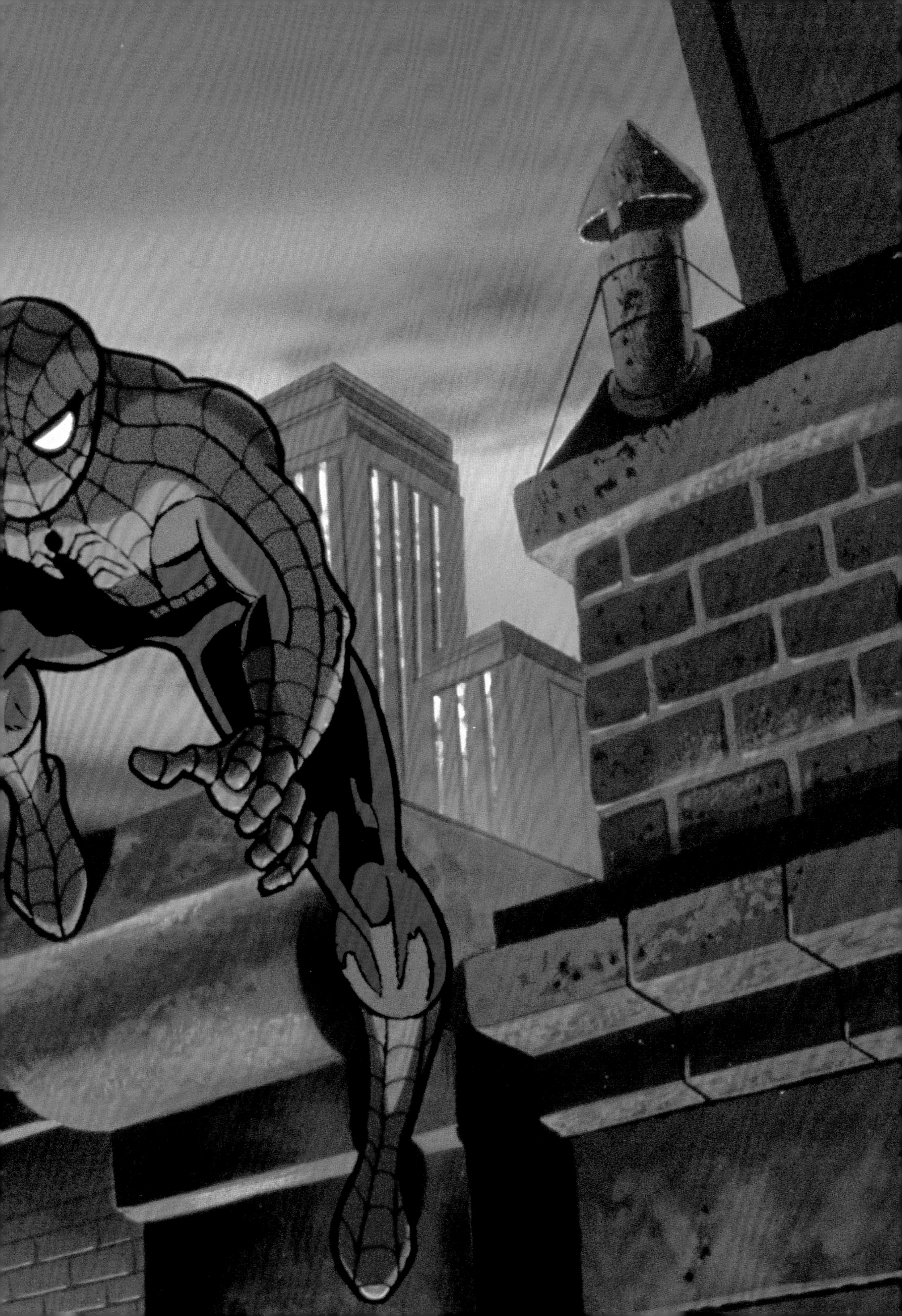

tracking his enemies Venom and Carnage. Society on Counter-Earth parallels that of the Earth, but there are a few big differences, notably that humans are the underclass, dominated by a race of animal-like humanoid mutants called Bestials. Spidey wears a new high-tech costume that consists of a blue-black and red body suit with a more stylized spider design and a transparent cape. Rather than keeping the costume under his street clothes in the time-honored fashion, Parker now uses remote control, which causes the suit to instantly materialize. The eyes in his newly designed spider mask also allow for infrared vision.

For Spidey fans, though, the biggest news of the decade was the 2002 release of Columbia Picture's big screen *Spider-Man*, one of the most eagerly awaited films in recent years.

Directed by Sam Raimi and written by David Koepp (with uncredited assists by Neil Ruttenberg, Scott Rosenberg, and Alvin Sargent, and utilizing elements from a 57-page treatment/script written in 1992 by James Cameron), the film stars the perfectly cast Tobey Maguire as the teenaged Peter Parker/Spidey, Kirsten Dunst as Mary Jane Watson, Willem Dafoe as The Green Goblin/Norman Osborn (whose flip-side personality as a streamline moderne gargoyle is chemically induced), James Franco as Harry Osborn, J. K. Simmons as Jameson, Rosemary Harris as Aunt May, and Cliff Robertson as Uncle Ben. *Spider-Man* depicts, for the first time in live action, the murder of Uncle Ben and the devastating effect it has on Peter have been depicted.

Plans for a *Spider-Man* feature had been in the works for nearly fifteen years before it landed at Columbia in 1999. Raimi, whose 1990 feature *Darkman* had a strong comic book atmosphere to it, won the plum assignment over such contenders as Tim Burton, Chris Columbus, and David Fincher. Raimi says his biggest challenge was "giving the thirty-nine years of *Spider-Man* readers what they wanted, but not necessarily what they expected."

(Previous spread) New York City was re-created inside a computer for 1995's "Spider-Man: The Animated Series."

(Above) 1999's "Spider-Man Unlimited" was set in an alternate world, with an almost-recognizable, but much less friendly, parallel New York.

(Opposite top) Spidey leaps into the future in the animated "Spider-Man Unlimited."

(Opposite bottom) Spidey (Tobey Maguire) shows off his bridge work in the 2002 film *Spider-Man*. (© 2002 Columbia Pictures Industries, Inc. All Rights Reserved.)

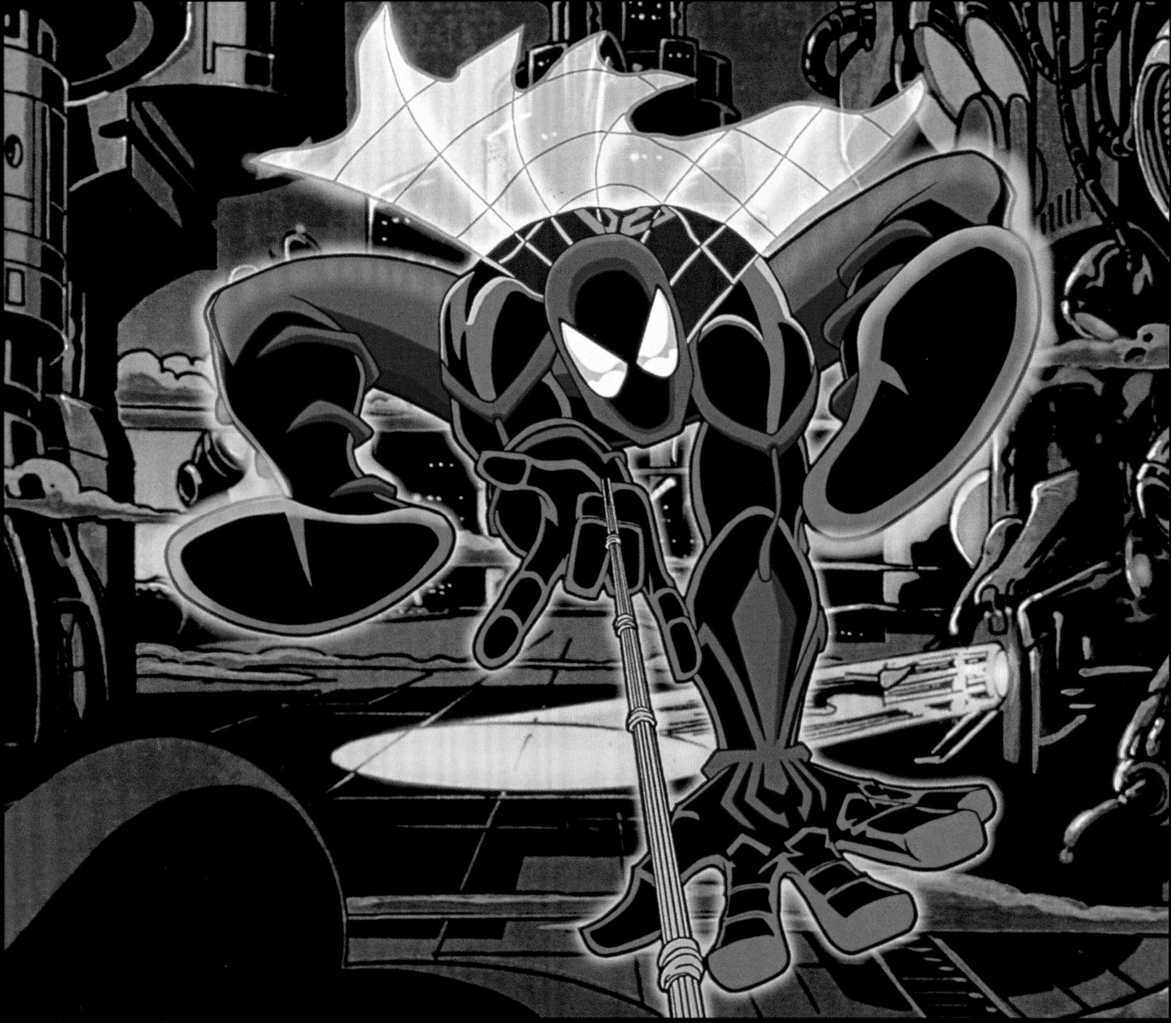

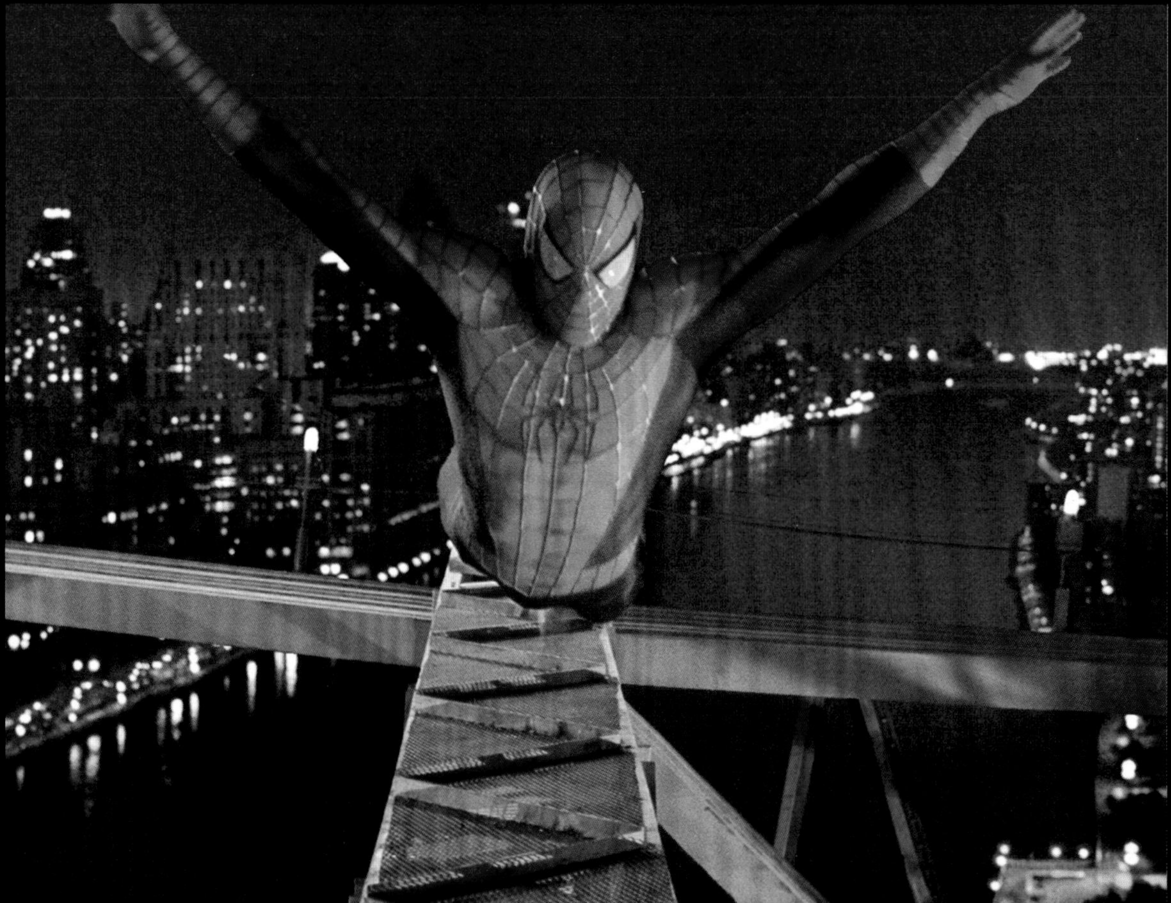

The film adheres fairly closely to the original mythology, as Peter is bitten by a DNA-mutated spider in his high school's science lab and develops super powers, though in this version that includes the ability to spin webs naturally, rather than creating a high-tech gizmo that shoots sticky filaments. "That was an idea James Cameron originally came up with in his 'scriptment,'" Raimi says. "I thought that was a great choice, because what was most important to me about the [Spider-Man] books I read as a young adult was that he was identifiable. The one thing that was hard for me to relate to was Peter Parker as super-genius."

To support the character's sense of normalcy, Raimi eschewed a comic-bookish look for the Peter Parker scenes. "I wanted to pay tribute to the character rather than the medium that delivered him," he says. However, for the scenes of Spider-Man in action, the director employed fast, kinetic camera movements to give a feeling of what it must be like to swing like Spidey.

Even though original wall-climber Fred Waugh was part of the film's stunt team, the most dramatic swinging and web crawling shots were accomplished through computer animation, with takeoffs and landings performed by a stuntman in the spandex Spidey suit hooked to sophisticated wire rigs, or by Maguire himself bouncing off a trampoline. "Anything that Tobey could do, he did do," Raimi confirms.

Released to enormous fanfare May 3, 2002, Spider-Man earned a whopping $114-million on its opening weekend alone, setting a Hollywood record, and the key creative team has already been signed for Spider-Man 2. It may have taken seventeen years to bring Spider-Man to the big screen, but having arrived, he is here to stay. There is even a new "Spider-Man: The Animated Series" in production, featuring Neil Patrick Harris as the voice of Peter/Spidey.

Nobody ever said being a superhero was easy, and no superhero has proven that more than Spider-Man.

(Opposite top) Spidey feels the Green Goblin's heat in the big-screen Spider-Man. (© 2002 Columbia Pictures Industries, Inc. All Rights Reserved.)

(Opposite bottom) Willem Dafoe soars high as the ghastly Green Goblin in Spider-Man. (© 2002 Columbia Pictures Industries, Inc. All Rights Reserved.)

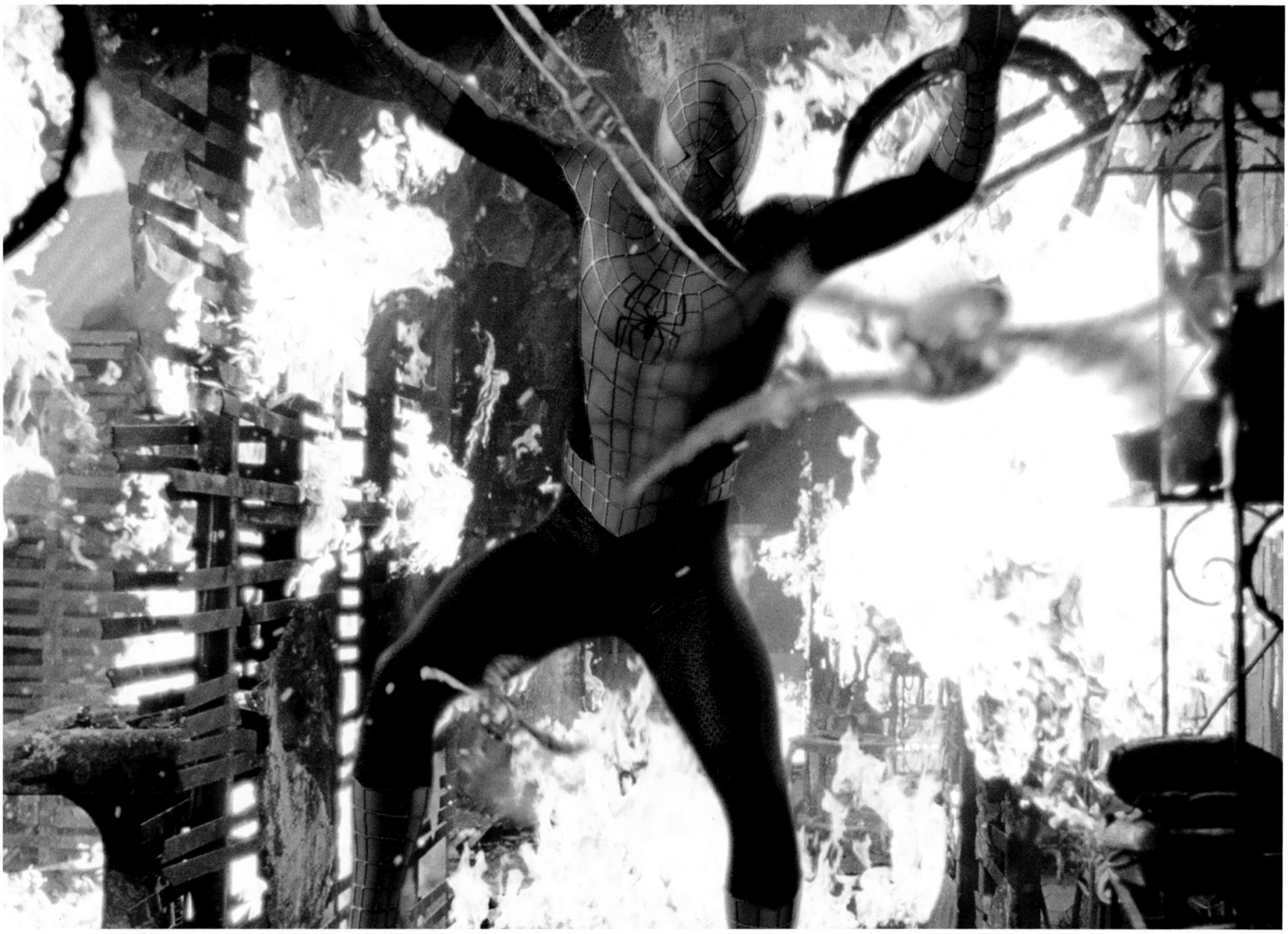

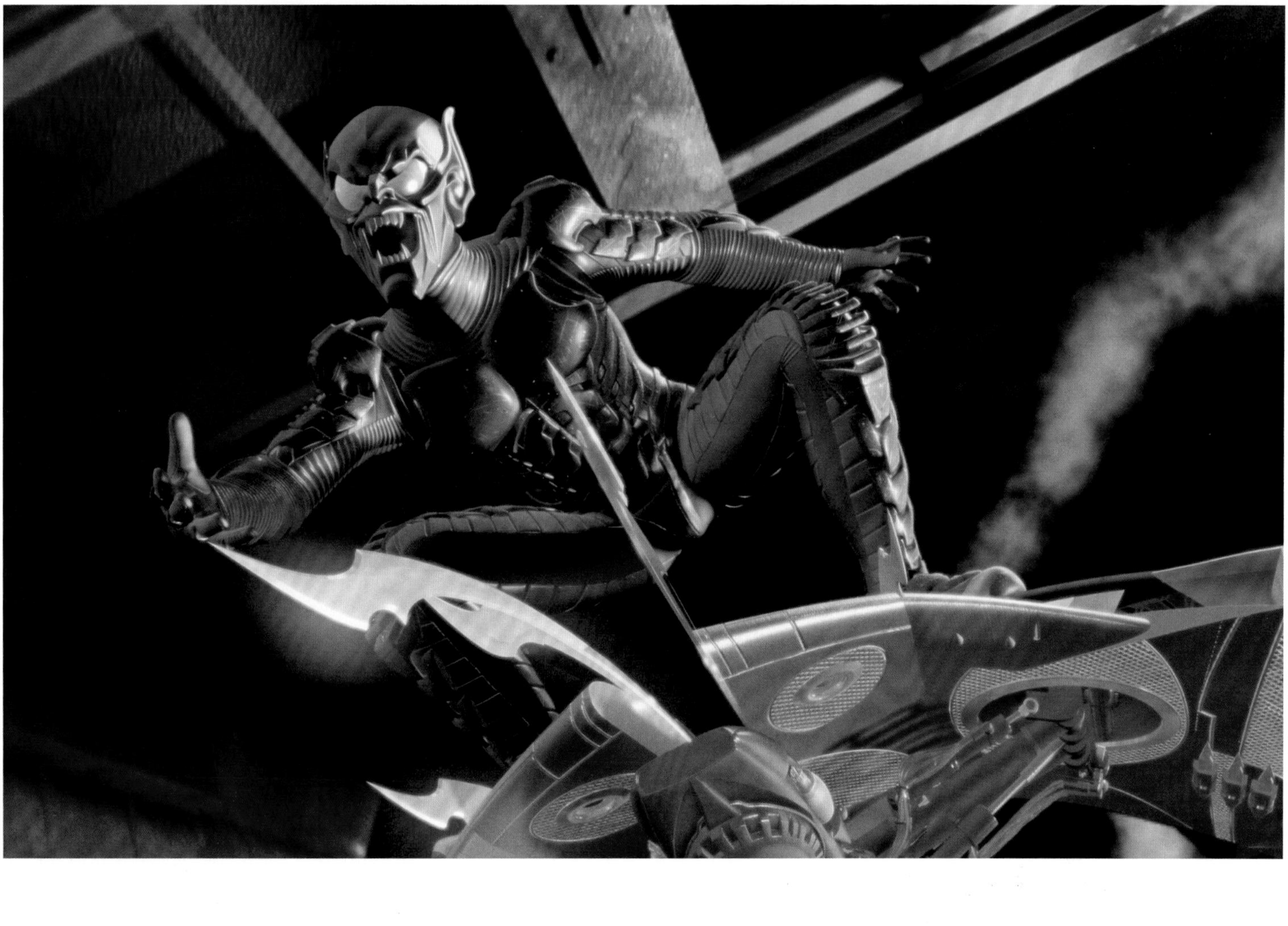

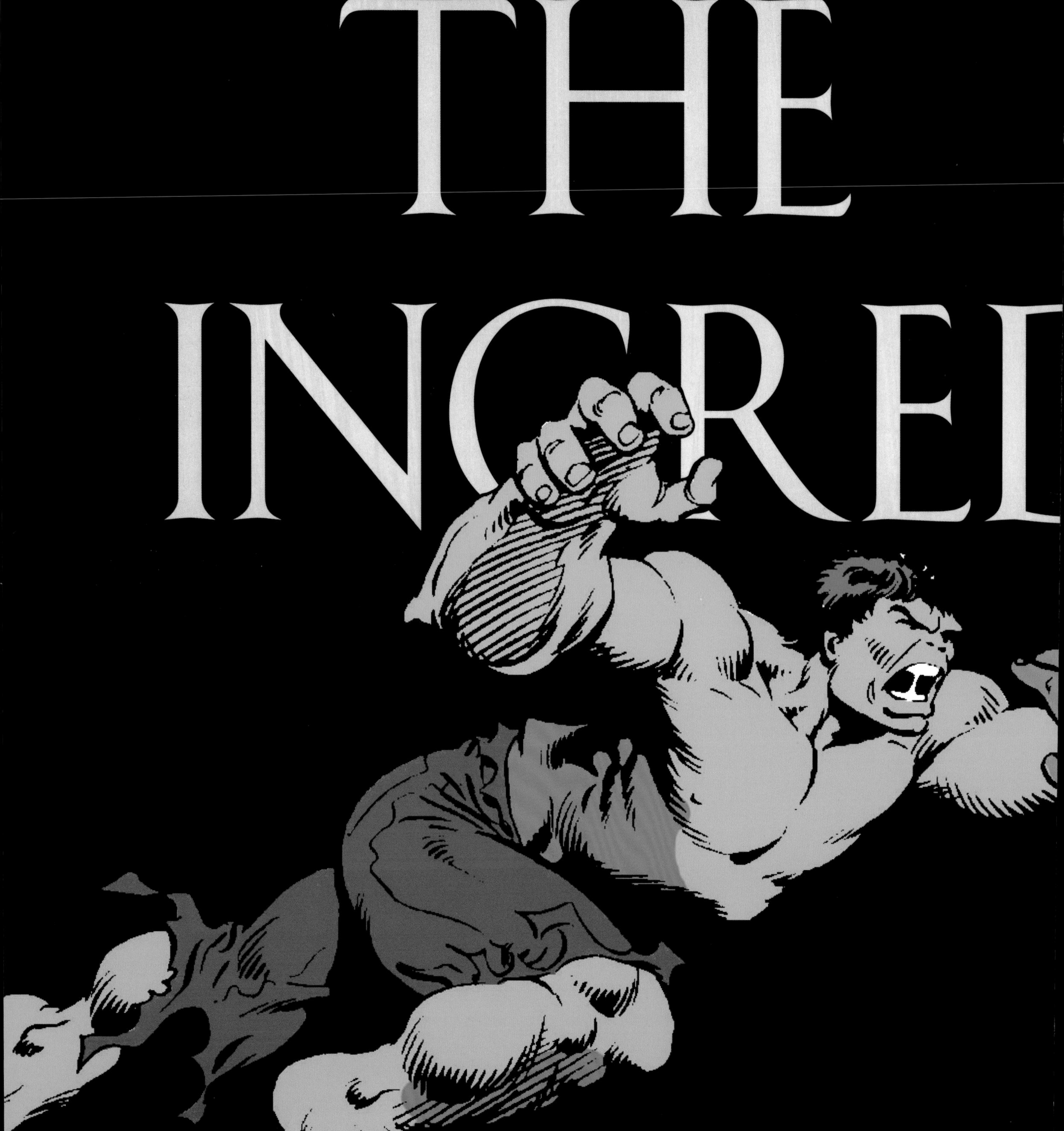
THE
INCRED

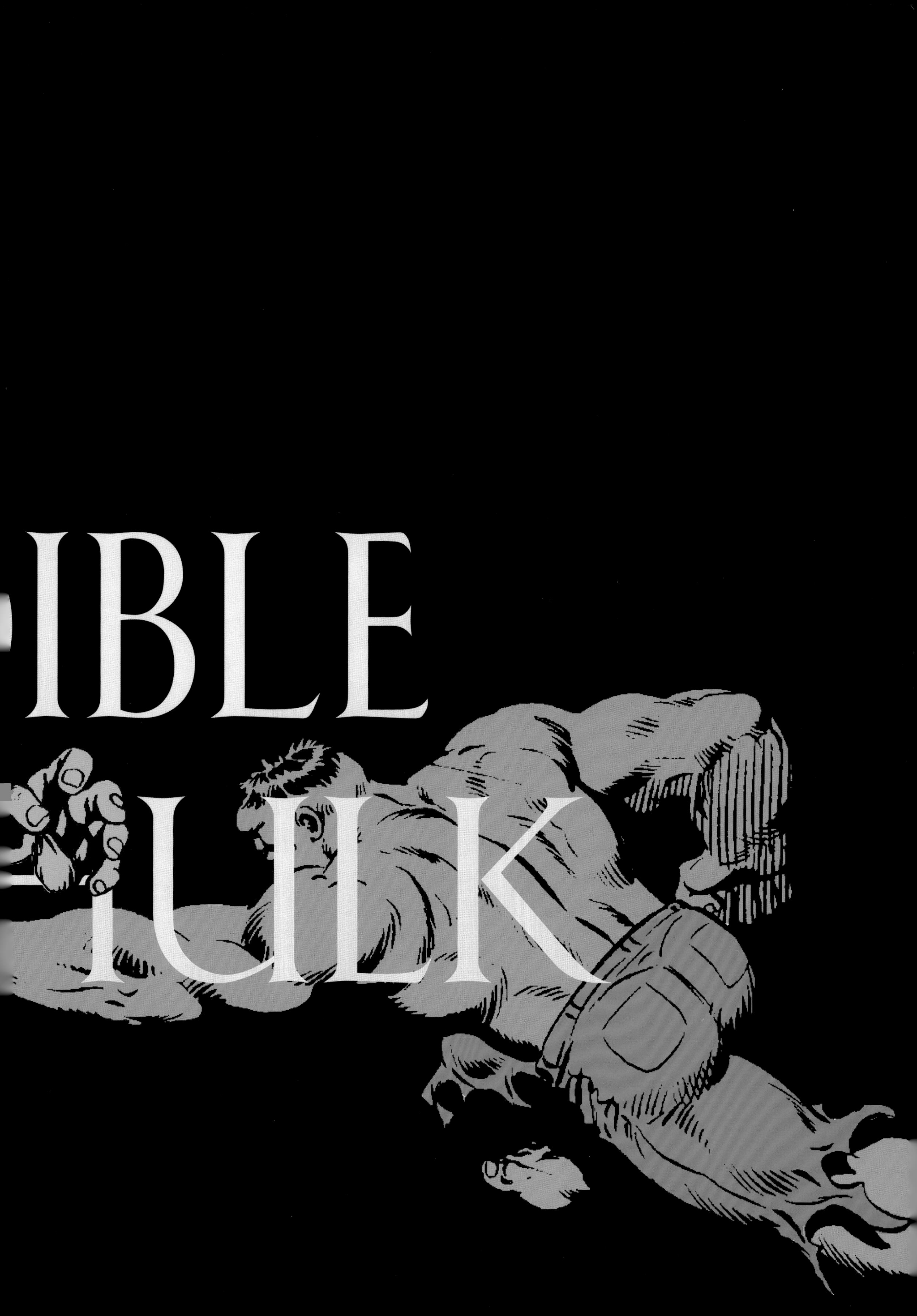

IBLE
ULK

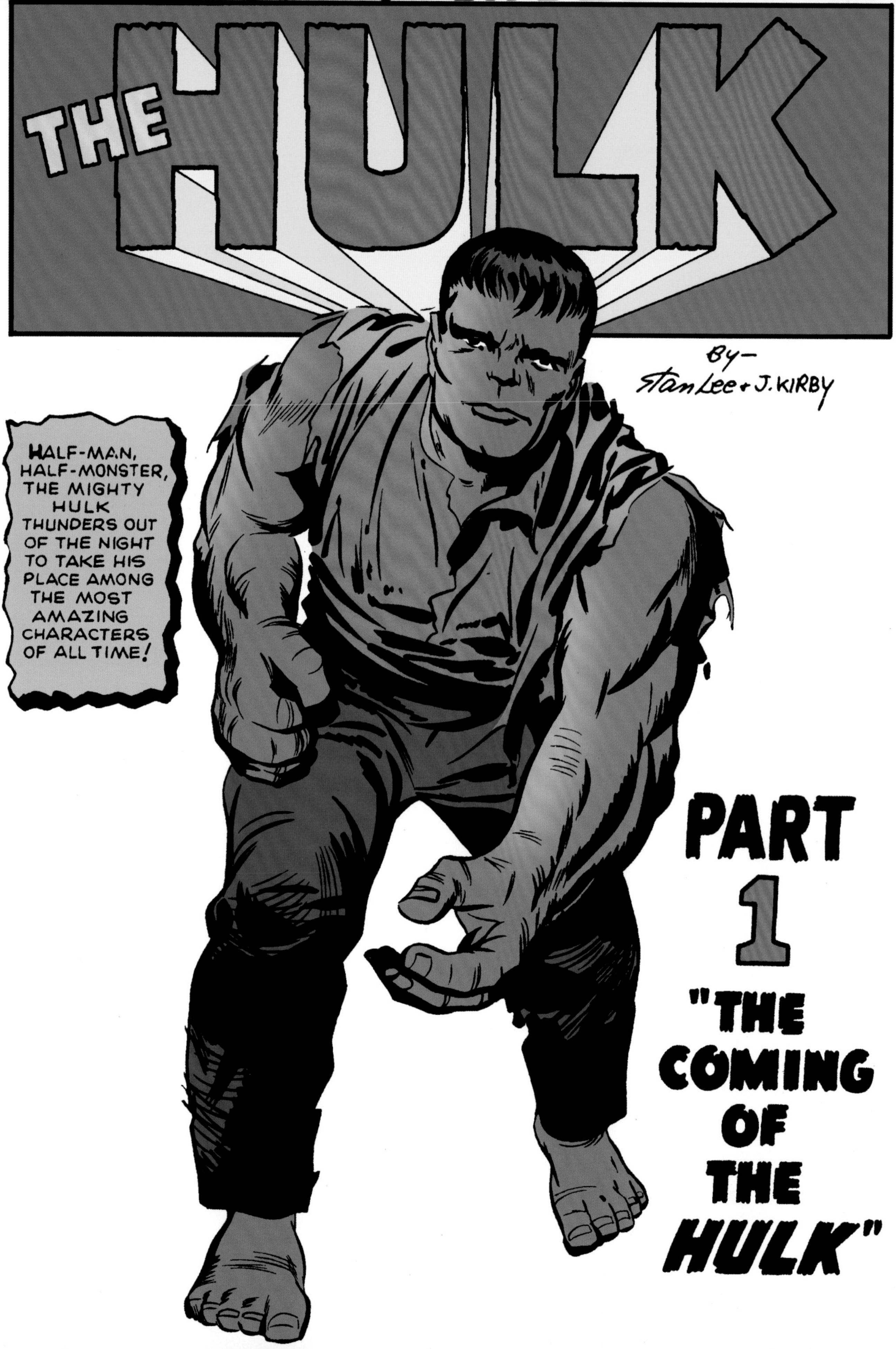
THE HULK
By— Stan Lee + J. KIRBY
HALF-MAN, HALF-MONSTER, THE MIGHTY HULK THUNDERS OUT OF THE NIGHT TO TAKE HIS PLACE AMONG THE MOST AMAZING CHARACTERS OF ALL TIME!
PART 1
"THE COMING OF THE HULK"

The Incredible Hulk

THERE! YOU'RE SAFE!
AND NOW I'LL---
AHHH
ALTHO' MANY MILES FROM BOMB ZERO, DR. BRUCE BANNER IS BATHED IN THE FULL FORCE OF THE MYSTERIOUS GAMMA RAYS!
THE WORLD SEEMS TO STAND STILL, TREMBLING ON THE BRINK OF INFINITY, AS HIS EAR-SPLITTING SCREAM FILLS THE AIR...!

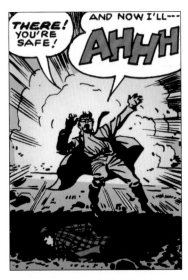

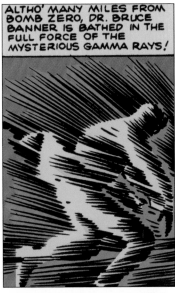

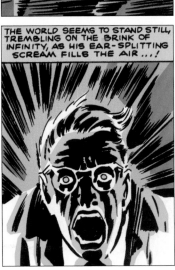

The terror and trauma of Bruce Banner's accidental pelting with gamma radiation are brilliantly captured by Jack Kirby in *Incredible Hulk #1*.

NOT SO JOLLY GREEN GIANT

Searching through the entire Marvel Universe, it would be difficult to find anyone who has experienced an existence as tumultuous, as tragic, even as doomed as Dr. Robert Bruce Banner. Banner's life was inexorably altered by coming into contact with the force of his own discovery, the lethal "G-bomb." That level of tragedy, however, was not uppermost in the mind of Stan Lee when he began to formulate the character as a superheroic follow-up to The Fantastic Four.

Having noticed that the fan mail Marvel had received about The Fantastic Four invariably singled out The Thing as the readers' favorite character, Lee began to think about a similarly brutish superhero. Drawing on the traditions of *Frankenstein* and *The Strange Case of Dr. Jekyll and Mr. Hyde*—both of which involve daring scientists whose creations run amok—Lee imagined the monster that became The Hulk. Kirby's design for the creature did in many ways resemble Hollywood's version of Frankenstein's monster, though not so much as to infringe on the copyrighted makeup.

Today one automatically thinks of The Hulk as green, but the character that debuted in *The Incredible Hulk* issue #1, published May 1962, was a dull gray color, a shade that proved nearly impossible to keep consistent in the printing. With input from the printer, the original gray Hulk was quietly forgotten (at least for a couple of decades), and by the second issue he had taken on his familiar emerald skin tone.

The saga of The Incredible Hulk begins in a secret military laboratory somewhere in the desert, where Dr. Bruce Banner is testing his creation, the G-Bomb, a deadly weapon created from harnessed gamma rays. As he tries to conduct the experiment, Banner is being assailed on all sides. Bellowing General Thaddeus "Thunderbolt" Ross is impatient for the test to get underway, while a fellow-scientist ominously named Igor is berating Banner for testing the bomb without having other scientists look at his figures and formulas, which are hidden back in Banner's room. "I don't make errors, Igor," Bruce coolly tells him.

The general's daughter Betty (who despite the name similarity is no relation to the Betty Ross of the early Captain America comics) attempts to defuse the tension in the lab. Betty is attracted to the mild-mannered Banner, who, unlike her father, "detest[s] men who think with their fists." (Many years later it would be revealed that there was a sound basis for this attitude: as a child, Bruce had been the victim of domestic abuse by his father, whose violence became so uncontrolled that the elder Banner actually killed Bruce's mother.)

Finally Bruce gives the go-ahead for the countdown, but peering at the test site through binoculars, he notices that a teenager in a jalopy has somehow gotten into the test range. Ordering Igor to halt the countdown, Bruce races out to chase the young man away. But Igor, who is in reality a Soviet spy, keeps the countdown going in the hopes that Bruce will be destroyed in the blast. Banner reaches the young man, Rick Jones, in time and pushes him to safety, but is rewarded for this heroic deed by taking the full brunt of the gamma radiation himself. Despite Igor's hopes, Banner does not die, and is instead hustled back to the base by Rick, an orphan, who now views Bruce as a kind of big brother. Back at the base, both Rick and Bruce are locked up in confinement. "They must be waiting for me to die," Bruce remarks, bitterly. But he doesn't die: he begins to change.

In this first transformation to the Hulk, Banner's intellect remains more-or-less intact, though he is inflamed with delusions of his own physical superiority, dismissing the mortals who attempt to capture him—even those who attempt to help him—as "fools" and "insects." "I'm glad it happened!" he roars, while looking at a photo of Bruce Banner, "I'd rather be me than that puny weakling in the picture!" Once he changes back, however, he describes the experience as a nightmare and is thankful it is finally over. He has no idea it is only beginning.

The second half of The Hulk's episodic debut story had The Hulk and Rick being abducted and taken

The Hulk's devoted friend Rick Jones tries to cure Bruce Banner of his affliction in *The Avengers* #3 (January, '64). It would be the first of many failed attempts.

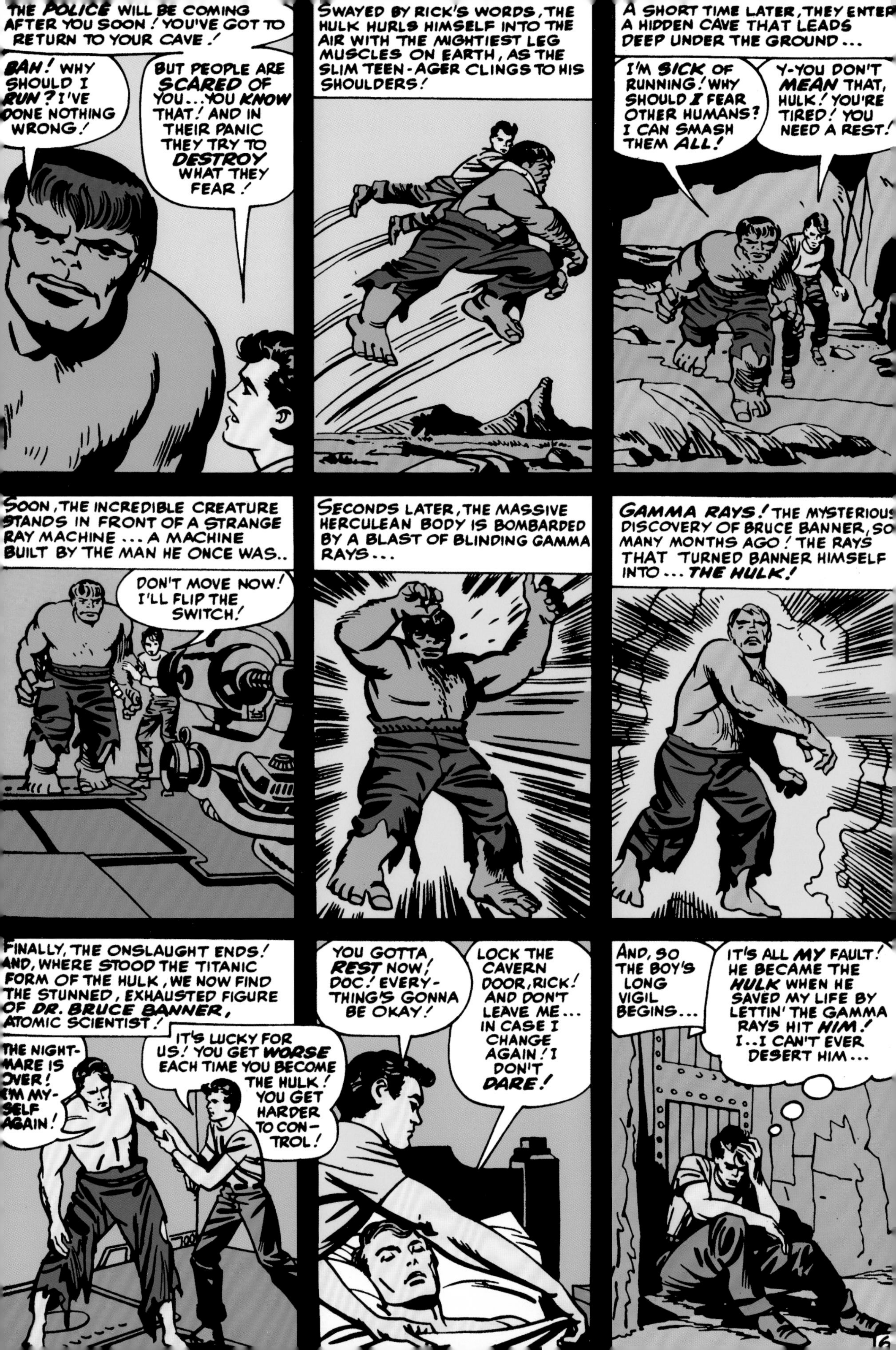

THE POLICE WILL BE COMING AFTER YOU SOON! YOU'VE GOT TO RETURN TO YOUR CAVE!
BAH! WHY SHOULD I RUN? I'VE DONE NOTHING WRONG!
BUT PEOPLE ARE SCARED OF YOU...YOU KNOW THAT! AND IN THEIR PANIC THEY TRY TO DESTROY WHAT THEY FEAR!
SWAYED BY RICK'S WORDS, THE HULK HURLS HIMSELF INTO THE AIR WITH THE MIGHTIEST LEG MUSCLES ON EARTH, AS THE SLIM TEEN-AGER CLINGS TO HIS SHOULDERS!
A SHORT TIME LATER, THEY ENTER A HIDDEN CAVE THAT LEADS DEEP UNDER THE GROUND...
I'M SICK OF RUNNING! WHY SHOULD I FEAR OTHER HUMANS? I CAN SMASH THEM ALL!
Y-YOU DON'T MEAN THAT, HULK! YOU'RE TIRED! YOU NEED A REST!
SOON, THE INCREDIBLE CREATURE STANDS IN FRONT OF A STRANGE RAY MACHINE ... A MACHINE BUILT BY THE MAN HE ONCE WAS..
DON'T MOVE NOW! I'LL FLIP THE SWITCH!
SECONDS LATER, THE MASSIVE HERCULEAN BODY IS BOMBARDED BY A BLAST OF BLINDING GAMMA RAYS...
GAMMA RAYS! THE MYSTERIOUS DISCOVERY OF BRUCE BANNER, SO MANY MONTHS AGO! THE RAYS THAT TURNED BANNER HIMSELF INTO... THE HULK!
FINALLY, THE ONSLAUGHT ENDS! AND, WHERE STOOD THE TITANIC FORM OF THE HULK, WE NOW FIND THE STUNNED, EXHAUSTED FIGURE OF DR. BRUCE BANNER, ATOMIC SCIENTIST!
THE NIGHTMARE IS OVER! I'M MYSELF AGAIN!
IT'S LUCKY FOR US! YOU GET WORSE EACH TIME YOU BECOME THE HULK! YOU GET HARDER TO CONTROL!
YOU GOTTA REST NOW, DOC! EVERYTHING'S GONNA BE OKAY!
LOCK THE CAVERN DOOR, RICK! AND DON'T LEAVE ME... IN CASE I CHANGE AGAIN! I DON'T DARE!
AND, SO THE BOY'S LONG VIGIL BEGINS...
IT'S ALL MY FAULT! HE BECAME THE HULK WHEN HE SAVED MY LIFE BY LETTIN' THE GAMMA RAYS HIT HIM! I..I CAN'T EVER DESERT HIM...
16

WHO IS RICK JONES?

5 SPECIAL COMICS INFORMATION

APPROVED FOR ALL READERS

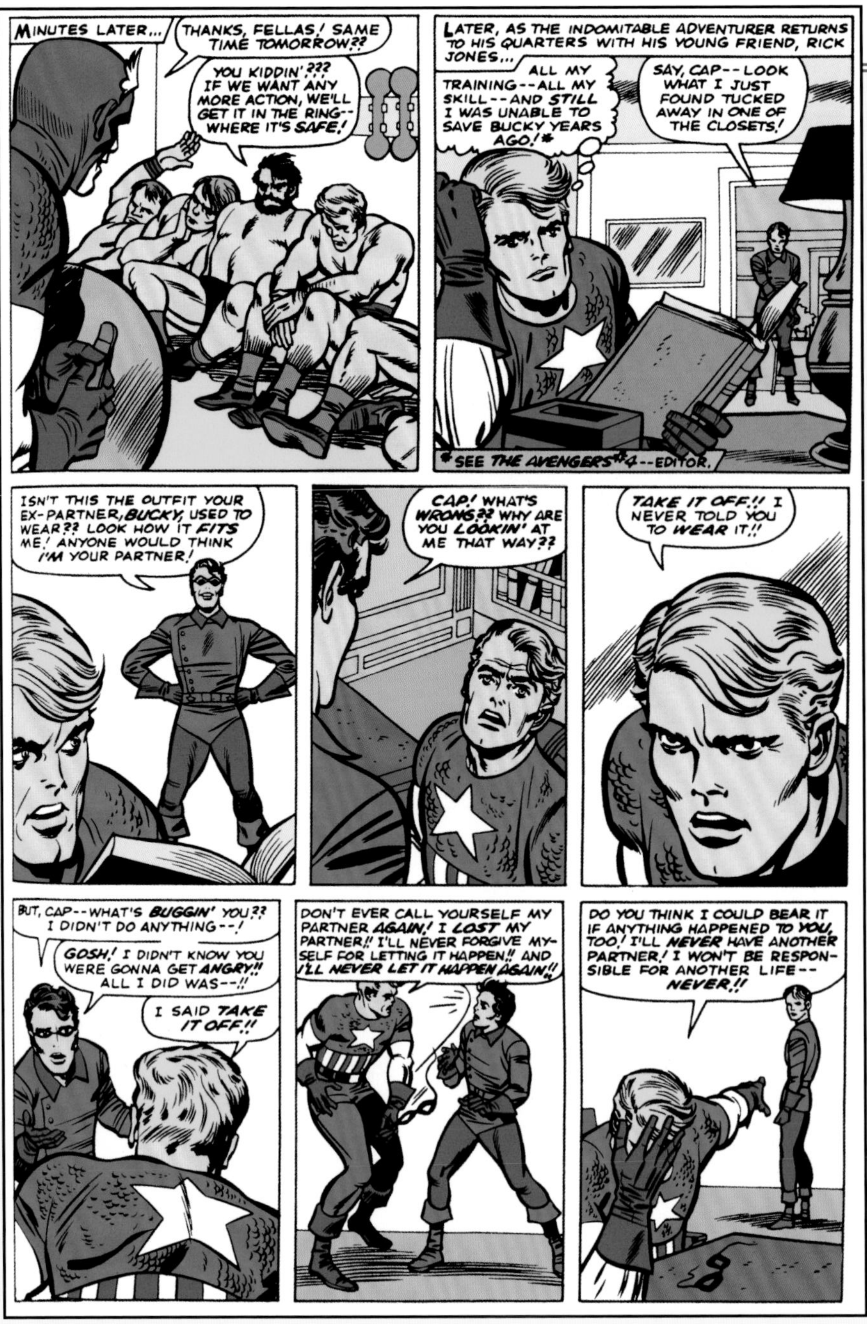
MINUTES LATER...
THANKS, FELLAS! SAME TIME TOMORROW??
YOU KIDDIN'??? IF WE WANT ANY MORE ACTION, WE'LL GET IT IN THE RING-- WHERE IT'S SAFE!
LATER, AS THE INDOMITABLE ADVENTURER RETURNS TO HIS QUARTERS WITH HIS YOUNG FRIEND, RICK JONES...
ALL MY TRAINING--ALL MY SKILL--AND STILL I WAS UNABLE TO SAVE BUCKY YEARS AGO! *
SAY, CAP--LOOK WHAT I JUST FOUND TUCKED AWAY IN ONE OF THE CLOSETS!
* SEE THE AVENGERS #4--EDITOR.
ISN'T THIS THE OUTFIT YOUR EX-PARTNER, BUCKY, USED TO WEAR?? LOOK HOW IT FITS ME! ANYONE WOULD THINK I'M YOUR PARTNER!
CAP! WHAT'S WRONG?? WHY ARE YOU LOOKIN' AT ME THAT WAY??
TAKE IT OFF!! I NEVER TOLD YOU TO WEAR IT!!
BUT, CAP--WHAT'S BUGGIN' YOU?? I DIDN'T DO ANYTHING--!
GOSH! I DIDN'T KNOW YOU WERE GONNA GET ANGRY!! ALL I DID WAS--!!
I SAID TAKE IT OFF!!
DON'T EVER CALL YOURSELF MY PARTNER AGAIN! I LOST MY PARTNER!! I'LL NEVER FORGIVE MYSELF FOR LETTING IT HAPPEN!! AND I'LL NEVER LET IT HAPPEN AGAIN!!
DO YOU THINK I COULD BEAR IT IF ANYTHING HAPPENED TO YOU, TOO! I'LL NEVER HAVE ANOTHER PARTNER! I WON'T BE RESPONSIBLE FOR ANOTHER LIFE-- NEVER!!

Captain America lashes out at Rick Jones, who tries to take Bucky's place, in *The Avengers* #7 (August 1964).

One of the most intriguing secondary characters in the Marvel Universe—if for no other reason, his ubiquity—is the young orphan Rick Jones, who was introduced in *The Incredible Hulk* issue #1. The footloose, wandering teenager is the catalyst for Bruce Banner's getting in the way of the gamma radiation and hulking out. Rick would become the Hulk's best friend and protector and years later, in 1986, he would take the bullet intended for Bruce Banner at the latter's traumatic wedding. But in between these two events Rick would also establish "The Teen Brigade," a group of superhero helpers first mentioned in *Hulk* #6, and in the mid-1960s, upon the Hulk's (temporary) disappearance, he would transfer his loyalties to Captain America, whom he called "the greatest guy I ever met!" In 1968 Rick linked with yet another classic hero, Captain Marvel, who was recreated as the alien, Mar-Vell, who channeled to Earth through Jones. With time, Rick outgrew his penchant for superhero-worship. But his unique position as a nexus point between several series and the *deus ex-Rickina* manner in which he was often used make one wonder exactly who Rick Jones might someday be revealed to be.

to Moscow by the Gargoyle, a Soviet scientist who has been grotesquely deformed through radiation poisoning. Banner is able to re-infuse him with radiation and reverse the disfigurement, and the grateful Gargoyle allows he and Rick to escape back to the U.S.A. On the return flight home, Bruce idly wonders if this might be "the beginning of the end of the Red tyranny."

The Incredible Hulk magazine lasted only six issues, though after a brief stint as a member of The Avengers, which reinforced the idea that The Hulk was too much of a loner and too mistrustful of others to be a team player, the character was revived on a regular basis in *Tales to Astonish*. (He fared somewhat better when teamed with fellow-loners Prince Namor and Dr. Strange as The Defenders in the 1970s.) The Hulk continued to astonish readers even after the title was changed to *The Incredible Hulk* in 1968. Since then, The Hulk has never looked back, though the life he shares with Bruce Banner has become increasingly difficult. Eventually The Hulk would lose the megalomanic intellect he demonstrated in his first adventure and devolve into a lonely, scorned, primal creature almost completely governed by emotions, particularly rage. The realization that the sudden release of suppressed rage was the trigger than caused the transformation between Banner and The Hulk was a leap forward in establishing a comic character that was uniquely troubled, as opposed to one who was just unlucky enough to get out of the way of a radiation shower.

The aura of tragedy that dogged Bruce Banner would achieve epic proportions. After years of courting Betty Ross, he finally married her in 1986, only to have the ceremony ruined when her father, now completely unhinged after a long period of growing instability, shows up and tries to shoot him. The former general's bullet hits best man Rick Jones instead, wounding him. Despite that, the ceremony continues. After suffering through what must count as the most difficult marriage in the history of comics, encompassing a tragic lost pregnancy and a period in which Ross left Banner to become a nun, Betty would die in 1998. Although as has been demonstrated, "death" in the Marvel Universe does not always come as the end.

In the 1990s, writer Peter David began to explore the bizarrely symbiotic psyche of Banner and The Hulk, and the results were stories of amazing complexity. At one point the troubled mind of Banner literally split into three, creating The Gray Hulk as a separate entity from both The Green Hulk and Banner. One story from 1991, facetiously titled "Honey, I Shrunk The Hulk," written by David and drawn by Dale Keown (pencils) and Bob McLeod (inks), has become a modern classic. In it, the gamma-altered psychologist Leonard Samson, a.k.a. Doc Samson, who had been helping The Hulk wrestle with his problems for some time, forced the three Banner/Hulk entities to confront the memory of Banner's abusive childhood, and ultimately fused them together into one personality: not Banner, but a poised and confident version of The Green Hulk. "Honey, I Shrunk The Hulk" typifies the quantum-leap that has occurred in comic book storytelling over the last couple of decades, taking a medium that was once governed by simple external conflicts between good and evil and replacing them by complex inner struggles within the darkness of one's own secret personality.

On a considerably lighter note, there is one more puzzling aspect of Banner's character that needs to be addressed: how he went from being Bruce Banner to *Robert* Bruce Banner. Given the character's history, it would not be surprising to learn that it was the manifestation of yet another identity crisis. The truth, however, is much simpler. "There was a television production executive named *Bob* Banner," explains Stan Lee. "I've known that name for years, and sometimes when I was writing a story, I would carelessly refer to Bruce Banner as Bob Banner. Then I'd get mail from the readers saying, 'Don't you know you the name of your own character?' So I took the cowardly way out and said his name is *Robert Bruce Banner,* just to get myself off the hook."

Bruce Banner and Betty Ross finally wed in *The Incredible Hulk* #319 (1986). Their happiness would be fleeting at best.

(Opposite) For a time The Hulk was split into two separate entities, one green and one gray—but both angry. From *The Incredible Hulk* #377 (1991).

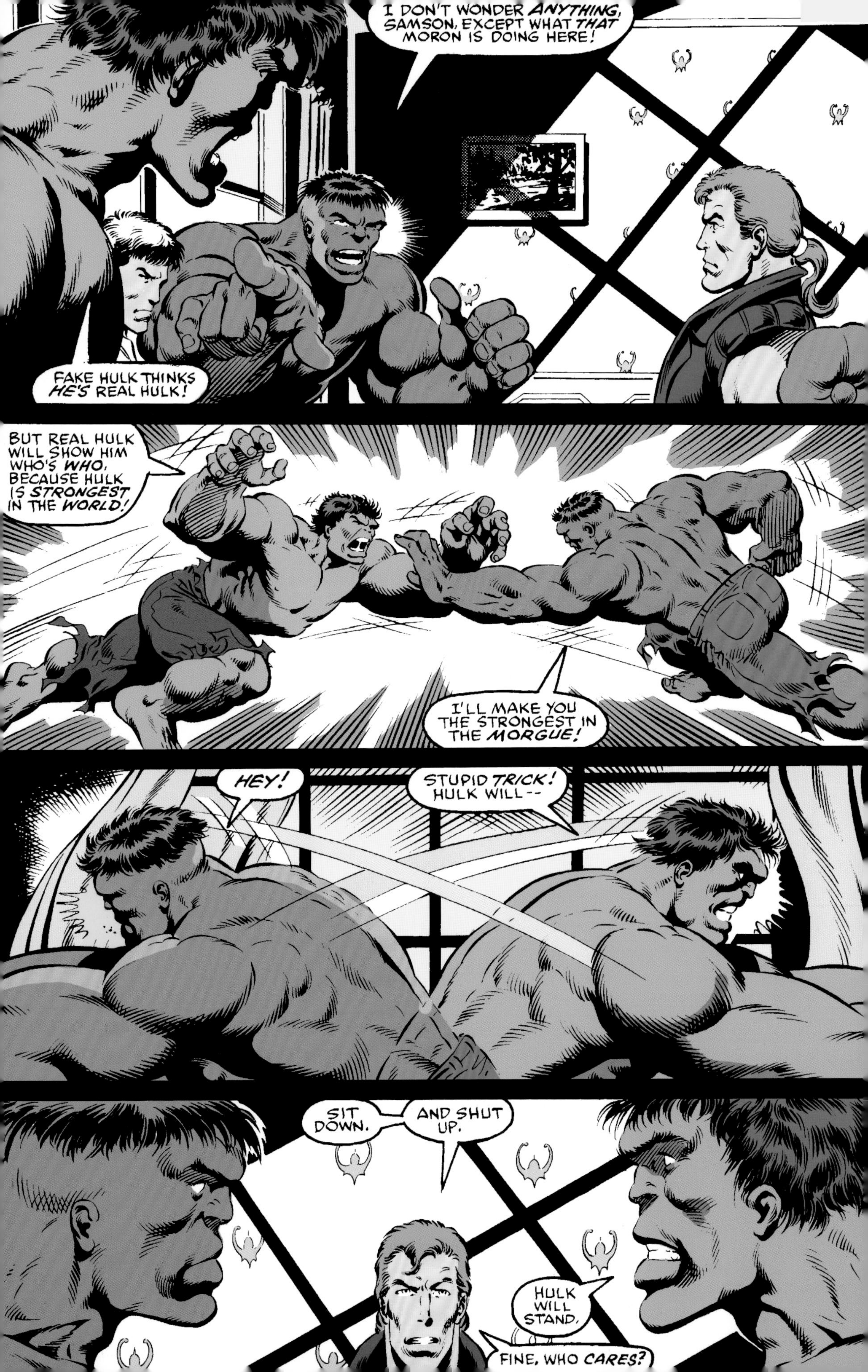
I DON'T WONDER ANYTHING, SAMSON, EXCEPT WHAT THAT MORON IS DOING HERE!
FAKE HULK THINKS HE'S REAL HULK!
BUT REAL HULK WILL SHOW HIM WHO'S WHO, BECAUSE HULK IS STRONGEST IN THE WORLD!
I'LL MAKE YOU THE STRONGEST IN THE MORGUE!
HEY!
STUPID TRICK! HULK WILL--
SIT DOWN.
AND SHUT UP.
HULK WILL STAND.
FINE, WHO CARES?

THE INCREDIBLE HULK IN THE MEDIA

Without question, The Incredible Hulk has enjoyed the most successful media existence of any Marvel superhero. A direct creative descendent of Dr. Jekyll and Mr. Hyde, the character's influence can be seen in other film characters as well, such as Troma's successful *The Toxic Avenger*. The green guy's television reign began on November 4, 1977, just six weeks after CBS had aired "Spider-Man," with the television film "The Incredible Hulk," produced, written and directed by Kenneth Johnson and starring Bill Bixby as the scientist (now rechristened *David* Bruce Banner) and a twenty-three-year-old professional body builder named Lou Ferrigno as The Hulk. Johnson's script was a major rethinking of The Hulk mythology. In the film, Dr. Banner is a research scientist at the private Culver Institute, working with a fellow-scientist Dr. Elaina Marks (winningly played by Susan Sullivan) to try and unlock the secret of the phenomenon of "super strength" that normal people demonstrate under conditions of extreme stress or danger. The two examine case study after case study of people who suddenly and mysteriously developed the strength to turn over a car or rip down a door in order to save a loved one in danger, or rescue themselves.

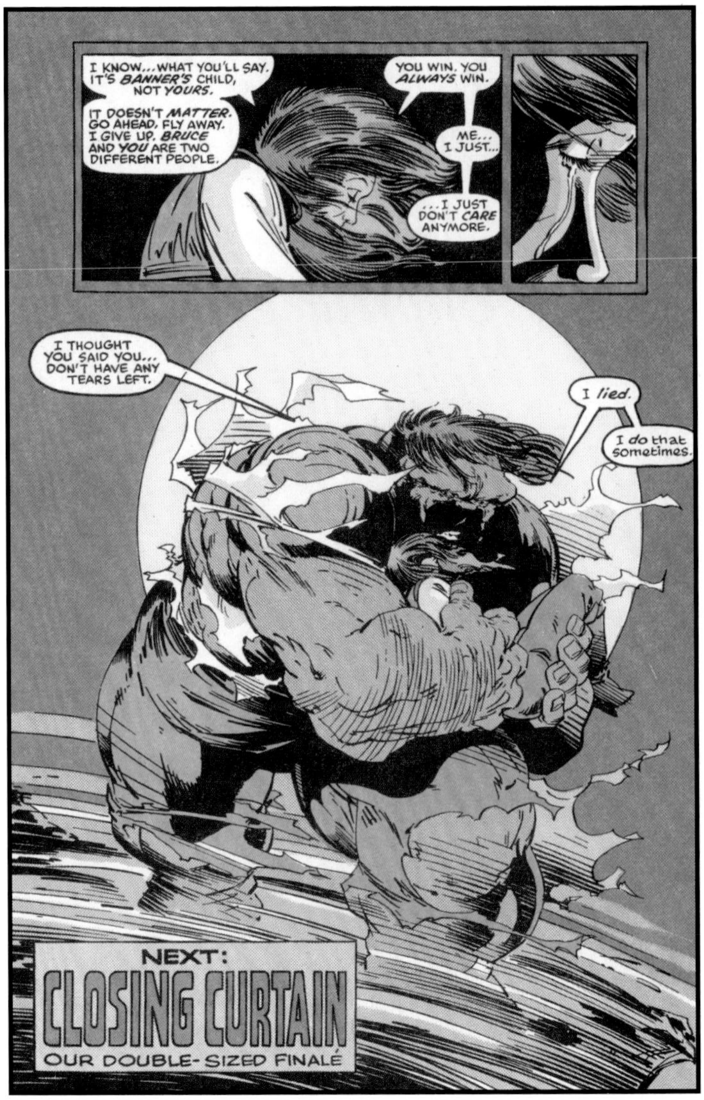
I KNOW... WHAT YOU'LL SAY. IT'S BANNER'S CHILD, NOT YOURS.
IT DOESN'T MATTER. GO AHEAD, FLY AWAY. I GIVE UP. BRUCE AND YOU ARE TWO DIFFERENT PEOPLE.
YOU WIN. YOU ALWAYS WIN.
ME... I JUST...
...I JUST DON'T CARE ANYMORE.
I THOUGHT YOU SAID YOU... DON'T HAVE ANY TEARS LEFT.
I lied.
I do that sometimes.
NEXT:
CLOSING CURTAIN
OUR DOUBLE-SIZED FINALE

Pregnant and troubled, Betty Banner is cradled in the arms of The Grey Hulk, one-third of her husband's fractured psyche in *The Incredible Hulk* #344 (1988).

Ostensibly this research is being conducted in order to figure out a way to consciously tap in to this strength, which exists latently in humans, but remains outside the realm of normal experience. But Banner has more personally felt motivation: some time earlier, he and his wife Laura had been in a car accident, from which Banner was thrown free, while Laura remained trapped inside the burning vehicle. Banner attempted to get her out, but was unable to summon up the strength to do so. Not only does the incident continue to haunt his dreams, but the case studies of normal people who were able to accomplish the very acts that he could not, fill him with bitterness, rage, and frustration. He has to know why he failed where so many others had succeeded.

The answer comes one day when a colleague recommends shutting down the lab's sensitive computer

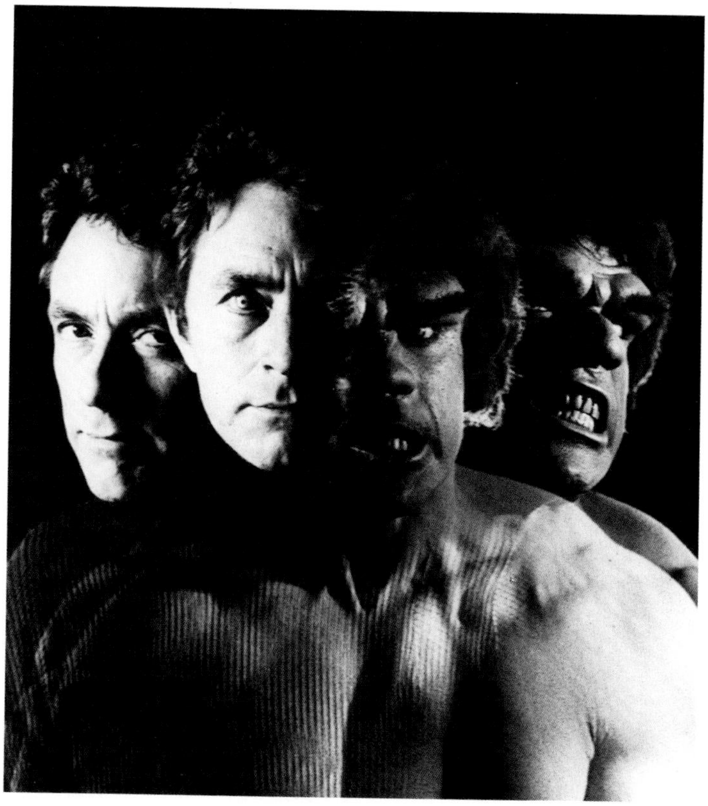

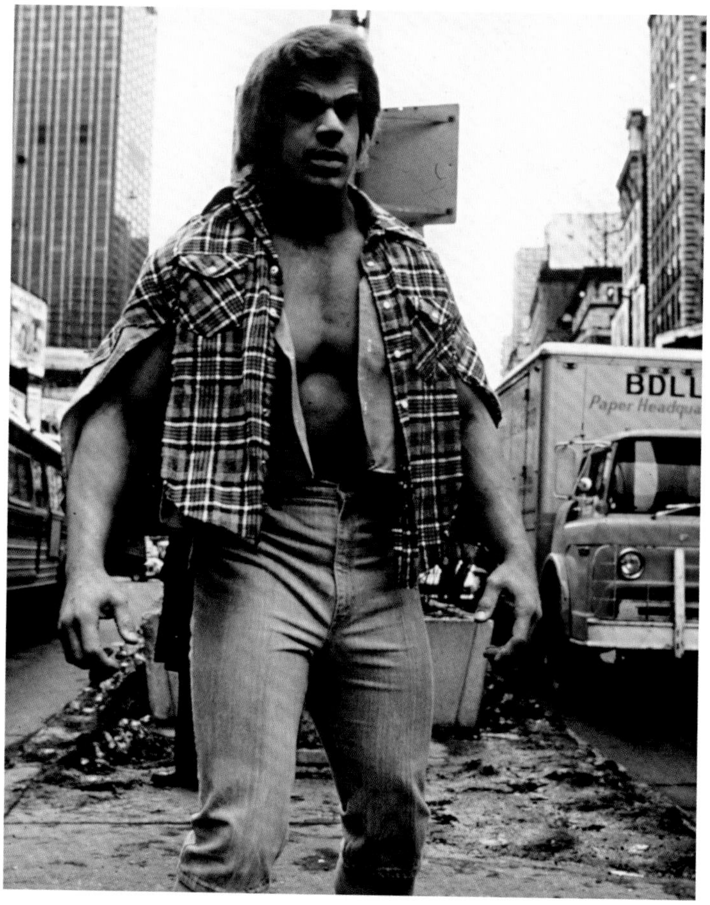
BDLL

(Top) Bill Bixby as "David" Banner transforms into The Incredible Hulk (Lou Ferrigno). The Hulk's television reign began in 1977 and lasted until 1990.

(Above) Hulk transformations were hard on costumes, as was the green makeup worn by Lou Ferrigno.

equipment because of unusually heavy gamma-ray interference caused by sunspots, and Banner suddenly realizes that these gamma rays might have acted as an external stimulus that triggered the instances of super strength. He charts the levels of gamma radiation that have hit the Earth for the past several years and juxtaposes it with the dates on which the super strength incidents of his test subjects occurred, and his conjecture is confirmed: in each instance the level of gamma radiation is abnormally high. In his own case, the gamma level was extremely low.

Anxious to test his findings, he enters the institute's radiation lab alone and prepares to bombard his body with 300,000 units of gamma radiation. Unfortunately, Banner does not realize that the machinery has recently been recalibrated, so instead of 300,000 units he gets close to *2 million* units, far above the safety level. But when the experiment appears to have no effect on him, he leaves the lab, greatly frustrated. While driving home through a blinding thunderstorm, Banner has a blowout and tries to change the tire in the rain, hurting his hand in the process. Suddenly, all the pent-up anger and frustration that he has been holding inside since his auto accident is released and Banner begins to transform: his eyes turn white, his arms begin to expand, ripping the seams of his clothing, his feet enlarge and tear through the stitching of his shoes. Naked (practically) to the elements, The Incredible Hulk is born. He proceeds to pulverize Banner's car in an exhibition of bestial rage.

Banner remains The Hulk even into the next day, when (in a scene highly reminiscent of the classic sequence from the original 1931 version of *Frankenstein*) he meets up with a little girl at the edge of a tranquil lake. Terrified, the girl leaps into the water to try and escape from the fearsome green creature, and The Hulk tries to save her by uprooting a tree and laying it across the water for the girl to grab onto. But the girl's cries alert her father, who shoots The Hulk, prompting the creature to pick the man up and throw him into the lake like a stone.

The Hulk lumbers away and reverts back to Banner, who has only a vague memory of possessing enormous strength and rage and who, amazingly, bears nearly healed scars from his recent gunshot wounds. Banner immediately goes to Elaina for help, and the two set up an experiment in hopes of resummoning the mysterious creature while Banner is safely locked inside a pressure chamber at the institute, which was designed to simulate the effects of being many fathoms under the water. Banner tries consciously to bring on the change, but he cannot. Only when he is asleep and having his recurring nightmare of the accident that killed his wife, and his failure to rescue her, does his rage once more explode like a volcano, triggering the transformation. Dr. Marks looks on, stunned, as The Hulk literally rips the pressure chamber apart from the inside, ultimately breaking out. But once he is out, she is able to approach him, managing to speak to the tiny part of The Hulk that is still Banner.

As though the realization that he could turn into a monster at any time while he is unconscious wasn't stressful enough, Banner finds that he and Elaina are being followed by a persistent tabloid journalist named Jack McGee (Jack Colvin), who smells a story in the reports of a monstrous, violent green giant, whom McGee links to Banner because of a Hulk-sized footprint that the police found in the mud beside Banner's ruined car. McGee continues to snoop, and even breaks into the lab (carelessly knocking over a jar of highly volatile chemical in the process), where he overhears Banner and Marks speaking about The Hulk. Banner discovers McGee and escorts him out of the lab, but while they are there the spilled chemical causes a fire to break out, endangering Elaina, who is still inside.

Banner rushes back to save her but cannot get inside, at least not until he transforms into The Hulk and breaks through a wall. The creature finds the injured scientist and carries her out, taking her to the safety of the nearby woods. But it is too late; Elaina is mortally wounded. With her last breath, she confesses her secret

Bodybuilder-turned-actor Lou Ferrigno did most of his Hulk stunts himself.

Just as the original gray Hulk in the comics had color consistency problems, the shaggy gray wig worn by Lou Ferrigno on television often photographed red or brown.

love for David Banner, and dies in The Hulk's arms, as the green one cries out in anguish.

David Banner and Elaina Marks have a dual funeral, which is attended by McGee, who now declares himself to be on the trail of the green monster that is believed to have "murdered" Banner and Marks. But after the mourners have gone, David Banner quietly steps up to the grave sites and confesses his previously unspoken love for Elaina. Then in what would become a recurring motif of every subsequent Hulk movie and television episode, Banner heads off down the road, alone, to the melancholy piano music of Joseph Harnell.

Shifting the emphasis away from The Hulk and putting it onto Banner and his problems helps to make "The Incredible Hulk" an emotionally resonant film that appealed to a wider audience than those who would have normally tuned in to see a monster movie or a comic book adaptation. Johnson delivers many fine directorial touches, including the silent montage of images from Banner's life with Laura (played by "Dark Shadows" alumnus Lara Parker) and her subsequent death, which recurs throughout the film as his tormenting dream. The picture is not "camped" or played for comedy, although there are little touches of humor, such as the moment when Banner tells the obnoxious journalist, "Mr. McGee, don't make me angry. You wouldn't like me when I'm angry." Bixby's delivery of the line not only got the desired laugh, but it launched another Marvel-related catch phrase in the process.

Given all of Johnson's labors and his dedication to the picture, it is surprising to learn that he was reluctant to take on the project. "I had just done 'The Bionic Woman,' and Frank Price came to me at the time they had acquired the rights to the Marvel superheroes and asked which of them I would like to do, and I said, 'Gee, none of them, thanks,'" Johnson recalls. What changed his mind was the realization that a piece of classic literature could be applied to The Hulk story—not the elments of *Frankenstein* and *Dr. Jekyll and Mr. Hyde* that were already there, but rather a book by Victor Hugo. "I was reading *Les Miserables* at the time, and so I had Jean Valjean and Javert, and the fugitive concept in my head, and I thought maybe there was an interesting way to take a little bit of Hugo and a little bit of Jekyll-and-Hyde and marry it to what I thought was a pretty ludicrous premise." Thus David Banner became the Valjean figure, a fugitive in his own land, forced to wander from place to place in a constant search of a temporary safe haven from which he could look for a cure for his affliction, all the while being stalked by the obsessive Jack McGee, who took on the role of Javert.

Once the concept was accepted, Johnson had one other problem with the original story. "The first thing I did was ask Stan Lee why he was green," Johnson says. "I mean, the color of rage is red, not green. He should be 'The Envious Hulk.'" Despite Johnson's entreaties, the color remained (and rightly so) though he did change another key element. "I couldn't deal with the name 'Bruce Banner,' Johnson says. 'It was just too cartoony, so I let 'Bruce' be his middle name and gave him 'David' as a first name, which had a little more reality to it."

Johnson was not alone in his reluctance toward the property. Bill Bixby was equally hesitant to take on a project based on a comic book, though he agreed after reading the script. The biggest challenge proved to be finding someone in Hollywood who would make a convincing Hulk. After interviewing dozens of bodybuilders, Johnson cast 7 2 actor Richard Kiel, who was already enjoying a personal triumph that year as the steel-toothed villain "Jaws" in the James Bond epic *The Spy Who Loved Me.* But after a week's filming with Kiel, both Johnson and Frank Price agreed that a change was necessary. "We decided that we really needed a more muscular kind of look, because it didn't look like what they thought they needed to sell," Johnson says. Kiel was dismissed (though one shot of him remains in the film: an overhead view of The Hulk as he looks up to the top of the tree by the lake) and Lou Ferrigno, the 6 4 , 225-pound former Mr. Teenage America, Mr. America, Mr.

The Man Who Would Be Hulk: 7 2 actor Richard Kiel was the first actor cast as The Incredible Hulk.

(Top) Ferrigno patiently endures the body paint that will turn him into America's favorite green giant.

(Above) Lou Ferrigno undergoes the application of rubber head and nose appliances, while a visitor, TV's Mister Rogers, looks on.

Universe (twice), and Mr. International, who had virtually no film experience, except for an appearance in the documentary *Pumping Iron*, became the once and future Hulk.

Ferrigno, whose achievements masked the fact that he suffered from hearing loss, had actually been a fan of Hulk comics as a child. "When I was a kid growing up, I used to read the comic books all the time," Ferrigno says, "and what I loved about The Hulk was the fact that he cares that he looked like a monster. That made the show successful." To play the character, Ferrigno endured a three-hour makeup ordeal, including full green face makeup and body paint, a prosthetic forehead and nose, white contact lenses, huge, oversized false teeth, and a scraggly green fright wig (though in the fourth season, Ferrigno would appear sans makeup as a body builder in an episode titled "King of the Beach"). Even after Ferrigno was on the set, his makeup problems were far from over. "The makeup was just a horrific nightmare!" Johnson says. "It came off on everything. I still have sweatshirts in my closet that have green smudges on them from twenty years ago."

But part of the magic of Hollywood is in not letting the smudges show, and "The Incredible Hulk" was a hit with audiences both in the United States and abroad, where it was released theatrically. The film's success prompted a feature-length sequel, "The Incredible Hulk Returns," which was also written, produced, and directed by Johnson, and which continued the *Les Miserables* theme by having McGee continuing on his quest to track down The Hulk and have him brought up on charges of murder. One shot in the film turned out to contain more realism that had been intended. The scene depicted a fairly common stunt in Hulk movies: the creature's crashing through a solid wall. Recalls Ferrigno: "The director said to me, 'We have one wall set up and you have to go through it, we can't replace it because we have budget and time problems, so just do the best you can.' So when he yelled 'action,' I kept pounding on this wall, and pounding on

it, and I said to myself, 'Jeez, what's wrong with this
wall? I'm killing myself!' And then I made it through.
Then I saw the nails sticking out of objects on the
floor, and the assistant director came over to me and
apologized because it was a real wall, it wasn't a fake
one! They made a mistake with the partition. And I
said: 'Thanks a lot!'"

Bixby, Ferrigno, and Colvin returned for their
roles as Banner, The Hulk, and McGee when "The
Incredible Hulk" became a weekly series in March of
1978. The show's first four episodes consisted of both
feature-length pilots cut into two-parters. Critics proved
to be somewhat resistant to the premise, which put
Bixby on the defensive. "I'm proud of the show and it
makes me angry that I have to keep apologizing for it,"
he told the *Los Angeles Times* (and whether or not
the reporter liked him when he was angry went
unmentioned). "We are not making a children's show.
We are making an adult show that children are allowed
to watch. There's a big difference." Viewers, however,
loved the show, and in its first season Emmy voters
proved that they were watching too by awarding guest
star Mariette Hartley with an Emmy for her performance
as Dr. Caroline Fields in a two-part episode titled
"Married," in which Banner weds Caroline, only to
see her become a victim of a deadly typhoon. The
two episodes were later cut together and released
theatrically in France under the title of *The Bride
of the Incredible Hulk*.

For three seasons audiences tuned in to see the
ongoing cat-and-mouse chase between the hunted,
David Banner, and the hunter, Jack McGee, who
eventually came to suspect that Banner and The Hulk
were one and the same, but who could not prove it. Its
popularity was such that for a time Lou Ferrigno as The
Hulk became a true media celebrity and popped up for
guest shots in other series. Ferrigno was even featured
on the venerable pre-schooler's show "Mister Rogers'
Neighborhood." By the fourth year, however, ratings had
begun to slip, and "The Incredible Hulk" was placed on

(Top) Lou Ferrigno lugs actress Laurie Prange in 1978's "The Incredible Hulk
Returns," the second feature-length pilot.

(Above) Banner and The Hulk confront each other during a hypnotic trance
in the two-part episode "Married" from 1978.

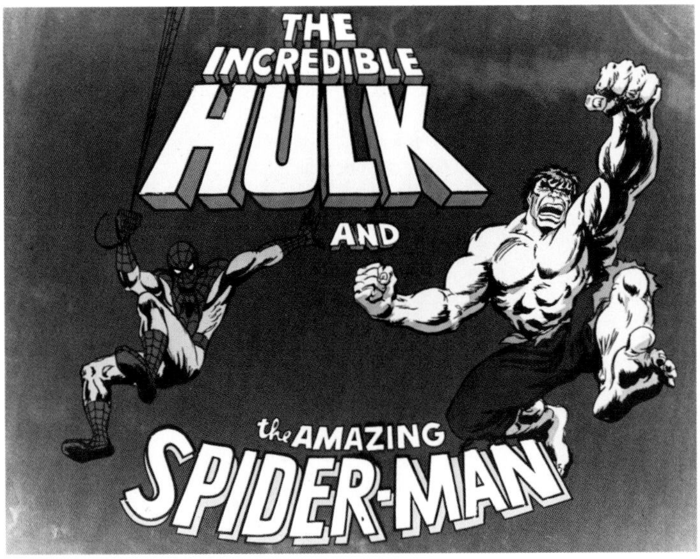
THE
INCREDIBLE
HULK
AND
the AMAZING
SPIDER-MAN

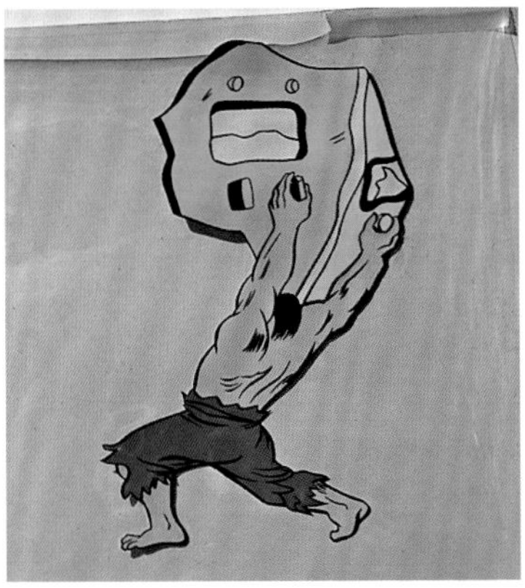

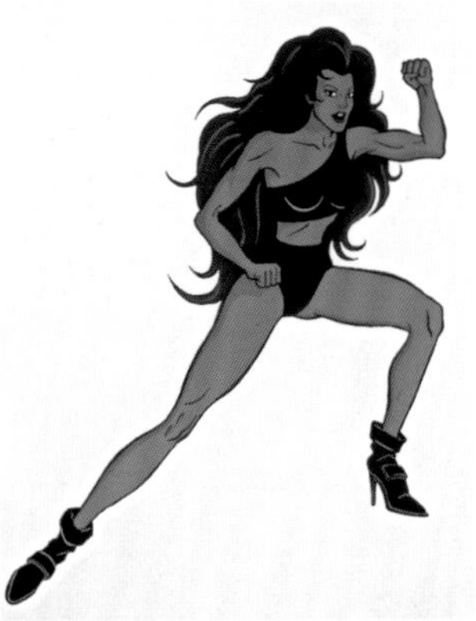

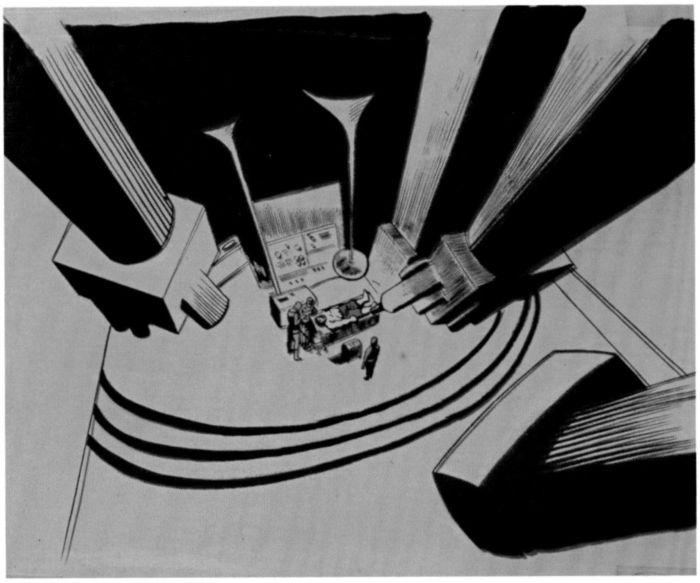

(Top) The Hulk and Spidey took to the airwaves in animation in 1982.

(Middle) Original Hulk animation cel from "The Marvel Superheroes" series in 1966. The "Savage" She-Hulk would in the course of a few years become the "Sensational" She-Hulk.

(Above) To make up for their lack of movement, the 1966 Hulk cartoons often employed dramatic staging.

hiatus in November of 1981. It returned in May of the following year, but only briefly, before being canceled in June 1982. That was hardly the end of The Hulk, however.

The Incredible Hulk turned up in animated form in September of 1982 as half of "The Incredible Hulk/Amazing Spider-Man Hour" on NBC's Saturday morning lineup. New half-hour "Hulk" episodes were combined with existing "Spider-Man" episodes of "Spider-Man and His Amazing Friends" to make the show. It was not the first time The Hulk had appeared in cartoon form: his adventures had earlier been chronicled as part of the animated series "The Marvel Superheroes" in 1966. Like "Amazing Friends," "The Incredible Hulk/Amazing Spider-Man Hour" seemed to be aimed squarely at a younger audience than those who read the comic books, and featured such fanciful storylines as "When Monsters Meet," in which The Hulk runs into the great-great-great-great-great-great-grandson of Quasimodo, the original Hunchback of Notre Dame (Victor Hugo had worked for the property once . . .).

The series also featured a character that had made her debut in the comics in 1980 under the moniker *The Savage She-Hulk*. The character origin of The She-Hulk is quite clever: successful criminal attorney Jennifer "Jen" Walters is Bruce Banner's cousin and one of the very few people who knows about his problem. When Jen is injured in an accident and requires a blood transfusion, Bruce willingly donates a pint. However, the lingering gamma radiation in his blood now infects Jen, causing her to turn into The She-Hulk. Unlike Bruce, though, Jen can control the transformations and retain her full mental capacity even while big and green. Because of this, she believes that she can someday help Bruce to learn to control his transformations.

That is the mythological origin for The She-Hulk. The actual creation of the character was mandated for a different reason. "After Lou Ferrigno did The Hulk on TV, they were afraid [Universal] might come out with a female Hulk," says artist John Buscema, who designed

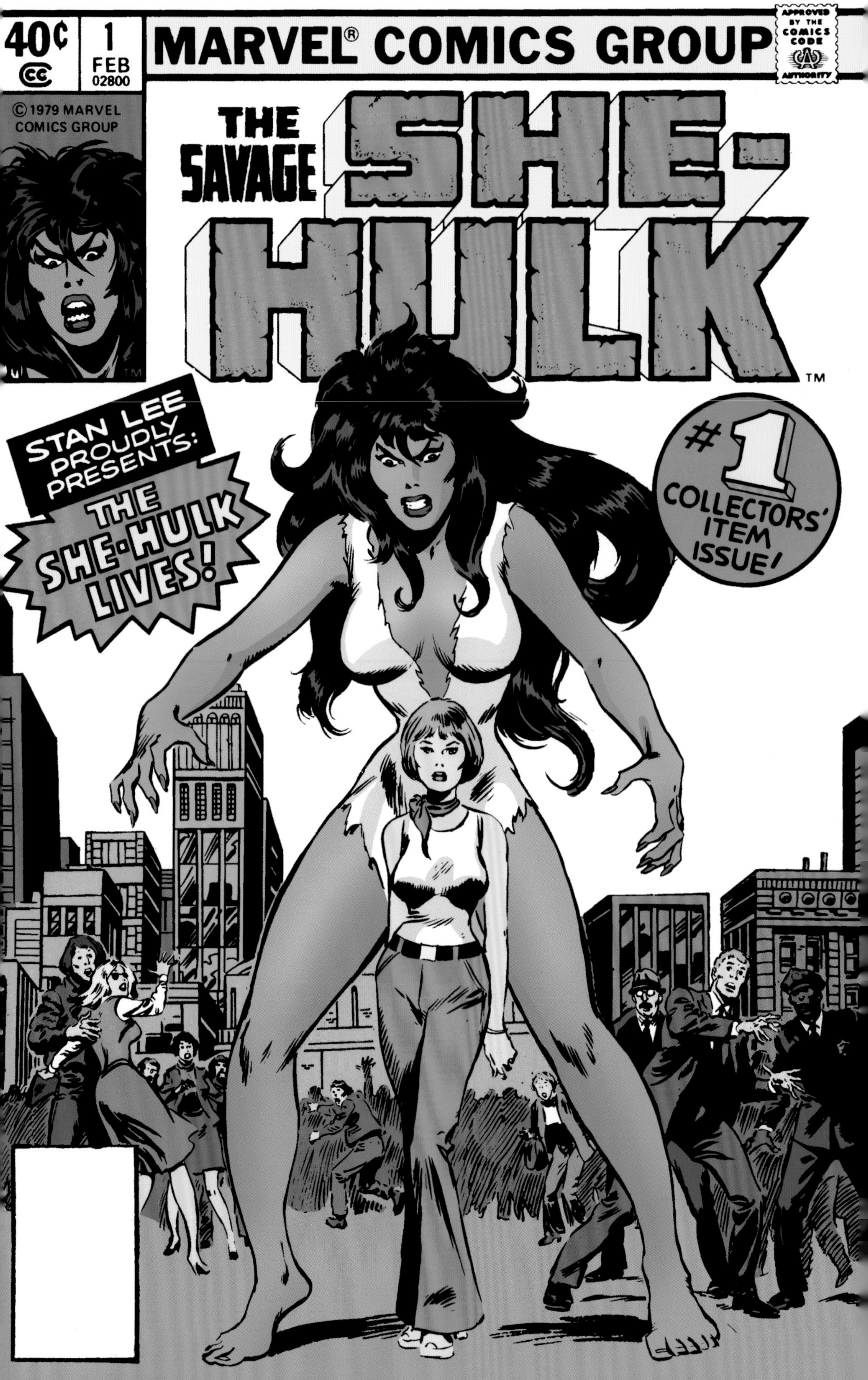

40¢
CC
1
FEB
02800
MARVEL® COMICS GROUP
APPROVED BY THE COMICS CODE AUTHORITY
© 1979 MARVEL COMICS GROUP
THE SAVAGE SHE-HULK™
STAN LEE PROUDLY PRESENTS:
THE SHE-HULK LIVES!
#1 COLLECTORS' ITEM ISSUE!

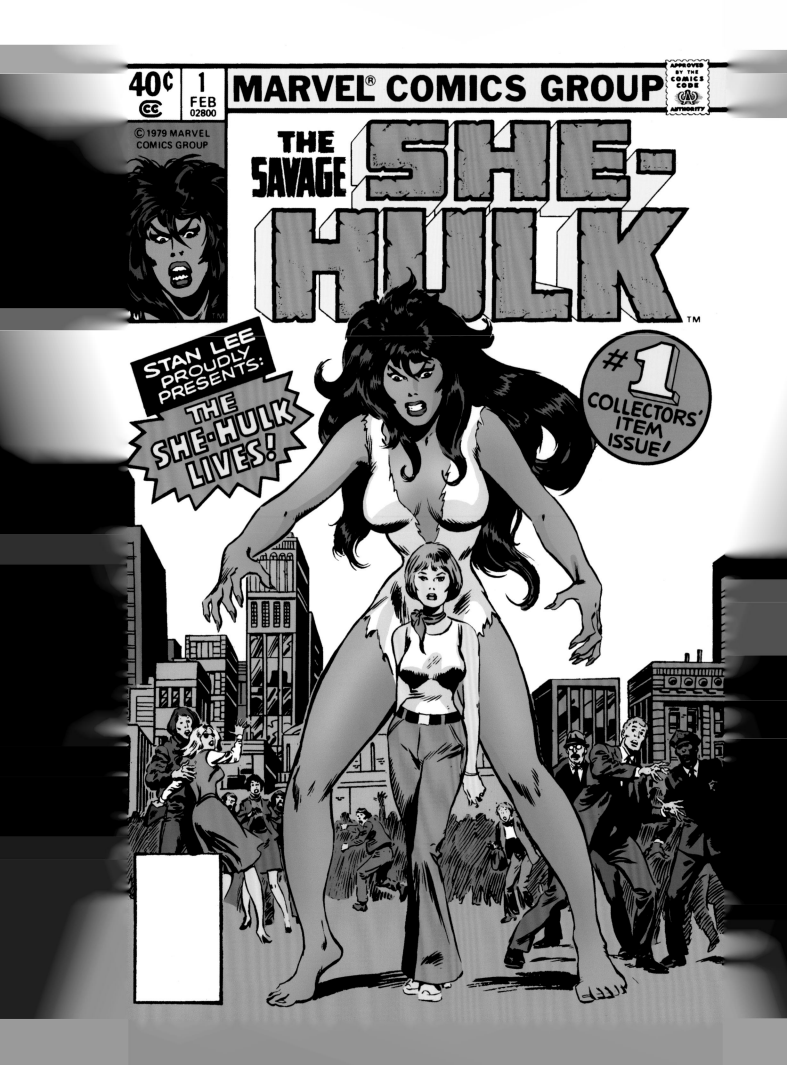

(Top) Eleven years after his first appearance as The Hulk, Lou Ferrigno came back to the role for 1988's "The Incredible Hulk Returns" (not to be confused with 1978's "The Return of The Incredible Hulk").

(Above) "The Incredible Hulk Returns" teamed Bill Bixby as Banner and Lou Ferrigno as The Hulk with Thor, played by Eric Kramer.

(Opposite) Savage in her first comic book incarnation, the She Hulk reappeared a decade later as "The Spectacular She-Hulk" in adventures that were more tongue-in-cheek.

the character. "So before the series produced one, they figured they would produce one at Marvel. They were protecting themselves." Initially there was talk of a "She-Hulk" television series as well as feature film to star statuesque actress Brigitte Nielsen, but neither materialized (though a makeup test of Nielsen was shot). It was ultimately up to the comics to revive the character in 1989. Taming her earlier savagery, artist and writer John Byrne took a more tongue-in-cheek approach for *The Sensational She-Hulk*.

NBC rebroadcast The Hulk halves of "The Incredible Hulk/Amazing Spider-Man Hour" during the 1984–85 season under the title "The Incredible Hulk."

After an absence of six years, the live-action "Incredible Hulk" team returned to the airwaves in 1988 with a new television movie titled "The Incredible Hulk Returns." While the movie was sold as a Hulk adventure, its real purpose was to serve as a pilot for another Marvel property, The Mighty Thor. The Hulk side of the story finds David Banner, now living under the name "David Bannion," working as a scientist at a genetics lab, where he has been instrumental in creating "the gamma transponder," a device that will create nearly unlimited energy as a result of accelerating the decay of gamma-radiated material, and which also has the potential of curing him. Banner's life had vastly improved during his television hiatus. He was enjoying a successful relationship with a fellow-scientist named Maggie Shaw (played by Lee Purcell) and his bestial side had been in remission for two years. While Banner still feared his inner Hulk, he was beginning to believe that a normal life might be possible. However, the unexpected appearance of The Mighty Thor (newcomer Eric Kramer)—whose threatening visage triggers a transformation—and the unwelcome reappearance in his life of Jack McGee, conspire to put an end to Banner's newfound sense of security.

If "The Incredible Hulk Returns" proved anything, it was that Bill Bixby was the perfect actor to play a comic book character since, like heroes on the

page, he appeared not to age. Bixby was fifty-four years old when the picture was filmed, yet he didn't look a day older than when he first took on the role eleven years earlier.

While "The Incredible Hulk Returns" did not succeed in spawning any more Thor projects, the same gambit was tried again the following year with "The Trial of the Incredible Hulk," a television film that featured the character of blind attorney Matt Murdock, alias Daredevil, played by Rex Smith. The title of the film is a little misleading, since the only time The Hulk actually appears in court is in a disturbing dream of David Banner's (and sharp-eyed viewers should have no trouble spotting Stan Lee as a terrified juror), but Banner—now bearded and working as a common laborer under the name "David Belson"—does end up under arrest for allegedly having assaulted a woman on a subway, a totally trumped-up charge. Only Murdock believes that he is innocent, though he is unable to persuade the hunted scientist to appear in court to clear his name. Banner's stubborn refusal is rooted in the fear that the stress of cross-examination will cause him to "hulk out." Eventually Banner is exonerated, and in his Hulk form he helps Murdock capture members of the criminal organization that framed him in the first place. But the film ends with Banner once more heading down that lonely road.

"The Trial of the Incredible Hulk" benefits from skillful direction by Bixby himself. The scene in the jail when David Banner's cell mate attempts to murder him, under orders from the big city crime boss who has framed Banner, is extremely well staged and very suspenseful. The script, by Gerald DiPego, also blends the characters of The Hulk and Daredevil together into one cohesive storyline naturally and seamlessly—something that The Hulk/Thor teaming did not quite manage to do.

The next Incredible Hulk television movie, aired on NBC in 1990, would be the last of the Bixby/Ferrigno collaborations. Titled "The Death of

(Top) A bearded David Banner "hulks out" in court in a dream sequence from "The Trial of The Incredible Hulk."

(Above) The Hulk has his day in court in "The Trial of the Incredible Hulk." Playing one of the jurors in this sequence was none other than Stan Lee!

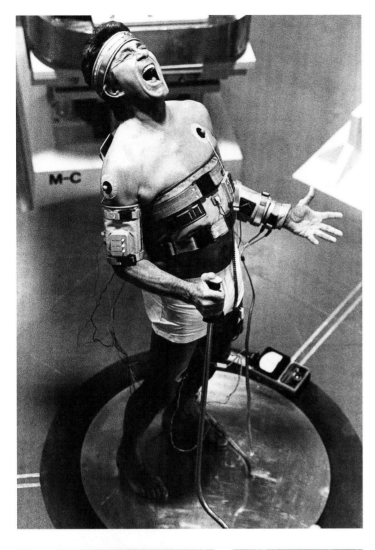

(Top) David Banner attempts another painful cure in 1990's "The Death of The Incredible Hulk."

(Above) Hulk vs. bulldozer in "The Death of The Incredible Hulk."

the Incredible Hulk," it was made by the same production team as "Trial," and once more directed by Bixby. Banner has now taken a job as a janitor at a nuclear laboratory under the name "David Bellamy." Instead of the beard he used to disguise himself in "Trial," Banner has adopted an intellectual disguise by pretending to be developmentally disabled. At night, though, he drops the *Rain Man* routine and sneaks into the lab and secretly works on the lab's main project, discovering the secret power of self-healing. Banner is eventually discovered by the project's leader, Dr. Pratt (played by Philip Sterling, who a dozen years earlier had co-starred in the television version of "Dr. Strange"), who takes him on secretly as a research partner.

But unbeknownst to either of them, agents of an enemy government (which is never specified, though "Soviet" could be inferred) are planning to steal the formula from the lab for their own government. A ruthless spymaster named Kasha (Andreas Katsula) forces a beautiful female ex-agent named Jasmin (Elizabeth Gracen) to pull the job. Unfortunately, she arrives at the lab, disguised as a female security guard, on the very night that Pratt is attempting to cure his new confidant and partner David Banner of his Hulk affliction by bombarding his brain with isotopes. The attempted theft is thwarted, as is the experiment to cure Banner. Now both fugitives, Banner and Jasmin are forced to remain together to survive. In spite of the chaos going on around them, they fall in love and plan to run off together, in essence, disappearing in order to start over again. It is a lovely thought, but one that is doomed. When Banner learns that Dr. Pratt has been kidnapped by the enemy agents, he knows that he must stay and try to rescue him, even if it means abandoning his final chance at personal happiness.

Using her skills as a spy, Jasmin helps Banner infiltrate the enemy stronghold and rescue the scientist, though in the final battle Banner transforms into The Hulk. In an attempt to prevent the leader of the terrorist organization from escaping in an airplane, The Hulk

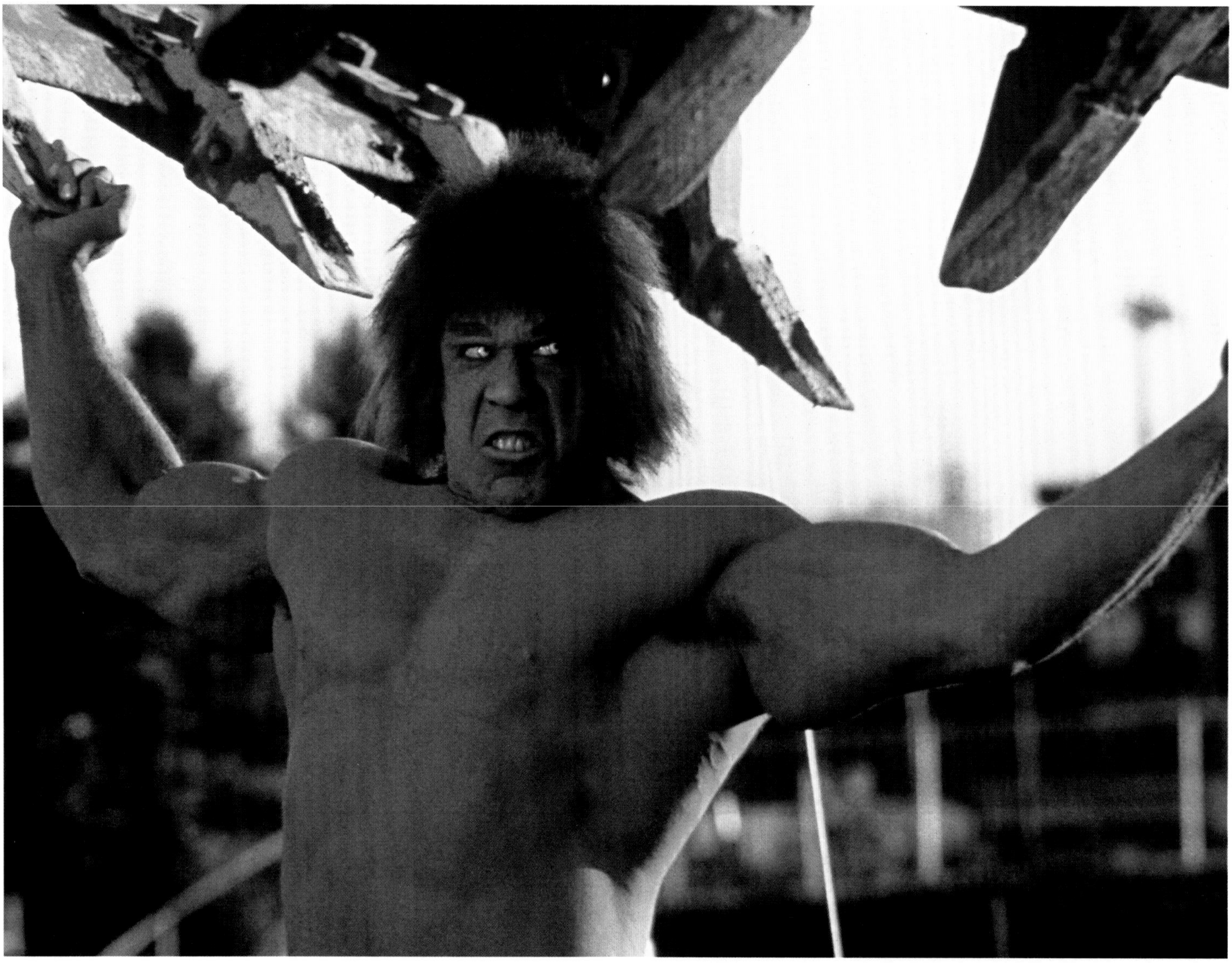

forces his way into the plane, just as it takes off. Gunfire inside the fuselage accidentally hits the fuel tank, causing the plane to explode. The enemy agents are killed instantly, but The Hulk survives, only to fall thousands of feet to the ground, slamming onto the tarmac with the force of a pile driver. Jasmin rushes to him, but it is too late. Even The Hulk's supernatural healing power cannot enable him to recover from the force of impact. For the last time, The Hulk transforms back into Banner, who utters, "I am free," and dies in Jasmin's arms. The lonely, troubled wandering of Dr. David Banner is over.

Surprisingly sexy by television standards of the time, "The Death of The Incredible Hulk" offered loyal Hulk followers the satisfaction of seeing David Banner find a few moments of happiness with his new love, however brief. It is also interesting that nearly thirty years after Banner's wishful speech about the end of "Red tyranny" in the first Hulk comic books story, Cold War sensibilities were still fueling Hulk storylines. But the chief distinction of "Death" as opposed to any of the

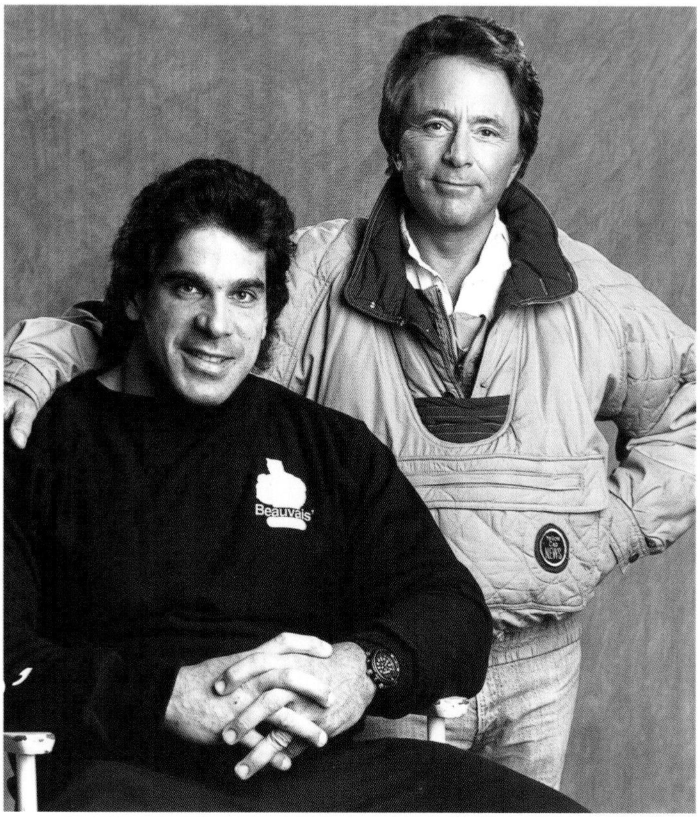
Beauvais'

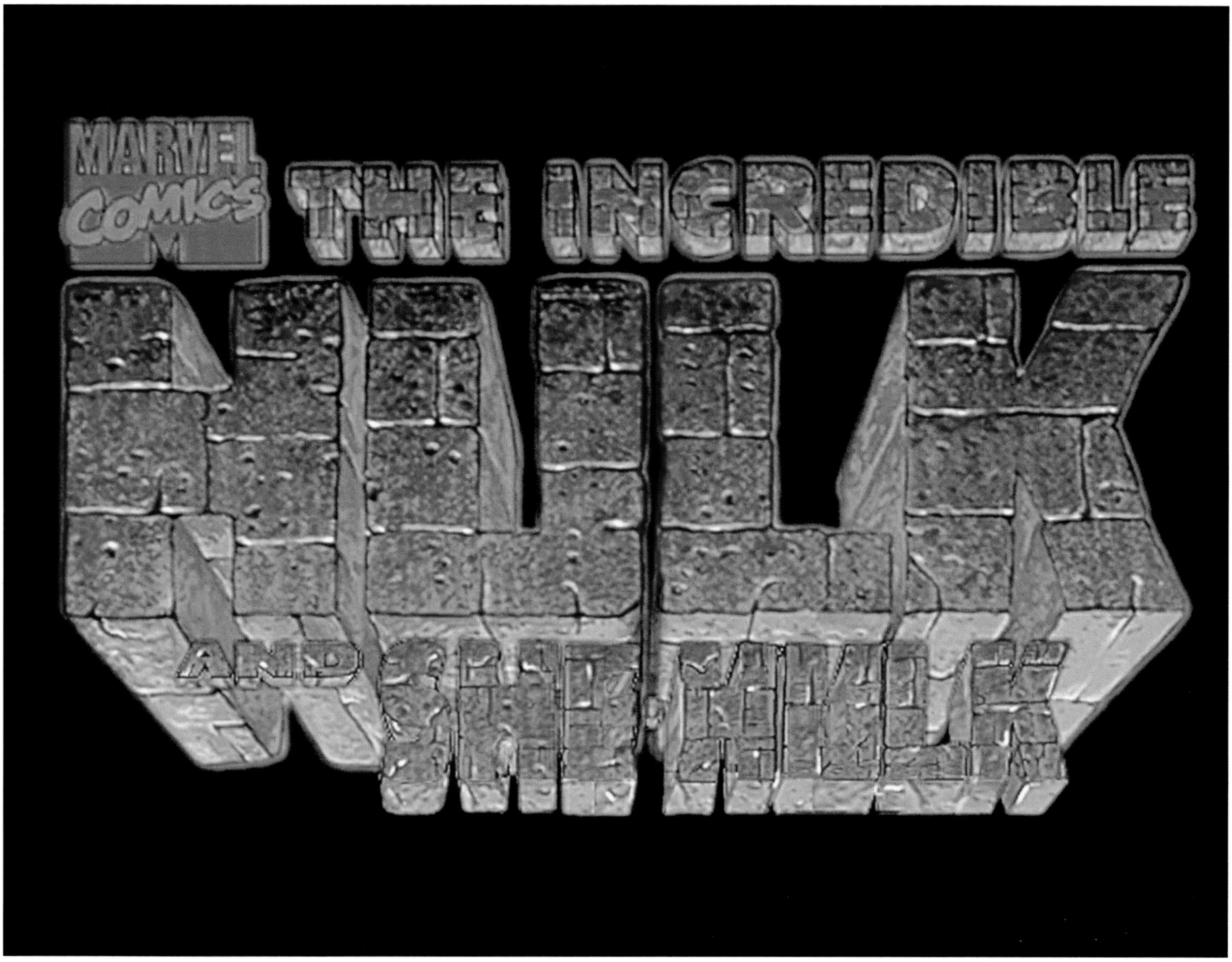
MARVEL COMICS
THE INCREDIBLE
HULK
AND SHE-HULK

"The Incredible Hulk" returned in animated form in 1996, and in 1997, co-billing was given to the She-Hulk.

(Opposite top) "The Death of The Incredible Hulk" presented the big green guy at his most frightening.

(Opposite bottom) Lou Ferrigno and Bill Bixby out of character. They were partners and friends through thirteen years of "The Incredible Hulk."

previous Hulk movies is that it offers the most completely fearsome depiction of The Hulk ever put on film. This is in part a result of modified prosthetic makeup, which minimized the rubber nose to create a more realistic look and utilized white, reflective contact lenses that make the character appear even more unearthly. But equally important is the fact that, in the course of thirteen years of Hulk duty, Lou Ferrigno had matured into a very skilled actor. His menacing grin as he mops up the floor with an army of opponents presents the terrifying image of a rampaging monster who enjoys the carnage he is creating.

Since the film is called "The Death of the Incredible Hulk," the ending is hardly a surprise, except to those who felt that The Hulk would somehow "die" leaving Banner alive. And that would seem to be the end. But amazingly, there were plans for another sequel. "We were going to come back with 'The Revenge of The Hulk,' where The Hulk has Banner's brain in him, meaning that David Banner sees himself as The Hulk,"

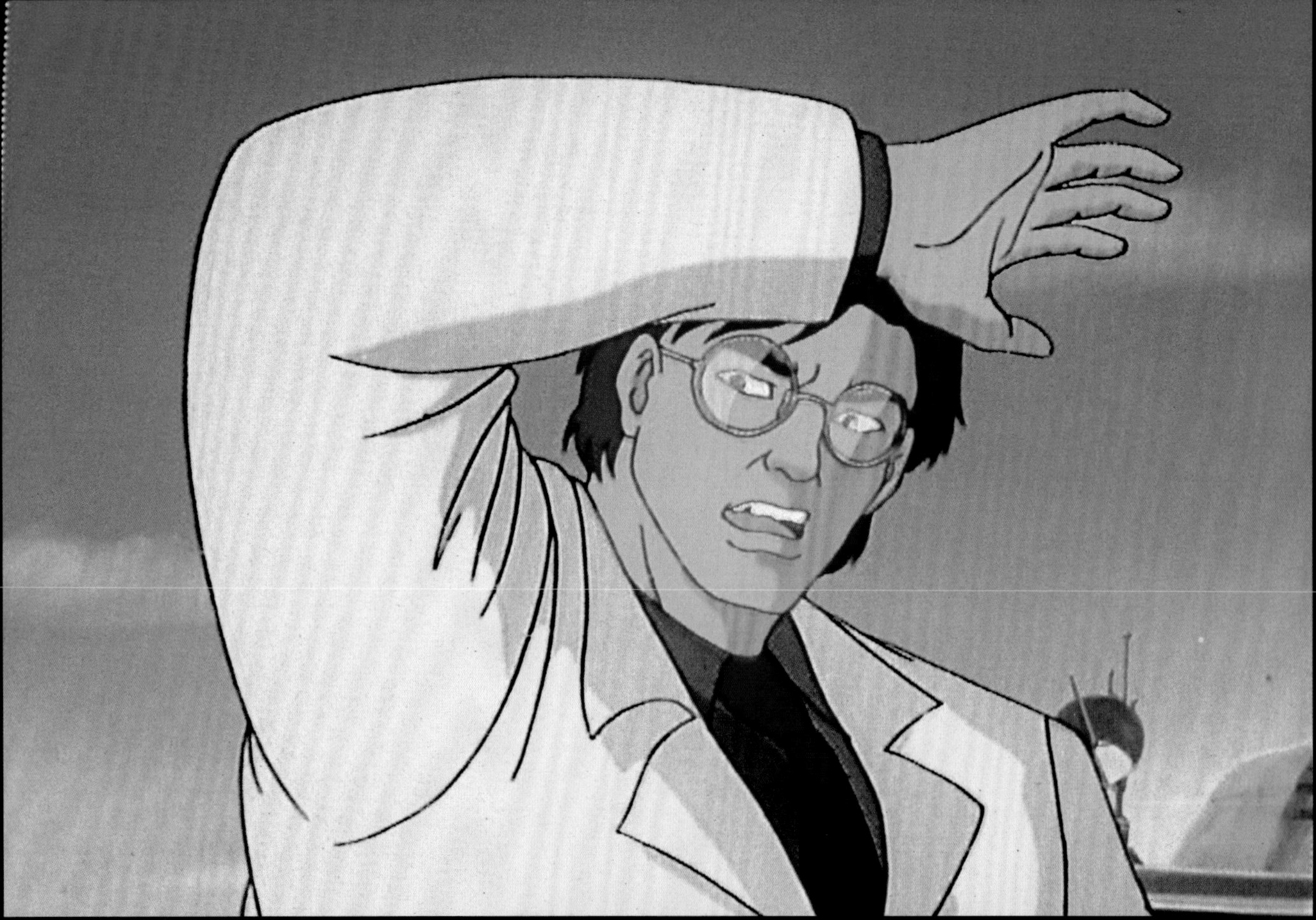

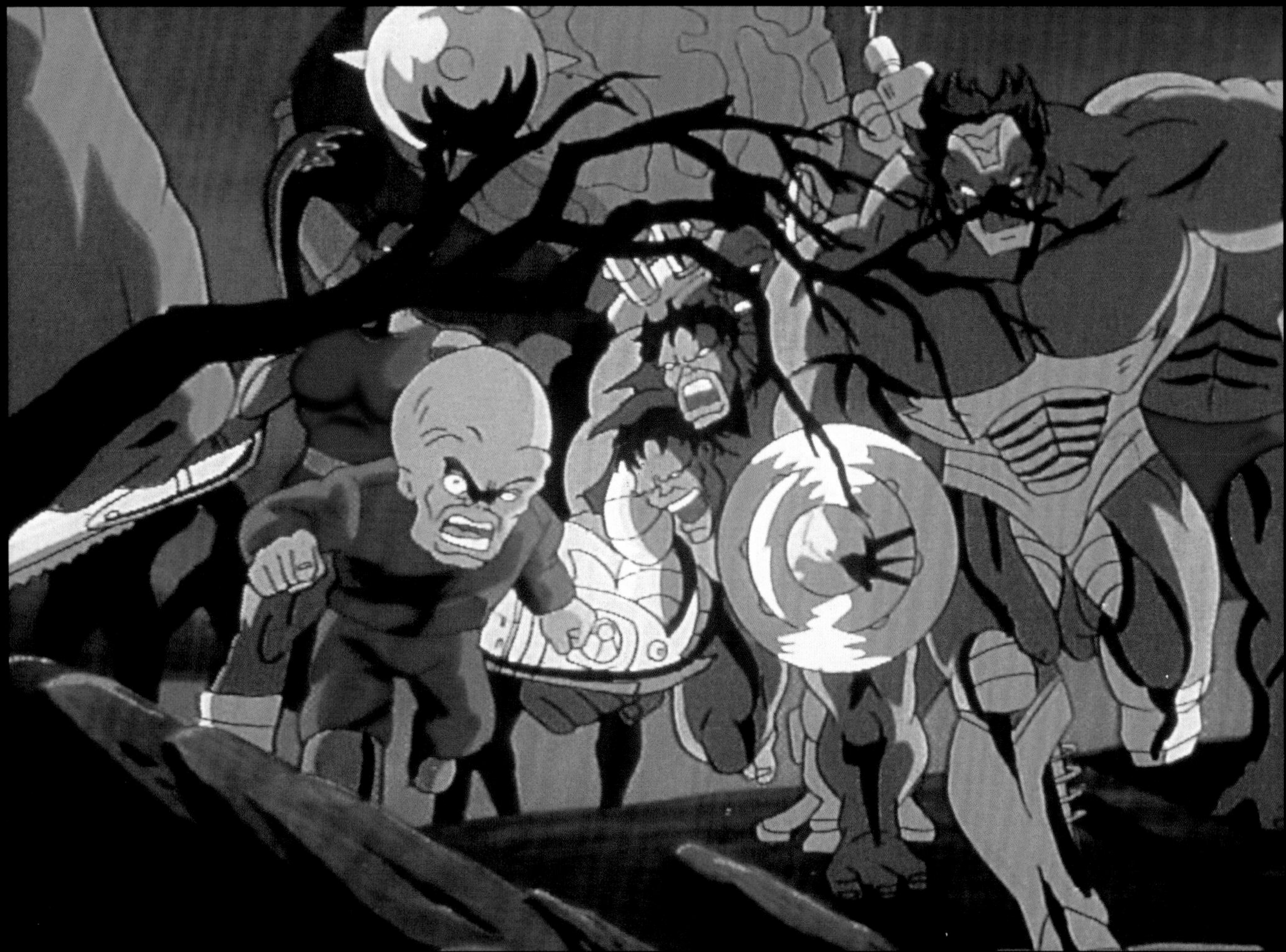

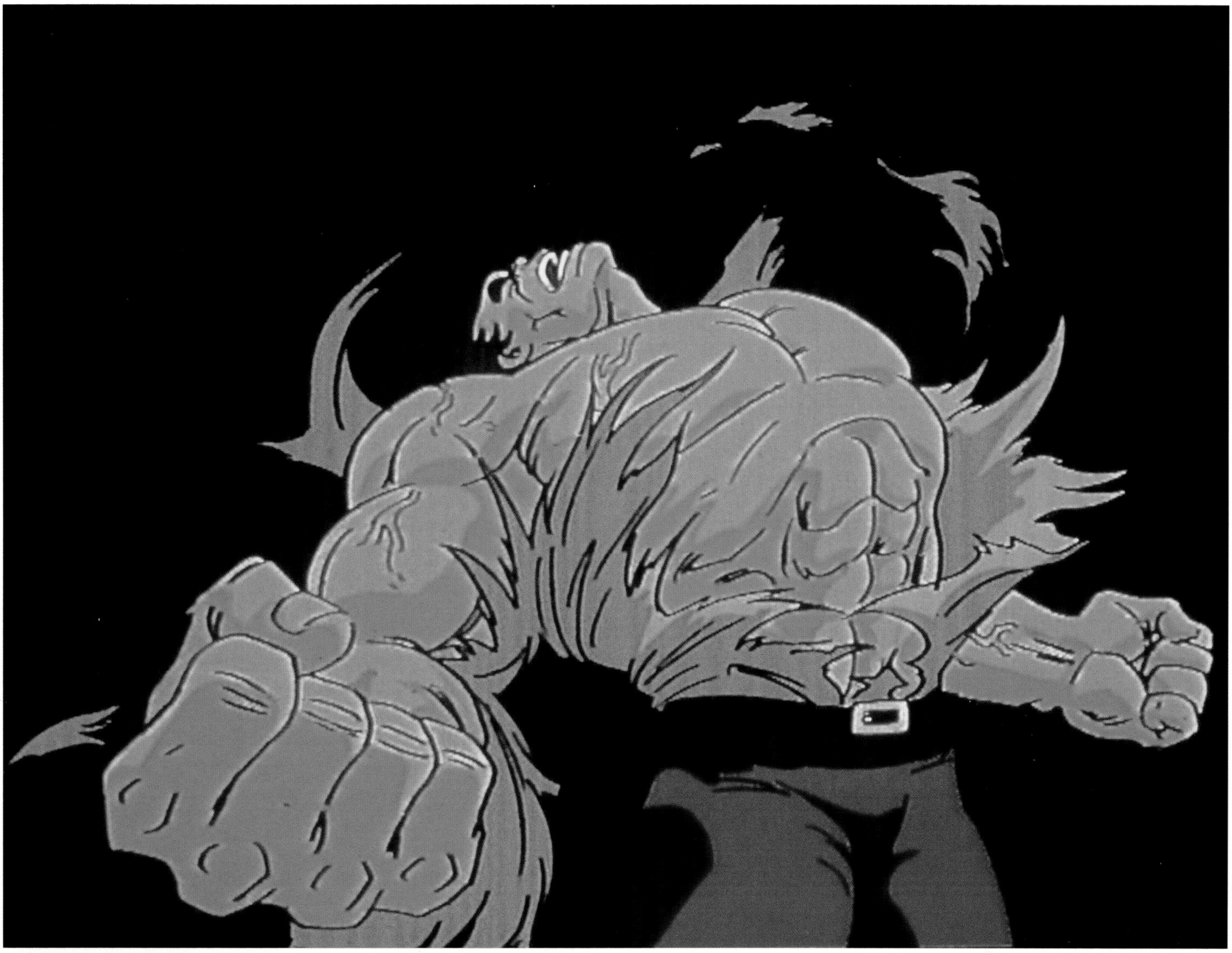

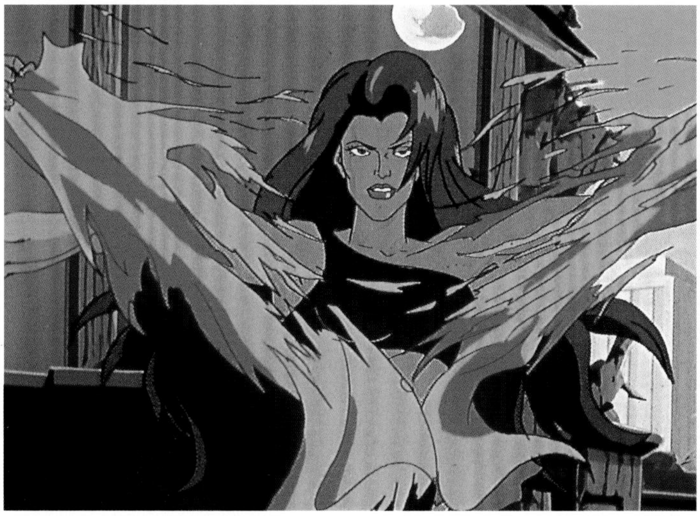

(Top) A dramatic transformation from the 1990s animated "The Incredible Hulk."

(Above) Unlike her cousin, Bruce Banner, Jen Walters could change into The She-Hulk at will (though she was equally hard on clothes).

(Opposite top) Dr. Banner (with stylish haircut) recoils from radiation in the animated "The Incredible Hulk."

(Opposite bottom) The Gargoyle was a perennial nemesis to The Hulk in the 1990s animated version.

says Ferrigno. "It was a great idea." Indeed, it was a great idea, and one that would have taken the character into an area that had been explored in The Hulk's comic book adventures. What kept the film from being made was a real life tragedy: executive producer, director, and star Bill Bixby was diagnosed with cancer. Bixby would succumb to the disease in 1993, at the age of fifty-nine.

That was not the end of Lou Ferrigno's association with the role, however. Having acted as the physical form of The Hulk for so many years, Ferrigno became the *voice* of the character for a new animated series titled "The Incredible Hulk," which debuted on the UPN Network in fall, 1996. Like "Spider-Man: The Animated Series" before it, "The Incredible Hulk" featured a full cast of characters from the comics, as well as an eclectic name-talent voice cast. Representing the side of right were Rick Jones (voiced by former "Beverly Hills, 90210" heartthrob Luke Perry), Betty Ross ("General Hospital" star Genie Francis), The She-Hulk (Lisa Zane), and Doc Samson (game show announcer Shadoe Stevens). On the side of evil were The Gargoyle, revived from The Hulk's very first adventure, who was now

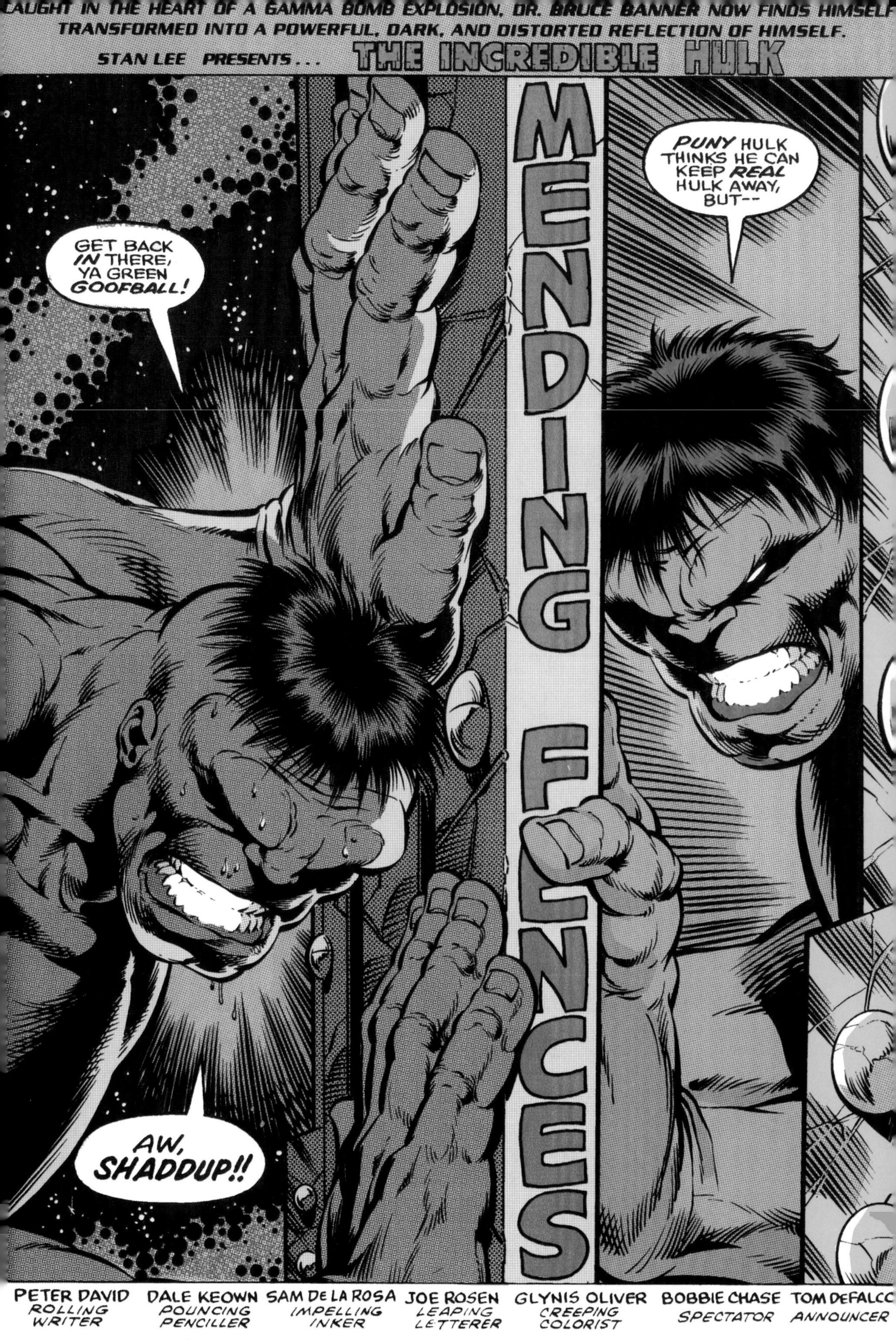
CAUGHT IN THE HEART OF A GAMMA BOMB EXPLOSION, DR. BRUCE BANNER NOW FINDS HIMSELF TRANSFORMED INTO A POWERFUL, DARK, AND DISTORTED REFLECTION OF HIMSELF.
STAN LEE PRESENTS... THE INCREDIBLE HULK
GET BACK IN THERE, YA GREEN GOOFBALL!
PUNY HULK THINKS HE CAN KEEP REAL HULK AWAY, BUT--
MENDING FENCES
AW, SHADDUP!!
PETER DAVID ROLLING WRITER
DALE KEOWN POUNCING PENCILLER
SAM DE LA ROSA IMPELLING INKER
JOE ROSEN LEAPING LETTERER
GLYNIS OLIVER CREEPING COLORIST
BOBBIE CHASE SPECTATOR
TOM DEFALCO ANNOUNCER

played for comic relief and allowed to fall madly in love with The She-Hulk (a passion that was unrequited with a vengeance), The Leader, an urbane, green villain with a hugely oversized brain (voiced by Matt Frewer, who would later appear in the live action "Generation X") and The Ogress, who was voiced by supermodel Kathy Ireland, of all people. Even The Gray Hulk showed up in a few episodes.

The graphic design of the series (which for its second season was retitled "The Incredible Hulk and She-Hulk") was several notches above the standard daytime animation fare, and a certain measure of relaxing in the standards and practices departments for children's programming in the mid-nineties (in conjunction with a newly implemented ratings system) allowed for The Hulk and She-Hulk to once more kick butt without risking the ire of watchdog groups—an element that had watered down cartoon adaptions of the character in the previous decade. The result was one of the best presentations of The Hulk ever done in animation.

Both as a character and a franchise property, The Incredible Hulk has proven indestructible. There are probably dozens of reasons as to why the primal green giant has transcended the comic book page to become the most successful media crossover character of the Marvel Universe, but when all is considered, it remains hard to dispute the assessment of Lou Ferrigno, who says: "You know, there's nothing like The Hulk."

Keeping up with recent developments in the comics, the 1990s version of "The Incredible Hulk" featured both the Green and Gray Hulks. (From *Incredible Hulk #373*)

X-

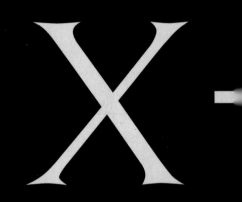

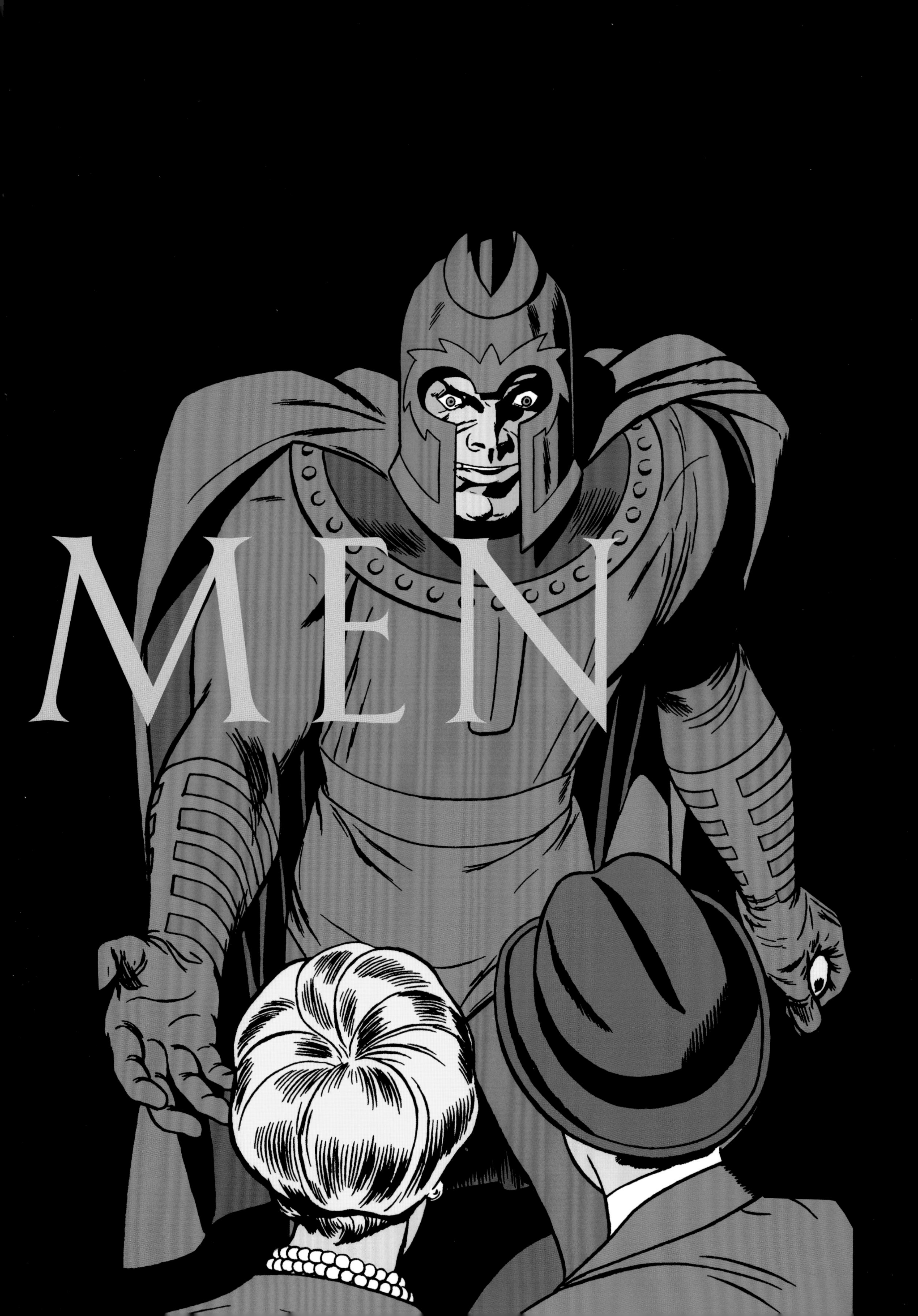
MEN

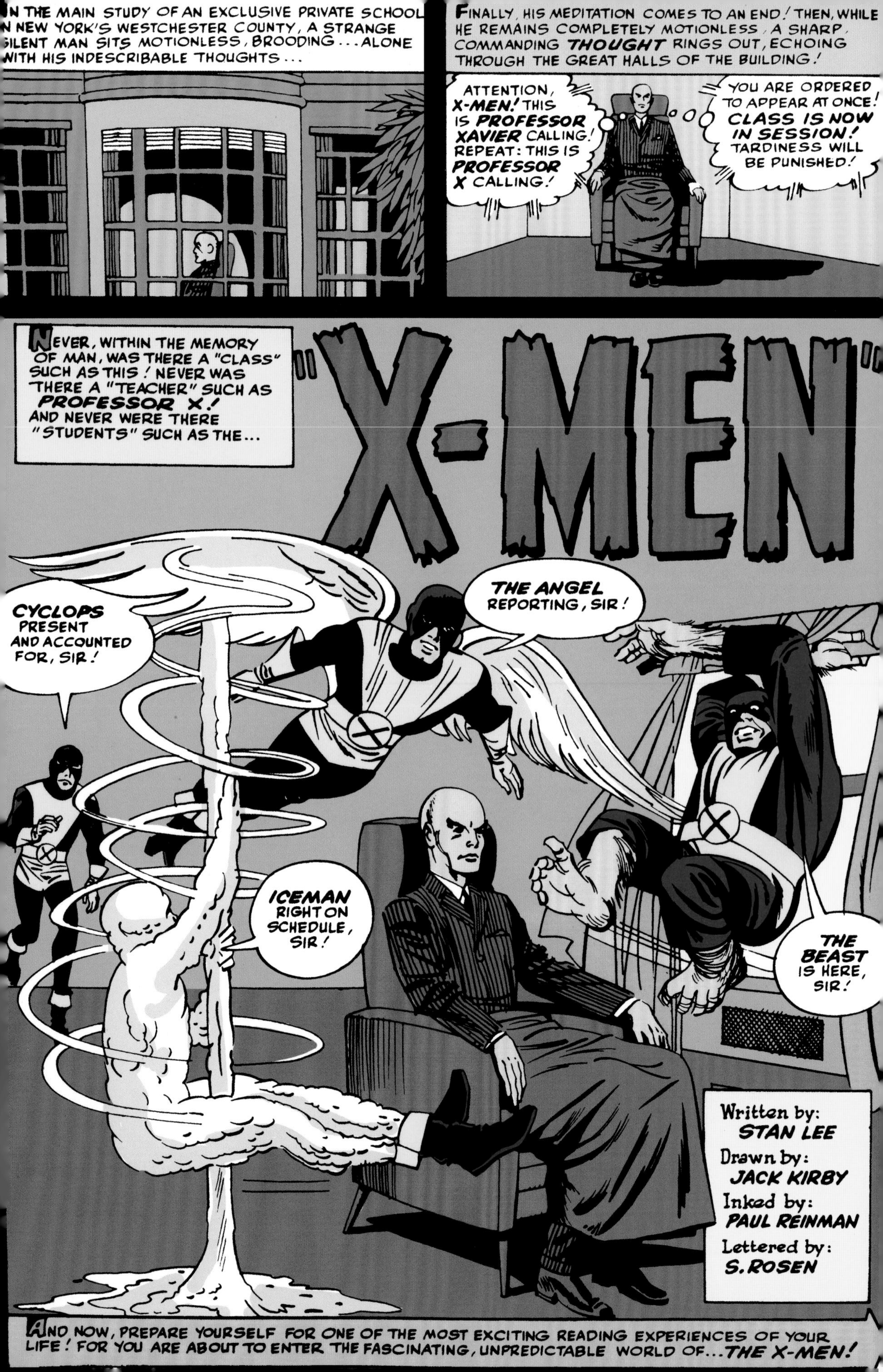
IN THE MAIN STUDY OF AN EXCLUSIVE PRIVATE SCHOOL IN NEW YORK'S WESTCHESTER COUNTY, A STRANGE SILENT MAN SITS MOTIONLESS, BROODING... ALONE WITH HIS INDESCRIBABLE THOUGHTS...
FINALLY, HIS MEDITATION COMES TO AN END! THEN, WHILE HE REMAINS COMPLETELY MOTIONLESS, A SHARP, COMMANDING THOUGHT RINGS OUT, ECHOING THROUGH THE GREAT HALLS OF THE BUILDING!
ATTENTION, X-MEN! THIS IS PROFESSOR XAVIER CALLING! REPEAT: THIS IS PROFESSOR X CALLING!
YOU ARE ORDERED TO APPEAR AT ONCE! CLASS IS NOW IN SESSION! TARDINESS WILL BE PUNISHED!
NEVER, WITHIN THE MEMORY OF MAN, WAS THERE A "CLASS" SUCH AS THIS! NEVER WAS THERE A "TEACHER" SUCH AS PROFESSOR X! AND NEVER WERE THERE "STUDENTS" SUCH AS THE...
"X-MEN"
CYCLOPS PRESENT AND ACCOUNTED FOR, SIR!
THE ANGEL REPORTING, SIR!
ICEMAN RIGHT ON SCHEDULE, SIR!
THE BEAST IS HERE, SIR!
Written by: STAN LEE
Drawn by: JACK KIRBY
Inked by: PAUL REINMAN
Lettered by: S. ROSEN
AND NOW, PREPARE YOURSELF FOR ONE OF THE MOST EXCITING READING EXPERIENCES OF YOUR LIFE! FOR YOU ARE ABOUT TO ENTER THE FASCINATING, UNPREDICTABLE WORLD OF... THE X-MEN!

X-MEN

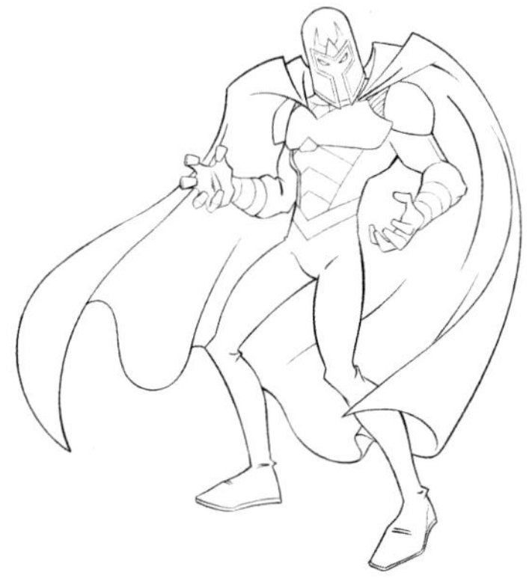

MUTANT MARAUDERS

One might have to go to the works of Charles Dickens to find a world of relationships as complex and a cast of characters as varied and curious as those that make up the ongoing saga of The X-Men. This fictional tapestry, which began with issue number one of *The X-Men,* September 1963, written by Stan Lee, pencilled by Jack Kirby and inked by Paul Reinman, introduced a potent new wrinkle into the Marvel Universe, the concept of *mutants.* Instead of being zapped by some form of radiation, which up to that point had been the explanation of choice for the acquisition of super powers, the majority of those who would become X-Men were born with their special abilities. It would eventually be revealed that a mutant gene located inside the brain was the factor that removed mutants from common humanity. As time went on, this concept would increasingly lend itself to allegory and become a metaphor for class and race agitation in modern society. But in 1963, a less complicated time for both America and the Marvel Universe, the focus was instead on excitement and action.

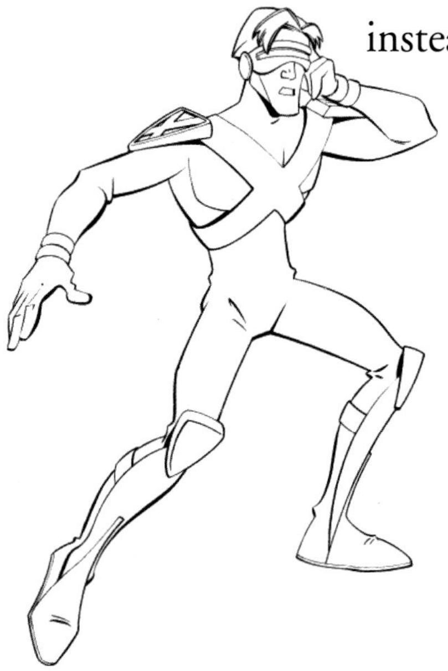

The Uncanny X-Men are called into action for the very first time, in the pages of *X-Men* #1 (September 1963).

Had Lee gotten his way all those years ago the comic book would have been titled *The Mutants.* But Marvel publisher Martin Goodman thought that was too complex a concept for the group that he envisioned as his target readers, small children (a demographic that would soon shift upwards). The eventual moniker, X-Men, was derived from the idea that each character had something "extra," or "X-tra," over regular mortals.

The new team of mutant crimefighters would be under the guidance and training of Charles Xavier, who also answers to "Professor X," a bald (from childhood, apparently), wheelchair-bound scientist who is a mutant himself, having advanced telepathic powers. The son of parents who worked on the first A-bomb tests (thus coming by his powers in the time-honored Marvel way), Xavier was a Korean War veteran who later became a

wanderer after his heart was broken by a woman named
Moira McTaggart, who years later would re-enter his life.
While wandering through Cairo, Egypt, Xavier ran afoul
of the deadly Amahl Farouk, the first evil mutant he had
ever encountered. After having barely defeated Farouk in
an "astral" battle, Xavier vowed to dedicate his life to
protecting mankind from evil mutants, as well as seeking
peaceful coexistence and tolerance between mutants and
humans. The fact that his legs were later crushed during
a fight in Tibet with an alien called Lucifer did nothing
to hinder his zeal and determination.

Returning to the states, Xavier set up a school for
"gifted youngsters" in Westchester County, New York,
all of whom he locates and identifies with the help of
an advanced computer called Cerebro. Xavier's goal is
to find young mutants and train them before they have
a chance to be lured to the dark side of the mutant
universe controlled by a supervillain called Magneto,
who holds powerful forces of magnetism. Because the
stakes are so high—X-Men are trained to battle the evil
mutants that are striving to take over the world—Xavier
is a stern taskmaster, putting his students through
rigorous survival training courses in the institute's
"Danger Room." At the same time, he is quick with
praise when his pupils do well.

Among the first group of students at the Xavier
school was Scott Summers, a.k.a. Cyclops, whose eyes
are like solar power storage units. When full they emit
powerful energy rays in a single beam (hence "Cyclops"),
which forces Summers to wear a ruby quartz lens over
his eyes at all times. Like so many others in the Marvel
Universe (notably Victor Von Doom, Rick Jones, Peter
Parker, and Ororo "Storm" Munroe), Scott was orphaned
at an early age, though unlike most, his parents were
abducted and taken as slaves by aliens of the Shi'ar
Empire. Years later his father, Christopher Summers,
would resurface as the outer space pirate Corsair.

Hank McCoy, another early student, is a
combination of brain and brawn wrapped up into one
ape-like package. His strength, acrobatic agility, and

"THEN, ROUNDING A CORNER..."
SO! IT IS YOU WHO HAVE TYRANNIZED THIS CITY! WHO ARE YOU--AND WHERE ARE YOU FROM?
MY TRUE PURPOSE YOU SHALL NEVER KNOW--BUT, ON THIS PLANET I CALL MYSELF ...LUCIFER!
AND NOW--THAT NAME SHALL BE THE FINAL THING YOU HEAR! PREPARE TO DIE--FOR DARING TO OPPOSE THAT WHICH NO MORTAL CAN COMPREHEND!
THAT GREAT SLAB--- RELEASED FROM ABOVE AT THE TOUCH OF A SWITCH! I--CAN'T DODGE--IN TIME!
"PINNED BENEATH THE INEXORABLE WEIGHT OF THE MASSIVE SLAB, I HEARD MY TORMENTOR'S VOICE THRU A MIST WHICH SEEMED TO BE ENVELOPING MY BRAIN..."
SO--YOU STILL SURVIVE! LIVE, THEN--PERHAPS IT IS FATED THAT YOU AND I MEET AGAIN ONE DAY!
OHHHH...!
"BEFORE MY EYES, A MOMENT BEFORE I LOST CONSCIOUSNESS, LUCIFER DISAPPEARED--INTO THE VERY WALL ITSELF..."
BUT, REMEMBER THIS--IT IS EVER THE STRONG WHO ARE MEANT TO RULE! AND WE ARE THE STRONG!
WHO DOES HE MEAN BY "WE"? IS HE ACTUALLY THE HERALD OF A FAR GREATER MENACE--FROM THE STARS?
THEN, AS THE PARALYZED MENTAL MUTANT CONCLUDES HIS STARTLING NARRATION...
THEN--THAT IS HOW YOU LOST THE USE OF YOUR LEGS YEARS AGO!
YES, JEAN! AND, IT IS YET ANOTHER REASON WHY I FOUNDED THE X-MEN!
FOR, I KNEW THAT ONE DAY MANKIND WOULD HAVE TO MEET THE RENEWED THREAT OF LUCIFER!
BUT, EVEN XAVIER DOES NOT FULLY REALIZE JUST HOW URGENT MANKIND'S PLIGHT TRULY IS! FOR, AT THIS VERY SECOND, BENEATH THE SOUTH-WESTERN DESERT...
IT IS DONE! I HAVE CONQUERED THE ONE EARTHLY MIND WHICH MIGHT HAVE DISCOVERED MY INTENTIONS IN TIME TO THWART THEM!
AND NOW, THE TIME DRAWS NEAR, WHEN MY RACE SHALL FULFILL ITS MISSION---ITS MAGNIFICENT DESTINY!

A battle with the alien Lucifer cost Professor X the use of his legs, as recounted in *X-Men* #20 (May 1965).

simian hands and feet cause him to be dubbed The Beast. In later years, Hank would become even more beast-like when an irreversible experiment left him dark blue and furry.

At sixteen, Bobby Drake, who takes the name Iceman, was the youngest of the original group. His mutant power enables him to lower the temperature within and outside his body, allowing him to become a being of solid ice, one who can create shields and missiles of ice and generate an ice slide over which he can propel himself.

The *rara avis* of the Uncanny X-Men, Warren Worthington III has bird-like attributes including wings and the power of flight, hence his team name The Angel. He is self-assured to the point of being cocky, and as a result occasionally risks making dangerous mistakes.

Into this boys club came beautiful, redheaded Jean Grey, who has amazing telekinetic powers. She adopts the name Marvel Girl. Jean and Scott would soon become a couple and weather the kind of long-term traumatic relationship that only superheroes can endure.

At first the group had matching costumes consisting of shirts, tights, and hoods of blue-black, over which were worn yellow vests and shorts, and a belt with a red "X" in a circle of the buckle, though in the case of Iceman, only his boots could be discerned through the frost. But even Lee seemed to have a problem with the convention of uniforms. In issue #1, he has an army official complain to the group: "Look, we're having enough trouble with *one* guy in a cornball costume! [Magneto.] Now, who or *what* are The X-Men?" In later years, as new X-Men were introduced, the focus of the stories would shift more toward the strong individual personalities of the group's members, which made the convention of identical costumes redundant.

The original X-Men found themselves pitted against such opponents as the Sub-Mariner, who in *X-Men* issue #6 (July 1964) toyed with the proposition of joining Magneto's Brotherhood of Evil Mutants, as well as an entire platoon of new villains, including the

Cyclops. Storm. Banshee. Nightcrawler. Wolverine. Colossus. Children of the atom, students of Charles Xavier, MUTANTS——feared and hated by the world they have sworn to protect. These are the STRANGEST heroes of all!

Stan Lee PRESENTS: THE UNCANNY X-MEN!™

CHRIS CLAREMONT / AUTHOR | JOHN BYRNE / PENCILER | TERRY AUSTIN / INKER | BRUCE PATTERSON / LETTERER | J. SHOOTER / EDITOR

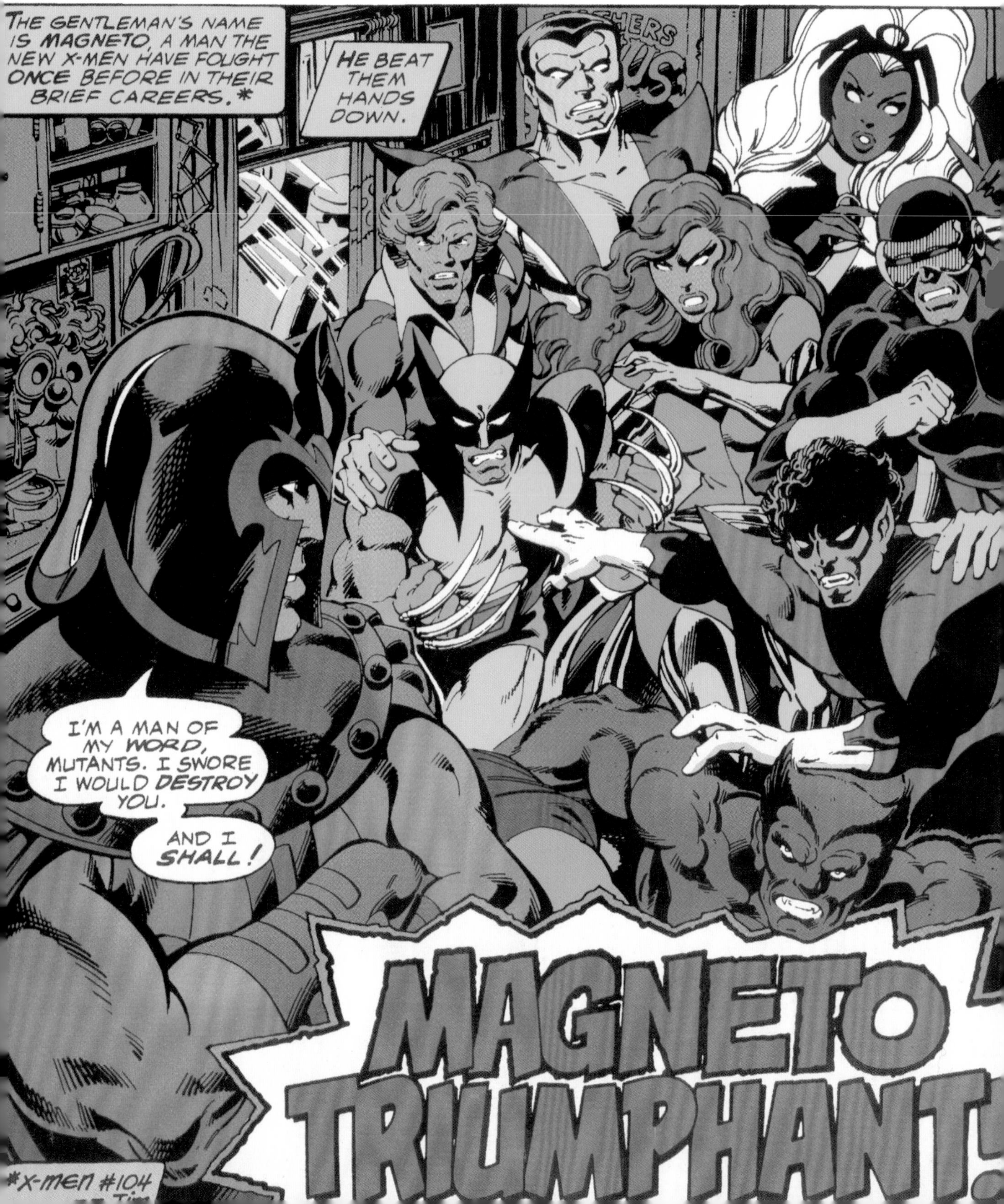

THE GENTLEMAN'S NAME IS MAGNETO, A MAN THE NEW X-MEN HAVE FOUGHT ONCE BEFORE IN THEIR BRIEF CAREERS.*
HE BEAT THEM HANDS DOWN.
I'M A MAN OF MY WORD, MUTANTS. I SWORE I WOULD DESTROY YOU.
AND I SHALL!
MAGNETO TRIUMPHANT!
*X-MEN #104

Scarlet Witch and Quicksilver, who were brother and sister; Mastermind; Pyro; The Juggernaut (who was actually Xavier's stepbrother Cain Marko); the Blob, an inhumanly obese, indestructible bad guy; Toad, a grotesque hunchback; and the Sentinels, a pack of marauding super-robots.

Towering over them all, however, was Magneto, whose lethally destructive magnetic powers were matched only by his ability to organize weaker villains and lead them into battle against Xavier's X-Men. Magneto would become one of Marvel's signature villains, and as was the case with so many of Marvel's captains of evil, over the course of time he would be given a complex history. Years after the character's creation it would be revealed that Magneto—whose real name is Erik Magnus Lensherr—spent part of his childhood in the concentration camp at Auschwitz. It was there that his perceptions of human monstrosity were formed, echoes of which he sees in modern society's intolerance toward mutants. The Auschwitz conceit, developed by writer Chris Claremont, is one of the grimmest nexus points between the Marvel Universe and real world ever devised.

In the mid-1960s Roy Thomas took over scripting duties from Lee, while a host of artists including Alex Toth, Jay Gavin, Werner Roth, and inkers Chic Stone, Vince Colletta, and Dick Ayers followed Kirby's lead. But despite the best efforts of all concerned, the series began to languish. A renaissance of sorts was staged when a rising star named Neal Adams took over the artistic duties in the late 1960s. Born in 1941 in New York, Adams had begun his career while still in his teens. By the time he arrived at Marvel, he had nearly a decade of experience in comic books and newspaper strips. Unfortunately, even Adams's best efforts were not enough to put X-Men back on solid footing. The last story of the original series was published in the March 1970 issue. Subsequent issues featured reprints of earlier stories. In 1975, however, a new group of mutants would arrive, and in a comeback the likes of which had never

Of all the X-Men's opponents, none ranked as high in power or popularity as the evil Magneto.

before been seen in the world of comics, *X-Men* would soar to incredible new heights.

The impetus for the return of X-Men came indirectly from Marvel's then-president Al Landau, who suggested creating a comic book that would feature superheroes from the various countries in which Marvel exported their magazines. Landau viewed the idea as a way of increasing sales in those countries. But Roy Thomas, who was then Marvel's editor in chief, immediately recognized it as a way of reviving X-Men. "I had always wanted to bring them back," Thomas says. "My idea was to have one or two of the established characters, Cyclops or Marvel Girl, let's say, and have them going around in this ship with a cloud around it, so people never actually saw it, that would hover over different places. The countries would have been Canada, South Africa perhaps, England, maybe Scandinavia, Germany, that kind of thing." Shortly thereafter, Thomas vacated the editor's chair, and in his absence the idea underwent alterations. "The idea of doing particular countries where we might sell comic books kind of got lost," Thomas says. "For instance, one of the new X-Men was from Kenya, and we weren't selling a lot of comics in Kenya."

Under writer Len Wein and artist Dave Cockrum, the new X-Men idea began to take shape. While new characters were being developed, it was decided that Cyclops would remain the key player from the old X-Men. Sean Cassidy, alias Banshee, an Irish ex-detective with a penchant for blarney as well as a mind-shattering sonic scream, who was introduced into the X-Men saga in 1967, was brought back, as was a modern-day Samurai named Shiro Yoshida who adopted the fighting name Sunfire because he can produce great heat. Like Xavier, Sunfire—who had first appeared in issue #64 in 1970—acquired his powers through the detonation of an atomic bomb, in this instance, the one the United States dropped on Hiroshima in 1945. Yoshida's mother was affected by the blast prior to his birth, and for this and other reasons he holds a deep mistrust toward anything American.

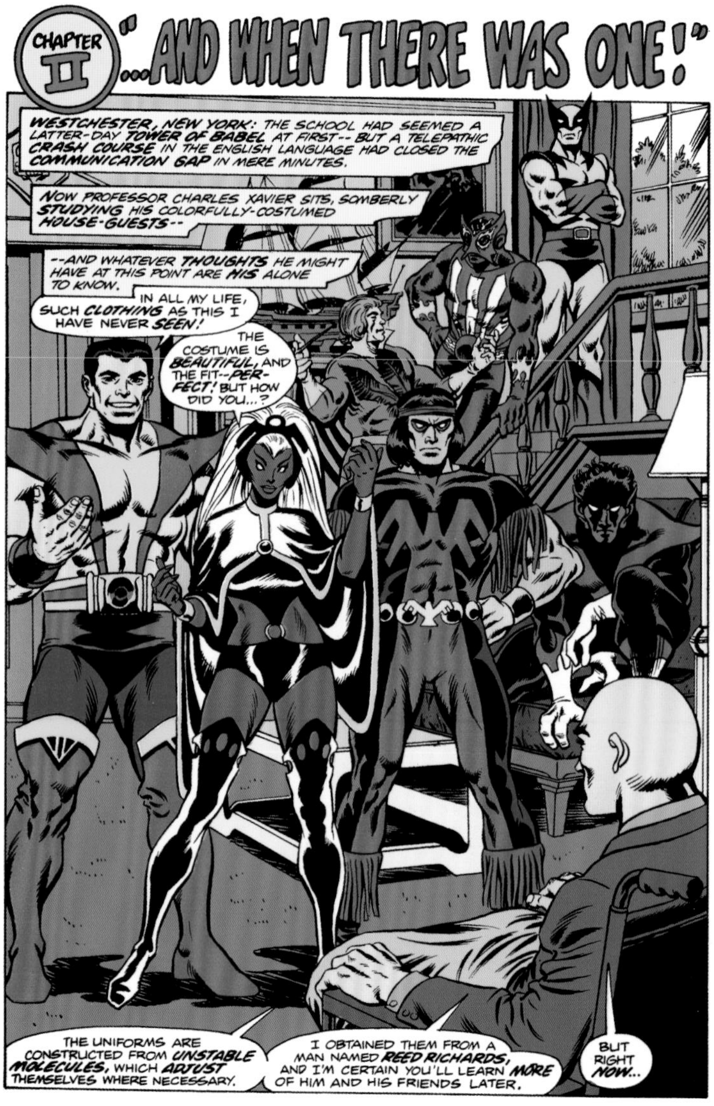
CHAPTER II
"...AND WHEN THERE WAS ONE!"
WESTCHESTER, NEW YORK: THE SCHOOL HAD SEEMED A LATTER-DAY TOWER OF BABEL AT FIRST-- BUT A TELEPATHIC CRASH COURSE IN THE ENGLISH LANGUAGE HAD CLOSED THE COMMUNICATION GAP IN MERE MINUTES.
NOW PROFESSOR CHARLES XAVIER SITS, SOMBERLY STUDYING HIS COLORFULLY-COSTUMED HOUSE-GUESTS--
--AND WHATEVER THOUGHTS HE MIGHT HAVE AT THIS POINT ARE HIS ALONE TO KNOW.
IN ALL MY LIFE, SUCH CLOTHING AS THIS I HAVE NEVER SEEN!
THE COSTUME IS BEAUTIFUL, AND THE FIT--PER-FECT! BUT HOW DID YOU...?
THE UNIFORMS ARE CONSTRUCTED FROM UNSTABLE MOLECULES, WHICH ADJUST THEMSELVES WHERE NECESSARY.
I OBTAINED THEM FROM A MAN NAMED REED RICHARDS, AND I'M CERTAIN YOU'LL LEARN MORE OF HIM AND HIS FRIENDS LATER.
BUT RIGHT NOW...

The "All-New" X-Men, introduced in 1975 by writer Len Wein and artist Dave Cockrum. Foreground, left to right: Colossus, Storm, Thunderbird, and Nightcrawler. On stairs, left to right: Banshee, Sunfire, and Wolverine. (From *Giant Sized X-Men #1*).

THE APACHE WERE MEANT TO BE HUNTERS, WARRIORS-- NOT SAD-EYED SIMPERING SQUAWS.
THEY WERE MEANT TO RUN FREE THRU THE CRISP PLAINS GRASSES, THE WIND BLOWING WILDLY THRU THEIR HAIR.
ONCE NOTHING COULD STAND BEFORE THE APACHE.
THE BISON THAT COVERED THESE PLAINS FELL LIKE RAIN BEFORE APACHE SKILL, APACHE BRAVERY--
--BUT NEVER DID ANY BISON FALL LIKE--THIS!
THERE, HORNED ONE--DO YOU SEE?
THERE IS STILL A MAN AMONG THE APACHE!
THOOM!

X-Men come and X-Men go, but the ill-fated John Proudstar, alias Thunderbird, was one of the few actual casualties in the group.

(Following spread) Ororo Munroe, a.k.a. Princess Ororo of Kenya, a.k.a. Storm, would have one of the most complex and fully developed backgrounds of any member of The X-Men.

Banshee and the anti-heroic Sunfire were placed into the mix with a new group of teenagers for a specific reason. "A subtext of the story [which would appear in *Giant Sized X-Men* #1 in 1975] was that it would be sort of an entrance exam for the new characters," says Dave Cockrum. "We brought in Banshee and Sunfire because we figured some people were going to have to fail the test. Then it turned out that we all liked Banshee and didn't want him to fail."

The new recruits chosen to join them were far more exotic and colorful than the original team. There was Kurt Wagner, a.k.a. Nightcrawler, an eerie, midnight blue, Satyr-like creature with a devil's tale and a talent for "transporting"—disappearing and reappearing to the accompanying stench of brimstone. When first spotted by Xavier in the village of Winzeldorf, Germany, the one-time carnival aerialist is being pursued through the night by angry, torch-wielding villagers (a scene right out of a Universal horror movie the 1990s).

In Kenya, Africa, Xavier recruits Princess Ororo, known to her people as the Goddess of Weather, which she has the ability to control, but who would take the name Storm. It would later be revealed that Storm and Xavier had actually met years before in Cairo, where the Harlem-born daughter of an American photographer and Kenyan princess was living by her wits on the streets, having been orphaned. At that time the six-year-old girl greeted her future mentor by lifting his wallet! At the age of twelve, though, an "inner need" caused Ororo to leave Cairo and walk for an entire year until she reached the Serengeti Plain, which she instinctively recognized as home. According to Cockrum, Storm was created by merging two earlier character concepts: The Black Cat, a woman who could change into a panther, and a male weather master called Typhoon.

Rounding out the new recruits were Peter Rasputin, a brawny farmhand from Lake Bailkal, Siberia, who has the ability to transform his body into living metal to become Colossus, and John Proudstar, an

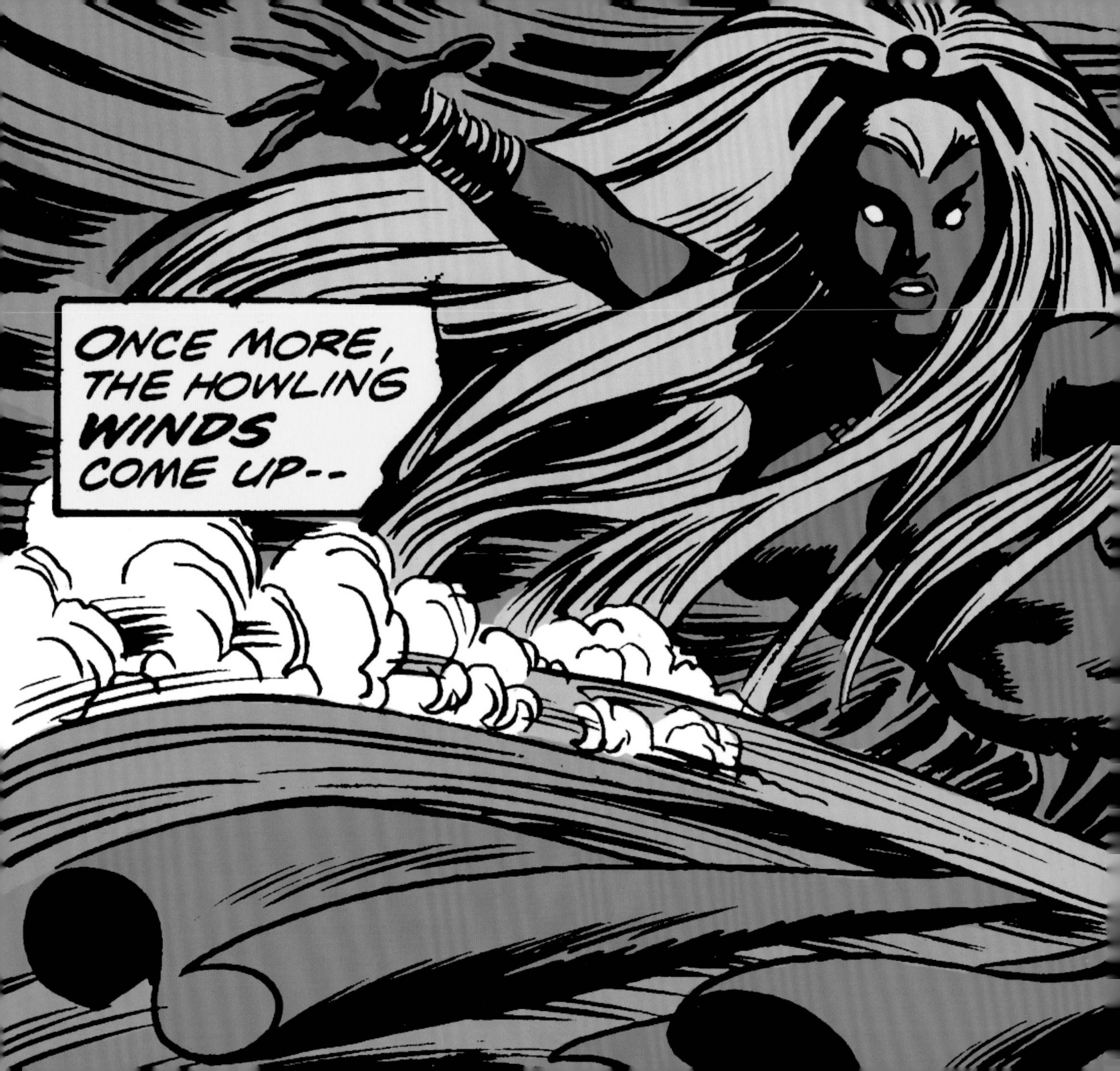
ONCE MORE, THE HOWLING WINDS COME UP--

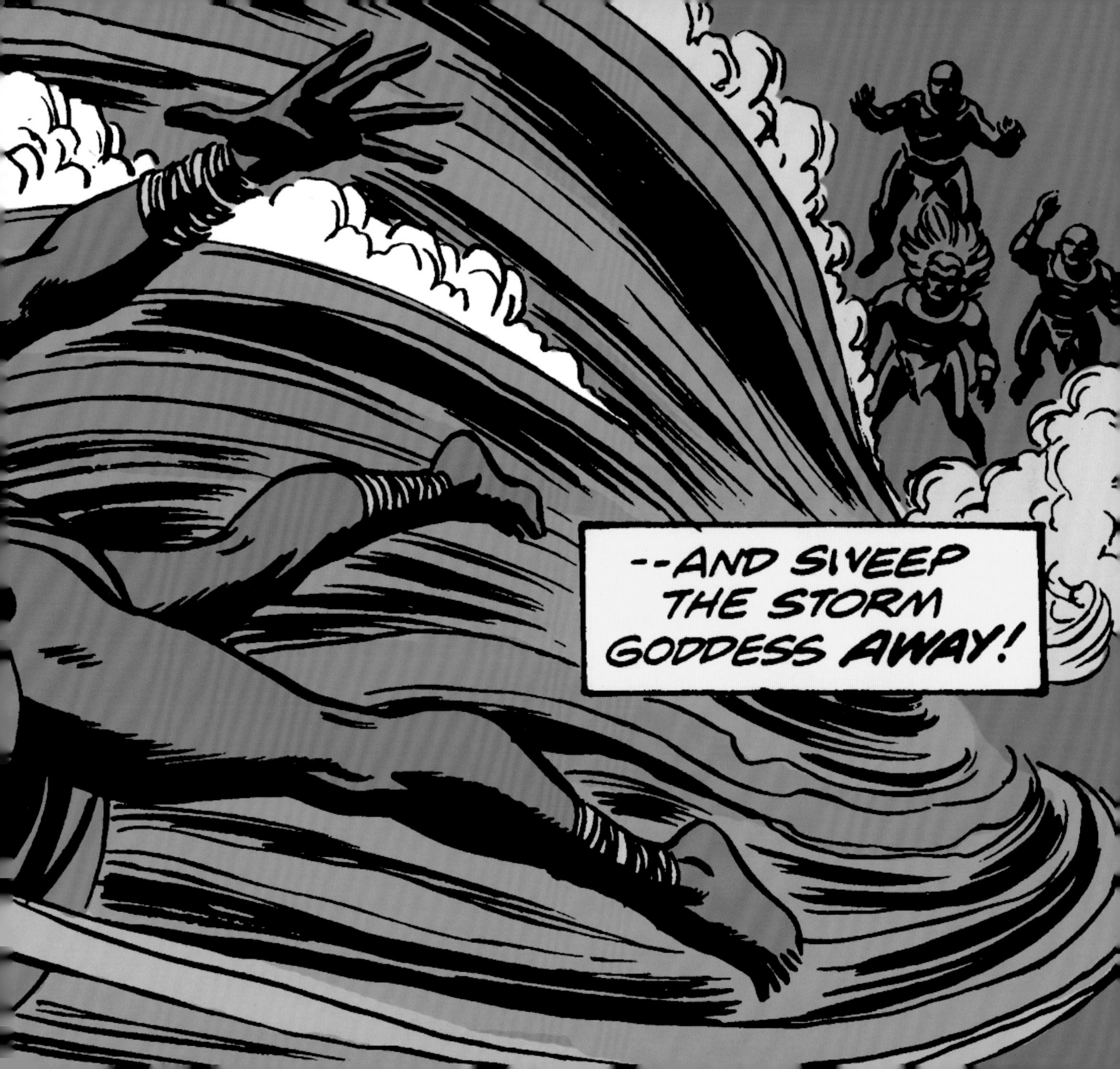
--AND SWEEP THE STORM GODDESS AWAY!

embittered Native American who possesses enough super strength and speed to outrun and tackle a buffalo. Nicknamed Thunderbird, Proudstar is as mistrustful as Sunfire and is disrespectful to boot, and Xavier has to trick him into leaving his Camp Verde, Arizona, home by casting aspersions on his bravery. "Thunderbird was supposed to fail the test, too," Cockrum notes, "but then we liked him too and kept him around." Thunderbird was kept around for two more issues, at which point he would defiantly go to his death as a way of proving to Xavier that he was a real man.

There was to be one more member of the team, a character that would grow to be one of the most popular in the entire Marvel canon: the mysterious, unruly, often disturbing figure called Wolverine. Known only by the name Logan, Wolverine is short (5'5" in full costume), but what he lacks in height he makes up for in attitude. He was discovered as a child living like an animal in the Canadian woods and was taken in by the government, for whom he became "Weapon X." His mutant powers include exceptionally acute physical senses and the ability to heal wounds almost instantly. This latter talent enabled Logan to endure the grisly "Weapon X" operation, in which powerful, retractable claws made of a strong alloy called adamantium were grafted onto his skeleton. Out of necessity, he has trained himself to withstand incredible amounts of pain. Moody and sullen, Wolverine is definitely in the anti-hero camp, but readers love him.

The new X-Men first meet in Professor Xavier's lab, each wearing a special costume created by The Fantastic Four's Reed Richards that "are constructed from unstable molecules, which adjust themselves where necessary." Their first mission is to find and recover the original X-Men, all of whom—except for Cyclops, who directs the expedition—have disappeared on the island of Krakoa (the Uncanny group now includes Scott Summers's brother Alex, a.k.a. Havok, and Lorna Dane, who as Polaris has super-magnetic powers). Soon they are on their way to the island, where Cerebro has

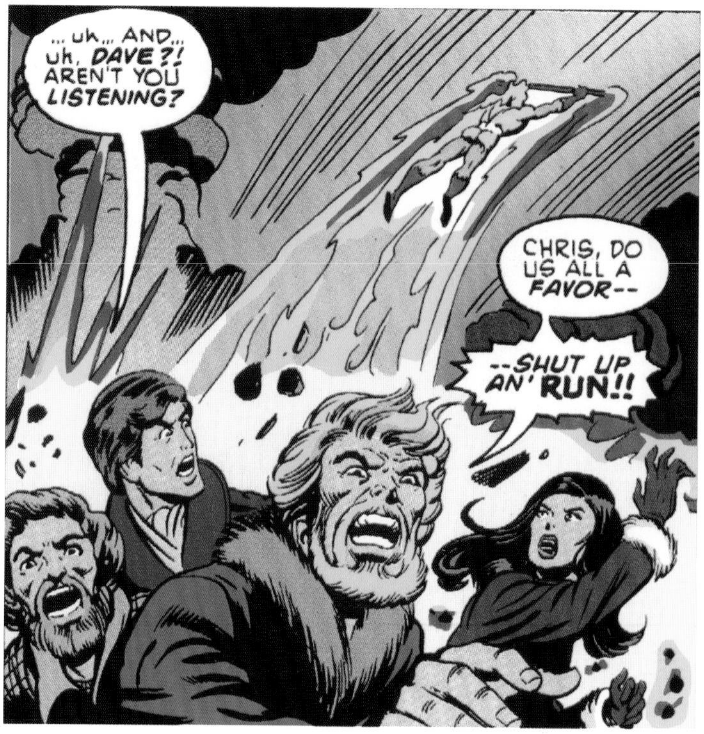
... uh... AND... uh, DAVE?! AREN'T YOU LISTENING?
CHRIS, DO US ALL A FAVOR--
--SHUT UP AN' RUN!!

Writer Chris Claremont and artist Dave Cockrum flee in terror from the menacing Firestorm in a joint gag appearance in *X-Men* #105 (June 1977).

CYKE, WE'RE RUNNIN' OUTA TIME-- WE GOTTA GO!
HOW FAR D'YOU THINK WE'D GET IN FIVE MINUTES, WOLVERINE-- BECAUSE THAT'S ALL THE TIME WE'VE GOT!
OUR ONLY CHANCE-- THE WORLD'S ONLY CHANCE IS TO TRY AND SHUT THE SYSTEM DOWN--
CYCLOPS, WHAT ARE YOU DOING!?!
WHA--? PROFESSOR, THE DOOMSMITH...
IS TOTALLY OUT OF COMMISSION! I'VE MENTALLY SCANNED THE SYSTEM-- YOUR BATTLE WITH THE ANI-MEN DESTROYED THE COMMAND RELAYS AND THE BACK-UPS...
BUT ENOUGH OF THAT--
--YOU MUST GET OUTSIDE THE MOUNTAIN, AND QUICKLY --YOU'VE AN X-MAN IN MORTAL DANGER!
YOU HEARD THE MAN, PEOPLE--
--MOVE IT!
AND THE X-MEN MOVE, AS ONLY X-MEN CAN...
...BUT EVENTS OUTSIDE ARE MOVING AS WELL, TOO FAR, TOO FAST.
YOU MADMAN--! YOU'LL KILL US BOTH!!
JOHN PROUDSTAR, GET OFF THE AIRPLANE, BEFORE IT'S TOO LATE!
BUTT OUT, BALDY --I'M THRU TAKIN' ORDERS--!
I'VE BEEN A LONER ALL MY LIFE, XAVIER --AN OUTCAST-- DUMPED ON BY EVERYBODY I MET--
--BUT I'M A MAN, XAVIER, A WARRIOR OF THE APACHE--
--AN' TODAY I'M GONNA PROVE IT!!
RAKT!
FOR GOD'S SAKE, LADDIE-- GET OFF THE PLANE!!

The sacrifice of Thunderbird from *X-Men* #95 (October 1975) demonstrated that the new X-Men were playing not just with danger, but with emotional reality.

detected an immensely powerful, unknown mutant. The new team barely acts like a team, hurling derogatory nicknames at each other, such as "Jap" and "Geronimo," but once faced with a common enemy, they manage to pull together and operate as a unit. The common enemy turns out to be the island itself, which because of atomic testing (what else?) mutated into a living entity, "The island that walks like a man!" Using their combined powers, the group manages to hurl the living landmass into outer space and saves the Uncanny team, but in the last panel they acknowledge that the world is now faced with a new challenge: "*What are we going to do with thirteen X-Men*?"

That problem was largely resolved in *All-New X-Men* issue #94, which was drawn by Dave Cockrum (pencils) and Bob McLeod (inks), and written by Chris Claremont, to whom Wein had passed the series. Born in 1950, Claremont was studying for a career as an actor when he began to write for Marvel in the early 1970s. In 1974 he was persuaded to put the greasepaint aside and officially join the company as an assistant editor and writer. Claremont's tenure as writer for *The X-Men* would be one of the longest associations between a writer and an individual title in Marvel history, and under his guidance the revitalized magazine would soar to the top by presenting, in Claremont's words, "a group of characters that [readers] embraced, rooted for, and wanted to see what happened next in their lives."

Issue #94 saw not only the perennially angry Sunfire bailing from the organization, but the original X-Men leaving as well. As Jean Grey explains to a shocked Xavier: "We were children when you took us in, Professor, scared and uncertain about who and what we were. You taught us, helped us realize our full potential. You helped us grow up . . . and that's just it, we've grown up. We're not children anymore, Professor. We have to live our own lives now." Only Scott Summers agrees to stay with the all-new team, even if it means losing Jean, in large part because he realizes that he cannot hide his dangerous mutancy as easily as the others. Cyclops

AND WHEN THE LATTICE DIES, THE NEUTRON GALAXY WILL BE FREE.
IN HER MIND'S-EYE, SHE WITNESSES THE POSSIBLE SHAPE OF THINGS TO COME.
NOTHING WILL BE SPARED AS THE POWER OF THIS NEAR-INFINITE MASS REACHES OUT ACROSS THE UNIVERSE...
...PULLING STARS AND PLANETS FROM THEIR ORBITS WITH MONSTROUS EASE--
--DESTROYING THEM ALL IN THE PROCESS.
FOR IS THIS NOT POWER ABSOLUTE? IS THIS NOT "THE END OF ALL THAT IS"?
SO MANY WORLDS, SO MANY LIVES, SNUFFED OUT IN THE TWINKLING OF AN EYE--WORLDS, SOLAR SYSTEMS, CLUSTERS, GALAXIES, MEGA-GALAXIES--
--ALL PLUNGE HELPLESSLY DOWN THE INSATIABLE GRAVITY WELL OF THE N-GALAXY, THEIR MASS ADDING TO ITS GRAVITY, GRAVITY ATTRACTING MORE MASS-- UNTIL REALITY ITSELF BEGINS TO TEAR APART.
SOMETHING HAS TO GIVE. SOMETHING DOES--IN AN EXPLOSION THAT SCATTERS STELLAR MASS OUT ACROSS A NEW, VIRGIN UNIVERSE.
WHERE THERE WAS DESTRUCTION, NOW THERE IS CREATION. AND WHERE THERE WAS DARKNESS, NOW THERE IS LIGHT. AND SOMEDAY... ONCE AGAIN... LIFE!
NO!
POWER FLARES FROM PHOENIX TO THE LATTICE, AND WHERE HER BEAMS TOUCH, THE SILVERY ENERGY STRANDS GLOW A FRACTION BRIGHTER.
SHE DOES HER BEST...

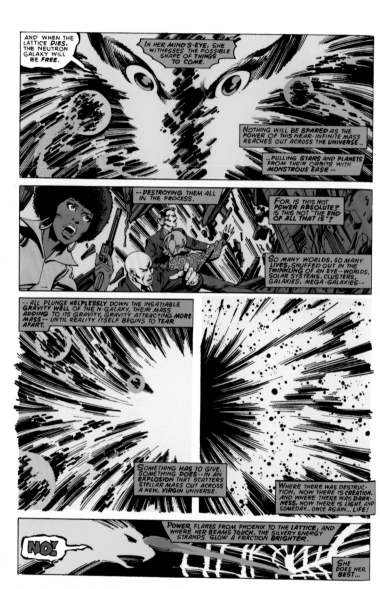

Jean Grey "dies" and is reborn as Phoenix in *X-Men* #108 (December 1976)

becomes the new team's leader and teacher, which is no easy task, particularly when dealing with hotheads like Thunderbird. When in the next issue Thunderbird sacrificed himself on the altar of testosterone, Cyclops is distraught, blaming himself for having pushed the young mutant too hard.

Eventually, Jean Grey would return to the magazine and in time she would undergo almost as much psyche-hammering as Bruce Banner, first "dying" and being reborn as Phoenix upon exposure to a solar storm (through which she was piloting the team to safety), and later crossing the line to the side of evil as Dark Phoenix, a fate from which she escaped by committing suicide! (*The Dark Phoenix* saga, which ran in issues #132 through 137 in 1980, would become yet another modern classic.) Still, Jean Grey managed to escape the Gwen Stacy Syndrome. Years later it would turn out that she had not been dead after all, but trapped in suspended animation. Jean and Scott would finally marry in 1994.

Xavier's former lover, Dr. Moira McTaggart, who had established a research laboratory for mutant studies in Scotland, would also become a member of the School for Gifted Youngsters, initially posing as its housekeeper.

After fifteen issues of clean, precise, and supremely energetic artwork, Dave Cockrum passed the pencil to John Byrne in issue #109. Born in England in 1950, but reared in Canada, Byrne was another example of a dedicated comic book fan who rose through the ranks of professionalism. Byrne's dynamic artwork wrung every drop of drama out of *The X-Men* and, coupled with Claremont's increasingly time-shattering storylines, would help to propel it to the top spot in the Marvel Universe in terms of reader popularity.

While the main track of X-Men (which now included thirteen-year-old Kitty Pryde) once more bore the designation "Uncanny," Claremont and McLeod had spun off a new title called *The New Mutants* in 1982. "We have an advantage over a book like *Spider-Man* because we can change the mix of characters, evolve and

(Opposite) An exquisite Virgil Finlay-esque rendering of a troubled Xavier by artists Dave Cockrum and Sam Grainger. (From *X-Men* #96)

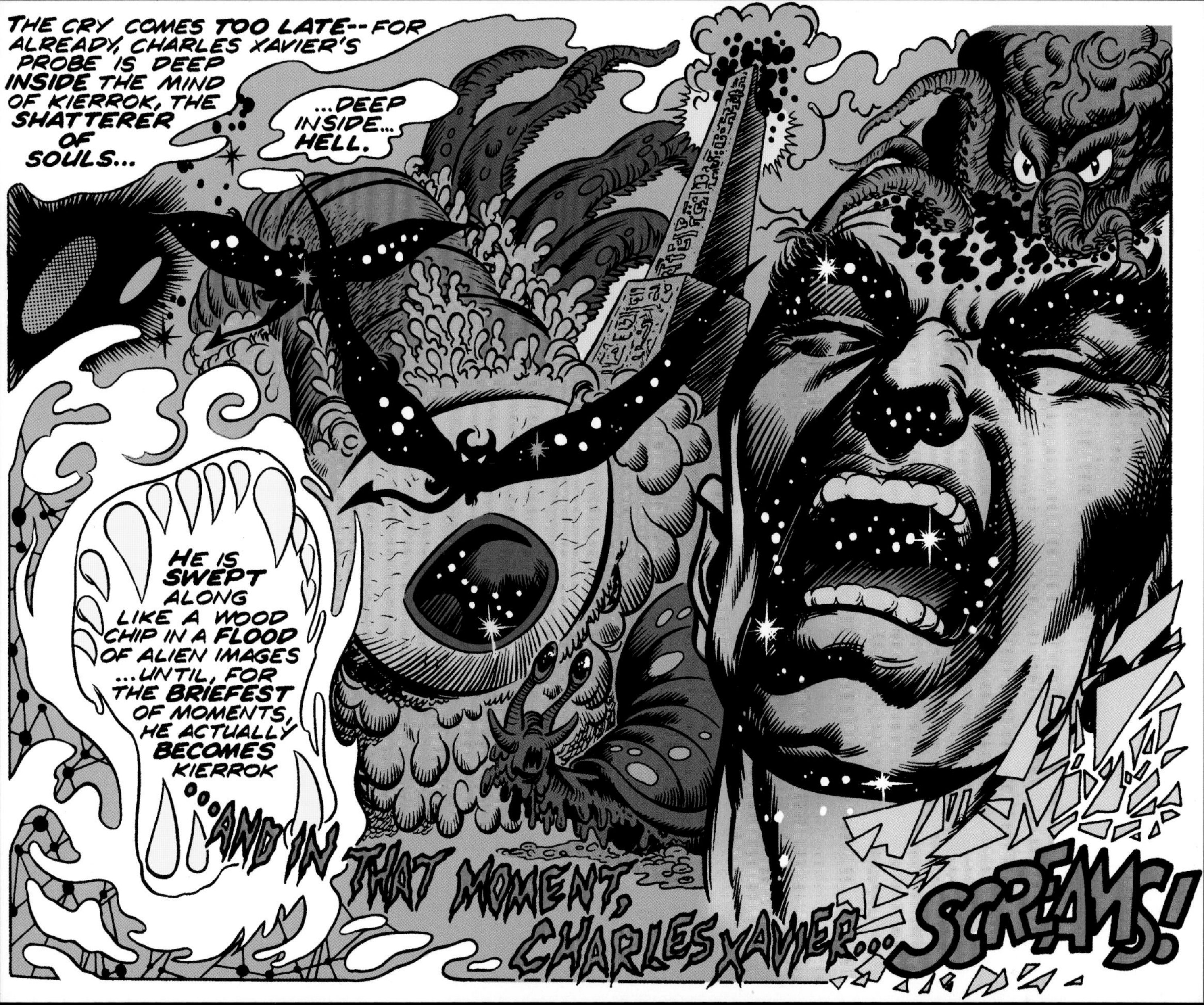
THE CRY COMES TOO LATE-- FOR ALREADY, CHARLES XAVIER'S PROBE IS DEEP INSIDE THE MIND OF KIERROK, THE SHATTERER OF SOULS...
...DEEP INSIDE... HELL.
HE IS SWEPT ALONG LIKE A WOOD CHIP IN A FLOOD OF ALIEN IMAGES ...UNTIL, FOR THE BRIEFEST OF MOMENTS, HE ACTUALLY BECOMES KIERROK
...AND IN THAT MOMENT, CHARLES XAVIER... SCREAMS!

bring in new people," says Claremont. "We're not restricted to one guy whose life cannot substantially change over the course of decades."

Turning again to the multinational idea, the cast of New Mutants included Karma, from Vietnam; Sunspot, from Brazil; Wolfsbane, a Scottish female werewolf; Mirage, a Native American; and Cannonball, an American. After a few years *The New Mutants* itself mutated into the edgier *X-Force*, which featured Boomer, Cannonball, Feral, Warpath, Domino, Cable, and Shatterstar. The original X-Men team came back in 1986 in *X-Factor* (with The Angel eventually emerging as Archangel), though by issue #71 a different team took over. Under the guidance of writer Peter David, the new *X-Factor* featured Havok, Polaris, Quicksilver (all of whom had experienced brushes with the dark side), Wolfsbane, and a new figure wryly called Strong Guy.

By the 1990s, X-Men was the best-selling comic book franchise in the world, both in terms of magazines and merchandise (and to date *X-Men* has racked up more than three-quarters of a *billion* dollars in sales of licensed products!). Things would get even better with the 1994 launch of *Generation X,* chronicling the adventures of a group of young mutants who were mentored by Banshee and, interestingly, a one-time nemesis of Xavier's called The White Queen. The new group included Jubilee, a.k.a. Jubilation Lee, a former X-Man; Mondo, from Samoa, who could take on the characteristics of any material or substance simply by touching it; Husk, a shape-shifter who was the sister of Cannonball; Skin, a Latino from the barrio of Los Angeles whose flesh could be stretched to extreme lengths; Synch, who could access the power of other mutants; Chamber, a half-faced mutant who could alter reality; and Penance, whose skin has a cutting edge. Tapping into the notion that even normal teenagers wrestle with feelings of "mutancy," *Generation X* quickly became one of Marvel's most popular titles, regular selling in excess of 200,000 copies per issue.

HEROES FOREVER

SPECIAL COMICS INFORMATION

6

APPROVED FOR ALL READERS

On September 11, 2001, the world became aware of real-life superheroes in its midst. Many of them were in uniforms, though instead of colorful tights and capes they wore rain slickers, firemen's helmets, and police blues. Some even wore street clothes, unaware of the secret heroic identities that resided within them.

Since New York City has long been home to both the Marvel Comics headquarters and the Marvel Universe, it is not surprising that the company would face the terror and tragedy of that day head on. The attacks on the World Trade Center were wrenchingly depicted in *Amazing Spider-Man* #36, written by J. Michael Straczynski and drawn by John Romita, Jr., and Scott Hanna.

More importantly, in February of 2002 the company launched issue #1 of *A Moment of Silence*, a special series saluting the heroes of September 11, from which all proceeds go to the Twin Towers Fund. That issue featured three stories without dialogue, one of which centered on real-life building inspector Tony Savas—the father of Marvel employee Tina Savas—who was killed in the collapse of the World Trade Center while helping others escape.

There is always an inherent danger in mixing real human tragedy with fictional characters, no matter how familiar those characters may be. But the combined talents of the artists, writers, and editors allowed Marvel to walk that line with taste and compassion, and to help make things a little better in a hurting city, in a hurting world.

Marvel's tribute to the heroes and victims of September 11 took many forms. (From left to right) Two lithographs created to raise funds for the NYC Police and Fire Widows and Orphans Fund: The Hulk stands watch at Ground Zero (Randy Queen with Sarah Oates and Brett Evans), and Captain America salutes true American heroes (Joe Jusko); Spider-Man witnesses the horror from *Amazing Spider-Man* #36; the Marvel special September 11 tribute collectible, *A Moment of Silence*.

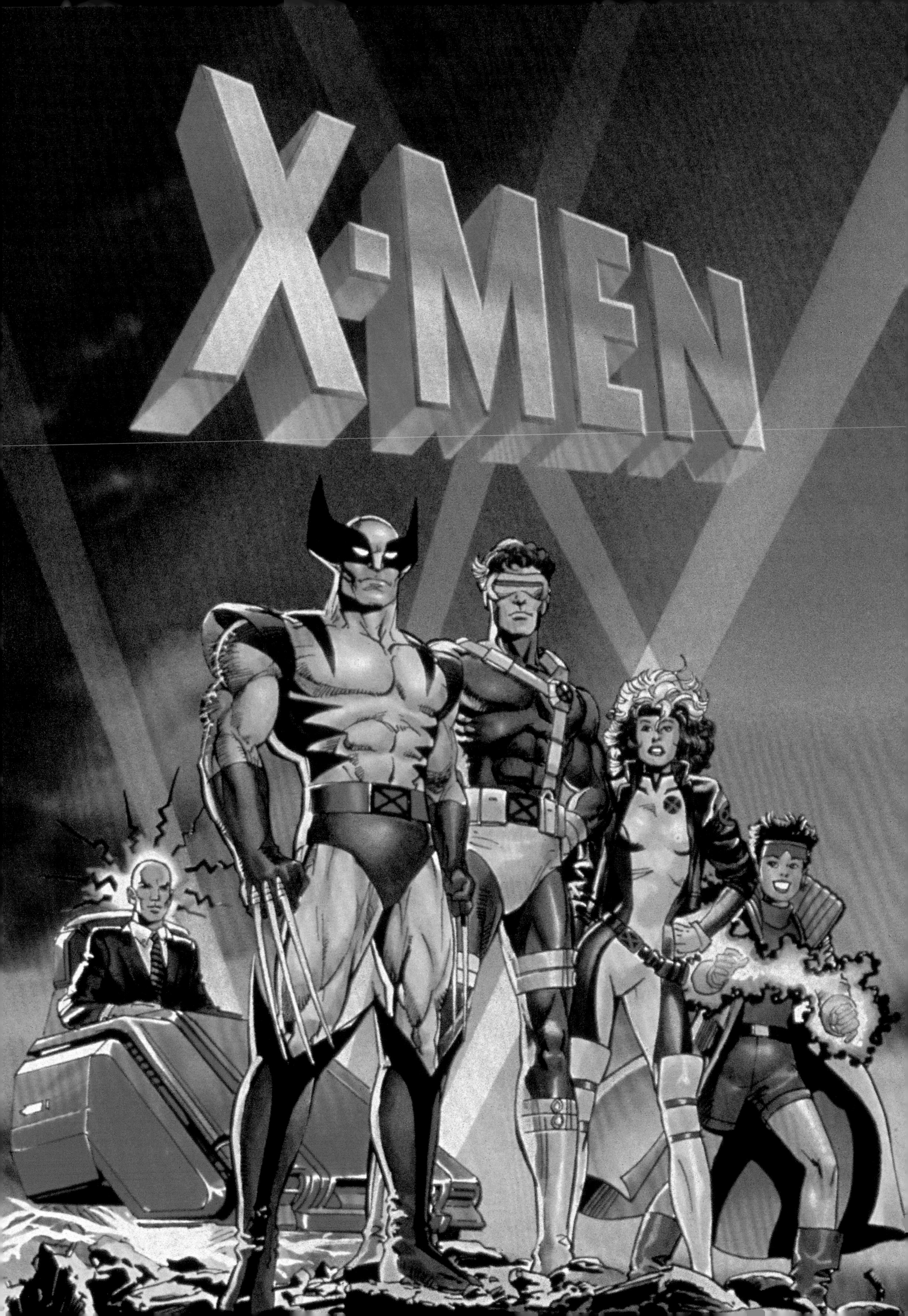
X-MEN

Meanwhile, the core X-Men team gained two new members, Rogue, who had the power to absorb the consciousness and abilities of others, and Gambit, who could infuse objects such as playing cards (his trademark) with power. Both are connected by mutual attraction and by somewhat shady pasts.

By the dawn of the new century, it was beginning to look like people in the Marvel Universe who were not mutants were becoming the minority!

X-MEN IN THE MEDIA

If within the last two decades it became increasingly hard to name the X-Men without a program, it was just as hard to get an X-Men program on television. Margaret Loesch, who was president and CEO of Marvel Productions from 1984 to 1990, tried repeatedly to launch an animated X-Men series, but each time encountered opposition from the networks. "What I kept running into, across the board, from all the networks, was that comics would not translate to television series, would not translate for kids, that comics were read by eighteen-to-twenty-four year-old men and they don't watch cartoons, and that they would have a very narrow appeal," Loesch says today. "Stan and I constantly went to the networks and pitched and repitched, and it was flabbergasting to me that, here we had the number one comic book of its day, with thirty-odd years of rich storytelling in its archives, and yet we were confronted with this mind set."

The impasse continued until 1992, when the young and audacious Fox Kids Network accepted the challenge of proving conventional network wisdom wrong, chiefly through the efforts of its founding president . . . Margaret Loesch. "I had a whole list of projects," Loesch notes. "I wanted to do X-Men first, I wanted to do Spider-Man second, I wanted to do Silver Surfer third, then I wanted to do The Avengers and Daredevil." During her tenure at Fox Kids, Loesch got her first three wishes. (An animated version of *The*

Many fans believe the 1992 animated "X-Men" to be the best animated adaption of a Marvel property ever done.

Avengers featuring a compendium of past team members, including Ant Man, The Wasp, Hawkeye, Wonder Man, The Vision, The Scarlet Witch, The Falcon, and Tigra, premiered on Fox in 1999.)

Years earlier, in 1988, right in the middle of all that concept pitching, an X-Men pilot was produced by Marvel Productions. Titled "Pryde of the X-Men," the half-hour show introduced Kitty Pryde into an existing team comprising Wolverine, Cyclops, Storm, Colossus, Nightcrawler, and The Dazzler, a.k.a. Alison Blair, who was a member of the team in the comics in the late 1980s. Kitty, who has the ability to pass through solid matter, "phasing," she calls it, is not quite sure what to make of the mutants who will become her teammates. In fact, she is uncomfortable even with the term "mutant," which she equates with "freak." She is particularly wary of the creepy Nightcrawler and the surly Wolverine.

Kitty, however, has little time to worry about her newly confirmed mutant status, since she is soon thrown into the middle of a pitched battle between Xavier's X-Men and Magneto's Brotherhood of Mutant Terrorists, a group that includes The White Witch, Juggernaut, the Blob, Pyro, and Toad. Magneto is particularly interested in Kitty, whom he corners while the others are battling it out, and offers her a spot on his team, which she instinctively refuses. Barring that, the wily Magneto has other plans: Kitty has been entrusted with the power circuit that is vital to the operation of Cerebro, and Magneto forces it away from her. Now armed with the power circuit, the supervillain captures the orbit of the comet Scorpio and redirects it on a collision course with earth, where, upon impact, it will raise a cloud of dust so great it will block out the sun, recreating the kind of atmospheric winter that is believed to have killed off the dinosaurs.

The X-Men quickly take off in a rocket ship which is launched toward "Asteroid M," Magneto's outer space base. Because of her inexperience (and the fact that Magneto has already gotten the better or her once), Xavier orders Kitty to stay behind at the school, but

(Top) Wolverine lost little of his edge in transferring to animation (though he did gain—and subsequently lose—an Australian accent).

(Above) Professor X mans Cerebro to find new mutants for TV's "X-Men."

(Top) Jubiliee joined the team in animation in 1992's "X-Men."

(Above) Jean Grey, sans her earlier Marvel Girl, Phoenix, or Dark Phoenix identities, was featured with other charter X-Men Cyclops and the Beast in the 1990s animated version.

she ignores his order and stows away, jetting off with the others to the asteroid. That turns out to be a good move since, with the help of Nightcrawler, she is able to break the contact of the beam on the comet and free it from its deadly path. Nightcrawler, though, is nearly killed in the process. This close call, coupled with the experience of working hand-in-hand with the demon-like mutant to save the world, softens Kitty toward her new partner. She decides she wants to become a full member of the team. The others—except for Wolverine, who cannot bring himself to trust her—welcome her as the newest X-Man. (And incidentally, never in history of X-Men has there been an attempt to differentiate between X-*Men* and X-*Women*.)

"Pryde of the X-Men," which was aired as an episode of the 1988 syndicated series "The Marvel Action Universe," proved that the property could successfully be translated to the small screen. While the characters were faithfully drawn, some liberties were taken, notably the decision to make Canadian-born Wolverine Australian. "At the time we heard about that we said, 'What? An Australian accent?'" recalls Tom De Falco, who was then Marvel's editor-in-chief. "Their response was, 'Well, a Canadian accent isn't interesting.' And we said, 'Hey, tough!'" Even so, the "Wolverine Dundee" voice remained.

It would take four more years for the authentic X-Men to show up in animation, but once it did, it became a history-making series. Produced by Marvel Films, Saban Entertainment, and Graz Entertainment, the series simply titled "X-Men" is thought by many to be the single finest translation of a Marvel property to film. The show benefitted from being made by animation artists and writers who were also diehard Marvel buffs. "I went after all of The X-Men aficionados and Marvel Comics fanatics in the industry who were also good directors and storytellers," says Stephanie Graziano, who was head of production for the series. "That included [producers] Will Meugniat and Larry Houston." (Along with Rich Hoberg and Larry Parr,

Meugniat and Houston had also produced and story-supervised "Pryde of The X-Men.") The combination of devotion to Marvel on the parts of the creative team, and experience in the trenches producing Saturday morning animation, allowed the filmmakers to successfully walk the tightrope that been prohibitively high for network execs in the past—maintaining fidelity to the characters and stories that were beloved by the core audience of Marvel, while making the show play for the traditionally younger Saturday morning crowd.

"They did a great job with translating the stories and not making people feel like it got watered down," says Graziano. "I've been in a taxi cab in another state and had the driver say how much he loved the stories, because they stuck right to the character lines from the book."

The cast roster for "X-Men," which premiered in the fall of 1992, included Wolverine (who now sounded suitably Canadian, which was not a stretch since the voice tracks were recorded in Canada), Cyclops, The Beast, whose alter ego, Hank McCoy, had become a respected doctor—or at least as respected as a mutant could be—Jean Grey, Storm, Jubilee, Rogue, and Gambit. Rather than try to maintain a full roster of eight superheroes in every show, different episodes spotlighted different characters, while others would fade into the background.

The universe into which the animated X-Men find themselves is one fraught with tension between the human and mutant classes, a tension that at times threatens to explode into open warfare, chiefly through the activities of a hate organization called "Friends of Humanity," whose agenda is to rid the world of mutants. At the other end of the spectrum are the outcast mutants called "Morlocks"—a concept and name taken straight from H.G. Wells's novel *The Time Machine*—who live underground in the subways and are enemies not only to the humans above ground, but also The X-Men. The series also explored the growing attraction Wolverine felt toward Jean Grey, and his rising jealousy of Scott

(Top) Despite his fearsome countenance, Dr. Hank "Beast" McCoy was a scholarly physician.

(Middle) Rogue was another new cast member for the 1990s "X-Men."

(Above) TV's animated "X-Men" often used Beast in storylines that explored the dangerous fear and hatred exhibited toward Mutants.

(Top) TV's "X-Men" contained unusually sophisticated storylines for Saturday morning animation, including a love triangle between Logan, a.k.a. Wolverine (seen here), Jean Grey, and Scott "Cyclops" Summers.

(Middle) As in his comics incarnation, Wolverine would remain one of the most popular X-Men on television.

(Above) Storm in action from the 1990s animation "X-Men."

Summers, to whom Jean remained both promised and devoted.

The instant success of the "X-Men" series had another effect: it launched the "upstart" Fox Kids Network to the top of the Saturday morning mainstream. "People think that what propelled Fox Kids to number one is 'Power Rangers,' but that is not true," says Loesch. "'Power Rangers' put us in the stratosphere, but we went from number three [network in the ratings] to number one because of one event: the premiere of 'X-Men.'" (And one can't help but wonder what influence the property had on another Fox series, a prime-time fantasy show that involved government agents, conspiracies, and a mysterious "Mr. X"—the wildly successful "The X-Files.")

"X-Men" remained in production for five years, a long life span for a Saturday morning cartoon series, then continued to air in reruns. It was enough to make the numbers two, three, and four networks wonder if they had perhaps miscalculated in turning the show down so many times.

A new generation of *homo superior* came to television in 1996's "Generation X," a rock-infused, live-action treatment of the teen-oriented magazine created by writer Scott Lobdell and artist Chris Bachalo. Produced by Marvel Films and MT2 Services, Inc., the $4-million project was designed as a pilot for either a weekly series or a string of "Generation X" two-hour movies. Either way, the goal was to translate the proven success of the comic book to television in hopes of capturing the burgeoning teen audience that had been created by MTV. The film, which aired on the Fox network February 20, 1996, established a world where mutants as a class of people are not simply scorned and hated by non-mutants, but are actually branded as threats to society. Unregistered mutants—most of them adolescents, since that is the age at which mutant powers begin to manifest themselves—are summarily arrested without due process and held in detention. The only alternative for this kind of threat is the Xavier School, which is now run by Sean Cassidy (played by Jeremy Ratchford) and Emma Frost (Finola Hughes), who possesses psychic powers that rival Xavier himself. (Interestingly, neither Sean nor Emma is identified in the film under their superhero names, Banshee and The White Queen.)

Through Cerebro, Emma and Sean have located and recruited Mondo (Bumper Robinson), Monet St. Croix/M (Amarillis), an invincible African-American superbrain who relishes her superiority over others; Kurt Pastorius/Refrax (Randall Slavin), who has x-ray and heat vision; and Arlee Hicks/Buff (Suzanne Davis), a girl-next-door type who is very sensitive about the fact that she possesses the hidden musculature of a Lou Ferrigno. Both Refrax and Buff were characters that had not appeared in the comics, but were created specifically for the film when the powers of Chamber, Synch, Husk, and Penance proved too complicated to capture on film. Into this mismatched mix the leaders introduce Skin, a.k.a. Angelo Espansoza (Agustin Rodriguez), whose stretching ability comes at the expense of great physical pain, and Jubilee (Heather McComb), who is still trying to get used to the electric power she has at her fingertips. The students make for a rather unruly bunch, and none of them get along very well, though because of their shared awkwardness at being the new kids, Angelo and Jubilee become fast friends, while Arlee gives the closest they will receive to a welcome.

Trouble from the outside comes on two fronts: the first is driven by the townie students from another prep academy who resent the Xavier students without even realizing who, or what, they are. The second and far more dangerous threat is launched by gonzo genius Russell Tresh (Matt Frewer), who five years earlier had been a member of a scientific team that also included Emma Frost and was working on a secret government research project involving young mutants. When Emma uncovered Tresh's plans to surgically remove the X-factor gene from a youngster and plant it in his own brain, the scientist was thrown off the project. Now embittered,

"Generation X"'s new mutants (clockwise from bottom): Jubilee (Heather McComb), Skin (Agustin Rodriguez), Refrax (Randal Slavin), Buff (Suzanne Davis), Mondo (Bumper Robinson), and M (Amarillis).

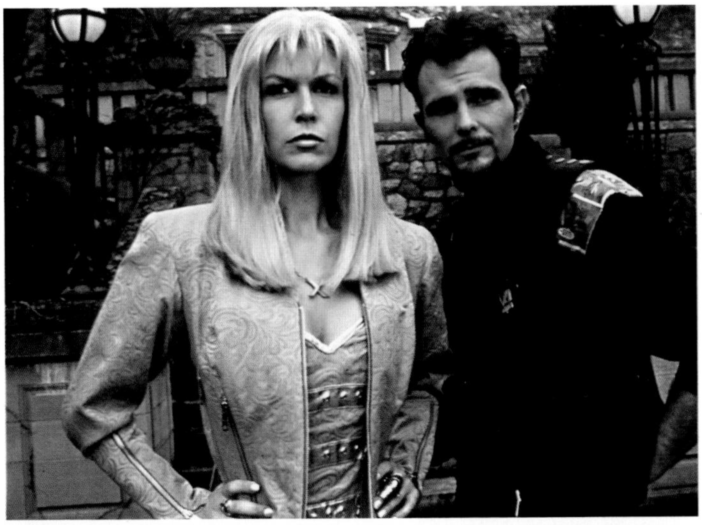

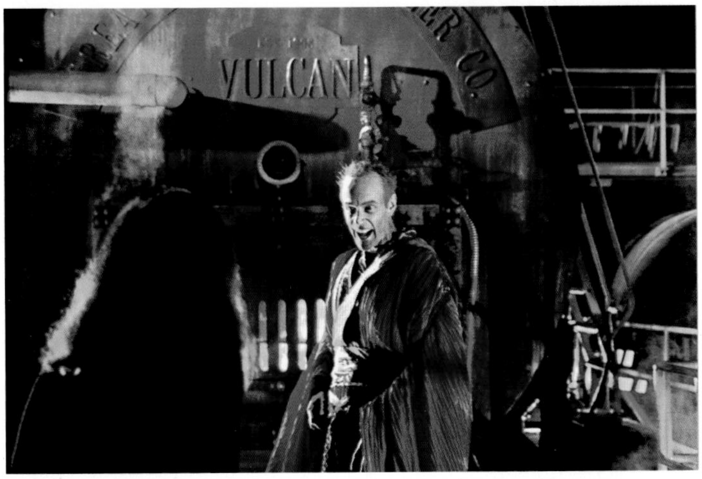
VULCAN

(Top) In "Generation X" Emma "White Queen" Frost (Finola Hughes) and Sean "Banshee" Cassidy (Jeremy Ratchford) run the Xavier Institute for gifted mutants.

(Above) The dangerous Russell Tresh (Matt Frewer) meets unwitting victims in their dreams.

not to mention hopelessly insane, Tresh is a rogue inventor seeking corporate funding to produce a machine that can invade people's dreams, which he proposes to use as a means of subliminal advertising. The concept is based on a dream chair device that Emma had constructed during her government service, and which Tresh has reconstructed in his home.

However, once Tresh has revealed himself to be too crazy even for the advertising business, his funding is cut and he is on his own. On a nocturnal journey through dreamland (during which time he plants the suggestion to commit suicide into the mind of his corporate benefactor), Tresh is surprised to find another mind-figure wandering around in the eerie netherworld. It is Angelo, who has discovered the original prototype of the dream chair in a secret room in the basement of the Xavier Institute, and is using it as a means of escape from a place he considers to be little better than a prison.

Not realizing how dangerous Tresh is, Angelo accepts him as a friend and fellow traveler, particularly when Tresh explains that he can influence the dreaming mind of a townie girl for whom Angelo has fallen. Angelo repays him by saving Tresh when his mind-figure is about to be pulled back to consciousness by a group of policemen, who have come to Tresh's house to arrest him for the death of his benefactor, only to find him asleep in the dream chair. Tresh's spirit is thus able to remain in dreamland, but it is now separated from his body, which falls into a catatonic state and is taken away to a hospital.

Tresh and Angelo continue to see each other in their dreams, and through the young man Tresh learns that his hated enemy, Emma Frost, is working at the Xavier Institute. He convinces Angelo to take a portable dream machine to the hospital in which his body is lying and reconnect his body and mind. Angelo does so, but no sooner is Tresh whole again than he abducts the boy and carries him off to his home laboratory and straps him in the dream chair, planning to pick up where he left off five years earlier by removing the mutant gene

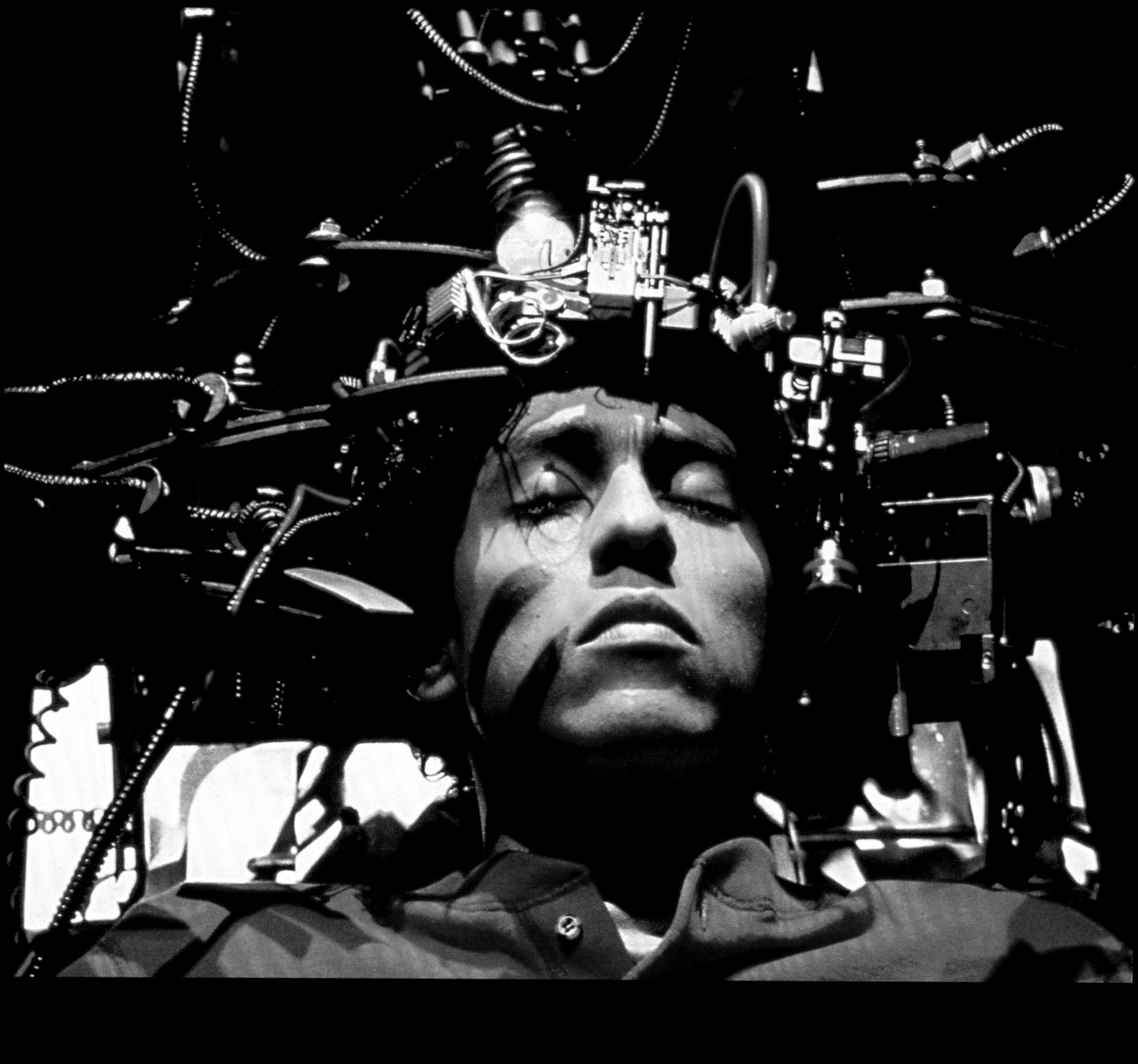

(Top) Sean and Emma clearly have more than a working relationship in "Generation X."

(Above) Buff (one of two characters created specifically for the "Generation X" television movie) steps into action, supported by Banshee and the White Queen.

(Opposite) Skin "escapes" through Emma Frost's forbidden dream machine in "Generation X."

(Following spread) Many Marvel fans were as eager to see the depiction of Cerebro (seen here) in *X-Men* as they were the main characters.

from Angelo's brain. Desperate, Angelo summons up all the powers he has acquired through taking Emma's class in telepathy and comes to Jubilee that night, begging for help. Once Emma and Sean have been informed of Angelo's predicament by Jubilee, they martial The Gen-Xers together to battle for the life of Skin.

Emma psychically opens the doorway between the normal plane of existence and the dream world, and the team goes on the offensive, though Tresh proves to be a more difficult foe than anticipated, since the amount of time he has spent in the dream dimension has prompted him to mutate on his own and become infinitely more powerful. It is ultimately Angelo who overcomes Tresh by wrapping the insane genius in his elongated arms and plunging into dream oblivion with him. For a while it appears that Angelo has perished as well, but he re-emerges from the void just in time to pass back through the doorway to reality. The physical body of Russell Tresh, meanwhile, has once more fallen into catatonia, an empty shell separated from his malignant consciousness . . . for the time being.

"Generation X" was an ambitious project for television, and one that benefitted from an intelligent script by Eric Blakeney (creator of the teen-oriented cop show "21 Jump Street") that pushed the concept of alienated teenagers to the extreme. For the most part the proceedings were taken seriously by the actors, particularly Ratchford and Hughes, who generated both conviction and tension (sexual and otherwise) as team leaders who struggle to remain in synch with each other while trying to maintain control over their difficult charges. Ultimately, though, the film is dominated by the performance of Frewer, who was encouraged by director Jack Sholder to soar as far over-the-top as possible as the wisecracking psychopath Tresh.

While "Generation X" did not spawn a mutant franchise for television, it proved that the X-Men mythos worked equally well in live action as in animation. The next film adaptation of X-Men, however, would effectively pave the way for a new era in Marvel-related cinema.

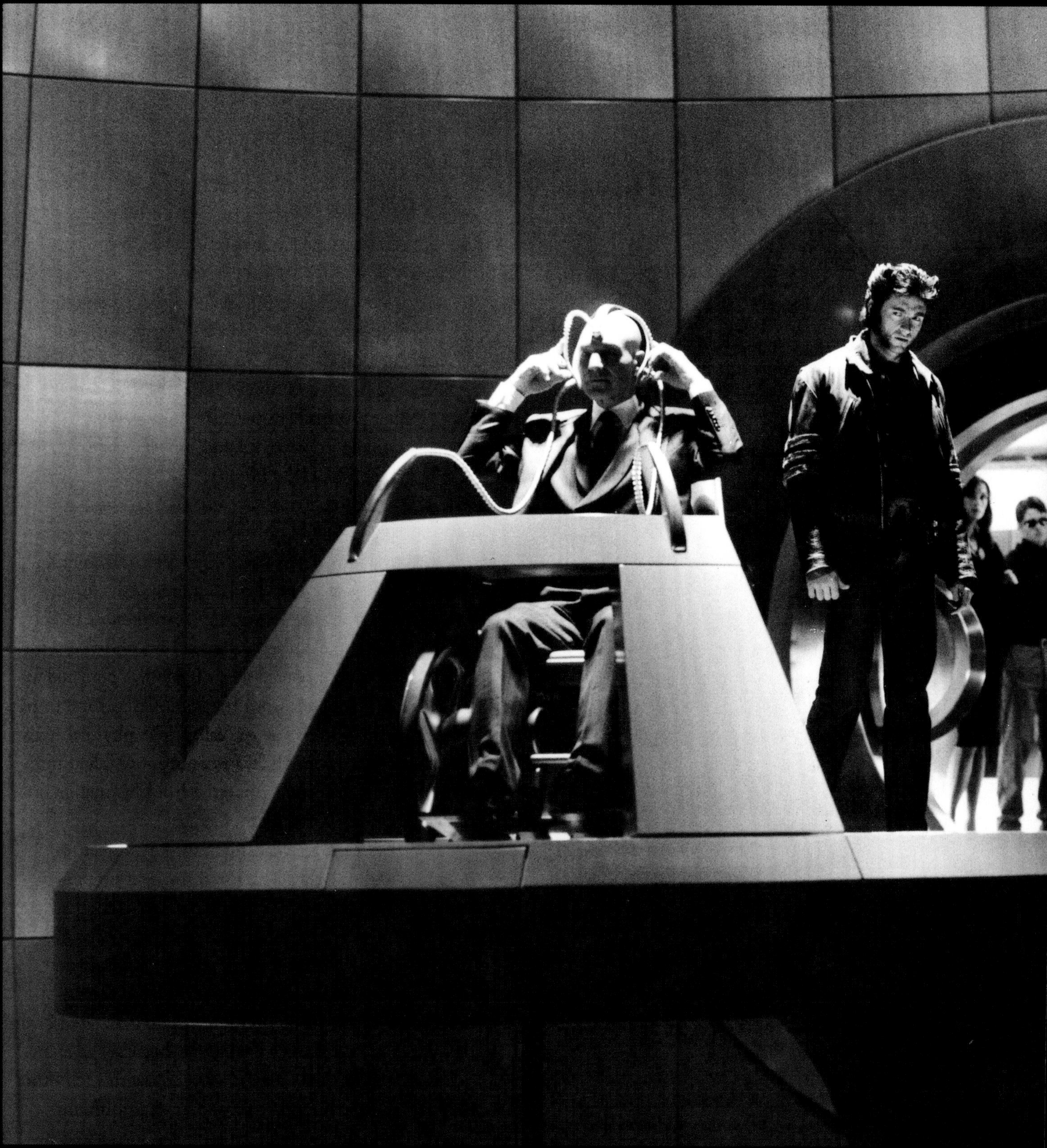

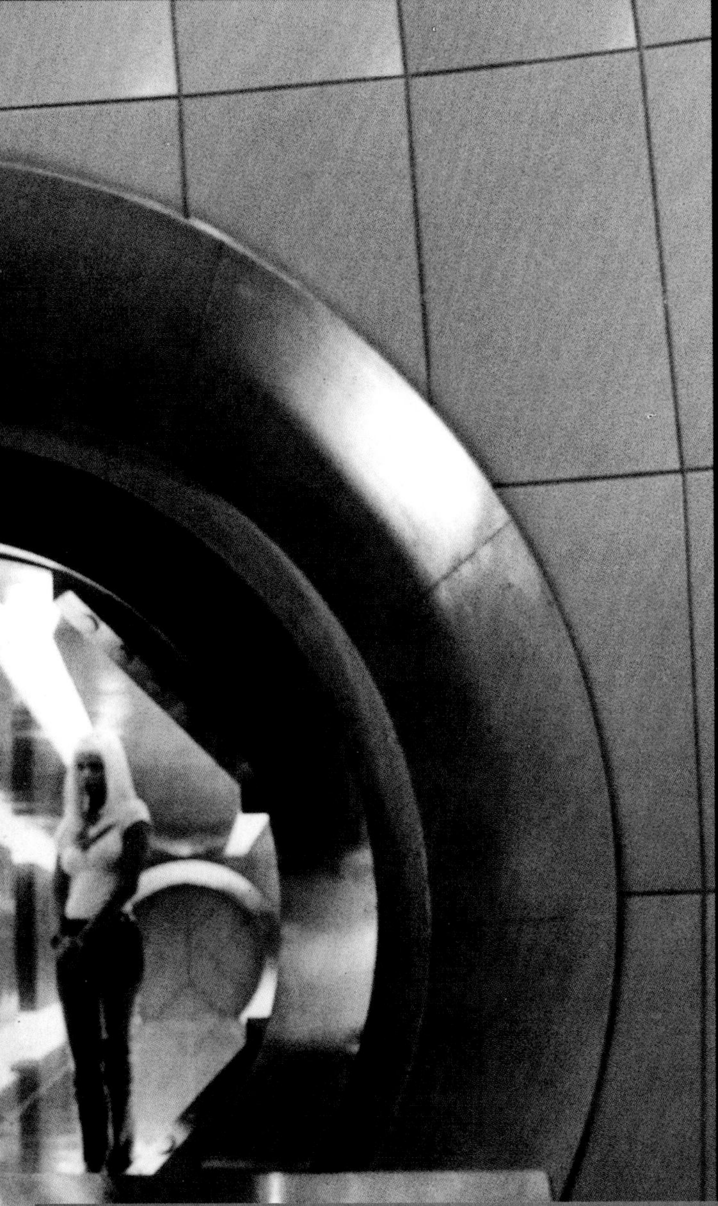

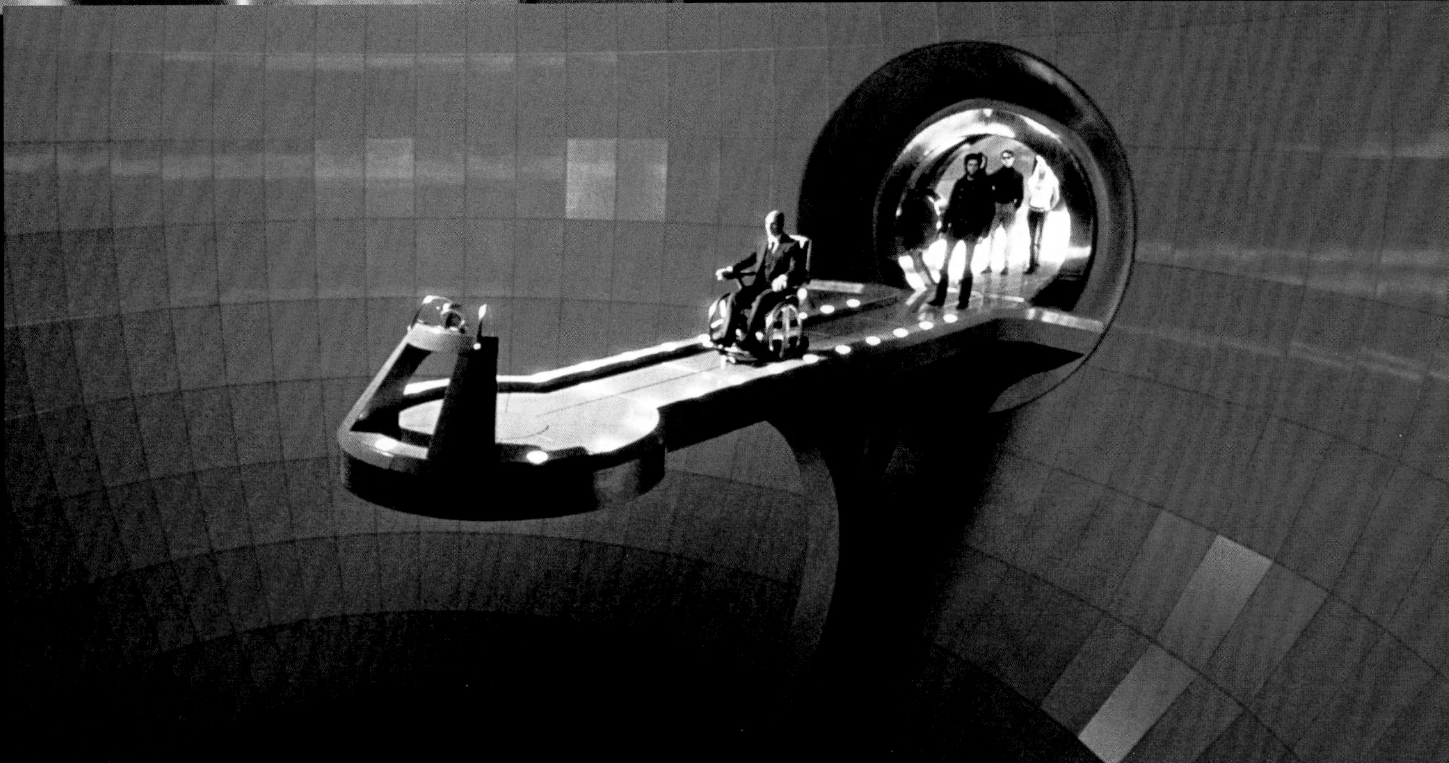

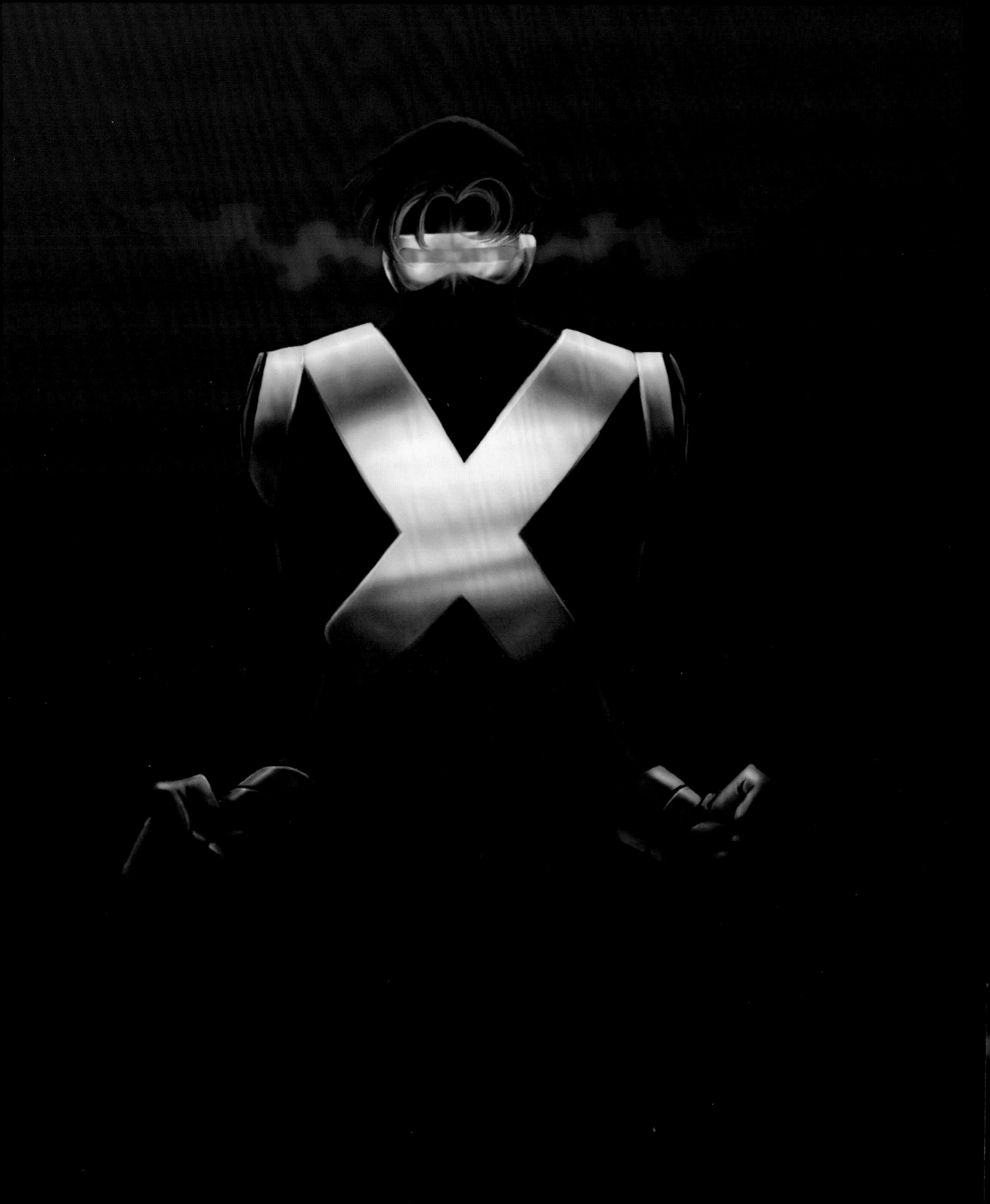

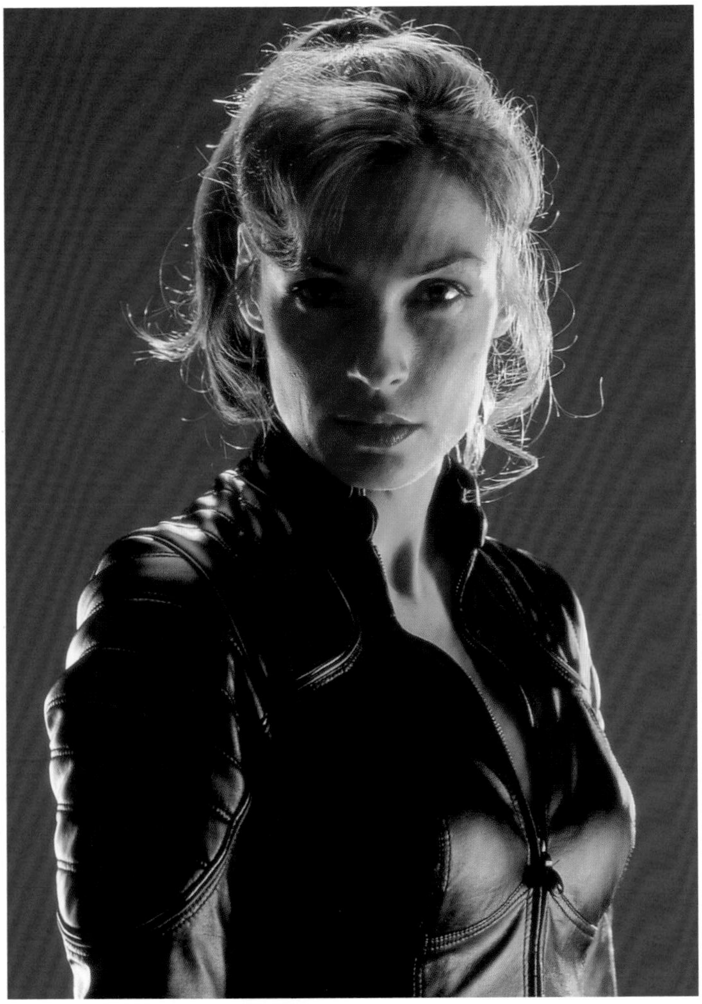

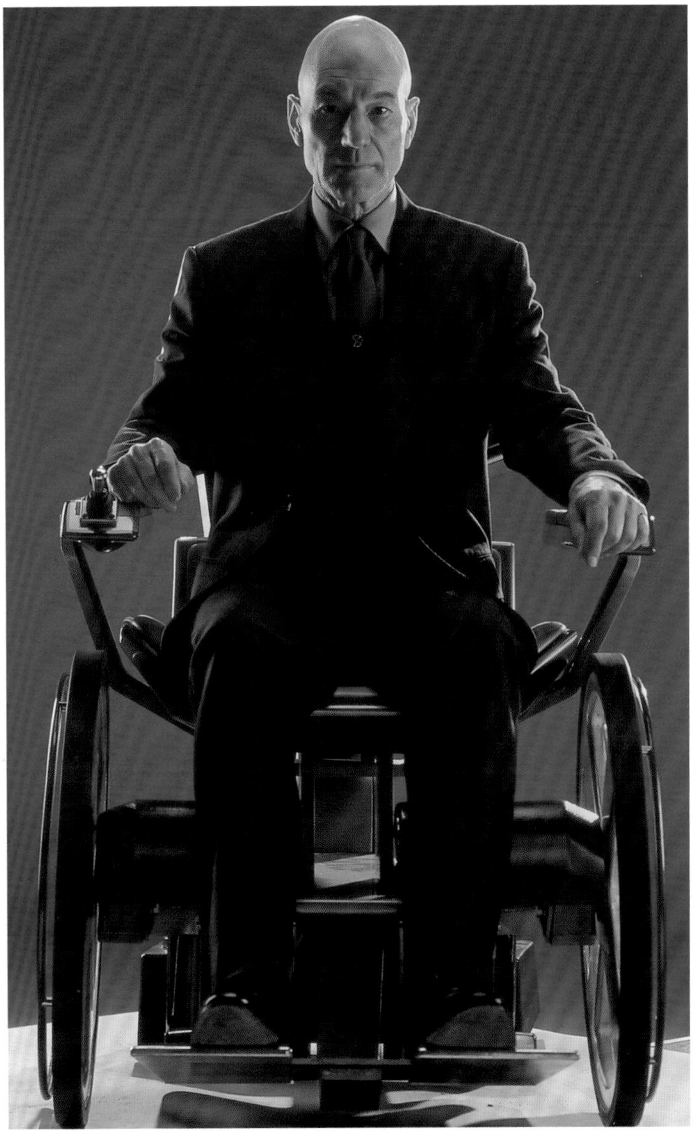

(Above) Famke Janssen as Jean Grey.

(Right) Perfect casting: Patrick Stewart as Professor Charles Xavier in 20th Century-Fox's big-screen *X-Men*.

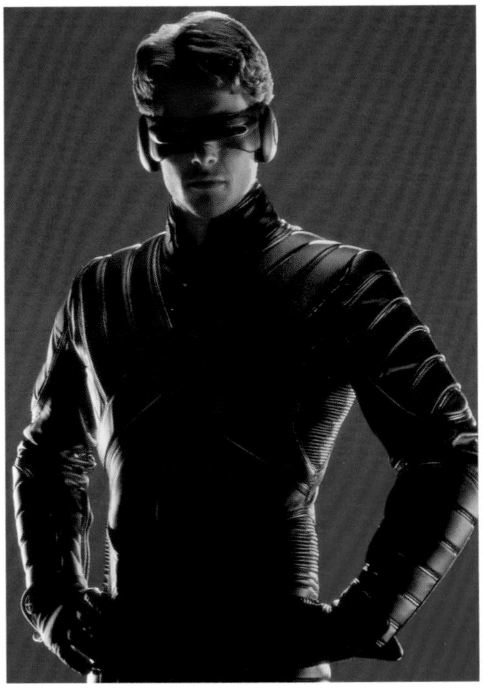

Actor James Marsden as Cyclops in *X-Men*.

20th Century-Fox's *X-Men,* which blazed into theaters on July 14, 2000, was one of the most eagerly awaited films of that year. For months prior to its release dedicated Marvel fans kept track of the production through news items on the Internet, hoping to get a glimpse of the characters, their new costumes (which consisted of matching leather jumpsuits with discrete "X" logos), even the Cerebro set. Filmed in Toronto on a budget of $75 million, which by present-day standards is actually a moderate price, *X-Men* was the biggest movie produced from a Marvel Comics property to that date. No less than eleven special effects houses were required to create more than five hundred special effects shots for the film.

Director Bryan Singer and screenwriter David Hayter (writers Christopher McQuarrie and Ed Solomon also worked on an earlier version of the script) pared down the four-decade roster of X-Men to come up with a lean, mean team for the movie. Cyclops (played by James Marsden), Jean Grey (Famke Janssen), and Storm

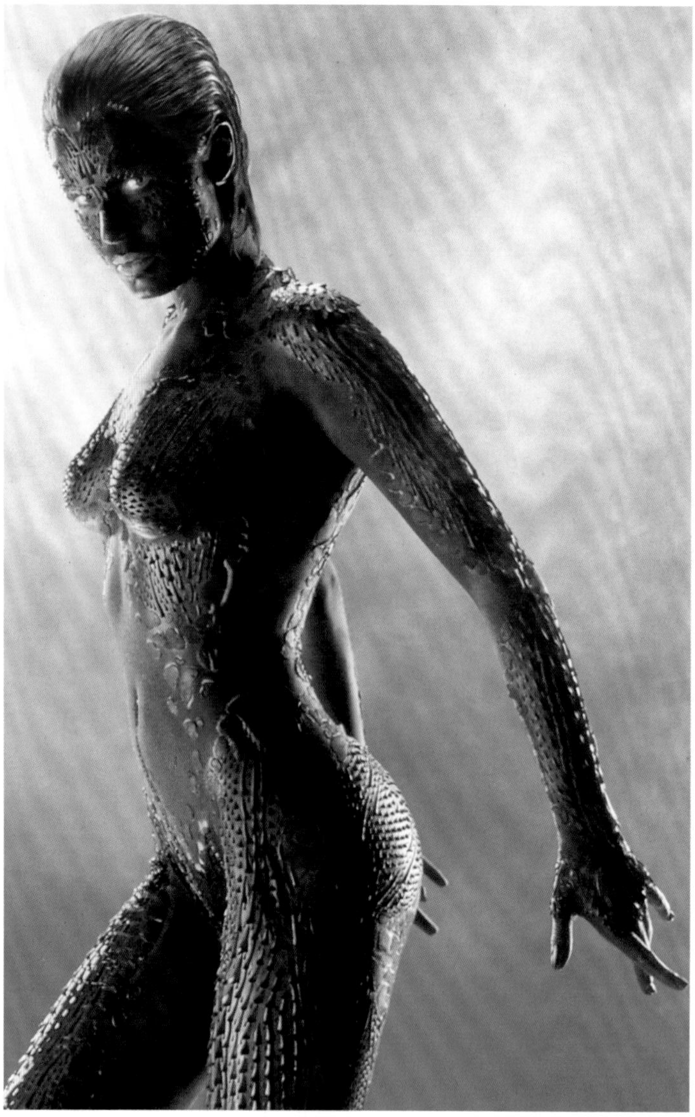

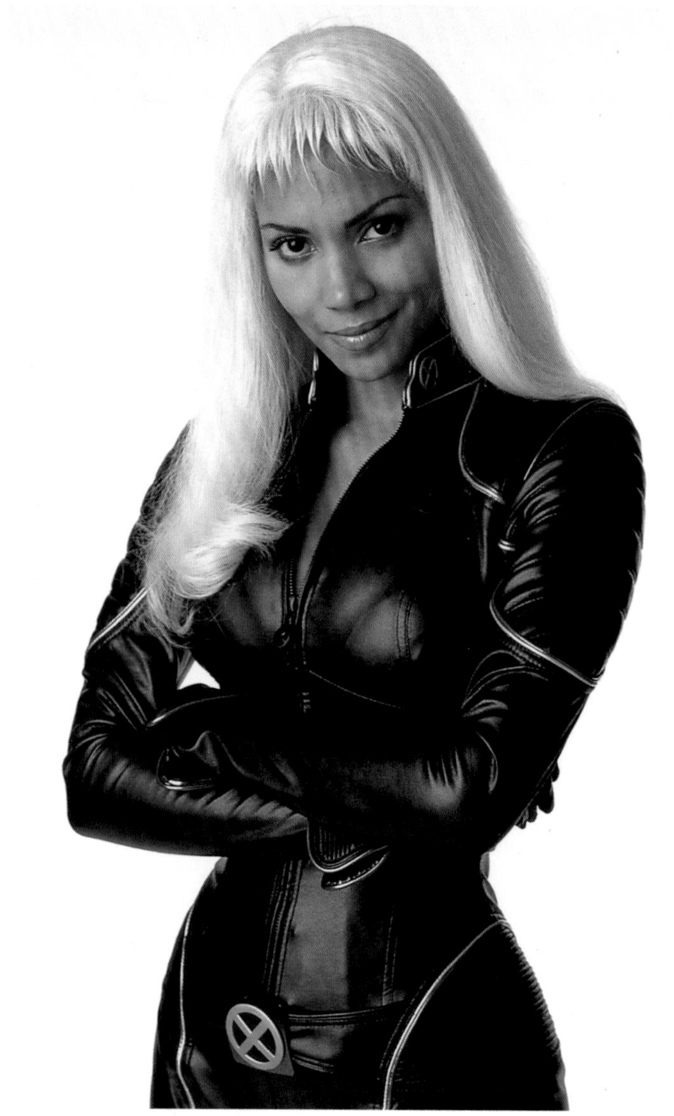

(Above) Halle Berry as Storm.

(Left) Rebecca Romijn-Stamos as the shape-shifting (but why would you?) Mystique.

(Halle Berry) formed the core group, into which Charles Xavier (Patrick Stewart, perhaps the perfect actor for the role from head to toe—particularly head), introduces Wolverine (Hugh Jackman, a last-minute replacement for Dougray Scott, who bowed out due to scheduling conflicts) and Rogue (Oscar-winner Anna Paquin). Longtime followers of X-Men will also recognize Jubilee, Kitty Pryde, and Bobby Drake in brief cameos at the Xavier School for Gifted Youngsters, and really sharp-eyed fans may be able to spot Stan Lee as a beachside hot dog vendor!

The natural enemies of the team are the Brotherhood of Evil Mutants, consisting of Sabretooth (played by 6' 10" former wrestler Tyler Mane), who is a baneful counterpart to Wolverine; Mystique (supermodel Rebecca Romijn-Stamos in a stunning ten-hour makeup job), who has the ability to morph into other forms; and Toad (stuntman and actor Ray Park, who gives the villain a wonderfully warped personality), whose remarkable leaping ability is augmented by a rope-like

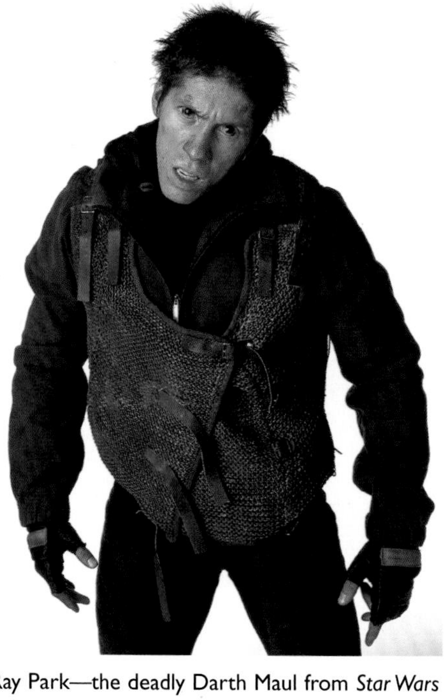

Ray Park—the deadly Darth Maul from *Star Wars Episode I: The Phantom Menace*—plays Toad.

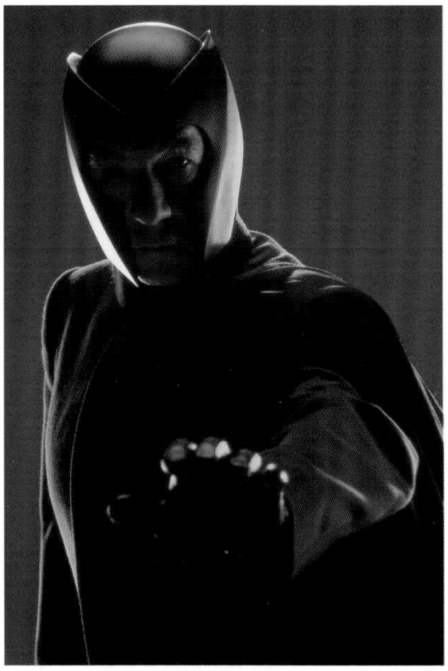

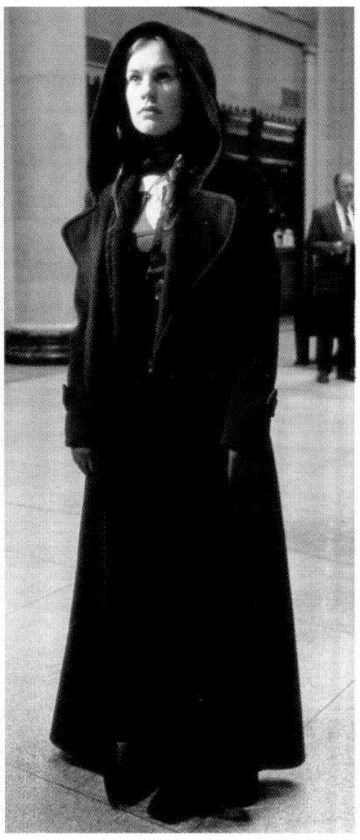

(Above left) Magneto in costume.

(Above center) The confused Marie, a.k.a. Rogue (Anna Paquin, pictured here), falls prey to the devious suggestions of Magneto, who needs her power to start his war on intolerant humans, in *X-Men.*

(Right) Reach out and kill someone—Sir Ian McKellen as Erik Lehnsherr, a.k.a. Magneto.

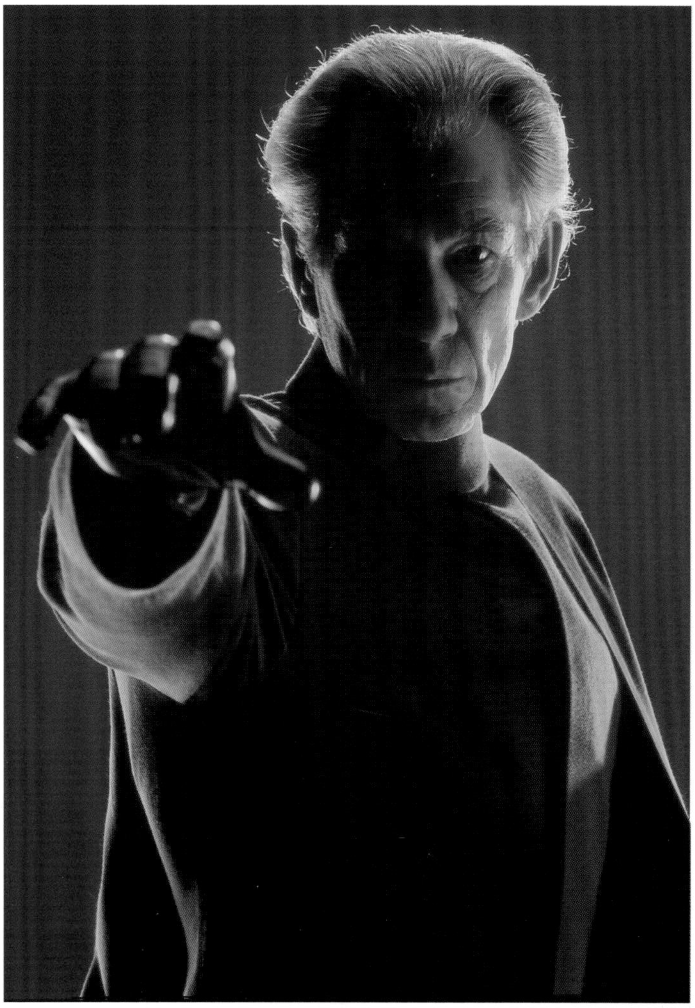

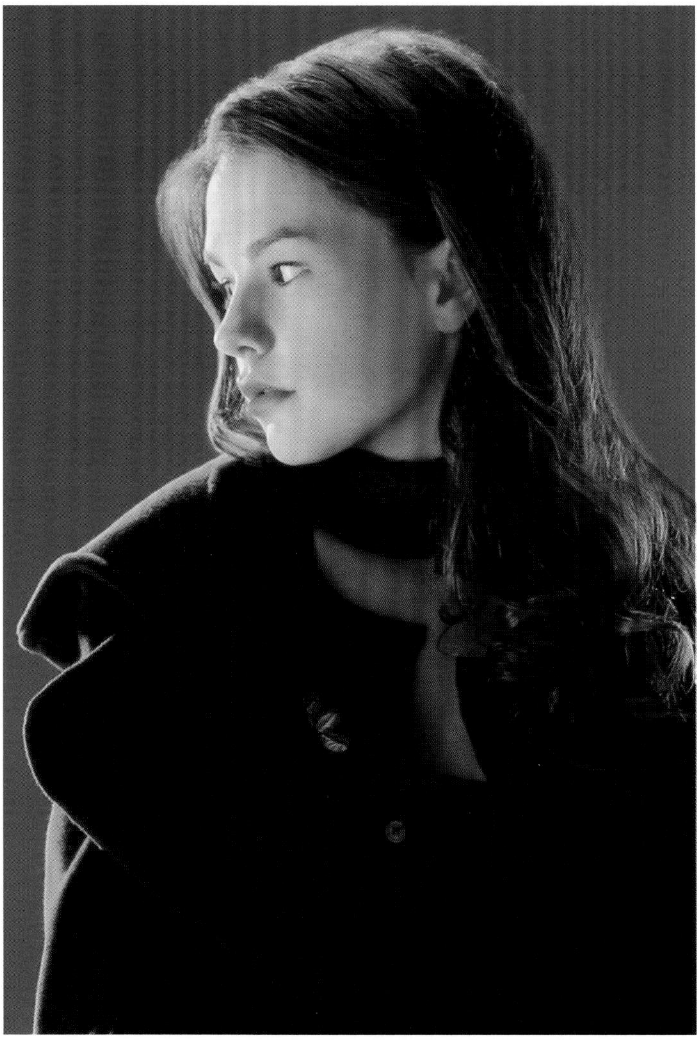

Academy Award–winning actress Anna Paquin as Rogue.

prehensile tongue. Leading this dangerous band is, of course, Erik Lensherr, a.k.a. Magneto, played by British classical actor Sir Ian McKellen.

Expanding upon a theme that had already been explored in the comic books and in recent film and animation adaptions, *X-Men* showed Xavier and his team not only having to deal with the dark side of mutanthood, but also the bigotry, fear, and hatred within normal human society. In the film, a wave of anti-mutant sentiment is being exploited by a United States senator named Robert Kelly (Bruce Davison), who is backing restrictive legislation against mutants. Jean Grey is called upon to testify before a Senate hearing on mutant registration, appealing to the senators to consider mutants not a separate race, but a stage of human evolution. This argument, though, does little to sway the McCarthyistic Kelly.

Part of the power of *X-Men* (both the film and the comic book property itself) comes from the fact that, philosophically, the ongoing war between the noble

(Above) Actor Hugh Jackman made a suitably dour, if rather tall, Wolverine.

(Left) Tyler Mane as the ferocious Sabretooth.

mutants and the evil mutants cannot be broken down in simple black-and-white terms. Xavier and Magneto are presented less as bitter enemies than as respectful, opposite sides of the same powerful coin. While Xavier struggles to achieve his lifelong dream of seeing mutants and non-mutants live side by side in society, Magneto's goal is to hasten the natural effects of evolution, which has governed humankind throughout its history, mandating that the strong overtake and eventually supplant the weak. "We are the future, Charles, not them [*homo sapiens*]; they no longer matter," Magneto tells his former friend at one point, effectively raising the conflict far beyond a simple good-versus-evil confrontation, to a battle for the future of Earth itself.

To advance what he believes is a coming battle between mutants and non-mutants, Magneto attempts to use radiation bombardment (what else?) to turn the leaders of the world into mutants, thereby ensuring that "our cause is their cause," a masterplot that requires the powers of the confused, teenaged Rogue, whom

(Opposite) The teenaged group as featured in TV's "X-Men: Evolution": Shadowcat (Kitty Pryde), Nightcrawler (Kurt Wagner), Jean Grey, Cyclops (Scott Summers), Rogue, and a new character, Spyke (a.k.a. Evan Daniels).

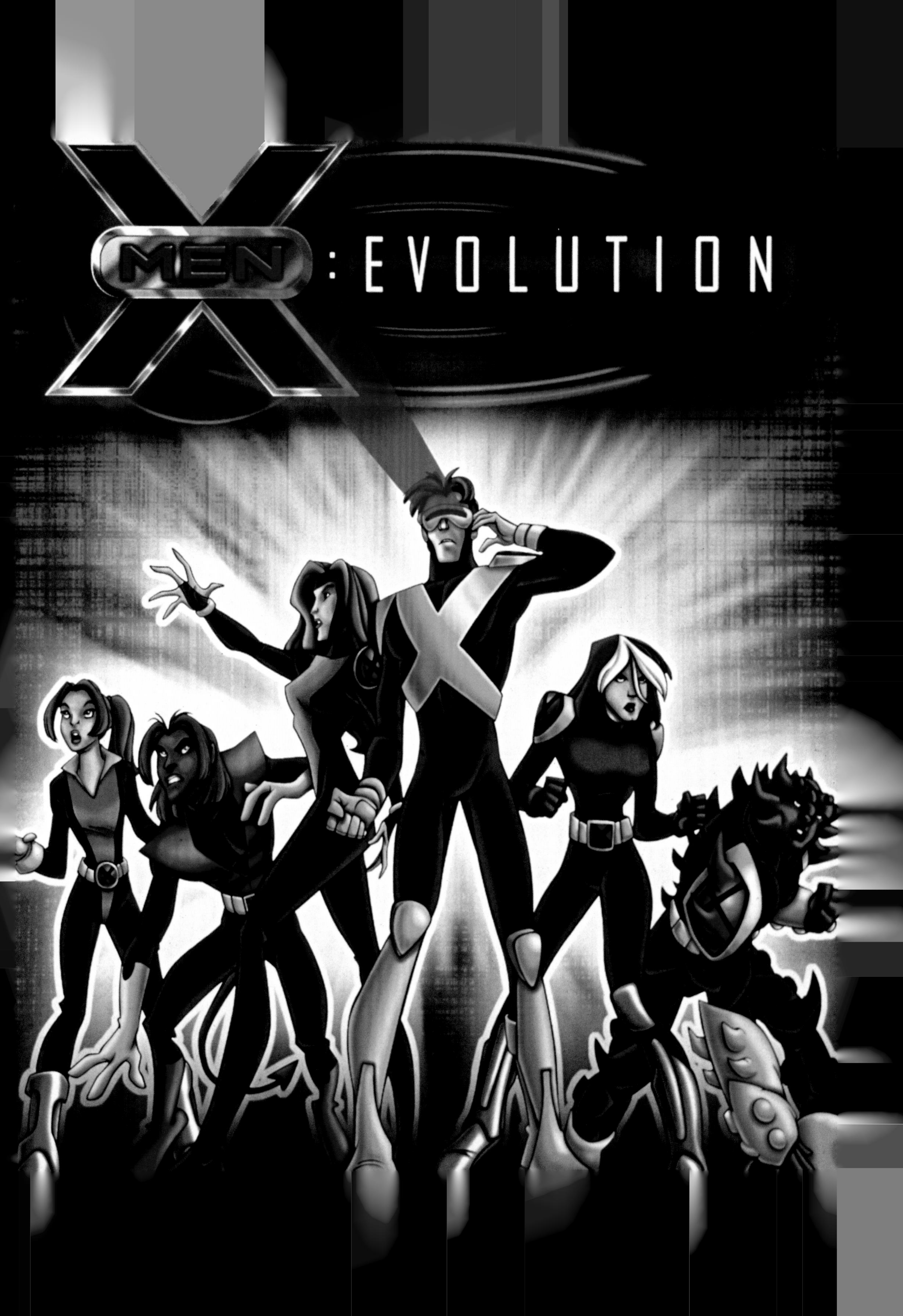
X-MEN: EVOLUTION

Magneto has kidnapped. In a high-voltage (if heavily
symbolic) climax set on the Statue of Liberty, Magneto
nearly succeeds in his plans, but he is stopped and the
young mutant is saved by Wolverine, who in the film
has shed his violently anti-social nature enough to
develop a protective bond toward Rogue.

From its bleak opening, which depicts young Erik
Lensherr watching his family herded into Auschwitz in
1944, to the final chess-playing confrontation between
Magneto and Xavier, *X-Men* paints its conflicts in tones
of dark gray. As portrayed by McKellen, Magneto
himself is not so much a figure of stark evil as a brilliant
but misguided victim of human cruelty, along the lines
of a Jules Verne anti-hero, such as Captain Nemo or
Robur the Conqueror. In light of the film's powerful
prologue, it is impossible not to feel at least a little
empathy for the character.

The character of Wolverine as depicted in
X-Men is likewise considerably softer than his comics
counterpart, and tantalizing hints are offered for his
history. After being examined by Jean Grey, for instance,
it is discovered that despite his youthful appearance,
Logan/Wolverine might actually be a senior citizen and
that the mutant has no conscious knowledge of his life
prior to the horrific surgical process through which his
skeleton was infused with adamantium. (And for the
record, Jackman's Wolverine appears taller than Cyclops.)

Ironically, Bryan Singer, whose previous films
The Usual Suspects and *Apt Pupil* were explorations of
evil in their own right, was initially reluctant to take the
project on, not wanting to do a comic book–inspired
movie. Ultimately, the intriguing philosophical
arguments between Xavier and Magneto became the
hook that lured him in. Even before Singer signed on
to the project, *X-Men* had spent some six years in
development and the screenplay went through myriad
versions, with writers Andrew Kevin Walker, Joss
Wheedon, and Tom DeSanto (who was also one of the
film's executive producers, along with Stan Lee, Avi Arad,
and Richard Donner) contributing different drafts.

(Above) The animated characters of the "X-Men Evolution." From top, L to
R: Kitty, Wolverine, Storm, Jean Grey, Rogue, and Sabertooth.

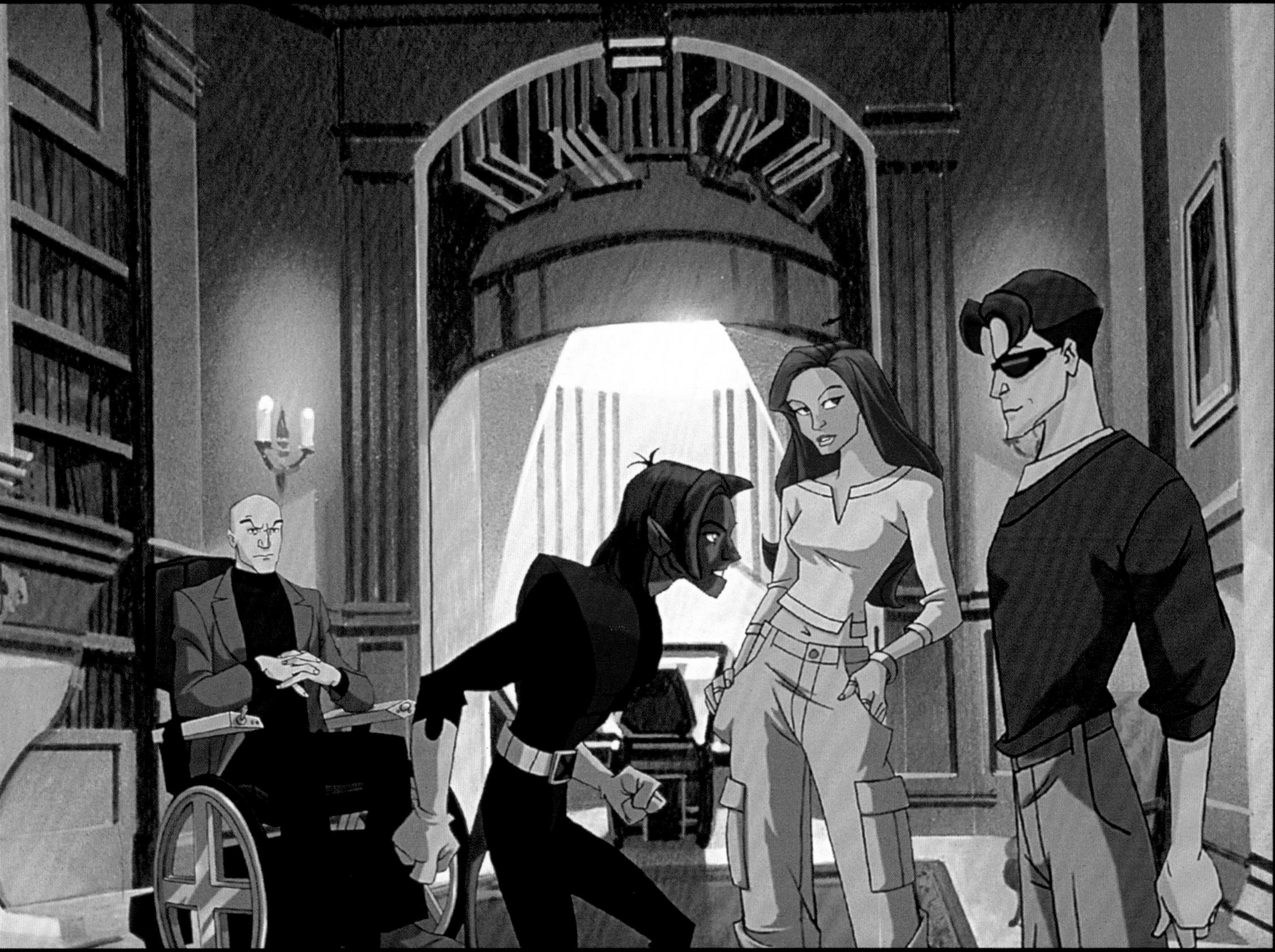

Professor X, Jean Grey, and Scott Summers keep watch over a restless Nightcrawler in "X-Men: Evolution."

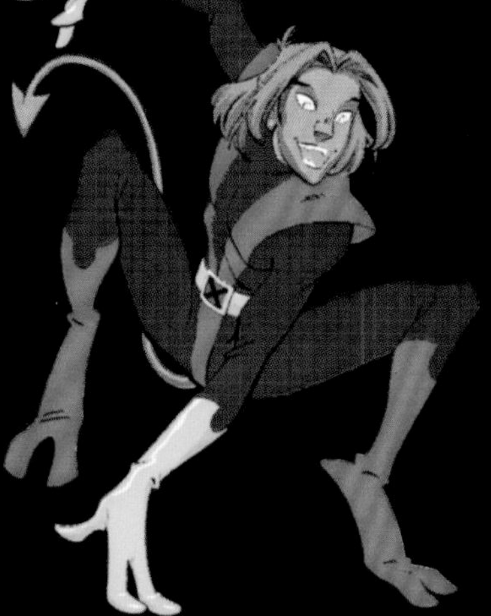

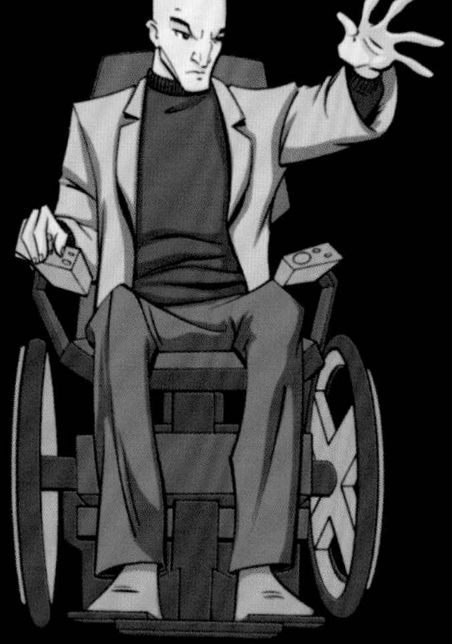

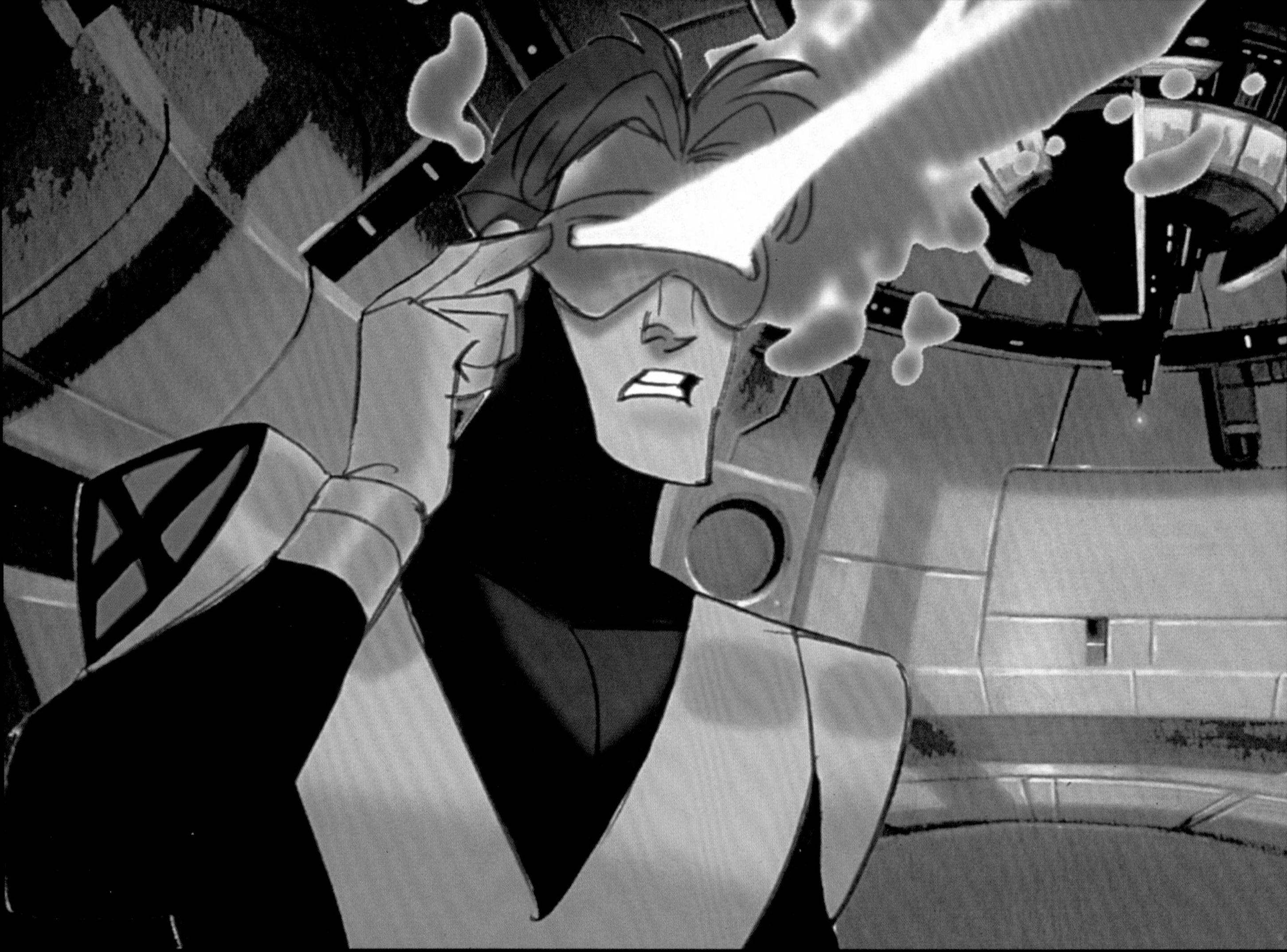

Cyclops powers on, from the animated "X-Men: Evolution."

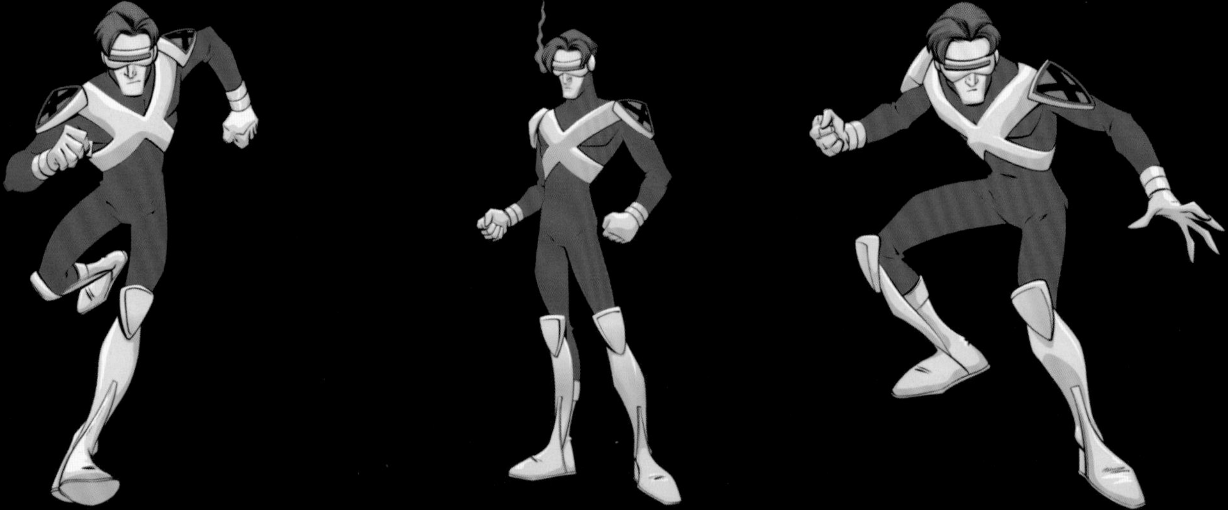

anything

Villainess Mystique, in animated form, from "X-Men Evolution."

But the time and care taken to develop the project paid off. *X-Men* (which was premiered on New York's Ellis Island) went on to earn more than $150 million at the box office in the U.S.—$54.5 million in its opening weekend alone, not only making it the centerpiece of the entire summer 2000 movie season, but the eighth highest-grossing opening in history.

While the *X-Men* film might arguably be the be-all of Marvel's mutant franchise, it is hardly the end-all. A brand new animated series titled "X-Men: Evolution" premiered on the Kids WB Network in the fall of 2000, timed to appear just as the theatrical run of *X-Men* was starting to wind down. The series, which is produced by Marvel Studios and Film Roman, is considerably different from the animated "X-Men" that had earlier aired on Fox, and only loosely connected to the feature film. "X-Men: Evolution" goes back to the comic book's roots by depicting several of the lead characters, Cyclops

The evil mutant Toad gets another re-design, this time as teen menace Todd Tolensky in the animated "X-Men Evolution."

and Jean Grey among them, as teenagers. But, unlike their comic book incarnations, who were confined to the relative safe haven of the Xavier School, the mutant teens in "X-Men Evolution" attend public high school, which forces them to try and conceal the very talents they are attempting to develop from their "normal" classmates.

"X-Men: Evolution" features a who's who of characters, both good and bad, from the nearly forty-year history of the comic book. In addition to Cyclops and Jean, Xavier's charges include Nightcrawler, Kitty Pryde (who is now also known as Shadowcat), Rogue, and a character created exclusively for the series, Evan Daniels, a.k.a. Spyke, who has superhuman bone-growth ability. Wolverine and Storm (who is Spyke's aunt) are also along for the adventure, though in the altered mythology of the show they are adults, not teenagers. The dark side of high school is represented by teenaged versions of Toad, the Blob, and Sauron, a character that was introduced into the comics in the late 1960s, who transforms into a fearsome pterodactyl-like beast. Like the Hulk, Sauron is an interesting twist on Jekyll and Hyde, in that his human form stands for good, while his reptilian side is pure evil. All of the villains (which in the series include the older Sabretooth and Juggernaut) take their orders from a mysterious leader who is never seen, but whose voice is heard. The identity of this shadowy figure was kept secret until the end of the show's first season, though it was not really difficult for fans to figure out who it was (hint: he has a "magnetic" personality).

"X-Men: Evolution" is indeed an evolution in terms of the mythology, but it serves to demonstrate the seemingly limitless vein of story and character potential that makes up the saga of "The X-Men."

(Opposite) Raven Darkholme transforms into Mystique in front of Todd in "X-Men: Evolution."

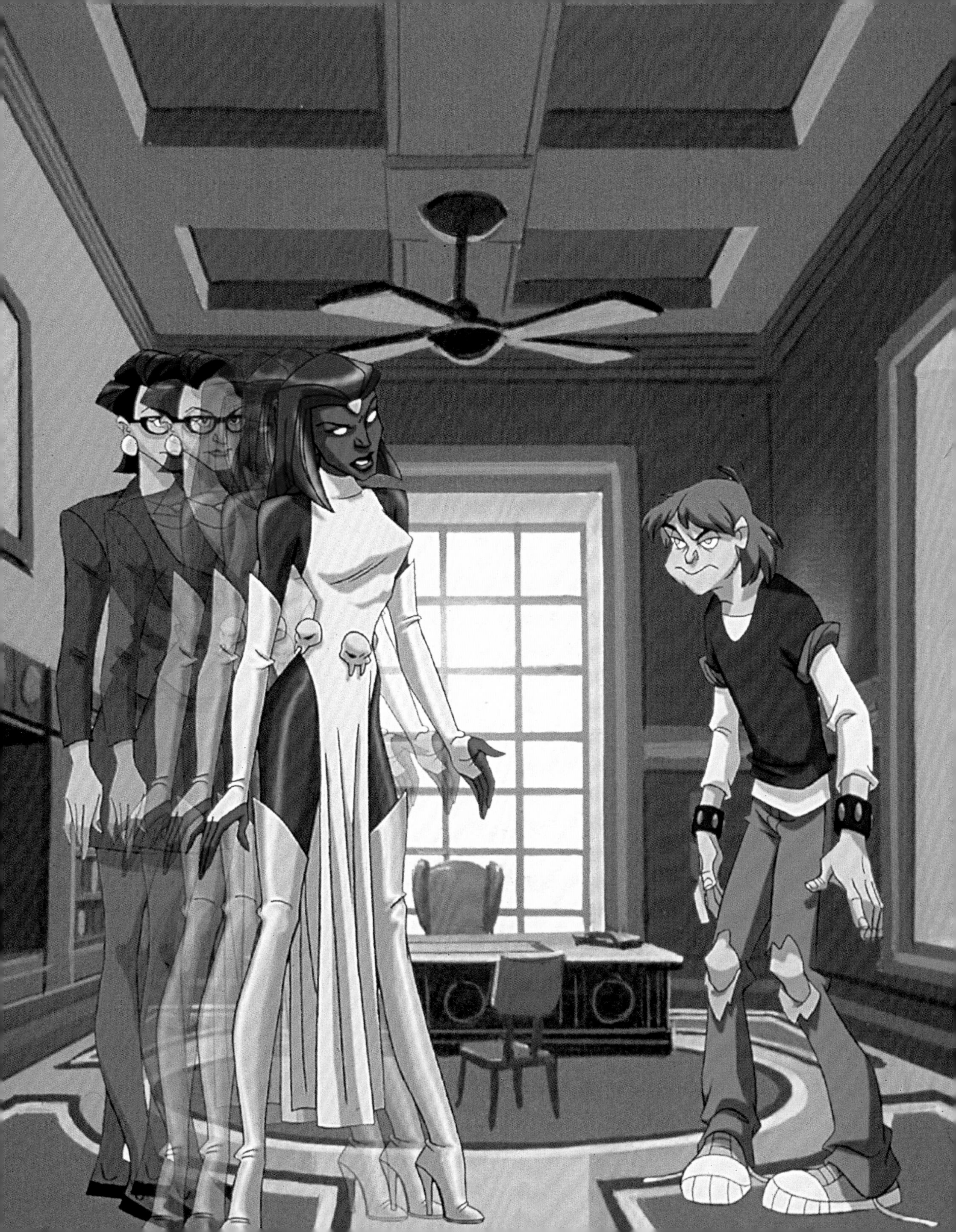

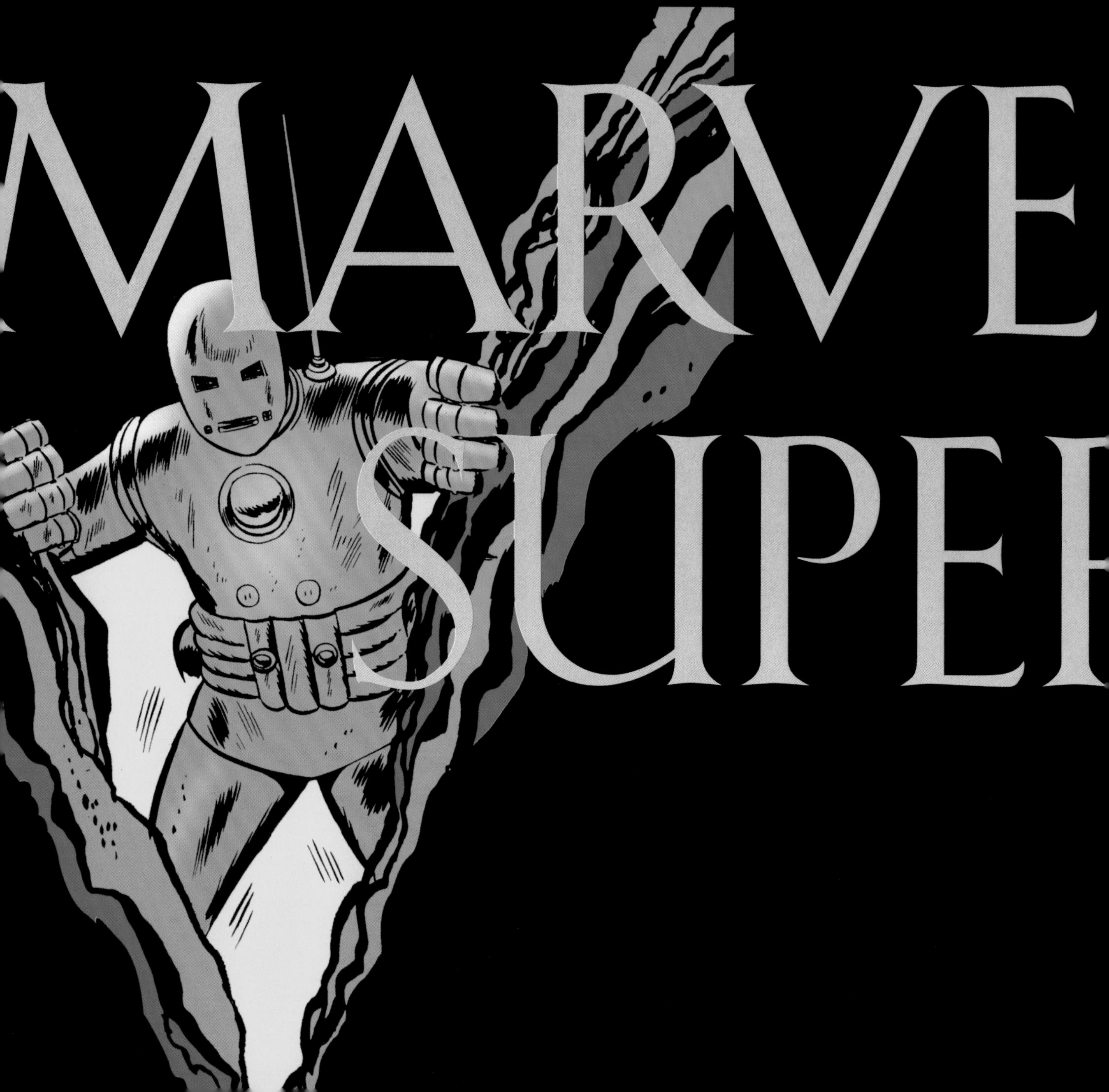
MARVE
SUPE

HEROES

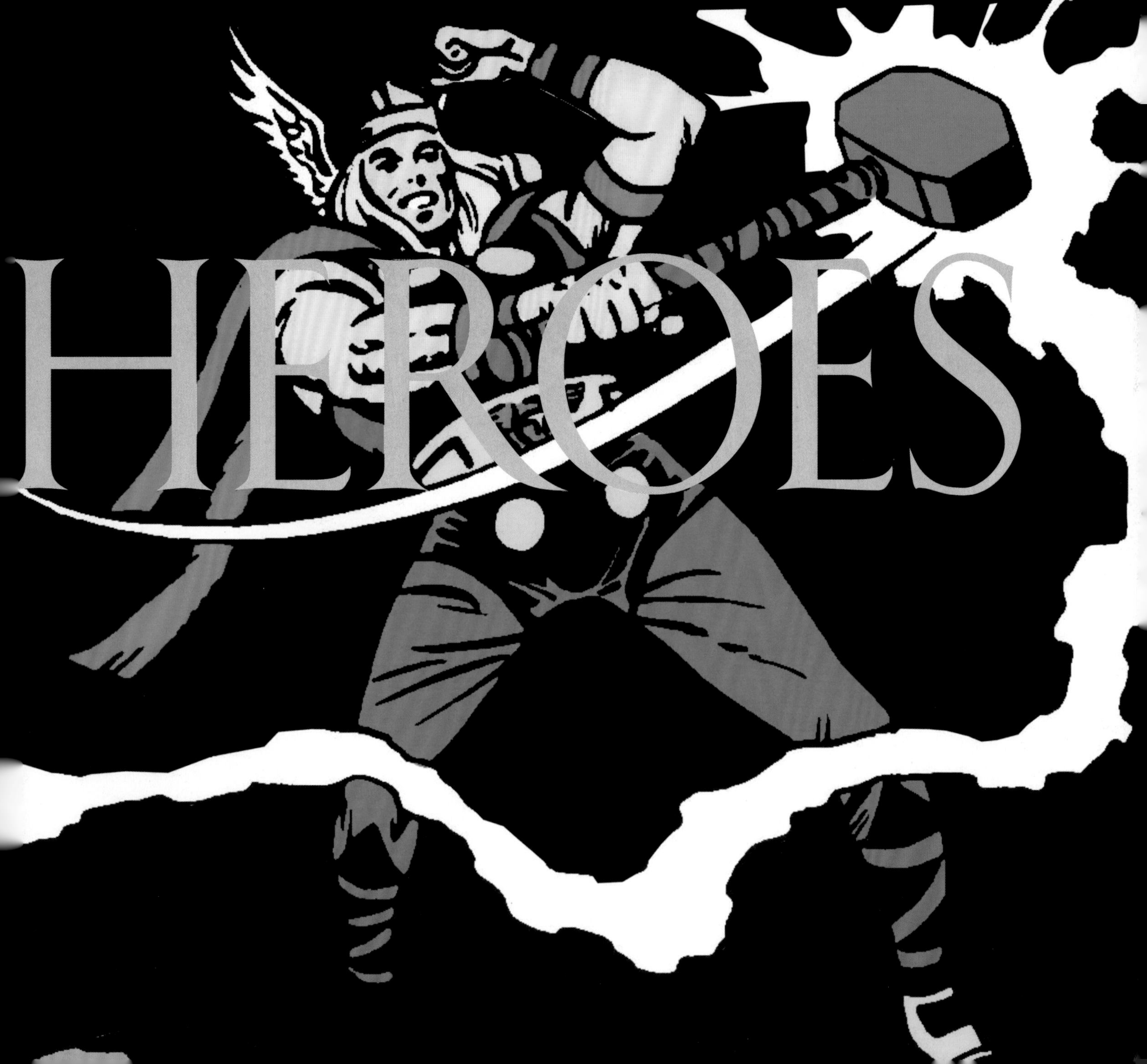

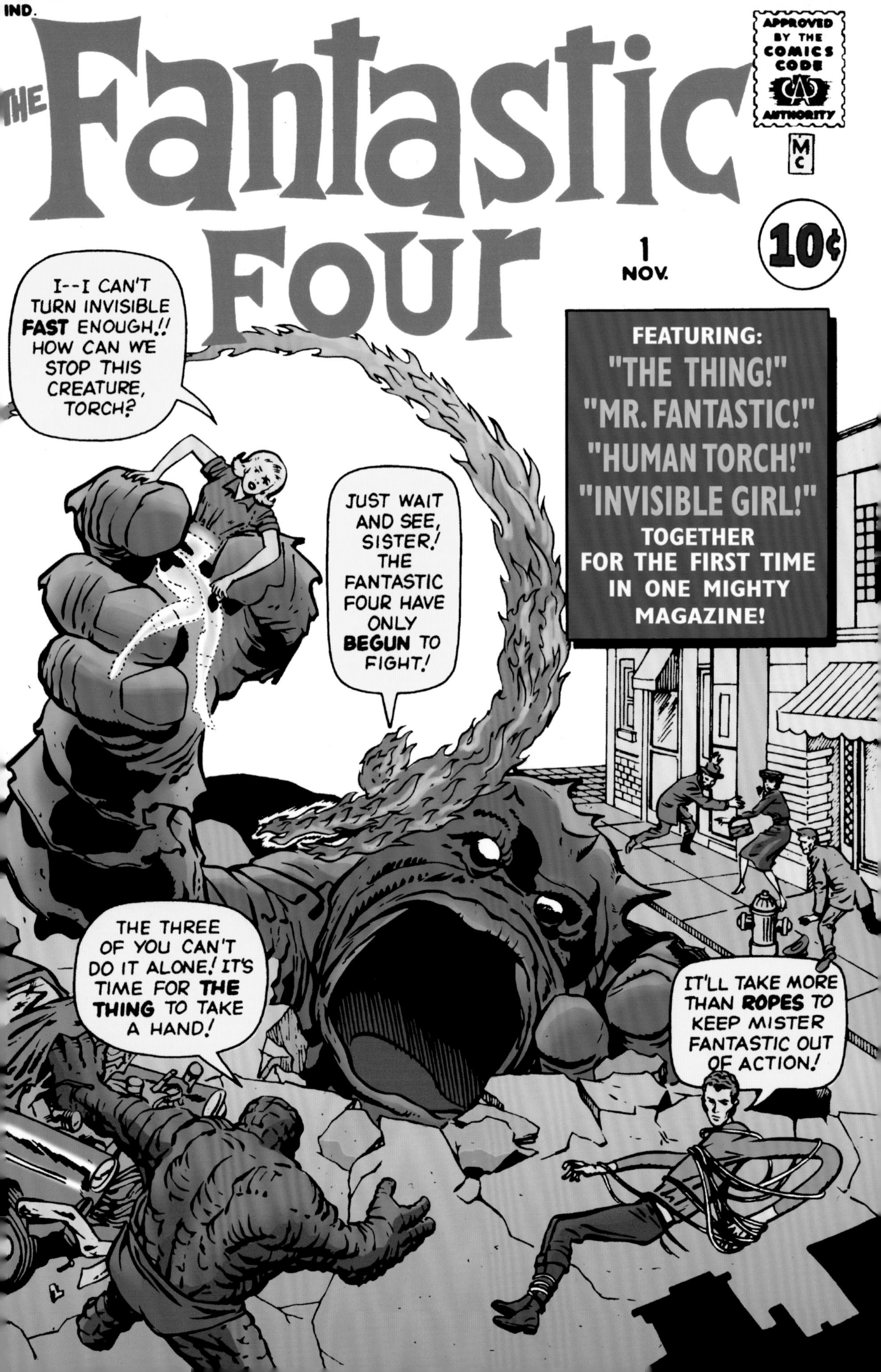
IND.
THE Fantastic Four
APPROVED BY THE COMICS CODE AUTHORITY
MC
10¢
1
NOV.
I--I CAN'T TURN INVISIBLE FAST ENOUGH!! HOW CAN WE STOP THIS CREATURE, TORCH?
FEATURING: "THE THING!" "MR. FANTASTIC!" "HUMAN TORCH!" "INVISIBLE GIRL!" TOGETHER FOR THE FIRST TIME IN ONE MIGHTY MAGAZINE!
JUST WAIT AND SEE, SISTER! THE FANTASTIC FOUR HAVE ONLY BEGUN TO FIGHT!
THE THREE OF YOU CAN'T DO IT ALONE! IT'S TIME FOR THE THING TO TAKE A HAND!
IT'LL TAKE MORE THAN ROPES TO KEEP MISTER FANTASTIC OUT OF ACTION!

MARVEL SUPERHEROES

ARRIVAL OF THE AVENGERS

The most amazingly creative and productive period in Marvel's history was between 1961 and 1964—three short years in which nearly all of its classic superheroes were introduced. It was a Platinum Age (or perhaps an Adamantium Age) that, if nothing else, proved that the boundaries of the Marvel Universe were unlimited.

THE FANTASTIC FOUR

Even though they have been somewhat overshadowed by the likes of Spider-Man and The Hulk, The Fantastic Four deserve a place of honor in the Marvel pantheon, because they were the characters that started it all. Like the Golden Age superheroes that had preceded them, The Four had strength, they had righteousness, and they had super powers. But unlike any character teams that had come before, they also had problems, worries, and arguments, just like real people. Little did readers of that debut issue in 1961 suspect that they were holding in their hands a bit of pop culture history in the making, for The Fantastic Four were not simply Marvel's first effort to revitalize the superhero genre in the 1960s, they were the impetus that set off the "Big Bang" itself.

FF issue #1 introduced to the world stern-faced, professorial Dr. Reed Richards, his levelheaded fiancé Susan Storm, Sue's hotheaded, impetuous younger brother Johnny, and Reed's best friend, the brawny, rough-edged, but highly intelligent Benjamin Grimm, in a story that was steeped in Cold War atmosphere. Richards is presented as America's secret weapon in the space race, which was then raging. He has created his own rocket ship and is striving to convince his friends and colleagues to accompany him "to the stars." It is not an easy task, since all are aware of the dangers involved, particularly the unknown consequences of being hit by "cosmic rays."

The fears of the team, as expressed by Ben Grimm, are justified: the rocket ship is bombarded by radiation, which causes it to crash back to earth. While

This is where it all started: the first issue of *The Fantastic Four"* (November 1961). Cover art by Jack Kirby (pencils) and Dick Ayers (inks).

the four are seemingly unharmed, they begin to evince strange talents: Sue becomes invisible, Johnny realizes that he can burst into flame and soar into the sky, Reed finds that his body now appears to be made of Silly Putty, and Ben changes into a rock-like beast with monumental strength. Initially startled by these developments, they pledge to use these newfound powers to help mankind, and dub themselves The Invisible Girl, The Human Torch, Mr. Fantastic, and The Thing, respectively.

The earliest FF stories were based in "Center City," which before long became a modern, recognizable New York. From their Manhattan headquarters in the Baxter Building, the Four battled equally fantastic adversaries such as The Mole Man, The Skrulls—a race of gargoylish, shape-shifting aliens—and The Sub-Mariner at his most virulent. Issue #3 introduced the team's uniforms—blue jumpsuits with a prominent "4" in a circular shield on the chest—which even The Thing attempted to wear, and the "Fantasticar," one of Reed's inventions, which enabled them to fly around the city. Initially resembling an airborne soapdish, the Fantasticar would later be given a much more streamlined design.

While the trappings of The Fantastic Four were fairly conventional for the genre (costumes, gadget-filled headquarters, fanciful vehicles), what set them apart from previous superhero teams were their personality foibles. Rare was the issue in which the grouchy-but-mordant Ben Grimm, whose battle cry of "It's clobberin' time!" became a signature catch phrase, didn't have it out with either Reed Richards (whom he delighted in calling "Stretcho," making the stuffy scientist sound like a forgotten Marx brother), or the flash-tempered Johnny Storm. Readers responded enthusiastically, and before long, the magazine was being hyped on the cover as "The Greatest Comic Magazine in the World!!"

Sweethearts Reed and Sue would eventually marry and have a son, Franklin (who from a very early age exhibited telepathic powers.) During her maternity leave from the group, Sue was replaced by Johnny's girlfriend,

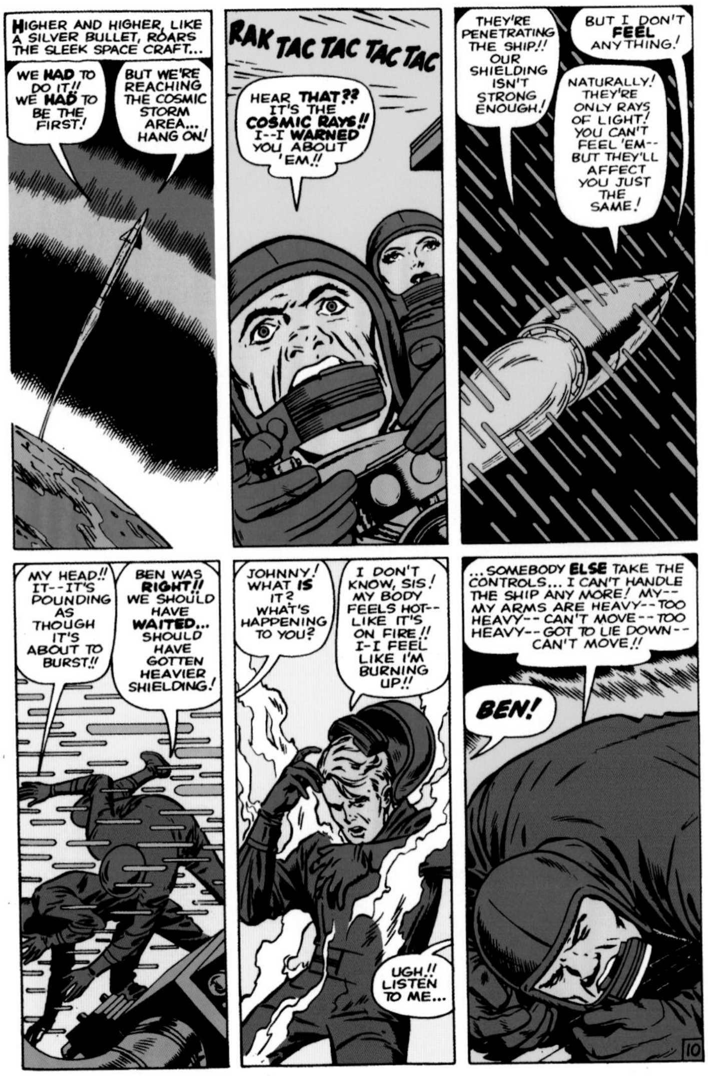
HIGHER AND HIGHER, LIKE A SILVER BULLET, ROARS THE SLEEK SPACE CRAFT...
WE HAD TO DO IT!! WE HAD TO BE THE FIRST!
BUT WE'RE REACHING THE COSMIC STORM AREA... HANG ON!
RAK TAC TAC TAC TAC TAC
HEAR THAT?? IT'S THE COSMIC RAYS!! I--I WARNED YOU ABOUT 'EM!!
THEY'RE PENETRATING THE SHIP!! OUR SHIELDING ISN'T STRONG ENOUGH!
BUT I DON'T FEEL ANYTHING!
NATURALLY! THEY'RE ONLY RAYS OF LIGHT! YOU CAN'T FEEL 'EM-- BUT THEY'LL AFFECT YOU JUST THE SAME!
MY HEAD!! IT--IT'S POUNDING AS THOUGH IT'S ABOUT TO BURST!!
BEN WAS RIGHT!! WE SHOULD HAVE WAITED... SHOULD HAVE GOTTEN HEAVIER SHIELDING!
JOHNNY! WHAT IS IT? WHAT'S HAPPENING TO YOU?
I DON'T KNOW, SIS! MY BODY FEELS HOT-- LIKE IT'S ON FIRE!! I-I FEEL LIKE I'M BURNING UP!!
UGH!! LISTEN TO ME...
...SOMEBODY ELSE TAKE THE CONTROLS... I CAN'T HANDLE THE SHIP ANY MORE! MY-- MY ARMS ARE HEAVY--TOO HEAVY--CAN'T MOVE--TOO HEAVY--GOT TO LIE DOWN--CAN'T MOVE!!
BEN!

The ill-fated rocket ship that turned a quartet of friends into the Fantastic Four. From issue #1.

(Opposite top) Sue Storm fashions the first FF costumes in The Fantastic Four #3 (March 1962).

(Opposite bottom) Wheras previous superhero teams were big happy families, personality conflicts characterized The Fantastic Four.

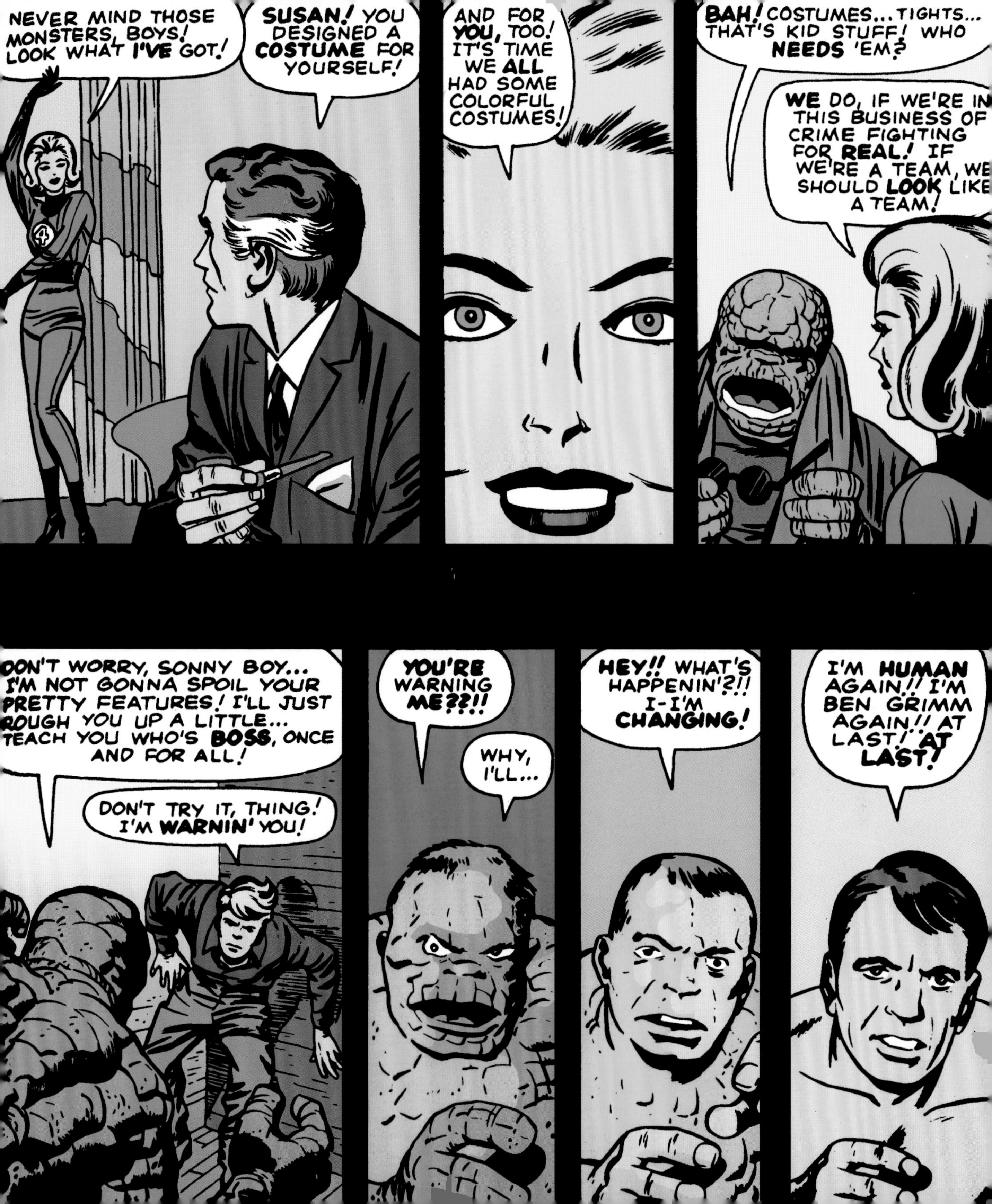
NEVER MIND THOSE MONSTERS, BOYS! LOOK WHAT I'VE GOT!
SUSAN! YOU DESIGNED A COSTUME FOR YOURSELF!
AND FOR YOU, TOO! IT'S TIME WE ALL HAD SOME COLORFUL COSTUMES!
BAH! COSTUMES... TIGHTS... THAT'S KID STUFF! WHO NEEDS 'EM?
WE DO, IF WE'RE IN THIS BUSINESS OF CRIME FIGHTING FOR REAL! IF WE'RE A TEAM, WE SHOULD LOOK LIKE A TEAM!
DON'T WORRY, SONNY BOY... I'M NOT GONNA SPOIL YOUR PRETTY FEATURES! I'LL JUST ROUGH YOU UP A LITTLE... TEACH YOU WHO'S BOSS, ONCE AND FOR ALL!
DON'T TRY IT, THING! I'M WARNIN' YOU!
YOU'RE WARNING ME??!!
WHY, I'LL...
HEY!! WHAT'S HAPPENIN'?!! I-I'M CHANGING!
I'M HUMAN AGAIN!! I'M BEN GRIMM AGAIN!! AT LAST! AT LAST!

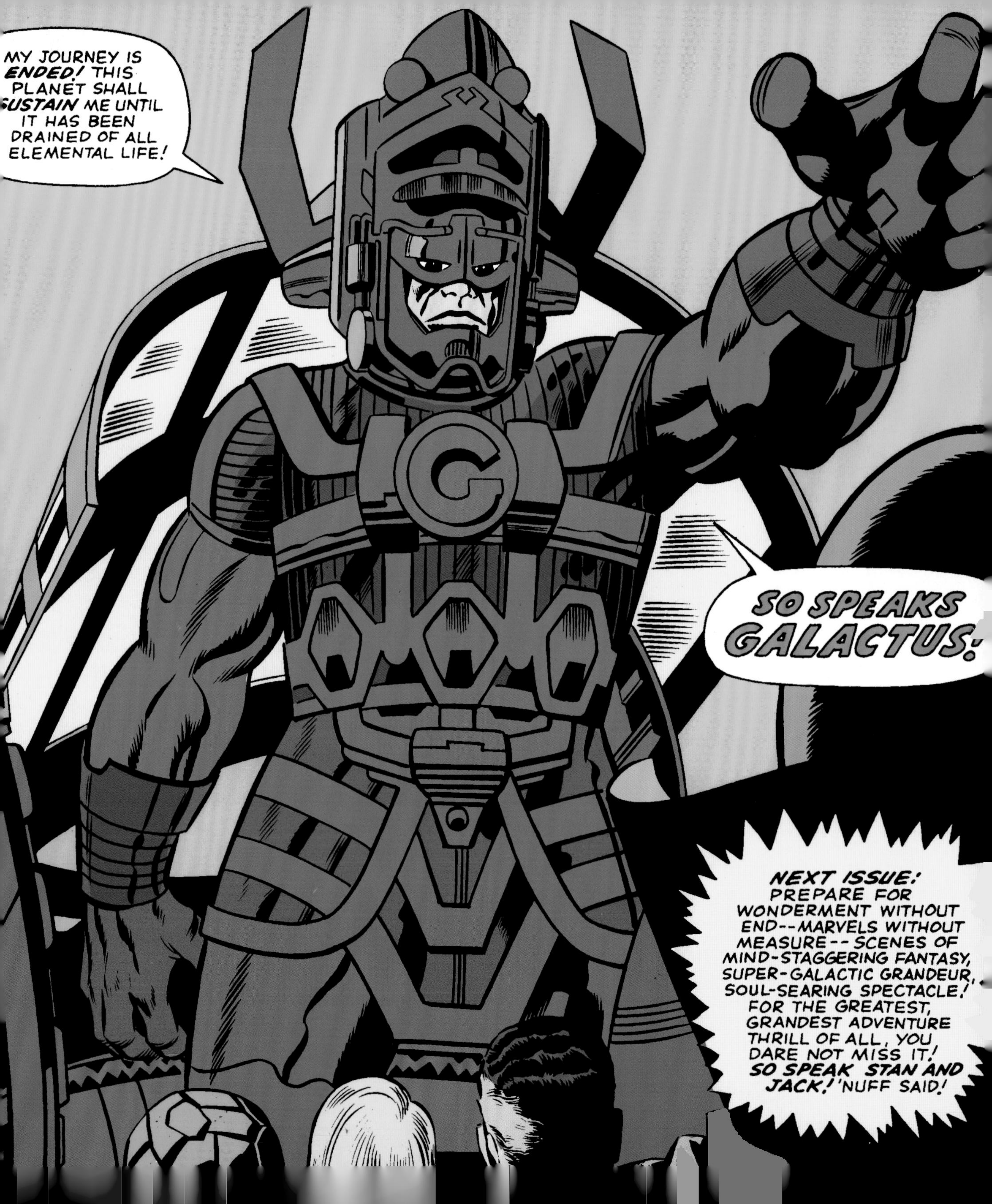
MY JOURNEY IS ENDED! THIS PLANET SHALL SUSTAIN ME UNTIL IT HAS BEEN DRAINED OF ALL ELEMENTAL LIFE!
SO SPEAKS GALACTUS!
NEXT ISSUE: PREPARE FOR WONDERMENT WITHOUT END--MARVELS WITHOUT MEASURE--SCENES OF MIND-STAGGERING FANTASY, SUPER-GALACTIC GRANDEUR, SOUL-SEARING SPECTACLE! FOR THE GREATEST, GRANDEST ADVENTURE THRILL OF ALL, YOU DARE NOT MISS IT! SO SPEAK STAN AND JACK! 'NUFF SAID!

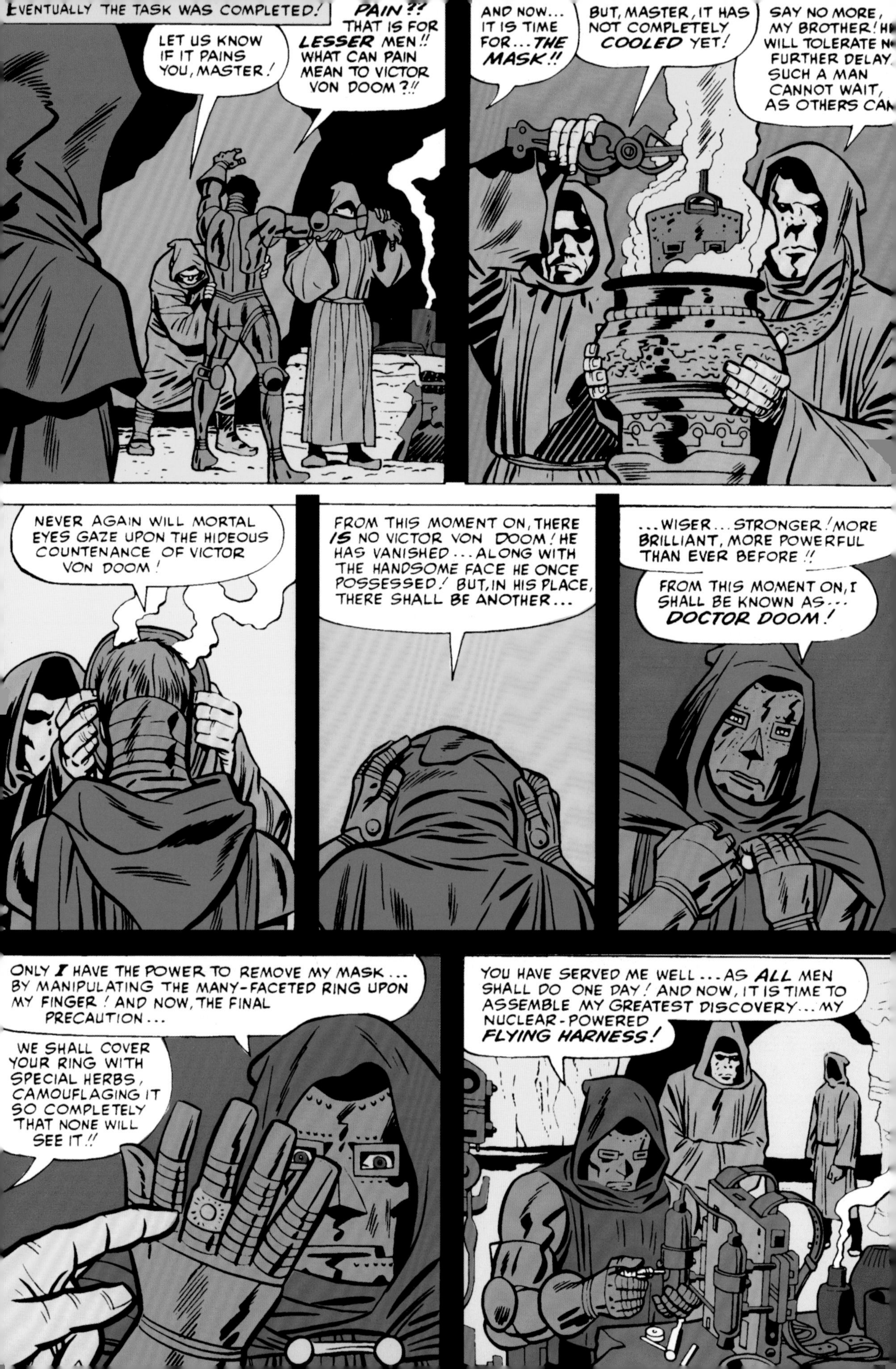
EVENTUALLY THE TASK WAS COMPLETED!
LET US KNOW IF IT PAINS YOU, MASTER!
PAIN?? THAT IS FOR LESSER MEN!! WHAT CAN PAIN MEAN TO VICTOR VON DOOM?!!
AND NOW... IT IS TIME FOR... THE MASK!!
BUT, MASTER, IT HAS NOT COMPLETELY COOLED YET!
SAY NO MORE, MY BROTHER! HE WILL TOLERATE NO FURTHER DELAY. SUCH A MAN CANNOT WAIT, AS OTHERS CAN
NEVER AGAIN WILL MORTAL EYES GAZE UPON THE HIDEOUS COUNTENANCE OF VICTOR VON DOOM!
FROM THIS MOMENT ON, THERE IS NO VICTOR VON DOOM! HE HAS VANISHED... ALONG WITH THE HANDSOME FACE HE ONCE POSSESSED! BUT, IN HIS PLACE, THERE SHALL BE ANOTHER...
...WISER... STRONGER! MORE BRILLIANT, MORE POWERFUL THAN EVER BEFORE!!
FROM THIS MOMENT ON, I SHALL BE KNOWN AS... DOCTOR DOOM!
ONLY I HAVE THE POWER TO REMOVE MY MASK... BY MANIPULATING THE MANY-FACETED RING UPON MY FINGER! AND NOW, THE FINAL PRECAUTION...
WE SHALL COVER YOUR RING WITH SPECIAL HERBS, CAMOUFLAGING IT SO COMPLETELY THAT NONE WILL SEE IT!!
YOU HAVE SERVED ME WELL... AS ALL MEN SHALL DO ONE DAY! AND NOW, IT IS TIME TO ASSEMBLE MY GREATEST DISCOVERY... MY NUCLEAR-POWERED FLYING HARNESS!

Crystal, an elemental who can mentally manipulate earth, air, fire, and water. Even Ben Grimm, embittered at being trapped inside the fearsome form of The Thing, found love through the sensitivity of blind sculptress Alicia Masters, stepdaughter of the villainous Puppet Master.

The Fantastic Four magazine would serve as the vehicle for introducing four of Marvel's most potent supporting characters: The Watcher, a benign, mysterious, otherworldly being who observes the actions of humans, as well as peoples on other planets; Galactus, a monstrous energy-devouring alien; The Silver Surfer, who began as Galactus's sentinel, but who quickly rose beyond supporting status to become a star character in his own right; and the ultimate villain Victor Von Doom, alias Doctor Doom.

If any one figure had to stand as the king of Marvel Supervillains, it is Doctor Doom, who was introduced in *FF* issue #5. The son of a gypsy woman who had been killed as a witch, and a doting, if fearful, father, Von Doom's brilliance was tempered by his thirst for forbidden knowledge. An experiment in college (where he was a classmate of both Richards and Grimm) resulted in an explosion that horribly disfigured him, physically and mentally, and forced him to hide forever behind a metal mask and medieval costume. As years went on he would blame Richards for this accident and devote himself to the tasks of destroying The Fantastic Four and taking over the world, plotting his schemes from a foreboding castle in the tiny European country he rules, Latveria.

Four decades after their creation, The Fantastic Four remain on the job, still fighting the never-ending battle to save the world . . . from Doom.

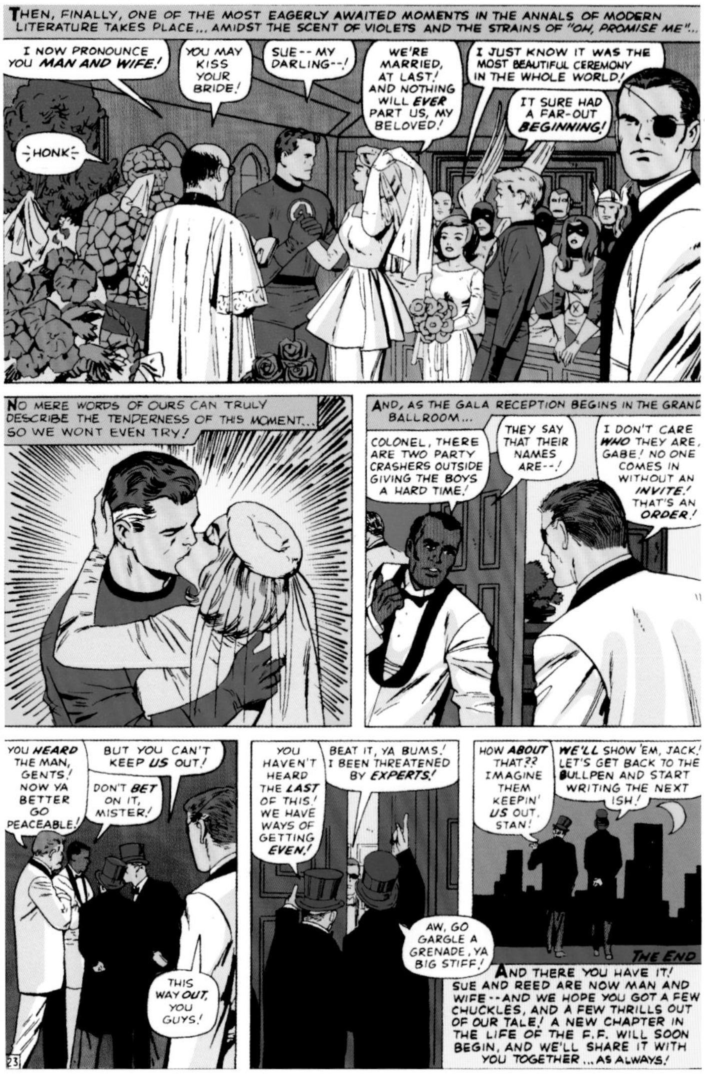
THEN, FINALLY, ONE OF THE MOST EAGERLY AWAITED MOMENTS IN THE ANNALS OF MODERN LITERATURE TAKES PLACE... AMIDST THE SCENT OF VIOLETS AND THE STRAINS OF "OH, PROMISE ME"...
I NOW PRONOUNCE YOU MAN AND WIFE!
YOU MAY KISS YOUR BRIDE!
SUE-- MY DARLING--!
WE'RE MARRIED, AT LAST! AND NOTHING WILL EVER PART US, MY BELOVED!
I JUST KNOW IT WAS THE MOST BEAUTIFUL CEREMONY IN THE WHOLE WORLD!
IT SURE HAD A FAR-OUT BEGINNING!
HONK
NO MERE WORDS OF OURS CAN TRULY DESCRIBE THE TENDERNESS OF THIS MOMENT... SO WE WONT EVEN TRY!
AND, AS THE GALA RECEPTION BEGINS IN THE GRAND BALLROOM...
COLONEL, THERE ARE TWO PARTY CRASHERS OUTSIDE GIVING THE BOYS A HARD TIME!
THEY SAY THAT THEIR NAMES ARE--!
I DON'T CARE WHO THEY ARE, GABE! NO ONE COMES IN WITHOUT AN INVITE! THAT'S AN ORDER!
YOU HEARD THE MAN, GENTS! NOW YA BETTER GO PEACEABLE!
BUT YOU CAN'T KEEP US OUT!
DON'T BET ON IT, MISTER!
THIS WAY OUT, YOU GUYS!
YOU HAVEN'T HEARD THE LAST OF THIS! WE HAVE WAYS OF GETTING EVEN!
BEAT IT, YA BUMS! I BEEN THREATENED BY EXPERTS!
AW, GO GARGLE A GRENADE, YA BIG STIFF!
HOW ABOUT THAT?? IMAGINE THEM KEEPIN' US OUT, STAN!
WE'LL SHOW 'EM, JACK! LET'S GET BACK TO THE BULLPEN AND START WRITING THE NEXT ISH!
THE END
AND THERE YOU HAVE IT! SUE AND REED ARE NOW MAN AND WIFE--AND WE HOPE YOU GOT A FEW CHUCKLES, AND A FEW THRILLS OUT OF OUR TALE! A NEW CHAPTER IN THE LIFE OF THE F.F. WILL SOON BEGIN, AND WE'LL SHARE IT WITH YOU TOGETHER... AS ALWAYS!
23

Reed Richards and Sue Storm tied the knot in *Fantastic Four Annual* #3. Compared to other wedded Marvel Superheroes, their marriage has been relatively problem-free.

THE FANTASTIC FOUR IN THE MEDIA

The Fantastic Four first blazed onto television screens in 1967, in an animated Saturday morning show produced for ABC by Hanna-Barbera. Comic book veteran (though a very infrequent Marvel Bullpenner) Alex Toth

(Previous spread left) The world-consuming behemoth Galactus was first introduced in *The Fantastic Four* #48 (1966).

(Previous spread right) Physically and mentally scarred Victor Von Doom assumes the persona of Doctor Doom, perhaps the ultimate Marvel supervillain. From *Fantastic Four Annual* #2 (1964).

DON'T WORRY, KID! YOU'RE SAFE AND SOUND! WE'RE ALL YOUR FRIENDS!
YOUR VOICE! YOU ARE THE STRONG, KINDLY ONE! BUT --YOU SEEM DIFFERENT NOW!
NO--WAIT! I-I WAS MISTAKEN! IT IS YOU-- IT IS THE SAME WONDERFUL MAN!
I'M BACK TO BEIN' THE THING AGAIN! IT MUST BE THAT CHEMICAL STUFF-- IT PROBABLY ONLY WORKS WHILE IT'S ON ME, BUT WHEN IT DRIES OFF, I GET BACK TO NORMAL! BUT THE CLINKER IS--SHE LIKES ME BETTER AS THE THING!

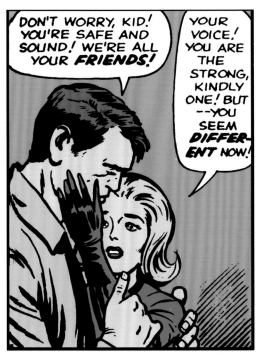

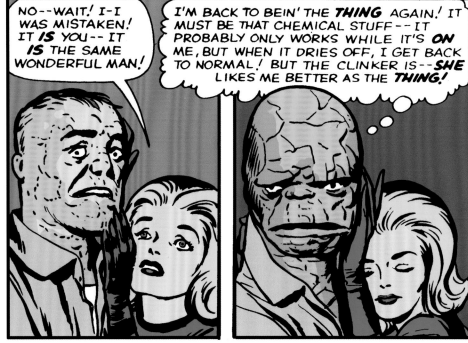

Love finds Ben Grimm in the form of blind Alicia Masters. From *The Fantastic Four* #8 (November 1962).

modeled the characters for their translation to limited animation. The series was notable for being one of very first "educational" cartoons on Saturday morning: in the middle of each episode, the action would stop long enough for Reed Richards to explain in simple terms such complex concepts as Einstein's theory of the universe or the construction of an atom. Movie actor Gerald Mohr provided the voice of Richards, while up-and-coming JoAnn Pflug (shortly to become a star in the movie version of *M*A*S*H*) voiced Sue, Jac Flounders portrayed Johnny, and cartoon veteran Paul Frees gave The Thing an amusing piratical delivery (Frees also voiced Doctor Doom). But despite the professionalism of the cast it was sometimes hard to get around such dialogue as, "We must hasten our return!" or "I must flee!" (The camp element might have come from the fact that the show's writers, Phil Hahn and Jack Hanrahan, normally wrote for such comedy shows as "Rowan and Martin's Laugh-In.") "The Fantastic Four" lasted two seasons.

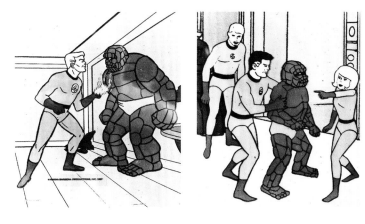

It would be a decade before the team returned to television, though once more it was as a Saturday morning cartoon series. "The New Fantastic Four," produced by DePatie-Freleng, premiered in the fall of 1978. It came with impressive credentials: Stan Lee and Roy Thomas wrote many of the scripts while Jack Kirby worked on storyboards. The designation "New" in the title referred to a new fourth member, a wisecracking robot named Herbie, who replaced Johnny Storm on the show. Why the sudden switch? "Irwin Allen [the sci-fi mogul behind TV's "Lost in Space" and "The Time Tunnel"] bought the rights to do a movie of 'The Human Torch,'" Lee explains. "He never made the movie but he had the rights, therefore we couldn't use The Human Torch in our cartoon. Since it was called 'The Fantastic Four,' we needed a fourth, and I didn't want to put a character in there that would contradict what the team had always been, so I figured we could get away with a robot."

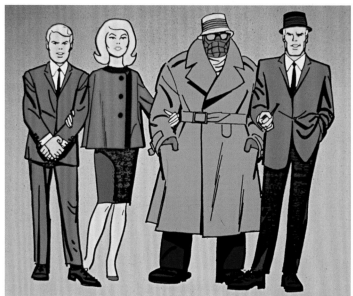

An invention of Reed's, the small, jelly bean–shaped Herbie (actually, HER-B, short for Humanoid Electronic Robot, B-Model) not only served as the team's mechanical housekeeper but also took over for Johnny as verbal sparring partner for The Thing (who was generally on his best behavior throughout this series).

"The New Fantastic Four" left the airwaves on September 1, 1979, and only three weeks later The Thing was back on NBC in what remains the most unusual packaging ever for a Marvel character, a Hanna-Barbera series called "Fred and Barney Meet the Thing." Fred and Barney were, of course, Bedrock's Fred Flintstone and Barney Rubble, who despite the title were seen in separate cartoon segments. In this version, The Thing had been changed back into a human through a scientific experiment, but instead of re-emerging as brawny, grown-up Ben Grimm, he becomes teenaged egghead "Benjy" Grimm, who takes time out from high school to fight crime. "Fred and Barney Meet the Thing" lasted under that title for two months before it was

Z-Z-1-2-3
ALL DIRECTIONS
ROBOT TALKS THRU SOUND BOX
4 FT. TALL IN RELATION TO HEIGHT OF AVERAGE MAN.
AIR JETS
JETS ENABLE Z-Z TO FLY · FLY AT GREAT SPEEDS
ALTHOUGH, CODE LETTERS "Z-Z" STANDS FOR ZERO-ZERO-ROBOT IS CALLED "ZEE-ZEE." "1-2-3" ARE COMMAND NUMBERS... WHEN YOU REPEAT NUMBERS, ROBOT PRODUCES EXTENSIONS HIDDEN IN BODY, WHICH CAN DO ANYTHING FROM VACUUMING THE FLOOR TO CONTROLLING A SPACE SHIP...
ZEE-ZEE DEFENDS ITSELF WITH CHEMICAL SPRAY HIDDEN IN HEAD UNIT... Z-Z-IS A CALCULATOR SECURITY GUARD, AUTOMATIC PILOT AND A GREAT COOK!

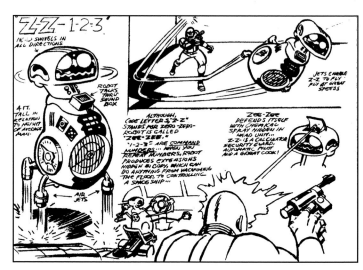

(Top left) Johnny Storm and The Thing try to settle their differences in animation, in 1967's "The Fantastic Four."

(Top right) The team leaps to action in limited animation in "The Fantastic Four."

(Middle) The Fantastic Four in street clothes from 1967's animated "The Fantastic Four."

(Above) Jack Kirby's original design sketch for "Z-Z-1-2-3," which evolved into Herbie the Robot.

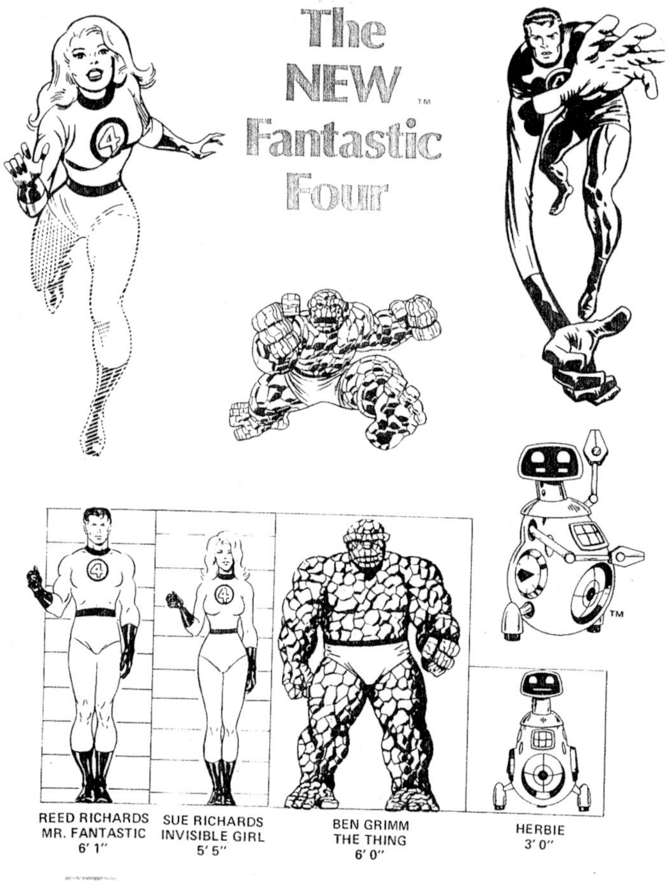
The NEW Fantastic Four
TM
REED RICHARDS MR. FANTASTIC 6′ 1″
SUE RICHARDS INVISIBLE GIRL 5′ 5″
BEN GRIMM THE THING 6′ 0″
HERBIE 3′ 0″

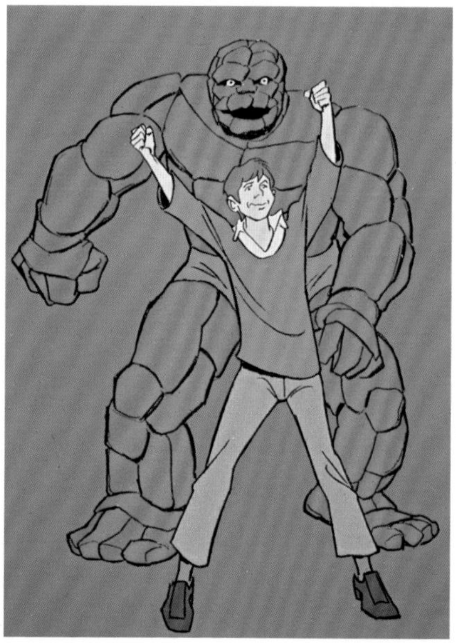

(Top) Advertising model sheet—complete with character heights—for a syndicated release of "The New Fantastic Four."

(Above) The Thing with teenaged Benjy Grimm, from "Fred and Barney Meet The Thing."

incorporated with "The New Shmoo," a half-hour series featuring Al Capp's shape-shifting newspaper strip character, to become the ninety-minute extravaganza, "Fred and Barney Meet the Shmoo." That version of the series ran until November 1980.

The Fantastic Four returned to animation in 1994 as one-half of "The Marvel Action Hour," produced by Marvel Films and New World Entertainment. The original four were once more united to face such enemies as Hydro-Man, Madame Medusa, and The Wizard. This time actor Chuck McCann, best known for his impersonation of comedian Oliver Hardy, provided the voice of The Thing.

To date there has been only one live-action adaption of The Fantastic Four, though it has become a modern legend that is known only to a small, hardy core of comic book and science fiction buffs. Titled *The Fantastic Four* (and not *Fantastic Four: The Movie,* as it is sometimes called), it was a full-length feature film shot in 1993, and starring Alex Hyde-White as Reed Richards, Rebecca Staab as Sue, Jay Underwood as Johnny, Michael Bailey-Smith as Ben (with stuntman Carl Ciarfalio taking over as The Thing), and Joseph Culp as Doctor Doom.

The story behind *The Fantastic Four* is as fascinating as the film itself, if not more so. It was the brainchild of German producer Bern Eichinger, whose previous films included *The Name of the Rose* and *The Never-Ending Story.* Eichinger bought the movie rights from Marvel through Neue Constantin Films, and planned to spend some $45 million on the project, making it a major production. But delays in getting the project started forced Eichinger into a corner: by the terms of the agreement, he had to be in production by the end of 1992, when the option expired, or else forfeit the rights. Eichinger decided to go forward with the project, but produce it as quickly and cheaply as possible. To that end he worked out a co-production deal with the legendary king of low-budget filmmaking Roger Corman, who was used to working around time and

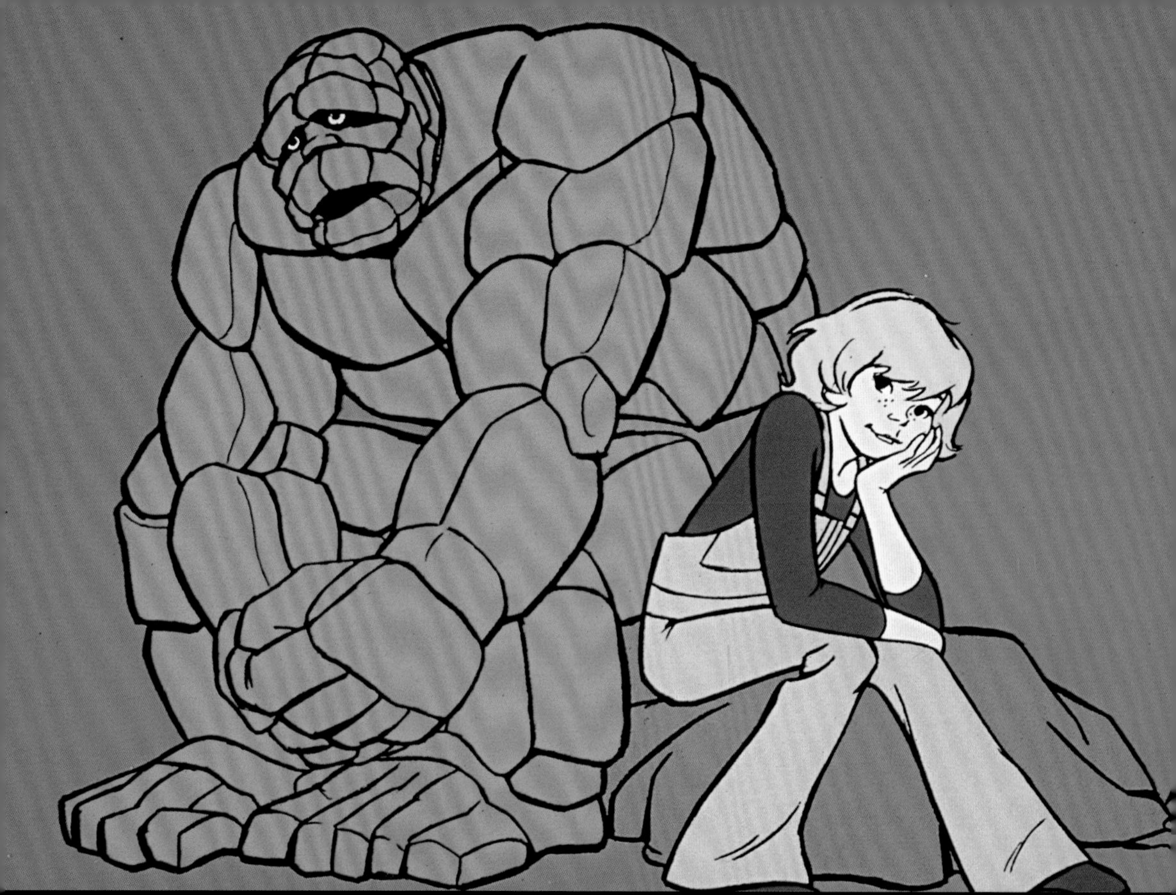

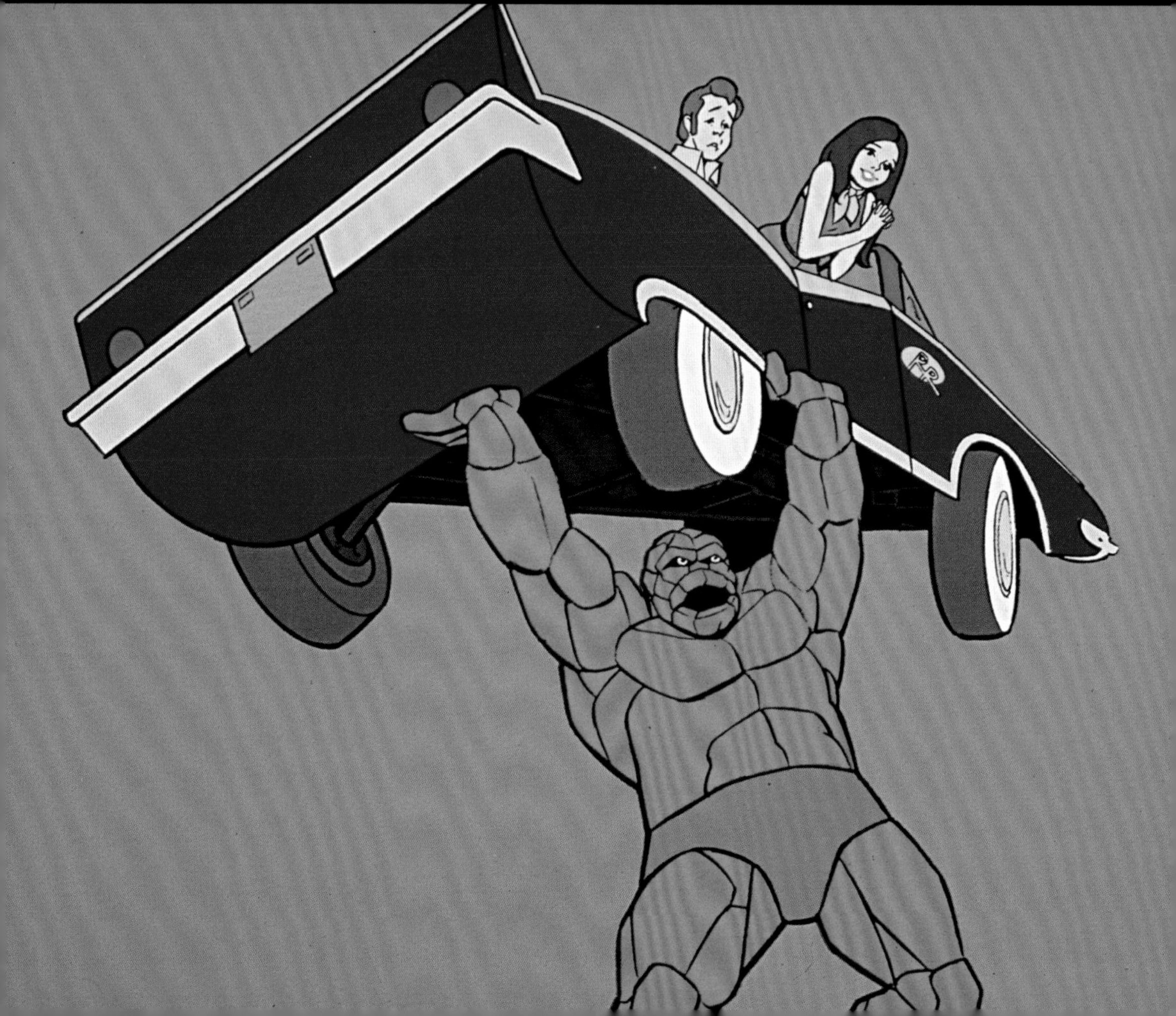

(Top) 1994's unreleased *The Fantastic Four* began with the college days of Reed Richards (Alex Hyde-White) and Ben Grimm (Michael Bailey Smith).

(Middle) Casting was one of the assets of the ill-fated *The Fantastic Four.* Left-to-right: Stuntman Carl Ciarfalio as The Thing, Rebecca Staab, Alex Hyde-White, and Jay Underwood as Johnny.

(Above) Richards and Grimm are puzzled that they have survived the crash of their rocket and have landed safely (and so, frankly, is the audience).

(Opposite top) Comedy was equally important to action in the animated "Fred and Barney Meet The Thing."

(Opposite bottom) Driver's Education, Thing style.

money constraints. (New York–based producer Lloyd Kaufman of Troma Films was also briefly considered.)

With little more than a finished script by Craig J. Nevius and Kevin Rock, director Oley Sasson began shooting on December 28, 1992—three days prior to the option's expiration date—at Corman's Concorde Studios in Venice, California. No corner was left uncut to stretch out the film's meager budget, which was announced as $2 million. Some who were connected with the project, though, speculate that it was closer to $750,000, an incredibly low sum for a feature film. Whenever possible, scenes were shot on existing sets from other Corman productions. Filming lasted twenty-eight days, after which the special effects teams took over to create more than one hundred effects shots.

By the fall of 1993, the PG-rated adventure was ready to go. *The Fantastic Four* recounted the origins of The Four and Doctor Doom and set them up as rivals for control of a "radioactive, comet-like energy source" called Colossus, which served as the primary conflict of the plot. A strange subplot had both The Four and Doom's minions caught up in the machinations of a bizarre, Fagin-like street criminal named The Jeweler.

Despite the minuscule budget, the film boasted good special effects, particularly a digitally rendered Human Torch in full burn, and a near-perfect Thing costume, complete with a fully articulated face mask, that was Jack Kirby's graphic vision brought to life. The acting of the leads was uniformly good, and while writers Nevius and Rock earned an E in science for allowing The Human Torch to outrun and intercept the end of Doctor Doom's laser beam, they contributed a clever addendum to the original mythology by postulating that the changes undergone by The Four were rooted in their character "defects." Thus Reed, who tends to stretch himself too thin, becomes a rubber man, while shy Sue disappears, hotheaded Johnny turns *really* hot, and Ben, who relies on brawn over brain, becomes a creature of brute strength.

The film was scheduled for a January 19, 1994, world premiere, not in Hollywood, but rather at the Mall of America near Minneapolis, Minnesota. Prompted by actors Hyde-White and Bailey-Smith, Concorde hired Hollywood public relations expert Jim Moore to create a notable, if unusual, publicity campaign that would have included having the stars ride on a float in the 1994 Tournament of Roses Parade! The film's trailer and its stars were big draws at comic book and sci-fi conventions. Posters were printed, and fans were poised and ready. Everybody, it seemed, wanted to see *The Fantastic Four,* but they would not get the chance. In a move that surprised nearly everyone, Eichinger paid Corman a cool million to get the film back, and then canceled all plans for its release, ostensibly because another, much more elaborate version of *The Fantastic Four*—much closer to the film that Eichinger had originally wanted to make—was by then in development with a major studio. As a result, *The Fantastic Four* went into the history books as the only movie that made a profit for its backer, in this case Roger Corman, without ever being released.

To this day *The Fantastic Four* has never been screened in public. Those who managed to see it often

(Top) As Doctor Doom, actor Joseph Culp mimicked the gestures drawn in the early days of the comic book by Jack Kirby.

(Above) The experiment of Victor Von Doom (Joseph Culp) goes awry, resulting in his becoming the nefarious Doctor Doom.

(Opposite) Doom holds Alicia Masters (Kat Green) hostage in his castle fortress.

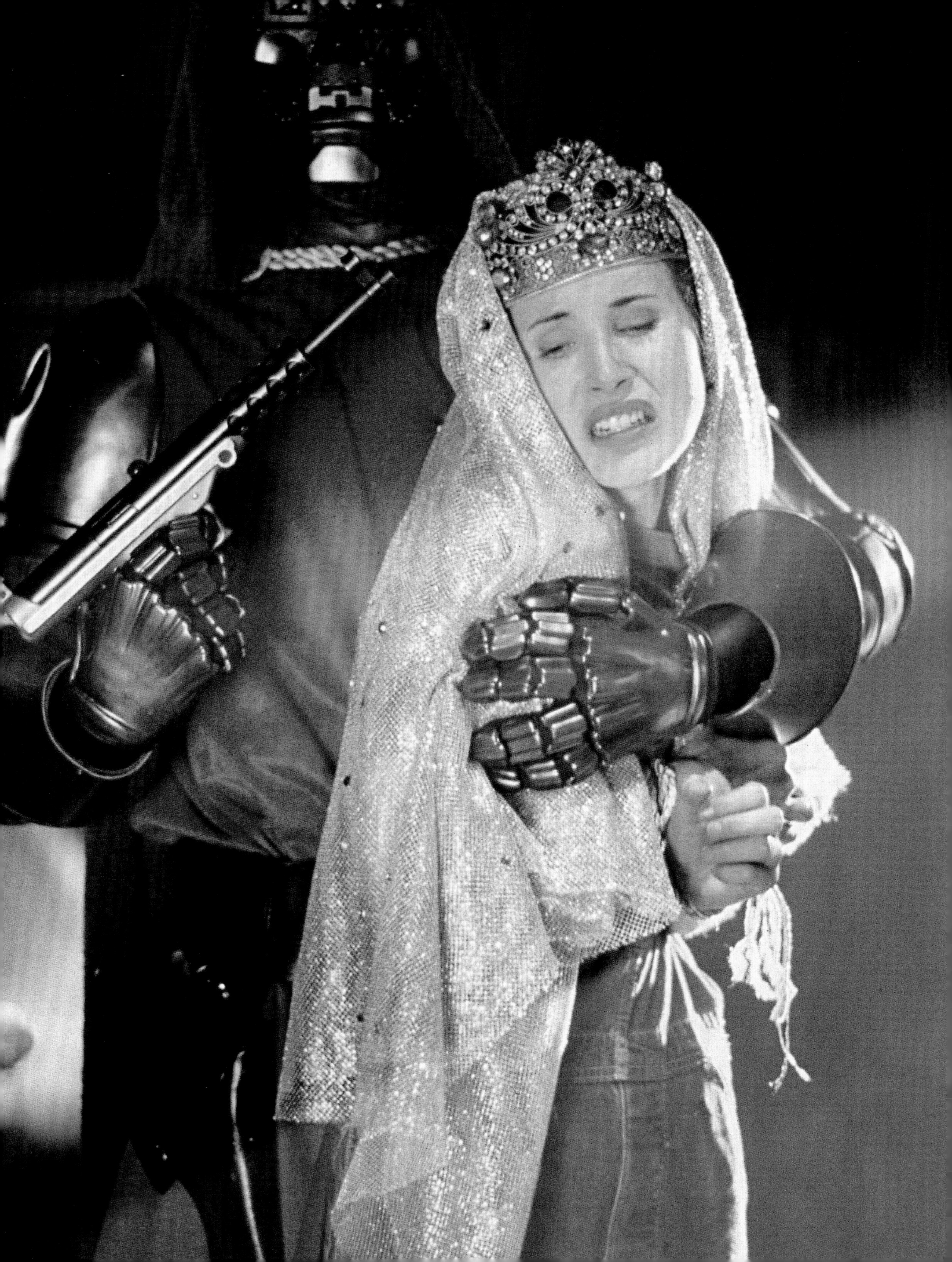

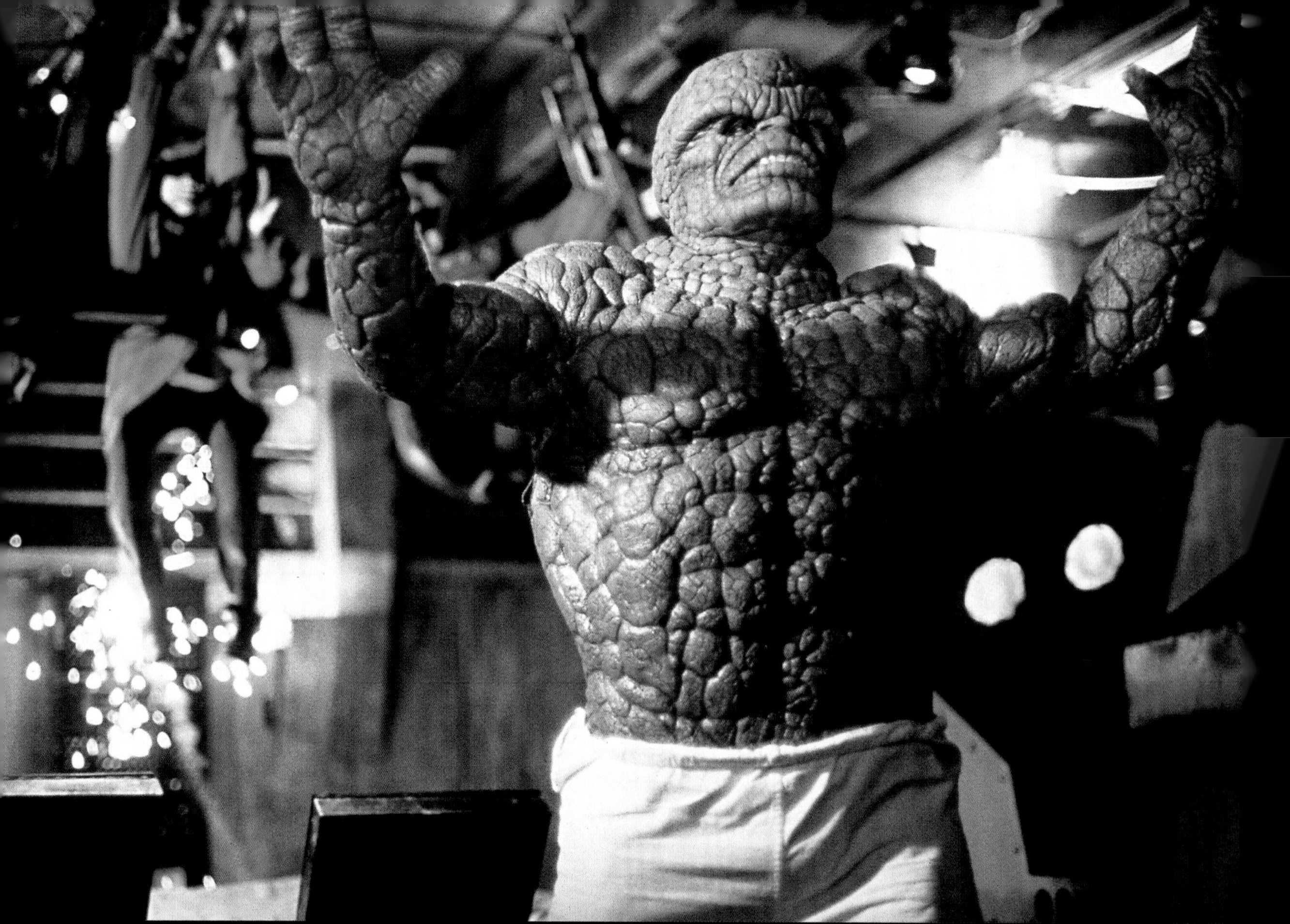

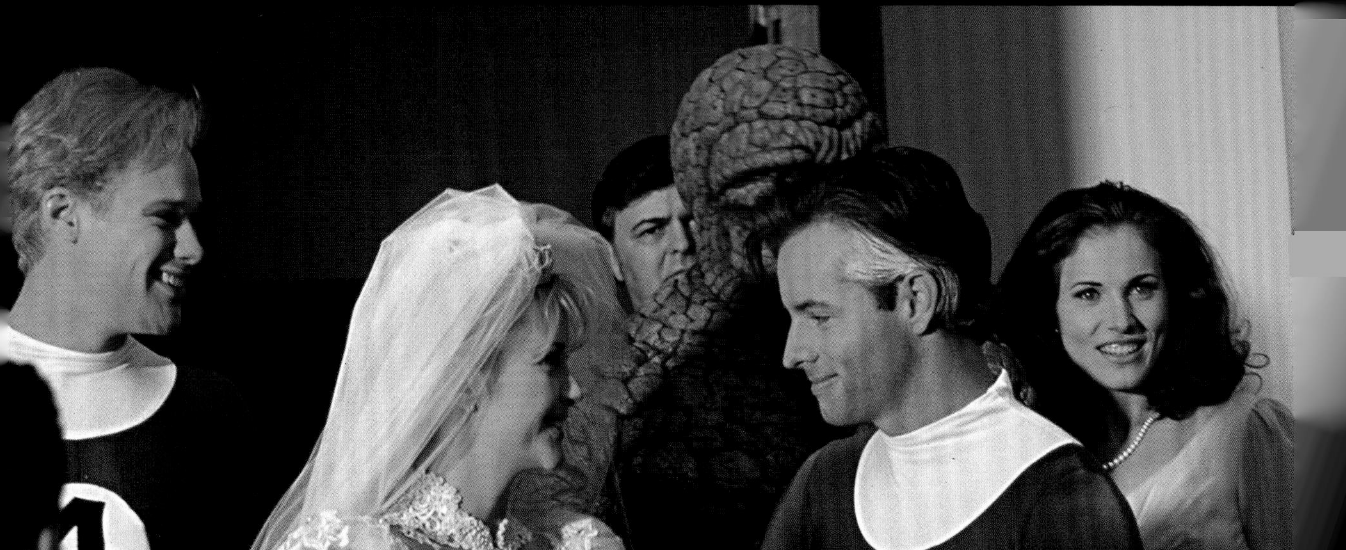

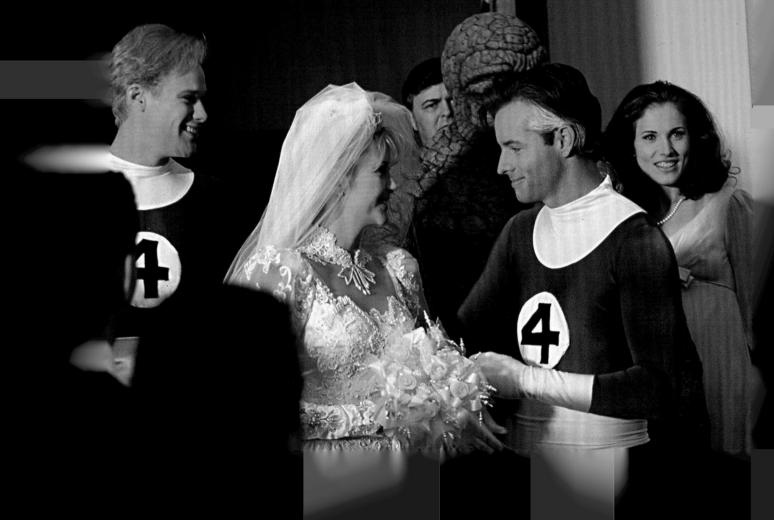

THEN, WITH HIS COLOSSAL STRENGTH, HE PROCEEDS TO WREAK HAVOC WITH THE UNDERWATER FLOTILLA!
PANIC REIGNS INSIDE THE SUB-TRAILERS
ALL HANDS AT BATTLE-STATIONS! RELEASE Nº 4 DEPTH-CHARGE! READY — FIRE!
IMMEDIATELY THE LETHAL "ASH-CAN" SPINS FROM THE DECK THRU THE MURKY WATER!
THEN —!
NAMOR, CAUGHT IN THE EXPLOSION, IS SENT TUMBLING GIDDILY ----
--- TO LAND SMACK AGAINST A BRICK BUILDING!
YEOW!

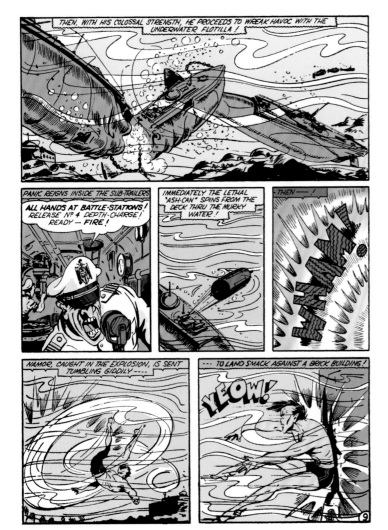

During wartime, Prince Namor was an Allied secret weapon. From *Marvel Mystery Comics* #26 (December 1941).

(Opposite top) "It's clobberin' time!" in 1994's *The Fantastic Four.*

(Opposite bottom) The wedding of Reed and Sue. A happy ending in *The Fantastic Four* did not translate to a happy ending for the movie itself.

defend it, on the basis of its budget, if nothing else. But the irony is that the film suffers from being too much like a comic book in its logic and plotting. What is acceptable on the comic page—such as depicting a scientist who builds his own rocket and invites his old school friends to come along for the ride—becomes fairly ludicrous when translated to the literalness of film.

How good or bad is *The Fantastic Four*? Perhaps Tom DeFalco, under whose editorial tenure the picture was made, sums it up best when he says, "I think it would have made a great syndicated television show. When you look at the final cut you can tell this was a labor of love, and I think if it was for the small screen it probably would have got a lot of laughs."

THE SUB-MARINER

While nearly all Marvel superheroes are forced to contend with a duality in their natures—everything from a secret identity to a borderline-split personality—Prince Namor, The Sub-Mariner, is unique in that his essential character and personality remain fixed. He is Prince Namor, period. But what makes the character so fascinating is that his sense of being, even something so basic as to whether he is a hero or a villain, alters radically depending on the point of view from which he is seen.

To his subjects in the undersea kingdom of Atlantis, Prince Namor is rightly regarded as a hero: brave, noble, regal, dedicated to his people, and never hesitant to defend them against any threat. To the terrestrial people of Earth, however—who in Namor's opinion *are* the threat—he is a powerful enemy, whose goal is to conquer the people of the land.

This richly complex character was created by Bill Everett in 1939, making The Sub-Mariner the first Marvel superhero. Prince Namor was part of a prehistoric race called *homo mermanus,* creatures that went back into the sea and evolved into an intelligent, water-breathing race rivaling the development of early humans. Over the centuries, they created a civilization,

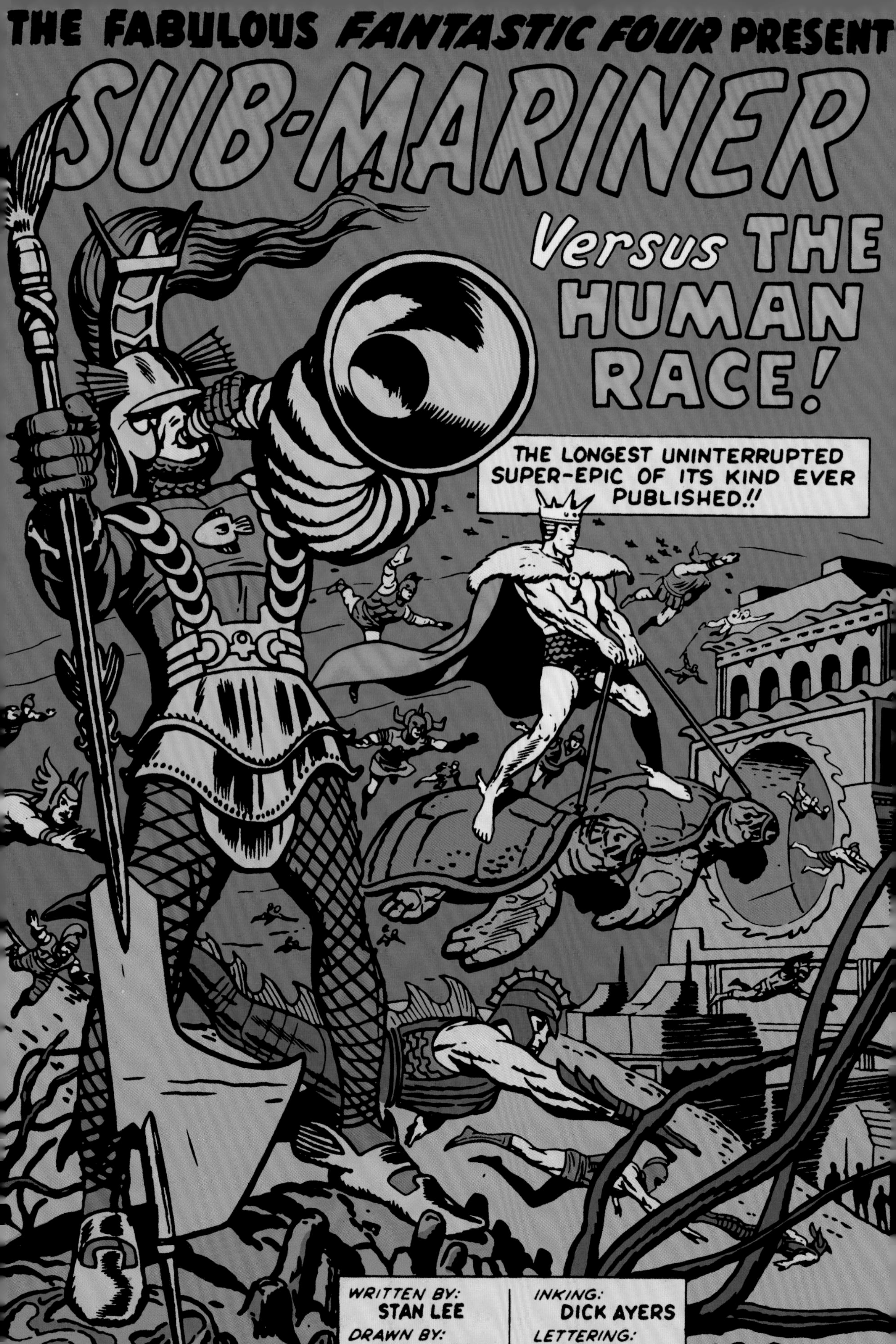
THE FABULOUS FANTASTIC FOUR PRESENT
SUB-MARINER
Versus THE HUMAN RACE!
THE LONGEST UNINTERRUPTED SUPER-EPIC OF ITS KIND EVER PUBLISHED!!
WRITTEN BY: STAN LEE
INKING: DICK AYERS
DRAWN BY: JACK KIRBY
LETTERING: ART SIMEK
COLORING: GLYNIS WEIN

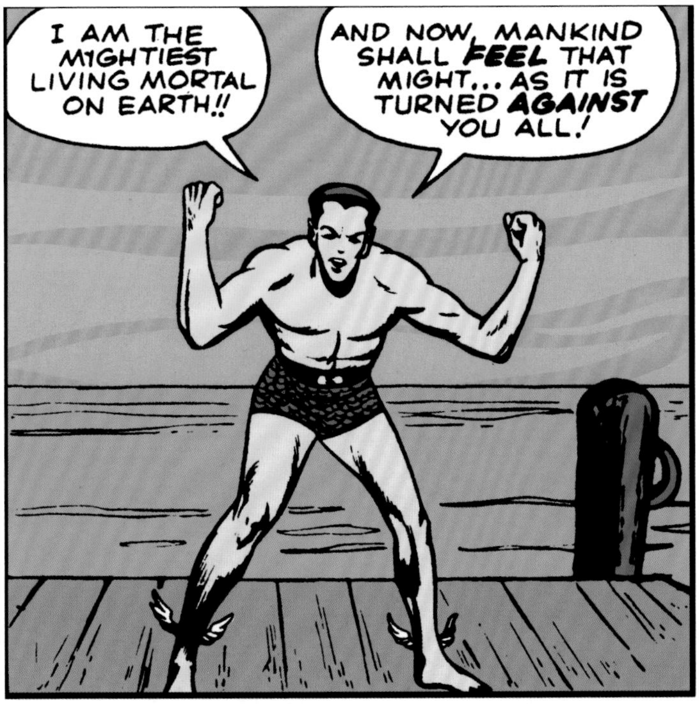
I AM THE MIGHTIEST LIVING MORTAL ON EARTH!!
AND NOW, MANKIND SHALL FEEL THAT MIGHT... AS IT IS TURNED AGAINST YOU ALL!

Revitalized in 1962, The Sub-Mariner was more of an anti-hero nemesis than ever. From *The Fantastic Four* #4 (May 1962).

(Opposite) Prince Namor was finally restored to his underwater throne in *Fantastic Four Annual* #1 (1963).

but also developed a taste for war. Although knowledge of this race is unknown to humankind for most of recorded history, the racial memory of *homo mermanus* remained with the terrestrials, leading to the universal legends of Atlantis.

Namor's duality of character stems from the fact that he is half-Atlantean, half-human. His father was Captain Leonard McKenzie, who, while commanding the icebreaker *Oracle* near the South Pole in 1920, disturbed the Atlanteans with the depth charges that were being used to shatter the ice. As a result, Thakorr, King of Atlantis, commanded his daughter, Princess Fen, to organize a scouting expedition to investigate the explosion. Personally taking charge of the operation, Fen (who took a potion that allowed her to breathe out of water for up to five hours), boarded the *Oracle,* and was discovered by Captain McKenzie, who quickly fell in love with her and married her. After several weeks, when Fen did not report back to Atlantis, the king feared the worst and sent a war party to the surface. In the ensuing battle, McKenzie was killed, though later Fen gave birth to Namor, the first of a new breed of humanoid amphibian.

Naturally able to breathe air for short periods of time, Namor could easily pass for a human, except for his unusually pointy ears and the tiny wings that adorn his ankles, which allow him to fly through the air. But despite his parentage, Namor has no love for the human race, though his stance softened somewhat during the war years, at least toward the Allied powers, whom Namor assisted in fighting against the Axis.

By the end of the 1940s, however, The Sub-Mariner's first official reign had come to an end. He was brought back in 1954, along with fellow Golden Agers Captain America and The Human Torch (the original, not Johnny Storm) for another short-lived run. It was only after Marvel's "Big Bang" in 1961 that The Sub-Mariner returned on a permanent level. The vehicle for his return was issue #4 of *The Fantastic Four,* published May 1962. In it, Johnny Storm, feeling unappreciated by

the rest of the team, storms out in a huff after yet another fight with Ben Grimm. With nowhere to go, he ends up in a Bowery flop house where he finds an old Sub-Mariner comic book. His consciousness now charged with tales of Prince Namor, Johnny quickly recognizes one of the bearded derelicts at the house as The Sub-Mariner himself, suffering from amnesia! (How Namor was able to survive on land breathing air for so long was not explained.) "Flaming on" as The Human Torch, Johnny picks Namor up, carries him over the sea, and drops him in, which shocks the memory back into the one-time prince. Once back in the water, Namor swims back to his undersea kingdom, only to find it destroyed. Naturally, he blames humans and their underwater radioactive testing, which only forges his hatred of humankind, and once again vows revenge on the world above. (Namor was, however, given a chance to show his softer side, by carrying a semi-human torch for Sue Storm.)

Eventually, Namor found his long-lost people (in a graphic novella published in 1963 as *The Fantastic Four Annual* #1), including his true love, Lady Dorma, who was by then promised to a traitorous warlord named Krang. Namor is crowned king of the mer-people, but soon learns that life as a ruler has its disadvantages, including the fickle nature of one's subjects. Early in his underwater reign, Namor found himself abandoned and rejected by the mer-people because of the affection he demonstrated for Sue Storm. Ultimately, Namor regained the trust of his people, and wed Lady Dorma, only to see her killed immediately after the ceremony.

THE SUB-MARINER IN THE MEDIA

If The Sub-Mariner has been one of the least visible of Marvel's A-list superheroes in other media, it is not for lack of trying. The mid-1950s found a number of Hollywood television producers looking around for superhero characters to exploit, in the wake of the hugely

(Top) The Sub-Mariner that never was: Actor Richard Egan was cast as Prince Namor in a proposed 1950s television series that sank.

(Above) Patrick Duffy as the Namorish "Man from Atlantis," a series that aired on NBC in 1977 and 1978.

(Top left to right) Original Namor cel from the "Marvel Superheroes" series. The animation in the 1966 Sub-Mariner cartoons was so limited that even the bubbles were sometimes stationary.

(Above) Lady Dorma lies unconscious in a cel set-up from 1966's "Marvel Superheroes."

(Following page) Don Blake miraculously changed into the Norse thunder god Thor for the first time in *Journey Into Mystery* #83 (August 1962).

popular "Superman" television series. Marvel (then Atlas), which had recently revived Prince Namor in magazine form, was courted by a group of investors with regard to adapting the character for television, with creator Bill Everett serving as series consultant. Actor Richard Egan, a popular, if stolid leading man of the time, was cast as Prince Namor, and underwater test footage was shot. After that the project fell apart for undisclosed reasons—not, it is safe to assume, because of the difficulty of shooting underwater sequences, as the popular series "Sea Hunt" would shortly prove.

Prince Namor finally arrived on television screens in 1966 in animated form, as part of "The Marvel Superheroes." Since the emphasis for the series was on superheroics rather than anti-heroics, the stories for Namor were largely confined to his underwater adventures as king of Atlantis, where he confronted such opponents as the nefarious Warlord Krang.

Due to budget restrictions, scenes of Namor soaring through the air or rising through the water were often not animated at all in the conventional sense, but were, rather, stationary paintings of Namor that were given the illusion of movement by passing them under the camera. In fact, in some scenes, the only actual animation was in the area of special effects, such as rising bubbles. But the graphics, which were taken directly from the original comic book art, showed off the staging and lighting to great advantage. (Many of the stories were taken directly from the comics as well, though when those ran out it was up to June Patterson to create original ones.) Actor John Vernon, who went on to star in Alfred Hitchcock's *Topaz* and later, *National Lampoon's Animal House,* as the venomous Dean Wormer, provided the resonant voice of Prince Namor.

Since then, no television or film adaptions of The Sub-Mariner have been made, though Namor's influence could certainly be detected in the popular NBC television series "The Man from Atlantis," which debuted as a television movie in March of 1977 and became a series in September of that year—the same

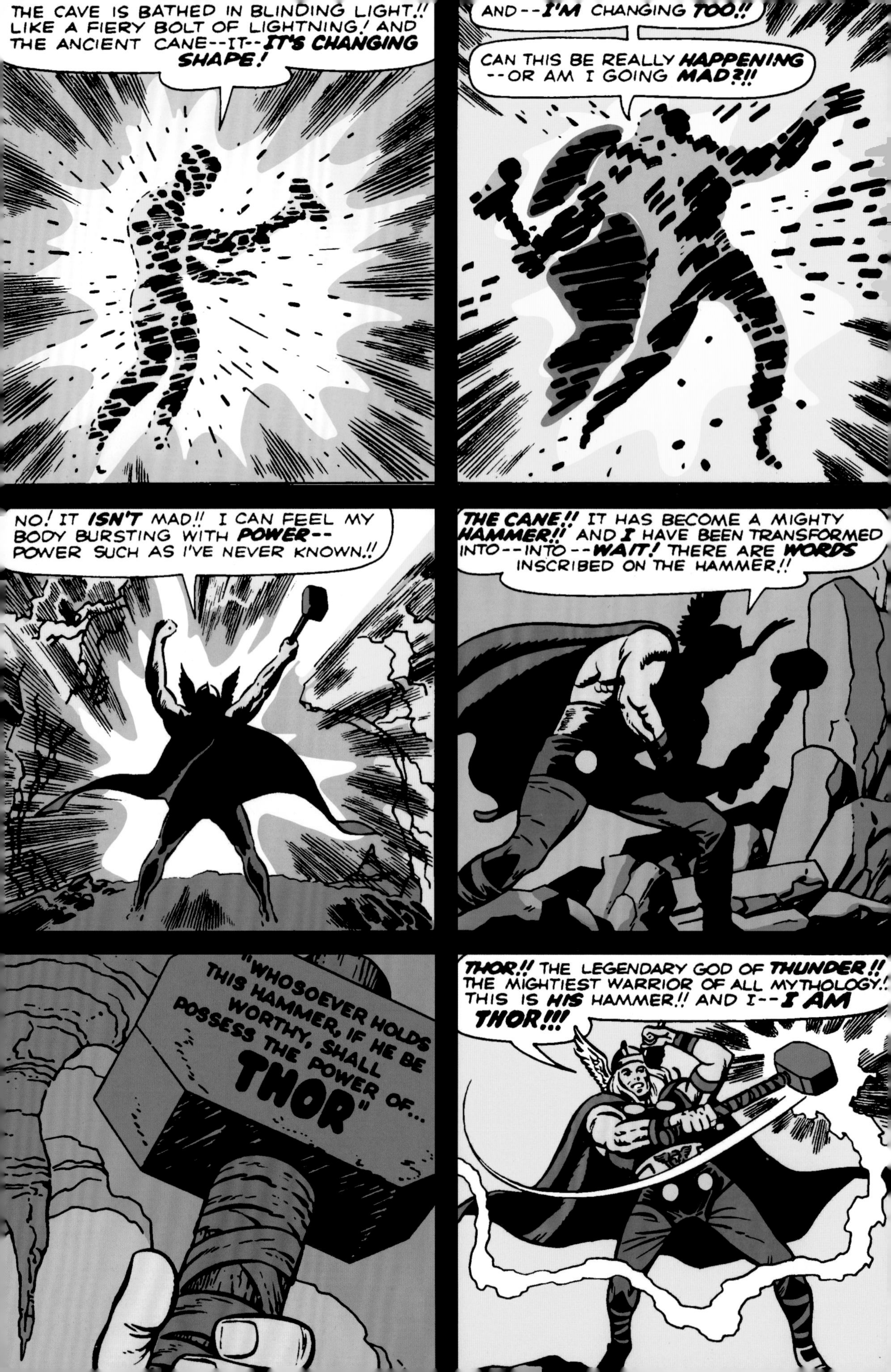
THE CAVE IS BATHED IN BLINDING LIGHT!! LIKE A FIERY BOLT OF LIGHTNING! AND THE ANCIENT CANE--IT--IT'S CHANGING SHAPE!
AND--I'M CHANGING TOO!!
CAN THIS BE REALLY HAPPENING --OR AM I GOING MAD?!!
NO! IT ISN'T MAD!! I CAN FEEL MY BODY BURSTING WITH POWER-- POWER SUCH AS I'VE NEVER KNOWN!!
THE CANE!! IT HAS BECOME A MIGHTY HAMMER!! AND I HAVE BEEN TRANSFORMED INTO--INTO--WAIT! THERE ARE WORDS INSCRIBED ON THE HAMMER!!
"WHOSOEVER HOLDS THIS HAMMER, IF HE BE WORTHY, SHALL POSSESS THE POWER OF... THOR"
THOR!! THE LEGENDARY GOD OF THUNDER!! THE MIGHTIEST WARRIOR OF ALL MYTHOLOGY! THIS IS HIS HAMMER!! AND I--I AM THOR!!!

BURI GREW WISE, AND STRONG, AND ONE DAY TOOK HIM A WIFE! THEN HE HAD A SON NAMED BORR! AND YEARS LATER BORR WAS MARRIED AND HAD THREE SONS OF HIS OWN! BUT OH, WHAT SONS THEY WERE! FOR ONE WAS NAMED -- ODIN!!!
ODIN!! CALLED THE ALL-FATHER! ODIN!! GREATEST OF ALL NORSE GODS! ODIN! SUPREME WARRIOR WHO SLAYED THE LAST OF THE ICE GIANTS, THUS BRINGING ABOUT THE FIRST TRIUMPH OF GOOD OVER EVIL!
ODIN, AND TWO BROTHERS SOON TURNED THEIR ATTENTION TO EARTH! FOR THERE WAS MUCH ABOUT EARTH THAT WAS BEAUTIFUL--MUCH ABOUT EARTH THAT THEY LOVED! AND SO, THEY SET A RING AROUND THE PLANET, AND THE MAGIC TREE YGGDRASILL GREW UP AND SPREAD ITS BRANCHES OVER EARTH, AND PROTECTED IT WHILE AWAITING THE COMING OF MAN!
NEXT ISSUE: WE SHALL GO BACK STILL FURTHER TO BRING YOU, IN FASCINATING DETAIL, THE BATTLE BETWEEN ODIN AND THE EVIL ICE GIANTS -- THE MOST EPIC BATTLE OF ALL TIME!
The END

IND.
12¢
JOURNEY INTO
MYSTERY
APPROVED BY THE COMICS CODE AUTHORITY
MC
85 OCT
I CHALLENGE YOU TO MATCH YOUR POWERS AGAINST MINE, THOR!
NEVER BEFORE HAS THE MIGHTY THOR FACED A FOE AS DANGEROUS AS LOKI, THE GOD OF MISCHIEF!!
TAKE THESE OTHER JOURNEYS INTO MYSTERY IN THIS GREAT ISSUE...
"FILBERT'S FRIGHTFUL FUTURE!"
"OFF-LIMITS!"
IT IS LOKI, MY SWORN ENEMY! HE HAS FOUND ME AT LAST!

(Top) Despite his heroic deeds on Earth, Thor's father, Odin, ruler of the Gods, was often hard to impress.

(Above) The evil trickster Loki was a perennial thorn in Thor's side.

season that Spider-Man and The Hulk made their live-action television debuts. The submergible hero of that series, Mark Harris (played by a pre-"Dallas" Patrick Duffy), was the last descendant of a lost race of Atlanteans, who had webbed fingers and toes, super-strength, and gills for underwater breathing. He could also stay on dry land for up to twelve hours. Even without the pointy ears, ankle wings, and attitude problem toward humans, Mark Harris was virtually Prince Namor's twin brother, right down to his Speedo.

THE MIGHTY THOR

Some superheroes are aliens, some are mutants, and some have been genetically altered in some form or other. There are even superheroes who are just plain "super," without much explanation as to why. But it is rare to find a superhero who is actually a god.

After the initial success of The Incredible Hulk, and fueled by the readership's growing taste for superheroes, Stan Lee sat down once more to puzzle over what kind of creation would be a fitting and natural follow-up. "We were looking for something bigger and stronger than The Hulk," Lee says, "and the only type of person that could be would have to be a god, so there we were. I figured, let's do a demigod, so to speak." Reasoning that Roman and Greek gods had been done ad infinitum both in and out of classrooms, he turned to Norse mythology, which was still largely untapped for consumption by the general public. It did not take long for Lee to come up with the name "The Mighty Thor." "I liked the name, I like adjectives for names, and The Mighty Thor sounded good to me." (For the record, a 1940 Fox Features Syndicate one-shot magazine called *Weird Comics* featured a superhero named Thor.)

Once again, Jack Kirby was called on for the artistic duties and Lee devised an outline of the plot. For the actual scripting, though, Lee turned to Larry Lieber. Among Lieber's contributions to the first Thor story was dubbing the demigod's magical hammer the "Uru hammer," which Lee initially believed was an actual kind of ancient weapon, a fact recovered from obscurity through diligent research. Some years later, according to Lee, Lieber confessed to simply making the name up. But like "The Mighty Thor" itself, it sounded good.

Thor's debut was in the pages of *Journey Into Mystery* #83, August 1962. The fanciful story centered around Dr. Don Blake, a frail, cane-toting physician who is vacationing on the coast of Norway. He happens to pick the wrong time for travel, however, as a space ship from Saturn suddenly lands and three aliens (who resemble the mysterious statues on Easter Island) step out, intent on invading Earth. Having stumbled upon the Saturnians, Blake attempts to flee, and ends up hiding out in a cave, where he discovers an ageless chamber that contains a rough-hewn walking stick. While attempting to use the stick to pry loose a boulder that is blocking the cave's exit, Blake strikes the stick against the boulder and immediately he transforms into The Mighty Thor. The cane similarly transforms, becoming the Uru hammer, which bears the quasi-Arthurian inscription: "*Whosoever holds this hammer, if he be worthy, shall possess the power of THOR.*"

Thor uses that power to defeat the aliens and send them home. He also teaches himself how to "fly" by swinging the hammer around with all his might, then letting go of it, but keeping a grip on the handle's leather strap so that it would pull him along through the air, a twist that delighted Lee. "The thing I was proudest of was the way I figured out how he could fly," Lee says. "I used to joke in college lectures and say, 'When Superman flies, he has no visible means of propulsion, but with Thor, we established a very sound scientific basis for the way he flies.'"

Future stories would flesh out Thor's otherworldly existence in Asgard, the realm of the gods, which is located at the edge of infinity across a "shimmering rainbow bridge." These would focus in particular on Thor's sometimes stormy relationship with his father, Odin, ruler of the pantheon of Norse gods and

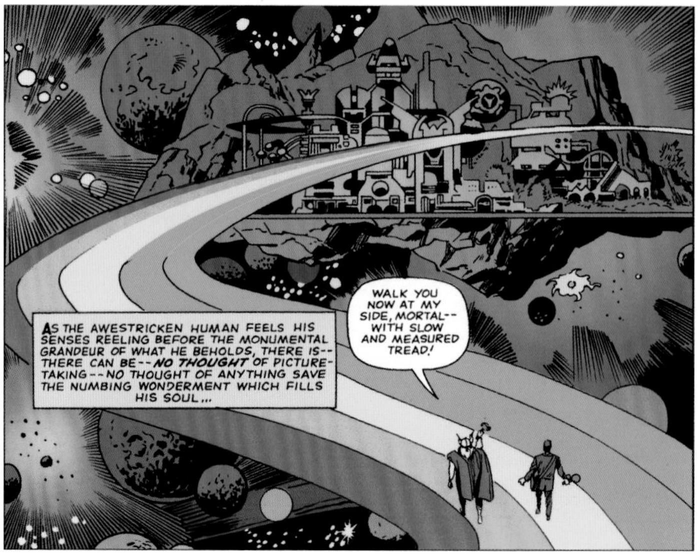
AS THE AWESTRICKEN HUMAN FEELS HIS SENSES REELING BEFORE THE MONUMENTAL GRANDEUR OF WHAT HE BEHOLDS, THERE IS-- THERE CAN BE--NO THOUGHT OF PICTURE-TAKING--NO THOUGHT OF ANYTHING SAVE THE NUMBING WONDERMENT WHICH FILLS HIS SOUL...
WALK YOU NOW AT MY SIDE, MORTAL--WITH SLOW AND MEASURED TREAD!

As time went on, Thor's comic book adventures increasingly took place in the mystical land of Asgard.

(Opposite) Another Marvel identity crisis: in the early 1990s, Eric Masterson became Thor.

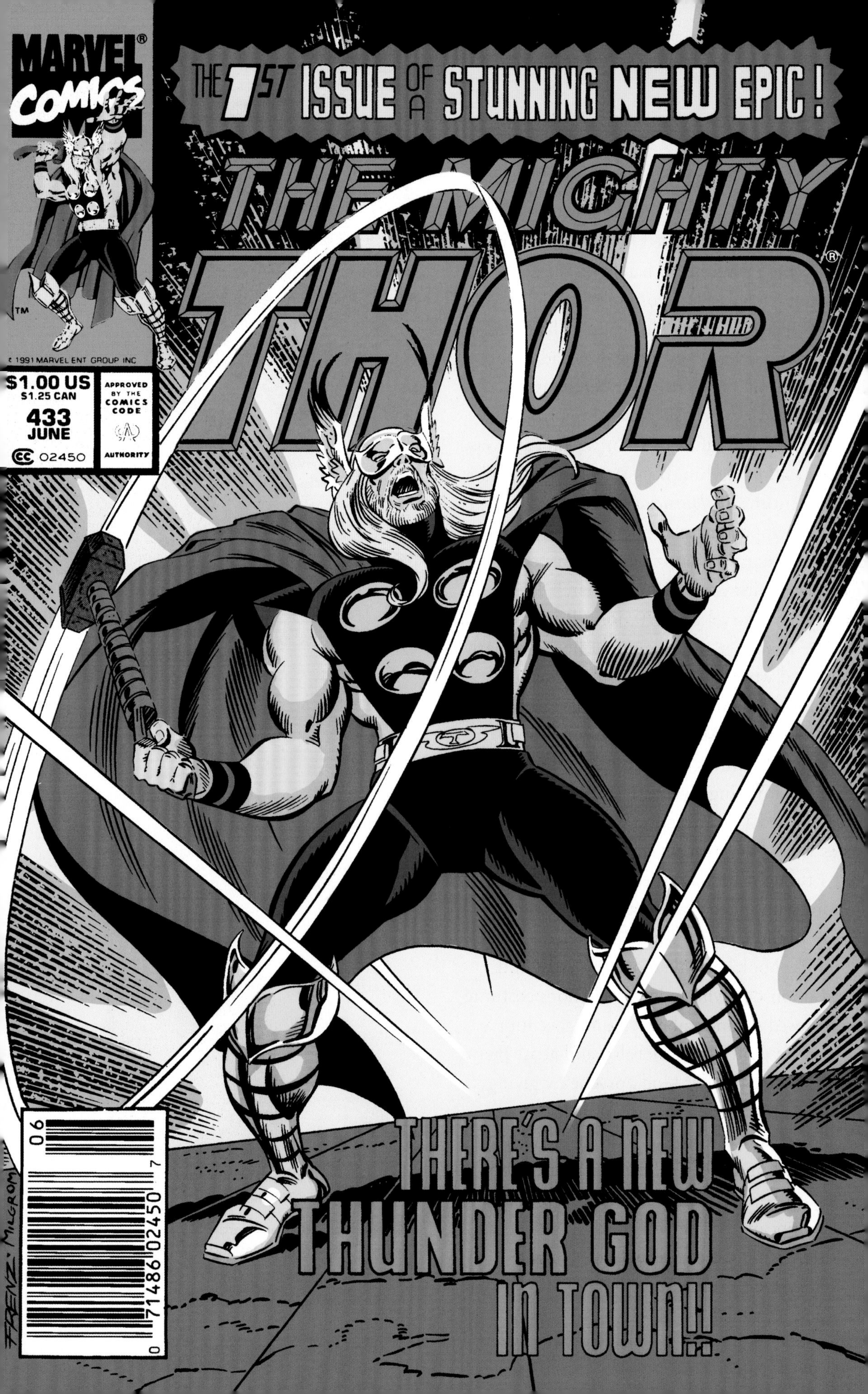
MARVEL COMICS
THE 1ST ISSUE OF A STUNNING NEW EPIC!
THE MIGHTY THOR
© 1991 MARVEL ENT GROUP INC
$1.00 US
$1.25 CAN
433
JUNE
02450
APPROVED BY THE COMICS CODE AUTHORITY
THERE'S A NEW THUNDER GOD IN TOWN!!
FRENZ/MILGROM

goddesses, and the problems caused by his half-brother Loki, whose trickster's personality barely disguises a penchant for genuine evil. Thor's origin mythology would be revised to reveal that Donald Blake had not really existed in the conventional sense, but had been a mortal incarnation of Thor created by Odin as punishment for his son, who had grown too arrogant. Thor's rediscovery of himself in the Norwegian cave was, in essence, Odin's allowing him back into the godly fold.

Thor's adventures in *Journey Into Mystery* (augmented by his appearances as one of The Avengers) became so popular that the magazine's title was changed to *The Mighty Thor* with issue #126, in March 1966. After Jack Kirby left Marvel in 1970, John Buscema took over drawing the character, an assignment he particularly relished. "I enjoyed working on Thor when he would be up in Asgard, because it gave me the Norse legends [to work with]," he says. "Also, I hate drawing cars, airplanes, buildings, anything mechanical, and up in Asgard I can draw anything I want. I was up there, don't tell me what it's like!" The attraction was noticed by other artists as well. "All [Buscema's] characters were fantastic, but I thought he was especially good on Thor," says Joe Sinnott, who inked Buscema's pencil art for the book, as he would later do with Ron Frenz.

In 1983 the book was taken over by artist and writer Walter Simonson (who redesigned Thor's costume to create an armored chain mail effect, and gave him a beard), and then by writer Tom DeFalco and artist Frenz, who complicated the Thunder God's psyche by giving him yet another human alter ego, architect Eric Masterson, who remained Thor for more than twenty issues between 1991 and 1993. Thor later returned to his familiar costume—the red cape with the winged helmet—and it appears that he will continue to battle evil on two different planes of existence, Earth and Asgard, for some time to come.

(Top) Actor Eric Kramer as Thor wielded the Uru hammer, but did not use it to fly in 1988's "The Incredible Hulk Returns."

(Above) From costume to attitude, the Thor seen in "The Incredible Hulk Returns" was a major departure from the comics character.

The Hulk and Thor put their differences aside long enough to defeat the bad guys in "The Incredible Hulk Returns."

THE MIGHTY THOR IN THE MEDIA

Along with The Incredible Hulk, Captain America, The Sub-Mariner, and Iron Man, Thor appeared as one of the regular rotating characters in the 1966 animated series, "The Marvel Superheroes," in faithful recreations from the comic books. These cartoons pitted Thor against such villains as The Grey Gargoyle and Zarko, and also touched on the growing romance between Dr. Donald Blake and his nurse, Jean Foster.

But if the "Marvel Superheroes" cartoons stuck religiously to the source material, Thor's next media appearance—a full twenty-two years later—came off as more of a travesty of the original character. While the television movie "The Incredible Hulk Returns," written and directed by Nicholas Corea (who had earlier served as supervising producer of the Hulk weekly series), had no trace of Thor in the title, the purpose of the film was to use highly popular, well-established TV characters— The Hulk and David Banner—as a vehicle for selling a prospective NBC series based on The Mighty Thor. The film introduced beefy actor Eric Kramer, who filled the bill physically as Thor and gamely played out the script's conception of the character, and featured Steve Leavitt in the role of Don Blake, who in a departure from the comic mythology has the power to summon up the Thunder God, but is not an alternate identity for him.

Thor and Blake are interwoven into the Hulk story by way of Blake's having been a former student of David Banner's. Even though Banner is officially listed as dead, Blake has searched for him, hoping his one-time professor can help him solve a problem. Blake explains that he recently had served as team doctor for a scientific expedition in Norway, during which time he discovered a secret cave that held a runestone, which, mysteriously, he found that he is able to read (how he developed this skill is left up in the air, though Blake at one point admits that he has long been fascinated by all things Viking). Deeper inside the cave was an ancient tomb containing the skeleton of a warrior in armor, complete with a Viking war hammer, which held an inscription

informing him that the tomb contained the body of a
great warrior (he is never referred to as a demigod) who
had been condemned by Odin to not enter Valhalla until
he had done a number of heroic deeds. When Blake
picked up the hammer, it became ablaze with blue
lightning-like energy. A cry of "Odin!" escaped his lips,
and Thor miraculously appeared. Don tells Banner that
he is the earthly channel for Thor, who is decked out
in ancient battle armor and furs, instead of the more
colorful costume from the comics.

To offer proof of his bizarre tale, Blake summons
Thor before Banner, and the Thunder God arrives in
such a bad and violent mood that the sudden tension
causes Banner to transform into The Hulk. The two
uncontrollable super beings battle it out to a draw.

It quickly becomes evident that Blake considers
his new charge to be a burden on his life, and at one
point sarcastically compares the brawny Viking to "a
Buick on stilts." Similarly, Thor has no affection for
Blake, nor does he enjoy his earthly existence; he does
Don's bidding simply because he has to.

Eventually, Blake and Thor come to an
understanding concerning their strangely paralleled
lives, while Banner has to work overtime to try and
keep the Viking off of the radar screen of journalistic
bloodhound Jack McGee, who is once more on Banner's
trail. Ultimately Thor and The Hulk team up to combat
a gangster named Le Beau who has been hired to kill a
friend of Banner's. The climactic fight with Le Beau's
minions ends amusingly as both superheroes run off and
hide, while the scrawny Blake remains behind to greet
the police and take responsibility for singlehandedly
subduing the army of criminals!

Not even Loki would recognize the version of
Thor that appears in "The Incredible Hulk Returns,"
though he would probably applaud his behavior. Rather
than fighting wrongdoing, or even striving to perform
deeds that are noble enough to persuade Odin to allow
him into Valhalla (no mention is ever made of *Asgard*),
this Thor is a party animal who is much more interested

Upon first donning his life-saving iron suit, even walking was a chore for
Tony Stark/Ironman (from *Tales to Astonish* #39 March 1963).

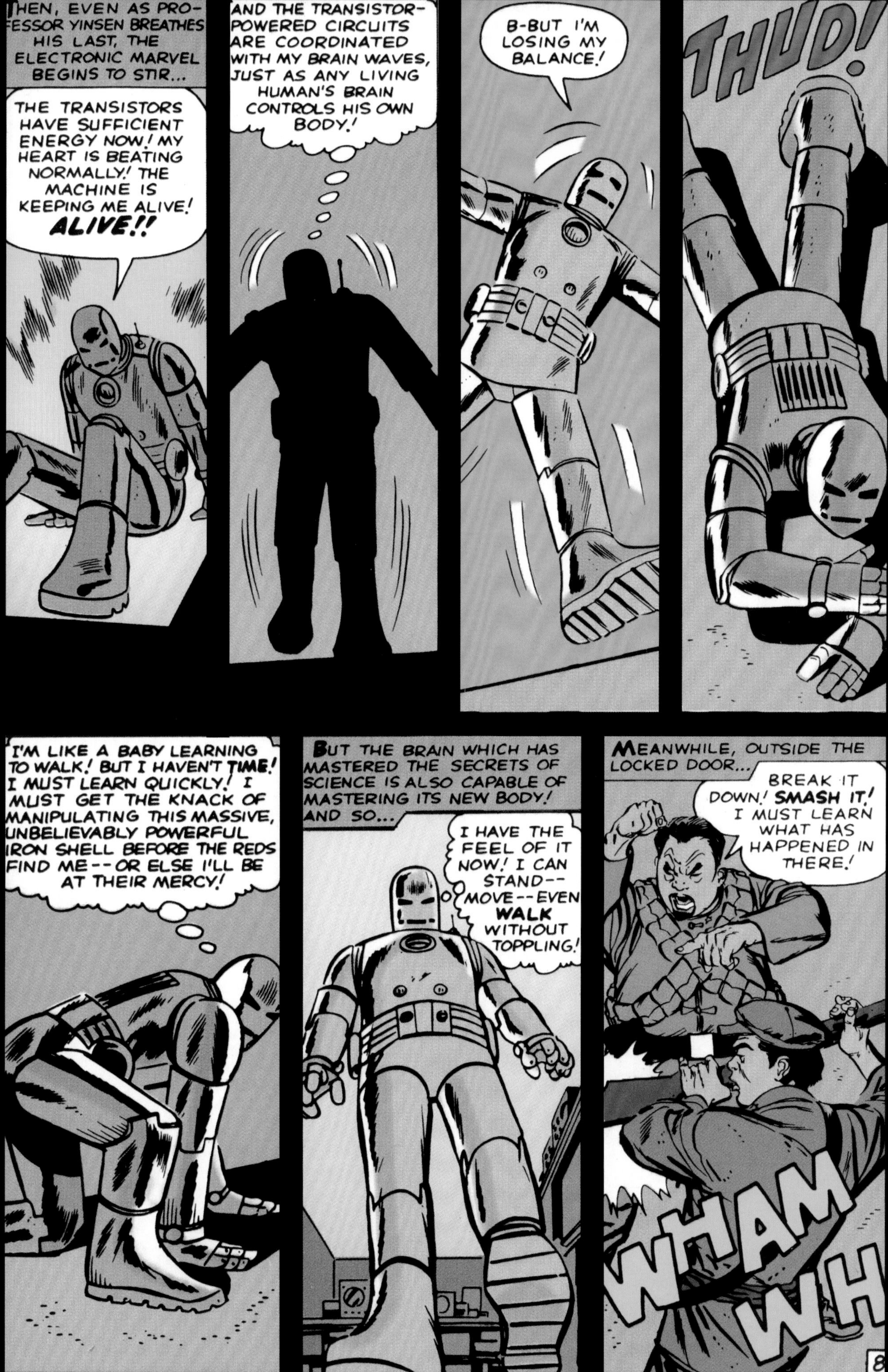
THEN, EVEN AS PROFESSOR YINSEN BREATHES HIS LAST, THE ELECTRONIC MARVEL BEGINS TO STIR...
THE TRANSISTORS HAVE SUFFICIENT ENERGY NOW! MY HEART IS BEATING NORMALLY! THE MACHINE IS KEEPING ME ALIVE! ALIVE!!
AND THE TRANSISTOR-POWERED CIRCUITS ARE COORDINATED WITH MY BRAIN WAVES, JUST AS ANY LIVING HUMAN'S BRAIN CONTROLS HIS OWN BODY!
B-BUT I'M LOSING MY BALANCE!
THUD!
I'M LIKE A BABY LEARNING TO WALK! BUT I HAVEN'T TIME! I MUST LEARN QUICKLY! I MUST GET THE KNACK OF MANIPULATING THIS MASSIVE, UNBELIEVABLY POWERFUL IRON SHELL BEFORE THE REDS FIND ME--OR ELSE I'LL BE AT THEIR MERCY!
BUT THE BRAIN WHICH HAS MASTERED THE SECRETS OF SCIENCE IS ALSO CAPABLE OF MASTERING ITS NEW BODY! AND SO...
I HAVE THE FEEL OF IT NOW! I CAN STAND--MOVE--EVEN WALK WITHOUT TOPPLING!
MEANWHILE, OUTSIDE THE LOCKED DOOR...
BREAK IT DOWN! SMASH IT! I MUST LEARN WHAT HAS HAPPENED IN THERE!
WHAM
WH

in eating, drinking, and making merry. It is hard to reconcile the regal superhero of the comics with the long-haired dude, clad in street clothes consisting of a suede shirt and jeans, who becomes the hit of a biker bar by swilling beer by the pitcher, arm-wrestling every Hell's Angel, and ogling every babe in sight. Purists notwithstanding, the idea of turning The Mighty Thor into a boorish, hedonistic Valley boy who is summoned and controlled by his opposite—a nerdy, obnoxious grad student—might sound like a hip, funny take on a classic character. The problem is that it just doesn't translate to the screen. Trying to conform the more inherently dramatic nature of the Hulk sequences with the goofball tone of the Thor scenes imposes a lightness on the Hulk side that robs the characters of their normal depth. Banner's patient amusement at the antics of Blake and Thor rings false in light of the fact that the two interlopers have not only destroyed the stability Banner had managed to eke out in his life, but have also ruined his chance of being cured. "The Incredible Hulk Returns" failed to generate interest in a weekly series starring The Mighty Thor, relegating the Thunder God back to Asgard to await a more worthy vehicle.

MEANWHILE, IN A PRIVATE, LOCKED ROOM, ANTHONY STARK UNDERGOES A SECRET LIFE-GIVING TREATMENT...
I'D HATE TO THINK WHAT WOULD HAPPEN IF I EVER FAILED TO CHARGE MY TRAN-SISTOR-POWERED HEART ACTIVATOR!
WELL, THAT'S ENOUGH FOR TODAY!... THE PHONE! IT MUST BE URGENT, FOR THEM TO RING ME IN HERE!
RRRIIINGGGGG
WHAT?? THE HULK STOLE MY MISSLE-GUN?!! BUT, THAT'S IMPOSS-- EH, HOLD EVERYTHING!!
I'LL SEND IRON MAN TO THE SITE IMMEDIATELY! HE'LL GET TO THE BOTTOM OF IT!
GOOD THING I GAVE MYSELF A COMPLETE CHARGE!
LUCKY THE MISSILES HAD NO NUCLEAR WARHEADS! THEY CAN'T DO ANY REAL DANGER! BUT WHAT CAN THE HULK BE UP TO!?? HE HASN'T BEEN ACTING LIKE HIM-SELF LATELY!!
WELL, THERE'S ONLY ONE WAY TO FIND OUT! MY BUILT-IN RADAR DEVICE REGISTERS AN UN-IDENTIFIED OBJECT AT THREE O'CLOCK, A HALF-MILE AWAY! AND I THINK I CAN GUESS WHO IT IS!!
IT IS YOU! I ALWAYS THOUGHT WE HAD MADE A MISTAKE ALLOWING YOU TO JOIN THE AVENGERS... NOW I'M SURE OF IT!
IRON MAN! REACTING JUST AS I HOPED HE WOULD! HOW EASY IT IS FOR THE SPACE PHANTOM TO SOW THE SEEDS OF DISTRUST AND HATRED AMONG MY VICTIMS!
I'LL ATTACK HIM! I'M SURE THE BODY I'VE IMITATED IS STRONGER THAN HIS!
11
As re-drawn by Jack Kirby for *The Avengers* #2 (November 1962), Stark's Iron Man costume was more flexible, but still bulky.

IRON MAN

All Marvel superheroes are, in some fashion, unique. Iron Man's uniqueness stems from the fact that the source of his powers, indeed, his entire crimefighting identity, comes from his costume. Not until Venom came along was a costume so important to the existence of a major character of the Marvel Universe, and then it would be for the side of evil.

Iron Man is distinctive in yet another costume-related way, since no other superhero before or since has gone through quite as many visual transformations. When he was first introduced in *Tales of Suspense* issue #39, in March 1963, Iron Man fought through a bulky, lead-colored costume that made him resemble a pewter golem. That quickly changed into an all-golden suit

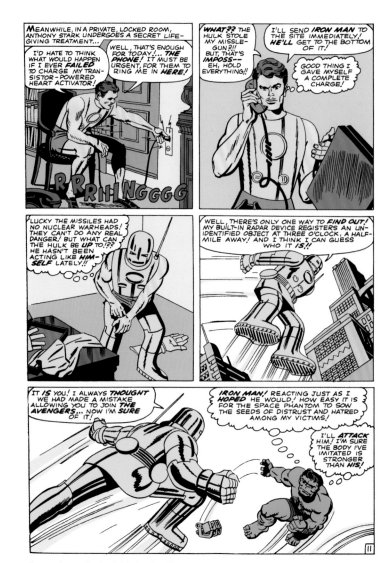

LOOK, DO I TELL YOU MY TROUBLES? I'VE GOT MY HANDS FULL RIGHT NOW! WHY DON'T YOU TRY THE MISSING PERSONS BUREAU ??
THANKS FOR NOTHING, SONNY! BUT THAT REMINDS ME...THERE IS ONE MORE PLACE I CAN TRY!

BUT SUDDENLY, THE KEEN EARS OF CAPTAIN AMERICA HEAR THE SOUND OF HEAVY BREATHING, AND...
HOLD IT!! LOOK... BEHIND US!! IT'S HIM AGAIN! IT'S... THE HULK!!
WE'VE GOT TO GET RID OF HIM!

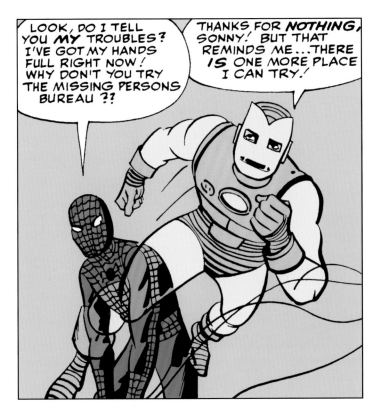

(Top) A streamlined Iron Man from *The Avengers* #3.

(Above) The continuing evolution of Iron Man: the "hockey mask" look from *The Avengers* #5.

(hence his enduring nickname "The Golden Avenger"), which was classier, but still bulky. From there, the suit became progressively sleeker, more muscular, and cast in two colors, red and gold. The iron costume continues to evolve, detail by detail, to this day.

Iron Man's hidden identity is Anthony Stark, a hugely wealthy industrialist, inventor, and playboy, the envy of men and the object of adoration by women ("the dreamiest thing this side of Rock Hudson," coos one redhead on the beach at the Riviera in that first issue), whose character was patterned after the even wealthier real-life inventor and playboy Howard Hughes. In his debut story, which was scripted by Larry Lieber and drawn by Don Heck, Stark is depicted in a location that was rarely seen in the world of comic books, the jungles of Vietnam. Stark is there to see first-hand a test of a device that he has created for the military, a tiny transistor that dramatically increases the power of a small magnet to the point where heavy munitions such as mortars can be carried through the jungle as easily as a flashlight. The test goes off without a hitch, but Stark, who is not trained for jungle warfare, trips over a booby trap that explodes and lodges a piece of shrapnel dangerously close to his heart.

Enter Wong-Chu, a "Red Guerilla tyrant" with a Mao Zedong haircut, who comes upon the injured Stark and realizes that he must be an important U.S. official. Wong-Chu takes Stark hostage with the intent of forcing him to use his talents on behalf of the Red Guerillas. Knowing it is the only way to save his life, the injured industrialist agrees to help Wong create a super weapon. But once in the enemy laboratory he begins work on a different project, the iron suit that will keep him alive once the shrapnel, which is moving through his chest toward his heart (a dramatic touch, even if it is impossible), has finally reached its destination. Working with another prisoner, a brilliant, elderly physicist named Professor Yinsen, whose books Stark had read in college, Stark installs electronic transistors in the suit, investing it with strength beyond human capacity. He also puts tiny jets on the bottom of its metal shoes, which enable him to fly.

As Iron Man, Stark escapes his captors and destroys Wong-Chu by blowing him up in his own ammo dump. But the story ends on a bittersweet note as Stark walks off, contemplating having to spend the rest of his life encased in a lifesaving iron vest.

In one sense, the problems faced by Iron Man as a crimefighter were nothing when compared to the problems faced by Tony Stark as a man. As years went on Iron Man would have to contend with such powerful foes as The Mandarin, an Oriental supervillain bred from the same stock as Timely's 1950s antagonist The Yellow Claw (who was revived in the mid-sixties as an enemy of Nick Fury); Titanium Man, a soviet version of Iron Man; and a host of colorful costumed criminals such as Blacklash, Stiletto, and The Beetle. But there was an extra pressure placed on him that most costumed crimefighters did not have to deal with, that being his weak heart. As an original member of The Avengers, he often had to sit out adventures or ignore calls to action because of his physical condition. Since he could not explain this to his teammates without revealing his secret identity (not only The Avengers but the world at large believes that Iron Man is Tony Stark's bodyguard), Iron Man occasionally had to endure the indignity of punishment from the team, usually in the form of expulsion for nominal periods of time, as a result of his apparent lack of team spirit.

Stark's real problems began in the late 1970s when pressures related to his business contributed to a growing problem with alcohol, which was a daring first for a comic book hero. Stark's descent into the bottle, which was in part a defense against his worsening business problems, including the attempt by S.H.I.E.L.D., the international espionage organization for whom Stark was chief gadget-master, to take over Stark International, and an assault by a ruthless criminal business rival named Justin Hammer, was chronicled in a now-legendary nine-issue run from 1979, written by David Michelinie with

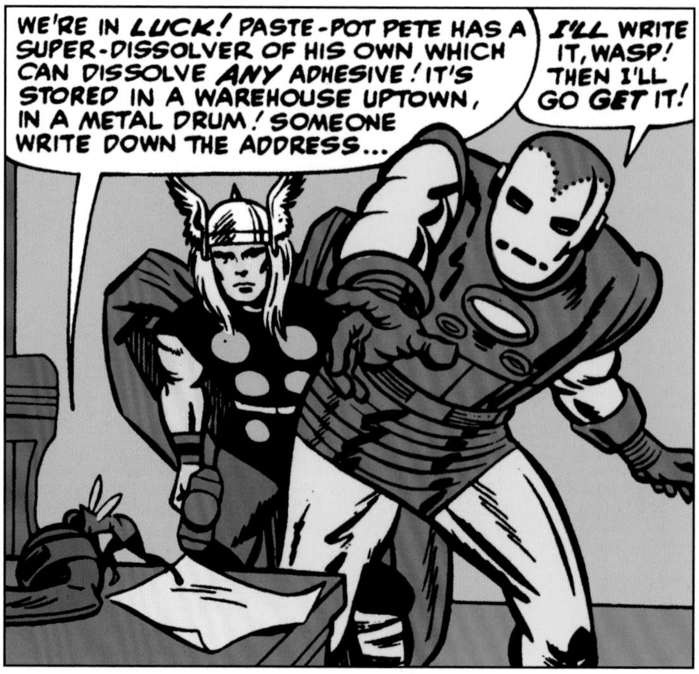
WE'RE IN LUCK! PASTE-POT PETE HAS A SUPER-DISSOLVER OF HIS OWN WHICH CAN DISSOLVE ANY ADHESIVE! IT'S STORED IN A WAREHOUSE UPTOWN, IN A METAL DRUM! SOMEONE WRITE DOWN THE ADDRESS...
I'LL WRITE IT, WASP! THEN I'LL GO GET IT!

After a few months of experimentation, the "standard" Iron Man look was finally formalized. From *The Avengers* #6.

(Opposite) Tony Stark's biggest enemy in the 1980s was the bottle.

When millionaire industrialist *Tony Stark*, inventor extraordinaire, garbs himself in solar-charged, steel-mesh *armor* he becomes the world's greatest human fighting machine...

Stan Lee Presents: THE INVINCIBLE IRON MAN®

DAVID MICHELINIE *writer/plot* / JOHN ROMITA JR. *pencil art* / BOB LAYTON *finished art/plot* / JOHN COSTANZA *letters* / BOB SHAREN *colors* / ROGER STERN *editor* / JIM SHOOTER *editor-in-chief*

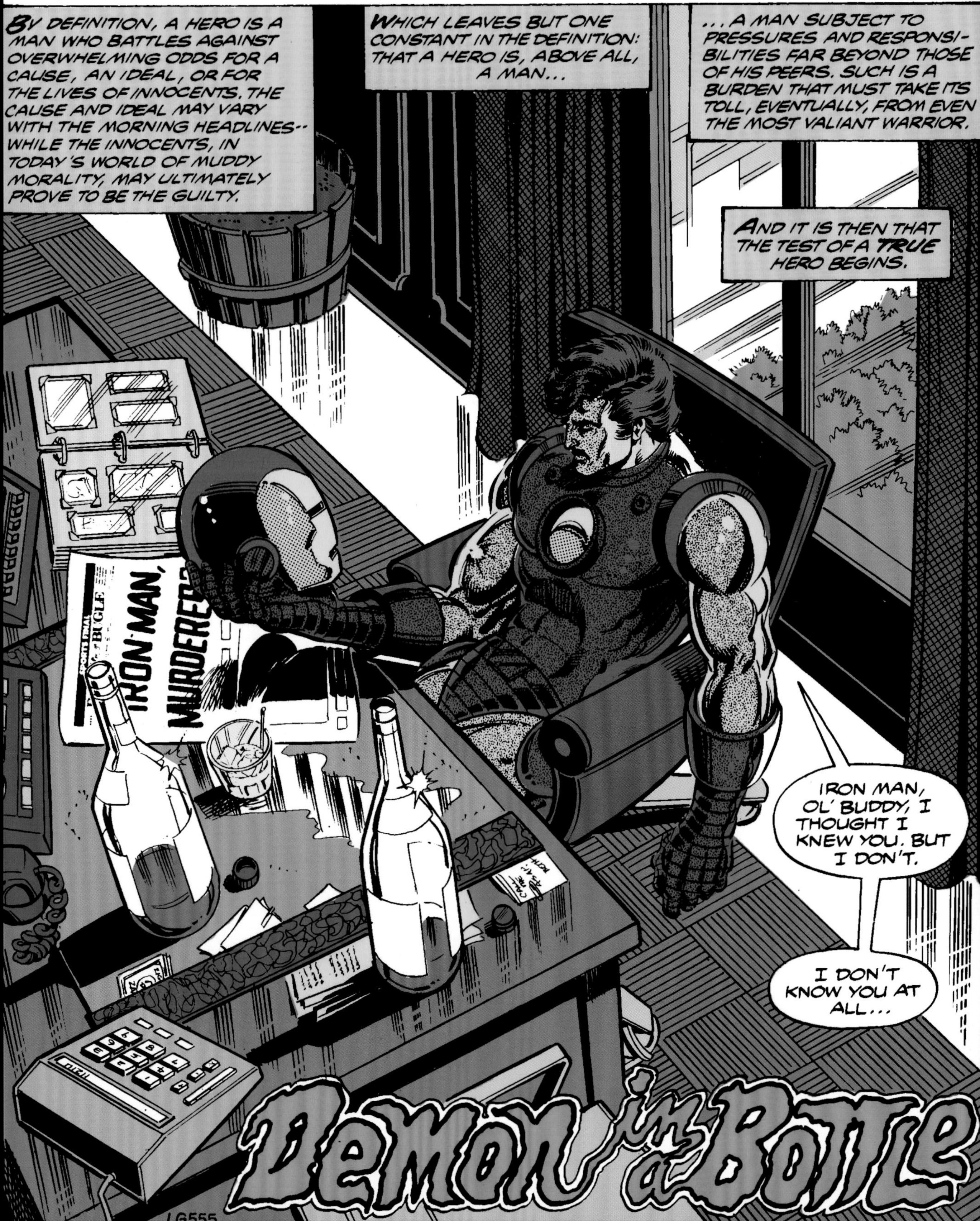
BY DEFINITION, A HERO IS A MAN WHO BATTLES AGAINST OVERWHELMING ODDS FOR A CAUSE, AN IDEAL, OR FOR THE LIVES OF INNOCENTS. THE CAUSE AND IDEAL MAY VARY WITH THE MORNING HEADLINES-- WHILE THE INNOCENTS, IN TODAY'S WORLD OF MUDDY MORALITY, MAY ULTIMATELY PROVE TO BE THE GUILTY.
WHICH LEAVES BUT ONE CONSTANT IN THE DEFINITION: THAT A HERO IS, ABOVE ALL, A MAN...
...A MAN SUBJECT TO PRESSURES AND RESPONSIBILITIES FAR BEYOND THOSE OF HIS PEERS. SUCH IS A BURDEN THAT MUST TAKE ITS TOLL, EVENTUALLY, FROM EVEN THE MOST VALIANT WARRIOR.
AND IT IS THEN THAT THE TEST OF A TRUE HERO BEGINS.
IRON MAN, MURDERER
IRON MAN, OL' BUDDY, I THOUGHT I KNEW YOU. BUT I DON'T.
I DON'T KNOW YOU AT ALL...
Demon in a Bottle

artwork by John Romita, Jr., and Bob Layton. (And those who find Hammer's image oddly familiar are onto something: Romita deliberate drew the character in the likeness of British actor Peter Cushing, a staple of Britain's *Hammer* Films). With the support of friend Bethany Cabe and James "Rhodey" Rhodes, his right-hand man, Stark finally beat the bottle, at least temporarily. He would continue to backslide for another several years, so much so that in the early 1980s, Rhodey Rhodes would don the Iron Man suit, fulfilling what everybody thought anyway, that it was an employee of Stark's inside the red and gold outfit. The extent to which the metal suit obscured the wearer was demonstrated by the fact that Stark was white and Rhodes African-American, an intriguing identity substitution that would have been impossible with most other superheroes.

In addition to being the most personally problematic of all Marvel heroes, Tony Stark has also been one of the most ubiquitous characters in the Marvel Universe, popping up in virtually every comic book line whenever an invention, device, or technological advancement was required. Technology has aided him on a more personal level as well, allowing for his heart to be repaired through surgery, making it no longer necessary to wear a metal shell in order to remain alive.

Fortunes come and fortunes go, and superheroes continue to change, evolve, and reestablish their identities. But if anything remains a constant within the Marvel Universe it is that Tony Stark is a survivor.

IRON MAN IN THE MEDIA

Iron Man's television career thus far has existed exclusively in animation. His first incarnation was in "The Marvel Superheroes," where he and Captain America, The Incredible Hulk, The Mighty Thor, and The Sub-Marine, all battled for justice on a shoestring budget. Even the voice-recording sessions reflected the

(Top to bottom) Original Iron Man cel from 1966's "Marvel Superheroes." Because of his mask, lip-movement animation was not required for the 1966 Iron Man cartoons. For the "Marvel Superheroes" cartoons, movement was simulated by passing a stationary cel past the camera. Iron Man has a big problem in the form of the Mandarin in a 1966 cartoon. (Note the absence of the Mandarin's mouth—it was animated separately.)

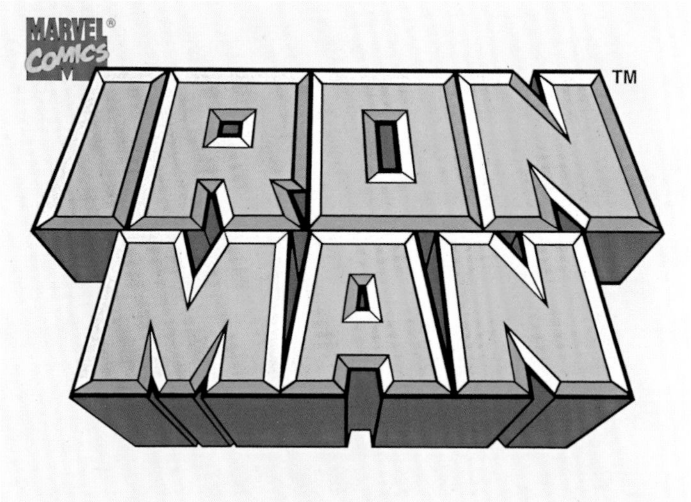
MARVEL COMICS
IRON MAN™

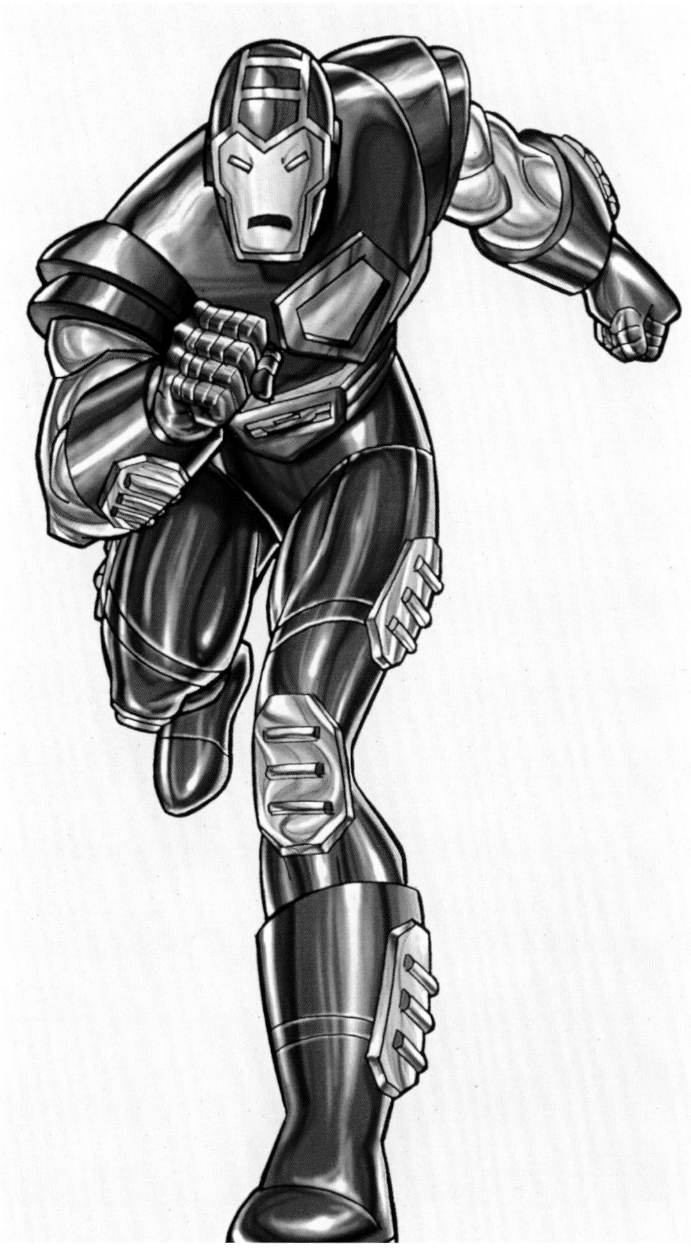

(Top) Iron Man returned to animation in 1994.

(Above) A sleek and powerful Iron Man from the 1994 animated series.

no-frills basis upon which the show was produced, according to actor John Vernon, who provided the melifluous voice for Tony Stark and Iron Man.

"The way we switched voices from Tony Stark to Iron Man was to put a styrofoam cup over the face!" Vernon recalls, with a laugh. "We did those very quickly with a minimum of rehearsal. We'd crank them right out."

As was the case with the other episodes of "Marvel Superheroes," original comic book art was used as the basis for the Iron Man cartoons, which proved to be a double-edged sword for the animators. On the one hand, additional time and money was saved on the character since Iron Man's mouth was hidden behind a rigid metal face, which made lip-synch animation unnecessary. On the other hand, the filmmakers found themselves challenged to try and keep up with Iron Man's ever-changing costume. "That threw us for a loop, because we had to start doing more and more artwork for ourselves," recalls producer Ray Patterson.

Indeed, watching these cartoons, it is hard to find two consecutive shots in which Iron Man looks the same. The eye openings in his mask change from square to round, the mask itself displays rivets in some scenes but not in others, and the mouth opening is sometimes a straight line and sometimes segmented. In one episode, titled "The Crimson Dynamo," Stark is seen changing out of his "lightweight" armor—which in the context of the story has been contaminated by radioactive material—and into the old, heavy golden suit, only to re-emerge a few scenes later in the lightweight armor once again. But if the kids watching the show back then cared about discrepancies, or even noticed them, they did not complain.

At the end of that series, Iron Man took a long hiatus from television, though Tony Stark continued to make guest appearances on such Saturday morning series as "Spider-Man and His Amazing Friends." Then in 1994, Iron Man triumphantly returned as one-half of the syndicated "Marvel Action Hour" (The Fantastic Four

OFF THE PAGE AND ONTO THE SCREEN

7 SPECIAL COMICS INFORMATION | APPROVED FOR ALL READERS

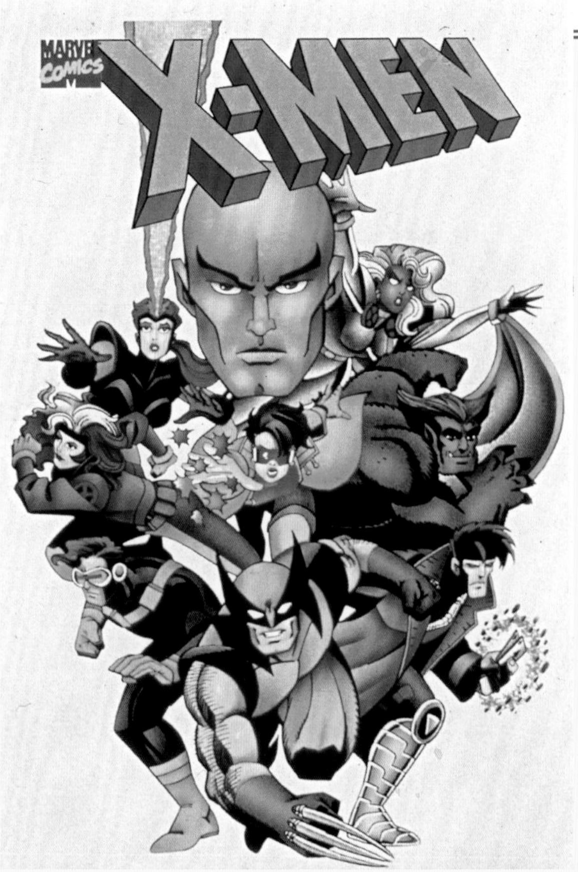
MARVEL COMICS
X-MEN

Comic books are drawn life and animation is drawn life, so it might seem like translating one to the other would be a simple task. Not always so. "Television is a different medium and you have to be able to design characters that are animatable and look good when they're moving," says Eric Rollman, president of production for Fox Family Worldwide, the entity that controls most of Marvel's small-screen properties. The adaptive process is not limited to the physical look alone; the characters themselves may also be revamped in relationship to the path they have taken within the comic books. A prime example of this is the 1994 "Iron Man" series that quite understandably sidestepped the subject of Tony Stark's battle with alcoholism. "The beauty of the Marvel characters is that we could do an Iron Man' series and just not go there [into the alcoholism]," says Rollman. "This is another world and another time in which Iron Man lived, and we do not even have to worry about what he's currently doing in the comic books. With the Marvel characters there are always surprises, always the unexpected, always the unknown, and I think that's why the characters are so interesting and have adapted so well to television and other media."

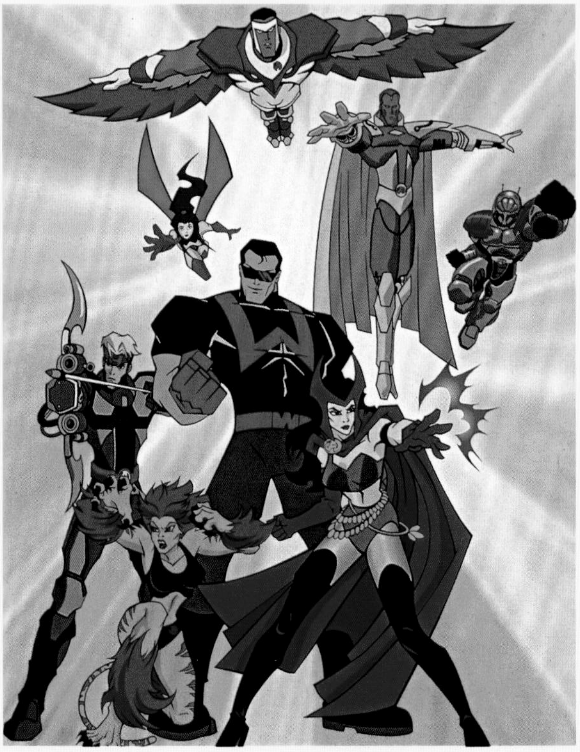

The 1990s saw a host of Marvel properties turned into animated television series, including: "X-Men" (top) and "The Avengers" from FOX KIDS. (™ © 2001 Saban)

comprised the other half), which for the first time featured Stan Lee not simply as supervising producer and narrator, but as an on-camera host in the tradition of Rod Serling in "The Twilight Zone"—something of a "Stan Lee Presents." "I'm thinking of changing my last name to 'Presents,'" Lee joked at the time, "Lee would be my middle name."

Another co-production of Marvel Films, New World Entertainment, and Saban Entertainment, the series featured actor Robert Hays (*Airplane!*) in the role of Stark/Iron Man, and offered a virtual one-stop-shopping compendium of the comic book's characters, from Rhodey Rhodes to the bizarre, Humpty Dumpty-ish villain Modok. One episode even featured the notorious Fin Fang Foom, a dragon-like creature from Marvel's pre-superhero bug-eyed-monster period of the late 1950s, that has become legendary, primarily because of its silly name. And if Fin Fang Foom wasn't enough, another episode featured President Bill Clinton and Vice President Al Gore! (It probably goes without saying that their voices were impersonated.)

A highlight of each episode was the elaborate transformation of Stark into Iron Man, which was accomplished via effects-laden animation that morphed into a realistic CGI sequence of Stark donning the mask, which appeared to fuse around his head. It stands as one of the first uses of computer animation in an animated series, which over the next several years would become more and more commonplace. (And this time, there were no continuity problems with the costume.)

The 1994 series was Iron Man's last, though he is not sitting around and rusting as far as Hollywood is concerned, and it is certain that he will be back.

DAREDEVIL

Every set of rules is destined to be broken at some point or other, and with the creation Daredevil, dubbed "the man without fear," Marvel successfully eschewed its own successful formula for creating comic book heroes, which

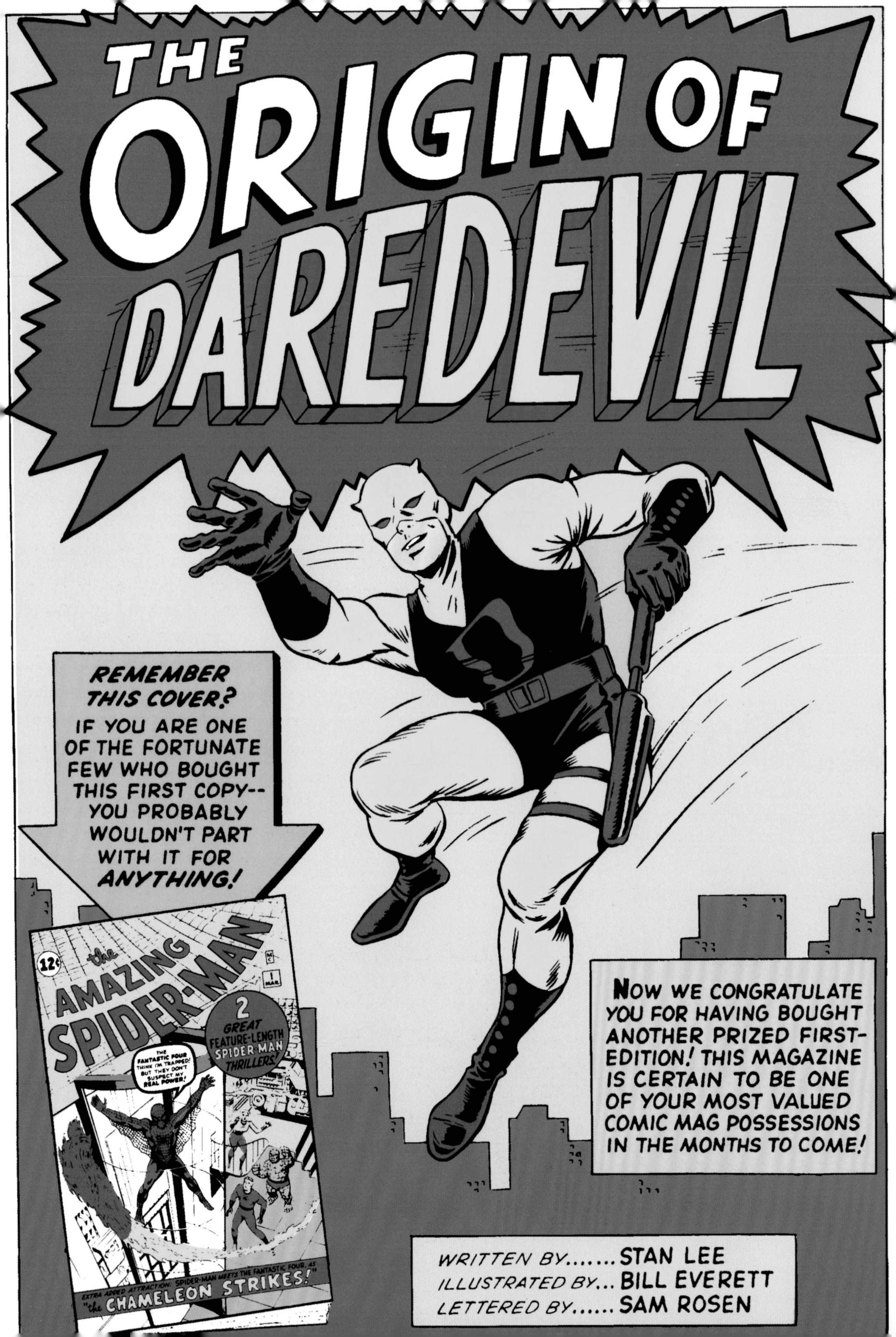
THE ORIGIN OF DAREDEVIL
REMEMBER THIS COVER? IF YOU ARE ONE OF THE FORTUNATE FEW WHO BOUGHT THIS FIRST COPY-- YOU PROBABLY WOULDN'T PART WITH IT FOR ANYTHING!
12¢
the AMAZING SPIDER-MAN
1 MAR.
2 GREAT FEATURE-LENGTH SPIDER-MAN THRILLERS!
THE FANTASTIC FOUR THINK I'M TRAPPED! BUT THEY DON'T SUSPECT MY REAL POWER!
EXTRA ADDED ATTRACTION: SPIDER-MAN MEETS THE FANTASTIC FOUR, AS "the CHAMELEON STRIKES!"
NOW WE CONGRATULATE YOU FOR HAVING BOUGHT ANOTHER PRIZED FIRST-EDITION! THIS MAGAZINE IS CERTAIN TO BE ONE OF YOUR MOST VALUED COMIC MAG POSSESSIONS IN THE MONTHS TO COME!
WRITTEN BY....... STAN LEE
ILLUSTRATED BY... BILL EVERETT
LETTERED BY...... SAM ROSEN

held that the best characters were those with recognizable problems. It is not that Daredevil is devoid of problems. In fact, he has what most people would consider a major one: he is blind. Furthermore, he lost his sight through the traditional Marvel way of an unfortunate encounter with radiation. But what sets Daredevil, who in reality is successful attorney Matt Murdock, apart from the pack is that he refused to treat his blindness as an affliction. As opposed to the worried, guilt-wracked Peter Parker and the bitter, combative Ben Grimm, Matt Murdock endures a series of devastating personal tragedies, including the deaths of his parents, and emerges remarkably free of crippling angst and personal demons . . . in the beginning, at least.

The blindness angle was inspired by a series of murder mysteries written in the 1940s by Baynard Kendrick, featuring a blind police captain named Duncan Maclain, whose exploits Stan Lee recalled while fishing around for a new superhero character in 1964. Lee was able to communicate his enthusiasm for a sightless superhero to artist Bill Everett, creator of The Sub-Mariner, whom Lee had been courting to return to Marvel. The result was published in its own magazine, *Daredevil* #1, August 1964. So confident was Lee that he had a winner on his hands that the magazine's first page was a reprint of page one of the first issue of *Spider-Man,* along with the proclamation: "Remember this cover? If you are one of the fortunate few who bought this first copy, you probably wouldn't part with it for anything! Now we congratulate you for having bought another prized first-edition! This magazine is certain to become one of your most valued comic mag possessions in the months to come!"

Hyperbole aside, the story that followed was an emotionally complex one. It told of eight-year-old Matt, who was being raised by his widower father, an over-the-hill prizefighter named Battling Murdock. Matt idolizes his dad and wants to follow in his footsteps, but the fighter wants his son to better himself instead. Encouraged to study at the expense of play time, Matt is

A brightly colored Daredevil bounded onto the scene in issue #1 of his own magazine in 1964.

BUT, IN THE NOW LONELY, DARKENED OFFICE, WHERE ONCE A BLIND LAWYER HAD STOOD, ANOTHER BEGINS TO TAKE HIS PLACE...
I'VE SECRETLY WORKED FOR MONTHS TO REDESIGN MY FIGHTING COSTUME -- TO MAKE IT MORE COMFORTABLE -- MORE DISTINCTIVE! BUT, I NEVER EXPECTED TO WEAR IT AGAINST SUCH A FANTASTIC FOE!
AND THEN, WITH THE SKILL OF A TRAINED ACROBAT, THE STEALTH OF A JUNGLE STALKER, AND THE COURAGE OF A-- DAREDEVIL, THE SIGHTLESS ADVENTURER TAKES TO THE ROOF-TOPS....!

(Above and opposite) Daredevil took on his familiar devilish appearance starting from issue #7, which pitted him against The Sub-Mariner (de riguer for any Marvel superhero of the time).

ridiculed by the more athletic students, who sneeringly call him "Daredevil" because he never participates in sports. Hurt and frustrated, Matt begins to secretly train himself physically, becoming a peerless acrobat, while maintaining his all-A status. Meanwhile, Battling Murdock signs a contract with a shady fight promoter called The Fixer, planning to put the money he makes from the fights toward Matt's college education. "This is the luckiest day of my life!" declares the pug, now rechristened "Kid" Murdock. He has no idea that fate is about to hit him below the belt.

While Murdock is celebrating his good fortune, Matt is witnessing a tragedy in the making: a blind man has walked into a line of traffic. Demonstrating superb reflexes, Matt jumps into the street and shoves the man out of the way of a truck (labeled "Ajax Atomic Labs Radio-Active Materials"), but a cylinder falls from the truck and splashes radioactive material onto Matt's face, blinding him. He is not bitter, however, particularly when he discovers that his other senses have been heightened to the point where he can read by feeling the imprint of the letters on a page and actually hear people's heartbeats (which enables him to detect when they're lying!). What's more, he can walk without help because of a strange tingling sensation that strikes whenever he nears solid objects.

Matt goes on to graduate from high school with honors and enters college, while his father continues to win fight after fight, not realizing that they have been rigged by The Fixer. But when it becomes Murdock's turn to take a dive, he refuses, since Matt is in the crowd watching. This betrayal of The Fixer would cost him his life, a murder carried out by one of the criminal's henchmen. This tragedy only spurs Matt to drive himself harder. He eventually graduates from college as valedictorian and opens a law firm with his college roommate Franklin "Foggy" Nelson and a gorgeous blond employee named Karen Page (who would blossom into Matt's love interest). But the pain of his father's death endures, and raises a vigilante feeling inside him.

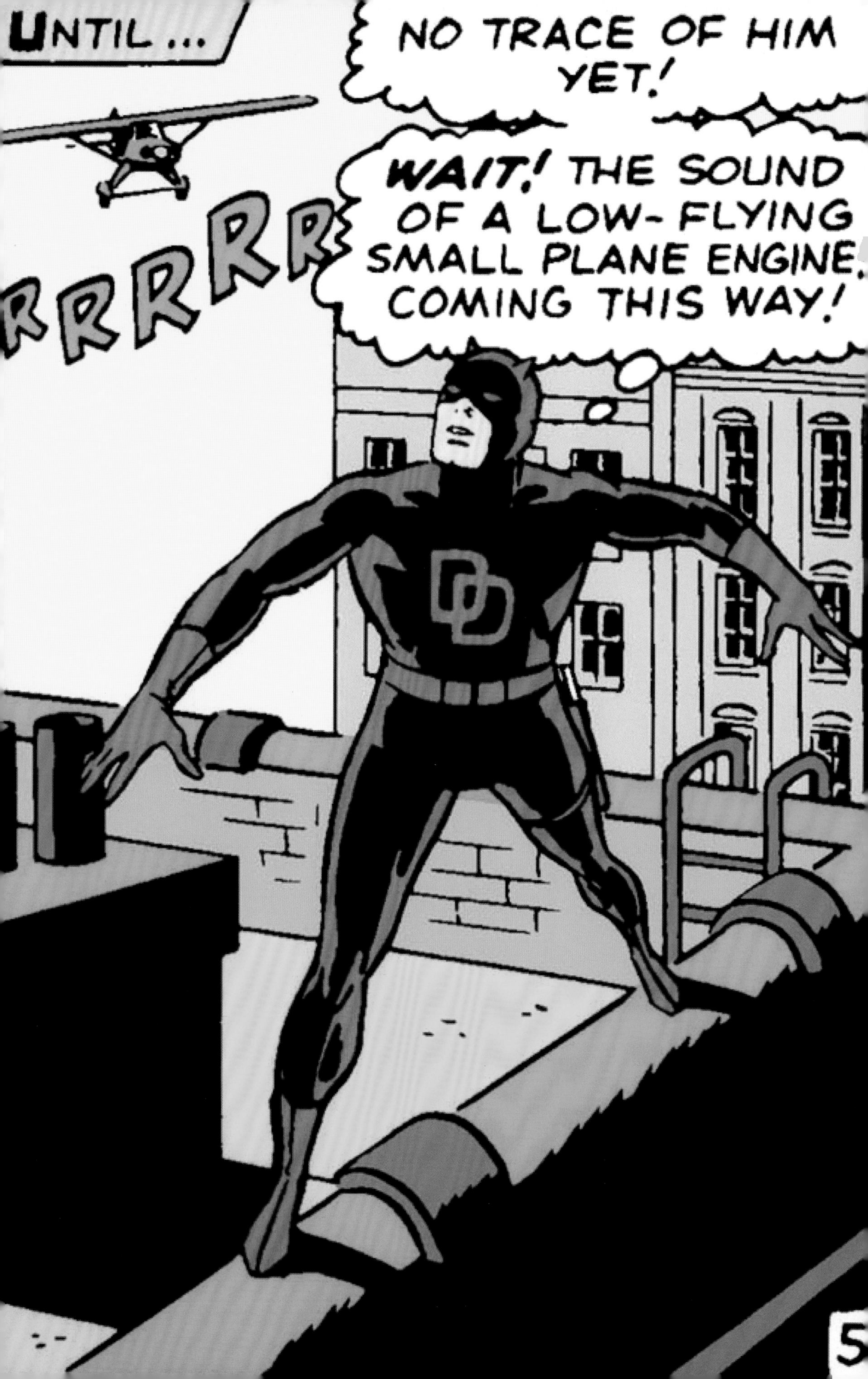
UNTIL ...
NO TRACE OF HIM YET!
RRRRRR
WAIT! THE SOUND OF A LOW-FLYING SMALL PLANE ENGINE. COMING THIS WAY!
5

Having promised his father that he would never become a fighter, Matt disguises himself through the costume and identity of Daredevil, "The Man Without Fear," and armed with the gadget-laden utility cane that would become a trademark, avenges his father's death by capturing The Fixer.

The first "Daredevil" story was indeed a winner. Lee's writing delivered more emotional power than usual and Everett's artwork possessed a gritty, noirish quality that perfectly captured the dark side of the street from which Matt Murdock rose. Everett would draw only this first Daredevil story, after which such distinctive artists as Joe Orlando, Wallace Wood, and Gene Colan would take over the character. Over the next five years, Daredevil would undergo many changes, both in costume—which was at first a yellow jumpsuit and hood with a red tabard overtop, replaced in *Daredevil* issue #7 by the sleeker, more mysterious all red suit with two interlocking "D"s on the chest—and disposition.

Later, under the hand of artist and writer Frank Miller, Murdock's former devil-may-care attitude turned increasingly dark as he was confronted with the ugliness of a world that he could no longer see, but could still experience. It was this outlook that colored his battles with such nemeses as the deadly femme fatale Elektra and the grotesquely obese crime lord Wilson Fisk, a.k.a. The Kingpin, a character first introduced in *Spider-Man* magazine.

Daredevil continues to fight for justice—by day, in the courtroom, and by night on the streets—with perhaps a bit less swagger than in his younger days, but still without fear.

FRONT VIEW
3/4 VIEW
SIDE VIEW
COLOR NOTES
COLOR NOTES
COLOR NOTES
FRONT VIEW
SIDE VIEW
BACK VIEW

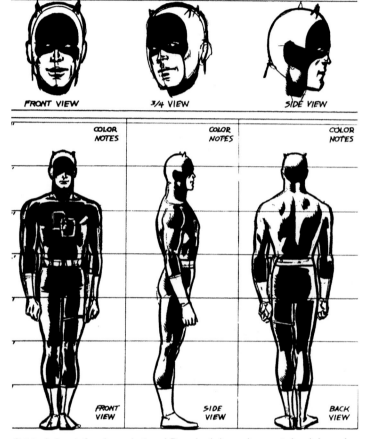

Original sketch for the redesigned Daredevil drawn by comic book legend Wallace Wood in 1964.

DAREDEVIL IN THE MEDIA

Daredevil's only appearance on film was in the 1989 NBC movie, "The Trial of The Incredible Hulk," directed by and starring Bill Bixby, with former teen-heartthrob Rex Smith as Matt Murdock. The film was a follow-up to the previous year's Hulk/Thor extravaganza,

Rex Smith as Daredevil and Lou Ferrigno as The Huk in 1989's "The Trial of the Incredible Hulk."

"The Incredible Hulk Returns," and like its predecessor it was intended as a pilot for a prospective Daredevil series, which never materialized. Not only is "Trial" a better film than "Returns," the script by Gerald DiPego manages to seamlessly blend the Hulk/David Banner side of the story with the Daredevil/Murdock side, which is no small accomplishment.

The story has David Banner wrongly arrested for an assault on a woman in the subway. Even the victim herself has identified him as the suspect, but only because she has been threatened by the minions of the city's powerful crime boss, Wilson Fisk (played with appropriate villainy—if less poundage—by Welsh actor John Rhys Davies). Fisk, a video-freak who controls his crime operation from the plush penthouse of his own high-rise, is making the threats in order to protect the real subway attacker, who is one of his employees. Crusading attorney Matt Murdock becomes involved because he realizes that Banner has been set up and he is convinced that Fisk is behind it. Murdock has been out to get Fisk for some time, but it is a lonely fight: almost every aspect of city government, from City Hall to the police force, is in Fisk's pocket.

That night Murdock changes into his Daredevil suit (which in the film is pretty unexciting, nothing more than a black leotard with a hood) and thwarts an attempt on the life of Ellie Mendez, the woman who was attacked. Under Murdock's protection, Ellie now tells the truth and confesses that she had been threatened. Banner is cleared, but Fisk has now become alerted to Daredevil's continuing interest in the case. To get rid of the nocturnal superhero, Fisk orders Ellie kidnapped, knowing that Daredevil will follow and try to rescue her. The criminal's plan is colorfully demented: he plans to ambush Daredevil and kill him, while videotaping the entire affair. Fisk then plans to show the videotape to a gathering of other crime bosses whose organizations he hopes to unify with himself at the head. The death of Daredevil is his means of demonstrating to the others his power and leadership skills.

Fisk's plan works insomuch as Daredevil is lured into the trap, arriving at an abandoned movie studio where he has been told Ellie is being held. Fisk's men use ear-shattering sound, which is magnified through Daredevil's super hearing, to immobilize him, then beat him senseless. However Banner (who is staying in Murdock's home and has learned that the attorney moonlights as Daredevil) has followed the superhero, having figured out that he was walking into a trap. Hearing the fight inside, Banner transforms into The Hulk and breaks into the building. He takes care of Fisk's thugs, and carries away the unconscious figure of Daredevil.

As bad as Murdock's physical injuries are, his state of mind has taken an even greater beating. It is the first time he has ever lost a fight and he is not taking the defeat well. Only the encouragement from Banner allows him to go back into training to rescue Ellie. Waiting until the other crime bosses arrive for Fisk's criminal confab, Daredevil and Banner break into Fisk's high-rise headquarters. Fisk meanwhile is playing the video of Daredevil's "death" for his guests, but just at the point where Fisk declares his victory, the real Daredevil bursts through the projection screen. The crime bosses scatter, and Fisk escapes from the top of the penthouse in a flying car, ready to fight another day.

Except for the drab costume, "The Trial of the Incredible Hulk" remains fairly faithful to Daredevil's comic book mythology, particularly in recounting the accident that robbed Murdock of his vision. The biggest departure is the absence of Matt's father and the entire prizefight angle, which was replaced by a subplot involving one good cop in a barrel of rotten apples who takes Murdock under his wing, and who even inspires the name "Daredevil." Rex Smith is very convincing as a sightless man—so much so that Matt Murdock out of costume comes off a more interesting character than Daredevil! Even so, "The Trial of the Incredible Hulk" is among of the best of the many Marvel-inspired television films.

"The Man Without Fear" was one of comicdom's greatest acrobats.

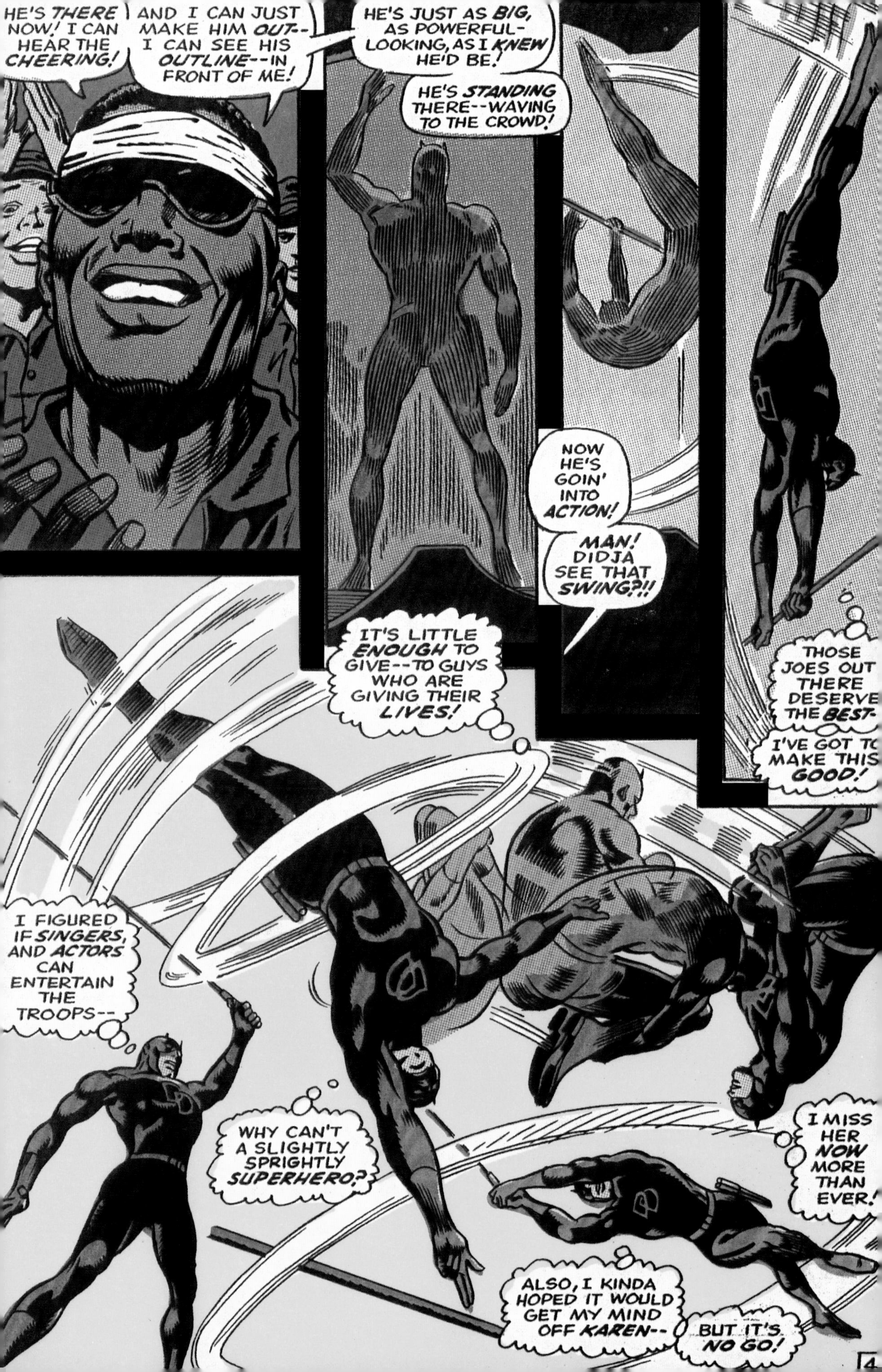
HE'S THERE NOW! I CAN HEAR THE CHEERING!
AND I CAN JUST MAKE HIM OUT-- I CAN SEE HIS OUTLINE--IN FRONT OF ME!
HE'S JUST AS BIG, AS POWERFUL-LOOKING, AS I KNEW HE'D BE!
HE'S STANDING THERE--WAVING TO THE CROWD!
NOW HE'S GOIN' INTO ACTION!
MAN! DIDJA SEE THAT SWING?!!
IT'S LITTLE ENOUGH TO GIVE--TO GUYS WHO ARE GIVING THEIR LIVES!
THOSE JOES OUT THERE DESERVE THE BEST-
I'VE GOT TO MAKE THIS GOOD!
I FIGURED IF SINGERS, AND ACTORS CAN ENTERTAIN THE TROOPS--
WHY CAN'T A SLIGHTLY SPRIGHTLY SUPERHERO?
I MISS HER NOW MORE THAN EVER!
ALSO, I KINDA HOPED IT WOULD GET MY MIND OFF KAREN--
BUT IT'S NO GO!
4

EXPAN
UN

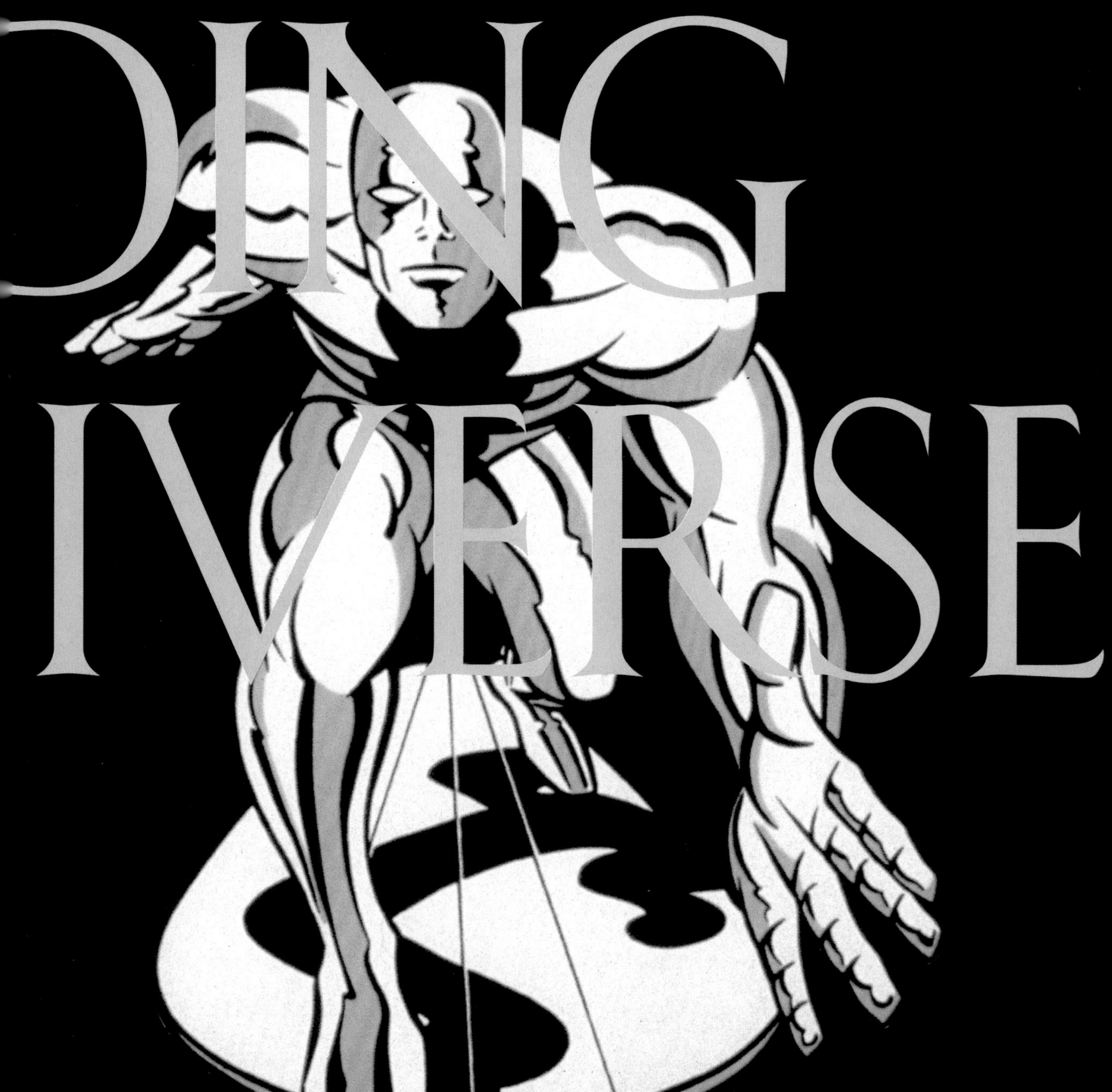
DING
IVERSE

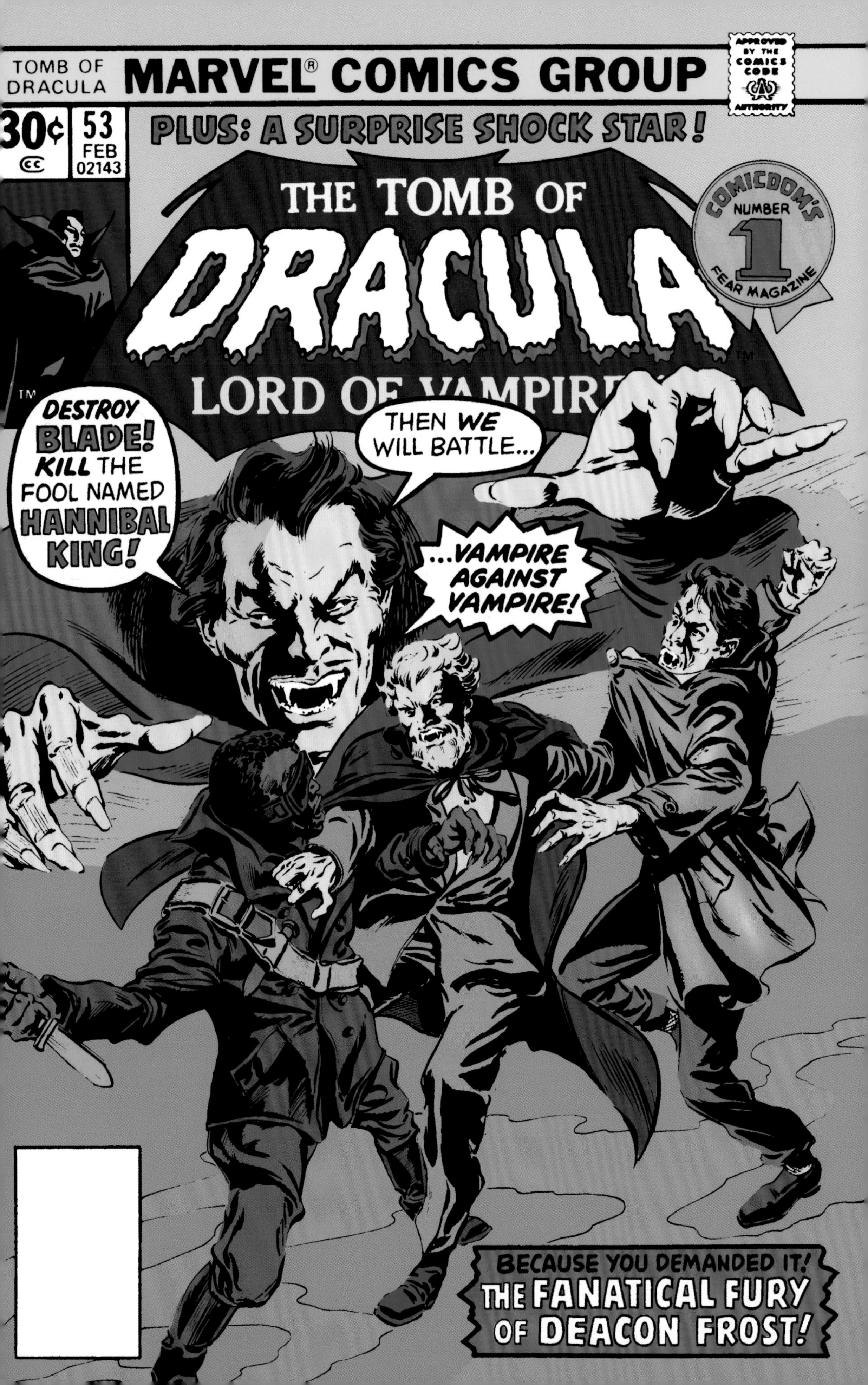
TOMB OF DRACULA
MARVEL® COMICS GROUP
APPROVED BY THE COMICS CODE AUTHORITY
30¢ CC
53 FEB 02143
PLUS: A SURPRISE SHOCK STAR!
THE TOMB OF DRACULA
LORD OF VAMPIRES
COMICDOM'S NUMBER 1 FEAR MAGAZINE
DESTROY BLADE! KILL THE FOOL NAMED HANNIBAL KING!
THEN WE WILL BATTLE...
...VAMPIRE AGAINST VAMPIRE!
BECAUSE YOU DEMANDED IT! THE FANATICAL FURY OF DEACON FROST!

THE EXPANDING UNIVERSE

HEROES ON EVERY HORIZON

Not all of Marvel's star characters, of course, fit neatly into the superhero mold. Some, in fact, do not fit neatly into *any* mold; rather they expand the limits of what can be done in the realm of comic book storytelling. To put it another way, some of the inhabitants of the Marvel Universe are simply ones of a kind, a quality that translates even into their film and television adaptions.

BLADE

It is ironic that the turning point for Marvel in terms of its feature film presence came from a movie that was based on one of the Universe's least known heroes, the African-American vampire fighter known as Blade. Blade was one of a group of vampire hunters featured in *Tomb of Dracula* magazine, a book that has achieved legendary status in the twenty years since its demise. Written by Marv Wolfman and drawn by Gene Colan (pencils) and Tom Palmer (inks), *Tomb of Dracula* ran from 1972 to 1979 and featured more sophisticated stories and dialogue than were often found in comics of that time.

The fact that Blade was black separated him from most other comic heroes of the time. "Not very much had been done in comics with black characters," recalls Colan, "so Marv thought of bringing a black character into it. I thought it was a very good idea." Blade was not Marvel's only African-American character: Luke Cage and "Black Panther" also set standards for minority heroes in comic books.

Often described as an erratic loner, Blade costumes himself in a brown and green combat outfit with green night goggles. Armed with wooden daggers, he carried on a nocturnal hunt for Deacon Frost, an elderly, white-haired bloodsucker who began life as a nineteenth-century German scientist who had developed an immortality serum distilled from a vampire's blood. Accidentally dosing himself, Frost got his immortality but at a cost: he became one of the undead. A century later, Frost killed Blade's mother just as she was about to

With the help of vampire Hannibal King and the outré hero known as the Son of Satan, Blade stakes his vampiric doppleganger, from *Tomb of Dracula* #53 (February 1976).

give birth to him, thereby creating a deadly vampiric *doppelganger* who grew up separate from Blade. The real Blade and the double were fused together at one point until fellow vampire hunters Hannibal King (himself a bloodsucker) and Daimon Hellstrom, alias "The Son of Satan," managed to separate the two entities and kill off the parasitic double. Eventually, Frost, who had created an army of thirsty *doppelgangers*, was destroyed by the vampire slayers.

In 1980, Japan's Toei Animation translated *Tomb of Dracula* into a two-hour television movie, which was notable for its adherence to Colan's artwork. Blade, however, did not appear in the film, the English version of which was retitled *Dracula, Sovereign of the Damned*.

Then in 1998, the character rose with a vengeance in New Line Cinema's *Blade*. Written by David S. Goyer, directed by Stephen Norrington, and starring Wesley Snipes, the film placed the character in a bleak post-modern world where the vampire underclass remains barely hidden below the surface of normal society. Even the vampire class is engaged in warfare between the old fashioned "purebloods"—born vampires who have learned to live alongside humankind—and "half-breeds," the young, violent, created vampires who want to take over and dominate the earth.

In the film, Blade begins life as Eric Brooks, born in 1967 to a dying, vampirized woman. Blade grows up half-human, half-vampire, and constantly struggles to contain his deadly parasitic nature. Working alongside a grizzled old arms maker named Abraham Whistler (Kris Kristofferson), who has created Blade's trademark titanium long sword, the black-garbed "Daywalker" fights his prey with the superhuman strength that is common to vampires, powered by his fanatical determination.

Meanwhile, Deacon Frost (played by Stephen Dorff as a drugged-out Gen-X slacker, miles removed from the Frost of the comics) is marshaling his army of half-breed vampires for a planned revolution, which turns on the second coming of the blood god La Magra.

Thrust into this war between vampires and

In the comics, Blade's blade was more modest than in the feature version.

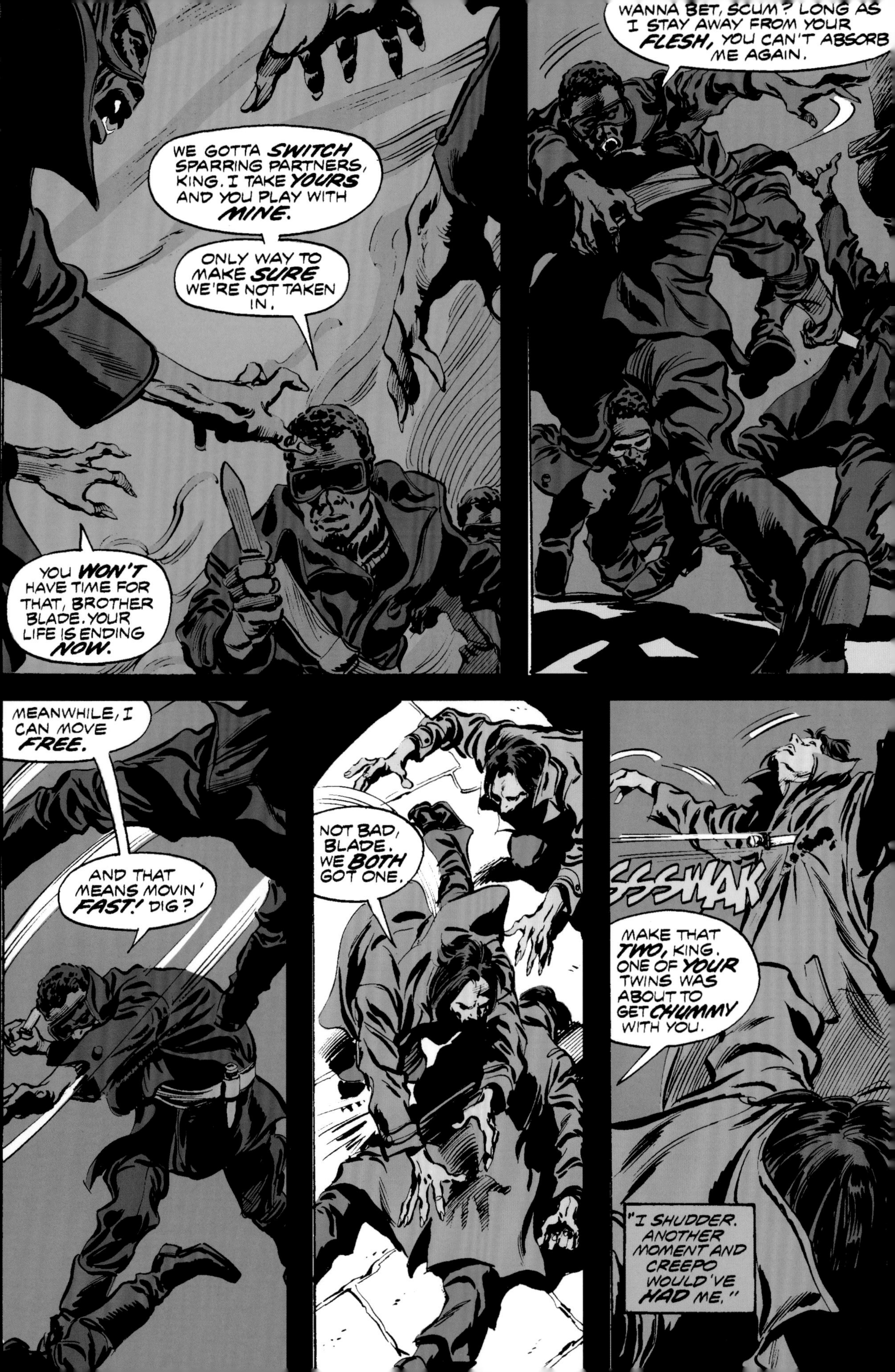
WE GOTTA SWITCH SPARRING PARTNERS, KING. I TAKE YOURS AND YOU PLAY WITH MINE.
ONLY WAY TO MAKE SURE WE'RE NOT TAKEN IN.
YOU WON'T HAVE TIME FOR THAT, BROTHER BLADE. YOUR LIFE IS ENDING NOW.
WANNA BET, SCUM? LONG AS I STAY AWAY FROM YOUR FLESH, YOU CAN'T ABSORB ME AGAIN.
MEANWHILE, I CAN MOVE FREE.
AND THAT MEANS MOVIN' FAST! DIG?
NOT BAD, BLADE. WE BOTH GOT ONE.
SSSWAK
MAKE THAT TWO, KING. ONE OF YOUR TWINS WAS ABOUT TO GET CHUMMY WITH YOU.
"I SHUDDER. ANOTHER MOMENT AND CREEPO WOULD'VE HAD ME."

humans is the beautiful hematologist Dr. Karen Jensen (N'Bushe Wright), who learns that vampires are virtually everywhere in society, even in positions of authority and power, and are aided by human servants. Karen develops a serum that will cure Blade of his vampirism, but at the cost of the superhuman abilities. After having the satisfaction of destroying Deacon Frost (in a martial arts fight scene as exciting as any ever filmed, with Snipes clearly performing a good deal of the action himself), Blade refuses the cure, knowing that his work fighting the evil warriors of the night is far from over.

Blade came about as a result of Wesley Snipes's desire to do a film based on Marvel's Black Panther. Marvel suggested that Snipes first consider Blade, and after reading a number of *Tomb of Dracula* comics, the actor agreed. "I wanted to do something that was edgy and tough and would give me back some of that *New Jack City* type of vibe," Snipes told the press at the time. "This was the perfect vehicle to do it in." In addition to taking the lead, Snipes signed on as co-producer through his Amen Ra Productions.

A pinnacle of 1990s high-tech action/horror films, *Blade* is one of the bloodiest and most violent films ever made, but underneath all the graphic gore is a surprisingly complex, even thought-provoking film that can be taken on an allegorical level. The human vampire wannabes who are identified through their brand-like tattoos are metaphors for street gangs, while the vampire "Council of Elders," which has quietly managed to gain control in the governments and police forces of all major cities worldwide, are stands-in for organized crime. There is also a dark strain of humor throughout the film, as typified by Blade's frustrated complaint to the police to stop shooting at him while he's trying to save the heroine.

The success of the film, which grossed $130 million at the box office worldwide, meant that Blade would return, and Snipes, Kristofferson, and writer Goyer did return for 2002's *Blade II*, which was set and shot in Prague. Director Guillermo Del Toro's stated goal was to

(Top) Actor Wesley Snipes as the title vampire-fighter in 1997's *Blade*. (© 1997 New Line Productions, Inc. All rights reserved.)

(Above) Blade the unflappable.

(Opposite top) Deacon Frost (Stephen Dorff, center) leading his deadly pack of vampire assistants.

(Opposite bottom) The final confrontation between Blade and Frost.

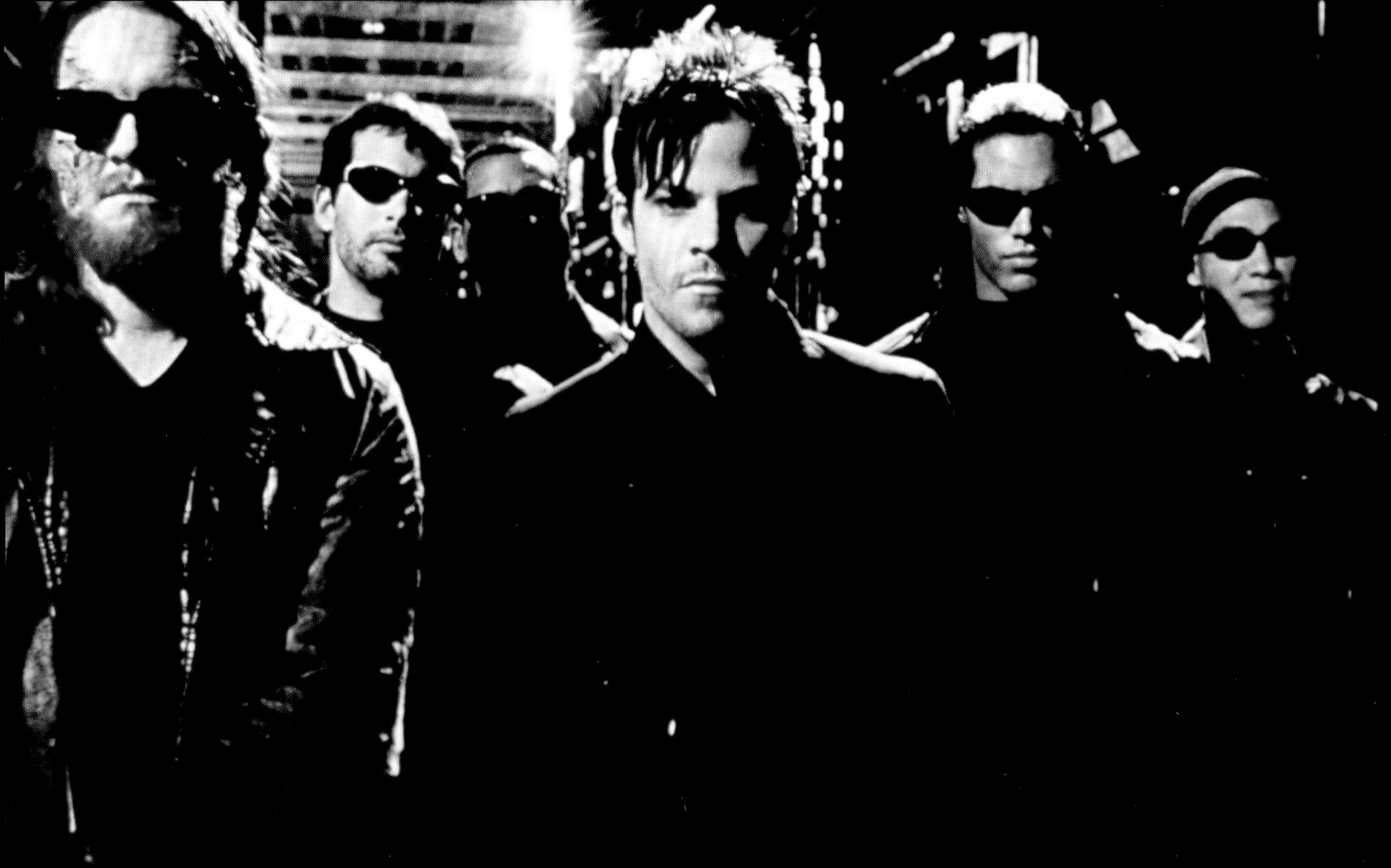

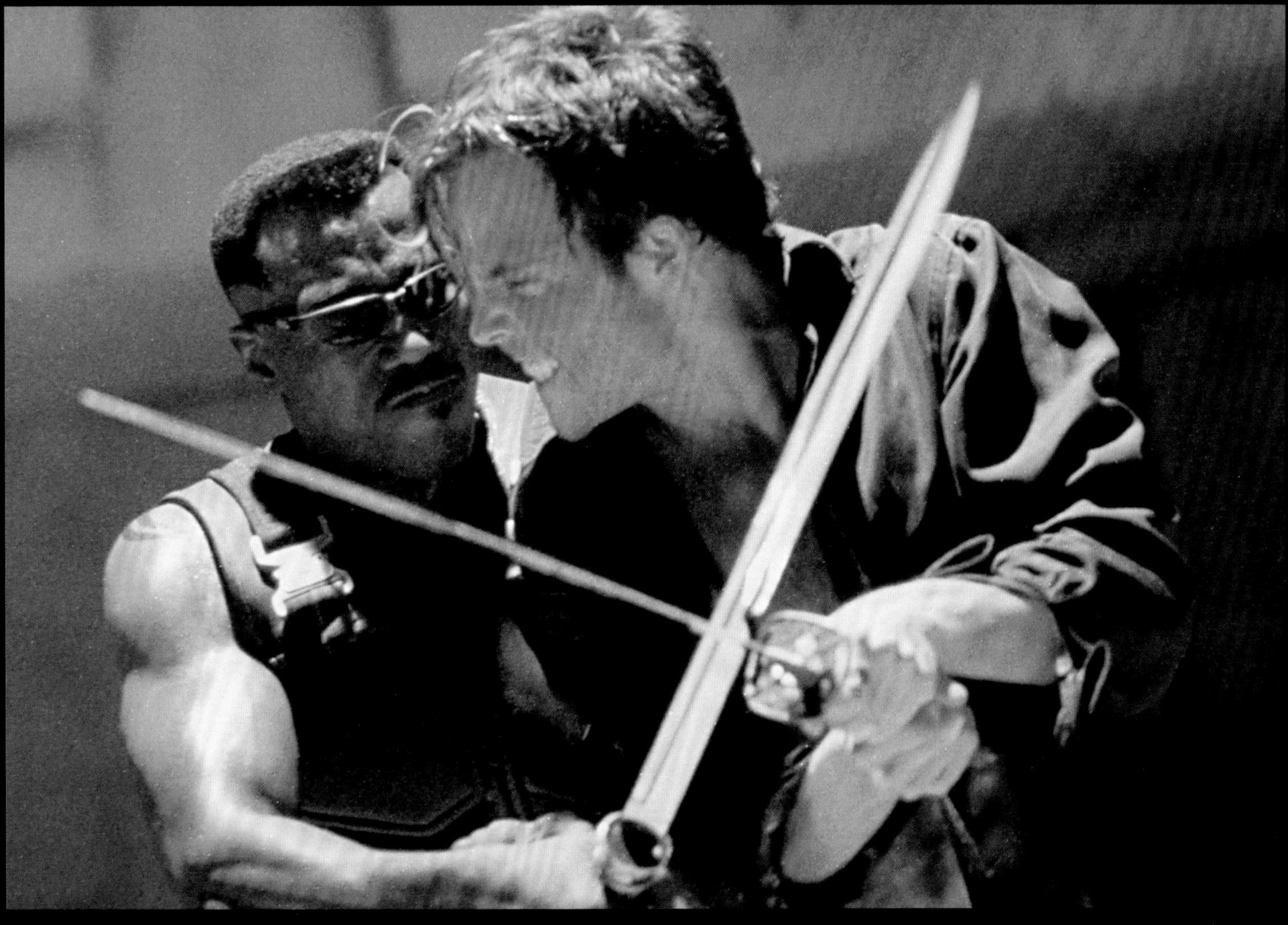

create a "kick-ass action movie," and he succeeded.

This time around Blade is assisted by a young electronics wonk called Scud (Norman Reeder), and together they hunt throughout Europe for Whistler, who appeared to die in the first film, but instead ended up undead. Eventually Blade finds him and forces him to undergo a cold-turkey cure back to humanity.

But there are bigger problems: an entirely new, nearly indestructible race of diseased parasites called Reapers, which feed on vampires, have been created through a rogue virus carried by a night monster named Nomak (Luke Goss). In a situation reminiscent of 1989's *The Punisher*, Blade finds himself being approached by his nemesis, the vampire overlord Damaskinos (Thomas Kretschmann), who suggests that they work together to defeat a common enemy. Reluctantly, Blade agrees to work with a street-tough force of vampire warriors called the Bloodpack, led by Damaskinos' beautiful daughter Nyssa (Leonor Varella) and characterized by the savage Reinhardt (Ron Perlman), who hates Blade.

They succeed in tracking down and destroying the Reapers, but soon the entire alliance is revealed to be a set-up. Once the Reapers are eliminated, Scud—who is revealed to be a double agent—betrays Blade to Damaskinos, who wants to learn the secret of Blade's invincibility in order to create a new race of genetically altered super vampires that can withstand silver, garlic, and daylight.

But the bitter, mistrustful Nomak, who is actually Damaskinos' first failed attempt at creation, is still alive. He turns on his creator and destroys him. In a wild, brutal fight (so wild that Snipes was stabbed through the hand during filming), Blade defeats Nomak, but not before the Reaper bites and infects Nyssa. To escape her horrible fate, she asks Blade to carry her into the sunlight, where she disintegrates in his arms.

Everything is cranked up to the max in *Blade II*, from the special effects to the high-flying martial arts action sequences (choreographed by Hong Kong action specialist Donnie Yen) to the settings, which graphically

(Top) Though natural enemies, vampire Nyssa (Leonor Varella) and Blade (Wesley Snipes) develop mutual respect and attraction in 2002's *Blade II*. (© 2002 New Line Productions, Inc. All rights reserved.)

(Above) Bloodpacker "Snowman" (fight choreographer/actor Donnie Yen) gets his kicks fighting a Reaper in *Blade II*.

Stunt wires facilitated the wild, high-flying battle between Blade and Nomak (Luke Goss) in *Blade II*.

evoke the character's comic book origins. The allegorical elements are downplayed this time in favor of action.

There are even echoes of classic films from an earlier era—not horror films, but Westerns! "There are a lot of Western elements in both films," David Goyer says. "I made no qualms about the fact that Whistler is very much supposed to be the aging gunslinger, passing his tools of the trade onto Blade." In this context, John Wayne, Walter Brennan, and Ricky Nelson from *Rio Bravo* can clearly be seen as prototypes for Blade, Whistler, and Scud.

Many critics felt *Blade II* was even better than its predecessor. So did the movie-going public, which bought $33-million worth of tickets during the film's opening weekend alone, ensuring that there will be a *Blade III*.

Once more, one of Marvel's least typical heroes served as the basis for one of the company's most successful films.

THE NEXT MORNING, ON A QUIET SIDE STREET IN NEW YORK'S COLORFUL GREENWICH VILLAGE...

I'M HERE TO SEE *DR. STRANGE!* HE DOESN'T KNOW ME, BUT---

DOCTOR STRANGE KNOWS ALL! ENTER!

SUDDENLY, A TALL, BROODING FIGURE APPEARS, WEARING A STRIKING AMULET AT HIS THROAT! THE COLD GREY EYES OF *DR. STRANGE* SEEM TO PIERCE THE MIST OF THE ROOM LIKE A KNIFE!

I-I HAD TO COME! I'M IN TROUBLE!

NATURALLY! ALL WHO COME TO ME ARE! *SPEAK...*

IT'S MY *DREAMS!* EVERY NIGHT I HAVE THE SAME DREAM---OVER AND OVER!! IT'S TERRIBLE! I CAN'T STAND IT!

CONTINUE...

IT'S ALWAYS THE SAME! A HAUNTING FIGURE, BOUND IN CHAINS APPEARS... IT STARES AT ME! IT NEVER STOPS! *NEVER!*

ENOUGH!

TONIGHT I SHALL VISIT YOU! I SHALL FIND THE ANSWER TO YOUR DREAM! NOW GO!

BUT *HOW??* HOW WILL YOU *DO* IT?

...BY *ENTERING YOUR DREAM.!!!*

!!!

LATER, ALONE IN HIS ROOM, *DR. STRANGE* SITS SILENTLY IN FRONT OF AN ANCIENT INCENSE BURNER, AS HIS PHYSICAL BODY GOES INTO AN EERIE TRANCE...

IT IS TIME FOR ME TO VISIT *THE MASTER,* FROM WHOM ALL MY POWERS STEM...

LIKE A FLEETING GHOST, HIS METAPHYSICAL SPIRIT LEAVES HIS MOTIONLESS BODY AND DRIFTS AWAY...

...BEING WITHOUT FORM OR SUBSTANCE, NOTHING CAN IMPEDE ITS FLIGHT! IT DRIFTS EFFORTLESSLY THRU THE BUILDING WALL...

...HIGH INTO THE SKY.. ACROSS THE VAST OCEAN ...ACROSS THE CONTINENTS... CONQUERING ALL OF TIME AND SPACE IN ITS SILENT FLIGHT..

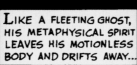
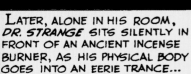

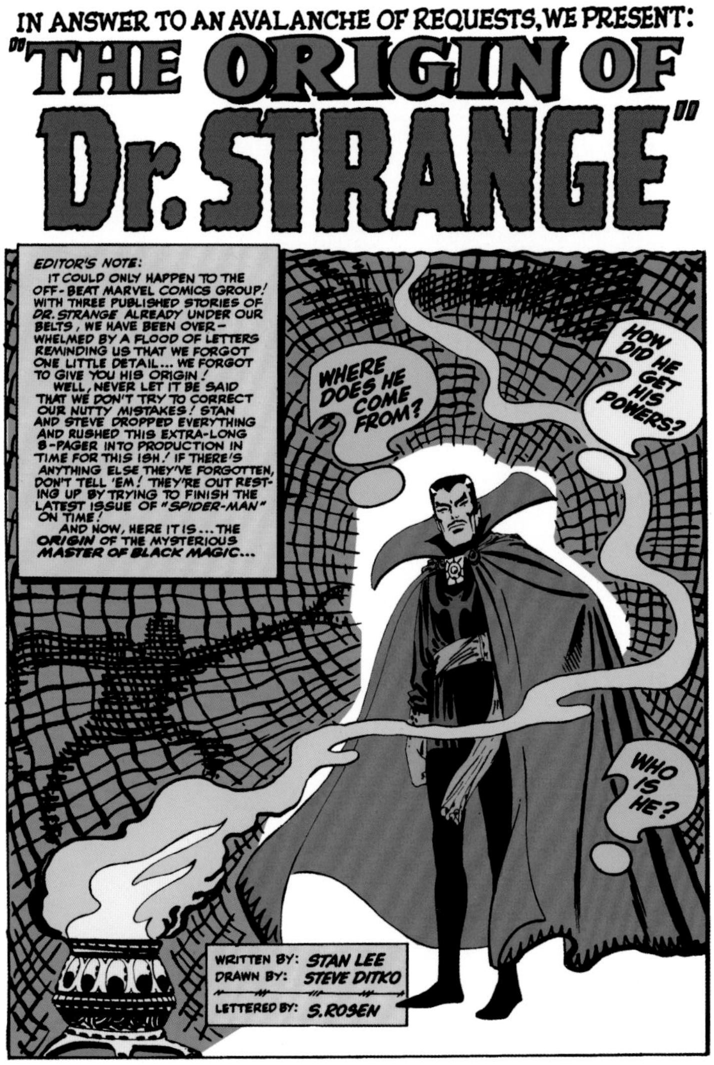
IN ANSWER TO AN AVALANCHE OF REQUESTS, WE PRESENT:
"THE ORIGIN OF Dr. STRANGE"
EDITOR'S NOTE: IT COULD ONLY HAPPEN TO THE OFF-BEAT MARVEL COMICS GROUP! WITH THREE PUBLISHED STORIES OF DR. STRANGE ALREADY UNDER OUR BELTS, WE HAVE BEEN OVER-WHELMED BY A FLOOD OF LETTERS REMINDING US THAT WE FORGOT ONE LITTLE DETAIL... WE FORGOT TO GIVE YOU HIS ORIGIN! WELL, NEVER LET IT BE SAID THAT WE DON'T TRY TO CORRECT OUR NUTTY MISTAKES! STAN AND STEVE DROPPED EVERYTHING AND RUSHED THIS EXTRA-LONG 8-PAGER INTO PRODUCTION IN TIME FOR THIS ISH! IF THERE'S ANYTHING ELSE THEY'VE FORGOTTEN, DON'T TELL 'EM! THEY'RE OUT RESTING UP BY TRYING TO FINISH THE LATEST ISSUE OF "SPIDER-MAN" ON TIME! AND NOW, HERE IT IS... THE ORIGIN OF THE MYSTERIOUS MASTER OF BLACK MAGIC...
WHERE DOES HE COME FROM?
HOW DID HE GET HIS POWERS?
WHO IS HE?
WRITTEN BY: STAN LEE
DRAWN BY: STEVE DITKO
LETTERED BY: S. ROSEN

Readers had to wait five issues before learning about Dr. Strange's origin. From *Strange Tales* #115 (December 1963).

(Opposite) Dr. Strange was never more mysterious than in his first appearance in *Strange Tales* #110 (July 1963).

DR. STRANGE

Ever since he first appeared in the pages of *Strange Tales* (in issue, #110, July 1963), Dr. Strange has defied easy categorization. He is not exactly a superhero, though at times he has taken on the mantle, and even the physical appearance, of one. Nor is he truly superhuman, although he can hardly be called an ordinary guy, either. He is neither a born mutant nor a man whose mind and body has been altered by radiation, though he does have powers that all other mortals do not possess.

Exactly who or what is Dr. Strange?

As first depicted by Steve Ditko, Dr. Strange was a completely inscrutable figure who had somehow acquired the power to step in and out of people's dreams. In his earliest tales, he is presented as a kind of private detective specializing in the arcane and eldritch, who wages battle against a spectral figure called Nightmare. A tall, tranquil figure dressed in black, with an orange sash and orange gloves, Strange wears an amulet that holds a metal eye, which opens to hypnotize others.

The secret origin of the Master of Mystic Arts was not revealed until *Strange Tales* #115 Dec 1963, at which time readers were introduced to the worldly Dr. Stephen Strange, a brilliant but self-centered physician whose skills as a surgeon are surpassed only by his arrogance toward others. When asked to participate in a research project, Strange snaps, "Sorry, I am not interested in charity work! When you're willing to pay me for my talent, I will listen!" But fate steps like an avenging angel and Strange's surgical career is ended when his hands were damaged in a car crash. Embittered and self-pitying, he becomes a derelict, wandering around the docks. There he overhears a sailor speaking of a legendary person called The Ancient One, who can cure any affliction through magic. Strange sets out to find him. After months of searching through India, a haggard Stephen Strange lurches into the abode of The Ancient One, who takes him in and teaches him not only humility, but mastery of black magic.

Despite its sinister connotation, the black magic used by The Ancient One is deployed for the benefit of mankind by keeping at bay the dark forces that are poised to take over an unsuspecting world. Of particular danger is the all-powerful Dread Dormammu, ruler of the Dark Dimension, whom a sinister fellow acolyte called Mordo is secretly attempting to summon. It is to this calling, saving mankind through mystic arts, that Dr. Strange now dedicates his life.

According to Stan Lee, the inspiration for creating Dr. Strange came from the old radio program "Chandu, The Magician" (which in turn was the basis for a 1932 serial starring Bela Lugosi), though heavy dollops of the cosmic "elder race" mythologies created by horror writer H. P. Lovecraft seem to have been thrown in for good measure.

The timing for such a character could not have been better: Dr. Strange arrived on the scene right at the beginning of a new wave of popular interest in the occult, a wave that would ultimately spawn the immensely popular novel *Rosemary's Baby* and its subsequent film adaptation. As time went on Dr. Strange was better outfitted for the part of a sorcerer, with a dramatic red-horned cape, giving him a faintly devilish appearance, and his adventures became increasingly wild, with the doctor zooming off into other worlds or other planes of consciousness, often to rescue his love interest, the Princess Clea, who hailed from the Dark Dimension.

After Ditko and Lee left the series, it seemed like every available member of the Marvel Bullpen took a crack at the character, including artists Bill Everett, Marie Severin, Gene Colan, Herb Trimpe, Dick Giordano, and Dan Adkins, and writers Roy Thomas, Steve Englehart, and Denny O'Neil. Under the guidance of Thomas and Colan, Dr. Strange was recast into a traditional superhero mold: a muscular figure in blue tights and a billowing red cape, with a ghostly "Vision"-like countenance. That version, though, was short-lived.

Strange Tales was rechristened *Dr. Strange* magazine in 1968, but the title was discontinued a year later. Dr. Strange has been brought back twice since, once in 1974 and in a longer running series that lasted

Actor Peter Hooten (left) assumed the title role in 1978's "Dr. Strange," with veteran actor John Mills as his mentor, Dr. Lindmer.

Little-known actor Peter Hooten beat out Patrick Wayne and Peter Fonda for the role of Dr. Strange.

from 1988 to 1996, in which he was billed as "Dr. Strange, Sorcerer Supreme." Despite his various incarnations, however, what readers most enjoyed about the character were his colorful, often alliterate oaths: "By the hoary hosts of Hoggath"; "By the Roving Rings of Raggadorr"; "By the vapors of Valtorr"; and "By the shades of the shadowy Seraphim," among them.

DR. STRANGE IN THE MEDIA

The same creative burst that brought The Incredible Hulk, Spider-Man, and Captain America to television in the late 1970s also resulted in the Master of Mystic Arts's only appearance on television, in the movie-cum-series pilot "Dr. Strange," executive produced, written, and directed by Philip De Guere.

The film's opening set the tone for what follows with the following Twilight Zonish invocation: *"There is a barrier that separates the known from the unknown. Beyond this threshold lies a battleground where forces of good and evil are in eternal conflict. The fate of mankind hangs in the balance and awaits the outcome. In every age and time, some of us are called upon to join the battle . . ."* The film then shifts to a strange, Hellish domain occupied by The Nameless One, a weird, tree-like creature with four glowing eyes (created through stop-motion animation), who is communing with his servant, Morgan Le Fay (played by Jessica Walter), instructing her to prevent the transfer of power that will take place in three days between the Earth's protective wizard and his successor. (And while Morgan LeFay may be evil, her scarlet *demonatrix* outfit is downright wicked, even by the loosening standards of 1970s television.) The demon tells Morgan that she will recognize the successor—who is not yet even aware of his destiny—by his ring, which bears the ancient mystic symbol for light.

The successor to elderly wizard Thomas Lindmer (veteran actor John Mills) is of course Dr. Stephen Strange (Peter Hooten), a resident in psychiatry at New York's East Side Hospital and in this treatment of the story a dedicated and caring physician—albeit one who often runs afoul of his stuffy, by-the-book supervisors—with an eye for the ladies. Both Strange and a young woman named Clea Lake (Eddie Benton, an actress despite her masculine-sounding name) are pulled into the cosmic tug-of-war between the seemingly frail Lindmer and the overconfident Morgan Le Fay, and at one point are forced to carry on the battle in the eerie astral plane ruled by The Nameless One.

It is eventually revealed that Lindmer knew Strange as a child and that Strange's father and the old wizard, who had recognized the boy's special gifts even then, had made a pact that Stephen would follow in Lindmer's footsteps, but even so, it is a choice that Stephen has to make himself. (This trapped-by-destiny approach differs from the comic book treatment of the character.) Initially he is reluctant, preferring the pleasures of normal Earthly existence far more, but after a final encounter with Morgan, he accepts his destiny. To do so, Lindmer informs him, means giving up forever "the pleasures of ignorance, of offspring, and easy death," but Strange accepts anyway and receives the guardianship of the light from a higher power. But the film makes it clear that the battle between Dr. Strange and Morgan Le Fay is far from over. In fact, it is only beginning.

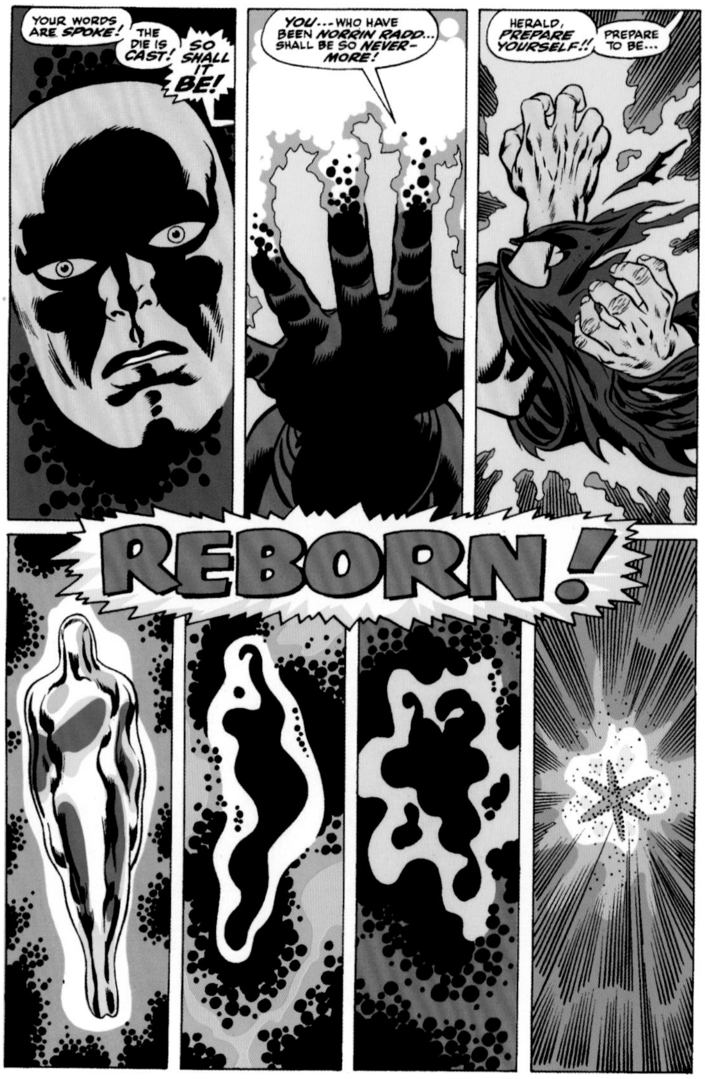
YOUR WORDS ARE SPOKE!
THE DIE IS CAST!
SO SHALL IT BE!
YOU...WHO HAVE BEEN NORRIN RADD... SHALL BE SO NEVER-MORE!
HERALD, PREPARE YOURSELF!!
PREPARE TO BE...
REBORN!

"Dr. Strange" is considered by some to be the best of the pack of Marvel-inspired pilots made by Universal in the late 1970s, in spite of its low budget (about $1 million) and a short shooting schedule (thirteen days), which seriously hampered the film's special effects, something that particularly distressed Philip De Guere. "We tried to use what was at the time a state-of-the-art front projection system, but it turned out not to work anywhere near as well as we had hoped," De Guere says. That technique, in which an artificial background image is projected overtop of the actors, creating an instantaneous matte, was employed for the scenes in which Strange and Clea fly into the psychedelic astral dimension. (For a demonstration of how far state-of-the-art television effects have come, just compare the

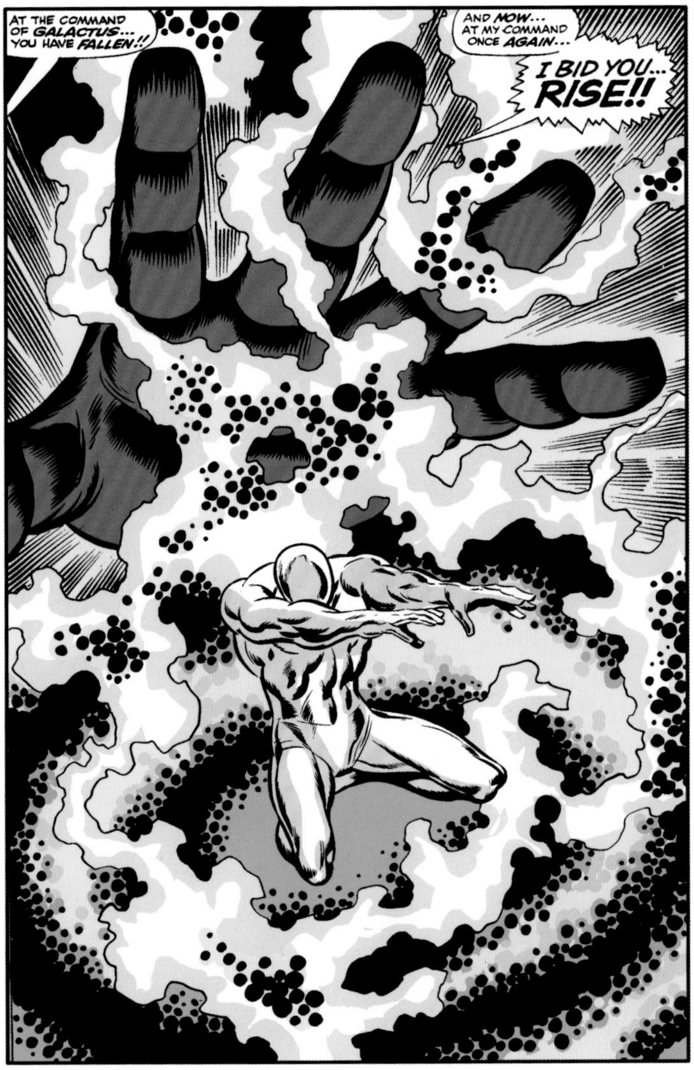
AT THE COMMAND OF GALACTUS... YOU HAVE FALLEN!!
AND NOW... AT MY COMMAND ONCE AGAIN...
I BID YOU... RISE!!

Norrin Radd is transformed into The Silver Surfer through the powerful artwork of John Buscema. From *The Silver Surfer* #1 (August 1968).

(Following spread) The Silver Surfer made an auspicious debut in *The Fantastic Four* #48 (1966).

interesting but low-tech astral plane scenes in "Dr. Strange" with the digitized dream/limbo sequences from "Generation X," made eighteen years later.)

But if the effects didn't work as planned, neither did the casting of Peter Hooten, who comes off as stiff and wooden, particularly against the elegant performances of Mills and Walter. "There were other candidates [for the role] like Patrick Wayne, who kind of looked like Dr. Strange, and we gave some consideration to Peter Fonda," recalls De Guere. "We felt that Peter Hooten was the right guy, partially because Frank Price, who was then head of Universal Television, showed the [audition] tape to his kids and his kids like Peter Hooten the best."

As for the dapper Mills, a major figure of the British postwar cinema who eight years earlier had taken home an Academy Award as Best Supporting Actor for the film *Ryan's Daughter,* De Guere says, "We were really graced with his presence." While the character of Lindmer is deliberately left mysterious, his name presents a tantalizing clue as to his possible identity when the "d" is removed from Lindmer and the syllables are reversed. Add to that the fact that the name "Morgan Le Fay" features prominently in Arthurian legend and the connection is strengthened.

"Dr. Strange" garnered disappointing ratings when it was aired over CBS on September 6, 1978, something that is often blamed on the fact that it ran opposite a re-broadcast of one of television's most notable productions, "Roots." Former Marvel editor and writer Roy Thomas recalls that a second "Dr. Strange" film was discussed at the time, which he was to have co-scripted, though nothing came of it. At least one person was glad that the project failed to launch a series: Phil De Guere. "At that point in the *zeitgeist* as it was reflected within Universal Television and CBS, everybody felt that everything had to be explained, that the subject matter couldn't simply be presented on its own terms," De Guere says. "I remember feeling that the show would be ponderous, that it would have the feeling of a lecture series more

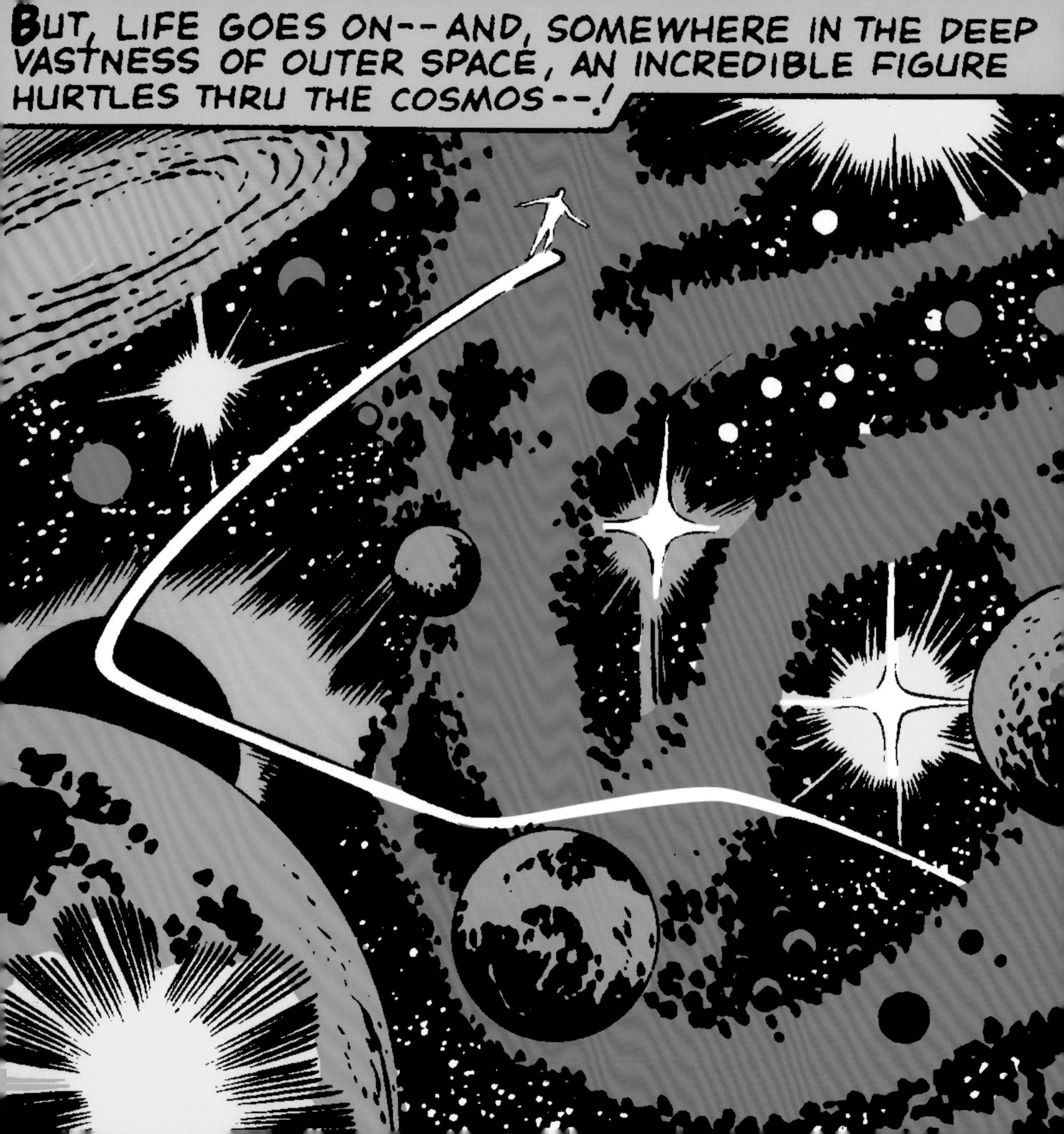
BUT, LIFE GOES ON--AND, SOMEWHERE IN THE DEEP VASTNESS OF OUTER SPACE, AN INCREDIBLE FIGURE HURTLES THRU THE COSMOS--!

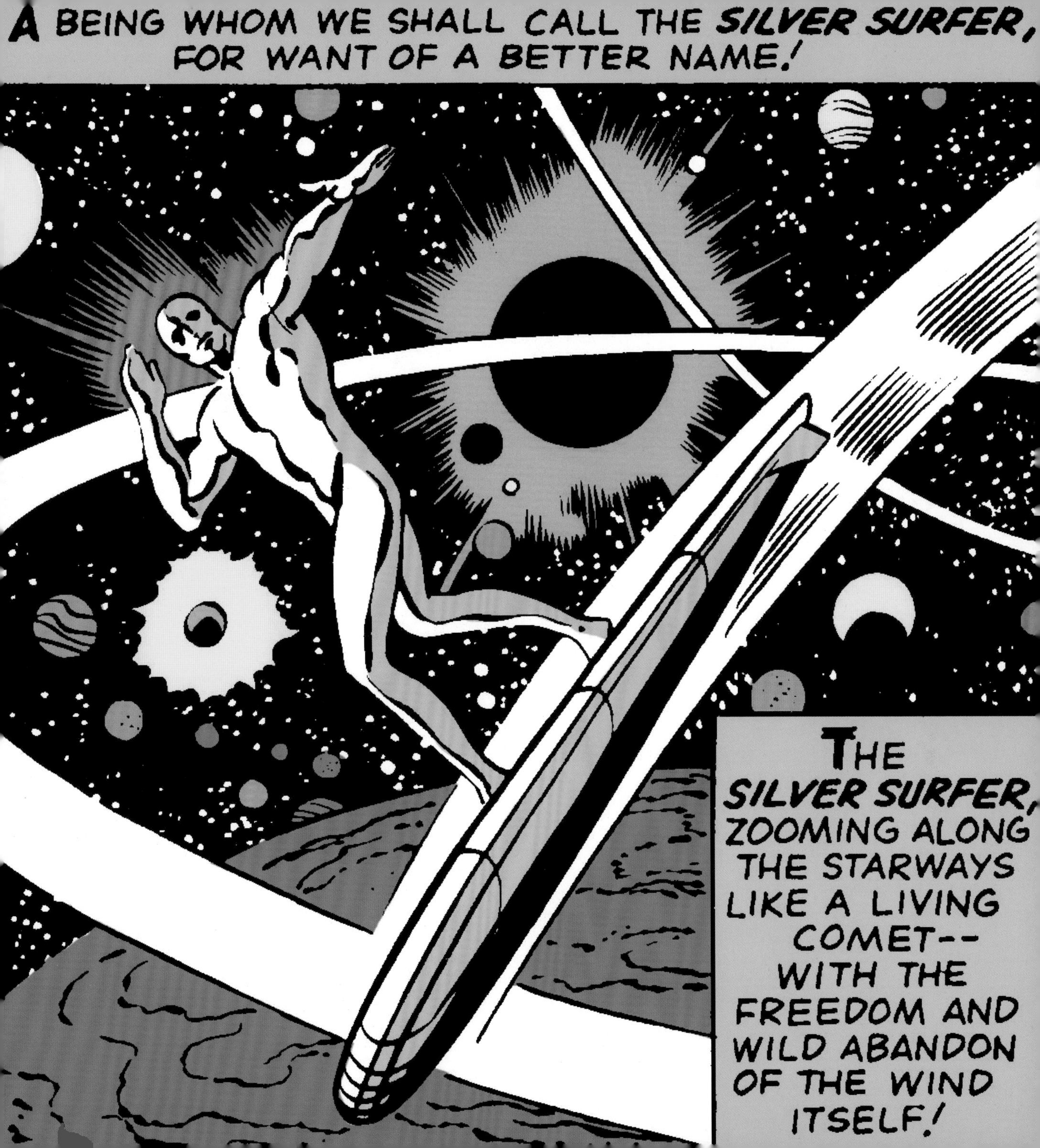
A BEING WHOM WE SHALL CALL THE SILVER SURFER, FOR WANT OF A BETTER NAME!
THE SILVER SURFER, ZOOMING ALONG THE STARWAYS LIKE A LIVING COMET-- WITH THE FREEDOM AND WILD ABANDON OF THE WIND ITSELF!

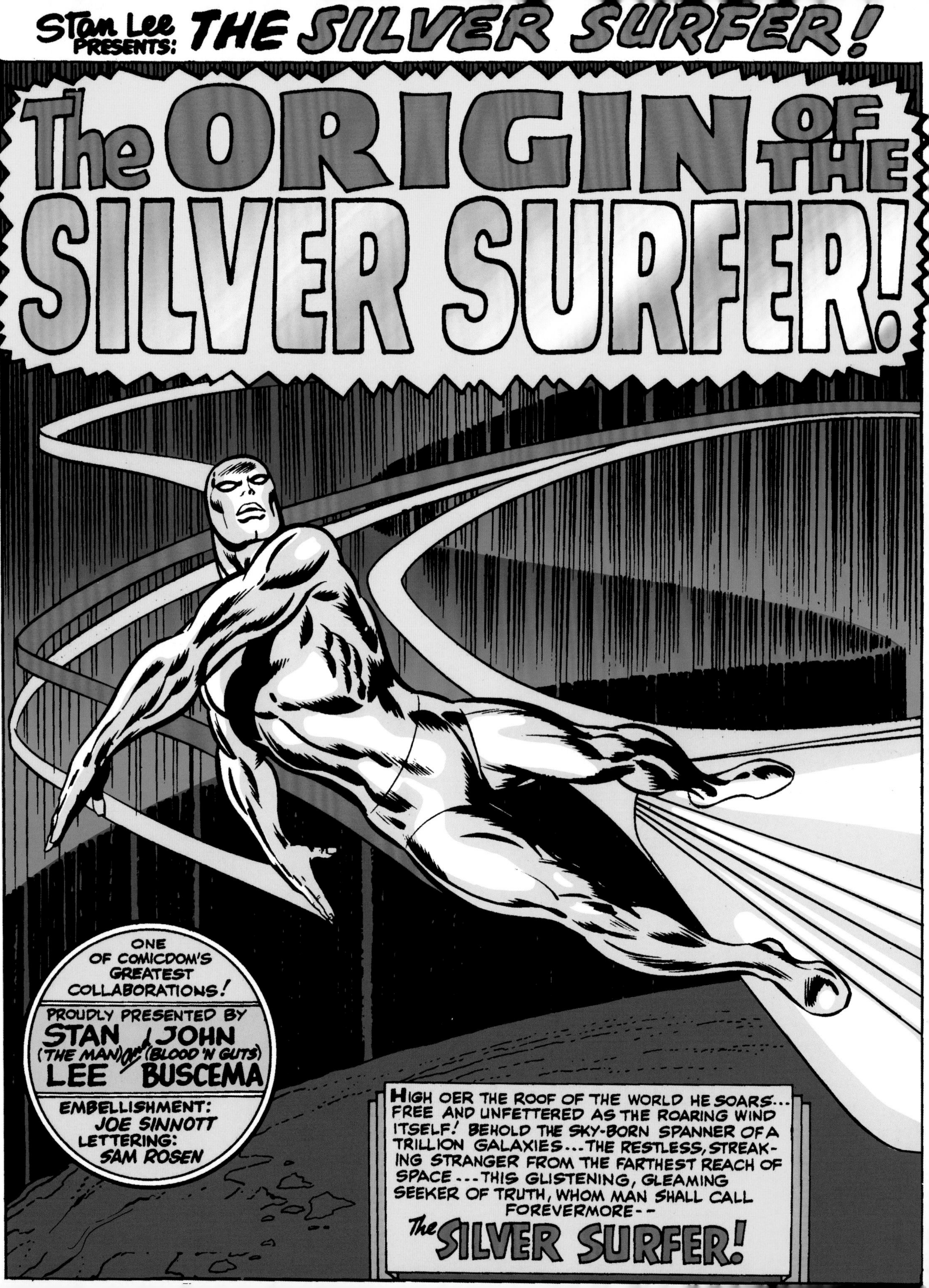
Stan Lee PRESENTS: THE SILVER SURFER!
The ORIGIN OF THE SILVER SURFER!
ONE OF COMICDOM'S GREATEST COLLABORATIONS!
PROUDLY PRESENTED BY STAN (THE MAN) LEE and JOHN (BLOOD 'N GUTS) BUSCEMA
EMBELLISHMENT: JOE SINNOTT
LETTERING: SAM ROSEN
HIGH OER THE ROOF OF THE WORLD HE SOARS... FREE AND UNFETTERED AS THE ROARING WIND ITSELF! BEHOLD THE SKY-BORN SPANNER OF A TRILLION GALAXIES... THE RESTLESS, STREAKING STRANGER FROM THE FARTHEST REACH OF SPACE --- THIS GLISTENING, GLEAMING SEEKER OF TRUTH, WHOM MAN SHALL CALL FOREVERMORE-- The SILVER SURFER!

than an adventure series if every single thing that was happening had to [be explained]."

Feature film adaptations of Dr. Strange were announced in 1983 and 1986, and again in 1993, at which time horror film director Wes Craven was connected to the project, but none of them were realized. One can only hope that before long, Dr. Strange will conquer his most persistent nemesis, The Horrible Hindrance of Hiatus.

THE SILVER SURFER

It was the classic show business cliché: the kid plucked from the chorus to become a star. Only it wasn't in a movie or Broadway show that this leap to stardom occurred, it was in the pages of *The Fantastic Four # 48*, in 1966, and the star-to-be was called The Silver Surfer.

The Surfer made his debut through a now-legendary three-issue story written by Stan Lee and drawn by Jack Kirby (pencils) and Joe Sinnott (inks) that has become known as *The Galactus Trilogy*. As conceptualized, the story was one that pitted The Fantastic Four against the destructive Galactus, an enormous, armored alien being who survives by draining the energy force from planets, without regard for who or what might be destroyed in the process. When Lee began to review Kirby's artwork, he noticed a sleek, metallic figure riding the cosmos on a surfboard to serve as Galactus's herald, searching the cosmos for new worlds for his master to consume. Recognizing a superhero when they saw one, Lee and Kirby began to build up The Surfer's role in the story until he became a major player.

The Silver Surfer began his planetary existence as Norrin Radd of the planet Zenn-La, a brooding, poetic malcontent and a restless spirit searching for understanding and adventure. When Galactus suddenly appears on Zenn-La, Radd is among the few of his planet willing to fight the intergalactic warrior. But in the end he opts instead for a bargain: if Galactus will

The Silver Surfer was one of the most stylish of all comic book heroes.

spare his home planet, Radd will serve him as his herald, roaming the universe to seek out safe planets, those with no advanced life forms, for Galactus to de-energize. Galactus agrees and encases Radd's body in a "life-preserving silvery substance" that shields him from heat, cold, and lack of oxygen, and proclaims him reborn as The Silver Surfer. Now transformed, Radd is forced to leave his love, Shalla Bal, behind on Zenn-La.

The Silver Surfer carries out his duties faithfully until he comes across the planet Earth. After an encounter with Ben Grimm's girlfriend Alicia Masters, the Surfer becomes fascinated by the imperfect human race and is persuaded to defy Galactus. With the help of the Surfer and the normally impartial Watcher, the Fantastic Four manage to drive Galactus away by threatening to use one of his own weapons, the "Ultimate Nullifier," against him. "The prize is not worth the battle," Galactus declares, and the Earth is saved. Incensed over the Surfer's betrayal, however, Galactus banishes him from his service and condemns him to remain on Earth by removing his space-time powers.

Eventually Galactus would try to reenlist the Surfer as his herald (as related in the 1978 Silver Surfer graphic novel by Lee and Kirby), employing the space-born temptress Ardina to lure him back, and while the Silver Surfer falls desperately in love with her, he cannot return to the service of Galactus. The Silver Surfer is destined to wander the earth, desperately trying to understand the humans that he must live alongside.

Working on The Silver Surfer seemed to inspire both Lee and Kirby to new heights. The character, in fact, might just be their signature masterpiece. Long a master at staging action, Kirby's work on The Silver Surfer was remarkable even for him, investing the character with lithe power and energy as well as an appealing, placid mystery. As for Lee's writing, even his panel texts soared off into a quasi-poetic realm that he rarely approached either before or since. "*High o'er the roof of the world he soars, free and unfettered as the roaring*

MEANWHILE ATOP ONE OF THE MOST INACCESSIBLE PEAKS IN EUROPE ...
WHAT AN INDESCRIBABLE THRILL! WHAT A GLORIOUS TRIUMPH!
WITHIN SECONDS WE'LL REACH THE VERY SUMMIT..!
WE'LL STAND WHERE NO OTHER LIVING BEING HAS EVER STOOD BEFORE.
WE'LL BE FAMOUS THROUGH-OUT THE WORLD!
A FEAT LIKE THIS MAY NEVER BE DUPLICATED AGAIN!
IT TOOK MONTHS OF PLANNING ... OF SACRIFICE ... BUT IT WAS WORTH IT!
WE'VE DONE THE IMPOSSIBLE!
BUT, WHEN THE FIRST MEMBER OF THE DAUNTLESS LITTLE EXPEDITION FINALLY REACHES HIS GOAL ... HIS STARTLED EYES BEHOLD ...
THERE'S SOMEONE.. HERE... BEFORE US...!
I HAVE LEARNED ALL THERE IS TO LEARN OF THE PLANET EARTH...
BUT... WHO?? WHAT..??
THE PLANET UPON WHICH GALACTUS HAS SENTENCED ME TO REMAIN.. FOREVER!*
AND NOW, THE TIME IS COME..
THE SILVER SURFER SHALL RETURN TO THE FEMALE HUMAN WHO HAD ONCE BEFRIENDED HIM!
*FROM THE NOW PRACTICALLY PRICELESS FANTASTIC FOUR #50.. SPECIFIC STAN.
I, WHO HAVE CRESTED THE CURRENTS OF SPACE... WHO HAVE DODGED THE METEOR SWARMS, AND OUT-DISTANCED THE FASTEST COMETS...
I MUST RESIGN MYSELF TO THIS PRISON WHICH MEN CALL EARTH... BECAUSE I DARED GIVE UP THE FREEDOM OF THE UNIVERSE TO AID THE HAPLESS HUMANS!
BUT, I MUST HAVE NO REGRETS! WHATEVER DESTINY AWAITS ME... I SHALL BE TRUE TO MY TRUST, THOUGH I AM A STRANGER IN A WORLD I NEVER MADE!

The Silver Surfer's probing, philosophical nature made him unique among superheroes. From *The Fantastic Four* #55 (October 1966)—artwork by Jack Kirby and Joe Sinnott.

(Top and Middle) The Silver Surfer made a graceful translation to animation in Fox Kid's 1998 series "Silver Surfer."

(Above) World-destroyer Galactus was created through computer animation in 1998's "Silver Surfer."

wind itself!" begins *The Silver Surfer* #1, *"Behold the sky-born spanner of a trillion galaxies, the restless, streaking stranger from the farthest reach of space, this glistening, gleaming seeker of truth, whom man shall call forevermore—THE SILVER SURFER."*

The Surfer was given his own magazine in 1968, with John Buscema ably taking over the artistic reigns from Jack Kirby (a situation that Kirby was not happy with), though sales levels implied that The Silver Surfer's time had not yet come. "We did sixteen or seventeen issues and each sold less than the previous issue," Buscema recalls. "Apparently the general public wasn't ready for that kind of character." At least not in the U.S. In France, the character was a huge success. It took a few more years for The Silver Surfer to catch on in the States, but once he did, the questing, self-reflective superhero would go on to become one of the most popular in the entire Marvel Universe.

THE SILVER SURFER IN THE MEDIA

Whatever it was about The Silver Surfer that so inspired the artists and writers of the comic books carried over into his only media translation to date, the Saturday morning animated series "Silver Surfer," which premiered in February of 1998 on the Fox Kids Network. Made by the same production team that had brought so many other Marvel characters to animation, Marvel Entertainment and Saban International, the sleek, high-tech look of the show was different from anything else on the air, thanks to the fact that it utilized computer-generated imagery to an extent not seen before in TV cartooning. Backgrounds, vehicles, spaceships, and special effects were all rendered in CGI. Even the imposing figure of Galactus was created entirely in the computer. "That was a very special show," says Margaret Loesch, who as head of Fox Kids Network supervised the development of the property. "The Silver Surfer was one of my favorite characters and in some ways it is probably the most interesting of all of Stan [Lee's] characters. We were really trying to do something different."

Regarding the computer-generated Galactus, Loesch adds, "The challenge with Galactus is that he's supposed to be huge, and how do you avoid making it look like a big cartoon character?"

The presentation of the Surfer changed only slightly from the comic book mythology. He was still the former Norrin Radd, who had bargained for the safety of his planet and loved ones at the expense of his freedom, but in the series Galactus erases Radd's memory upon transforming him into the Silver Surfer as a way of maintaining control over him. (An early 1990s revision of the comic book origin story revealed that Galactus had altered Radd's personality to eliminate his moral compunction over destroying worlds). In the battle with Galactus over the destiny of Earth, in which a rollerblading teenaged girl named Frankie Raye takes on the task of convincing the Surfer to defend the planet, the Silver Surfer regains his memory and rebels (ultimately, Frankie transforms into Nova and becomes Galactus's new herald). As revenge for his defiance, Galactus does not banish him to Earth, but instead hides the Surfer's home planet of Zenn-La, forcing the Surfer to search the cosmos, wandering from planet to planet like a modern-day Ulysses in search of his home.

Throughout the course of thirteen episodes-worth of intergalactic journeys, the Silver Surfer comes into battle with the evil Thanos; Nebula, the beautiful but dangerous leader of a band of space pirates; The Kree, under the rule of Supremor, and the cruel Skrull. But despite its distinctive graphic look that can only be described as *cool* and its thoughtful scripts, "Silver Surfer" was not the kind of huge hit that Fox Kids had enjoyed with the earlier "X-Men" and "Spider-Man" series. Then again, Loesch says she never expected that it would be. "It was like an art film," she says. "It wasn't that commercially successful, but to a small group it was very successful."

(Top) Norrin Radd—soon to be The Silver Surfer—and his Shalla Bal confront danger on their home planet of Zenn-La in 1998's "Silver Surfer."

(Above) To save his planet from destruction, Norrin Radd (right) surrenders his freedom to Galactus in "Silver Surfer"'s two-part origin episode.

(Opposite) The Questor of the Cosmos, the Silver Surfer.

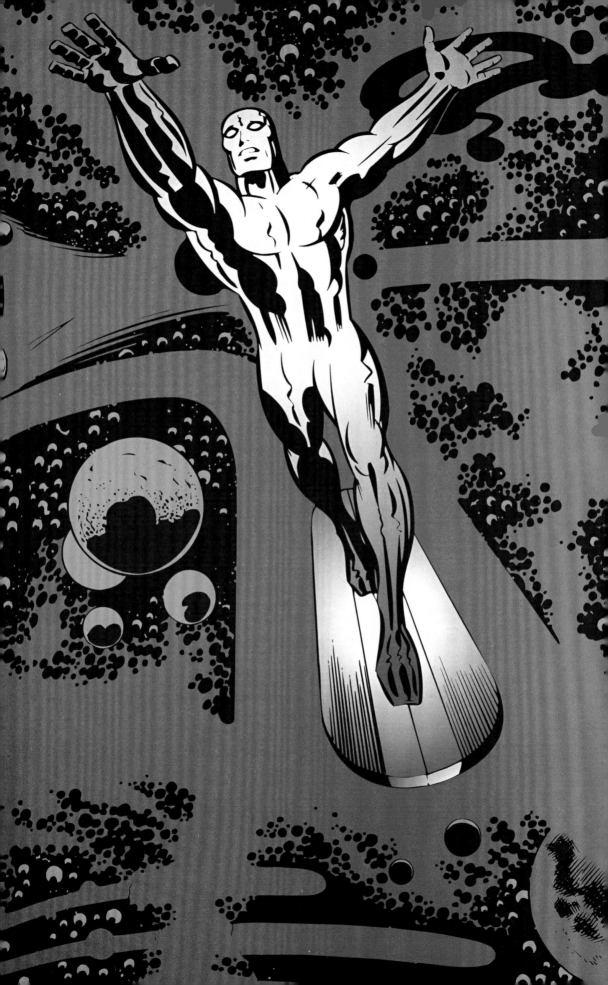

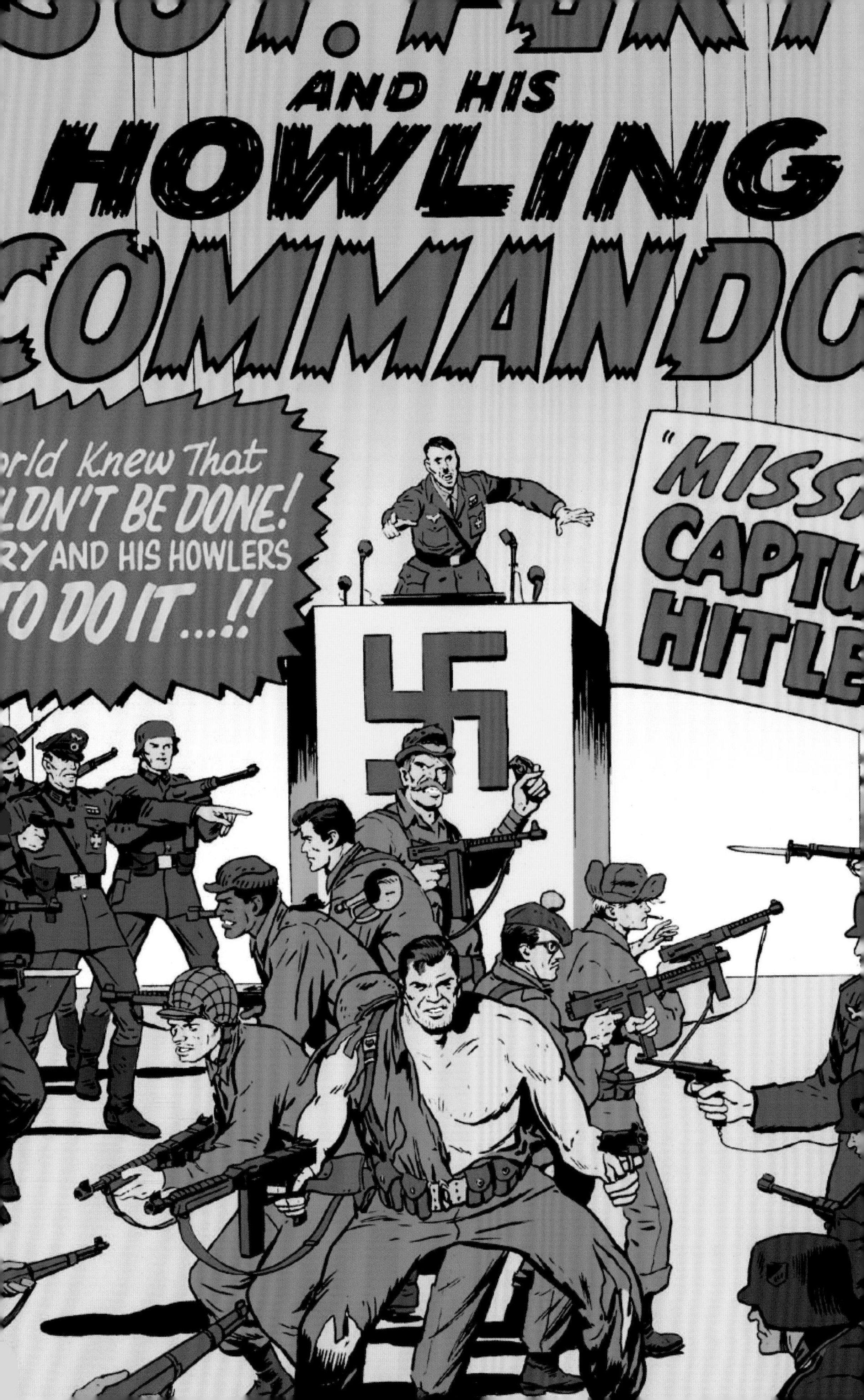

AND HIS
HOWLING
COMMANDO
orld Knew That
LDN'T BE DONE!
RY AND HIS HOWLERS
TO DO IT...!!
"MISS
CAPTU
HITLE

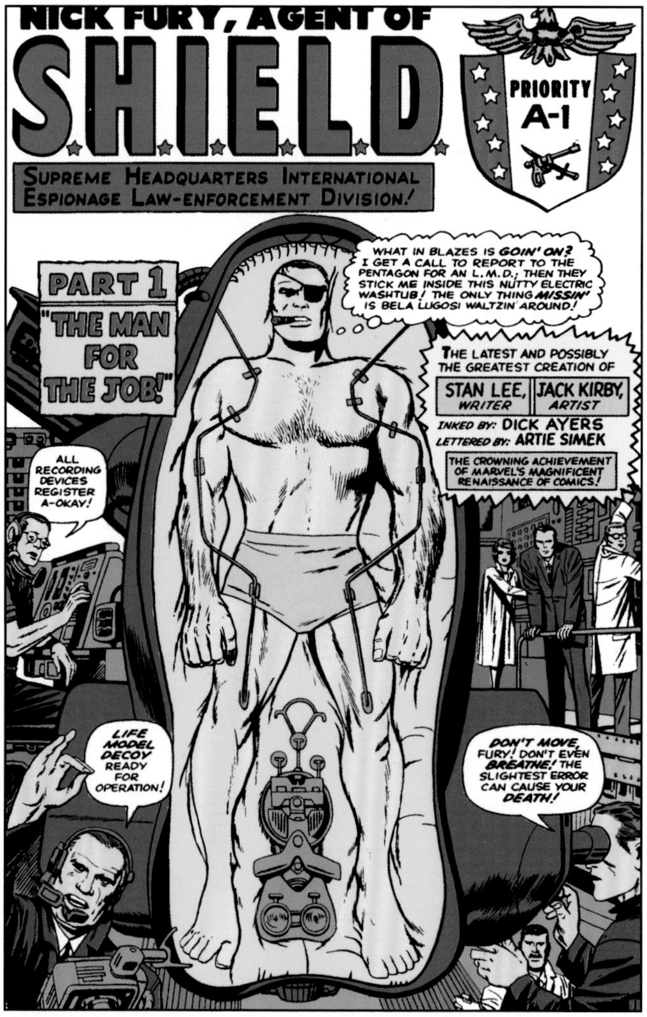
NICK FURY, AGENT OF
S.H.I.E.L.D.
PRIORITY A-1
SUPREME HEADQUARTERS INTERNATIONAL ESPIONAGE LAW-ENFORCEMENT DIVISION!
PART 1 "THE MAN FOR THE JOB!"
WHAT IN BLAZES IS GOIN' ON? I GET A CALL TO REPORT TO THE PENTAGON FOR AN L.M.D.; THEN THEY STICK ME INSIDE THIS NUTTY ELECTRIC WASHTUB! THE ONLY THING MISSIN' IS BELA LUGOSI WALTZIN' AROUND!
THE LATEST AND POSSIBLY THE GREATEST CREATION OF
STAN LEE, WRITER
JACK KIRBY, ARTIST
INKED BY: DICK AYERS
LETTERED BY: ARTIE SIMEK
THE CROWNING ACHIEVEMENT OF MARVEL'S MAGNIFICENT RENAISSANCE OF COMICS!
ALL RECORDING DEVICES REGISTER A-OKAY!
LIFE MODEL DECOY READY FOR OPERATION!
DON'T MOVE, FURY! DON'T EVEN BREATHE! THE SLIGHTEST ERROR CAN CAUSE YOUR DEATH!

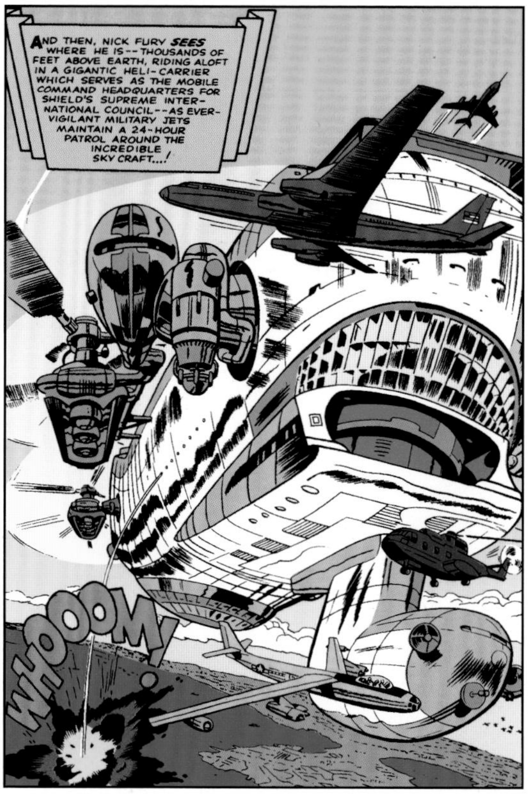
AND THEN, NICK FURY SEES WHERE HE IS--THOUSANDS OF FEET ABOVE EARTH, RIDING ALOFT IN A GIGANTIC HELI-CARRIER WHICH SERVES AS THE MOBILE COMMAND HEADQUARTERS FOR SHIELD'S SUPREME INTER-NATIONAL COUNCIL--AS EVER-VIGILANT MILITARY JETS MAINTAIN A 24-HOUR PATROL AROUND THE INCREDIBLE SKY CRAFT...!
WHOOOM!

(Top) Fury gets replicated in his first Cold War adventure. From *Strange Tales* #135 (August 1965).

(Above) S.H.I.E.L.D.'s flying fortress as drawn by Jack Kirby (who had a positive genius for rendering machines and gadgets). From *Strange Tales* #135.

(Opposite) Before he was a 1960s secret agent, Nick Fury was leader of a World War II brigade called the "Howling Commandos."

NICK FURY, AGENT OF S.H.I.E.L.D.

The arrival in 1965 of Nick Fury, late of the Central Intelligence Agency, recently promoted to take a leading role in the international organization Supreme Headquarters International Espionage Law-Enforcement Division—better known as S.H.I.E.L.D.—effectively killed two birds with the same stone at the Marvel offices. One was to satisfy readers who wanted to know the current whereabouts of Sgt. Fury, whose World War II exploits in the magazine *Sgt. Fury and His Howling Commandos* were flying off the newsstands each month. Second, it allowed the company to capitalize on the spy craze that was sweeping the 1960s, spurred by the success of the cinema's James Bond and television's "The Man From U.N.C.L.E."

The cigar-chomping, nail-tough, wartime commando was introduced in 1963 and got his promotion "twenty years" later in *Strange Tales* #135, published in August 1965, in a story from Lee and Kirby (with Dick Ayers, who was then handling the pencils for *Sgt. Fury,* inking). Sporting a black eye-patch like a modern pirate, Nick Fury, now a colonel, has been chosen by the president of the United States himself to lead S.H.I.E.L.D.'s fight against HYDRA, a deadly organization of fanatics whose collective goal is to take over the world. Word of Nick's appointment has already gotten to HYDRA (whose shadowy members dress in green suits and head masks with yellow "H"-shaped straps on the front) and assassins are dispatched to kill him.

Seeing five S.H.I.E.L.D.-constructed robotic duplicates take bullets that were intended for him convinces Fury of the need to declare war on HYDRA, though the plain-talking soldier has doubts that he is the right man for the job. He is finally persuaded to take the commission by S.H.I.E.L.D.'s gadget master, Tony Stark, whose incredible devices include a Porsche that converts into a flying car and fires missiles from the rear, and a gigantic "heli-carrier" that hovers above the clouds and houses S.H.I.E.L.D.'s international headquarters. Fury

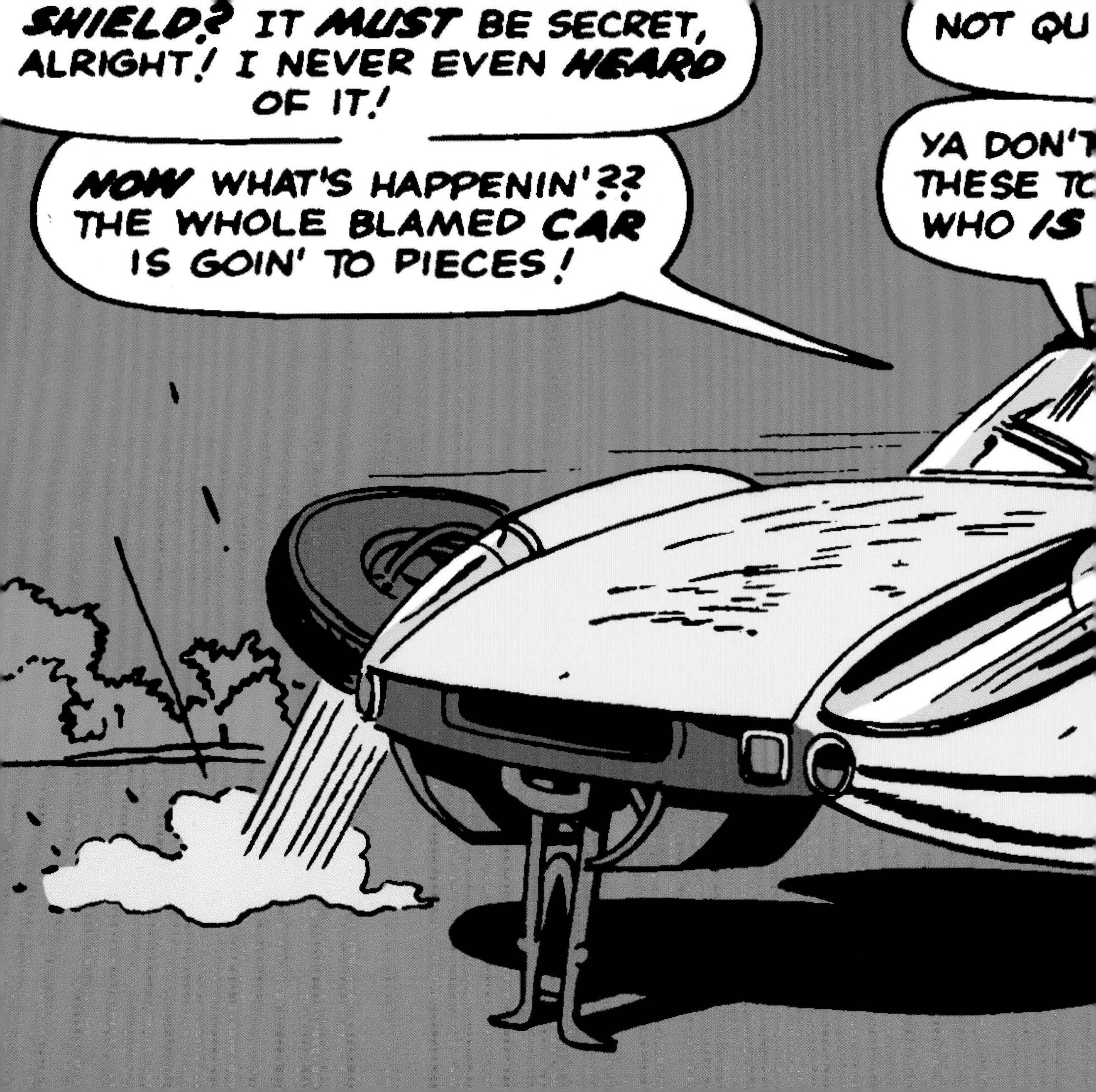

SHIELD? IT MUST BE SECRET, ALRIGHT! I NEVER EVEN HEARD OF IT!
NOW WHAT'S HAPPENIN'?? THE WHOLE BLAMED CAR IS GOIN' TO PIECES!
NOT QU
YA DON'T THESE TO WHO IS

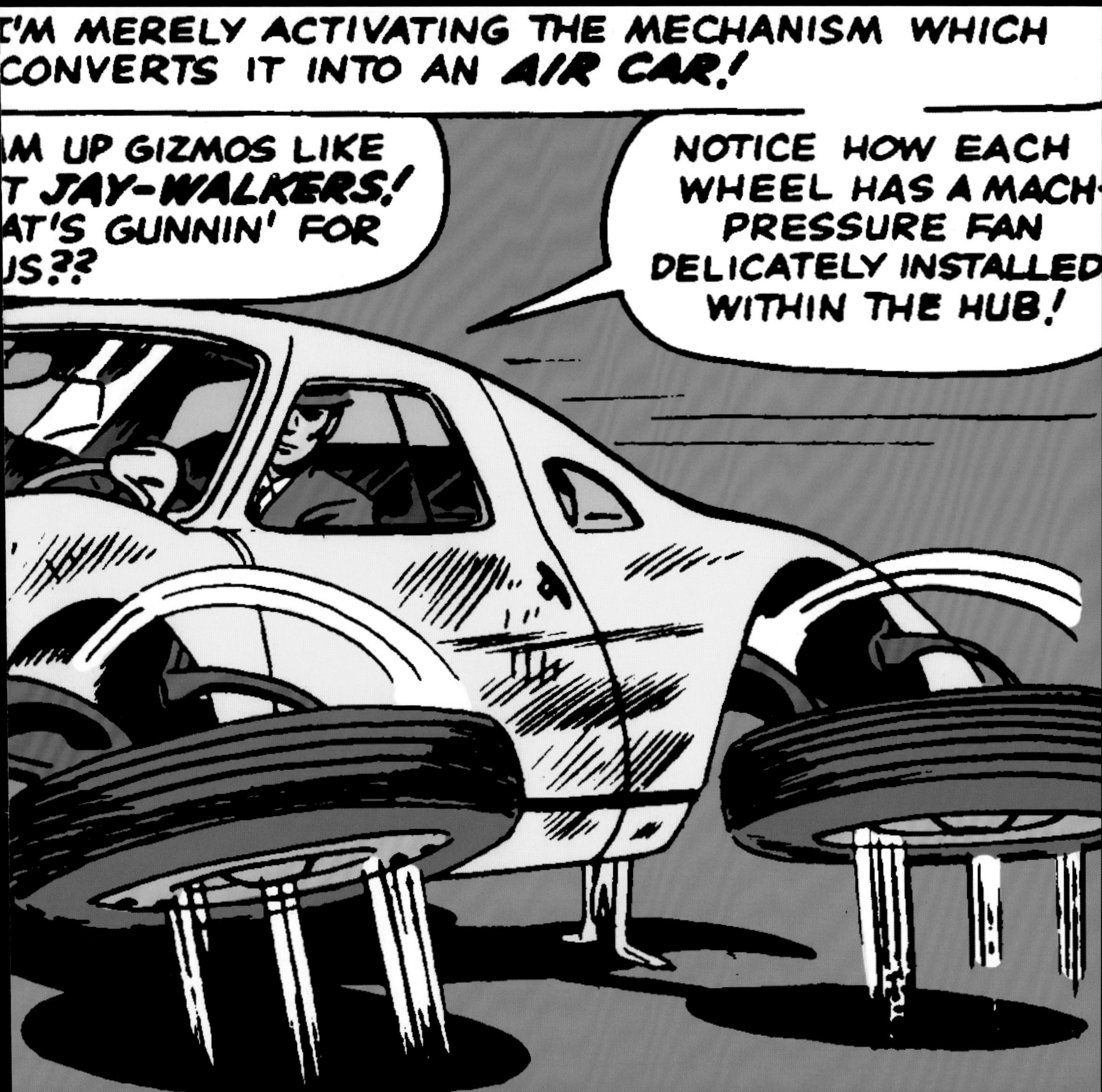
I'M MERELY ACTIVATING THE MECHANISM WHICH CONVERTS IT INTO AN AIR CAR!
M UP GIZMOS LIKE T JAY-WALKERS! AT'S GUNNIN' FOR US??
NOTICE HOW EACH WHEEL HAS A MACH- PRESSURE FAN DELICATELY INSTALLED WITHIN THE HUB!

quickly proves his mettle by discovering a wire under his chair that leads to a bomb. Deploying his combat-trained reflexes and quick thinking ability, he rips the chair out of the floor and shoves it through a porthole of the heli-carrier, where it detonates safely below the sky craft. If there were any doubt before, there is none now: Nick Fury is the only man alive to lead S.H.I.E.L.D. in its battle against HYDRA.

Fury received his own magazine, *Nick Fury, Agent of S.H.I.E.L.D,* in June 1968, and many of his subsequent adventures were guided by artist and writer Jim Steranko, whose striking, innovative style often employed panoramic scenes to create a cinematic effect. Born in 1938 in Reading, Pennsylvania, Steranko (who in later years would go only by his last name) joined Marvel in 1966 and divided his time between comic books and work as an advertising and motion picture artist. His tenure was brief—barely three years—though he would return in the 1970s to edit the first several issues of Marvel's in-house fan magazine *FOOM.*

In the years to come, Fury would discover that the head of HYDRA was his old World War II enemy Baron Wolfgang von Strucker, a key figure in the Third Reich (it would also be revealed that Fury's stubborn refusal to age was the result of his having been exposed to an anti-aging serum called "the Infinity Formula").

Nick Fury remains on the job today, having far out-distanced such one-time contemporaries as U.N.C.L.E.'s Napoleon Solo. He's a little grayer now, though still rock-hard, still sporting the eye-patch, and sometimes working alongside another hero from "the good war," Captain America.

NICK FURY IN THE MEDIA

Colonel Fury's only film appearance to date was in the television movie "Nick Fury, Agent of S.H.I.E.L.D.," which aired on the Fox Television Network in 1998. Written by David Goyer (who had also scripted *Blade* that same year) and directed by Ron Hardy, the film

(Top) Actor David Hasslehoff made a surprisingly convincing Nick Fury in 1998's "Nick Fury, Agent of S.H.I.E.L.D."

(Above) Sandra Hess as The Viper, David Hasslehoff as Nick Fury, and Lisa Rinna as Val from "Nick Fury, Agent of S.H.I.E.L.D." It's easy to see which girl Nick ends up with.

(Previous spread) Another of Fury's spy devices was a transforming Porsche (how James Bond can you get?).

(Opposite) No matter how badly outnumbered or surrounded, Fury and his Commandos always lived to fight another day. And another...

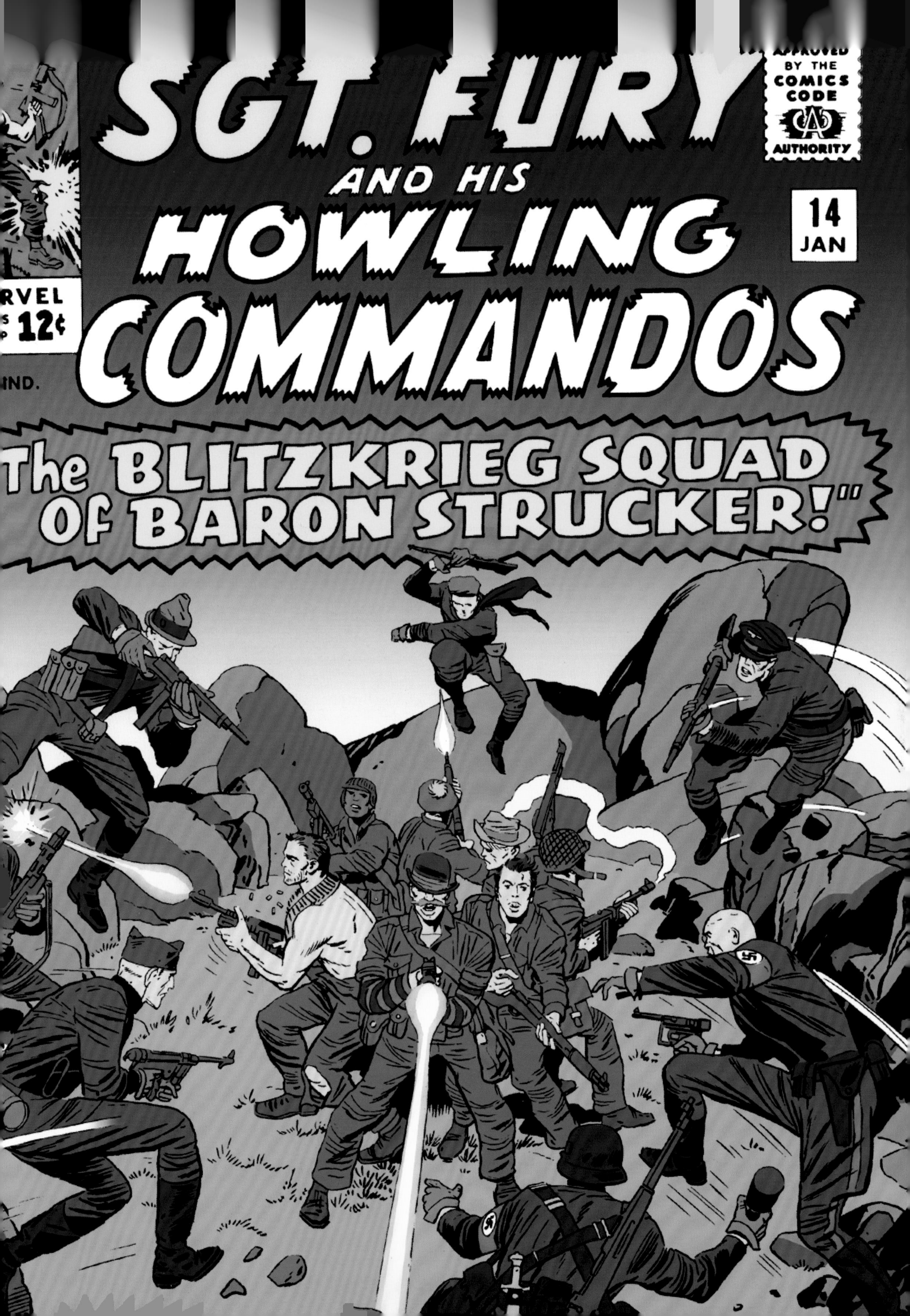
SGT. FURY
AND HIS
HOWLING
COMMANDOS
APPROVED BY THE COMICS CODE AUTHORITY
14
JAN
RVEL
12¢
IND.
"The BLITZKRIEG SQUAD OF BARON STRUCKER!"

starred David Hasselhoff as Fury and Sandra Hess as a sexy blonde supervillainess called The Viper.

Five years after he has been retired and put out to pasture by S.H.I.E.L.D.—chiefly because he was not diplomatic or politically correct enough to function in a post–Cold War world—Nick Fury is summoned back to active service by the president himself to once more take on HYDRA, which has reared its ugly multiple heads, years after it was thought to be extinct. As he returns to his old job, however, Fury is acutely aware of the changes five short years have wrought. The floating fortress is now a no-smoking environment, and Fury finds he has to fill out tax forms before he can be reactivated! In his five-year hiatus Nick has not developed any talent for respecting authority, and now he is even more discomforted to learn that he will be working on a special mission with his former lover, Val—short for Contessa Valentina de Allegro Fontaine (played by Lisa Rinna)—with whom he broke up with his retirement.

But whether his officious superior officer General Jack Pincer likes it or not (and he doesn't), it is agreed that Fury is the only person who has a prayer of stopping Andrea Von Strucker, alias The Viper. The daughter of the deceased Nazi Baron Von Strucker, The Viper is attempting to bring HYDRA back to its former glory. With her weakling brother, Werner, Andrea has stolen the preserved body of her father that was being safeguarded by S.H.I.E.L.D. in order to distill from his DNA what was to have been Hitler's greatest weapons, The Deathshead Virus, a highly deadly germ that produces an agonizing death and leaves the victim with a horrible death grin. Baron Von Strucker himself died of the virus, and with the aid of another ex-Nazi scientist named Dr. Zola, The Viper can extract it.

In a chance confrontation, The Viper gives Nick a kiss of death that infects him with the virus. She then demands $1 billion in cash, or else she will launch missiles containing the virus to target New York City (leaving one to wonder if The Viper saw "Captain America II" on TV as a little girl). Despite his weakening

MARVEL
#1 FIRST ISSUE OF AN UNLIMITED SERIES!
THE PUNISHER
75¢ US
1
JULY

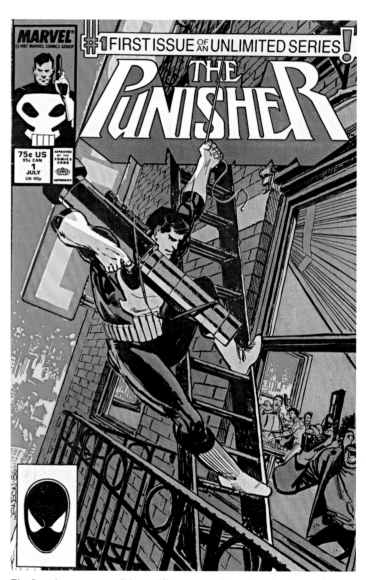

The Punisher was one of three different magazine series that featured the vigilante character in the 1980s.

(Opposite) The Punisher made his debut on the wrong side of the law in *Amazing Spider-Man* #129 (February 1974).

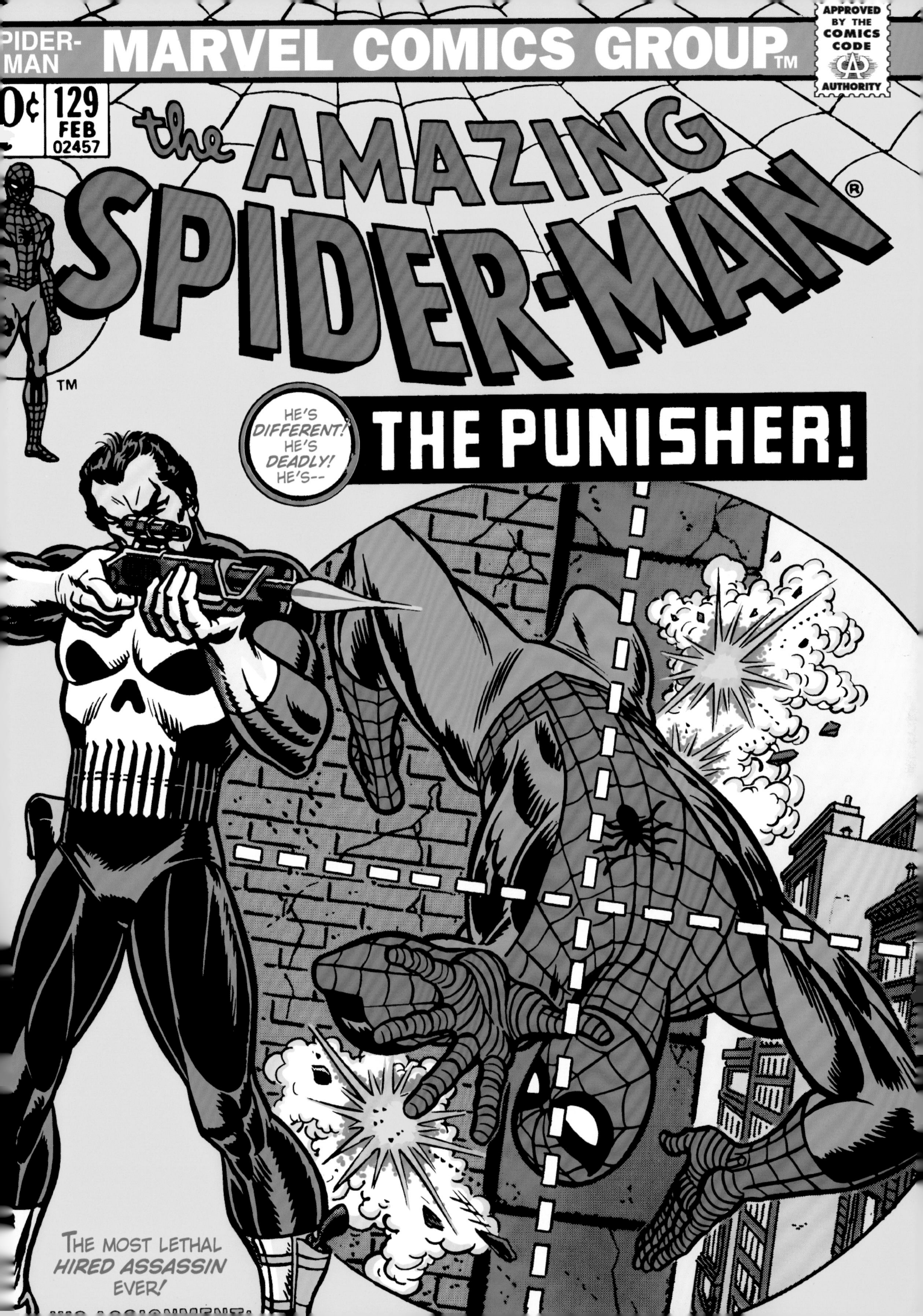

SPIDER-MAN
MARVEL COMICS GROUP
APPROVED BY THE COMICS CODE AUTHORITY
20¢ 129 FEB 02457
the AMAZING SPIDER-MAN
HE'S DIFFERENT! HE'S DEADLY! HE'S--
THE PUNISHER!
THE MOST LETHAL HIRED ASSASSIN EVER!

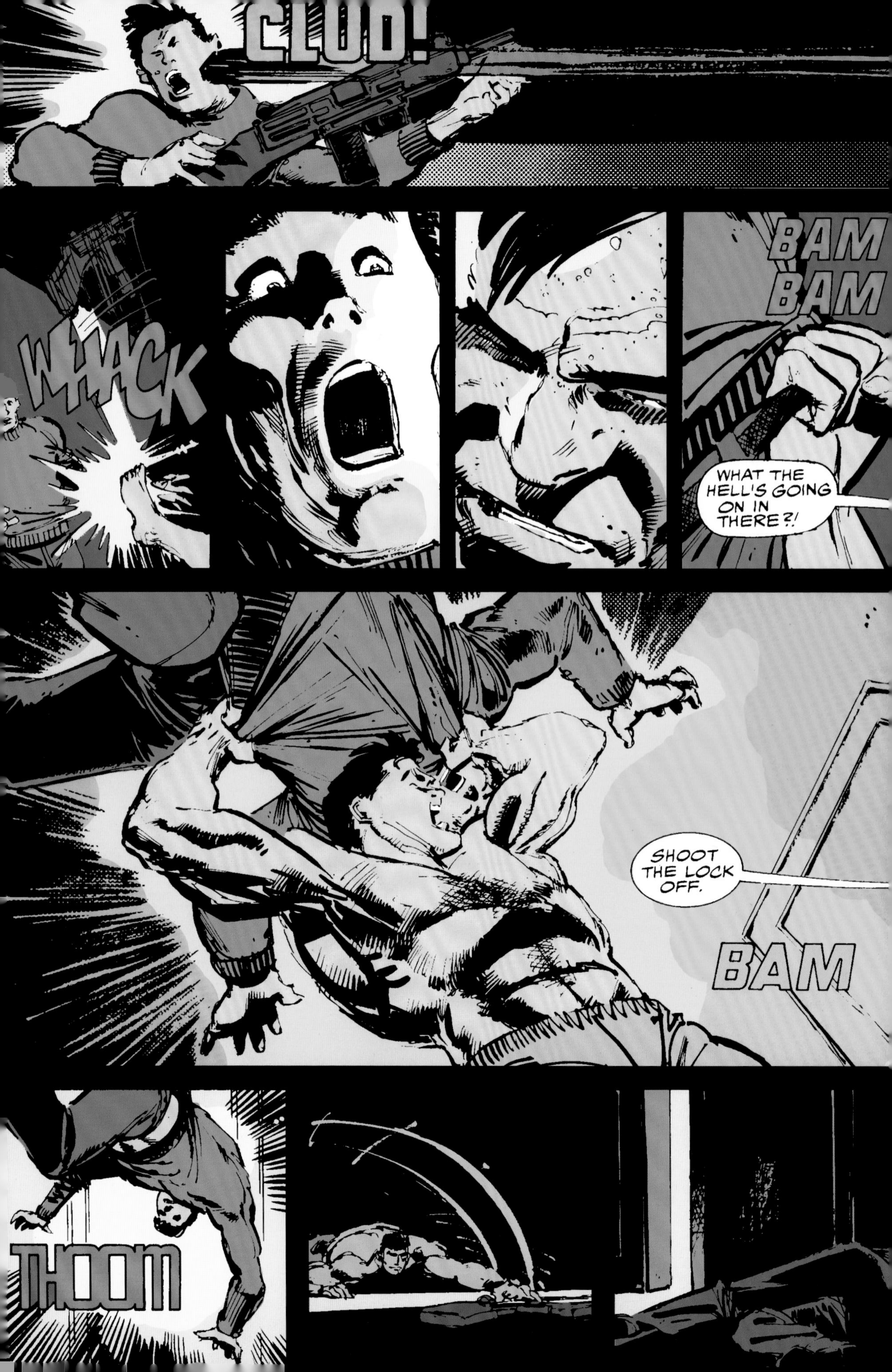
CLUD!
WHACK
BAM
BAM
WHAT THE HELL'S GOING ON IN THERE?!
SHOOT THE LOCK OFF.
BAM
THOOM

(Top) Dolph Lundgren as Frank Castle, alias The Punisher, in 1989's "The Punisher."

(Middle) Lt. Berkowitz (Louis Gossett, Jr.) tries to talk sense into his former partner, but it is a lost cause.

(Above) Castle gets tough with a member of the Yazuka in "The Punisher."

(Opposite) As demonstrated on this page from *The Punisher* #1 (July 1987) dialogue was not an all-important element for the character.

condition, and the fact that he can only count on forty-eight hours to live, Nick accepts the challenge of tracking down The Viper, destroying what exists of HYDRA, and taking a sample of her blood from which it might be possible to produce an antidote to the virus. Nick and his team do indeed manage to achieve all their goals except for one: capturing The Viper. She manages to escape, and is reunited with her father, whom she has returned to life. Nick understands that the current battle against HYDRA has only just begun.

"Nick Fury, Agent of S.H.I.E.L.D." benefits from elaborate sets and special effects, particularly the computer-animated supersonic planes that carry Nick and his team to and from S.H.I.E.L.D. space station–like headquarters. The film's biggest asset, however, is the performance of David Hasselhoff, who looks every inch the part and perfectly captures the innate toughness of the character, while managing to leaven it with humor. Hasselhoff approaches the role seriously and manages to sell such lines as: "Let's go kick some HYDRA butt!" and "I've got eight million other lives to worry about right now, I'm running a little low on Hallmark moments." For those who know the actor only through "Baywatch," his performance is eye-patch-popping.

THE PUNISHER

"Anti-hero" does not begin to describe The Punisher.

Created in 1974 by writer Gerry Conway and artist Ross Andru, The Punisher, a.k.a. Frank Castle, first appeared in an issue of *The Amazing Spider-Man* as an antagonist, if not an outright bad guy. Castle was a Vietnam veteran who was on a picnic with his family in Central Park, when they inadvertently witnessed a mob hit. Castle's wife and children were murdered by the mobsters as a result, though he survived the attack and went on to identify the killers, who were ultimately tried but not convicted. Fueled by bitterness and hate, Castle became The Punisher, a vigilante clad in a black suit with a death's head on the chest, silver boots and gloves, and a weapon belt, who sought vengeance against those criminals who manage to escape traditional justice.

For a time, The Punisher's quest to be the ultimate judge, jury, and executioner all in one actually drove him into temporary insanity, from which he eventually emerged. But sane or not, The Punisher's vigilante actions are disdained and repudiated by some of the Marvel Universe's more upright, law-abiding superheroes, including Daredevil, who in his daytime guise as legal eagle Matt Murdock strove to bring Castle to justice.

Readers seemed to have fewer qualms with the character, and by the mid-1980s The Punisher was one of Marvel's most popular characters, with three different Punisher titles appearing every month, which were soon supported by a full line of toys, including a five-inch action figure with "real machine gun sounds." While still morally ambiguous, he reflected—even defined—the saber-rattling political tenor of the times, and was most often seen as a dark force on the side of right, battling international drug lords and other "untouchable" criminals. Given the nature of the character, it is a safe bet that The Punisher is not destined to turn up any time soon on network television, and certainly not in animation (unless it was for the more adult-oriented animation that has been featured on premium cable channels), so it is no surprise that The Punisher's only media adaptation has been as a feature film. *The Punisher,* directed by Mark Goldblatt from a script by Boaz Yakin, was filmed in the summer of 1988 in Sydney, Australia, under the auspices of New World Pictures' Australian production banner, Down Under. It was a $10 million production that was designed to be the first of a series of films. Due to financial problems, however, it was destined to be the only film produced by the company.

In *The Punisher,* 6' 6"-Swedish action star Dolph Lundgren portrays Frank Castle, a policeman whose family was blown up in a car, a deadly explosion meant

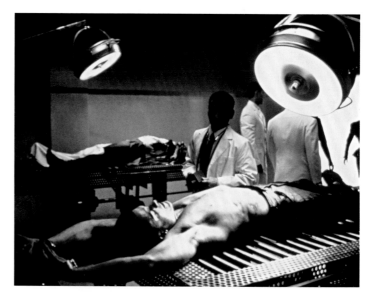

(Top) Captured by the deadly Lady Tanaka (Kim Miori, seen in silhouette in background), Castle is tortured.

(Above) Castle with his weapon of choice, aiding his sworn enemy Gianni Franco (Jeroen Krabbe). The truce would not last for long.

Frank Castle with police detective "Sam" Leary (Nancy Everhard). By the end of "The Punisher," Castle is bruised and bloody, but he's still not beaten.

for him. An organized crime boss named Dino Moretti was to blame. The authorities, however, believe that Frank was in the car with his family (apparently no one thought to count the bodies) and he is officially listed as dead. However, Castle's former partner, Lt. Jake Berkowitz (played with conviction by Louis Gossett, Jr.) suspects that Frank is not only alive but doing duty as the shadowy vigilante killer who has wiped out more than 125 organized crime figures in the past five years. What Berkowitz—who heads the police's Punisher task force—does not know is Castle's whereabouts: he is living a bleak, solitary existence in the sewers hidden beneath the city, through which he zips around on a motorcycle.

Castle is drawn aboveground by the very people he has sworn to destroy, the mob, under the leadership of Gianni Franco (Jeroen Krabbe). The organized crime forces are reeling from the sudden intrusion of a powerful Japanese organization called the Yazuka, which is under the direction of The Lady Tanaka (Kim Miori), an icily beautiful but completely ruthless crime boss. To force the American crime families to bend before her, she kidnaps all their children and holds them for ransom. Franco has no choice but to appeal to The Punisher to help them recover the children, which Castle agrees to, remembering his own family. While Berkowitz tries to track down his old partner, Castle helps the crime network win their bloody war with the Yazuka. Castle eventually does prevail, managing to kill both Lady Tanaka and Gianni Franco before retreating once more into the sewers.

There is hardly a stationary moment in *The Punisher* as Castle almost psychically anticipates his enemies' approaches and dispenses his personal brand of justice, which is summed up by his motto, "If you're guilty, you're dead." And Castle lives by his words: in the course of the film people are shot, stabbed, hung, crucified, tortured, and run over with cars. It is almost more than even a hardened policeman like Lt. Berkowitz can take: "What the hell do you call 125 murders in five

(Following page) Howard received his own magazine in 1976.

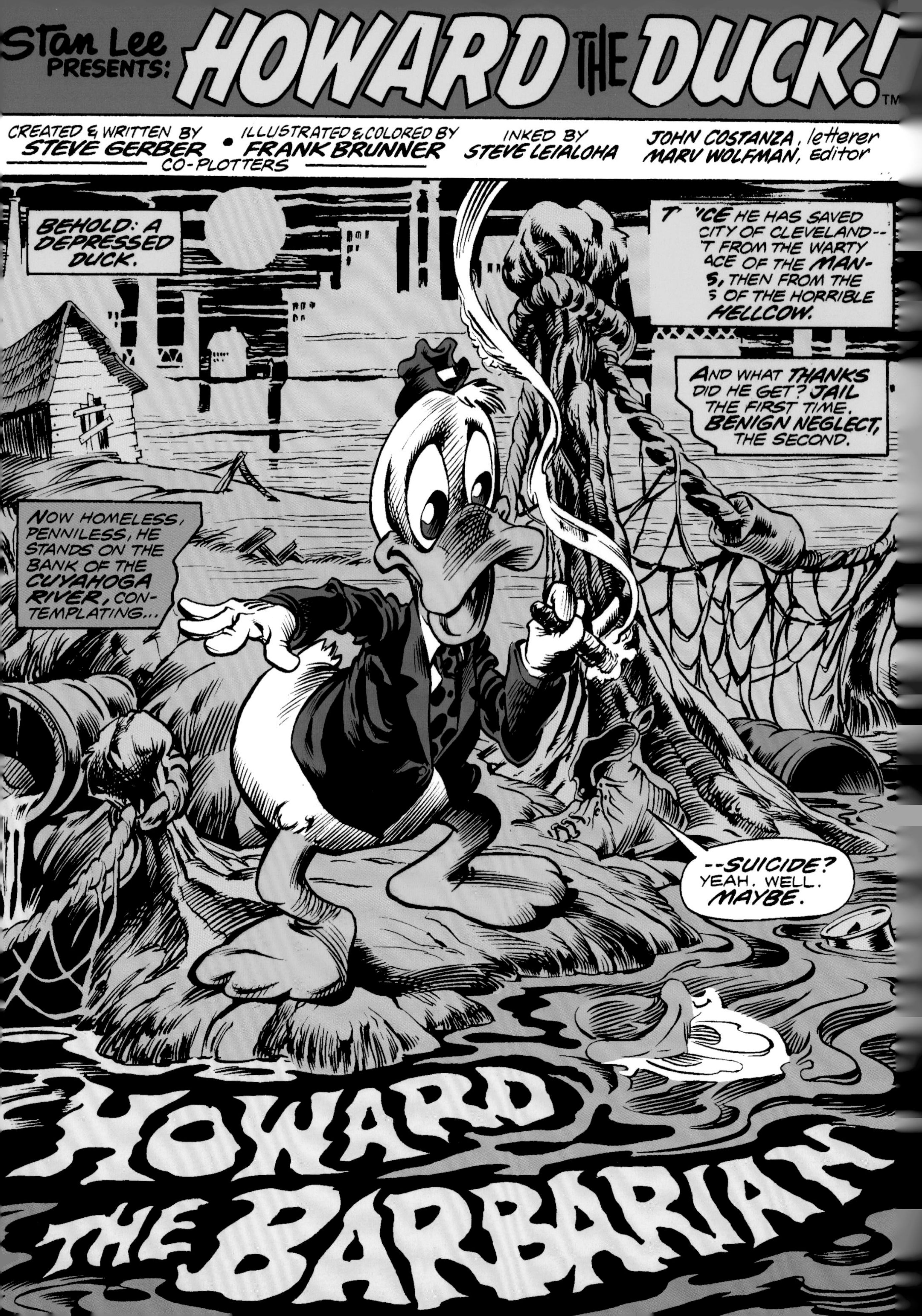

Stan Lee PRESENTS: HOWARD THE DUCK!™
CREATED & WRITTEN BY STEVE GERBER • ILLUSTRATED & COLORED BY FRANK BRUNNER
CO-PLOTTERS
INKED BY STEVE LEIALOHA
JOHN COSTANZA, letterer
MARV WOLFMAN, editor
BEHOLD: A DEPRESSED DUCK.
HE HAS SAVED CITY OF CLEVELAND-- FROM THE WARTY ACE OF THE MAN- THEN FROM THE OF THE HORRIBLE HELLCOW.
AND WHAT THANKS DID HE GET? JAIL THE FIRST TIME. BENIGN NEGLECT, THE SECOND.
NOW HOMELESS, PENNILESS, HE STANDS ON THE BANK OF THE CUYAHOGA RIVER, CONTEMPLATING...
--SUICIDE? YEAH. WELL. MAYBE.
HOWARD THE BARBARIAN

(Top) The four faces of Howard the Duck as chronicled in issue #15 of *FOOM*. Left to right: Howard's first appearance, drawn by Val Mayerik and Sal Trapani; a noirish Howard from Frank Brunner and Steve Leialoha; attitude to spare, courtesy of John Buscema and Leialoha; and a picture of disgruntlement by Gene Colan and Leialoha.

(Above) Performer Ed Gale in a $2 million-dollar duck suit in 1986's *Howard the Duck*.

years!" he screams at Castle when he finally catches up with him. "Work in progress," Castle deadpans.

Moral ambiguity is, of course, the entire point to the character. But in *The Punisher* Castle comes off as little more than a robotic killing machine, devoid of any emotion, even vigilante outrage. Not only does this make it harder to justify his actions, it makes it harder to distinguish him from the killers he is killing. Had the filmmakers put Castle in a Punisher suit (as it is, he is usually seen in a grubby black outfit weighed down with weapons and ammo belts), it might have established enough of a visual metaphor for Castle's demented quest for vengeance to make the character work.

The Punisher was ready for release in 1989, but financial problems from its studio caused it to be sold and shelved, at least in the United States. The film was released in theaters in England and Europe. Its one and only 35mm screening in the U.S. was a noncommercial one staged for the Los Angeles Comic Book and Science Fiction Convention on July 8, 1990. After that, *The Punisher* went directly to home video.

HOWARD THE DUCK

In Hollywood circles, one still is forced to use hushed tones when saying *Howard the Duck*. Universal's 1986 adaption of writer Steve Gerber's off-the-wall comics character is still considered a buzzword for uncontrolled, overblown filmmaking and an object lesson in how the mighty—in this case George Lucas—can belly flop. There just isn't any polite way of saying it: *Howard the Duck* was one of the biggest motion picture disasters of all time.

How did a popular, funny comic book idea unfairly get transformed into a metaphor for the ultimate Hollywood flop?

Howard the Duck's first comic book appearance came in a "Man-Thing" story from the comic book *Fear* in December 1973. At the time it was little more than a joke perpetrated by artist Val Mayerik, who had Howard

suddenly pop up out of nowhere to complain that
Man-Thing didn't know the meaning of the word
absurdity. Readers, however, did. So did Gerber,
Man-Thing's writer, who further developed the character
of the tough-talking, cigar-chewing canard and ushered
him into his own magazine, *Howard the Duck,* which
premiered in January 1976.

Howard was a pugnacious, cynical duck from
outer space who was "trapped in a world he never
made," as the cover of every issue proclaimed. Only
in the presence of knockout redhead Beverly Switzler,
whom he habitually called "Toots," did he reveal his
downier side. Howard's opinion of the human race in
general—"hairless apes," he called them—fell somewhere
in between puzzlement or annoyance, depending on his
mood. Gerber used Howard's adventures, both in the
comic book and in the short-lived newspaper strip
drawn by Gene Colan, which was launched in 1977,
as an opportunity for satire directed both toward the
comic book genre and society in general, and readers
responded, making Howard an immensely popular
character, albeit one with a shelf-life. By 1979,
However, Howard-mania had faded and the comic
book ceased publication.

HOWARD THE DUCK IN THE MEDIA

No Marvel character—probably no comic-related
character of any kind—arrived on the Hollywood scene
with as much fanfare and brouhaha as Howard the
Duck . . . and therein lies a major part of the tale. After
having been inundated with updates about the filming
of *Howard the Duck* during its production, most critics
were not able to separate the film itself from the hype,
and in particular could not (or would not) get past
the amount of money that it took to bring the story
to the screen.

Things were far duckier a few years earlier, in
1980, when the property was originally optioned from
Marvel by producers Peter Shannaberg, Morrie

(Top) *Howard the Duck* writer/director Willard Hyuck poses with a bevy of
duck extras.

(Above) If nothing else, 1986's *Howard the Duck* demonstrated the flying
technique of ducks.

(Top) Lea Thompson as Beverly tries to rescue Howard from entrapment in a world he never made.

(Above) Keeping Howard out of trouble is not easy.

Eisenman, and Peter Coffin. They announced an $8 million production that ultimately fell through because of an unsatisfactory script ($8 million would ultimately be the advertising budget for the spent on *Howard the Duck* six years later).

Enter George Lucas, who had an affection for the character of Howard, and obtained the rights in 1984 and, with his associates Gloria Katz and Willard Hyuck, brought the property to Universal, which was then headed up by Frank Price, the man who had brought Captain America, The Hulk, Spider-Man, and Dr. Strange to television a decade earlier. At first everything appeared to be clicking: a casting call went out for little people to play Howard in a $2 million suit, while the studio announced it was seeking a hot comedy actor of the ranks of Chevy Chase or Dan Aykroyd to provide the voice for Howard. At one time Robin Williams was rumored to be on tap for the role, though the performer eventually chosen by Katz and Hyuck, who were writing, directing, and producing the picture, was the lesser-known Chip Zien. Ed Gale won the role of Howard's body, with Margarita Fernandez and Felix Silla (better known as Cousin Itt from TV's "The Addams Family) serving as "stunt ducks."

Budgeted at $20 million, filming started in October of 1985, in Northern California and Cleveland, Ohio. By the time the film had wrapped, the budget had nearly doubled to $37 million, due in part to a number of logistically difficult and costly sequences, such as the one in which Howard creates chaos by piloting an ultra light plane through the middle of a small town. To film that sequence, the filmmakers ventured out of the studio and took over the main street of Rio Vista, California, a small town in the northern part of the state. Despite the cost overruns, the studio remained convinced it had a major hit on its hands. An exhaustive marketing campaign was launched, including a telephone info access line—1-900-415-DUCK—which gave out info on Howard, the first time a phone campaign had been used to promote a film. A headline-making billboard that featured a 3-D inflatable duckbill and cigar emerging from an egg was erected over the Sunset Strip in Los Angeles. The media buzz remained strong, and in July of 1986, audiences finally got the opportunity to see the film they had been hearing about for months.

Howard the Duck begins in a parallel universe, on a two-mooned world remarkably like Earth, except that it is inhabited by waterfowl. While in the comfort of his home in "Marshington, D.C.," Howard is suddenly wrenched out of his world and sucked through a cosmic vortex to land in an alley in Cleveland, Ohio. He quickly meets Beverly Switzler (Lea Thompson), a young woman who is the lead singer of a struggling band called The Cherry Bombs, who takes Howard home with her. Through a science student friend, Phil Blumberg (Tim Robbins), Howard is introduced to Dr. Walter Jenning (Jeffrey Jones), who is in charge of the astrophysics lab for a company called Dynatechnics. As it turns out, Howard is on Earth because of Jenning, who was testing a device called a laser spectroscope, which was supposed to measure the density of the gasses around Alpha Centauri. Instead, the beam was accidentally directed to Howard's planet, where it caused a cosmic vortex to open up in the duck's living room. By reversing the spectroscope, however, Jenning believes he can send Howard back home, which is the best news Howard has received since he first arrived. Howard bids a sentimental goodbye to Beverly as he prepares to go.

Unfortunately, another lab explosion causes Jenning to lose control of the spectroscope again, and this time, an evil entity identified as a Dark Overlord of the Universe arrives through the vortex and inhabits Jenning's body. As the parasitic alien takes control, Jenning becomes obsessed with opening the way for all of the Dark Overlords to come to Earth and overtake it. After numerous fights, car crashes, and airplane pursuits, the Dark Overlords are thwarted and sent back to their galaxy, and Howard—who has been stranded on Earth due to the destruction of the spectroscope—decides to make the best of it with his human love, Beverly.

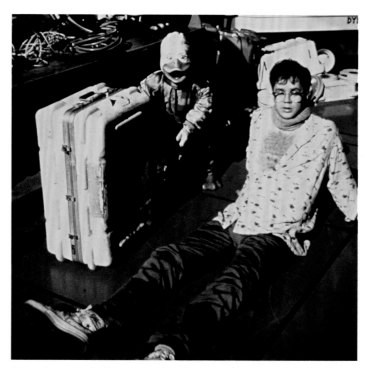

An explosion at the Dynatechnics lab floors Phil Blumberg (Tim Robbins) and nearly signals the end of the planet (but not the movie) in *Howard the Duck.*

Howard's expression seems to indicate he's just seen his own movie.

Fans of the character in his comic book and newspaper strip incarnations were universally disappointed by the film's treatment of the character. In the comics Howard was brusque, cynical, and sometimes nasty—that was what made him funny. But in the film he is winsome and cuddly. In the comics, when Beverly and Howard finally make it into bed, Howard remarks, "What the heck, I guess it's destiny, Toots." In the film, as Beverly attempts to seduce Howard, the duck turns coy and embarrassed and offers a stammered refusal.

Another problem was story construction. Due to the script's episodic nature, Howard's story is effectively concluded halfway through, at which time the story of Dr. Jenning and the Dark Overlords takes over (and Jeffrey Jones's slow transformation into the Dark Overlord is both believably scary and outrageously funny in a way that Howard himself is not). For the entire second half of the film, Howard's role could have been filled by a little girl, a chimp, a robot, or any other creature that would look out of place piloting an airplane.

Howard the Duck took in only $15 million at the box office in the United States. It performed somewhat better in foreign markets, where it was retitled *Howard, A New Breed of Hero,* but still fell far short of studio expectations. No one was more affected by the film's failure than Frank Price, who was forced out as vice president/director and chairman of MCA's Motion Picture Group and President of Universal, in large part because of the losses sustained on *Howard the Duck.*

Except for "Duckman," a well-received animated series created by underground cartoonist Everett Peck, which premiered on the USA Network in 1994, no one in Hollywood has been brave enough to venture into the raucously opinionated waterfowl genre. But given the advancements that have been made in computer animation technology, a trend that Marvel is currently capitalizing on in its slate of film projects, it would be possible to revive Howard using a digital duck that could be made to look exactly like the comic book version.

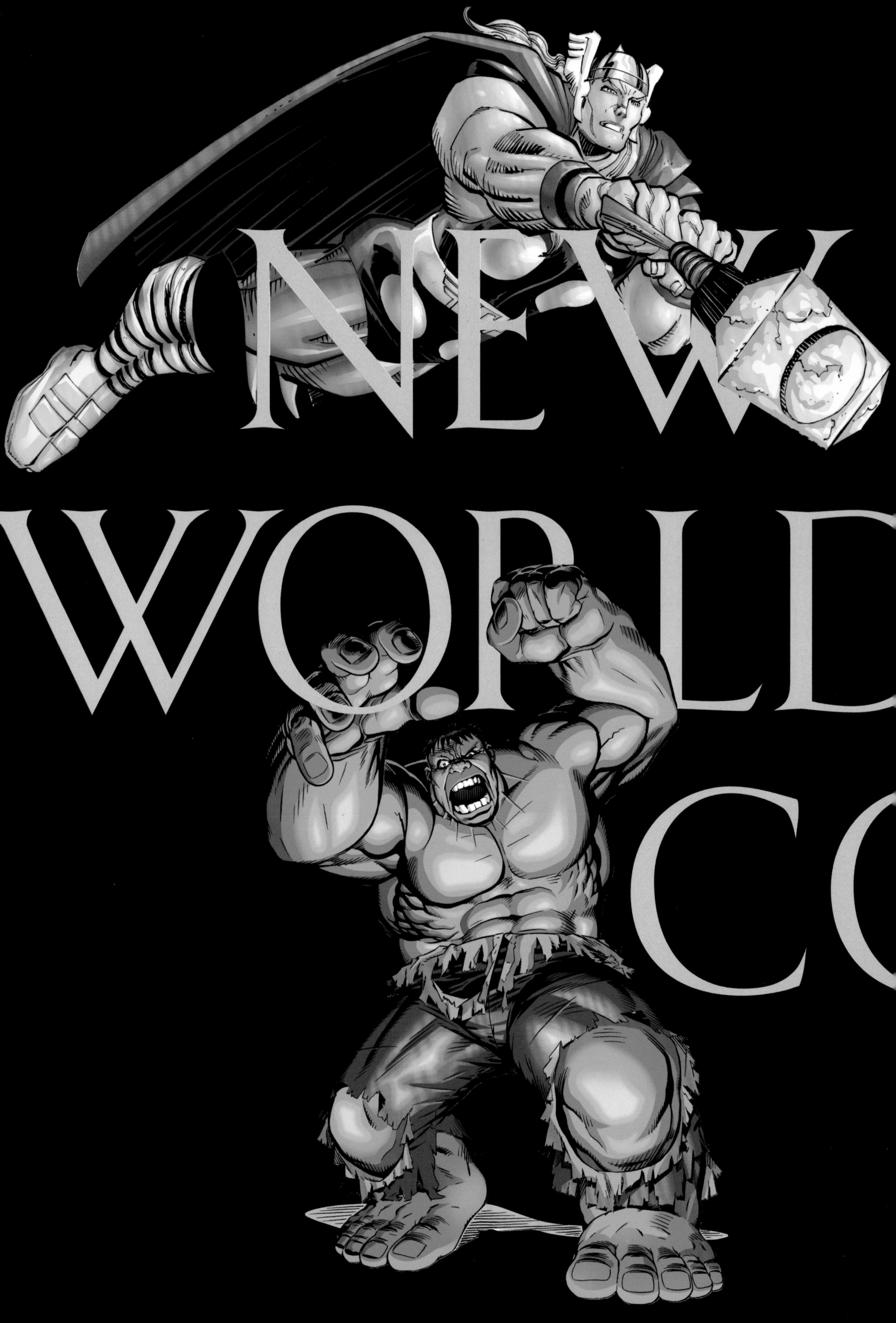
NEW
WORLD
CO

S TO
NQUER

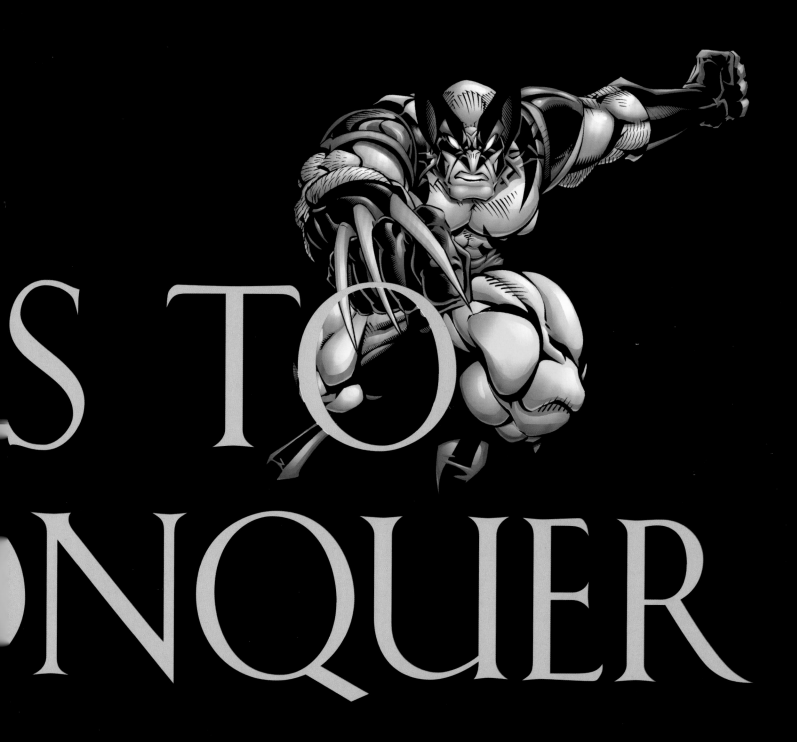

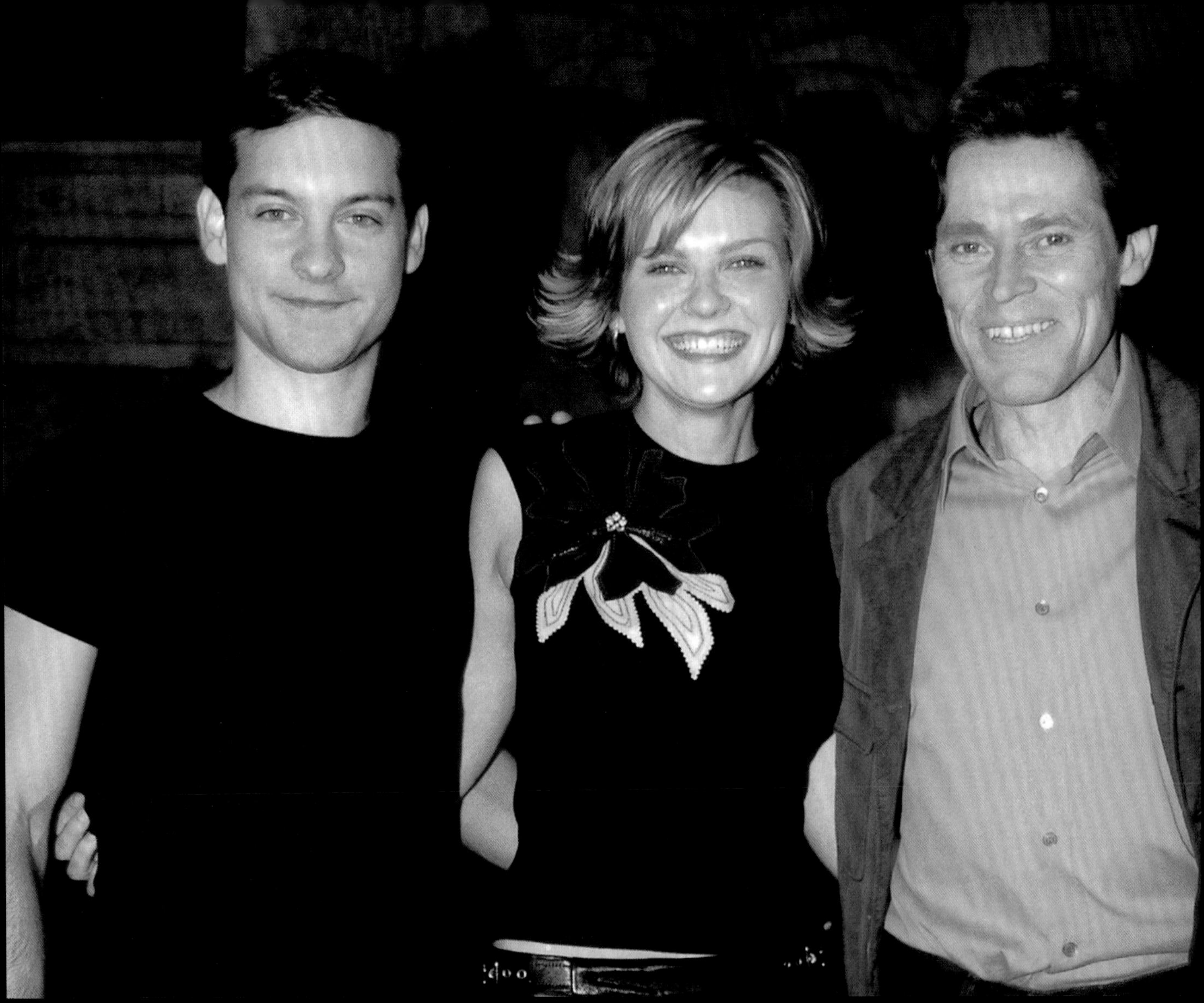

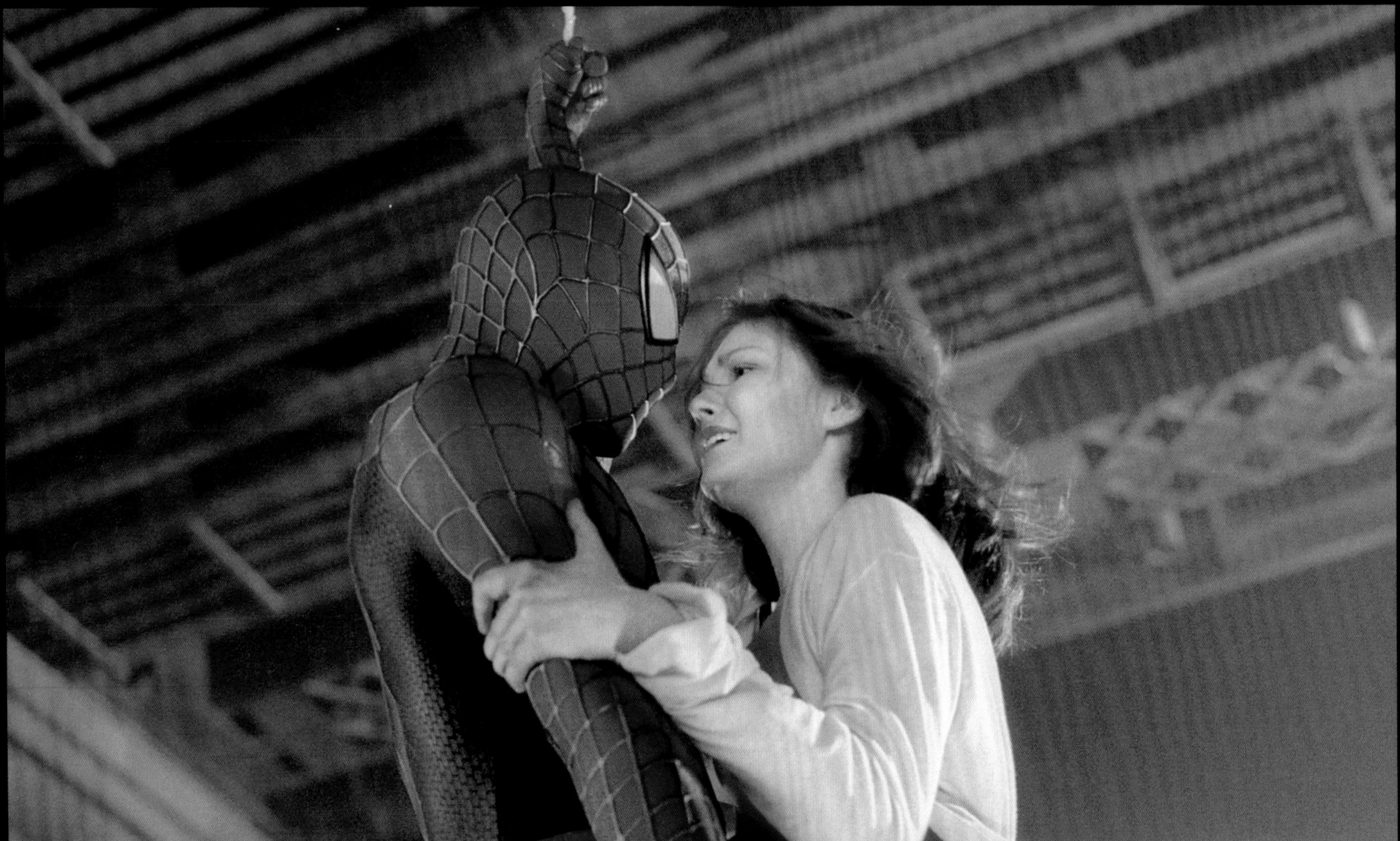

New Worlds to Conquer

Given its amazing history of storytelling and the sheer number and diversity of its characters, it should come as no surprise that the Marvel Universe has proven to be a rich vein of material for entertainment producers. But even such high-profile film productions as *Blade*, *X-Men*, and *Spider-Man* represent only the tip of the proverbial iceberg. The next few years will see a tidal wave of Marvel-related entertainment, in part, because the time is finally right.

(Opposite top, left to right) Tobey Maguire, Kirsten Dunst, and Willem Dafoe were all smiles at the January 2001 press conference announcing them as the lead actors in *Spider-Man* that debuted in May 2002. (© Eric Charbonneau/BEI)

(Opposite bottom) Kirsten Dunst, as Mary Jane Watson, is clearly caught up in Tobey Maguire's web in the 2002 *Spider-Man*. (© 2002 Columbia Pictures Industries, Inc. All rights reserved.)

"It takes a long time to prepare markets and properties," says Marvel Media president and CEO Avi Arad. "We are not in the licensing business of taking a movie, going to a studio, and saying, 'Here, take this and do something with it.' We produce our own movies in a way. We develop the story and the script hand-in-hand with the studios and usually bring the talent to the table."

Principal photography on 20th Century Fox and New Regency Enterprises' big-screen version of *Daredevil* began in March of 2002. Written and directed by Mark Stephen Johnson, the film stars Ben Affleck as the title hero, Jennifer Garner as Elektra, a femme fatale martial arts assassin with a connection to organized crime, Michael Clarke Duncan as plus-sized crime boss Wilson Fisk, a.k.a. The Kingpin, Colin Farrell as the Kingpin's psychotic triggerman Bullseye, Jon Favreau as Matt's friend Foggy Nelson, Joe Pantoliano as Urich, an investigative reporter on a Jack McGee-like quest for the truth about Daredevil, and David Keith as Matt's doomed father, here named Jack "The Devil" Murdock. Young Scott Terra plays Matt as a twelve-year-old. In a nod to the current Hollywood's craze for Hong Kong-style action, Daredevil will be depicted as a martial arts master as well as an acrobat. Cheung-Yan Yuen, who staged the kicks for such films as *Charlie's Angels* and *Iron Monkey*, signed on as action director, though for the more extreme action, CG house Rhythm & Hues is creating a digital Man Without Fear. The film will also utilize "virtual sets"—background settings created on the computer. *Daredevil* is slated for a January 2003 release.

Just one week before *Daredevil* began shooting, principal photography also began in L.A. on *The Hulk* (no "Incredible"), a project that had been in development at Universal on and off for a number of years. Perhaps to ensure a smooth production after such a bumpy development phase, director Ang Lee—best known for *Crouching Tiger, Hidden Dragon*—staged a Chinese blessing ceremony on the sound stage on the first day of filming, March 18, 2002. "The whole cast and crew, producers, Ang, and myself were there, and we actually had an ancient Chinese ceremony for everybody to be well and successful," says Arad. "It was touching and emotional and unifying and spiritual, and it gives you an idea of the man who is making the movie." (Lee is also a longtime Hulk fan.)

After much casting speculation, Australian actor Eric Bana won the role of Dr. Bruce Banner. *The Hulk* cast also includes Jennifer Connelly as Betty Ross, Sam Elliot as General Ross, and Nick Nolte as Dr. David Banner, Bruce's father. The story has Banner working in an Army nuclear research laboratory and getting "gammatized" (one version of the script written by David Hayter—who joined writers Michael France and Michael Tolkin on the project—also had Sam Stern, "The Leader" of the comics, and a scientist named Jennifer Sussman becoming radiated), then going on a cross-country rampage pursued by the Army and a villain named Creel. Scheduled for a June 2003 release, the film will present a Hulk unlike any we've yet seen: one created entirely through computer animation. Work on a digital Hulk actually began in the late 1990s at Industrial Light and Magic (ILM), the special effects house that created the Oscar-winning miracles for such films as *Star Wars* and *Terminator 2: Judgement Day*. ILM researched and developed animation systems to create the CG Hulk, and, had development of the film continued at that time, it would have resulted in the first completely computer-generated humanoid lead character in motion pictures. The project was then back-burnered,

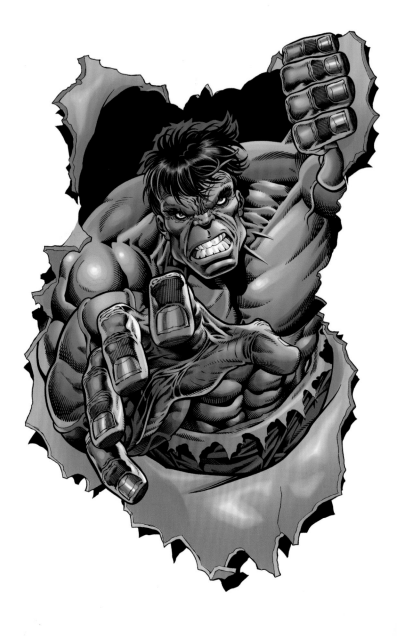

though ILM was able to apply the research it had done for the creation of the digitally disintegrating Im-Ho-Tep in the hit 1999 remake of *The Mummy*. Now with *The Hulk* back on track, ILM is able to utilize three additional years of technological development for state-of-the-art character creation, which includes incorporating Bana's facial features (or a Hulkish rendering of them) on the animated character.

The success of *X-Men* of course ensured a sequel, so director Bryan Singer and the principal cast are reuniting for *X-Men 2* (sometimes called *X2*), which began filming in May 2002 for release in May 2003. Writers David Hayter and Zak Penn worked independently on the script, which adds Nightcrawler to the team that had previously included Cyclops, Wolverine, Rogue, Storm, and Jean Grey. Ian McKellen is returning as Magneto, though this time the Sentinels will be added to the list of problems for the X-Men. This impressive slate of films is only the beginning: the long-promised "real" film version of *The Fantastic Four* has been scripted and has a target release date of 2004; a new version of *The Punisher*, currently planned as a direct-to-video, has been written by Michael France; and *Iron Man*, *Captain America*, *Dr. Strange*, and *The Silver Surfer* are all in development.

But those only cover the Marvel Universe's A-list of heroes. There are an estimated 4,700 character properties that have emerged from the House of Ideas, and if the success of *Blade* proved anything it is that many of those second-tier characters, while not as well known as Spidey or the X-Men, have outstanding film potential. "Who would have thought Blade would have turned out to be a successful movie franchise?" asks David Goyer, who has brought more Marvel heroes to the screen, big and small, than any other screenwriter. "There's no reason other [secondary] characters couldn't also be successful franchises."

Marvel has joined with Paramount Pictures to bring Deathlok to the screen, a film based on the cyborg manhunter from the 1970s that was revitalized in the early 1990s by comic writers Dwayne McDuffie and Gregory Wright. And as part of its comprehensive joint venture deal with Artisan Entertainment, Marvel is developing *Iron Fist*, based on the martial arts hero. Stuntman and actor Ray Park, who played Toad in *X-Men* has been announced for the lead role. A feature treatment of Steve Gerber's Man Thing is also in the works. Also in development is *Ghost Rider*, based on Mike Ploog and Gary Friedrich's 1970s treatment of the night vigilante with the flaming death's head (as opposed to the 1990 comics redo by writer Howard Mackie), which plans to re-team David Goyer and director Stephen Norrington from *Blade*. In fact, Goyer's *Ghost Rider* script was written in between completing that film and his work on the 1998 TV movie "Nick Fury: Agent of S.H.I.E.L.D." The story concerns biker Johnny Blaze, who makes a deal with the Devil—here personified as a man named Stark—in order to save the life of his fiancé (in the comic book version it is Johnny's stepfather). But as often happens with these sort of arrangements, there is a catch. Johnny ends up cursed by Stark to live forever and at night turns into a spirit of vengeance. "The script kind of has the feel of *Once Upon a Time in the West* with Johnny Blaze in place of Charles Bronson," Goyer states, further likening Johnny's uncontrollable nocturnal personality to Lon Chaney's predicament in *The Wolf Man. Ghost Rider* is being prepared for a 2003 release.

While feature films may currently represent the company's highest profile, Marvel continues to explore other media outlets, both existing technology— such as video games—and developing technology. "There is no area of business in which our characters will not be represented," confirms Arad.

As we continue to chart our way through the first decade of the new millennium, one thing seems clear: the Marvel Universe is real, it is vital, and it is here to stay.

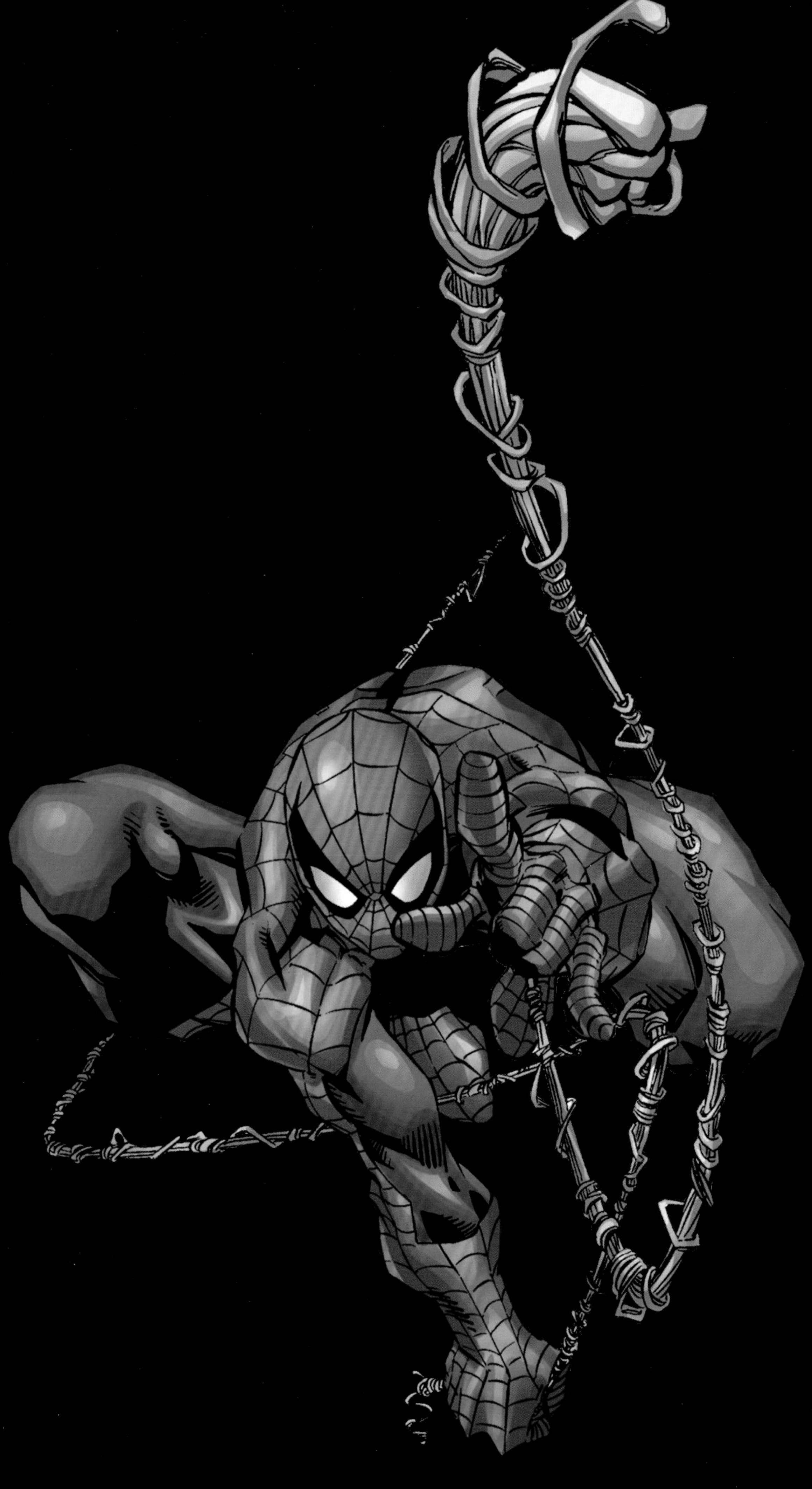

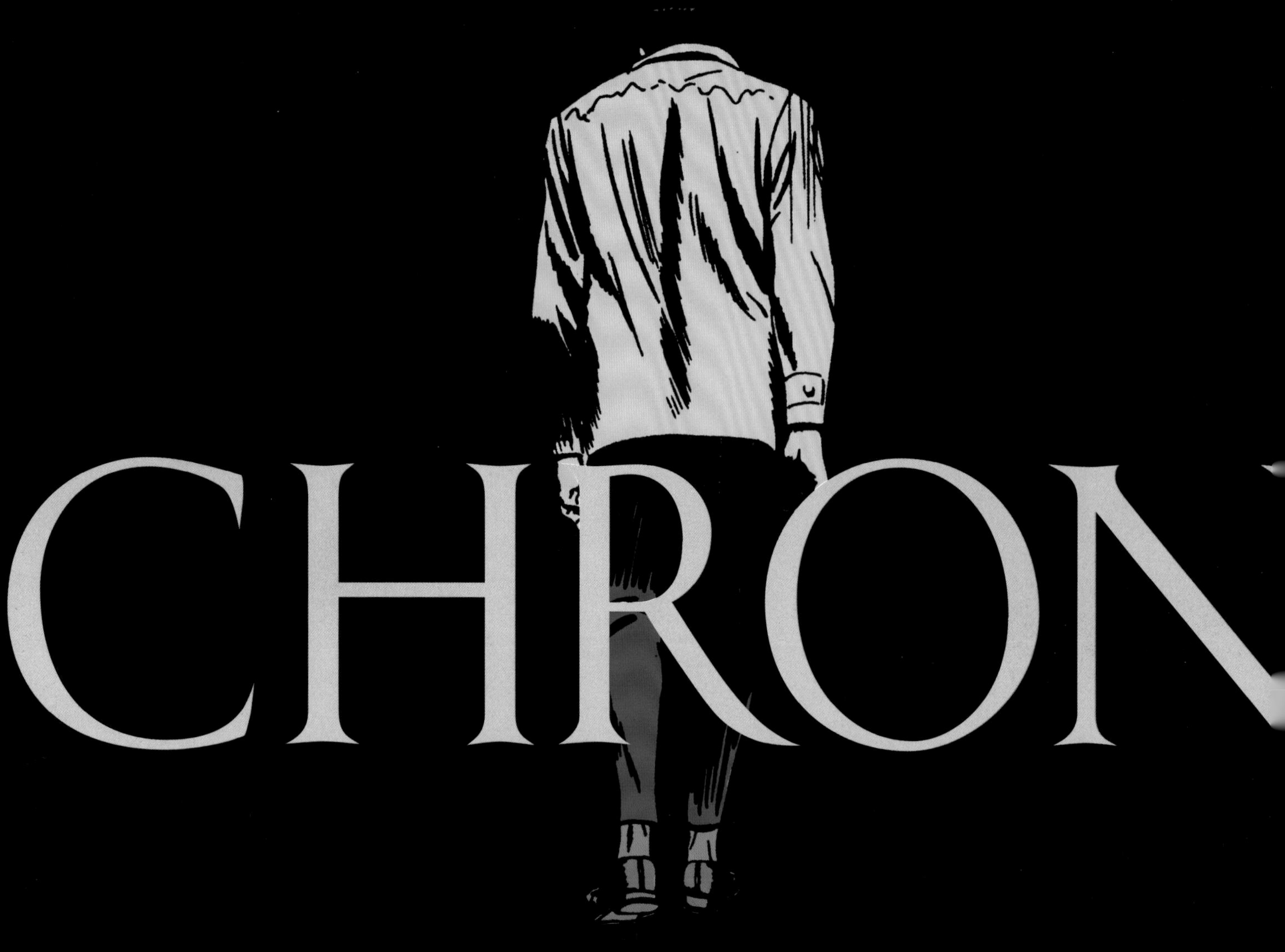
CHRON

OLOGy

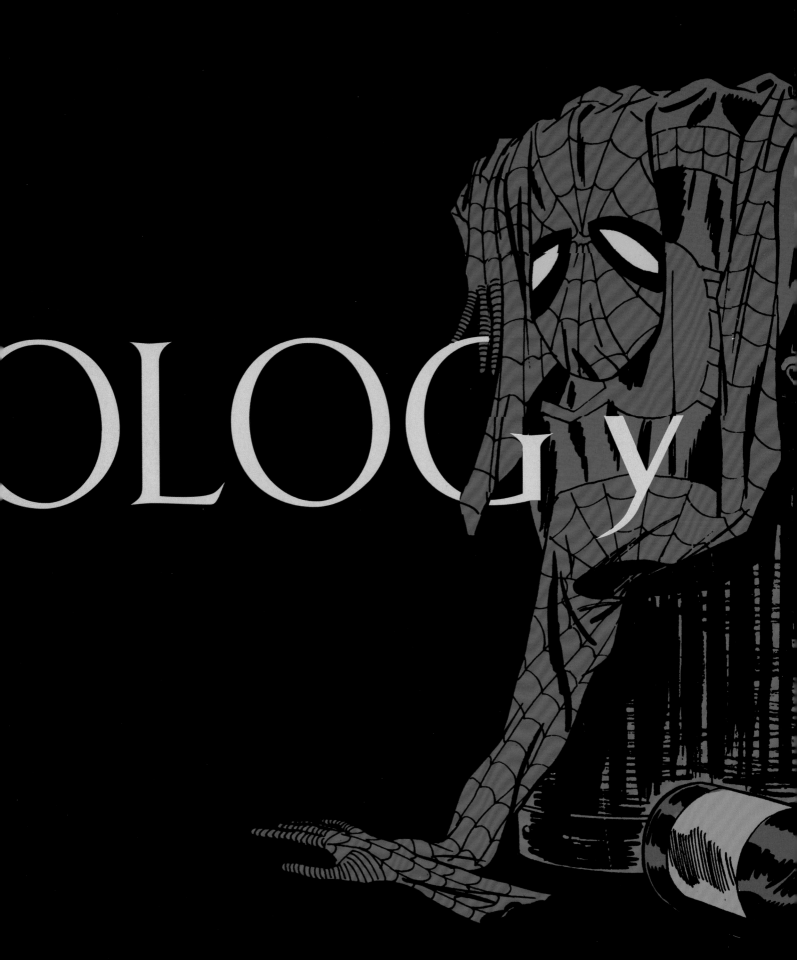

CHRONOLOGY

1932 Martin Goodman and partner Louis Silberkleit form Western Fiction Publishing. The pulp magazine *Complete Western Tales* is started.

1934 Martin Goodman becomes sole owner of Western Fiction Publishing.

1938 Goodman's company adopts the name Red Circle Magazines.

Issue #1 of pulp magazine *Marvel Science Stories* (August).

1939 Bill Everett's The Sub-Mariner debuts in *Motion Picture Funnies Weekly*, produced by the comic packaging house Funnies, Inc.

Martin Goodman adopts business name of Timely Publications.

Artist/writer Joe Simon joins Timely to develop new characters.

Seventeen-year-old Stanley Martin Lieber joins Timely staff as a proofreader and copywriter. He signs his work in comic books "Stan Lee."

Issue #1 of *Marvel Comics* published in October. It features Carl Burgos's The Human Torch, Paul Gustavson's The Angel, Bill Everett's The Sub-Mariner, and Al Anders's The Masked Raider.

Marvel Comics becomes *Marvel Mystery Comics* with issue #2.

1940 Jack Kirby joins Timely's staff as artist.

1941 Issue #1 of *Captain America* by Joe Simon and Jack Kirby published in March.

Issue #3 of *Captain America*, published in May, contains text filler "Captain America Foils the Traitor's Revenge," the first published work of Stan Lee.

The Sub-Mariner gets his own eponymous magazine.

Editor Joe Simon and art director Jack Kirby leave Timely over a dispute with publisher Martin Goodman. Stan Lee is appointed editor.

1942 Stan Lee enters U.S. Army and is replaced as editor by Vince Fago.

1943 Republic's fifteen-chapter serial *Captain America* is produced; the first chapter plays in theaters in December.

1944 Issue #1 of *Miss America*, a title that courts the teen girl audience. Subsequent titles include *Nellie the Nurse* and *Millie the Model*.

Dick Purcell, star of Republic's *Captain America*, dies of a heart attack in Hollywood at age thirty-eight.

1945 *USA Comics*, featuring Captain America, ceases publication, a sign of a dip in the popularity of superheroes.

Stan Lee returns to Timely as editor.

1946 For the first time Captain America, The Sub-Mariner and The Human Torch are featured together in the same story in issue #19 of *All Winners Comics*, setting the stage for myriad later character teamings.

Artist Gene Colan joins Timely.

1947 The designation "Marvel Comic" or "A Marvel Magazine" starts to appear sporadically on comic book covers.

Issue #1 of *Justice*, the first of a series of crime and law enforcement titles, launched by Timely/Marvel.

1948 Issue #1 of *Two Gun Kid*, the first of a series of Western titles, launched by Timely/Marvel.

Issue #1 of *My Romance*, the first of a long series of romance comics, launched by Timely/Marvel.

Artist John Buscema joins Timely.

1949 *The Sub-Mariner* ceases publication.

Marvel Mystery Comics becomes *Marvel Tales*.

Issue #74 of *Captain America's Weird Tales*, the last issue to feature Cap. The title would be discontinued with issue #75.

1950 Issue #1 of *Marvel Boy*, which would only last two issues.

Issue #1 of *War Comics*, first in a line of combat titles.

1951 Publisher Martin Goodman creates his own distribution company, Atlas News Company; Atlas becomes the moniker for the publishing company as well.

Artist Joe Sinnott joins Atlas.

1953 Captain America, The Human Torch, and The Sub-Mariner are revived in the pages of *Young Men* #24, which paves the way for their return in their own magazines.

Serial *Captain America* is re-released in theaters as *The Return of Captain America*.

1954 Publication of the book *Seduction of the Innocent* by Fredric Wertham, M.D., argues that comic books are ruining the minds of youth, and as a result the Senate Subcommittee to Investigate Juvenile Delinquency is convened in April.

The Sub-Mariner is revived, picking up with magazine issue #33.

The Human Torch is revived, picking up with issue #36.

Captain America is revived (under the banner *Captain America. . .Commie Smasher!*) with issue #76.

Artist John Romita (Sr.) joins Atlas.

Artist Don Heck joins Atlas as a freelancer.

1955 The Comics Code Authority is created to approve every comic book story published in the United States.

Bill Everett, who had revived *The Sub-Mariner* in 1953, leaves Atlas.

1956 Artist Steve Ditko joins Atlas as a freelancer. Jack Kirby returns to Atlas on a freelance basis.

1957 Atlas's distribution operation is folded and publisher Martin Goodman signs with American News Company for distribution.

1958 Issue #1 of *Tales To Astonish*.

Atlas artist Joe Maneely is killed at age thirty-two in a commuter train accident.

Artist/Writer Larry Lieber joins Timely.

1961 Issue #1 of *The Fantastic Four* (November) detonates "The Big Bang" that results in the Marvel Universe.

1962 Issue #1 of *The Incredible Hulk* (May).

Spider-Man introduced in *Amazing Fantasy* #15 (August).

The Mighty Thor introduced in *Journey Into Mystery* #83 (August).

The Sub-Mariner is revived in *The Fantastic Four* #4 (May).

1963 Iron Man introduced in *Tales of Suspense* #39 (March).

Dr. Strange introduced in *Strange Tales* #130 (March).

Spider-Man gets his own magazine, *The Amazing Spider-Man* (Issue #1, March), in which he meets The Fantastic Four.

The Hulk appears in *The Fantastic Four* #12 (March), which, along with *The Amazing Spider-Man* #1, sets the stage for future crossovers that hallmark the Marvel Universe.

Nick Fury debuts in issue #1 of Sgt. *Fury and His Howling Commandos* (May).

Marvel magazines receive the official designation "Marvel Comics Group" on their cover.

Issue #1 of *The Avengers* (September), featuring Thor, Hulk, Ant-Man, and Iron Man.

Issue #1 of *X-Men* (September)

1964   Issue #1 of *Daredevil* (June), drawn by Bill Everett.

1965   Marvel's official fan club "The Merry Marvel Marching Society" (M.M.M.S.) launched.

Nick Fury joins the Cold War as "Agent of S.H.I.E.L.D." in *Strange Tales* #135 (August).

Writer Roy Thomas, a fan of comic books, joins Marvel staff as a writer.

Gene Colan returns to Marvel.

1966   The Silver Surfer and Galactus introduced in *The Fantastic Four* #48 (March), the first of a three-issue series known as *The Galactus Trilogy.*

Journey Into Mystery retitled *Thor* with issue #126 (March).

Black Panther's (first black superhero) first appearance in *Fantastic Four* #54.

Steve Ditko leaves Marvel over creative differences.

John Buscema returns to Marvel after a sabbatical as an advertising artist.

Artist/writer Jim Steranko joins Marvel.

Krantz Films' "The Marvel Superheroes" animated series premieres in syndication.

1967   Issue #1 of Marvel's self-spoofing *Not Brand Ecch* (August).

"The Fantastic Four" animated series from Hanna-Barbera premieres on ABC.

"Spider-Man" animated series from Krantz Films and Grantray-Lawrence premieres on ABC.

1968   Tales of Suspense renamed *Captain America* for its 100th issue (April).

Tales to Astonish renamed *The Incredible Hulk* with issue #102 (April).

Iron Man receives his own magazine with *Iron Man* #1 (May)

Prince Namor receives his own magazine with *The Sub-Mariner* #1 (May).

Modern-day Nick Fury receives his own magazine with *Nick Fury, Agent of S.H.I.E.L.D.* #1 (June)

The Silver Surfer receives his own magazine with *The Silver Surfer* #1 (August).

Strange Tales renamed *Doctor Strange* with issue #169 (June).

"Spectacular Spider-Man," a two-issue newstand comic magazine (the first issue was black and white, and the second color).

1969   Jim Steranko leaves Marvel.

1970   The last new story of the original *Uncanny X-Men* published in issue #66 (March).

Jack Kirby leaves Marvel.

Writer Gerry Conway joins Marvel.

1971   The Comics Authority is challenged head-on with a three-part anti-drug story in *The Amazing Spider-Man*, issues #96–98. As a result, these three issues are released without the Comics Code seal on the covers.

Marvel gets cover story of *Rolling Stone* for September 16th issue.

Savage Tales #1, is the first of a line of black and white magazines for mature readers (May).

1972   Issue #1 of *Tomb of Dracula* (April)

Bill Everett returns to *The Sub-Mariner,* the character he created in 1939.

Martin Goodman retires. Stan Lee leaves post of editor in chief to become Marvel publisher. Roy Thomas is promoted to editor in chief.

1973   Bill Everett dies in February at age fifty-five.

John Romita, Sr., appointed Marvel's art director.

Writer Len Wein begins association with Marvel.

First issue of *FOOM* (Friends of Ol' Marvel) fan magazine is published, under editorship of Jim Steranko.

"The Death of Gwen Stacy," a landmark two-issue story published in *The Amazing Spider-Man* issues #121 and 122 (June and July).

Howard the Duck first appears in *Fear* #19 (December).

1974   The Punisher makes his debut in *The Amazing Spider-Man* #129 (February).

Issue #1 of *Spidey Super-Stories,* a joint venture with the Childrens Television Workshop (October).

Wolverine introduced in *The Incredible Hulk* #180 (October).

Roy Thomas vacates editor's chair; Len Wein takes over.

Writer Chris Claremont joins Marvel.

1975   "All-New" X-Men are launched in *Giant Sized X-Men* #1.

James Galton becomes president of Marvel.

Len Wein exits editor's chair; Marv Wolfman takes over.

1976   Issue #1 of *Howard the Duck* (January).

Marv Wolfman exits editor's chair; writer Gerry Conway takes over temporarily. Ultimately writer Archie Goodwin takes over as editor in chief.

Jim Shooter joins company as associate editor.

Jack Kirby returns to Marvel.

Former Marvel Girl Jean Grey becomes Phoenix in *X-Men* issue #101 (October).

1977   Spider-Man newspaper strip is launched in January.

Artist John Romita, Jr., joins Marvel.

Universal's "Spider-Man" television movie airs on CBS in September.

Universal's "The Incredible Hulk" television movie airs on CBS in November.

1978   Stan Lee relocates to California to head up the film and television development.

Jim Shooter becomes Marvel's editor in chief.

Artist John Byrne joins Marvel.

"The Incredible Hulk" television series from Universal premieres on CBS in March.

"Spider-Man" television series (also known as "The Amazing Spider-Man") from Universal premiers on CBS in April.

Issue #1 of *Spider-Woman* (April).

Toei's "Spider-Man" series for Japanese television premieres in May.

"Dr. Strange" television movie from Universal airs on CBS in September.

"The New Fantastic Four" animated series from DePatie-Freleng premieres on NBC in September.

1979   Universal's "Captain America" television movie airs on CBS in January.

Landmark nine-issue *Iron Man* series chronicling Tony Stark's battle with alcoholism begins in issue #120 (March).

"Fred and Barney Meet the Thing" animated series from Hanna-Barbera premieres on NBC in September.

"Spider-Woman" animated series from DePatie-Freleng premieres on ABC in September.

Actress Mariette Hartley receives Emmy Award for her performance in two-part episode of "The Incredible Hulk."

"The Incredible Hulk" newspaper strip is launched in October.

Universal's "Captain America II" television movie airs on CBS in November.

"Fred and Barney Meet the Thing" becomes component of "Fred and Barney Meet the Shmoo" in December.

1980　Marvel Productions, Ltd., is formed
　　　Issue #1 of *The Savage She-Hulk* (February).
　　　"Captain America II" rebroadcast on CBS as "Captain America" in June.
　　　Landmark "Dark Phoenix Saga" runs in *X-Men* issues #132–137 (April–September).
　　　Toei Animation's feature-length adaptation of "Tomb of Dracula" aired on Japanese TV.

1981　"Spider-Man and His Amazing Friends" animated series from Marvel Productions premieres on NBC in September. A syndicated version of "Spider-Man" is produced by the same unit simultaneously.

1982　Marvel launches subsidiary Epic Comics.
　　　The New Mutants published as "Marvel Graphic Novel" #4.
　　　"The Incredible Hulk" TV series canceled in June after successful five-year run.
　　　"The Incredible Hulk/Amazing Spider-Man Hour" animated series from Marvel Productions premieres on NBC in September.

1983　Fan magazine *Marvel Age* launched.

1984　Carl Burgos, creator of the original Human Torch, dies in April at age sixty-four.
　　　Secret Wars twelve-issue limited series launched (May).
　　　Spider-Man abandons traditional costume for new black outfit.
　　　"The Incredible Hulk" animated series from Marvel Productions premieres on NBC in December.

1986　Issue #1 of *X-Factor* (February).
　　　Bruce Banner and Betty Ross marry in *The Incredible Hulk* #319.
　　　The Hulk once more becomes gray, his original color.
　　　Universal's feature film *Howard the Duck* is released in July. Most wish it hadn't been.

1987　Jim Shooter vacates editor's chair; Tom DeFalco becomes new editor in chief.
　　　Peter Parker and Mary Jane Watson marry in *The Amazing Spider-Man* "Giant Sized AnnuaL." A publicity wedding is staged in New York's Shea Stadium with Stan Lee officiating and actors standing in for Spidey and M.J.
　　　Issue #1 of *The Punisher* (July).
　　　Debut of the Spider-Man balloon in Macy's Thanksgiving Day Parade.

1988　Universal/New World Pictures' "The Incredible Hulk Returns" television movie airs on NBC in May.
　　　Artist Todd McFarlane takes over Spider-Man with issue #300, and returns Spidey to his traditional costume.

"The Marvel Action Universe" animated series from Marvel Productions/Orion Pictures/New World Entertainment premieres in syndication in October.
　　　Issue #1 of *Wolverine* (November).

1989　Universal/New World Pictures' "The Trial of The Incredible Hulk" television movie airs on NBC.
　　　Issue #1 of *The Sensational She Hulk* (May).
　　　Investor Ronald O. Perelman buys Marvel.

1990　Terry Stewart becomes president of Marvel.
　　　Issue #1 of *Spider-Man* (new series) becomes best-selling comic book in history, selling more than 2 million copies.
　　　Marvel begins long-term partnership with Toy Biz.
　　　Universal/New World's "The Death of The Incredible Hulk" television movie airs on NBC.
　　　New World's feature film *The Punisher,* completed in 1989, is released on home video.

1991　Forty percent of Marvel is taken public.

1992　*Captain America* feature film, shot in 1989, is released on home video.
　　　"X-Men" animated series from Marvel/Saban/Graz premieres on Fox in October.

1993　Actor Bill Bixby, television's David Banner, dies at age fifty-nine.
　　　Unreleased feature film *The Fantastic Four* shot in Los Angeles.

1994　Jack Kirby dies in February at age seventy-six.
　　　Issue #1 of *Generation X.*
　　　X-Men's Scott Summers and Jean Grey are married in *X-Men* (Second Series) #30.
　　　"The Marvel Action Hour" animated series from Marvel/New World premieres in syndication in September. The "Hour" is made up of "Iron Man" and "The Fantastic Four."
　　　Tom DeFalco vacates editor's chair; Bob Harras takes over.
　　　The first episode of "Spider-Man: The Animated Series" airs in a sneak preview in November.

1995　"Spider-Man: The Animated Series," a co-production of Marvel/New World/Saban/Graz, premieres as a weekly series on Fox in February.
　　　Peter Parker's Aunt May dies in *The Amazing Spider-Man* #400 (but not forever).

1996　Marvel Films' "Generation X" television movie airs on Fox in February.
　　　"The Incredible Hulk" animated series from Marvel/New World premieres on UPN in September.
　　　Marvel merges with Toy Biz in (unsuccessful) attempt to avoid bankruptcy. Company files for Chapter 11 protection on December 27, 1996.

1997　In June, bondholder Carl Icahn takes control of Marvel. Joseph Calimari becomes president of company.

1998　"Silver Surfer" animated series from Fox/Saban/Marvel premieres on Fox in February.
　　　Twentieth Television and Marvel Films' "Nick Fury, Agent of S.H.I.E.L.D." airs on Fox.
　　　New Line Cinema's feature film *Blade* opens in theaters in August and earns $17 million in its opening weekend.
　　　Stan Lee creates own company, Stan Lee Media, to develop individual projects, while remaining Marvel's CEO emeritus.

1999　Marvel Superhero Island attraction opens at Universal Studios Escape in Orlando, Florida, in spring.
　　　Spider-Man: On Stage premieres at England's Butlins Family Resorts.
　　　"Spider-Man Unlimited" animated series from Saban premieres on Fox in September.
　　　"The Avengers" animated series from Saban premieres on Fox in October.

2000　Artist Gil Kane dies at age seventy-three.
　　　Marvel partners with Artisan Entertainment for deal that will develop fifteen character franchises for movies, television, direct-to-video films and Internet projects.
　　　20th Century-Fox's feature film *X-Men* opens July 14 and earns more than $100 million in its first two weeks.
　　　"X-Men Evolution" animated series premieres on Kids WB! in November.

2002　Artist John Buscema dies in January at age seventy-four.
　　　New Line Cinema's *Blade II* opens in March.
　　　Long awaited *Spider-Man* feature from Columbia Pictures opens May 3.
　　　New "Spider-Man: The Animated Series" premiers.

2003
　　　20th Century Fox's *Daredevil* opens in January.
　　　20th Century Fox's *X-Men 2* to open May 2.
　　　Universal's *The Hulk* feature to open in June.
　　　Ghost Rider feature scheduled to open.

INDEX

Page numbers in *italics* indicate illustrations.